History of the Ninth Regiment

Col. Thomas Cass, the Ninth Massachusetts Volunteer Infantry's first commander. *(Library of Congress)*

The

HISTORY

of the

NINTH REGIMENT

MASSACHUSETTS VOLUNTEER INFANTRY

June, 1861–June, 1864

Daniel George Macnamara

With an introduction by Christian G. Samito

FORDHAM UNIVERSITY PRESS
New York
2000

The Irish in the Civil War, No. 7
ISSN 1044–5315

Library of Congress Cataloging-in-Publication Data

Macnamara, Daniel George, 1839–1900.
    The history of the ninth regiment, Massachusetts Volunteer Infantry, June, 1861–June,1864 / Daniel George Macnamara ; with an introduction by Christian G. Samito.
        p.   cm.— (The Irish in the Civil War, ISSN 1044-5315 ; no. 7)
    Originally published: Boston : E.B. Stillings, 1899.
    Includes bibliographical references and index.
    ISBN 0-8232-2055-9 (hardcover)—ISBN 0-8232-2056-7 (pbk.)
    1. United States. Army. Massachusetts Infantry Regiment, 9th (1861–1864)   2. Massachusetts—History—Civil War, 1861–1865—Regimental histories.   4. United States—History—Civil War, 1861–1865—Participation, Irish American.   5. Irish American soldiers—Massachusetts—History—19th century. I. Samito, Christian G. II. Title. II. Series.
    E513.5 9th.M33   2000
    973.7′41—dc21   00-029379

Printed in the United States of America
00   01   02   03   04   5   4   3   2   1

THE IRISH IN THE CIVIL WAR
Lawrence F. Kohl, series editor

1. Lawrence F. Kohl with Margaret Cossé Richard, eds., *Irish Green and Union Blue: The Civil War Letters of Peter Welsh, Color Sergeant, 28th Massachusetts.*
2. William Corby, C.S.C., *Memoirs of Chaplain Life: Three Years in the Irish Brigade with the Army of the Potomac.* Edited by Lawrence F. Kohl.
3. James P. Sullivan, *An Irishman in the Iron Brigade: The Civil War Memoirs of James P. Sullivan, Sergt., Company K, 6th Wisconsin Volunteers.* Edited by William J. K. Beaudot and Lance J. Herdegen.
4. Capt. D. P. Conyngham, A.D.C., *The Irish Brigade: And Its Campaigns.* Edited by Lawrence F. Kohl.
5. St. Claire A. Mulholland, *The Story of the 116th Regiment: Pennsylvania Volunteers in the War of Rebellion.* Edited by Lawrence F. Kohl.
6. Christian G. Samito, ed., *Commanding Boston's Irish Ninth: The Civil War Letters of Colonel Patrick R. Guiney, Ninth Massachusetts Volunteer Infantry.*

CONTENTS.

ACKNOWLEDGMENTS.

No work such as this is done without the help of others. I am indebted to a number of people who aided me in preparing this edition of Daniel Macnamara's regimental history of the "Fighting Ninth" Massachusetts Voluntary Infantry.

I would like to thank Lawrence F. Kohl for his valuable advice and suggestions concerning my introduction, as well as his obtaining several of the photographs reprinted in this volume. Professor Kohl is not only a top scholar but also a true gentleman, and it is always a pleasure working with him. I would also like to thank Fordham University Press for its continued interest in the Irish-American experience during the Civil War.

The staffs of the National Archives, Library of Congress, United States Army Military History Institute, and the Massachusetts Historical Society graciously made many important photographs and documents available for my use.

James Mahoney, curator of the College of the Holy Cross's Rare Books, Special Collections and Archives, aided my research into the Ninth Massachusetts with good humor and great warmth. Working with him has added greatly to my enjoyment of studying the Ninth Massachusetts.

I am grateful to Henry Roberts for providing me with a copy of a Ninth Massachusetts soldier's diary, along with other research leads and his great interest in and support for this project in general. Robert Bateman sent me valuable information concerning his ancestor, the famous Fenian Timothy Deasy, and Steven Hill shared some of his great knowledge on Civil War flags with me. Brian Caputo gave me permission to reproduce a photograph of his ancestor, James F. McGunnigle, in addition to many enjoyable conversations and his enthusiastic support of my research. From our mutual interest in the Ninth Massachusetts, Mike Shotwell and I have grown to be good friends as well as collaborators on an article concerning the regiment at Gettysburg.

John F. McCormack provided me with several photographs from his collection as soon as he learned that I was working on this edition. William Prince granted me permission to reproduce a photograph of his currently at the United States Army Military History Institute.

I should also like to thank my parents and family for their love and encouragement of my writing, and all my friends for their good company and fellowship.

INTRODUCTION TO THE 2000 EDITION.

When rebellion erupted and President Abraham Lincoln called for volunteers to restore the Union, many Irish-Americans around Boston answered his summons. For some, feelings of patriotism and devotion to their adopted country motivated them to enlist. Others wished to strike against what they viewed as an illegitimate government supported by an Irish enemy, England, while still more sought adventure or the economic security of a soldier's monthly salary. Thomas Cass, former commander of an Irish-American militia company, organized these civilian-soldiers into Massachusetts's first ethnic regiment. Six companies from Boston and one each from Salem, Milford, Marlboro, and Stoughton excitedly gathered, using Faneuil Hall as their first barracks. On May 12, 1861, the men, mostly laborers, were transported to Long Island in Boston Harbor to begin training at Camp Wightman.

That they were civilians and unused to military discipline quickly became apparent. One observer found a "sentry . . . patrolling with bare feet + a pipe in his mouth," and another time, officers left Camp Wightman without leave to visit a nearby unit. Yet amid the open fields of the island, Cass began forging his regiment into a formidable fighting force by drilling the unit and instilling a sense of discipline in his troops. By the time the regiment returned to Boston to be mustered in as the Ninth Massachusetts Volunteer Infantry, the rough citizens had become soldiers, holding themselves with military bearing and feeling pride at seeing their green Irish flag flutter next to the Stars and Stripes.[1]

On June 25, 1861, more than a thousand Irishmen left Boston to fight in what everyone assumed would be a brief, glorious war. Three years later, only a portion of the original volunteers remained with the regiment. Hundreds of their comrades had fallen at previously unknown places named Gaines' Mill, the Wilderness, and Spotsylvania. Cass lay in a Boston cemetery, dead of wounds received while commanding his regiment at Malvern Hill. His replacement, Patrick R. Guiney, returned home to recuperate after a bullet destroyed his eye at the Wilderness.

---

[1] George D. Wells to Governor John A. Andrew, Boston, May 16, 1861, in Andrew Collection, Massachusetts Historical Society, Boston, Massachusetts. Daniel G. Macnamara, *The History of the Ninth Regiment Massachusetts Volunteer Infantry* (Boston: E. B. Stillings & Co., 1899), 6–15, 22–25, hereafter cited as *History of the Ninth*.

The regiment proved it had become a finely honed weapon, but Irish valor came at a cost—the Ninth Massachusetts suffered the highest losses of any Federal regiment at Gaines' Mill. During its service in the Army of the Potomac's Fifth Corps, the unit lost 209 men killed or mortally wounded, ranking it thirty-first in the entire Union Army in that category and earning its sobriquet, the "Fighting" Ninth.[2]

A shared Irish heritage identified the men of the Ninth and provided them with a source of pride. Shortly after First Manassas, an officer addressed Capt. Edward Fitzgerald in front of other members of the regiment, saying, "It is strange that when your countrymen undertake to do anything they do it wrong." "There is one thing about it," Fitzgerald quickly shot back, "They stand their ground in a fight—they don't run," and the officer rode off to "peals of Irish laughter." When a new flag replaced the tattered Irish green banner after the Seven Days' Battles, Guiney sent the old one back to Massachusetts's governor for preservation, writing, "Sometimes when all else looked vague and battle-fortune seemed to be against us, there was a certain magic in the light of this old symbol of our enslaved but hopeful Ireland, that made the Ninth fight superhumanly hard."[3]

While securing a reputation as a hard-fighting regiment, the Ninth Massachusetts also added its Irish Catholic identity to the Army of the Potomac. The privations and dangers of military service heightened the importance of religion to the Irishmen, and except for brief intervals, the unit had a chaplain assigned to it. While outside Washington in the early days of the war, the men constructed a small altar where Mass could be celebrated, and some participated in evening spiritual readings. The most famous photograph of the Ninth Massachusetts shows Cass and his men crowded around a chapel tent marked by a cross, with regimental chaplain Rev. Thomas Scully posing in his religious vestments. As the Ninth turned out during one alarm, Scully went to each company as the men bent on one knee to make an act of contrition and receive absolution.[4]

---

[2] William Fox listed that the regiment suffered at least 231 casualties at Gaines' Mill and 137 at the Wilderness, with 209 killed or mortally wounded during its term of service. Macnamara listed the casualties even higher, at 252 for Gaines' Mill and 150 for the Wilderness. William Fox, *Regimental Losses in the American Civil War* (Albany: Albany Publishing Company, 1889), 3, 11, 430, 445. Macnamara, *History of the Ninth*, 131, 377.

[3] Patrick R. Guiney to Jennie Guiney, Arlington Heights near Washington, D.C., July 31, 1861; Patrick R. Guiney to Governor John A. Andrew, Camp near Sharpsburg [sic], Maryland, October 22, 1862, in Christian G. Samito, ed., *Commanding Boston's Irish Ninth: The Civil War Letters of Colonel Patrick R. Guiney, Ninth Massachusetts Volunteer Infantry* (New York: Fordham University Press, 1998), 30, 144.

[4] Rev. Thomas Scully from Arlington Heights, Virginia, August 12, 1861, in *The Pilot*, August 24, 1861. Patrick R. Guiney to Jennie Guiney, Arlington Heights near Washington,

For the war's first Christmas, the Irishmen adorned their camp with evergreens and bedecked their tents with crosses and wreaths. Father Scully celebrated High Mass on a sunny Christmas Day, and that night officers of the Ninth joined with other officers from their brigade in a jovial celebration featuring delicacies from Washington. However, the Saint Patrick's Day festivities were the ones that the Boston Irishmen most anticipated. In 1863 the Irish Ninth decorated each company street in camp with an arch of holly and evergreens. For the special day, Colonel Guiney set aside the officers of the regiment to allow the men to elect officers from the ranks. After breakfast on a bright, sunny day, Guiney delivered an oration on Saint Patrick's life and the Irishmen's duties to both Ireland and the United States. Several other speeches gave way to cheers for Major Generals McClellan and Joseph Hooker, President Lincoln, Colonel Guiney, Ireland, America, and Massachusetts. Then the men were dismissed to receive the first of three whiskey rations and participate in various games. Some tried to climb a greased pole having fifteen dollars and a ten-day furlough at the top (no one succeeded), while others attempted to catch a greased pig and competed in various foot and sack races. Horse racing ensued after a midday meal, followed by a mock parade in which the enlisted "commander" of the regiment parodied Guiney's manner of drilling the regiment, while a crowd of spectators watched the display. The following year, the celebration was even larger, with all Irishmen in the division given leave to revel in the Ninth's camp.[5]

Their Irish and Catholic identity made the men of the Ninth Massachusetts stand out among the regiments of the Army of the Potomac, not only for their personality but because they enlisted in the first place. Initially, the notion that many Irish-Americans, especially those from Boston, would be staunch fighters in the Union war effort seemed improbable. Years of nativist hostility had culminated in the American Party, which sought to curtail the influence of immigrants in the United States. More commonly known as the Know-Nothings, this party achieved great success within Massachusetts and for a time controlled the governorship and both houses of the state legislature. By 1860, Know-Nothingism had declined

---

D.C., July 31, 1861; Patrick R. Guiney to Jennie Guiney, Miner's Hill, Virginia, February 18, 1862, in Samito, *Commanding Boston's Irish Ninth*, 30, 74.

[5] Unfortunately, the horse racing stopped when Quartermaster Thomas Mooney's horse collided with that of the surgeon of the Thirty-second Massachusetts. While the doctor got up with a broken or dislocated arm, both horses were killed, and Mooney was rendered unconscious. He died of his injury on March 27, 1863. Timothy Regan diary, December 23, 1861; March 16, 17, 1863; March 16, 17, 1864. *The Pilot*, January 11, 1862; March 28, 1863. Macnamara, *History of the Ninth*, 65–66, 278–79, 430. Michael Macnamara, *The Irish Ninth in Bivouac and Battle* (Boston: Lee and Shepard, 1867), 74–75, 179, hereafter cited as *Bivouac and Battle*.

as a party, but its sentiments survived, and many former adherents joined ranks with the Republican Party.

The tension between Yankee Protestants and Catholic newcomers went back for decades but was greatly exacerbated by a massive influx of immigrants starting about fifteen years earlier. When the potato rot devastated Ireland in 1845, the ensuing famine stimulated emigration to the United States. Many of the impoverished, unskilled immigrants landed in Boston, needing immediate employment, and they accepted manual-labor jobs offering poor wages and working conditions. Most settled in slums in the North End and Fort Hill districts, where families packed into crowded, dilapidated apartments, and an unsanitary environment, fostered epidemics. The combination of hard labor and terrible living conditions led some to find solace in the local groggeries, where people could gather and cheap whiskey flowed freely.[6]

While the Democratic Party supported immigration and religious and social freedom, nativist hostility toward immigrants, anti-Catholicism, temperance, and abolitionism marked the Republicans. Boston's Protestant Yankees became anxious at the flood of Irish Catholic immigrants and feared their loyalty to foreign religious leaders such as the pope. The immigrants' strong ties to their native country and clamors for United States involvement in Ireland's quest for independence reinforced this apprehension.[7]

The puritanical impulses of temperance activism and abolitionism within the Republican Party further pushed Irish-Americans into the arms of a Democratic Party willing to welcome them as voters. Many Irish-Americans disliked the temperance movement. For a large number, drinking at the local groggery was their one opportunity for social interaction and release from the squalor of their existence. The association of Irish Catholics with drunkenness led some temperance activists to manifest further nativist hostility against the newcomers.[8]

---

[6] Oscar Handlin, *Boston's Immigrants 1790–1880: A Study in Acculturation*, rev. and enl. ed. (Cambridge: The Belknap Press of Harvard University Press, 1979), 60–61, 115, 121. Dennis P. Ryan, *Beyond the Ballot Box: A Social History of the Boston Irish, 1845–1917* (Rutherford, N.J.: Fairleigh Dickinson University Press, 1983), 85. Thomas H. O'Connor, *The Boston Irish: A Political History* (Boston: Northeastern University Press, 1995), 65. Robert H. Lord, John E. Sexton, and Edward T. Harrington, *History of the Archdiocese of Boston*, 3 vols. (New York: Sheed & Ward, 1944), 2:453–54. Thomas H. O'Connor, *Fitzpatrick's Boston, 1846–1866* (Boston: Northeastern University Press, 1984), 84.

[7] Joel H. Silbey, *A Respectable Minority: The Democratic Party in the Civil War Era, 1860–1868* (New York: W. W. Norton & Co., Inc., 1977), 24–25. Eric Foner, *Free Soil, Free Labor, Free Men: The Ideology of the Republican Party Before the Civil War*, repr. ed. (New York: Oxford University Press, 1995), 227–29. O'Connor, *Boston Irish*, 69–70. Edward M. Levine, *The Irish and Irish Politicians* (Notre Dame, Ind.: Notre Dame University Press, 1966), 63.

[8] Handlin, *Boston's Immigrants*, 121, 134. Foner, *Free Soil, Free Labor, Free Men*, 241–42. Levine, *The Irish and Irish Politicians*, 93.

Abolitionism threatened Irish-Americans on several levels. The prospect of millions of freed slaves migrating north and competing for already scarce labor alarmed workers barely able to support their families. While white Irish lived in misery in Boston's slums and exhausted themselves in securing a livelihood, they viewed free blacks not with empathy as another wronged group but as a threat to their jobs and tenuous social position. *The Pilot*, organ of Boston's Irish population, once questioned, "[W]here the white find it difficult to earn a subsistence, what right has the negro to either preference, or to equality, or to admission?" In turn, many blacks expressed antipathy toward Irish immigrants, referring to them as "white niggers," as these immigrants displaced free African Americans from the job market in Northern cities. Taking notice of many Irish-Americans' pro-slavery bias, some abolitionists took a nativist stance, which in turn further antagonized Boston's Irish population. As early as 1839, *The Pilot* warned that abolitionists were "bigoted and persecuting religionists . . . [desiring] the extermination of Catholics by fire and sword."[9]

The eagerness displayed by Boston's Irish militia companies in helping enforce the Fugitive Slave Law further enflamed abolitionist hostility toward them. The best-known case came in May, 1854, when the runaway slave Anthony Burns was apprehended in Boston. Opposition to sending him back to the South ran high, and officials, fearing a riot, called out the militia to prevent mob violence. While many native militia companies declined to participate, several Irish units deployed, to the chagrin and anger of abolitionists. Among them was the Columbian Artillery, led by Capt. Thomas Cass, which took a position by the Court House. A letter in the *Liberator* later protested, "Irishmen, instead of shedding the tear of pity [for Burns], hardened their hearts, and did the business of the oppressor"; another periodical noted, "Where there is base, vile work to be done for slavery, there is your Irish Catholic . . . ready for business."[10]

Nativist hostility and resentment over such active Irish support of the Fugitive Slave Law led Know-Nothing Governor Henry J. Gardner to disband all militia companies composed of foreigners in 1855. The Colum-

---

[9] *The Pilot*, September 23, 1839; July 20, 1861; February 15, 1862; August 16, 1862. Handlin, *Boston's Immigrants*, 133. Joseph M. Hernon, Jr., *Celts, Catholics, and Copperheads* (Columbus: Ohio State University Press, 1967), 65.

[10] Recently, Noel Ignatiev held the Irish as "the Swiss Guards of the slave power." Noel Ignatiev, *How the Irish Became White* (New York: Routledge, 1995), 162. Albert J. Von Frank, *The Trials of Anthony Burns* (Cambridge: Harvard University Press, 1998), 72. Macnamara, *History of the Ninth*, 2–4. Tyler Anbinder, *Nativism and Slavery* (New York: Oxford University Press, 1992), 89. *Liberator*, September 19, 1854, quoted in Anbinder, *Nativism and Slavery*, 89. *Dedham Gazette*, July 1, 1854, quoted in John R. Mulkern, *The Know-Nothing Party in Massachusetts: The Rise and Fall of a People's Movement* (Boston: Northeastern University Press, 1990), 65–66.

bian Artillery reorganized as a civic organization led by Cass in order to maintain its existence. Upon Lincoln's summons for volunteers to restore the Union, it became the core around which to form the regiment that would become the Ninth Massachusetts. Exacerbated by Irish hostility to abolitionism and temperance, anti-immigrant sentiments were further fueled as the number of foreign-born voters in Massachusetts exploded in the first half of the 1850s. The allegiance of Irish-Americans to the Democratic Party fed Republican antagonism, and some blamed the Irish vote for presidential candidate John C. Frémont's defeat in 1856. Massachusetts Know-Nothings managed to amend the state constitution to require a two-year period following naturalization before newcomers could vote in elections.[11]

Irish-Americans openly displayed hostility to much of the Republican agenda, and few would have expected them to demonstrate an enthusiastic response to Lincoln's call to arms. Democrat Stephen Douglas garnered overwhelming support from the Irish community in the 1860 presidential contest, as *The Pilot* argued that no Catholic should vote for Republican candidate Abraham Lincoln. Lincoln won the election, however, and his party swept into control in the North, precipitating the secession of Southern states.[12]

Yet, devotion to the Union and the Constitution governing it inspired many of Boston's Irish-Americans to rally to their adopted country's defense. The *Irish American* claimed that it was the duty of immigrants to defend the Constitution they swore to uphold, and *The Pilot* argued that the "war of the North is a just one." Some Irish-Americans saw the war

---

[11] During the period 1850–55, the Irish accounted for nearly half the total increase in the Massachusetts population, and the foreign-born vote grew at an explosive 194.6 percent. In 1855, extreme nativists in the state legislature attempted to exclude foreigners from exercising any suffrage or office-holding rights. Know-Nothing Governor Henry Gardner proposed a twenty-one–year period following naturalization before immigrants could vote, and the legislature adopted it along with an act requiring passage of a literacy test prior to voting. Two more passages were required before the measure became an amendment to the state constitution, and in 1856 the legislature reduced the waiting period from twenty-one to fourteen years. Radical Republicans managed to lower the period to two years before the people of Massachusetts approved the amendment in an 1859 referendum. Many radical Republicans opposed the measure as detracting attention from the more important issue of slavery, fearing that such anti-immigrant laws would deter German voters in the western states from supporting the party. O'Connor, *Boston Irish*, 70. Handlin, *Boston's Immigrants*, 204. Foner, *Free Soil, Free Labor, Free Men*, 230–31, 250–51. Hernon, *Celts, Catholics, and Copperheads*, 64. Macnamara, *History of the Ninth*, 2–4.

[12] In the north, Republicans took 14 of 18 governorships, 102 of 146 seats in the U.S. House of Representatives, and 29 of 36 seats in the Senate. Silbey, *Respectable Minority*, 18. O'Connor, *Fitzpatrick's Boston*, 186. Florence E. Gibson, *The Attitudes of the New York Irish Toward State and National Affairs, 1848–1892* (New York: Columbia University Press, 1951), 105.

as an opportunity to increase the spirit of patriotism and cooperation in both the general and the Irish-American communities, as *The Pilot* argued, "This same war has already made us love our country better than ever we did before; it will correct the corruption of all our political proceedings. . . ." They hoped that Irish valor in the war would prove their loyalty and surmount the misgivings and disdain of nativists.[13]

Other factors also helped motivate Irish-Americans to fight. The Catholic Church's position that government must be lawfully established helped check Irish-American support of the illegitimate Southern rebellion. England's pro-Confederate stance also antagonized Irish Catholics, who refused to be on the same side as Ireland's oppressor. *The Pilot* exclaimed, "When England takes part with the South, she can have no possible good in view. . . . When we Irish are side by side with England in any quarrel, we *must* be in the wrong. It is the natural instinct of our race to hate the English side, and take the other; and if the southern States of America have England for their backer, they must look on it as a thing of fate to have Ireland for their foe." Economic conditions also made army service a viable option for many unemployed laborers struggling to avoid starvation. Thus, while most Irish did not want freedom for the slaves and maintained their affiliation with the Democrats, many came forth to fight for the preservation of the Union.[14]

Whatever some may have thought of them, Irish-Americans fought well. Despite skepticism as to their loyalty and questions as to their worth, Irish-Americans bled and died in defense of their adopted country. In a postwar speech, Guiney once challenged his audience, "Go up to the State House and you will find the torn and faded banners of the Ninth Regiment, and so long as they remain there no man will ever be heard to say that the Irish people living in Massachusetts are enemies of the republic."[15]

Throughout its service, the Ninth Massachusetts occupied a prominent role in the public eye. Local ceremonies honored the Irish volunteers before they journeyed to the seat of war. A few days before joining the regiment in Boston, the Fitzgerald Guards of Salem (later Company F of the Ninth Massachusetts) attended Mass together, after which its commis-

---

[13] *The Pilot*, November 2, 1861. *Irish American*, April 20, 1861.

[14] Sectionalism greatly influenced these sentiments, as Irishmen in the South enthusiastically fought for the Confederacy. *The Pilot*, June 8, 1861 (quoted); July 20, 1861; October 26, 1861. *Irish American*, January 11, 1862. David Conyngham, *The Irish Brigade and Its Campaigns*, ed. Lawrence Frederick Kohl, repr. ed. (New York: Fordham University Press, 1994), xvi. Handlin, *Boston's Immigrants*, 208–9. O'Connor, *Fitzpatrick's Boston*, 187.

[15] Speech in Patrick Robert Guiney Scrapbook, Dinand Library Archives, College of the Holy Cross, Worcester, Massachusetts, quoted in Samito, *Commanding Boston's Irish Ninth*, 252.

sioned officers each received a revolver and the company accepted a splendid silk banner of the Stars and Stripes. On the Guards' departure from Salem, the town's brass band and an escort led the company to the train depot, where hundreds gathered to say farewell.[16]

A similar event occurred for the regiment as a whole on the early afternoon of June 24, 1861, the day before it left for Washington, D.C. Following weeks of training, the Ninth Massachusetts debarked at Long Wharf to find an escort of various Irish societies, numbering up to perhaps a thousand men, and Gilmore's Band playing "Saint Patrick's Day." The streets and windows of nearby buildings were packed with cheering onlookers as the escort preceded Cass, atop a spirited charger, and his men on their march up State, Court, Tremont, and Beacon Streets to the State House. There, Governor John A. Andrew received the Ninth Massachusetts and presented it with the state colors, proclaiming in his speech that "the United States knows no distinction between its native born citizens and those born in other countries." His statement stood in stark contrast to the nativist impulse of recent years and the hostility that led to the two-year amendment and disbandment of the Columbian Artillery. After Cass's response, the Ninth Massachusetts paraded behind Gilmore's Band through the Boston Common to the cheers of observers and enjoyed a meal provided by the city government. Before marching back to the wharf to return to Long Island, Boston's Mayor Joseph Wightman inspected the men. Despite the patriotism and sentiments of solidarity between native and immigrant, some in the crowd persisted in manifesting their disdain, and one exclaimed upon the Ninth's departure, "There goes a load of the Irish rubbish out of the city."[17]

Flags provided a symbolic link between the soldiers and the Bay State communities they left behind. Friends delivered a Federal banner, and the widow of ex-Mayor Harrison Gray Otis donated a magnificent green silk Irish flag to the Ninth Massachusetts before it departed for Washington. Several weeks later, the boys of Boston's Eliot School forwarded another Stars and Stripes to the regiment in the field. An accompanying letter expressed "their appreciation of the self-sacrificing devotion" of the Irish soldiers and cited the interest and pride the boys felt in what they called "our regiment." The bond and gratitude displayed through these flag presentations was mutual and moved both civilians in Boston and their soldiers of the Ninth. After the Seven Days' Battles, when Colonel Guiney

---

[16] *Salem Advertiser* quoted in *The Pilot*, May 25, 1861.

[17] *The Pilot*, June 29, 1861; August 24, 1861. *Boston Courier* quoted in *The Pilot*, July 6, 1861. Macnamara, *History of the Ninth*, 22–25.

returned the battle-worn regimental color to Governor Andrew in exchange for a new banner contributed by supporters in Boston, he did so with the sentiment, "The memories which cluster around these shreds are indeed very dear to us. We need not ask Your Excellency to hold them sacredly."[18]

Furthermore, friends and family back in Massachusetts closely followed the movements and experiences of the Ninth Massachusetts through Boston's newspapers. Serving Boston's Irish community, *The Pilot* printed many articles and letters concerning the unit for readers who devoured information about their absent loved ones. From July 13, 1861, to August 2, 1862, the Ninth's Michael A. Finnerty served as the paper's correspondent, and his frequent letters provided detailed news to those at home. Other newspapers, such as the Boston *Post* and Boston *Journal*, also reported on events of importance to members of the Ninth and even published letters and articles discussing the regiment's internal political controversies.[19]

As the expiration of the Ninth Massachusetts Volunteer Infantry's term of enlistment drew near, Bostonians once again turned out to receive their Irish regiment. Early on June 15, 1864, a throng of family, friends, and curious onlookers crowded around Worcester Depot as the train bearing the veterans of this regiment arrived in Boston. Joy at the reunion with loved ones and a spirit of pride and patriotism filled the air, but an unspoken sadness also permeated the scene. After breakfast at the Beach Street barracks, the men formed a column, and loud cheers filled the air as Guiney rode to the head of his regiment. With its "tattered and smoke stained colors" unfurled, the Ninth Massachusetts marched to Faneuil Hall in the oppressive heat. Throngs of onlookers filled the route, and the national flag hung outside many homes. Medallions entwined with the colors of the United States and Ireland and bearing the names of Cass, Guiney, and various battles in which the unit had participated bedecked Faneuil Hall, and the upper galleries were packed with mothers, fathers, sweethearts, and children of the veterans. Mayor Frederick W. Lincoln

---

[18] Michael Macnamara felt such gratitude that he dedicated his *The Irish Ninth in Bivouac and Battle* to "Madam Harrison Gray Otis," praising her as "The Patroness of the Ninth Regiment." *The Pilot*, June 29, 1861. S. W. Mason to Col. Thomas Cass, Boston, September 10, 1861, in *The Pilot*, October 12, 1861. Col. Patrick R. Guiney to Governor John A. Andrew, Camp near Sharpsburgh [*sic*], Md., October 22, 1862, in Samito, *Commanding Boston's Irish Ninth*, 143–44. O'Connor, *Fitzpatrick's Boston*, 194–95. James Bernard Cullen, ed., *The Story of the Irish in Boston* (Boston: James B. Cullen & Company, 1889), 228.

[19] *The Pilot*, July 13, 1861; August 2, 1862. Boston *Post*, April 14, 1863; April 17, 1863; May 16, 1863; September 8, 1863; September 9, 1863; September 15, 1863. Samito, *Commanding Boston's Irish Ninth*, 184–85.

and Massachusetts Adjutant General William Schouler addressed the soldiers, and Colonel Guiney reflected on the military record of the "Fighting" Ninth. Perhaps some of the soldiers and family members shed a tear, in disbelief at the regiment's return to Boston or in remembrance of a joking friend who went off to war in 1861, never to return to his home state. The feeling of accomplishment must have been powerful as Guiney told the men, "[Y]ou did it," and, "[T]he great praise belongs to you for what the Ninth did."[20]

The man who fought with and later recorded the deeds of the "Fighting" Ninth, Daniel G. Macnamara, was born in Boston on April 12, 1839. His father, also named Daniel, was born on January 4, 1807, in Thomond, North Munster, in Ireland, and became a mason. In February, 1830, he married Mary Hickey in Limerick, and the couple emigrated to America, reaching Boston in the spring of 1833. Over the years, they raised a family of four boys and two girls. Young Daniel received a public-school education and at the age of sixteen took a job teaching penmanship and bookkeeping. He grew up a handsome man, standing five feet eleven and a half inches tall, with light hair and gray eyes. However, the attack on Fort Sumter changed the Macnamara family forever, as Daniel and two older brothers decided to join in the effort to suppress the Confederacy.[21]

Daniel and Michael H. Macnamara, a law student, set to work raising a company for the Irish regiment authorized by Governor John A. Andrew. Their eldest brother, James W. Macnamara, had chosen the life of a seamen at the age of seventeen. During seven years in the merchant marine, he voyaged to different ports and became a navigator. Overseas when the rebellion broke, James rushed back to support the Union upon hearing the news. He originally planned to enlist in the cavalry but, upon finding two of his brothers recruiting Irishmen for their unit, joined their effort.[22]

The Macnamara brothers played a major role in the exploits of the Ninth, despite a disagreement with Colonel Cass. Since the brothers worked to organize Company E, Michael planned to be its captain, James its second lieutenant, and the youngest, Daniel, its first sergeant. However, on the day the regiment mustered in, Cass replaced Michael with John R. Teague, and Michael accepted the position of first lieutenant.

---

[20] *The Pilot*, June 25, 1864.

[21] Both of Macnamara's parents lived into their eighties and were buried at Holyhood Cemetery, Brookline. Boston *Post*, April 6, 1900. Daniel G. Macnamara Pension Record; James Macnamara Pension Record, National Archives, Washington, D.C. Macnamara, *History of the Ninth*, 416–17.

[22] Macnamara, *History of the Ninth*, 417–18.

Similarly, James was deprived of his lieutenancy in favor of Timothy Lee and mustered in as sergeant. Continued tensions with Cass led Michael to act disrespectfully toward the colonel, who placed him under arrest on August 6, 1861. Michael was dismissed by court-martial, to date from September 10, on charges of willfully disobeying orders, deserting his post, violating a promise to a superior officer, using language unbecoming a gentleman and an officer, assaulting the adjutant while he was trying to discharge his duty, and exhibiting conduct detrimental to military discipline and order. After Cass's death, Guiney assumed command of the regiment in August, 1862, and Michael reenlisted as a private. By July 1, 1863, he had risen to the rank of quartermaster sergeant and served in that capacity until mustered out of service with the rest of the Ninth.[23]

Colonel Guiney commended both James and Daniel for their meritorious and gallant services. James was seriously wounded and captured on the skirmish line at Gaines' Mill, but after exchange he recuperated and rose to the rank of captain. While leading Company I at the Wilderness, he suffered a mortal wound. Daniel served as commissary sergeant and eventually rose to become regimental quartermaster.[24]

After mustering out, Michael returned to the front as a war correspondent, observing events through Appomattox. Admitted to the bar in 1867, he published a regimental history of the Ninth Massachusetts that year, and, on July 8, Rev. Bernard McFeeley of Boston officiated at the marriage of the twenty-nine-year-old Michael to twenty-one-year-old Mary Jane Upton. Eventually, estranged relations with his wife led him to leave for a life of wandering as a newspaper reporter. He claimed to have served as a correspondent during a Fenian raid on Canada, where he was captured and served eighty days in a Montreal prison.[25]

---

[23] Michael H. Macnamara Service Record; Michael H. Macnamara Pension Record, National Archives, Washington, D.C. Macnamara, *History of the Ninth*, 19, 417–19. *Massachusetts Soldiers, Sailors, and Marines in the Civil War*, compiled by the Adjutant General of Massachusetts (Norwood: Norwood Press, 1931), 1:635, 648.

[24] On September 2, 1864, Mary Macnamara applied for a mother's pension after the death of her son James. While her husband, Daniel Macnamara, was still alive, he could not work due to physical inability and loss of eyesight. She received the pension dated December 29, 1865. James Macnamara Pension Record, National Archives, Washington, D.C. Macnamara, *History of the Ninth*, 418–20.

[25] The Fenian Brotherhood was the American branch of the Irish Revolutionary Brotherhood, an organization devoted to liberating Ireland from British rule. This militaristic association grew during the Civil War, aided by Britain's generally pro-Confederate posture. Following that conflict the Fenians carried out several attacks on Canada, notably on New Brunswick, Ontario, and Quebec, hoping to force Irish independence by invading Britain's North American territories. After Michael's death, his younger brother John denied that he had had any involvement with the Irish society. However, *The Pilot* reported that he had participated and been captured in the 1870 Fenian invasion of Canada. W. S. Neidhardt,

Afterward, he went to Chicago to work for various daily newspapers for several years. In 1883 he met a younger widow, Edna Tennyson, who had been born in Ireland of English parents. After living together for a year, Michael explained to her that he was a widower who had had a wife in New York. He said he could not marry her in religious rites because he was Catholic, but he drew up and signed a marriage contract. This relationship proved tempestuous as well, and Michael left her several times.[26]

The couple continued on despite uneasiness between the two until Michael's mental state completely collapsed. On May 8, 1897, after a spree of drunkenness and brawling, Michael administered opium to himself and committed suicide, leaving Edna penniless. Meanwhile, Michael and Mary had never divorced, and as late as March, 1914, Mary Macnamara still lived in New York City and drew a pension. The matter of Michael H. Macnamara's two wives led to an investigation nearly a decade after his death.[27]

Fenianism in North America (University Park, Penn.: The Pennsylvania State University Press, 1975), 7, 16. Michael H. Macnamara Pension Record, National Archives, Washington, D.C. *The Pilot*, May 15, 1897. Macnamara, *History of the Ninth*, 418–19.

[26] A blue-eyed woman of light complexion and hair, Edna Tennyson (or possibly Sweikard) was either a clerk in a hotel or store or an organist in an Episcopal church in Chicago. In 1885 Michael traveled to Arizona with his brother John, and upon their return to Kansas City, Missouri, where the latter resided, Edna was waiting for him. Tensions were again exacerbated when Edna found out about Mary from a letter she found in Michael's clothing, probably sometime in 1888. Apparently, his first wife had written to request he sign a deed so that she could sell some property. By 1889 the couple resided in Kansas City. Michael went to Oklahoma Territory that year to write about the opening up of that territory but returned to Kansas City after Edna pursued him. On September 9, 1891, he sought a military pension, claiming he was unable to support himself because of "Rheumatism, Kidney disease, chronic Diarrhoea, Disease of Bowells [sic], liver, spleen, disease of eyes, and resulting general emaciation," along with wounds in the head and right leg. By December 31, 1892, he had returned to Oklahoma Territory, signing that he was a resident of the town of Guthrie. Michael again requested aid on May 27, 1893, claiming he contracted chronic diarrhea from exposure and bad diet at Bealton Station, Virginia, which caused piles from which he had suffered since the war, rheumatism that had developed while marching in wet weather by Stoneman's Switch, and a wound from a shell fragment in the head and nose during the fighting at Fredericksburg. On March 3, 1894, Michael appeared before a notary public and swore that he knew of no member of the Ninth Massachusetts who could verify the alleged head and neck wound from Fredericksburg. The statement, written by the notary public, claims that he was in Perry, Oklahoma Territory, and that "he does not know if there is a man of his regiment living today and if there is he is ignorant of his whereabouts. . . ." Michael did not wish contact be made with Daniel, although after his death, Edna mentioned she knew he had a brother working in the Boston Custom House. Eventually, he obtained a job, and possibly residence, at the Oklahoma Soldier's Home in Guthrie, but by September, 1895, Edna was at Leavenworth, Kansas, and persuaded him to return once again. Michael H. Macnamara Pension Record, National Archives, Washington, D.C. Macnamara, *History of the Ninth*, 419.

[27] The couple rented a room at the Willard Hotel, 314 West 9th Street in Kansas City in July, 1896. Michael spent much time in the bars there and continued his association with

Daniel's life took a very different path from that of his older brother. After his enlistment in the Ninth expired, he found employment as an accountant in the army's quartermaster and commissary departments. Following the war, he went with the Twenty Fifth corps to Brownsville, Texas, a town on the Rio Grande. He reentered the service there as a lieutenant on April 25, 1866, served in the foreign occupation of Mexico, and mustered out on November 26 of that same year. He returned to Boston and studied law for a year before taking a position at the Boston Custom House on November 1, 1867.[28]

On June 1, 1876, Daniel married twenty-seven-year-old Margaret A. Graham, who had been born in Boston of Irish parents. The ceremony took place in Cambridge, with the former chaplain of the Ninth Massachusetts, Rev. Thomas Scully, presiding. Daniel also maintained close ties with Civil War comrades, serving as adjutant of the Ninth Massachusetts Militia Regiment in 1868–69. During the 1880s, he held multiple terms as president of the Society of the Ninth Regiment Massachusetts Volunteers, an organization composed of veterans of the "Fighting" Ninth. The highlight of the association's activities was a yearly reunion, such as that

---

Irish independence movements. He and Captains Thomas Phelan and Waters were known as the "Three Guardsmen," and people called him "Major," although after his death one newspaper reported that he had never held rank higher than captain (and that only before the Ninth mustered in on June 11, 1861). On May 7, 1897, Michael drew his pension check and drank it away, returning to his room in the Willard Hotel in Kansas City with his face cut and bruised from a barroom brawl. He slept a while and then left, returning drunk at 11:00 the night of May 8. Edna scolded Michael for squandering their money as he undressed and lay down. She saw him fumble with a bottle but failed to realize that he was administering opium poisoning to himself. When Michael's breathing became affected, she called her landlady and others who notified the police, and he died at the police station in Kansas City. After his death, a letter was found on Michael's body from Joe Speyer, editor of a Kansas City paper, demanding that he return money obtained under "false pretense." During the 1896 presidential campaign, Macnamara had approached Speyer and told him of his poverty. Speyer had given him a job and advanced him twenty-eight dollars, to be paid out of his pension check. However, Speyer had learned of Michael's drunken spree and written the letter in which he had called him a liar and a swindler and threatened to have him arrested. Meanwhile, Edna had stood by Michael as he abused and impoverished her, drinking away whatever money he found. She mourned his death, wearing a worn calico wrap. She was destitute, as he had even pawned her clothing, and the landlady of the Willard Hotel allowed her to stay a few months until she got back on her feet. One newspaper account stated that he left her an envelope containing his Grand Army of the Republic badge and that on the front he had written, "My darling, my Edna, my wife. Goodbye." In June, 1899, Mary J. Macnamara was living at 114 East 32nd Street in New York City and still resided there in 1914. Upon his death, Michael carried no life insurance, and Mary owned no real or personal property and had no income other than that from her own labor. Michael H. Macnamara Pension Record, National Archives, Washington, D.C. Macnamara, *History of the Ninth*, 419.

[28] Daniel G. Macnamara Pension Record, National Archives, Washington, D.C. Boston *Post*, April 6, 1900. Macnamara, *History of the Ninth*, 418–20.

held on August 29, 1888, at Revere Beach, outside Boston. The veterans gathered while younger people enjoyed the festive atmosphere and steam toboggan rides, merry-go-rounds, slides, and sporting events. At 11:00 the soldiers convened at a nearby hotel for elections, a meal, and various speeches and literary exercises. In 1889 a granite monument to Colonel Cass was erected in the Boston Public Garden, and Macnamara delivered an oration at the dedication ceremony.[29]

On September 20, 1898, the surviving members of the Ninth gathered once again for a ceremony in the Boston Public Garden. Sculptor Richard E. Brooks had crafted a bronze replacement of the stone likeness of Cass, and after the colonel's daughter unveiled the work, Macnamara spoke eloquently in remembrance of the officers and men of the "Fighting" Ninth, hoping that "their memories live forever green in the hearts of the people of our great republic." He continued,

> Civil and religious liberty is our birthright, and it is the corner stone of the republic. Those who love the Union will foster and perpetuate it. Only the enemies of our great country will seek to destroy our liberty. The models for our civil government are to be found in the teaching of the great and immortal Washington and in those of his able colleague, Jefferson. If war must come, let us emulate the steadfast bravery and magnanimity of Grant. The blessings of freedom and self-government which God has vouchsafed to us we should freely share with the oppressed of all lands who may come under the protection of our flag.

Macnamara finished his speech by reviewing Cass's life and summarizing the service of the Ninth Massachusetts.[30]

By this time, Daniel had taken on the role of historian of his regiment and was engaged in writing a definitive history of the "Fighting" Ninth, working, over the span of several years, before and after business hours of the Custom House. He finally saw it published in 1899 but did not live long afterward. While at the Custom House at nine o'clock in the morning of April 5, 1900, Macnamara was stricken with apoplexy, an uncontrolled

---

[29] By at least October 30, 1891, the couple moved into a house at 40 Alleghany Street in suburban Roxbury, and Daniel applied for an invalid pension on account of rheumatism contracted at Fredericksburg and Stoneman's Switch. The Ninth Massachusetts was stationed near Fredericksburg and Stoneman's Switch during the winter of 1862–63. The disability was not sufficient under the 1890 pension laws, and his request was denied. Daniel G. Macnamara Pension File, National Archives, Washington, D.C. *Irish World and American Industrial Liberator*, September 15, 1888. *The Pilot*, November 16, 1889. Boston *Post*, April 6, 1900.

[30] Untitled newspaper clip, September 21, 1898.

bleeding into the brain today commonly referred to as stroke. Taken to the Emergency Hospital, he died of the cerebral hemorrhage at six o'clock that evening. Reverend Scully, former chaplain of the Ninth Massachusetts, rose from his own sickbed to be by the side of his old friend, and Reverends Frawley and Barrett were also present. An obituary reported that "many business men who had been recipients of his kindly attention for years came to the hospital to see him when they found his office chair vacant." The funeral was held on April 9, the body escorted from Macnamara's house to the Mission Church by twenty members of the Ninth Regiment Association and Grand Army of the Republic. Many floral arrangements were donated, and the church was packed with friends and members of the many groups with which Macnamara had been associated. Reverend Frawley presided over the funeral Mass, and Scully delivered a moving eulogy before the body was interred in Holyhood Cemetery in Brookline, Massachusetts.[31]

The couple had never had children, and at his death Daniel left a widow, one surviving brother, and a married sister. In 1901 Margaret had an adopted "daughter" between twelve and fourteen years old living with her, although she did not formally legalize the relationship. She lived until the age of ninety, dying of myocarditis and arteriosclerosis on May 30, 1936, and was buried in Holyhood Cemetery as well.[32]

Of the three Macnamara brothers who served with the Ninth, two survived the war and both chronicled their experiences and those of the regiment. Michael's *The Irish Ninth in Bivouac and Battle*, published in 1867, was the first book-length account of the Ninth Massachusetts. The book was different from Daniel's later work, being much shorter and less formal and offering more anecdotal information. Based largely on his personal diary, Michael's clearly expressed his opinions and biases. The book

---

[31] Daniel Macnamara had been a past commander of Grand Army of the Republic Post 15, Colonel of the Montgomery Guards, President of the Old Ninth Regiment Association, and a member of the Irish Charitable Society, American Irish Historical Society, and other organizations. Macnamara, *History of the Ninth*, x. *The Pilot*, April 14, 1900. Boston *Post*, April 6, 1900.

[32] When Daniel died, Margaret Macnamara inherited the house at 40 Alleghany Street, valued at $5,000, vacant lands in Kinsley, Kansas, worth $728, $2,000 in the bank, and her husband's life insurance policy of $2,000. After paying for his burial and other expenses, she had $1,000 of the insurance money left. By 1911, she was residing at 160 Longwood Avenue, Roxbury. Daniel's surviving brother, John, did not serve in the Ninth Massachusetts. Daniel G. Macnamara Pension Record, National Archives, Washington, D.C. Boston *Post*, April 6, 1900.

sought both to exalt the accomplishments of the regiment as well as reaffirm the Irish contribution to the Union's victory, though doing so at the expense of being a detailed regimental history.[33]

The emotional impact of nativist hostility still affected Michael, and one of his primary objectives was to demonstrate the loyalty and valor of the Irish. His preface opened by announcing his "desire to show the world how well the Irishmen, exiled from their native land by the ruthless system of English law practised in Ireland, can serve their adopted country in the day of her trial. . . ." Later he reiterated, "It is a proud reflection of the Irishmen of this generation, that, when the fidelity of his people was tested, their allegiance was as good a guarantee as birth and native blood to the nation which had trusted in and protected them."[34]

Michael viewed battle as the vehicle by which the men of the Irish Ninth brought honor to their homeland as well as vindicated their right to be active participants in the activities of the Republic. At Hanover Court House, "Irish valor proved itself victorious," and at Gaines' Mill, the immigrants "showed themselves worthy of the land which gave them birth and of maintaining the honor of their adopted country." Thus, in recording his history, Michael often glorified the actions of the Ninth in grandiose phrases. For example, before the regiment went to Washington, he wrote, "In no camp in the State of Massachusetts could there be found a more hearty desire, or a regiment who worked more strenuously to achieve military perfection than the Ninth." The horrors of war did occasionally make their way into Michael's narrative, such as his description of camping among the bones and skeletons of fallen comrades and enemies while bivouacking on the old Manassas battlefield in October, 1863.[35]

Elsewhere in his book, Michael asserted that Irish troops were superior to Yankees. He maintained that Irishmen readily volunteered while most native Americans haggled over the details of their enlistment, that there existed a noticeable "distinguishing characteristic of the Irish recruit in painful contrast with the sordid exactations of some native soldiers." In praising the Irish soldier, Michael wrote, "The Irish recruit is . . . a very rapid learner, and more readily grasps the principles of a movement than the soldiers of other nations." Pride in this Irish-American identity in-

---

[33] Macnamara, *Bivouac and Battle*, 5.

[34] Ibid., 5, 29.

[35] Similarly, he displayed a partisan opinion of Southerners, writing that, "Cleanliness, regularity, and *refined* discipline are noticeable attributes in the sturdy Northerner of America. And if this distinguished peculiarity is proof of blood and breeding inferior to the *pseudo* 'chivalry' of the South, let us accept the token of inferiority, and be unto the Giver of all things devoutly thankful." Ibid., 27, 91, 104, 230–32, 234.

spired Michael and his countrymen in their fight, both to prove themselves worthy of their new country and to defeat the Confederacy. The sight of the "green flag, side by side with the starry banner," was a moving image to the men of the Ninth Massachusetts.[36] Michael refrained from addressing the internal discord that occasionally wracked the Ninth Massachusetts. Despite his troubled relationship with Colonel Cass, Michael did not mention his ouster from the captaincy of Company E. While agreeing that Cass was a "rigid disciplinarian," he observed that during the training of the regiment, Cass displayed evidence "of fine soldierly qualities, which, with cultivation, promised noble fruit." Later in the book, he illustrated how Cass attempted to bolster morale in the regiment by complimenting the men, and upon recounting his death deemed him "our lamented and gallant colonel."[37]

Michael's views on the issues of the war diverged from those of his countrymen. He looked down upon blacks as a lesser people, occasionally calling a black woman "wench" and referring to a black boy as having the "agility of a monkey." Nonetheless, Macnamara seems not to have held the same hostility toward African Americans as other Irish-Americans felt and went so far as to value abolitionist John Brown as "gallant." This was due, perhaps, to firsthand encounters with slavery. He criticized minstrels on the basis of his personal observation, that "though we have seen nearly all kinds of negroes, and have had a genuine plantation boy in our own service, we have never yet met with any who can so approach the absurdities, in action, feature, or distorted language, so unsparingly thrust upon the general public by these pseudo darkies." His strongest commentary came after encountering an eighty-year-old black man who had worked his entire life as a slave, his strength sapped from a now withered body. Macnamara recalled feeling that such was a terrible life, that this "was the idea that crossed our crude, free, northern mind, and we felt, more than ever, in heart and principle, an uncompromising enmity to human slavery."[38]

Michael also criticized the Copperhead movement and other efforts to undermine the Union war effort. Although many Irish people participated in the draft riots of mid-July, 1863, Michael condemned such behavior:

---

[36] Macnamara mentioned this point elsewhere, that the national flag "always fluttered proudly in the front of the fight, side by side with our 'Irish green.' " Ibid., 16–19, 52, 68, 79.

[37] Ibid., 26, 38, 47–48, 62–63.

[38] Ibid., 58, 59, 133, 152, 219–21.

. . . when the "draft was commenced," we fervently wished we were at home to help enforce it. When we learned of the disgraceful New York riots, how heartily we wished for a chance to give those fellows a taste of our quality, and show them how the Irish Ninth could charge; but, as none of these gratifying duties were vouchsafed us, we would drop the discussion of the subject with maledictions on the copperheads, who were considered infinitely more contemptible than the crawling viper— the thing from which they have received their name.[39]

Michael's book is not an outstanding source of information about the Ninth Massachusetts's military experience. However, it remains a valuable text because it provides an Irish-American's commentary on political issues during the Civil War, from firsthand encounters with slaves to the Copperhead movement. Furthermore, it reveals the deep scars nativism left on the Irish community.

While *The Irish Ninth in Bivouac and Battle* provided interesting insights and stories about both Michael Macnamara and his unit, Daniel realized that another history of the Ninth Massachusetts had to be written to supply a more complete and historical record of his regiment's service. In his preface, he explained that since his brother's work was composed when war records were unattainable, it could not provide the detail necessary to memorialize the achievements of the unit. Decades later, Daniel consulted official documents, accounts, and letters when researching *The History of the Ninth Regiment, Massachusetts Volunteer Infantry*, and before his preface placed a certification of accuracy signed by twelve fellow comrades from the regiment. While echoing his brother's ethnic pride and many of his political tenets, Daniel's book diverged from Michael's in placing greater emphasis on accurate detail and adopting a more scholarly tone.[40]

Despite their participation in the Civil War and demonstrated loyalty,

---

[39] Copperheads were Northern Democrats opposing Lincoln and continuation of the war, supporting a compromised peace with the Confederacy instead. *The Pilot* argued these Peace Democrats were "the only true representatives of Republican freedom today in this country" and predicted, "[T]ime will vindicate the justice of their conduct." Other Irish-American soldiers expressed sentiments similar to Michael Macnamara's, however. See Peter Welsh to Margaret Welsh, Bloomfield, Va., July 22, 1863; Peter Welsh to Margaret Welsh, In camp near Kelly's Ford, Va., August 2, 1863, in Lawrence Frederick Kohl, ed., *Irish Green and Union Blue* (New York: Fordham University Press, 1986), 113–15. See also Patrick R. Guiney to Jennie Guiney, Berlin, Md., July 16, 1863, in Samito, *Commanding Boston's Irish Ninth*, 203. Macnamara, *Bivouac and Battle*, 217–18. O'Connor, *Fitzpatrick's Boston*, 209–12. *The Pilot*, April 4, 1863. For more information on the Copperheads, see James McPherson, *Battle Cry of Freedom* (New York: Oxford University Press, 1988), 494, 591–98, 761–73.

[40] Macnamara, *History of the Ninth*, vi–viii.

active disdain toward Irish Catholics survived at this late date, and Daniel wrote in part to combat these persistent nativist sentiments. Reformers promoting temperance, women's rights, and clean city governments were angered at immigrants they perceived as combating every reform movement. In New York, Mayor Abram S. Hewitt attacked the appropriateness of flying a flag adorned with a shamrock over City Hall on Saint Patrick's Day, insisting that "America should be governed by Americans." Henry F. Bowers, a lawyer who thought Catholic conspiracies existed on every side, founded the American Protective Association in Iowa in 1887. While never achieving the success of ante-bellum nativist organizations, the group raised a fearful cry at the flow of new immigrants. In 1895, however, prominent Massachusetts Senator George F. Hoar attacked the organization and its agenda in a speech at Clark University in Worcester. In a published letter, Hoar further argued that Irish Catholics had contributed greatly to the United States and were a resource, not threat, to liberty.[41]

Daniel Macnamara addressed this new manifestation of nativism in his writing, showing that Irish-Americans had already proven their fidelity to the United States. He claimed that the Ninth's achievements were "only partially recognized in history" and went on to argue that "it can be said without egotism, that in patriotism, in valor, in love for the American flag, the Constitution, and the Union of the United States, the Catholic Irish-American soldiers take no second place, and the survivors stand today in the front rank to uphold, as they did in war, all the principles of true American citizenship." Macnamara noted how nativism even influenced histories of the Civil War, citing, for example, how William Powell slighted the participation of the Ninth Massachusetts in his massive *The Fifth Army Corps*.[42]

Macnamara reiterated his pride in Irish support for the Union in recounting the early days of the regiment, agreeing with his brother's work in recalling that "Patriotism and love of country was as publicly prominent in the voices and hearts of the Irish-American citizens as it was in the native born. All vied with each other in their feverish haste to volunteer. . . ." Discussing the mustering in and presentation of flags to

---

[41] The American Protective Association was primarily a secret organization centered in the Midwest. Members took an oath never to vote for a Catholic, employ one if a Protestant could be found, or strike with them. John Higham, *Strangers in the Land*, rev. and em. ed. (New Brunswick, N.J.: Rutgers University Press, 1988), 41, 62–63. George F. Hoar, *Autobiography of Seventy Years*, 2 vols (New York: Charles Scribner's Sons, 1903), 1:282–93.

[42] Macnamara, *History of the Ninth*, ix, 373.

the Ninth Massachusetts, Macnamara quoted Governor Andrew's statement of unity between the native and foreign born and reported "the general appearance and conduct of the Ninth that day was a great credit to
their countrymen." He further emphasized the dedication to the Union
that Irish-Americans felt, that they "laid down their lives, proved to the
country that they were terribly in earnest and fully meant all that they
professed."[43]

According to Macnamara, the men of the Ninth found identity and
pride in their Irish background. On review, "Every man held his head well
up, showing lines of tanned and determined Irish faces." While the Ninth
was on board a steamer transporting the men to the Peninsula in 1862,
the vessel's captain had the Irish flag hauled up to the main truck, providing a sentimental and symbolic point in the book: "Cheers from hundreds
of Irish throats greeted the green flag of Erin as it fluttered and snapped
its folds in the strong breeze like a thing of life suddenly set free. For the
time being many Irish hearts were swelling with pride and pleasure at
such an unusual sight. As a flag raising it was emblematic of the lifelong
desire of their hearts, i.e., 'freedom for Ireland.' "[44]

In addressing this theme of Irish participation, Macnamara also con-
tended that Irish participation in the Union war effort and the shared
experience of combat service helped lessen the tensions between native and
immigrant. Early in the war, as the regiment marched to Arlington
Heights, Virginia, troops bivouacking nearby called out, "Three cheers for
the Ninth Massachusetts!" at which Macnamara and others recalled the
scorn of Know-Nothingism experienced but a short time earlier. A particular friendship grew between the Ninth Massachusetts and another regiment in their brigade, the Sixty-second Pennsylvania Infantry.
Macnamara recalled that they "joined in our little festivities and we engaged in theirs. They participated in our celebrations on Saint Patrick's
day with as much zest as 'those to the manner born.' " Gen. Joseph
Hooker and his staff participated in the Irish Brigade's 1863 Saint Patrick's Day celebration, and the following year visitors from brigade and
division headquarters and other regiments came and were entertained at
the holiday celebrations held by the Irish Ninth.[45]

Gerald Linderman found that some veterans used positive memories

---

[43] Similarly, he wrote when Cass was wounded, "When he fell in honorable battle at the
head of his regiment after four hundred and more of his brave officers and men were killed
and wounded, he and they sealed their devotion to the republic." Macnamara, *History of the
Ninth*, 5, 23–25, 183.

[44] Ibid., 64, 75.

[45] Ibid., 43–44, 60, 283, 365

of the conflict "in compensation for the insufficiencies of their civilian lives. Wartime camaraderie might be employed as a palliative for peace-time feelings of isolation; combat excitement for peacetime boredom; the life-and-death issues of war for civilian inconsequentiality; the constant movement of campaigning for peacetime immobility." As Oliver Wendell Holmes told the Harvard graduating class in 1895, "War, when you are at it, is horrible and dull. It is only when time has passed that you see that its message was divine. . . . Out of heroism grows faith in the worth of heroism." By the 1880s and 1890s, distance from the war allowed many veterans to engage in the military revival partially responsible for the writ-ing of Macnamara's book. In addition, the outbreak of the Spanish-Ameri-can War led many Civil War veterans to again experience the martial spirit and patriotic fervor they felt upon volunteering nearly four decades ear-lier.[46]

When the Civil War erupted, the values of courage and honor occu-pied a central place in the mind of volunteer soldiers, who believed there was no better way to demonstrate one's character than to act with valor in combat. According to Linderman, such bravery had to "be a fearless courage," and while enlisted men needed to prove their mettle, officers felt an even greater expectation to excite the fortitude of their men by "positive demonstration." Courage helped ensure success in combat, but also amel-iorated the sting of defeat and protected men from the brutal shock of violence.[47]

Thus, Macnamara praised brave action and contempt for death. He often employed an epic style, portraying battle as simultaneously brutal and violent, yet glorious. "When it is considered that on the one hand there is glory and victory and on the other death and ignominious defeat," he wrote, "the true soldier will without hesitation go forward to win or die." Macnamara honored Southern courage at Gaines' Mill, that the "bravery of the continued charges of the enemy against our lines in the face of a terrific fusilade of shot and shell was most remarkable, plunging forward as they did, through their own disordered lines, over their own

---

[46] Even those who reached the pinnacle of success engaged in this conception. While Oliver Wendell Holmes, Jr. experienced disenchantment during the war, by 1885 the horrors of battle seemed far removed. He proudly displayed his sword and regiment's banner in his study and in 1895 expressed the sentiment quoted here. Even those who feared that glorifi-cation of the Civil War would make future conflict seem more attractive displayed this train of thought: Clara Barton delivered speeches with "military phraseology . . . in the heroic mold," and William Tecumseh Sherman described war in knightly terms to a veterans' re-union in 1890. Gerald Linderman, *Embattled Courage* (New York: The Free Press, 1987), 280–84.

[47] Ibid., 8, 11–12, 20, 61–64, 147–48.

dead and wounded, with unrelenting strides seeking for victory or death."
He recalled the valor of both sides at that battle, the "bravery even to
confront slaughter at the cannon's mouth; repeated instances of an utter
contempt of death; closeness of contact in bloody battle seldom
equalled. . . ." Sometimes, battle descriptions seem almost as if taken from
the *Iliad*, as men "fell dead and wounded on both sides like grain before
the reaper's sickle," killed by "death-dealing missiles."[48]

In embracing bravery's importance, Daniel sharply censured those
who, in his opinion, failed to display it. When Confederate artillery shelled
the camp at Harrison's Landing the night of July 31, 1862, Macnamara
deemed the cannoneers "poltroons" whose "cowardly style of warfare did
not coincide with vaunted Southern chivalry." Along with many of his
comrades, he criticized sharpshooters as firing at everything, charging,
"Many a brave fellow, wounded at the front, bit the dust from a sharpshooter's cowardly bullet while limping faint and weary to the hospital in
the rear, when he least expected it." Looting and undisciplined behavior
especially angered Macnamara. He denounced "Lee's vandals . . . taking
all they could reach to keep their half clothed bodies warm during the chilly
nights" during the Maryland campaign, and condemned the destruction of
Fredericksburg by the "Goths and vandals" of the Union army.[49]

Nonetheless, while viewing brave charges as glorious, Macnamara realized that conflict could be brutal and sorrowful, that "[w]ar means, if
anything, the slaughter . . . of men, soldiers." While admiring the bravery
of Southern assaults on the Federal lines at Mechanicsville, Daniel also
admitted that "the slaughter they received from the fire of our troops was
deplorable. . . ." And on the night before Antietam, "the rank and file . . .
were deep in slumber, resting their tired bodies on mother earth, dreaming
perchance of home and kindred. It was the last night of life for many
thousands in both armies, for their young and manly forms tomorrow
night would lie dead and scattered over the great field of slaughter in
victory for one side, and defeat for the other."[50]

At times, Daniel's descriptions of the horrors of war could be starkly
realistic, even ghastly. He described the work of surgeons following a battle, how they extracted bullets and amputated limbs, conveying that the
"pyramid of arms and legs that had been lopped off were [*sic*] a gruesome
sight to behold." At Gaines' Mill, Daniel's brother James received a leg
wound and was captured by Confederates. During his captivity, he had to

---

[48] Macnamara, *History of the Ninth*, 42, 123–24, 135, 375.

[49] Ibid., 175, 221–22, 262, 266.

[50] Ibid., 41, 112, 210–11.

The Glorious 9th!

IRISHMEN

To the Rescue!

Irish Americans of Massachusetts!

The indomitable valor and bravery which distinguished your ancestors on many a bloody battle-field in past ages, have descended to you untarnished. Your fellow countrymen of the 9th Massachusetts Regiment have proved at "Hanover Court House," at "Mechanicsville," at "Gaines' Mill," and at "Newtonville," that it has not degenerated. They are worthy inheritors of the courage and prowess of the heroes who fought at "Clontarf," at "Beal-an-ath-Buidhe," at "Limerick," at "Landen," at "Cremona" and "Fontenoy."

The Union and future glory of this great sanctuary of freedom is in danger. A host of Southern traitors seek to destroy our free democratic government, and erect upon its ruins a contemptible and Despotic Aristocracy.

Irish valor and bravery, have, to a great extent, thus far, impeded the march of these native Vandals, and driven back their superior numbers in dismay. Wherever the "chivalry" of the South have dared to encounter, on an open field, our Irish braves, they have found to their cost that Irishmen, as of old, are still invincible.

No Regiment in the service of the United States, has earned more imperishable glory than the 9th Regiment Massachusetts Volunteers, and its late gallant and heroic Colonel. The fortunes of war have thinned its ranks: it must not be allowed to perish for want of brave men to fill up its numbers. The honors it has earned you can share. The living heroes of the 9th are still "eager for the fray." They pant to be led once more against the enemy—the enemy of human freedom—the enemy of mankind. They long to avenge their brave compatriots.

"We swear to revenge them !—no joy shall be tasted,   Our halls shall be mute, and our fields shall be wasted,
The harp shall be silent, the maiden unveil,   Till vengeance is wreaked on the liberticides' head."

They call upon you from the banks of the James to fill up their ranks, to share with them the laurels of the past and the glory of the future. Will you not respond to their call?

"Our green flag flutters o'er us,
The friends we've tried are by our side,
And the foe we hate, before us !"

The City of Boston has voted a

Bounty of $100!

In addition to thirty-eight dollars allowed by the United States, for every volunteer who joins the 9th Regiment, to defend the best and freest government ever vouchsafed to man. In joining the Ninth, you join your own gallant kith and kin. You will be led to the battle-field by officers of your own ancient race, who have proved themselves inferior to no others of our grand army. Here, too, the

FLAG OF IRELAND!

Is carried side by side with the Starry Banner, and Irish bravery will obtain the credit it deserves. The laurels you win will deck your own brows—others will not obtain the credit which belongs to you. And while your prowess and invincible valor shed aditional lustre on

The Stars and Stripes!

They will cast a bright ray of glory on the

GREEN FLAG!

and the unconquerable nationality it represents.

In this Regiment you will have

A CHAPLAIN OF THE OLD FAITH

To minister to your spiritual wants and dispense the priceless blessings of religion.

Your families will be provided for by the BOUNTY OF THE STATE, and you will receive in Pay, Rations and Clothing, an allowance more than that for which many of you toil at laborious drudgery, equally, if not more dangerous, than the field of honor and glory.

The nation provides also a handsome pension for you if disabled, and for your wives and little ones if you fall at the post of duty. What employer, let us ask, does the like?

Our brave countrymen, hitherto, have rushed to the battle-field without bounty, with little hope of reward. Can YOU hesitate NOW, when such ample provision is made for you and yours?

Let the ranks of the glorious 9th be at once manned by heroes, worthy successors of those who have fallen, and fit companions of the veterans still eager for the fight. This Regiment is yours. Its history—its glory—its past—its future, are yours, and shed a lustre not on you only, but on the Irish race. The only power in Europe which supports the South is your ancient enemy, the Government of England.

"Then onward your green banners rearing!   On our side is virtue and Erin,
Go flash every sword to the hilt;   On theirs is the Saxon and guilt."

☞ The Sum of $138,00! ☜

Will be paid to each volunteer as soon as mustered into service. Pay and Rations from enlistment.

Transportation for volunteers, over any of the railroads to Boston, furnished to those wishing to join.

The undersigned has received full power from the City Government of Boston to recruit the ranks of the 9th REGIMENT to its full quota.

☞ All applications for enlistment to be made at the

Headquarters, 112 Washington Street, Boston,

Over Little & Brown's Bookstore, to

Capt. B. S. TREANOR,

OR HIS AUTHORIZED AGENTS.

J. E. Farwell & Co., Steam Job Printers, 37 Congress Street, Boston.

A recruitment poster. (*Massachusetts Historical Society*)

Colonel Cass surrounded by officers and men of the Ninth Massachusetts. (*U.S.A.M.H.I., Carlisle Barracks, Pennsylvania*)

Chaplain Scully, celebrating Mass at Camp Cass, Arlington Heights, Virginia. (*U.S.A.M.H.I., Carlisle Barracks, Pennsylvania*)

Col. Patrick R. Guiney, second commander of the Ninth Massachusetts Volunteer Infantry. (*College of the Holy Cross Rare Books, Special Collections and Archives*)

Men of the Ninth Massachusetts' Cow Bell mess. (*Francis T. Miller's* The Photographic History of the Civil War)

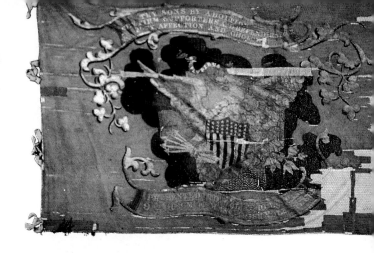

First Irish regimental flag, which saw heavy fighting during the Peninsula campaign.

Second Irish regimental flag.

Third Irish regimental flag, given to the Ninth by Brig. Gen. Thomas F. Meagher.

The Pilot.

"I have sworn obedience to the Republic, and I know no other flag than the Stars and Stripes."—*Archbishop Hughes*.

Boston, Saturday, July 26, 1862.

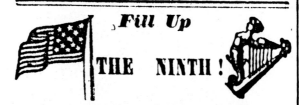

Fill Up **THE NINTH !**

It is an imperative duty upon the Irish residents of Boston to recruit this regiment to its full extent.— It has been reduced by hard fighting to three or four hundred effective men out of ONE THOUSAND. No Regiment from the old Bay State—and no Regiment in the Army—has suffered more than the Ninth.— The scarcely cold body of their late commander(Col. Cass), calls upon them from the grave where he sleeps to fill up the regiment to its full amount. Let the Irishmen of Boston see that it is done. The regiment has earned imperishable renown in the war for the Union. It is glory enough for any man to have inscribed on his tomb—I died a member of the Massachusetts Ninth Irish Regiment.

FILL UP THE NINTH !

Father Scully a Prisoner.

Recruitment advertisement in the Boston *Pilot*.

Sketch of the Ninth's encampment near Yorktown, Virginia, on April 10, 1862, by E. S. Hall.

Guiney with twelve of his officers, dated 1863, Culpepper, Virginia. The officers are identified, from left to right, seated: 1st Lt. Timothy Deasy, Lt. James O'Donnell, 1st Lt. William R. Bourke, 1st Lt. Daniel G. Macnamara, 2nd Lt. William A. Plunkett; standing, Adjt. Michael W. Phalen, Col. Patrick R. Guiney, Surgeon James F. Sullivan, 1st Lt. Bernard F. Finan, 1st Lt. Patrick E. Murphy, Capt. Michael Flynn, Capt. Martin O'Brien, and Capt. Timothy R. Bourke. (*U.S.A.M.H.I., Carlisle Barracks, Pennsylvania*)

Lt. Col. Robert Peard.
(*U.S.A.M.H.I., Carlisle Barracks, Pennsylvania*)

Lt. Col. Patrick T. Hanley.
(*U.S.A.M.H.I., Carlisle Barracks, Pennsylvania*)

Maj. John W. Mahan.
(*U.S.A.M.H.I., Carlisle
Barracks,
Pennsylvania*)

Capt. James W. Mac-
namara and Capt.
Christopher Plunkett.
(*U.S.A.M.H.I., Carlisle
Barracks,
Pennsylvania*)

Chaplain Thomas Scully. (*U.S.A.M.H.I., Carlisle Barracks, Pennsylvania*)

Lt. Michael A. Finnerty, the Ninth's correspondent with the Boston *Pilot*. (*U.S.A.M.H.I., Carlisle Barracks, Pennsylvania*)

Lt. Timothy Deasy, a prominent Fenian following the Civil War. (*U.S.A.M.H.I., Carlisle Barracks, Pennsylvania*)

Capt. Patrick W. Black. (*U.S.A.M.H.I., Carlisle Barracks, Pennsylvania*)

Capt. Michael Scanlan.
(*From the collection of*
John F. McCormack)

Lt. John F. Doherty.
(*U.S.A.M.H.I., Carlisle*
Barracks,
Pennsylvania)

Capt. James F. McGunnigle. (*From the collection of Brian Caputo*)

Capt. Jeremiah O'Neil. (*U.S.A.M.H.I., Carlisle Barracks, Pennsylvania*)

Lt. James O'Neil.
(*U.S.A.M.H.I., Carlisle Barracks, Pennsylvania*)

Drummer boy John J. Benden. (*From the collection of William J. Prince, U.S.A.M.H.I., Carlisle Barracks, Pennsylvania*)

Monument to Colonel Cass at the Boston Public Garden.

Monument to the Ninth Massachusetts on Big Round Top, Gettysburg, Pennsylvania.

pour turpentine into his wound to drive out maggots and combat gangrene, a painful process graphically described in the book. During his account of Fredericksburg, Macnamara movingly depicted a soldier suffering from battle stress, with shaky hands and nervous exclamations at the horror of the dead around him. Daniel recorded that wounded soldiers burned in woods that had caught fire during the Battle of Chancellorsville and that on October 18, 1863, the regiment slept on the old Manassas battlefield among the skulls and skeletons of fallen soldiers.[51]

Perhaps one of the saddest passages in the book is that describing the return of Ninth Massachusetts veterans to their old camp on Miner's Hill, following months of campaigning in Virginia. There, Macnamara and his comrades recalled the former days, when the regiment was full of men anxious for action and unbloodied by the maelstrom of the Seven Days' Battles. Now the men felt the pain, sorrow, and loneliness of those they left behind, and even the desolate campsite itself seemed to ask the question, "Where are the men who lived here? why are they not with you?"[52]

Daniel Macnamara's political opinions diverged from those of most Irish people, although it is important to consider that he wrote more than three decades after the war and time may have influenced the feelings he articulated. In recounting the meeting between Irishmen of the Ninth Massachusetts and slaves at Arlington Mansion, he condemned slavery and movingly expressed how the destiny of these slaves was connected to the Union army, which would deliver the shackled into freedom. "We ourselves felt then that the day of deliverance for the negro slaves of our land was near at hand," and he wrote that the confidence of the men in the ultimate Federal victory "was never shaken" from that time. In describing a review by President Lincoln, Macnamara recalled that "every eye was kindly, lovingly turned towards him. His tall form and silk hat as he sat on horseback were ever in their mind's eye. His face was engraved on their hearts."[53]

Nonetheless, Macnamara shared in the soldier's enthusiasm for the army's former commander, Maj. Gen. George McClellan. He recalled the confidence that pervaded the Army of the Potomac when he rode among the men, and praised his unceasing labors to hone that army into a well-organized, well-trained fighting weapon. Further, he defended McClellan's choice not to pursue Lee's army after Antietam, citing the defeats of Burnside and Hooker and the length of time it took Grant, with "unlim-

[51] Ibid., 119, 140, 260–61, 294, 348–49.
[52] Ibid., 199–201.
[53] Ibid., 45, 284.

ited resources" and "supreme control," to capture Lee's army. He saw, in McClellan's removal, the action of an honest president manipulated by the schemes of intriguing politicians.[54]

With ethnic pride a major theme of the book, it is little surprise that Macnamara openly displayed hostility toward England and support for Fenianism. He recalled a member of the Ninth under fire at Fredericksburg exclaiming, "If it was not for a few ambitious Southerners, who are backed by British interests to destroy our republic, the Union of States would be all right and you and I, and all the rest, would be living in peace with our families and friends around us in the good old State of Massachusetts."[55]

Macnamara saw the Canadian border, "with its English backing," as a haven during the Civil War for those who did not support the Union. A circle of the Fenian Brotherhood formed and met within the Ninth Massachusetts, and following the war, several officers and men participated in activities in Ireland and Canada to support Irish freedom. Yet England, " 'the dark mother of the penal laws,' " wrote Macnamara, "still holds Ireland in her cruel grasp." He further warned that the "United States would, indeed, be recreant to its traditions, history and principles, if at any time it joins Tory England in her covert schemes for conquest, or as the crafty statesmen put it, 'for extending civilization to the benighted people of the earth.' "[56]

The most important and prominent of the Ninth's Fenians was Timothy Deasy (also spelled Dacey), whose story Macnamara included in his regimental history. Deasy attained the rank of first lieutenant in the Ninth and received a wound at the Wilderness. As a Fenian overseas, he led an uprising at Millstreet, County Cork, and was later assigned to oversee activities in Liverpool. At three o'clock in the morning on September 11, 1867, Col. Thomas J. Kelly and Deasy were arrested by the English while loitering on the street after a meeting of Fenian officers in Manchester. Both were brought before a magistrate, and the case was remanded for a week while a rescue attempt was organized. On September 18, the two prisoners were being transferred from the Manchester Court House to the county jail in a police van, handcuffed, separated, and guarded by twelve unarmed police officers. As the van passed under a railway arch, thirty

---

[54] Ibid., 60, 221, 236.

[55] Ibid., 260.

[56] When possible, Macnamara passed remarks demeaning the English. An example comes in recounting a skirmish after Antietam, in which the One hundred-eighteenth Pennsylvania Infantry was armed with "defective Enfield (English) rifles." Ibid., 223, 339, 361–62.

Fenians armed with revolvers stopped it, shot one of its horses, and called for the prisoners' freedom. When this request went unheeded, the small mob shot Sergeant Charles Brett dead inside the van, took his keys, and released Kelly and Deasy. Despite a reward of three hundred pounds for their recapture, the liberated Irishmen escaped to America while three Fenians were executed for Brett's death. In recounting the episode, Macnamara maintained they suffered as martyrs, dying a death "as patriotic as though they fell on the battlefield. Their memory will live forever green in the Irish heart."[57]

Though aspiring to write a perfectly accurate book, Macnamara did not always achieve this goal. The most glaring and inexplicable error in the work comes in his treatment of the Ninth Massachusetts's role at Gettysburg. As the regiment neared Gettysburg with the rest of its brigade on July 2, the Ninth was detached to serve on skirmish duty on Brinkerhoff Ridge northeast of town. When the Irishmen rejoined their brigade later that day, its remaining regiments had already endured the carnage of the Wheatfield. However, Macnamara recorded that the Ninth spent all of July 2 on Big Round Top, engaging in skirmish duty and helping to fend off the attack of Maj. Gen. John Hood's Confederate division. Actually, it was not until the evening of July 2 that the Ninth joined Col. William S. Tilton's brigade and deployed on the northeast side of Big Round Top. With their colors planted on a large boulder in the center of the regimental line, the men took cover behind a breastwork of rocks and engaged in skirmish duty, remaining in this position on July 3 and 4. The official reports of the Ninth's division and brigade commanders confirm this, as does a postwar letter written by Guiney to Joshua Chamberlain describing the actions of the Bay Stater's men that day, Michael Macna-

---

[57] The British arrested twenty-six men for the murder of Brett, and five were convicted on capital charges. Two turned state's evidence, but the other three were executed on November 23, 1867. The next day, the Irish of New York City held a funerary procession for the "Manchester Martyrs." On November 22, 1992, the eve of the 125th anniversary of the execution of the Manchester Martyrs, a Memorial Mass was celebrated for Captain Deasy at St. Mary's Church in Lawrence, Massachusetts, and a monument to him unveiled in the Immaculate Conception Cemetery in that town. Among the participants were Robert J. Bateman, former National Historian of the Ancient Order of Hibernians and Deasy's great-grandnephew, Mayor Raymond Flynn of Boston, and other dignitaries, reenactors, and family members. *Captain Timothy Deasy Patriot-Irish American On the Occasion of the Unveiling of a Memorial*, November 22, 1992. Ricard O'Sullivan Burke, article published in the *Gaelic American*, quoted in John Devoy, *Recollections of an Irish Rebel* (New York: Chas. D. Young Company, 1929), 239–43. Leon O Broin, *Fenian Fever: An Anglo-American Dilemma* (London: Chatto & Windus, 1971), 193–94, 196. Mabel Gregory Walker, *The Fenian Movement* (Colorado Springs: Ralph Myles Publisher, Inc., 1969), 154–55. Macnamara, *History of the Ninth*, 361.

mara's book, and the regimental history of the Thirty-second Massachusetts Infantry.[58]

Personal bias also affected the manner in which Macnamara treated various tensions within the regiment. Some officers were hostile toward Colonel Guiney due to his superior social status and outspoken support for Lincoln and emancipation. These individuals brought him up on various charges and once signed a petition against him. Macnamara chose not to record the issue, either out of friendship to Guiney or a desire to present the Ninth Massachusetts in a more favorable light. Another omitted incident occurred in the fall of 1862, when friends in Boston donated a new Irish flag to the Ninth Massachusetts to replace the original, tattered in the fighting on the Peninsula campaign. When Guiney announced he would send the old color back to Boston, where it would be cherished and preserved, several officers opposed this move and even removed the battle-scarred banner from Colonel Guiney's tent, but the entire affair is absent from Macnamara's book. Yet he did record a controversy in which two officers from the Ninth extended their leaves of absence by claiming medical necessity, depriving other officers of the privilege of a leave upon their return. Petitions were signed by officers of the Ninth to have the "delinquents" brought to justice, and Macnamara condemned their "selfish and ungentlemanly behavior."[59]

Furthermore, Macnamara remembered Colonel Cass's actions toward his brothers and openly displayed his bitterness. He praised Cass as a man of "remarkable soldierly qualities," one whom the "regiment had

---

[58] Originally, the Thirty-second Massachusetts was to be detached for this duty, but its colonel requested it be excused for lack of experience in skirmishing, and the Ninth was dispatched instead. In June, 1885, a granite monument to the Ninth was dedicated off Sykes Avenue on the northern slope of Big Round Top, where the regiment spent the evening of July 2, and July 3 and 4. This was a prime location of the battlefield as compared to the obscure position on Brinkerhoff Ridge. Macnamara, *History of the Ninth*, 319–20. *The War of the Rebellion: A Compilation of the Official Records of the Union and Confederate Armies*, 128 vols. (Washington, D.C.: Government Printing Office, 1880–1901), vol. 27 pt. 1:601–2, 610. Patrick R. Guiney to Joshua Chamberlain, October 26, 1865, quoted in Samito, *Commanding Boston's Irish Ninth*, 201. Macnamara, *Bivouac and Battle*, 195. Francis Parker, *The Story of the Thirty-Second Regiment Massachusetts Infantry* (Boston: C. W. Calkins & Co., 1880), 165–66. Harry W. Pfanz, *Gettysburg: Culp's Hill and Cemetery Hill* (Chapel Hill: The University of North Carolina Press, 1993), 116–17, 154.

[59] Guiney was a lawyer whose outspoken support for Lincoln and the abolition of slavery contradicted the political sentiments of most Irish-Americans. On October 8, 1867, when Guiney wished an increase in his pension due to disability from the wound suffered at the Wilderness, Daniel Macnamara was one of the witnesses who signed the request. For more on the tensions between Guiney and others, see Samito, *Commanding Boston's Irish Ninth*. Patrick R. Guiney Pension Record, National Archives, Washington, D.C. John King to "Friend John," Sharpsburg, October 14, 1862, located in Patrick R. Guiney Military Service Record, National Archives, Washington, D.C. Macnamara, *History of the Ninth*, 277.

full confidence in . . . as a brave and able soldier, and a discreet and trusted commander," although he could be "arbitrary in his manner" and "severe in his decisions and discipline." However, Macnamara criticized the changes in rank that Cass made before the regiment mustered into service. While admitting that "the colonel had the welfare of his regiment at heart," Macnamara claimed the changes had "a lasting ill effect on the regiment," depriving some of their "rightful positions" with a "spirit of unfairness." Later, he harshly judged Cass's activities as "political clap-trap and favoritism." Four commissioned officers left during Cass's tenure but reenlisted upon his death. One was Michael Macnamara who, Daniel remarked in understated fashion, departed after "extended and disagreeable altercations" with Cass. Daniel failed to mention that Cass brought Michael up on charges that led to his court-martial and dismissal.[60]

Whatever its flaws, Daniel Macnamara's book is the standard history of his regiment and a valuable source of information about it. Frank J. Flynn relied extensively on it when writing his *"The Fighting Ninth" for Fifty Years and the Semi-Centennial Celebration*, a much smaller work published in 1911 to review the regiment's history and chronicle a celebration held in Boston to honor the fiftieth anniversary of the mustering in of the Ninth Massachusetts. Flynn's book largely summarized Daniel Macnamara's work, then discussed the regiment's postwar history. Following the Civil War, the Ninth reconstituted itself within the Massachusetts militia, with Guiney serving as the unit's first colonel from May 20, 1866, to April 24, 1868. The various companies were scattered across Boston until April, 1891, when they occupied an armory on East Newton Street as their central meeting place. On May 11, 1898, the Ninth Infantry Massachusetts Volunteer Militia was mustered into the service of the United States for the Spanish-American War, where it lost many men to disease in Cuba.[61]

Daniel Macnamara wrote to commemorate the brave actions of his regiment and emphasize the loyalty Irish-Americans demonstrated to their adopted country in its time of need. Furthermore, he wrote *The History of the Ninth Regiment, Massachusetts Volunteer Infantry* with sensitivity, including the human aspect by describing why Irish-American civilians volunteered for military service and became soldiers for the Union. While

---

[60] Macnamara, *History of the Ninth*, 2, 20, 90, 183, 201, 417, 419. See pages xx–xxi, xxvii of this edition for more on the relations between Colonel Cass and Michael Macnamara.

[61] Flynn's book concluded with a discussion of the parade and celebration held on June 11, 1911, to commemorate the fiftieth anniversary of the Ninth's mustering in and reprinted several speeches delivered at a banquet that day. Frank J. Flynn, *"The Fighting Ninth" for Fifty Years and the Semi-Centennial Celebration* (Boston: n.p., 1911), 49–52.

a granite monument to the "Fighting Ninth" stands on Big Round Top, Macnamara's book serves as a living memorial. Largely forgotten in the literature of the Civil War, it records the deeds and spirit of the Boston Irishmen who fought and died at Gaines' Mill, Malvern Hill, and the Wilderness. While supplying information on the maneuvers and battles of a combat regiment, it also provides insight into what motivated a community of ethnic soldiers to fight for their adopted country, what ideals they valued in leaders and themselves, and how these civilians evolved into a veteran military force. Macnamara's words are those of a man who served three years in the field, lost a brother in battle, and proved his devotion to both Ireland and the United States by word and deed.

CHRISTIAN G. SAMITO

History of the Ninth Regiment.

THE

HISTORY

OF THE

NINTH REGIMENT

MASSACHUSETTS VOLUNTEER INFANTRY

SECOND BRIGADE, FIRST DIVISION, FIFTH ARMY CORPS

ARMY OF THE POTOMAC

———

JUNE, 1861 — JUNE, 1864

By

DANIEL GEORGE MACNAMARA,

First Sergeant, Company E ; Commissary Sergeant, N.C.S. ; Second Lieutenant,
First Lieutenant, Quartermaster,

NINTH MASSACHUSETTS VOLUNTEERS.

———

BOSTON, MASS. :

E. B. STILLINGS & CO., PRINTERS, 55 SUDBURY STREET.

1899.

DEDICATED TO THE

Officers and Soldiers of the Ninth Regiment, Massachusetts Volunteers,

FROM

BOSTON, SALEM, MILFORD, MARLBORO
AND STOUGHTON.

The Ninth Regiment was Recruited in April, 1861.

Organized May 3, 1861.

Mustered Into Service June 11, 1861.

Mustered Out of Service June 21, 1864.

Committee on History, Etc.

We the undersigned, officers and soldiers of the Ninth Regiment Massachusetts Volunteer Infantry, hereby certify that we have reviewed the manuscript history of the Ninth Massachusetts Volunteers, written by Lieut. Daniel G. Macnamara, and testify that the events portrayed coincide with our personal knowledge, and that the work as a whole meets with our approbation.

The roster of the Ninth Regiment, accompanying it, was prepared under our supervision, and is as correct as can be obtained at the Adjutant-General's office, Massachusetts.

(Signed)   PATRICK T. HANLEY,
Lieut.-Colonel and Brevet Colonel.
GEORGE W. DUTTON,
Major.
REV. THOMAS SCULLY,
Chaplain.
TIMOTHY O'LEARY,
Captain.
MARTIN O'BRIEN,
Captain.
PATRICK E. MURPHY,
1st Lieutenant.
JOSEPH MURPHY,
1st Lieutenant.
LAWRENCE CUNNINGHAM,
Co. F.
BARTHOLEMEW KELLEHER,
1st Sergeant, Co. A.
JOHN F. DONOVAN,
Sergeant Co. H.
THOMAS MALLAHAN,
Corporal Co. D.
CORNELIUS J. CARMODY,
Cos. H. and A, Secretary.

Committee on History and Roster,
Ninth Massachusetts Volunteers.

PREFACE.

In writing the history of a three years' regiment of the war of 1861-65, which served in the Army of the Potomac, one is obliged to keep up the connection in the brigade, division, corps and army, to which it was attached, by a thread of narrative which must necessarily permeate the whole army association. To do otherwise would make but a monotonous story of the bare individual life of a regiment. The writer has, therefore, endeavored, in a way, to keep up the army connections of which the Ninth Massachusetts Volunteers was a fractional part. He would, however, crave the indulgence of the officers and soldiers — readers — who have passed through any or all of the scenes depicted, if to their mind's eye, or memory, they differ from their standpoint or knowledge of events; for, be it remembered, no two men ever viewed the same scenes in their experience alike. If a generally correct connection is recognized it is about all that can be asked. The writer feels that too much praise cannot be given to the regiments with which the Ninth was brigaded. The 62d Pennsylvania, to which it was particularly attached by strong ties of friendship; the 4th Michigan, 14th New York, the 32d and 22d Massachusetts, while often mentioned, have not received here the meed of praise they deserve. Where omissions are noticed the reader will lay it to a lack of exact or minute knowledge of events, the fault being with the head and not the heart. To each of these regiments a brave and gallant history attaches, second to none in the service.

The Ninth Massachusetts Volunteers differed from the majority of regiments in several ways. Its officers and soldiers were Catholics; by birth Irish or Irish descent. In the main they were adopted citizens. While professional and business men and master mechanics were represented among its officers, the mechanic and the hardy handed sons of labor composed the great majority of its fighting

material. Very few of its men were on detached duty, so that the
rank and file were always strongly and fully represented throughout
its entire service of active duty in the field.   Its career from the commencement was marked by rigid discipline.   That sturdy old " West
Pointer," Gen. Wm. Tecumseh Sherman, was the first of its brigade
commanders.   He was followed in succession by soldiers from the
same school, Gen. Fitz John Porter, Gen. George W. Morrell and
Gen. Charles Griffin.   In the corps there was a division of regular
army regiments.   Their rigid discipline enhanced the *morale* of the
volunteer regiments of the Fifth corps.

In preparing a book of this nature the writer is deeply impressed
with the great responsibility which he incurs in the undertaking. His
mind is further imbued with the fact that a history — even so small a
thing as the history of a volunteer regiment — should be truthful, unbiased and accurate.   Many years have passed since the close of that
terrible conflict of 1861–65.   In the meantime it has been the writer's
fortune to come in possession of papers, records, etc., that bear on
many of the events through which the Ninth regiment passed.
Although these occurrences are written for publication at this seemingly late day, the reader is reminded that they come from the pen of
one who served during all the term of the Ninth regiment's enlistment
both as a non-commissioned and a commissioned officer; so that the
scenes portrayed are simply pen pictures of a regiment that marched,
bivouacked and battled for three years at the front, in the Army of
the Potomac, during its campaigns in Virginia, Maryland and Pennsylvania.

A book entitled " The Irish Ninth in Bivouac and Battle " was
written on the field during the service of the regiment by the writer's
brother, and a small edition was published in Boston in 1867.   At the
time of writing it, war records were incomplete and unattainable.   It
served a purpose in its day; but it is not a work that is satisfactory to
the survivors, or that renders justice, in statistical and general detail,
to a body of Irish-American Catholic soldiers such as the Ninth Massachusetts Volunteers are entitled to.   That the Ninth regiment has, for
a small body of infantry, a patriotic and a glorious record — from the

earliest days of the war until the backbone of the rebellion was broken
— and one that has been but partially recognized in history, no one
familiar with its brave achievements will deny. Its survivors of the
present day realizing that their regiment's history ought to be fully and
properly written, if only for future reference, have urgently prevailed
upon the writer to undertake the arduous task. Thus urged his wish
will be — when with great diffidence he lays down his pen at the end —
that his earnest and unselfish labor of love for his comrades has done
justice, in all truth, to the patriotic record of the " Gallant Ninth."

It can be said without egotism, that in patriotism, in valor, in love
for the American flag, the Constitution and the Union of the United
States, the Catholic Irish-American soldiers take no second place, and
the survivors stand today in the front rank to uphold, as they did in
war, all the principles of true American citizenship. It is a fact that
every organization of our great army of 2,200,000 men, to a more or
less extent, contained Catholic soldiers. The writer is not confining
his estimates to any one country but he includes all nationalities which
served in the volunteers and regulars, for about all the nations of
Europe and America were represented. Remember likewise, that
whole companies, regiments and brigades were of the Irish nationality
Catholic. They were not confined to the rank and file alone, but were
represented among the generals, and field and line officers of the army.
Catholic chaplains were frequently met with in camp, in hospital, and
on the battlefield. That they always held the love and esteem of the
Union army goes without contradiction.

And what can be said in praise, that will do justice to its fullest
extent, of our Catholic Sisters of Charity? Words of commendation,
however inadequate, are left to the soldiers; to the sick and the
wounded, and to the friends of the dying soldiers, who without regard
to race or religion, received the kind and attentive care of these Christian women. In their ministrations, mark how unobtrusive, gentle
and diligent they were; performing their self-imposed duties by day
and by night, in all kinds of weather; battling, as it were, with all the
hardships and miseries of war. Fortunate indeed, in their sufferings,
were the comrades who received their nursing and attendance. Their

presence alone was a blessing.   Untold thousands of wounded, dying
soldiers, brought in fresh from the battlefields, during our fratricidal
war, were nursed and tended with a mother's care, and the last sad
moments of these young departing soldiers — far away from their
beloved and anxious relatives — were soothed and tenderly watched,
as their brave young lives prematurely ebbed away until their eyes
were closed in death, by these children of God, perchance the only ones
to witness their heroic deaths; and then to write their last parting
words to their loved ones at home.   The end of another quarter of a
century, or so, will have seen the last of the soldiers of the war, who
are daily passing over to the silent majority; then the Catholic ceme-
teries distributed over this broad land can give an approximate number
of that faith who offered their lives and services in defence of the
Republic to the end that the UNION should remain forever indivisible
under one flag, one country, one people, speaking one language.

In closing this preface the writer wishes to say that this book has
been prepared and written at regular times before and after business
hours.   After several years of such labor the time of its completion
has been anxiously looked forward to with the hope that it may be of
some benefit to his country and to humanity.

The reader is requested. not to mistake a statement of facts for a
criticism on the conduct of the war or the action of its army commanders, for the latter intention is far from the writer's mind.

THE AUTHOR.

CONTENTS.

NOTE.

It was the intention of the writer to publish short biographical sketches of the commissioned officers of the Ninth Massachusetts Volunteers, but the difficulty encountered in obtaining proper material for that purpose — there being some seventy-six officers to look after, most of whom are deceased — rendered it next to an impossibility to do so. It was with regret that the writer was obliged to abandon this matter.

THE AUTHOR.

CHAPTER I.

RECRUITING AND ORGANIZING A REGIMENT.

THE COLUMBIAN ARTILLERY — CAPTAIN CASS — COMPANY B, 5TH M.V. M.,
SURRENDERS ITS CHARTER — THE COLUMBIAN ASSOCIATION — OPINIONS
OF SECRET POLITICAL SOCIETIES BY GENERAL GRANT AND PRESIDENT
LINCOLN — MEETING TO RAISE A REGIMENT — FORT SUMTER — 6TH
M.V. M. IN BALTIMORE — RECRUITING IN BOSTON, SALEM, MILFORD,
MARLBORO AND STOUGHTON — CARE OF RECRUITS — FANEUIL HALL
"BARRACKS"— EXAMINATIONS — CAMP AT LONG ISLAND — OFFICERS'
ROSTER — A COMPETITIVE DRILL — SUNDAY IN CAMP — READY FOR
MUSTER-IN — STRENGTH OF A COMPANY AND REGIMENT — RUMORS.

" And thou, my country, write it on thy heart,
Thy sons are those who nobly take thy part;
Who dedicates his manhood at thy shrine,
Wherever born, is born a son of thine."
Rev. Dr. VAN DYKE

" Shall I ask the brave soldier who fights by my side
In the cause of mankind, if our creeds agree?
Shall I give up the friend I have valued and tried,
If he kneel not before the same altar with me?
From the heretic girl of my soul should I fly,
To seek somewhere else a more orthodox kiss?
No, perish the hearts, and the laws that try
Truth, valor, or love, by a standard like this! "
THOS. MOORE.

BEFORE entering directly into the history of the Ninth Regiment,
Massachusetts Volunteers, it is deemed necessary to introduce
the reader to local matters of minor importance which occurred
several years before the breaking out of the rebellion. The object in
doing so is to bring together the connecting links which led up to the
formation of an Irish-American regiment in April, 1861.

Many years previous to the rebellion there existed in the city of
Boston Company B of the 5th regiment (artillery) Massachusetts

Volunteer Militia. This company was more familiarly known as the
"Columbian Artillery," and it dated its organization as far back as
1798. Its armory was situated in the North End, and, in its day, it
was considered one of the finest American companies in the State
militia.

About the year 1850 it grew lax in discipline and suffered from
general financial mismanagement. Many of the young men of the early
Irish families, which had settled in the North End, were then invited to
join the company, which they did, until it was mostly composed of Irish-
Americans of the Catholic faith. The company, with its new membership, had now assumed an active and flourishing existence; in fact, a
new life had taken possession of it. Its members when on parade, in
full dress uniform, wearing tall bearskin hats, were a remarkably fine
looking body of soldiers, and were acknowledged to be — by many
influential citizens — a great credit to the militia. Indeed, many of the
best known and highly respected Irish-American business men of that
day and generation were on its muster-roll; and, as it always proved,
none were more prompt, with full ranks, to respond to the call of the
State than the members of the Columbian Artillery. It was their
highest aim to do their whole duty by obeying and enforcing the laws
of the land, whether as soldiers quelling slave riots; or on parade; or
on the muster-field; or as citizens of the Commonwealth. That they
were faithful in their allegiance, and thoroughly patriotic, was subsequently shown during the war when they laid down their lives in defence
of the flag of their adopted country.

In 1854 the Columbian Artillery had for its commander Capt.
Thomas Cass. He was a man of remarkable soldierly qualities which
were enhanced by a strong sense of discipline. By close attention to
military affairs, hard study and constant drill, he was enabled to pass
through all the grades in the company to that of captain. Under his
direction the "Columbians" had attained a most excellent membership
from "the foreign element," and for a militia company the discipline
and drill was of a high order. The company was in a most prosperous
condition when the following event occurred which drove them out of
existence as a militia company.

Jan. 9, 1855, the message of the new Governor elect of Massachusetts, Henry J. Gardner, was read before both branches of the
legislature in General Court assembled. Paragraph No. 5 of the
address announced the intention of the Governor " to disband all military companies composed of persons of foreign birth." In consequence
of this announcement the Columbians held a meeting with the following
result :—

Jan. 9, 1855.

To His EXCELLENCY, HENRY J. GARDNER,
Commander-in-Chief.

Sir: In consequence of what we consider to be a grievous insult to the members of Company B, Fifth Regiment of Artillery, and others now in the service of your Excellency, in paragraph marked No. 5 of your address to the legislative bodies of Massachusetts, at a meeting held in said company's armory on Tuesday evening the 9th inst., Captain Cass in the chair, sixty members being present, it was unanimously voted to surrender the charter of said company forthwith, and Captain Cass is hereby authorized to inform the Commander-in-Chief of said vote.

(Signed) THOMAS CASS,
Captain Company B, Fifth Regt. of Artillery.

Attested :
HUGH MCCAFFERTY, *Clerk.*

The officers of the company resigned their commissions, and, on the disbandment of the organization, formed it into a civic body under the name of the Columbian Association, for literary and military purposes.

All right-minded Christian people must admit that secret political societies, which from time to time permeate American politics, are a curse to the republic, and are liable at any and all times to lead to riot and bloodshed. But when they are led by such a high official as the Governor of a State, all good citizens must tremble for the results.

In General Grant's memoirs, page 213, Vol. I., he says, among other things : " But all secret, oath-bound political parties are dangerous to any nation, no matter how pure, or how patriotic the motives and principles which first bring them together. No political party can, or ought to, exist when one of its corner-stones is opposition to freedom of thought, and to the right to worship God according to the dictates of one's own conscience, or according to the creed of any religious denomination whatever."

President Lincoln in writing on this subject goes on to say :—

" I am not a Know-Nothing ; that is certain. How could I be? How can any one who abhors the oppression of negroes be in favor of degrading any classes of white people? Our progress in degeneracy appears to me to be pretty rapid. As a nation, we began by declaring that ' all men are created equal.' We now practically read it, ' All men are created equal, except negroes.' When the Know-Nothings get control, it will read, ' All men are created equal, except negroes and foreigners — and Catholics.' When it comes to this, I shall prefer emigrating to some country where they make no pretence of loving liberty — to Russia, for instance, where despotism can be taken pure and without the base alloy of hypocrisy. ABRAHAM LINCOLN."

(Works of Abraham Lincoln, by John G. Nicolay and John Hay, Vol. I., page 218.)

That religious liberty is one of the vital principles on which the perpetuity of republican freedom in the United States rests, is as true as the fact that civil liberty is impossible without it.

During the years which followed, the Columbian Association continued to flourish under the direction of Captain Cass and his subordinates. On the breaking out of the rebellion, and when the militia regiments of Massachusetts were rallying to the support of the U.S. government, a meeting of prominent Irish-American citizens was held in Boston with the view of recruiting a regiment to aid in the suppression of the Southern rebellion. Captain Cass was selected as the colonel for the new Irish-American regiment.

Proper authority having been obtained from Governor Andrew recruiting commenced at the armory of the Columbian Association on Sudbury street. Company A of the new regiment was promptly recruited and organized, and named the Columbian Guards. It was the nucleus around which nine more companies quickly formed and organized into a regiment.

The officers who rallied to the support of Captain Cass in his patriotic efforts to recruit and organize an infantry regiment, were professional and business men of good standing. They were earnest, energetic and patriotic citizens, full of soldierly ardor in their desires to defend the flag of their adopted country, and to preserve intact the union of States.

The news of the firing on Fort Sumter caused a thrill of surprise in every patriotic heart, that language is impossible to describe. Political differences were thrown to the winds, and all loyal citizens united in the cry, " THE UNION MUST AND SHALL BE PRESERVED." Massachusetts hastened the 6th regiment, M.V.M., on to Washington. While hurriedly passing through Baltimore it was fiercely assailed by a secession mob. The firing on both sides resulted in three of the soldiers of the 6th M.V.M. being killed and several slightly wounded, and eleven of the mob being killed and many others of them wounded. This event, following so quickly on the fall of Fort Sumter, caused still greater consternation throughout the country, and more particularly in Massachusetts where the friends of the murdered soldiers lived.

The incentive for recruiting was now redoubled, as all doubts of a peaceful settlement of the secession movement had vanished from the minds of the most credulous. Volunteer companies were rapidly forming throughout the loyal States, and the " Old Bay " State was second to none in its patriotism and in its determined activity. Money was appropriated and contributed to carry on the war with a lavish hand, until $40,000,000 could be counted on from the Union States. Since the first gun was fired on our flag at Fort Sumter it could be said that the cities throughout the North had suddenly become universal recruiting stations. Hardly had the call of the President been issued for 75,000 troops before it was filled, and a hundred thousand more were ready to volunteer.

Everywhere could be seen then the young men, and the middle-aged, ready and anxious to don a uniform and shoulder a musket in order to fight for the " old flag " and the preservation of the Union. Patriotism and love of country was as publicly prominent in the voices and hearts of the Irish-American citizens as it was in the native born. All vied with each other in their feverish haste to volunteer, and go at once to the seat of war, that they might boast in future years how they had a hand in putting down the rebellion; for it was the belief of many, at this time, that the war would be over before they could have a chance to get to the front and go into battle.

In the meantime recruiting for the new Irish-American regiment was rapidly advancing in the city of Boston, which, together with a company, each, from Salem, Milford, Marlboro and Stoughton, would furnish ten companies.

The six companies which were then recruiting in Boston had as a nucleus, besides the Columbians, ex-members of the disbanded Emmet, Shields, Sarsfield and Jackson Guards. Each new company in the city had a separate rendezvous. Recruits were boarded and lodged as near to their company headquarters as accommodations offered. Under charge of non-commissioned officers, they reported each morning for roll-call and drill.

A liberal private fund was subscribed by many of the patriotic citizens of Boston to meet the expenses of raising a regiment. Patrick Donahoe, Esq., publisher of the Boston *Pilot*, was the treasurer, and under his energetic management sufficient money was obtained to carry the regiment along generously until it was mustered into the U.S. volunteer service.

Drilling the new recruits by squads, platoons and companies, took place in armories, vacant halls and stores, such as the localities then offered. These primary exercises were carried on without either guns or uniforms. The enthusiasm of the recruits to learn a soldier's duties supplied all deficiencies in this respect for the time being. Owing to the excitement of the times many of the new recruits were impatient to go into camp and prepare to leave for Washington, D.C., or the seat of war; anywhere, in fact, so as to get out of the city as citizens, and into a soldier's uniform. From these causes of discontent we lost many good men whose desire for active service took them into the navy, and into other regiments already in camp, which were expecting early calls to the front. This state of affairs in our embryo regiment rendered it advisable to rendezvous in camp, or at least, under one roof. In order therefore to put the men under some restraint all the companies were ordered to Faneuil Hall as a temporary barracks. Here it was that, for the first time, our regimental guard-mounting took place, and regular guard duty was instituted.

Nearly all the enlisted men in Faneuil Hall were novices in regimental military affairs. Owing to this lack of experience, during the ceremony of guard mounting, many amusing mistakes occurred; as time wore on, however, this interesting daily event was very creditably performed. The " Officer of the Day " was looked upon as a most important personage; all, in fact, from the colonel to the private, were imbued with the importance of their military duties. The desire to enlist was so great, by the youthful element, that young fellows, who aspired to be soldiers, and who were refused on account of their juvenile appearance, would climb the spout outside of Faneuil Hall, and get in through the window at the risk of falling some twenty feet to the sidewalk. They would then watch for an opportunity to join the ranks of some company in line. As they could not disguise their youthful appearance they were soon discovered and hustled out the door and forbidden to again enter the building. Guards had to be finally stationed at the windows to prevent these incorrigible youngsters from forcing their way into the hall.

It was at this hall that Company H — the Davis Guards of Milford — under the command of Capt. Robert Peard, first joined the regiment. They were dressed in a neat militia uniform of dark green, fully armed and equipped, and made a fine appearance. As the company marched upstairs and into the hall, with fife and drum, it was enthusiastically received, and cheered by all the companies present. First Sergeant Patrick E. Murphy gave at once, on the great floor of the hall, an exhibition drill of Company H. His thorough command of the company, and the manner in which it went through its movements, elicited great praise from all present, and soon established its reputation as a superior body of soldiers. He followed the manœuvres with a well executed drill in the manual of arms. At the close the company was given three rousing cheers by its audience of delighted comrades, who were now more anxious than ever to don a uniform and go into camp.

Our close confinement in Faneuil Hall, at this time of the year, was very irksome and our accommodations were quite unsatisfactory; but, as we were in daily expectation of going into camp at Long Island, Boston Harbor, every one felt disposed to accept the situation of affairs without murmuring. Furthermore it was generally known that the State authorities were likewise anxious to place the regiment in good wholesome quarters. In the meantime, and in order to give the men some good air and exercise, the colonel ordered all the companies to assemble on Boston Common for drill each evening. These outings were productive of great good, both in drill and exercise, and in aiding to keep the men in good health and spirits.

In accordance with the law and regulations of the State regarding the militia, it was required that each company elect its own officers, and that, preliminary to being commissioned, they must appear before a duly appointed Board of Militia Officers for examination as to their qualifications and fitness for military duty. At this time the recruiting and formation of new companies, in various regiments, was so rapid that a large number of line officers were newly elected and awaiting examination. It was a matter of daily occurrence to find them in large numbers in the rotunda of the State House, awaiting to be called before the " Board." Many of these newly elected officers had never served in the militia; and those among them who had seen military service could not boast of it, as their knowledge of tactics was, to say the least, very limited. As for Scott's Manual, most of them had never seen the work. Groups of these aspirants for military glory might have been seen — in the light of the windows — looking intently over each other's shoulders at an " instructor," holding in his hand a piece of paper with a parallel line drawn across its face representing, as it were, a company of soldiers, with certain dots, at intervals, showing the position of the captain and that of the 1st, 2d, 3d and 4th lieutenants — the militia had four lieutenants to a company in those days — and the position of the 1st, 2d, 3d, 4th and 5th sergeants. The " instructor "— always an aspirant for a commission— would point out as requested from time to time, with an unnecessary amount of volubility, the places of each of these company officers. Crammed with this information and more, perhaps, of a like nature in tactics which could be gleaned from militia experts (?), they waited with bated breath to be called up for examination! So great a demand was made on the august " Board " that, at times, all the officers of a company would be called in together. However much, or little, these aspirants for military fame knew of tactics and the strategy of war, none, as far as the knowledge of the writer goes, were rejected. It was probably just as well to allow all to pass, as it was only *pro forma* and perfunctory, for it was found on later experience that men of very inferior ability and education were selected and commissioned who gave neither time, labor nor money, in recruiting and organizing the companies and regiments to which they were attached. Personal and political influence, and other indirect ways, were the principal qualifications that raised, alas! too many incompetents into commission in the volunteer service.

It is food for thought to the reader to know that Gen. Ulysses S. Grant, at the outbreak of the war, offered his services to the Governors of four different States, and they were rejected. When a West Point graduate, a veteran captain of the Mexican war, and a soldier of fifteen years' experience, passed through such trials as he relates in his memoirs before obtaining a colonel's commission in a volunteer regiment, then the meritorious volunteer, without influence of any kind, you may imagine, stood a poor show for proper recognition from those who held political leadership or personal and other influence. Political appointments of officers in the volunteer army (and their name was legion), with their incompetence, neglect of duty and peculations, were no insignificant factors in prolonging the war, and in sacrificing valuable lives in battle.

As the time approached to leave Faneuil Hall for Long Island we had the pleasure of receiving another uniformed company. It marched into the hall, with the martial music of fife and drum, under the command of Capt. Edward Fitzgerald, and hailed from the historic city of Salem. Company F was received with cheers which lasted several minutes. After a short rest the 1st sergeant, Michael W. Phalen, gave an exhibition drill in company movements. All the evolutions were well executed, and received great applause from the young soldier spectators. The manual of arms was well done and brought much praise to the instructor, Sergeant Phalen. This fine appearing uniformed company of young stalwart men from Salem increased the enthusiasm of the others present for camp life and an opportunity for active service in the field.

On the 12th day of May, 1861, tents having been pitched on Long Island for a regiment of ten companies, the battalion was transferred by steamer *Nellie Baker* to that healthy camp in the harbor. The regiment being still in the nominal service of the State, each company was entitled to one captain and four lieutenants. Having passed through the necessary company elections, and the ordeal (?) of examination, all the officers, including the field officers — which were elected by the line — were commissioned by the Governor, May 3, 1861, and the regiment was designated the 13th Massachusetts Volunteer Militia. For the information of the reader the following roster of officers of our thirty-eight days regiment is appended.

OFFICERS' ROSTER OF THE 13TH M.V.M.

Colonel, Thomas Cass.
Lieutenant-Colonel, C. G. Rowell.
Major, Robert Peard.
Surgeon, Dr. P. A. O'Connell.
Chaplain, Rev. Thomas Scully.
Adjutant-Lieutenant, George W. Perkins.
Quartermaster-Lieutenant, Michael Scanlon.

COMPANY A.
Captain, James E. Gallagher.

1st Lieutenant, Frank O'Dowd.   *3d Lieutenant*, John F. Doherty.
2d Lieutenant, Michael F. O'Hara.   *4th Lieutenant*, Patrick Early.

COMPANY B.
Captain, Christopher Plunket.

1st Lieutenant, Patrick T. Hanley.   *3d Lieutenant*, H. J. Sweeney.
2d Lieutenant, John H. Walsh.   *4th Lieutenant*, Timothy Lee.

COMPANY C.
Captain, William Madigan.

1st Lieutenant, John W. Mahan.   *3d Lieutenant*, Patrick W. Black.
2d Lieutenant, Edward McSweeney.   *4th Lieutenant*, John Clancy.

COMPANY D.
Captain, James J. Pendergast.

1st Lieutenant, Archibald Simpson.   *3d Lieutenant*, Nicholas C. Flaherty
2d Lieutenant, John H. Rafferty.   *4th Lieutenant*, William Carr.

COMPANY E.
Captain, Michael H. Macnamara.

1st Lieutenant, James E. McCafferty.   *3d Lieutenant*, Edward Denny.
2d Lieutenant, James W. Macnamara.   *4th Lieutenant*, Daniel G. Macnamara,

COMPANY F.
Captain, Edward Fitzgerald.

1st Lieutenant, Timothy O'Leary.   *3d Lieutenant*, James O'Rourke.
2d Lieutenant, Philip E. Redmond   *4th Lieutenant*, Thomas Fallon.

COMPANY G.

Captain, John Carey.

1st Lieutenant, John M. Tobin
(transferred from Co. H).

2d, 3d and 4th Lieutenants, no record
of election or commissions.

COMPANY H.

Captain, Jeremiah O'Neill.

1st Lieutenant, Timothy K. Roach.   3d Lieutenant, John M. Tobin (trans-
2d Lieutenant, Timothy Burke.   ferred to Co. G).
4th Lieutenant, William H. Armstrong.

COMPANY I.

Captain, Bernard S. Treanor.

1st Lieutenant, Patrick R. Guiney.   3d Lieutenant, Simon S. Rankin.
2d Lieutenant, Richard Nugent.   4th Lieutenant, Michael Flynn.

COMPANY K.

Captain, George W. Dutton.

1st Lieutenant, James E. McGunnigle.   3d Lieutenant, Joseph Ford.
2d Lieutenant, Charles Willey.   4th Lieutenant, John Toomey.

Subsequently the captains, 1st and 2d lieutenants, in most instances, received recompense for their services from May 11 to June 11, 1861. The 3d and 4th lieutenants never received pay, as such, from the State or nation. The writer desires, therefore, as a part payment, to record here to their great credit their gratuitous services to their country; for like all low grade officers they did more than their share of work. On that account they are deserving of this passing remembrance. When the 13th M.V.M. was merged into the Ninth Massachusetts Volunteers, June 11, 1861, the 3d and 4th lieutenants, generally speaking, enlisted as non-commissioned officers.

The transferrence of the regiment from Faneuil Hall to Long Island was, indeed, a great blessing to all parties interested. The freedom of the island, with its green fields, pure salt air and bright sky, infused new life into both officers and men. The camp of wall tents was well laid out, and presented a clean and spacious appearance; and, as it was situated towards the south shore of the island, ample room was given for a fine, grassy parade and drill ground. The close proximity to the city, which was about six miles distant, afforded easy transportation for all necessary supplies, and for the general transaction of business pertaining to the growth and welfare of the regiment. The camp was named " Camp Wightman," in honor of the mayor of Boston. In a short time officers and men were assigned to their respective quarters. Muskets — of the sixty-nine calibre — equipments, overcoats and blankets, were furnished to all the companies.

A picket was established along the shore, and a guard posted around the camp, so that practically, on the first day of our arrival, we began to feel, with some pride, that our real soldiering days had at last commenced. Among the novelties of camp life the reveille impresses the recruit with more or less pleasure. The shrill notes of the fifes, and the martial beat and roll of the drums, as they play in unison at early daylight, strike on the soldier's ear while he sleeps and gradually awakens his senses with music which on the instant seems to him as he listens to be the sweetest he ever heard ; suddenly and without warning it ceases, and very abruptly he is reminded by the 1st sergeant's order to : " Fall in, company." In a few moments he is up and dressed and in line to answer the " roll-call," and begin his labors for the day. Promptness at morning roll-call is one of the recruit's first lessons in discipline. The regiment, among its other good qualities, had a fine corps of drummers and fifers. It now seems to the recollection of the writer that the finest reveilles we ever enjoyed were those played during our encampment on old Long Island.

Company drill, guard mounting, battalion drill and dress parade were the incessant rounds from day to day. It seemed as though no one could get enough of it. The execution of " charge bayonets," by our unusually long battle-line, on the double-quick, with an Irish yell loud and long, was worth going miles to see. As it subsequently proved, no foe in " Dixie's Land " could withstand it, and the writer verily believes that no man of the regiment ever after lost the inspiration which he received at Long Island, whether charging bayonets on the enemy, or elsewhere. Scott's Tactics was, at that time, the authority for all drills. Nearly all of our battalion movements were executed in " double-quick " time. Apparently it became a favorite order with the colonel; and it generally proved to be very warm work, particularly on rising ground. The double-quick movement tried the mettle of the regiment at first very severely, but there was scarcely a murmur against it, unless we except the resignation of one or two officers whose avoirdupois was too great to stand the daily strain on their systems imposed by this hardest of hard drills.

The ambition to become proficient in the manual of arms now characterized the whole regiment, and when one or more experts held a drill in the manual on the parade ground, hundreds would assemble and closely watch every movement in order to get " points." The nearest man to perfection in the manual of arms in the regiment — or anywhere else for that matter — which the writer ever saw at any time, was Lieut. James E. McCafferty of Company E. (This gallant officer, when captain of Company I, was subsequently killed in action at the battle of Gaines' Mill, Va.) His movements with a musket were like clockwork, or, as some put it, like an automaton, and his fancy drill movements were the admiration of all beholders. When a boy he was a "marker" and carried the guidon in the Pulaski Guards of South Boston, and it may be said that he grew to manhood with a musket in his hand. Those were the days of the old smooth bore, sixty-nine calibre, buck and ball, muzzle-loading musket of Mexican war fame. He told the writer that he had always taken great pleasure in going through the manual, and in order to become as perfect in the drill as possible he would stand before a full-length mirror in the armory, with the tactics open for reference, and there practice almost daily for hours in order that every motion should be made according to "Scott." By this hard and constant work for years he became an expert drill-master without an equal.

There was in camp, at this time, Sergeant-Major Teague, and he got it into his head that he could drill with a musket full as well as, if not better than, Lieutenant McCafferty. He announced that feeling in an audible manner to some of our officers. This resulted in a challenge, and in a few days a competitive drill was brought about between the two. On the appointed afternoon for the match the parade ground was alive with a standing audience from the regiment. On this occasion 1st Sergeant P. E. Murphy of Company H was selected by the referee as drill-master. Sergeant-Major Teague opened the ball and the drill-master put him through a very creditable drill in the points selected. He handled his musket with that expertness which is only gained by long practice and study. At the finish the sergeant-major received a generous round of applause. After the plaudits and talk had subsided Lieutenant McCafferty stepped to the front, with a smile of confidence on his face, which, by the way, was adorned with a large black mustache. His slight, yet firm and well-knit form was the perfect picture of a soldier, as he stood with his musket at attention. As the orders fell from the mouth of the drill-master every movement of the lieutenant was simply perfect. The crowd was so still and watchful that one could almost have heard a pin drop. It was a fine exhibition of how correctly a thorough expert could handle a musket. At the close of the final order a deafening shout of applause went up from the spectators, which continued for some minutes. His opponent was among the first to recognize and acknowledge his defeat and he became lost in admiration for the " little lieutenant." The champion thereupon entertained the soldiers with a fancy drill with the musket which emphasized the fact that he was a most expert drill-master. From that hour his championship was never excelled in the regiment. Taken all together it was a pleasant and instructive affair. It inspired, as it were, others to practice, and for many days afterwards individual manual drill was to be seen at seasonable times all over camp. It was remarkable to notice the rapidity with which the men of the regiment acquired proficiency in the manual of arms and in the school of the company during a few weeks' time; particularly when it is remembered that the great majority of them had but little previous training in military tactics. It has been often brought to the writer's attention during his experience, that recruits who are practically new in musket or rifle drill are more easily taught the manual of arms correctly than those who have acquired a smattering of it in an incorrect and occasional manner. This may be explained from the fact that the raw recruit is willing and anxious to learn under a patient instructor, while the partially-taught soldier thinks, or feels, that, in his own conceit, he knows it all, and chafes under instruction and repeated correction. It invariably turns out, in time, that the raw recruit proves to be in every way the best and most obedient soldier; while the former man, in addition to being an indifferent soldier, is generally spoiled for effective service.

As the intricacies of battalion movements began to unfold and become clearer by the aid of books and the daily field instruction of our persevering colonel, the interest of both officers and men deepened and expanded to such an extent that the marked proficiency of the regiment in marching, wheeling and turning, etc., was plain to the most casual observer.

Sunday was a day of rest, with the exception of guard mounting, dress parade and other necessary duties of camp life. A part of the day was devoted to the reception and entertainment of relatives and friends. Their arrival was looked forward to with much pleasure. Fathers, mothers, sisters, brothers, wives, sweethearts and friends, intermingled with their own throughout the regiment during the day. As time wore on each Sunday was deemed to be our last on Long Island, and when the hour arrived in the evening for the departure of our visitors to the city, many affecting farewells took place, as though for the last time. The strong hand-shake, the fervid " good-by," and " God bless you " of the men; and the kiss, the smile and the tear of the women, as if for the final parting, made these departures more

depressing and sad than our young, light-hearted Irish-American soldiers would wish each other to know.   But the feeling was there, disguise it as they would in a measure by laughing and joking and much
assumed mirth; for the time did come, and that shortly, when very
many of our men were to part from dear ones to meet no more on
this earth.

A few weeks after our arrival at Long Island another regiment,
in embryo, came there and encamped to the west of ours, and quite a
little distance over the hill.   It was, in addition to being only partially
recruited, greatly lacking in many ways, so much so that, eventually, it
was disbanded.   At the time of its arrival it was designated the 14th
M.V.M.

Several of the line officers of the Ninth were soon on visiting terms
with the officers of the 14th, and as their calls in that direction took
place at night, it was customary, although against orders, to leave
camp without permission.   By some means they generally obtained
the countersign so that for a short time everything went along smoothly.
These visits became somewhat frequent, and the number indulging in
them gradually increased, so much so that one night the colonel learned
very suddenly that quite a number of his line officers were absent from
camp.   He thereupon changed the countersign, and gave strict orders
to the officer of the day to allow no one to pass the guards into camp
unless he or they gave the new countersign.   Having ascertained the
whereabouts of the absentees, and the direction they would be likely
to take on their return to camp, he, in company with his staff officers,
sauntered forth to quietly watch along the line for the return of the
delinquents in order to arrest and teach them a lesson in discipline.
It was late in the evening when the party started to return from
the camp of the 14th, wholly unconscious of the disagreeable surprise
in store for them.   As they talked quite loud among themselves, as
they walked along, it was very easy to tell the exact direction in which
they were coming.   The guard, knowing that the colonel was near,
was very much on the alert.   With military precision he came to a
charge bayonets — he must have been one of the old Columbians —
and in a loud voice — an unusually loud tone — cried, "Halt!
Who goes there?"   The party were so astonished at such a peremptory and unexpected challenge that they all halted on the instant,
within twenty feet of the sentinel, and ceased talking.   The spokesman,
however, quickly recovered his speech and breath and replied: "Friends
with the countersign!"   The guard promptly ordered: "Advance one
and give the countersign."   Thereupon one of the officers advanced

and gave the old countersign, but the sentinel refused to recognize it. The group of delinquents having by this time recovered from their amazement began to parley with the guard, but he firmly refused to allow them to pass unless they gave the correct password. Suddenly one of the lynx-eyed men in the group descried the colonel in the background, and said to the rest of his comrades in a hoarse undertone: "By Jove! There's the colonel." Colonel Cass heard the exclamation, and finding he was discovered, ordered the guard to allow the party to pass into camp, at the same time saying, as they came over the line: " Gentlemen, you are my prisoners." The officers who had the misfortune to get arrested were quite dumbfounded and crestfallen. All their fun of the evening was turned into semi-serious sadness as they were individually inspected by the colonel with a lantern, which he held up to their faces to ascertain beyond a doubt their identity in the darkness. After enjoying their discomfiture for a while the colonel mildly lectured them on the impropriety of their conduct — absence from camp without leave — and then dismissed them with the warning: " Don't let me catch any of you again out of camp without leave!" These same officers subsequently discovered that the rigidity of discipline in the U.S. Volunteer Service was different in degree from that of the militia; the mildness of it being much in favor of the latter service, and, as they looked back on their tour of duty at old Long Island, they felt that its happy days had fled all too soon.

Three weeks of hard and constant work, spent by Colonel Cass and his subordinate officers in organizing, disciplining and drilling the regiment, brought it into the month of June, 1861. All doubts about being sent to the seat of war had now vanished since the day— May 24, 1861 — that our army had marched over the Potomac river into Virginia and taken possession of Alexandria and of Arlington Heights. The regiment was now looking forward to the day when it would be mustered into the United States Volunteer Service. A new gray uniform was also being made, and new muskets, equipments, knapsacks, haversacks, canteens, etc., were shortly to be issued to the regiment. About this time the regiment on the hill — 14th M.V.M. — having failed to meet the requirements expected of it by the Commonwealth, was disbanded, then and there, by order of the Governor. Many of the men of the 14th on gaining their freedom came into our camp and sought to enlist. Company commanders, on consultation with the colonel, were authorized to weed out, in their judgment, any poor material they had, provided better men could be obtained. So the weeding process was quietly gone through with in nearly every company simply

for their improvement.   In a short time it was accomplished, not without regret, and all the poor disappointed and discharged ones were,
much against their wishes, transported to Boston proper, free to enlist
again if they desired.   It was not long, however, until these discharged
men had all the opportunity to serve their country if they wished.   In
a few days after this event orders were received by the colonel to have
his regiment ready for muster into the United States Volunteer Service
on the morning of June 11, 1861, each company to have a maximum
strength of

1 Captain
1 First Lieutenant
1 Second Lieutenant
1 First Sergeant
4 Sergeants
8 Corporals
2 Musicians
1 Wagoner
82 Privates
———
101 Total strength officers and men.

Maximum strength of regiment :

1 Colonel
1 Lieutenant-Colonel
1 Major
1 Adjutant
1 Quartermaster
1 Chaplain
1 Surgeon
1 Assistant Surgeon
1 Sergeant-Major
1 Quartermaster-Sergeant
1 Commissary Sergeant
1 Hospital Steward
24 Brass Band
1010 Ten Companies
———
1046 Total strength of regiment.

The news of this order for muster into the United States Volunteer Service was hailed with joy by the regiment generally.   Rumors
that radical changes in the officers of some of the companies, and
particularly the fact that the 3d and 4th lieutenants must enlist, or be
dropped altogether, caused much trepidation throughout the regiment.
Many of the 3d and 4th lieutenants finally enlisted as non-commissioned
officers, while others went out of the service of the regiment altogether.

CHAPTER II.

DEPARTURE OF THE NINTH MASSACHUSETTS.

MUSTERED INTO THE U.S. SERVICE — OFFICERS ROSTER — CHANGES IN OFFICERS — ORDERED TO THE STATE HOUSE — GOVERNOR'S ADDRESS — OUR COLOR-BEARERS — ON THE COMMON — REVIEWED BY THE MAYOR — DEPARTURE FROM LONG ISLAND — MEETING THE "QUAKER CITY" — "MASKED BATTERY" AT MATHIAS POINT — POTOMAC RIVER AT NIGHT — MAN OVERBOARD — ARRIVAL AT THE ARSENAL YARD — AT MASS ON SUNDAY — VISIT FROM PRESIDENT LINCOLN — SURGEON PINEO'S LETTER — MARCH TO EMMART'S FARM — WORK IN AN INFANTRY REGIMENT — TWO MEN WOUNDED — VISIT FROM COLONEL CORCORAN OF THE 69TH NEW YORK — ACCIDENT TO COL. P. T. HANLEY, WHEN A LIEUTENANT — THE SKILL OF ASST.-SURGEON P. A. O'CONNELL.

"Swiftly our pleasures glide away,
Our hearts recall the distant day
With many sighs:
The moments that are speeding fast
We heed not, but the past, the past
More highly prize."

LONGFELLOW.

ON Tuesday, June 11, 1861, the sun dawned for the last time on our 13th Regiment M.V.M. It sprung into existence as a militia regiment on the 3d day of May, 1861, and it lived in the history of the Commonwealth long enough to produce a regiment of volunteer infantry over one thousand strong and, as its subsequent history proved, the Ninth Massachusetts Volunteers was as fine a fighting regiment as ever marched in the whole Union army.

Bright and early on that Tuesday morning, after reveille, the men were all astir preparing for muster-in. At the appointed hour of ten o'clock A.M. each company stood under arms in its company street, awaiting its turn to be duly sworn into the United States Volunteer Service. Companies A, B and C, respectively, were duly mustered and sworn in. In Company D there was trouble. The captain and his 1st lieutenant were deposed. New officers, named by the colonel, were on hand to take their places. The rank and file of Company D

2

did not take kindly to the change and at first refused to be mustered. After considerable parleying they submitted to the colonel's choice of officers and were then duly mustered in. In Company E a new captain and a new 2d lieutenant were assigned. The old captain was appointed 1st lieutenant and, as he accepted the reduction in rank without a murmur, the trouble that was brewing in the ranks quickly subsided. The company was then duly mustered in. Companies F, G, H, I and K, respectively, quickly followed in the ceremony of muster-in, and thus the Ninth Regiment Massachusetts Volunteers sprung into existence for three years' service, or during the war. The following is the roster of the first commissioned officers of the

NINTH MASSACHUSETTS VOLUNTEERS.

Colonel, Thomas Cass.
Lieutenant-Colonel, Cromwell G. Rowell.
Major, Robert Peard.
Surgeon, Peter Pineo.
Assistant Surgeon, Patrick A. O'Connell.
Chaplain, Rev. Thomas Scully.
Adjutant, George W. Perkins.
Quartermaster, John Moran.

COMPANY A (Columbian Guards), BOSTON.

[Many of the members of this Company belonged to the old Columbian Artillery, which was established in 1798.]

Captain, James E. Gallagher.
1st Lieutenant, Michael Scanlan.   *2d Lieutenant*, Michael F. O'Hara.

COMPANY B (Otis Guards), BOSTON.

[Named in honor of that patriotic lady, Mrs. Harrison Gray Otis of Boston, Mass.]

Captain, Christopher Plunkett.
1st Lieutenant, Patrick T. Hanley.   *2d Lieutenant*, Patrick Walsh.

COMPANY C (Douglas Guards), BOSTON.

[Named after the Hon. Stephen A. Douglas of Illinois, candidate for President in 1860.]

Captain, William Madigan.
1st Lieutenant, John W. Mahan.   *2d Lieutenant*, Edward McSweeney.

COMPANY D (Meagher Guards), BOSTON.

[Named in honor of Thomas Francis Meagher, the Irish orator and exile, afterward General of the " Irish Brigade," 2d Corps, Army of the Potomac.]

Captain, Patrick R. Guiney.
1st Lieutenant, William W. Doherty.   *2d Lieutenant*, John H. Rafferty.

COMPANY E (Cass Light Guard), BOSTON.

[Named in honor of Colonel Thomas Cass, Commander of the 9th Regiment Mass. Vols.]

Captain, John R. Teague.

1st Lieutenant, Michael H Macnamara.   *2d Lieutenant*, Timothy F. Lee.

COMPANY F (Fitzgerald Guards), SALEM.

[Named in honor of Lord Edward Fitzgerald, the Irish patriot and martyr.]

Captain, Edward Fitzgerald.

1st Lieutenant, Timothy O'Leary.   *2d Lieutenant*, Philip E. Redmond.

COMPANY G (Wolf Tone Guards), MARLBORO.

[Named in honor of Theobald Wolf Tone, the Irish patriot and martyr, and one of the principal founders of the " United Irishmen."]

Captain, John Carey.

1st Lieutenant, John M. Tobin.   *2d Lieutenant*, Archibald Simpson.

COMPANY H (Davis Guards), MILFORD.

[Named in honor of Thomas Osborne Davis, the Irish poet and patriot. Originally organized at Milford in 1858.]

Captain, Jeremiah O'Neil.

1st Lieutenant, Thomas K. Roach.   *2d Lieutenant*, Timothy Burke.

COMPANY I (McClellan Rifles), BOSTON.

[Named in honor of General George B. McClellan, the 2d Commander of the Union Army.]

Captain, James E. McCafferty, Jr.

1st Lieutenant, John H. Walsh.   *2d Lieutenant*, Richard P. Nugent.

COMPANY K (Stoughton Guards), STOUGHTON.

[Named after the town of Stoughton, Mass., where they were recruited.]

Captain, George W. Dutton.

1st Lieutenant, James F. McGunnigle.   *2d Lieutenant*, John C. Willey.

During the muster-in of the Ninth Massachusetts Volunteers, the following changes were made in some of the companies as the roll was called : —

First Lieutenant Frank O'Dowd was deprived of his position in Company A. He afterwards enlisted as color sergeant. Quartermaster Michael Scanlan was appointed 1st lieutenant in O'Dowd's place. John Moran was appointed quartermaster in place of Scanlan. Captain James J. Pendergast was deprived of his position in Company D and left the regiment. First Lieutenant Patrick R. Guiney of Company I was appointed captain of Company D in place of Pendergast. First Lieutenant Archibald Simpson was deprived of his position in Company D and transferred to Company G as its 2d lieutenant. William W.

Doherty was appointed 1st lieutenant in Company D in Simpson's place. Captain Michael H. Macnamara was deprived of his position in Company E and appointed 1st lieutenant in the same company. Sergeant-Major John R. Teague was appointed captain of Company E in place of M. H. Macnamara. First Lieutenant James E. McCafferty of Company E was appointed captain of Company I in place of Bernard S. Treanor, who previously resigned and left the regiment. Second Lieutenant James W. Macnamara was deprived of his position in Company E. He afterwards enlisted as color sergeant. Fourth Lieutenant Timothy F. Lee of Company B was appointed 2d lieutenant in Company E in place of J. W. Macnamara. Patrick Walsh was appointed 2d lieutenant in Company B in place of John H. Walsh, appointed 1st lieutenant in Company I when Patrick R. Guiney was appointed captain in Company D. The officers in the above mentioned list who were deprived of their positions and continued in the regiment, were, in time, again commissioned. For further information consult the roster in the last part of this book.

That the colonel had the welfare of his regiment at heart and believed that in making these changes they were for the best interests of his command, no one who knew him will deny. It can be said in all truth, without any feeling in the matter at this late day, that he realized later that these changes had a lasting ill effect on the regiment. Those who were deprived of their rightful positions felt it keenly and they were shocked at the spirit of unfairness which they never imagined existed until the blow fell on their unsuspecting heads. On the other hand, several of those who were benefited by the changes in their favor, failed to appreciate the kindness; indeed, in several instances, it was repaid with ingratitude. The result was, in a degree, that an indefinable friction was produced and it continued to increase as time sped on and lasted, spasmodically, during the service of the regiment. Experience proved that it would have been better not to have interfered with the results of company officers duly elected. No unbiased mind will deny that one company was as much entitled to its duly elected officers as another. It would have been better for the regiment and for all concerned if this fact had been recognized from the first and acted on accordingly; particularly so when a question of merit or ability was not considered on either hand when the changes were made. These individual differences among officers did not, however, at any period in the service, affect the *morale* of the regiment.

The duty of mustering in the regiment having been duly performed by the United States mustering officer, Captain Marshall, all matters pertaining to the management of the command, although returning somewhat into the groove in which they had been running, were imperceptibly tightened, for in fact a certain amount of extra restraint and discipline seemed to have taken hold of every one in authority. Orders were given in a peremptory tone; less deference and more authority were exhibited toward the enlisted men, so that each and every one in a subordinate position began to feel that the " iron rule of military discipline " was about to be rigidly enforced. The rigidity of discipline could now be noticed and felt when on duty more than at any other time.

On the morning of the 12th of June army rations were issued. After living, as it were, on the fat of the land up to this time, the change to army rations was unexpected and wholly unwelcomed. It was much like substituting husks of corn for milk and honey. After the first dinner there was trouble in the camp. Nearly all the companies were grumbling, not only deep, but loud. All had good appetites and, like Oliver Twist after his first bowl of soup, many were calling for " more "; but, like Oliver Twist, they couldn't get it for the reason that they had eaten their rations. The majority of the men of the regiment lacked experience in this matter of rations, with the exception of an old soldier or sailor here and there, who had seen service in the past and knew what was coming. As these veterans expressed it: " The boys have n't got their regimental bellies on yet; wait a few months and their rations will be more than they will care to eat." The discontent, however, became so great that it soon reached the colonel's ears. He thereupon ordered up all the 1st sergeants and inquired into the matter very thoroughly. Some few of the sergeants who had but little trouble with their men, gave their experience in dealing out rations and the manner in which their company cooks managed the culinary department. From this investigation it was decided to instruct the company cooks to make more soup, even if it was necessary to make it thinner; to slice the meat into smaller pieces and the bread into thinner slices. The coffee, too, was considered too strong and by making it weaker there would be more of it. It was urged that economy could be practised by soaking rations over night, such as beans, rice and other stuff; by this process the food would increase in size if not in weight! When the 1st sergeants returned from the colonel's quarters the men concluded that " something was up," so quiet reigned until the next day. When rations were issued at dinner, the men, after getting their heads together, said there was " quantity, but not quality "; that it was " too thin." No doubt that is how that hackneyed expression originated. However, whether it was " too thin " or not, there seemed to be more general satisfaction in camp regarding rations thenceforward. Of course all the growlers were not hushed nor ever could be, for some men would find fault out of pure " cussedness " until the end of their lives, and many of the poor fellows came to a premature end in the service long before they expected it.

The arrival of new gray uniforms, of good material, muskets, equipments, etc., served to warn us that the day of our departure for the seat of war was drawing near. As most of the men of the regiment had not left camp since their first arrival on Long Island, and as a great demand was being made for passes to the city, the colonel considered it advisable to grant the whole regiment one day's furlough in Boston and vicinity, that they might bid farewell to relatives and friends before their final departure. Most of the men returned to the camp on time and many more did not. After being penned in, as it were, for so long a time — some six weeks — which in the retrospect seemed like so many months, it was hard to blame the delinquents for extending their jollification. Many of them went to their homes a good way out of town. In a few days, however, every man was reported present for duty. There were none sick and the regiment, as a whole, was in fine condition. Preparatory to leaving the State the colonel was ordered to report with his command, in light marching order, at the State House, in order to receive the State flag and be reviewed by the Governor.

Tuesday forenoon, June 25, 1861, the regiment, fully uniformed, armed and equipped, boarded the steamer *Nellie Baker* and shortly after landed at Long Wharf, greeted by an immense crowd of people.

Headed by Gilmore's Band and Mooney's Juvenile Drum Corps and escorted by various Irish societies of Boston, numbering 800 men, the Ninth proceeded to march up State street. The route to the State House, on both sides of the streets and sidewalks, was one mass of people — men, women and children. The reception accorded the regiment all the way was most enthusiastic; it was an ovation of continued cheers and hand-clapping. On reaching the State House, on Beacon street, the crowd was so dense that the men found difficulty in marching through it; line was formed after awhile and the Governor shortly appeared, surrounded by his staff officers, State officials and others.

As the Governor stood on the steps near the sidewalk, holding the flag at rest, he delivered the following speech : —

" *Mr. Commander:* I thank you, and through you, this splendid regiment, which you, sir, have the honor to command, and which the Commonwealth of Massachusetts is proud to register among the first six regiments of its volunteer contingent; for the happy opportunity of a few moments' interview, and for the parting congratulations between us on the eve of your departure for the seat of war.

" The progress of the enlistment of your men and the appointment of the time of your departure, have been the subject of the deepest solicitude. I understand, sir, that, like yourself, a majority, if not nearly all of your command, derive their origin, either by birth or directly by descent, from another country than this.

" As religion makes no distinction in the human family, so the United States of America knows no distinction between its native born citizens and those born in other countries. In one common tide flows the blood of a common humanity inherited by us all, and into our hearts, by the inspiration of the Almighty, has been breathed a common understanding.

" To you and all your soldiers, from all the inhabitants of this land today begins an indebtedness which it will take long to discharge, and by future generations will you be remembered. Inspired, sir, by the purposes of patriotism, you, as adopted citizens, will know no other allegiance than that due to the United States of America, now the mother of us all.

" I now put into your hands, as I have in the hands of regiments that preceded you, the State ensign of this Commonwealth. You already bear with you the Stars and Stripes, but I would have you recognized wherever you go as coming from this State, where you have your homes. When you look on the Stars and Stripes you can remember that you are American citizens; when you look on this venerable ensign you can remember your wives and families in Massachusetts.

" Take this as a pledge of affectionate care from the State of your kindred and homes, and of the sincere and undying interest which its people feel and will ever feel for you. In the utmost confidence in your patriotism and valor we send you forth as citizens of Massachusetts, assured that her honor will never be disgraced by the countrymen of Emmet and O'Connell."

This speech of the Governor was received with great enthusiasm and many cheers.

Colonel Cass replied to it in a brief and feeling manner.

The State flag was received by Color Sergeant Frank O'Dowd, who was flanked on the right by Color Sergeant J. W. Macnamara, bearing the Stars and Stripes, and on the left by Color Sergeant Edward McDonald, carrying the Irish flag. The two latter flags were presented to the regiment the day previous by its friends. They were both made of beautiful silk. On one side of our Irish flag of green was a scroll with the following inscription in letters of gold : —

THY SONS BY ADOPTION ;

THY FIRM SUPPORTERS AND DEFENDERS

FROM

DUTY, AFFECTION AND CHOICE.

In the centre was the American coat of arms, eagle and shield. Beneath it in letters of gold was inscribed : —

PRESENTED TO COLONEL THOMAS CASS,

NINTH REGIMENT MASSACHUSETTS IRISH VOLUNTEERS.

On the reverse side was the Irish harp. Its strings in ground color denoted the " Red, White and Blue," surmounted by thirty-four stars, surrounded by a wreath of shamrocks. Over the harp was the legend : —

As aliens and strangers thou didst us befriend.
As sons and true patriots we do thee defend.

Below the harp were two wolf dogs and the motto :

Gentle when stroked,
Fierce when provoked.

Underneath all was our National motto :

THE UNION MUST AND SHALL BE PRESERVED.

At the close of the State flag presentation the crowd was forced back from the centre of the street. The regiment, led by Gilmore's Band, etc., then proceeded, in column of companies, to march past the reviewing officer, Governor Andrew. Under the inspiring music of the brass band it passed down Beacon street with the full ranks of each company filling the street from curb to curb. It never presented a finer appearance than when it wheeled, company after company, at the Charles street gate, onto the parade ground on Boston Common. Without egotism in saying it, the general appearance and conduct of the Ninth that day was a great credit to their countrymen. After stacking arms the men partook of a bountiful collation. At three o'clock line was formed and the regiment marched in review before

Mayor Wightman, thence continued on the route back to Long Wharf, still followed and surrounded by the immense concourse of friends, admirers and spectators, who cheered lustily from time to time as it marched along. Having safely boarded the *Nellie Baker*, without an accident thus far, the return trip was taken to the old campground on Long Island, there to spend one night more before the final departure on the morrow.

At reveille, Wednesday, June 26, 1861, the Ninth Regiment was all astir with a full realization of the importance of the day. It was now ready to leave Long Island, fully uniformed, armed and equipped, in heavy marching order, in response to the call of the President of May 3, 1861, for volunteers for three years' service, or during the war, to aid by force of arms in putting down the rebellion against the National government and to suppress secession in the South. This was the most serious and most important move that the regiment had yet made since its muster into service. As the morning advanced our friends and relatives began to arrive from the city to say their last farewell. And, indeed, it proved a lasting farewell on this earth to a great many of our brave fellows who still believed that the war would soon cease and that they would, in a measure, enjoy a sort of " picnic " for a few months, after which they were to return home full-fledged heroes, crowned with the laurel wreaths of victory. Underlying these light estimates of the situation, however, there was a deep-seated patriotism and love for the Union. That " the Union must and shall be preserved " meant to them all that that motto implied. The Stars and Stripes must continue to wave for all time over the whole United States, North, South, East and West.

These were the expressed and heartfelt sentiments of our Irish-American volunteers. The subsequent battles in the near future, where they with thousands of others laid down their lives, proved to the country that they were terribly in earnest and fully meant all that they professed.

The hour — 2 o'clock P.M. — for embarking on the transports had arrived. The command, " Forward, march! " was given, and, to the martial music of the drum corps, the regiment crossed the parade ground for the wharf. With much hand-shaking, good-byes and kissing, mingled with unbidden tears, hastily muttered prayers and the waving of handkerchiefs — the hour was too serious for cheers — the companies slowly made their way to the different gangways and marched on board the steamers, which, in a few days, would carry them to the long-looked-for field of action.

The steamer *Ben de Ford* carried the colonel, officers and men, to the number of 664; the steamer *Cambridge* carried the lieutenant-colonel, officers and men, to the number of 204; the steamer *Pembroke* carried the major, officers and men, to the number of 154: a total of 1022 men. Each vessel carried, besides, its complement of army wagons and horses, quartermaster's and commissary's stores, ammunition, medical stores, baggage, etc.

A brass band of twenty-four pieces, under the leadership of Bandmaster Michael O'Connor, was to accompany the regiment, but, as it was not fully organized and equipped at the time of sailing, it was left behind in order to get in readiness. It subsequently joined the regiment in a few weeks in charge of Commissary-Sergeant Patrick W. Black. This increased the regiment to 1046 men, all told.

The three government transports, *Ben de Ford*, *Cambridge* and *Pembroke*, were old-fashioned freighters and, outside of their saloons and cabins, were unfitted for the purpose of transporting so large a number of men for so long a journey. One day was more than long enough to be confined on board of those rolling and pitching vessels. Although the weather was warm and the sea comparatively calm, yet these small boats managed to keep up an unpleasant motion during most of the trip of four days, which brought to many of the men that unpleasant feeling known as sea-sickness.

As the steamers with their living freight sailed into the channel towards Long Island lighthouse, a last sad farewell was given by many a one to our camp of deserted tents, still in view, that would know us no more forever. Guard-mounting in a modified form was held on the deck of the *Ben de Ford*, and as much military discipline as the nature of the surroundings would allow was likewise kept up. The writer being at that time 1st sergeant of Company E, soon learned that that non-commissioned officer was a very important personage. The "First Sergeant's Call" was quite a familiar one during the voyage, so much so that the sergeant-major had a drummer at his elbow at all times for the sole purpose of issuing and repeating many very trivial orders. All the business of the companies seemed to have shifted from the commissioned officers of companies onto the shoulders of the 1st sergeants. The sergeant-major appeared to have assumed, in a measure, control of the colonel's and adjutant's prerogatives; an assumption that he wielded with all the serio-comic dignity of a martinet, such as can be found only in a foreign army. In hunting up their men, as the nature of the situation obliged them to do, the 1st sergeants soon became familiar with every hole and corner of the dark and dirty interior of the ribbed-bound steamer on which we were doomed to live and perform a soldier's duty for nearly four consecutive days. During a constant service of three years it is safe to say that nothing transpired in the way of duty to equal, in the same space of time, the disagreeable effects of that never-to-be-forgotten voyage to Washington. It is a great mistake, not to say blunder, to transport troops by sea when the facilities are at hand to carry them overland or on the march. On land the men are healthier, fresher, cleaner and better in every way; while by sea the reverse of this situation is the result. Our voyage for the first two days was otherwise uneventful, as we steamed on our way along the coast and up the Chesapeake. The weather continued pleasant and naturally grew warmer as we went south. Many of our men were so uncomfortable in the hold of the vessel that they were allowed to rest and sleep on deck and in out of the way places, where they could get the air; even the boats which hung in the davits were utilized as bunks. All covering appeared to be superfluous.

After we entered the Potomac river on the evening of the 28th of June we were hailed by a large steamer which towered far above our little craft. It was said to be the *Quaker City*. As our boat slowed up the commander of this armed vessel cautioned the colonel of the Ninth to be on the lookout on the next day as he was passing Mathias Point, for it was reported that the enemy had taken possession of that place on the 27th instant and very likely had planted a masked battery there. That if such were the facts we would be fired upon and, perhaps, receive a warm reception. This information created a breeze of excitement. Buck and ball cartridges were at once issued and every man ordered to load his musket and hold himself ready for action at a moment's notice. If attacked, Colonel Cass intended to make a landing and assume the aggressive. Each of the transports carried one small cannon. Ours was also loaded for action.

At daylight every eye was turned to the south bank of the Potomac, trying to discern the exact location of Mathias Point on the Virginia shore. The captain of our transport, who was familiar with the river, pointed the place out to the colonel. It was quite a distance ahead of us and situated at a prominent bend in the stream. The soldiers were now all ordered to go below out of sight and await orders. Everything was perfectly quiet on board as we steamed over the placid waters of the broad Potomac. No sign of life was apparent on either bank nor in the woods and fields that skirted the shore. As we drew nearer the point of land which was supposed to conceal the enemy, not a sound was heard nor a sign of life to be seen there. If the Confederates intended to open fire on our boat there would never be a better opportunity, for we were then directly in range of the " masked battery." As we passed the point every one began to breathe freer and to talk louder. The men were then allowed on deck and the suppressed excitement of the day died away. Not having been fired upon we concluded that the much-talked-of battery had not been put in position.

It was subsequently learned that there was good ground for our supposed danger. On the 27th of June the *Thomas Freeborn*, a small side-wheel steamer, made an attack on Mathias Point, where a considerable force of Confederates were picketted, although no batteries had as yet been erected. In this attack Commander James H. Ward was assisted by two boats from the *Pawnee*, under Lieutenant Chaplin. A landing was effected by the party led by Commander Ward in person, and after some skirmishing the Confederate picket was driven in; but upon the approach of the main body of the enemy a retreat was ordered to the boats. Commander Ward was mortally wounded and four men seriously wounded. Immediately after this affair the Confederates constructed a formidable battery at that point.

Brigadier-General Holmes of the Confederate army had that very day — June 27 — called on his government for two 32-pounder rifled cannon, to use at Mathias Point on the river. Had the place been fortified with this heavy ordnance by the enemy, who at that time might have easily held it, much damage might have been done to our transports, going so far, even, as to sink one or all of them. As it was, the place was held by the enemy, but we sailed along without any further excitement.

The night of the 28th had closed upon us very warm and still. The dark banks along the river were visible only by their intense blackness against the horizon. The firmament was cloudless to the eye and beautiful in its greatness, with its myriads of bright, twinkling stars. No unusual sounds disturbed the stillness of the midnight hour. Nothing could be heard, except the semi-muffled noise of the steamer's machinery in its regular motions and the gurgle and ripple of the dark water of the Potomac as it lightly dashed from the bows along her sides. Suddenly the stillness was broken by a loud splash in the water, as if some heavy body had dropped into the river, accompanied by a human cry of despair. Those on deck who were awakened by the startling shriek — or already awake — rushed to the side of the boat from whence the sound proceeded, but nothing could be seen or heard of any one in the river; only the recollection of that heavy splash and the cry of distress was left to tell us that some one of our men had fallen overboard to his death. Evidently our unfortunate comrade was no swimmer, for he failed to come to the surface. Many watched and listened intently for the least sign of a man in the water, in instant readiness with the boat to rescue him from a watery grave, but he had sunk to rise no more.

On inquiry among the sleepers just awakened, it was at that time of night pretty well established that the unfortunate man was one of the comrades in a boat which hung in the davits on the port side. He slept near the gunwale on the outside and very likely arose in his sleep and rolled over, or lost his balance and fell out. His name was Owen W. Garland of Company E. At roll-call the next morning a thorough search was made throughout the vessel until it was conclusively settled that he was the victim of the unfortunate accident. The writer knew him well, having enlisted him. He was a young man from Lowell about nineteen years of age, pleasant and quiet in manner, with a full smooth face, fair complexion and medium height. The comrades of the regiment and in his company particularly, expressed deep sympathy at his untimely end.

The day following this accident was Saturday, June 29, 1861, the last day of the voyage. Much pleasure was manifested when the city of Washington appeared in the distance. Late in the afternoon all on board were prepared to land; and the reader may feel assured that the rank and file were highly pleased as the last hour on board the *Ben de Ford* and on the other vessels approached. The officers on board had, comparatively speaking, a good passage. They occupied the staterooms in the saloon of the boat and sat down to regular meals at the table, so that the poor quarters and rations of the men were something that they did not have to put up with. By sundown we were alongside of the wharf in the United States Arsenal yard, and marching off the vessels.

The whole regiment bivouacked in the Arsenal yard and on the wharf that night. After a sound and refreshing sleep on Southern soil, for the first time in our soldier lives, we were awakened by the sounds of the reveille; at least many of us were, for we soon perceived that a majority of our regiment had disappeared. Even the colonel for a moment was at a loss to account for the absence of so many men. He was soon informed, however, that very early in the morning our reverend chaplain, Father Scully, had marched off with them to attend early mass, if they could find a Catholic church near at hand in Washington city. We were satisfied that they succeeded in their pious endeavor, for it was an hour or more before they returned to camp to tell of their pilgrimage.

After the regiment had partaken of its frugal breakfast of coffee and hardtack, and was slowly preparing to leave the Arsenal grounds, President Lincoln appeared and cordially greeted the colonel and his regiment. The following letter received by the writer a few years ago from our first surgeon will, no doubt, give the reader a good idea of the President's call on us.

WEST SOMERVILLE, MASS., July 13, 1891.
MY DEAR MACNAMARA:
    A notice of the reunion of the Old Ninth is received, and it would be a great pleasure to be able to be with you; but illness forbids. It is more than thirty years since we sailed from Boston Harbor and landed at Washington, when Abraham Lincoln, of blessed memory, came down to the wharf to meet us and welcome us, and tell us his joy at our presence, and said pleasant words to us. I can see him now with his cheerful voice and manner. As the years go by we learn to love him more and more; and the brave comrades of the years following — both the living and the dead — are nearer to us as the time passes. I would send affectionate greetings to each and every one of the old regiment that made for itself a glorious history.
                    Sincerely yours,
                        PETER PINEO,
                        Formerly Surgeon 9th Mass. Vols.

Doctor Pineo went out with the Ninth regiment as its surgeon. In a few months' time he was promoted respectively brigade, division and corps surgeon, and finally lieutenant-colonel and medical inspector of the army. He was a gentleman of fine appearance, address and education, and, during the short time that he remained with the Ninth, won the esteem and life-long friendship of both officers and men. Duing his lifetime he took great pride in claiming membership in the regiment and in attending, when his health would permit, its annual reunions in later years. He died in Somerville, Mass., Sept. 10, 1891, aged sixty-seven years.

The colonel having received orders to go into camp on Emmart's farm, at once marched his regiment for that place. It was some miles out in the suburbs in the direction of Seventh street. While on the way a heavy southern shower came up, which in a short time drenched every one to the skin. On the route through the muddy and, at that time, filthy streets of Washington, there was scarcely a person to be seen. It appeared to us then as though the city was deserted; but we learned subsequently that the secession spirit was so strong among the southern natives that they actually detested the sight of Union troops. They were puzzled and appalled at the constant arrival of such a large number of " Yankee " regiments " invading " southern soil. To show their contempt for us generally they made it a point to keep out of sight as much as possible. We soon arrived at our destination and found that we were to occupy a camp in which the tents were already pitched. It had been previously occupied by a regiment which had lately moved and camped on the other side of the Potomac river. Our new quarters were on elevated ground and well covered by large shady trees. Everything appeared perfectly clean and wholesome; and the recent heavy shower, which had subsided on our arrival, added to its bright appearance. Several regiments from other States were encamped in our vicinity, so that we were not affected by any lonesome feelings such as new troops in a strange place might be expected to feel. The arrival at a fixed camp, on the contrary, after a four days' sea voyage, seemed to have a particularly lively effect on the regiment, generally, after breaking ranks.

A breach of discipline was exhibited by a frequent discharge of muskets that had been loaded since our affair at Mathias Point. One man started the racket by an accidental discharge of his piece in the air. Others joined in until the random firing, from the right wing to the left, became quite lively and exhilarating. The colonel sent his mounted officers through the camp to stop the firing and preserve order. After much galloping to and fro, and shouting orders to " Cease firing! " the horsemen succeeded in restoring order, but not until nearly every man had emptied his charge of buck and ball. The fact of the matter was, the regiment knew that the first thing in order would be an inspection, and before cleaning their muskets they would have to draw the charges, so they were only too quick to take the hint and fire them off as the easiest and quickest way out of it. There was no other reason for this inadvertent breach of discipline. On the following day, however, an extra hour was added to the battalion drill as punishment and a reminder that the colonel intended to maintain proper discipline in the regiment at all times.

The main line of work in an infantry regiment devolves on the colonel, the adjutant, the sergeant-major and the 1st sergeants of the companies. The orders, standing and otherwise, of the colonel, are enough to keep these officers busy from early morning till night. The rest of the regiment are the auxiliaries which are moved in detail by the former. The adjutant or his sergeant-major starts the drum corps to beat reveille. The 1st sergeants begin the day with the familiar order of " Fall in, Company, for roll-call." Shortly after that is " Surgeon's Call "; then the sick, in charge of the 1st sergeants, call on the doctor for treatment. The captain and his 1st sergeant make out the morning report, which accounts for the whereabouts of every man. It is imperative that this duty be accurate and sent to the adjutant's office at an appointed hour in the morning. Regimental reports are transmitted and consolidated by the various assistant adjutant-generals, until they reach army headquarters and finally the war office, Washington. It was thus that every man in our large army was accounted for daily when practical. In the meantime breakfast is disposed of. Either before or after the frugal matutinal meal, company drill and fatigue duty takes place. The whole camp must be cleaned and swept daily, wood must be furnished for cooking purposes; guard mounting and picket details must be attended to. After that a morning parade " To the colors " is held, or, instead, company or battalion drill, or both, takes place. We sometimes had all three. Dinner at noon is followed, perhaps, by more fatigue duty. In the afternoon company and battalion drills take place. The day closes with dress parade. In time of war no man knows what the night may bring forth to arouse one from slumber. In the meantime the adjutant is having any number of " First Sergeants' Calls," to deliver orders and instructions to them. The company books must be kept; clothing, etc., and rations must be looked after and supplied, with other minor details too numerous to mention. Fortunate is the company in time of war which has a 1st sergeant who is a thoroughly competent officer. It can get along fairly well without its captain or its lieutenants, but it cannot get on at all without the watchful care of the 1st sergeant. He is the foster-father of the men of his company; he knows their strong points and their weak ones; he knows when they are sick and when they are shamming; he is their confidant in all their troubles, both in camp and at home; although necessarily severe at times, from the nature of his office, he never loses their respect, friendship and obedience. To maintain proper discipline he divides his company into four permanent sections, and places one sergeant and two corporals in charge of each section. Each sergeant divides his section into two divisions and places a corporal in charge of each. In this manner, through his non-commissioned officers, the 1st sergeant can keep the run of all his men. His discipline must be regular, strict, and, above all, impartial in all his calls for duty; otherwise the multifarious duties that devolve upon him would, in a short time, lead to a partial demoralization in his company and cause him no end of worry and annoyance.

The daily routine of camp duty, drills, guard and picket, kept the regiment busy. The weather was exceedingly hot during the day. A cotton hood, called a havelock, was issued to each man to keep the sun from burning him. It went on over the head and neck, but it proved to be a very uncomfortable piece of head gear and, after wearing it once or twice on battalion drill, it was ever after discarded.

A ripple of excitement was created one forenoon, at this camp, at company drill. Two men, named, respectively, Edward Collins and James Malcolm of Company E, were shot; one in the leg and the other in the shoulder. No report of firearms was heard. It was declared that the shots came from the forests that stood off in the distance. The news of the shooting coming to the colonel's notice, he ordered a couple of companies to scour the woods for the enemy (?) After an exciting chase they returned to camp and reported no enemy in sight, but had discovered a detachment from a New York regiment out there target shooting. Conclusions were at last arrived at that the bullets which hit our men came from this party; the fact that the enemy had no footing on this side of the river added to that decision.

A short time after our arrival at this camp we received an informal visit from Col. Michael Corcoran, commanding the 69th New York National Guard — an Irish-American regiment from New York city — in the three months' service, then doing duty at Arlington, Va., where they were engaged in building the famous fort afterwards known in the service as Fort Corcoran. He and his regiment were already quite famous among the Irish-Americans of the country on account of their refusal to parade in New York City in honor of the Prince of Wales, who was at that time — 1860 — on a travelling tour through the principal cities of the United States. Colonel Corcoran was at that time placed in military arrest for that act of insubordination, but on the breaking out of the rebellion the charges were quashed and he was honorably released from arrest and sent with his gallant regiment to the city of Washington on the first call for troops.

His appearance in our camp created much interest amongst us as he passed down the line of company streets, from the right wing to the left, and back to Colonel Cass' headquarters. We were sorry to hear subsequently that he was taken prisoner at Bull Run, where his brave regiment under his command did some hard fighting. The enemy held him in reprisal for nearly a year. On being exchanged he was promoted a brigadier-general, his commission to date from the day of his capture, July 21, 1861. He afterwards organized a brigade known as the " Corcoran Legion." On Dec. 22, 1863, he was thrown from his horse and fatally injured near Fairfax Court House, Va. He was born in Ireland; at the age of twenty-two he emigrated to New York and became one of its prominent citizens. At the time of his accidental death he was thirty-six years of age. By his untimely death the country lost a gallant general who was greatly lamented by all who knew him.

While on regimental drill one day at this camp, an accident of a serious nature befell Colonel Hanley, who was at that time the first lieutenant of Company B. In changing direction at double quick time, Company B was obliged to jump a ditch in their front. When the colonel made the jump he held his scabbard — the sword still remaining in its sheath — in his left hand. By the motion of his hand in going over the ditch the sword leaped from its scabbard and struck the opposite bank of the ditch hilt first. As the colonel alighted on the ground he received the sharp point of the blade in his left leg, just above the knee, on the inside, passing through the flesh diagonally to the depth of seven inches ; the point protruded on the opposite side. He instantly caught the weapon in his right hand and pulled it forth ; in doing so he unintentionally twisted the blade and thus the wound became still more dangerous. It is hardly necessary to say that he was laid up quite a while from this accident, but was most fortunate in having the constant attendance of Assistant Surgeon P. A. O'Connell of the regiment, whose great skill and care brought his patient around again all right. The surgeon afterwards told Colonel Hanley that he greatly feared that his leg would have stiffened at the knee and rendered him a cripple for life. But, thanks to the skill and care of the doctor, the colonel recovered the full use of his wounded leg, which, in after years, enabled him to render brave and valuable service to his regiment and country.

CHAPTER III.

THE FIRST BATTLE OF BULL RUN.

THE CRY "ON TO RICHMOND"— PREPARING FOR THE CONFLICT— THE
FIRST BATTLE OF BULL RUN — THE NEWS OF DEFEAT — PROMINENT
OFFICERS ENGAGED — CONFEDERATE GENERAL JOHNSTON'S FORCES
ARRIVE — THE TURNING POINT IN THE BATTLE — THE PANIC IN THE
REAR — THE RETREATING TROOPS IN WASHINGTON — CASUALTIES ON
BOTH SIDES — THE NINTH MASS. VOLS. RECEIVES MARCHING ORDERS
— ARRIVAL ON THE "SACRED SOIL" OF VIRGINIA — RECEPTION OF
THE NINTH — GEN. ROBERT E. LEE'S PLANTATION AND SLAVES —
CLEARING GROUND FOR A CAMP AT ARLINGTON — LIFE ON THE PICKET
LINE — COLONEL CASS AND THE SERGEANT — ARMY ON THE INCREASE
— FELLING TREES — THE NINTH BUILDS A FORT — FORT CASS.

" Careless seems the great Avenger; history's pages but record
One death-grapple in the darkness 'twixt old systems and the Word;
Truth forever on the scaffold, Wrong forever on the throne,—
Yet that scaffold sways the future, and, behind the dim unknown,
Standeth God within the shadow, keeping watch above His own."
JAMES R. LOWELL

A FTER the first two weeks' encampment at Emmart's farm it was
noticed from day to day that the troops in our vicinity began to
move away, so much so that up to the 18th day of July every regiment around us had gone over Long Bridge or Aqueduct Bridge to
the other side of the Potomac, until an army of 35,000 men, of all
arms, was under command of General McDowell, whose army headquarters had been established at Centreville.

The blue U.S. army uniform had not, as yet, been issued to
volunteers, and these troops had left home in their old militia uniforms
of various patterns, or in those furnished them by their States. One
or two of the New York organizations appeared in the gaudy Zouave
dress. In fact, our own regiment wore a handsome gray uniform at
that time. So that our new army, so hurriedly brought together at

Bull Run, was notable for its varieties in uniforms and guns, and in its lack of trained organization.

Since the day that the Union forces were thrown onto the south side of the Potomac river and placed under the command of General McDowell, the enthusiasm throughout the North continued to increase; and the war cry, " On to Richmond," from millions of non-combatants, was resounding through the land. This public cry for action at the seat of war became in time, as it were, irresistible. This unreasonable demand for war was the topic of all conversation everywhere. The old war veteran General Scott was wholly opposed to any active operations against the enemy with an unorganized army of three months' men, " raw soldiers," as they were called, whose terms of service had already nearly expired. But public sentiment, it seems, was not to be gainsaid.

The Southern army had concentrated on the south side of that insignificant stream known as Bull Run, under the command of General Beauregard, whose headquarters were at Manassas. His united forces numbered some 32,000 men. After five days' manœuvring and skirmishing on both sides the battle of Bull Run commenced, and terminated in partial defeat and disastrous rout to some of the Union troops. The advantage gained by the enemy proved to be of doubtful import. Indeed, it may properly be designated a drawn battle.

On the afternoon of Saturday, July 20, 1861, the Ninth Massachusetts received orders to be in readiness to move at a moment's notice. Three days' rations, ammunition to make up forty rounds, and new canteens, were issued. As night set in the regiment was on the march towards the Potomac; but before reaching Long Bridge the order was countermanded and we returned at once to our old camp. On our arrival the colonel formed his regiment into square and in a short speech thanked his officers and men for their promptness and other good qualities. We were now held as a part of the reserve force in and around Washington which did not participate in the battle of the following day, July 21, 1861.

On Sunday, as the battle was in progress, we could hear in our camp the firing of the distant artillery. The faintness of the sounds only added to our anxiety and restlessness. That whole day we were consumed, so to speak, with longing desires for definite news from the front. Rumors of victory were rife in the early part of the day, only to be contradicted later by the doubtful news of defeat; but all the time nothing definite reached us. As night came we clung to the hope that our army had been successful. The fact that we had not again been called upon to march to the front led us to believe that our first great battle had been fought and won. We were elated at the thoughts of a great victory for our arms. But to our minds our pleasure was marred as we remembered that we had no share in the fight. We wondered somewhat why it was that we were obliged to remain inactive when so many of our comrades were battling for the Union. The morning of the 22d of July dawned upon us when the startling news of defeat was heard all around camp. Many of the disorganized troops in our immediate vicinity had returned to their old camps to tell the sad tale and how their regiments " had been all cut up (?)."

It is hardly necessary here to enter into the many details that belong to the history of the first battle of Bull Run. That the advanced movements of the Union army towards the plains of Bull Run and Manassas, which culminated in the desperate and desultory fighting of Sunday, the 21st of July, were undertaken and carried out with the utmost bravery by *those engaged*, cannot be denied. The persistent courage displayed in that battle by many of the infantry and artillery organizations *at the front* was of such a character as to challenge the admiration of the subordinate commanders under whose eyes and directions it took place. That the latter were competent to judge of the situation it is only necessary to mention the names of some of those officers who afterwards held prominent positions in the army : Gen. W. T. Sherman, Generals Fitz John Porter, Heintzelman, Burnside, Hunter, and others. On the Southern side under General Beauregard were Generals Thomas E. Jackson (Stonewall), Longstreet, Ewell, J. E. B. Stuart, etc , and Gen. Joseph E. Johnston, who reinforced General Beauregard with his army in the afternoon and became the ranking general.

It was subsequently learned that at Bull Run thousands of slaves were employed by the Southerners in the construction of earthworks, as teamsters, as cooks for the army, as laborers in the quartermaster's, commissary's and ordnance departments. In a word, all the Southern whites were to do the fighting and all the Southern blacks to do the drudgery. It will be seen that this state of affairs virtually added at least a million of black men to the army of the Confederacy. On the other hand similar labor in the Union army was performed by its own soldiers, thus materially decreasing our fighting ·forces in many ways. Hard work was added to hard fighting.

General Beauregard's line of battle extended eight or nine miles, beginning on his right at Union Mills and covering the country on his

left as far as Stone Bridge. His plan of battle was to defend his
selected and fortified positions from assault. General McDowell
having assigned his divisions in accordance with his plan of attack,
moved forward at 2 o'clock Sunday morning and crossed Bull Run at
several points at an early hour, with 18,000 troops. Most of the three
months' regiments' terms of service had nearly expired, in fact, that
very day, and the day before several regiments from different States
left the field for their homes; although urgently requested by the War
Department to remain until the battle was decided, they positively
refused because their time was up. The enemy, as before stated,
fought on the defensive and were strongly protected by earthworks,
forests and some few houses that were scattered here and there on the
field. The Union troops were principally in the open country during
their assaults on the enemy's position. From half past ten A.M. until
half past three P.M. the battle continued with varying success in our
favor. After that time — 3 o'clock — it was undoubtedly in favor of
the Southern forces, owing to the fact that large reinforcements had
arrived on the field under command of Gen. Joe Johnston. This was
the turning point. The report that the enemy had a fresh army in the
field spread like wildfire to the rear of the Union lines and started
the panic. Every living thing in the rear began to move towards the
Potomac river at once. Hundreds of vehicles containing politicians,
officials and spectators, became panic stricken and, in their mad,
foolish haste to reach the city of Washington, mixed in with army
wagons, artillery and thousands of soldiers; the latter so inextricably
intermingled and demoralized that all organization was lost among
them. The roads and by-ways were blocked and the fields were
covered with moving masses. Hundreds of excited mounted men of
every description drove hither and thither in their endeavors to cover
ground to the rear and thus assisted in making the demoralization
complete. Repeated floating rumors of an advancing enemy tended
from time to time to wedge the fleeing crowds into an immovable mass
of excited humanity. In time the roads became freer and the vehicles
containing the non-combatants did not spare their horse-flesh when the
opportunity offered to seek safety in flight.

Our forces at the front having ceased to be the aggressors, were
in the meantime falling back behind Bull Run. The enemy's cavalry
made several ineffectual attacks on some of our retreating infantry, but
was handsomely repulsed and soon ceased to appear. A strong rear
guard was established in which the regular army regiments formed a
prominent part. At sunset the excitement occasioned by the retreat

had died away. That evening General McDowell abandoned his headquarters at Centreville. Most of the army returned to their old camps and bivouacked for the night, while thousands of stragglers remained on the south side of the Potomac until daylight next morning. The following short extract from General Sherman's official report of the operations of his brigade at Bull Run will be of interest to the reader.

* * * * * * * * * * *

" But about 9 o'clock at night I received from General Tyler, in person, the order to continue the retreat to the Potomac. This retreat was by night and disorderly in the extreme. The men of different regiments mingled together and some reached the river at Arlington, some at Long Bridge and the greater part returned to their former camps at or near Fort Corcoran. I reached this point at noon next day and found a miscellaneous crowd crossing over the aqueduct and ferries. Conceiving this to be demoralizing I at once commanded the guard to be increased and all persons attempting to pass over to be stopped. This soon produced its effect. Men sought their proper companies and regiments, comparative order was restored, and all now posted to the best advantage."

The 13th New York, Colonel Quimby, and the 69th New York, Colonel Corcoran, two Irish-American regiments, were attached to General Sherman's brigade at Bull Run.

As the enemy did not make an offensive and determined pursuit it led to the belief by prominent officers present that their forces at the close of the battle were about as demoralized as our own. The Union lines had ceased their aggressive warfare in broad daylight with several hours to spare, in the long days of a hot July, for further battle. The Southerners accepted this cessation of hostilities as an acknowledgment of defeat on our part and were apparently only too glad of an opportunity to cease fighting and claim a fruitless victory.

A few miles from our locality on Monday morning, July 22, in the rain that was falling, the retreating men, in various styles of uniforms and in a disorganized manner, were tramping over Long Bridge into the city of Washington. They were seeking for a place of rest and shelter and as many as were able were making haste to reach their old camps around the city and in its suburbs, which only a week or so before they had left as organized regiments, eager to meet the enemy and now as eager to get away from it in an opposite direction. As the day advanced these remnants of a disorganized army increased in numbers. Now and then a broken regiment, with many of its officers, moving rapidly along, presented a woe-begone and used-up appearance, wet, muddy and grim, but yet looking stern, silent and determined. Before, behind and alongside these were stragglers in squads and other groups of once gallant companies. The sidewalks along the route presented a lively scene of idle spectators. The windows of dwellings were filled with the faces of men, women and children, gazing in silence at the tramping Union soldiers, now without bands of music, drums and fifes or waving flags. The " Secesh " element at this time was predominant and their countenances showed unconcealed pleasure at the condition of our demoralized passing army of stragglers in their thousands. Only a few days ago they were a part of a glorious appearing army of men in all the panoply of war. In a short space of time they had transformed themselves into an armed mob, worn out with a long and dreary march, insufficient food and drenched to the skin. Hundreds halted by the wayside to rest and eat and drink the food and coffee that was supplied by friendly hands along the route. Many fell asleep as they eat in the rain and rested on the sidewalks, doorsteps, vacant lots, anywhere and everywhere, it mattered not to them, for it was impossible to keep awake, so tired and foot-sore, aye, and heart-sore, were they. Some were without guns and equipments, others while fast asleep held the guns that they would not part with as they seemed determined to keep them for use again in the near future to retrieve the laurels so recently lost.

In a few hours the vicinity of our camp was alive with our defeated comrades ; many were wounded, some dangerously, others slightly, and all were wet, weary, foot-sore and grievously disappointed. As the men of the Ninth viewed their return and gazed on the scenes around them and listened to the stories of the fight and the retreat, their faces put on a long, stern and sad look, full of sympathy for the defeated. That our own regiment was still in the prime and strength of its manhood was to us, under all the circumstances, a source of pride and consolation, for we felt then that the time would yet come when we would engage in battle and do our utmost to retrieve the honor of the Union army.

Casualties in the Union army at Bull Run, July 21, 1861, were : —

Officers killed	19
Enlisted men killed	462
Officers wounded	64
Enlisted men wounded	947
Officers missing	40
Enlisted men missing	1176
Total	2708

Casualties in the Confederate army at Bull Run, July 21, 1861, were : —

Officers killed	25
Enlisted men killed	362
Officers wounded	63
Enlisted men wounded	1519
Officers missing	1
Enlisted men missing	12
Total	1982

The general clamor of the Union people to send the army " On to Richmond " was obeyed, and it yielded the bitter fruit of defeat. The government, although humiliated at the condition of military affairs, was neither dismayed nor disconcerted, for President Lincoln acted bravely and promptly, seconded as he was by the old hero, General Scott. The worst fears of General Scott were fully realized, for he did not wish to commence operations with an untrained and unorganized army, composed mostly of short term men who, to use the words in the official report of General McDowell, " When the army moved forward into battle these troops moved to the rear to the sound of the enemy's cannon."

The Confederacy had six months' start of the United States government in organizing its army and equipping it with the property taken from government arsenals. Added to this was the incentive of defending their homes and firesides, as they believed then and termed it, from the " Northern invaders." It was deplorable that the brave men who fought and fell at the first battle of Bull Run were not supported by an army of equal valor; but events proved to our cost that we had no such army and that time alone was required to produce one. The government, therefore, without loss of time, set itself to work to organize an army to meet the emergency. It is alleged, rightly, by all disciplinarians, that a true soldier is, to all intents and purposes, a machine, subject to the directions of his superior officers. A good soldier must and will obey all orders without question or hesitation, even at the instant sacrifice of his life. If he has not made up his mind to die, as it were, at a moment's notice, in the discharge of his duty at all times, then he has not attained that spirit of discipline to which all good soldiers should aspire. War means, if it means anything, the slaughter, so to speak, in a measure, of men, soldiers; and the army which is taught this stubborn fact without mincing matters, is, with proper leadership, always bound to be victorious, for the simple reason that the rank and file have determined to " do or die." When a regiment is ordered to charge on a battery which all the while is sending a destructive fire into their lines, and, to a man, the regiment has made up its mind to capture the enemy's guns or die in the attempt; there is little doubt of complete success, in fact, no doubt, for the assault is only a question of pluck and endurance. If the foe in defense of its artillery is equally determined, then it all lies on the side of the resolute fighters whose discipline has reached the acme of true soldiers. If in the charge, on the other hand, it proves that the soldiers have not reached this high state of training and they falter, break and retreat, the chances are that the slaughter which overtakes them will be greater from the destructive fire poured into their retreating ranks than if they had pushed forward bravely and fought and won. When it is considered that on the one hand there is glory and victory and on the other death and ignominious defeat, the true soldier will without hesitation go forward fighting to win or die.

On the following day, Tuesday, July 23, 1861, the Ninth received marching orders. The regiment at that time was in possession of fifteen four-horse army wagons, the same that we brought from Boston. The historical six-mule army teams were then unknown to us. At a later period we made their acquaintance and at a time when our wagons were greatly reduced in numbers. In the memory of the writer our fifteen wagons were then insufficient to carry our baggage, camp and garrison equipage, quartermaster's and commissary's stores, medical supplies, etc., so that after we arrived at our final destination several trips were required to complete the removal of all regimental effects. A comparison of this " move " with those which we went through with afterwards, when each regiment was allowed only two wagons, will give the reader an idea of our rapid reduction in field transportation. When at a later period these two wagons were laden with the regiment's effects, the residue left over was, regardless of consequences, made a bonfire of.

At a late hour in the afternoon the Ninth Regiment moved from camp at Emmart's farm in heavy marching order at a route step, without music, with the aforesaid fifteen four-horse army wagons bringing up the rear at a respectable distance. As the regiment passed through the streets of Washington in the direction of Long Bridge, it attracted much attention. There were no cheers, no enthusiasm. The people just stood on the sidewalks and surveyed us. Our ranks were full; our men were young, lithe, active and buoyant, and over a thousand strong. As they marched in four ranks they covered considerable ground and gave the impression of a brigade instead of a regiment. The light gray colored soft hats and neat fitting gray uniforms gave them an appearance of strength and solidity which occasioned many complimentary remarks from the friendly bystanders. As we marched over Long Bridge it appears that " Bull Run " Russell, the correspondent of the London *Times*, reviewed us in person, and in writing to his journal afterwards said that we were an Irish regiment from the colonel to the drummer boy; that shoulder to shoulder we covered more ground than any regiment he had ever seen.

By the time we reached the " sacred soil " of Virginia darkness had fallen upon us. The roads were much cut up by heavy wheeling and tramping on the days just past, and irregularly so. The reddish-brown clayey mud was likewise cloggy, and it would stick to an army shoe like a brother; so much so that it greatly impeded our march and the darkness also aided in retarding our progress. It was no child's play to carry a musket, a well-filled knapsack, a haversack containing three days' rations, a canteen full of water, and equipments with forty rounds of buck and ball cartridges, aggregating a weight of forty pounds or more per man, over heavy and recently rain-soaked country roads which had been traveled on for days by our Bull Run army until they presented the appearance of a ploughed field more than anything else we can imagine. As we approached Arlington Heights we could see on the distant sky the reflections of bright lights from many camp-fires. In a short while we were tramping along in the midst of them. They were bright blazing logs along the openings in the woods. The appearance of these immense wood fires was quite exhilarating to our regiment. As soon as our presence became known to the troops that were bivouacked along our line of march, they appeared at the great openings in the forest and cheered us to the echo. " Three cheers for the Ninth Massachusetts! " greeted our surprised ears so often as we moved along that we were as much astonished as we were pleased. It was to us a most delightful reception and one that will last in our memories as long as we live. It was a greeting in the wilderness from our comrades in arms which came from their hearts and was given with great good-will. Our valor on the battlefield was still untried, yet our fame as an Irish-American regiment, from whom great things were expected, had that day preceded us; expectations, it can be said, which were not subsequently disappointed. As we tramped along and passed beyond these bright and cheering scenes our minds naturally reverted to the old " Know Nothing " days; to the time when the

" Know Nothing " governor proclaimed * * * * " That the honor of the American flag should be confided only to those who are born on the soil * * * * they alone can justly be required to vindicate its rights " * * * *. As these thoughts flashed through our minds it looked to us then as though the Irish-American Catholic citizens of the United States were vindicated. We had no resentment in our hearts; we were then Catholic Christian soldiers whose love for the Union and the Stars and Stripes, our flag, our country, was above all and over all, and with God's assistance we would prove it with our lives on the battlefield against all foes, foreign or domestic, as did our countrymen during the Revolution and subsequent wars.

At length we left the road and took to the woods and up the heights we went, halted in a short time, formed column of companies, stacked arms and went into bivouac. After responding to the inevitable " First Sergeant's Call," the guard detail was made and the guard mounted and posted around our camp. The sweet sound sleep which soon overtakes the tired soldier after a toilsome march at length prevailed throughout the regiment. It was our first night to bivouac in the woods under a starry sky on the " sacred soil " of Virginia. We were aroused from our sound sleep in the early morning by the sweet music of the reveille. On surveying our surroundings we found that we were near the Robert E. Lee mansion, with many of the plantation slave quarters and the slaves themselves in our vicinity. Also near by was the family cemetery, in and around which many of us had unknowingly slept during the night. The owner of this large mansion on the heights, which commanded a view of the city of Washington, the Potomac river and a good part of the surrounding country, was now far away, acting the part of a general in the Southern army. By his own volition all his ancestral landed possessions — his mansion, his plantation and slaves — were now in the hands of the government which he had deserted with the intention of destroying. As future events determined he was doomed to hold and occupy them nevermore. Today on these grounds, which once resounded with the stern voice of the overseer and echoed with the snap of the slave-driver's whip, and which were wet with the blood and sweat and tears of the despised negro slaves, there sleep the heroes of the Union army in their thousands, showing, in that silent city of the dead, monumental evidence for all future time that the Union was saved and the accursed institution of slavery forever swept from the land of the great republic of the United States of America.

" But never yet was city fortified
    Like that sad height above Potomac's tide;
    There never yet was eloquence in speech
    Like those ten thousand stones, a name on each;
    No guards e'er pressed such claims on court or king
    As these Prætorians to our Senate bring;
    The Army of Potomac never lay
    So full of strength as in its camp today ! "

          *   *   *   *   *   *   *   *   *   *

    " Here proud Columbia bends with tear-stirred mouth,
      To kiss their blood-seal, binding North and South,
      Two clasping hands upon the knot they tied
      When Union lived and Human Slavery died ! "

                                        JOHN BOYLE O'REILLY.

After a breakfast of standard morning rations — army coffee and
hardtack — we brushed and cleaned up generally as well as army life
would permit and packed our knapsacks preparatory to moving to a
permanent campground. In the meantime, while awaiting the order
to march, many of us loitered around the Lee mansion and the slave
quarters and held conversation with some of the slaves, learning for the
first time many practical lessons from the living subjects themselves
of the degradation of human slavery, which gave us food for thought
on their aimless, animal-like life. It was for them to eat, work, sleep
and die, after generating others to follow on in the same darkness and
ignorance and Godless existence, in order that idle masters might live
a life of luxurious ease. These simple, harmless children of nature had
lived and died in their bondage from generation to generation, looking
forward for freedom; freedom which was hoped for but never came
until their eyes beheld the Union soldiers. How or when it was to
reach them they did not know, but their crude ideas and instinct taught
them that now, if ever, it was near at hand. They knew through that
same instinct that, although the Union soldiers were the enemies of
their master and his kind, they were still their friends and in some
unaccountable way connected with their future destiny, and would in
time lead them out of the house of bondage. We ourselves felt then
that the day of deliverance for the negro slaves of our land was near
at hand, and, with the assistance of the Almighty, whose creatures we
were, that the slaveholders' days were numbered. Our confidence in
the final victory of the Union army from that hour, during the following
years of terrible warfare, was never shaken.

The shrill notes of the bugle sounding the assembly called us to our places. In our march from the heights we repeated our experience of the day before and in a roundabout way reached the immediate vicinity of Fort Corcoran in the afternoon. From the plains where we halted we had a good view of the hillside whereon we were to pitch our permanent camp. It was now Wednesday, the 24th day of June, 1861, and here we were to remain until September 28 following.

That afternoon is memorable in the minds of the 1st sergeants of the regiment on account of the great amount of " double-quick " duty performed by them in answer to the numerous " calls " of the sergeant-major. About two hundred yards from the ground where we were halted temporarily he took up his position near the colonel's quarters. One roll and four taps of the drum, three times repeated, about every fifteen minutes or so, kept the 1st sergeants on the run back and forth to supply details of men for fatigue duty. By judicious management one detail for fatigue duty under charge of an officer or two would have answered all purposes and relieved the regiment of much annoyance and friction, besides giving every one else a chance to attend to their personal and company affairs. This easy and proper method, however, would not suit our active sergeant-major at all. It would not impress the colonel and others with his untiring activity in pushing things around headquarters or show his subordinate non-commissioned officers his authority over them. The inoffensive man of fifty years who was adjutant at that time, moved about apparently paralyzed at the way his sergeant-major was rushing everything, and seemed satisfied that he was relieved of all care while he occasionally hob-nobbed with other officers who were taking things easy.

On the following morning we took possession of our hillside camp-ground. The regiment fell to work like pioneers in clearing the virgin soil of its undergrowth and other accumulations, besides felling trees here and there for company streets. Our tents were soon erected and that night our soldiers slept under canvas.

Being now in the face of the enemy as it were, we at once commenced to perform real picket duty. At Munson's Hill and vicinity, several miles south of us, the Southern army was encamped and strongly intrenched. About one hundred and fifty men from our regiment were detailed every twenty-four hours for picket. About the same number were likewise detailed for camp guard. It was customary then to put three men together on each picket post, thus giving each man two hours' picket and four hours off; at the end of the twenty-four hours each man would have performed eight hours' watching.

Our front and flanks were thus protected from any surprises by a long connecting line of pickets by our different regiments. The enemy was guarded in like manner about a mile or so away. Picket duty was not only monotonous through the day, but at night it was irksome and lonely, particularly after twelve o'clock. Added to this the nights at times in Virginia were very chilly, owing to the heavy fall of dew which would towards morning actually drip from the leaves of the trees like rain in a light shower. Our pickets were posted so as to command a full view if possible of their front and flanks without exposure to the enemy. When practicable the picket line was posted along the edge of the woods or behind the rail fences which were numerous at that time on the plantations and along the roads. Sometimes artificial obstacles were erected in order to seclude the picket from observation, where he could see and not readily be seen. Pickets were generally in hailing distance of each other and were allowed to make themselves comfortable, barring fires of any kind. The latter order was not always stringently enforced if the distance between the lines was very great. Pickets generally for their own personal protection were careful not to attract the attention of the enemy. At times, though, both lines became very friendly as the war progressed. Picket friendliness was supposed to be unknown (?) to the officers of the picket. When night fell upon the lonely sentinel and while his comrades slept, he would peer into the darkness and watch and listen for the cause of any and all sounds which might strike his ear. With ready musket in hand he would bend forward with strained eyes to see and challenge any and all comers. The monotonous and irregular jingle of a distant cow-bell would be a source of uneasiness to him, thinking, perhaps, it was the ruse of a stealthy foe to distract his attention and spring upon his post from another quarter than from whence the sound proceeded. The sudden flight and sharp cry of some night bird would startle his senses as he listened to the plaintive notes of a distant whip-poor-will; or he could see, in his somewhat excited imagination, in the distant shadows of a clump of trees or bushes, the wily foe creeping forward through the long grass to surprise and capture, or perhaps kill him, if perchance he ceased to be wakeful and vigilant. Rainy or stormy weather was no addition to one's comfort on picket. As the army profited by experience it led to detailing whole regiments for three days' picket duty. This was a great improvement on the old way, for it made life on the picket line more endurable. The knowledge of a strong reserve to fall back on in case of attack made the hours of the sentinel on duty seemingly shorter; when relieved he could return to the companionship of his comrades on the reserve, posted as it was behind a house or two or some other sheltered place, where small fires could be kept burning if required for warmth and cooking purposes.

After many days of hard and constant labor our camp on the hillside was made quite picturesque and habitable. The colonel and his officers spared no pains or labor in doing everything for the comfort of the regiment. On one occasion the colonel was directing the sergeant of the pioneer squad how to perform a certain piece of bridge work near his headquarters. The sergeant — a large, strongly built, florid complexioned man, with a full red beard and bushy red hair — failed to catch on to the colonel's idea, although he worked hard and earnestly to follow instructions; work as he would he could not fulfil the colonel's plan. Losing all patience the colonel ordered all hands to cease labor and, as he looked the sergeant full in the face, exclaimed : " I wonder what fool made you a sergeant !" At this astonishing remark the sergeant, who was, likewise, gazing expectantly into the colonel's face, seemed for a few seconds dumbfounded, but by a strong effort of will he rallied and with a serious and impatient expression on his flushed and perspiring face, replied : " Faith, Colonel, it was your own four bones that did it." The earnest manner of the sergeant and the sparkle of his bright brown eyes as he partially leaned forward, together with his quick and unexpected reply, seemed to modify the colonel's stern manner and with the faintest of smiles on his face he said in a quiet tone as he moved away, " Sergeant, go ahead with your job and do it your own way, but don't be all day about it." When the colonel got out of earshot, the men who witnessed the scene had a hearty laugh over it, and many a witty joke with the sergeant — who was likewise well pleased with himself — telling how he got the better of the colonel. Much fun and innumerable jokes, tricks and witty sayings were of daily occurrence at this camp, more so than at any others in subsequent years ; owing perhaps to the reason that nothing very serious had as yet happened to mar the high spirits and good nature of the regiment generally. In order to appreciate these pleasantries one must be present and see the men, hear their voices and note their manner of action and delivery, together with the expressions which play on their faces ; then to hear the loud ringing laughter and the running comments of those who enjoyed a good witty saying. Language is impossible to portray it ; and when it is attempted the pith of the fun is lost. The writer during all his service failed to find any of the " stage Irishmen," or such as we read about in English and American novels with their unheard of " brogue " and inane buffoonery, yclept wit.

The writer noticed likewise among the negro slaves a total lack of the so-called " nigger minstrels." While some of the slaves would dance and sing (?) and occasionally engaged in a " butting " match, they did so in a natural way without anything " stagey " about it. You can teach a person to make an ass of himself before an audience for pay; for money unprincipled persons can be found who will give degrading imitations of their own nationality; and even go so far as to caricature their parents and friends. Writers and actors who engage in that kind of business if denied patronage would turn their talents into a more commendable direction.

Our supply of good wholesome rations — including soft bread — was more than enough to satisfy the hungriest man in the regiment. The remark made at Long Island, that, " in a few months your rations will be more than you will care to eat " was now verified. The health of the men during our stay at this camp was excellent. Our army was now always on the increase. Only long-term regiments were encamped on the south side of the Potomac. All the forts were fully garrisoned, and the tented field met the eye in every direction, occupied as it was by infantry, artillery, cavalry and engineers.

The daily drilling commenced in the early morning, and ended at early evening with dress parade. As the colonel continued in his " double-quick " movements, our battalion drill of two hours in a hot southern sun each afternoon was indeed hard work. " Charge bayonets " in line of battle for a couple of hundred yards both front and rear —" right about "— was one of the features of our drill, and, as it was accompanied by the usual prolonged yell, it attracted considerable attention from some of the other regiments which did not practice that sort of drill. As we had none of our men on detached duty the unusual length of our regimental line on parade was also a matter of favorable comment by others.

Far to the front and south of Arlington Heights, and off on our right flank were large belts of wooded country. In order to obtain a clear view for the guns in the forts in case of an attack, it was deemed imperative to fell all of these trees. Our regiment was supplied with axes, and, together with other troops, it commenced the work. The trees were cut about three feet from the ground, and all made to fall with their branches toward the enemy. The work occupied many days, and, as it was a great change from incessant drilling, our men took to it as to a pastime. After the work was finished for miles in every direction, it made a great change in the phase of the surrounding country, and the appearance of thousands of dead trees all lying in the same direction added greatly to the desolate looks of this war afflicted vicinity. Many of these trees were trimmed and pointed and laid down for abatis around the forts and across the roads. When this work was thoroughly completed we were again detailed as a regiment for other "fatigue duty." The chain of forts that were planned to encircle the south bank of the Potomac for the better protection of the capital, were as yet uncompleted. One of these forts was given to the Ninth to build; as we were to do it without other assistance much pride was manifested by both officers and men in the undertaking. This interesting work was under the direction of Captain Alexander of the U.S. Engineer Corps. It occupied many weeks in building and was composed of earth and stockade. It mounted five guns on front and flanks. The rear was protected by a stockade with small portholes for infantry firing. Inside the fort good quarters were built for the use of the garrison. It likewise contained a bomb-proof magazine, and, in case of assault, bomb-proofs for the men. Captain Alexander complimented the Ninth on building as fine a fort as any in the circle. In about two months from the day it was begun it was garrisoned by a detachment from the regiment for a short time. Our fort was first named Fort Ramsay, but in justice to the regiment which built it, General McClellan issued General Orders No. 45, Nov. 16, 1861, which changed the name to Fort Cass. This order, though coming somewhat late, was greatly appreciated by Colonel Cass and his regiment, and was accepted as a deserved recognition of labor faithfully performed.

CHAPTER IV.

GENERAL McCLELLAN, COMMANDER U.S. ARMY.

MAJ.-GEN. GEO. B. McCLELLAN — BIOGRAPHICAL SKETCH OF HIS LIFE — GENERAL SHERMAN'S BRIGADE — OUR BRIGADE COMMANDER ORDERED WEST — SUCCEEDED BY GEN. FITZ JOHN PORTER — CONFEDERATE FORCES — FORWARD MOVEMENT — UNION REGIMENTS FIRE INTO EACH OTHER — A NIGHT IN THE WOODS — AT MINER'S HILL — FRIENDSHIP BETWEEN THE 62D PENNSYLVANIA AND THE 9TH MASSACHUSETTS — GENERAL SCOTT SUCCEEDED BY GENERAL McCLELLAN — CHAPLAIN FATHER SCULLY'S " BIG CHAPEL TENT " — THE GRAND REVIEW — STRENGTH OF THE UNION FORCES — CHRISTMAS IN CAMP — DEATH OF LIEUTENANT-COLONEL PEARD — RECONNOISSANCES — ARMY OF THE POTOMAC ORGANIZED.

" In thy holy need, our Country, shatter other idols straightway;
Quench our household fires before us, reap the pomp of harvests low;
Strike aside each glad ambition born of youth and golden leisure,
Leave us only to remember faith we swore thee long ago !"

* * * * * * * * * *

" If we be thy burden-bearers, let us ease thee of thy sorrow;
If our hands be thine avengers, life or death, they shall not fail;
If thy heart be just and tender, wrong us not with hesitation:
Take us, trust us, lead us, love us, till the eternal Truth prevail !"

LOUISE IMOGEN GUINEY.

IN selecting a commander to organize a new army the President's choice fell upon Gen. George Brinton McClellan. By a brief reference to his antecedents it will be seen that no better selection could have been made.

General McClellan was born in Philadelphia, Dec. 3, 1826. He entered West Point in June, 1842, and graduated second in the class of 1846. He went at once into active service in Mexico as a second lieutenant. At the close of the Mexican war he was brevetted captain for meritorious services. He was then sent to West Point and devoted himself to the study and instruction of military engineering. During the Crimean war he was sent abroad to study and report on European systems of warfare. On his return he issued a work on "The Armies of Europe." In 1857 he resigned from service in the army and engaged in successful railroad engineering, holding, in the meantime, prominent positions in U.S. railroad corporations up to the breaking out of the rebellion. He accepted a commission as major-general of volunteers, May 10, 1861, and was assigned to the Department of Ohio, Indiana and Illinois. He was subsequently commissioned a major-general in the regular army, May 14, 1861, and placed in command of all the troops in West Virginia. There he engaged, defeated and captured the Confederate forces under General Pegram, July 11 and 12, 1861. This short and successful campaign preserved West Virginia to the Union cause. For this service he received the thanks of congress.

Four days after the battle of Bull Run President Lincoln ordered General McClellan to take command of all the forces in the Military Departments of Washington and Northeastern Virginia, with headquarters at Washington, D.C. The troops in the departments mentioned numbered less than 50,000 infantry, a small body of cavalry and nine field batteries, imperfectly equipped. It included, also, all the fortifications on the south side of the Potomac river. The defenceless condition of the capital was referred to by General McClellan in the following language: "Many soldiers had deserted, and the streets of Washington were crowded with straggling officers and men, absent from their stations without authority, whose behavior indicated the general want of discipline and organization. * * * * All was chaos and despondency; the city was filled with intoxicated stragglers and an attack was expected. The troops numbered less than 50,000, many of whom were so demoralized and undisciplined that they could not be relied upon even for defensive purposes. Moreover, the term of service of a large part had already expired, or was on the point of doing so. * * * * Sufficient and fit material of war did not exist. The situation was difficult and fraught with danger." As it was only six days after the battle of Bull Run, and as many thousands of the short-term troops were still in and around the city of Washington, preparatory to their return home for muster-out, this bad condition of affairs can be charged principally to the results that inevitably followed the demoralization which began at the disastrous close of that battle. In a short time the provost marshal by rigid service brought order out of chaos, and, as it was afterwards claimed, Washington soon became one of the most quiet cities in the Union.

The new levies of long-term volunteers — infantry, artillery and cavalry — were rapidly arriving in Washington, and as fast as they were found to be thoroughly equipped they were transferred across the Potomac. The infantry was formed into brigades, which generally consisted of four regiments each. August 4, 1861, the Ninth Massachusetts Volunteers was assigned to Brig.-Gen. William Tecumseh Sherman's brigade. The brigade was composed of the Ninth and 14th Regiments Massachusetts Volunteers, 41st Regiment New York and 4th Regiment Michigan Volunteers. Hamilton's Battery E, 3d U.S. Artillery, and Company I, 2d U.S. Cavalry, were also attached. The 2d Maine, 2d Wisconsin and 13th New York regiments were stationed at Fort Corcoran, at General Sherman's headquarters.

The authorities in Washington were now easily alarmed. If any unexpected or slight infantry firing occurred it was made the immediate cause of telegraphic inquiry. In the early mornings, at company drill, in going through the motions of loading and firing muskets, it occasionally happened that those who had returned from picket neglected to withdraw the charge of buck and ball, and would on drill discharge their pieces, alleging that they forgot they were loaded. General Sherman issued strict orders to stop it, and, for a time, they were obeyed, but now and then there would be a slight break. One morning the writer noticed a middle-aged officer strolling leisurely about the parade ground with his coat open all the way in front and his hands clasped behind his back. At this time the companies of the Ninth were drilling in various parts of the field, when suddenly one of them, in going through the motions of loading and firing, discharged two muskets within a second of each other. The elderly looking gentleman above mentioned moved leisurely towards the company and asked: "Who commands this company?" The captain saluted with his sword and replied, "I do, sir." "Captain, this firing must be stopped; you will report to your colonel in arrest," said General Sherman, for it was he. This episode passed from mouth to mouth until the whole brigade knew of it. The delinquent captain, although soon released with a reprimand, took good care thenceforth to inspect his company's muskets before commencing company drill. Neither he nor any other company commander disobeyed the order against firing after that.

During the short time that General Sherman commanded our brigade he won the respect and esteem of his whole command. We knew him to be a patriotic professional soldier — a "West Pointer"—who had distinguished himself at the late battle of Bull Run as the colonel of the 13th U.S. Regulars and as the commander of a brigade during that battle. August 24, 1861, General Sherman was ordered, much to our regret, to the Department of the Cumberland, where he continued to render distinguished service, and was later on promoted major-general of volunteers.   The writer has in his possession an autograph letter from General Sherman, the sentiments of which are characteristic of the man and will be of interest to the reader.   The following is an exact copy : —

HEADQUARTERS ARMY OF THE UNITED STATES, }
WASHINGTON, D C , June 15, 1882. }

DAN'L G. MCNAMARA, *Secretary Reunion 9th Mass. Vols.*, Woburn.

My Dear Sir : I beg to acknowledge receipt of your kind letter of June 12 inst., inviting me to attend the Reunion of the old Ninth Massachusetts, to be held at Woburn on the 21st inst.

I cannot possibly come because I have already been absent too much of late, and as Congress is drawing to its close, we in Washington consider it a critical period of the year.

Well do I recall the old Massachusetts Ninth in those trying days of 1861, when for a short period it fell under my command at Fort Corcoran; about nine hundred bright, intelligent young men, well equipped and well commanded (by Colonel Cass, if I remember right), fresh from their New England homes, and anxious to do a full measure of the awful work before them.   And now you tell me that only two hundred and seventy remain alive.   If these will now meet and cast their thoughts across our broad continent, they will realize that their fallen comrades have not died in vain, but are almost to be envied that they sleep now well in their honored graves, and leave us, their survivors, to plod along a few short years, and then to pass the dark river into the same sleep of eternity.

I always encourage these reunions, whether of armies, corps, divisions, brigades or regiments, not so much for the revival of our own pleasant and sad memories, but because they teach the lessons of patriotism to the youth of this land, who must very soon take our places and hold the ship of state on her glorious course through the Sea of Time.

Thanking you for the compliment, and begging to be remembered to the survivors of the good old regiment, I am with great respect,

Yours truly,

W. T. SHERMAN.

During all the brilliant career of this great general he always stood near to the volunteer soldiers, and in his subsequent illustrious life he dearly loved to meet them on all occasions and to call them comrades. It is needless to say that his friendship was reciprocated by them all. General Sherman was born Feb. 8, 1820, and died, honored and lamented by the republic, Feb. 14, 1891.   The following anecdote will give the reader an idea of the kindly nature of General Sherman : Five officers of the Ninth, desiring to visit the city of Washington, obtained passes from the colonel for forty-eight hours' leave.   The road from the camp to the bridge was heavy with mud, and, altogether, was very bad walking.   By some influence they obtained an ambulance and very comfortably rode over to the bridge. On presenting their passes they were informed that all passes must be countersigned by General Sherman. After talking the matter over it was decided that Captain O'Leary — one of the party — should proceed to General Sherman's headquarters at Fort Corcoran, and take all the passes with him and get them signed. The captain, but recently promoted, was dressed in a brand new uniform and cut quite a dash as a volunteer officer. On arriving inside the fort he saw a tall man standing near by, without any insignia to distinguish his rank, whose style of dress, with one leg of his trousers in his boot and generally careless looks, did not come up to the captain's idea of a brigadier-general. In fact, he supposed him to be a man-of-all-work around the place. Beckoning with his raised hand and finger to the man, who was looking towards him, the captain said, " Come here, my man." The man came forward as requested, and the captain said again as he stopped in front of him, " Can you direct me to General Sherman's headquarters? " " What do you want of General Sherman? " the man inquired. On receiving this answer to his question the captain impatiently exclaimed, " What in —— and —— is it your business? " following up this query with quite an indignant look at the supposed audacity of the stranger. Without seeming to notice the blunt question addressed to him he proceeded to direct the captain by a circuitous route over to the general's quarters. Then the stranger moved off quickly in another direction. After carefully picking his steps to avoid muddying his shiny shoes or soiling his nice new trousers, the captain reached the desired headquarters, and, meeting the assistant adjutant-general, tried to prevail on him to countersign the five passes. The adjutant was affable and smiling, evidently pleased at something, and said : " Oh, no, captain, the general is right inside there ; you go right in and he will sign your papers." The captain boldly walked into the inner tent and was dumbfounded as he beheld the man with whom he had the colloquy outside. It was the general himself sitting at his desk. He noticed the surprise and confusion of his visitor, but cheerily said : " Well, captain, what can I do for you? " When the captain found his voice he very meekly stated his errand. The general took the passes, looked them over and said : " How long is it, captain, since you were in Washington? " Not waiting for a reply, he continued, " But what in —— and —— is it my business ! " He then signed the papers, and, as he handed them back, pleasantly bid the abashed captain good-day. Years afterwards the captain met General Sherman and recalled the incident just related. The general inquired : " Are you the captain I met on that occasion? Yes, I remember it well, and had many a good

laugh over it, telling to others my meeting with a captain of the Ninth
Massachusetts. I think, captain, you learned a good lesson from that
interview." The captain assured him that he had, for he never forgot
the well-merited rebuke.

Brigadier-General Fitz John Porter succeeded General Sherman in
command of our brigade. General Porter was a graduate of West
Point. He saw service as a lieutenant at the age of twenty-four in the
Mexican war, and for gallant and meritorious services was brevetted
major. May 14, 1861, he was promoted colonel of the 15th regiment,
U.S. infantry; May 17, 1861, he was appointed a brigadier-general of
volunteers on the recommendation of General McClellan. General
Porter, on assuming command of his brigade, caused it to be increased
by the addition of the 2d Maine and 13th New York regiments, then on
duty at Fort Corcoran. These two latter regiments had been in the
battle of Bull Run. A misunderstanding with the authorities regarding
their term of service was the cause of much trouble.

The great work undertaken by General McClellan of organizing
the Army of the Potomac was undergoing rapid development. The
Department of Washington and Northern Virginia, the Valley of the
Shenandoah, the whole of Maryland and Delaware were united into one,
and denominated the Department of the Potomac, under command of
General McClellan, with headquarters in Washington. Engineers,
topographical engineers, medical department, quartermaster's department, subsistence department, ordnance department, provost marshal's
department, signal corps, telegraphic department, brigades and divisions of infantry, parks of artillery, squadrons of cavalry, etc., were all
assuming proper formations preparatory to their final organization in
the near future into brigades, divisions and army corps, all to be
led as one great army, by one master mind, in the near future, against
the enemies of the Union. Frequent inspections and reviews in detail
without number of all branches of the army had been made by General
McClellan in person, and under his vigilant care and direction the herculean task of organizing the Army of the Potomac was rapidly
approaching completion.

The close proximity of the enemy's lines to the Potomac river was
the occasion of recent continual alarms. General Longstreet, with an
advanced division of some 10,000 men, was in possession of a great
expanse of beautiful country in our front, and, as our army increased,
our picket lines were often extended in the direction of the enemy.
This apparent encroachment occasioned some resistance every time they
were obliged to fall back with their pickets. Skirmishes of this nature,

however, had a tendency to accustom our soldiers to the presence of the enemy. Besides giving them confidence under fire it likewise, in a measure, educated them in the art of war.

On several occasions during our encampment at Arlington Heights the enemy raided our newly-advanced picket lines. At one time the attack was made by a piece of artillery from which shell were thrown into our lines. As it was the first time for the picket to experience a shell fire it created among them considerable excitement. On this particular occasion one hundred and fifty men were detailed from the Ninth to reinforce the picket, which was found to be somewhat demoralized. At other times, as we established a more advanced line, an incessant infantry picket fire would be kept up by the enemy. When these alarms reached headquarters the Ninth would be generally ordered out on reconnoissance. We always returned without a skirmish, as the enemy evidently had no intention of moving on our lines. While at Arlington Heights the following men were reported

WOUNDED ON PICKET.

Sergt. Wm. Kerr, Co. C . . .	no date
Patrick Sheridan, Co. B . . .	no date
John Cosgrove, Co. C . . .	Aug. 16, 1861
Cornelius Creden, Co. F . . .	no date
James Dempsey, Co. F . . .	no date
Joseph H. Monaghan, Co. F . .	no date

The strength and organization of the army had so rapidly increased that it became necessary, for a better formation of the new divisions, to advance and occupy the fine country in our front, which was held by the enemy. On Saturday afternoon, Sept. 28, 1861, our new and badly directed movement commenced. The Ninth Massachusetts took up the line of march, in heavy marching order, with two days' cooked rations in haversacks, for the enemy's lines in the direction of Monson's Hill, a distance in a direct line of seven miles or so.

Although we had occupied our old campground at Arlington only eight weeks — it seemed like months in the retrospect — we left it with feelings of regret. We were obliged to part with many souvenirs which added in the past to the comforts of camp life, in the way of camp beds, tents, floors, utensils, etc., which must at such times be abandoned forever. Such was the lot of the rank and file. With the officers it was at that time somewhat modified, owing to their privilege of baggage transportation.

This particular march was not very tiresome, but it was slow and roundabout, and, as darkness fell upon us, it became monotonous. To a certain degree it was an unexpected movement and it struck us as lacking in method and direction. It was quite gloomy, tramping by night, and as we entered a piece of woods from off the road the chill of the night air was anything but comfortable. Not having received any definite orders up to this time the colonel brought the Ninth to a halt. It was generally understood that we were somewhere near Monson's Hill, but how near or who were in our front no one seemed to know.

After the colonel threw out a picket line he did the next best thing to do and that was to remain still and wait. To the sagacity and patience of Colonel Cass that night, without doubt, many of his regiment owed their lives. He held his command in that piece of woods till daylight. Then, and not till then, orders were sent him. We stood in line, shivering from the dew that fell and from the chill air that swept all night through the spruce trees. At about an hour after midnight volleys of musketry broke forth on our left and front. In a short time quietness again prevailed, only to be again disturbed by more volleys of musketry in quick succession; after that ceased a few shots now and then were fired in an irregular way. This affair covered about three-quarters of an hour, as it seemed then. The rest of the night passed slowly by without noise or incident. The morning came at last, and we soon learned that our own troops had been firing into each other. This news created much indignation, for every one of us felt that some one had blundered.

The night just past was particularly dark and cheerless. About midnight three or more demoralized cavalry men came dashing down the road and firing their revolvers, and meeting the 69th Pennsylvania, Colonel O'Kane, cried out: "Look out, boys, here they come," and continuing their headlong course, these cavalry men were soon far to the rear. The 69th Pennsylvania soon after this report saw in the road in their front what they supposed were the enemy's skirmishers, and the same that the excited cavalrymen were fleeing from, so they at once opened fire on them and drove them back. The skirmishers disappeared into the woods and a regiment concealed there returned the fire, which immediately became general between the two regiments. The other regiment proved to be the 71st Pennsylvania, in command of Lieutenant-Colonel Wistar. It lost four killed and fourteen wounded. The 69th Pennsylvania lost one killed and two wounded. The reader will be surprised, if nothing more, to learn that both of the above-named regiments belonged to the same brigade, which was commanded by Col. E. D. Baker of the 71st Pennsylvania.

A surprise was in store for the Ninth. When it became light enough to see at a distance we discovered to our right and immediate front a battery of six pieces of field artillery ready for action, and pointed directly towards the piece of woods wherein we had passed such an uncomfortable night. It was about two hundred yards distant, and, as we afterwards learned, ready to open fire on us if we advanced in that direction during the night. From the orders they had heard given in our regiment during the first part of the night they knew that some large bodies of troops were in the woods, and taking the benefit of all doubts in their minds, concluded we were the enemy. Colonel Cass was asked by General Porter what he would have done if the battery had opened fire. He replied that he would have charged on it with his regiment and captured it. His answer was correct. It would undoubtedly cost us many lives, not to say what might have happened to the battery. The stupidity, not to use a harsher term, of this part of our advance did not strengthen our opinion or confidence in volunteer commanders of brigades, and as time went by we lost our confidence in most of them altogether.

After partaking of a soldier's breakfast — hardtack and coffee — the regiment marched to Miner's Hill, where it went — as it afterwards proved — into permanent camp for the winter. Miner's Hill is the smallest of a range of hills in this vicinity. Hall's Hill is next in rear, then Upton's, then Monson's, the two latter to our left, facing south. Monson's Hill is the most prominent and the highest. Our division took possession of Hall's and Miner's Hills and environments. Our regiment camped on the south slope of the hill, which here gradually ran to an incline, and finally to a level surface, which answered for a parade ground. Our view in this direction was intercepted by the embankment of a road which led to Fall's Church, a town some three miles to our left. Over the brow of Miner's Hill, to our rear, was an open country leading in the direction of Hall's Hill, where the 22d Massachusetts Volunteers was encamped. This intermediate ground, containing hundreds of acres, was used for company, regiment and brigade drills. The place was infested with rabbits when we arrived. On company drill they had a demoralizing effect on some of the more excitable of our men. Sometimes drill was suspended for a while and permission given the men to hunt them. As no firing was allowed the game generally escaped, but the fun and diversion of the chase was harmless and gratifying. The use of blank cartridges on battalion drills finally drove the rodents away, besides making birds and all other living things very scarce.

On our right flank the woods were abundant for camp use. On our left flank the 62d Pennsylvania Volunteers encamped. An unusual friendship grew up between the Ninth and 62d, which continued throughout our whole service. The comradeship of the rank and file was even stronger than that between the officers of both regiments. Even at this late day it is pleasant to contemplate these kindly feelings, which were shown not only in camp, but on the march and on the battlefield. They joined in our little festivities and we engaged in theirs. They participated in our celebrations on Saint Patrick's day with as much zest as " those to the manner born." It was thus we went through the hardships of our soldier life, " Sharing each other's sorrows; sharing each other's joys."

New tents were issued by our quartermaster to the whole regiment. Wall tents for the field, staff and line officers and " A " tents for the men. The " A " tent was so called from its shape and appearance to the block letter A. Wall tents were likewise given to the sergeants of each company, one tent to a company. Excavations were made the size of the base of the A tent, and lined up with hewn plank. Two bunks were built, one on each side, each to hold two men; chimneys composed of mud and sticks were built at the back. The floors were also laid with hewn plank. When all was complete the quarters of the men, and of the regiment as a whole, were quite comfortable even in the coldest of weather. The mud produced in rainy weather was one disagreeable feature in our winter quarters; but of course we must have some drawbacks, even in the best of camps.

Under the influence of an open country and a wider field than any which we had up to this time experienced, our ideas and feelings, as it were, seemed to expand. The spirit of patriotism sunk deeper into our hearts. We now felt more than ever that a great war was before us. We gradually learned that our foes were strongly organized and determined to fight us over every inch of territory as we advanced toward their capital. We never lost sight of the fact, however, that with our immense resources victory must in the end crown our arms with success. But just how far off the end was no one could surmise. The confidence in General McClellan and the enthusiasm manifested whenever he rode amongst us, was great, not to say unbounded, and it permeated the whole body of the Army of the Potomac. His untiring interest in everything pertaining to the organization of a perfect army impressed the soldiers with the idea that their young commander was a man of great force of character and a trustworthy leader.

The retirement, on his own request, of Lieut.-Gen. Winfield Scott* was announced to the army Nov. 1, 1861, in a well-deserved laudatory General Order, No. 94, by the President, who at the same time directed that Maj.-Gen. George B. McClellan assume command of the Army of the United States, with headquarters in the city of Washington.

Gen. George W. Morell, a regular army officer, now commanded our brigade. Gen. Fitz John Porter, likewise a regular, commanded our division. Corps formations were not as yet organized. Drilling on a more extended scale than ever was carried on continually. Brigade drills were frequent. Inspections, specially ordered, were more thorough and exacting. Having a great scope of country special attention was given to skirmish drill. "McClellan's Bayonet Exercise" drill was likewise taken up and entered into with great zest by the Ninth. In all battalion drills Colonel Cass continued to follow up all his movements in double-quick time. The regiment got so well used to these quick methods that our brigade drills in common and quick time were light work to us. Our men were robust and enjoyed rude health. There were exceptional cases of light sickness, but no deaths had occurred in camp. We were in fact as healthy a regiment as one would wish or expect to see.

Our chaplain, Father Scully, was indefatigable in his efforts in looking after the moral and spiritual welfare of the regiment. In order

---

* The following is a very brief synopsis of the eventful career of Lieut.-Gen. Winfield Scott. He was born in Petersburg, Va., on June 13, 1786. Educated at William and Mary College, he studied law and was admitted to the bar in 1806. In 1808 he was appointed a captain of light artillery in the U.S. Army. During the war of 1812-14 he was promoted lieutenant-colonel, brigadier general and brevet major-general. He was noted for his great skill and bravery, and at the close of the war he was appointed a major-general, and awarded by Congress with the thanks of the nation and a gold medal. He subsequently spent many years in Europe studying the science of war, and was the author of "Military Manuals and Tactics." On his return to active service he was engaged for many years in quelling our Indian troubles. During the war with Mexico he commanded the United States Army and achieved brilliant successes. He was the unsuccessful candidate of the Whig party in 1852 for President in opposition to Gen. Franklin Pierce.

The war of 1861 found General Scott, at the age of 75 years, in command of the United States forces, and faithful to the Constitution, the Union and the Flag. He nobly fulfilled his duty as commander until old age and its concomitant infirmities obliged him to retire, with the continuance of the full pay and emoluments of a lieutenant-general, and give place to a younger and more vigorous man. He lived to see the surrender at Appomattox, and to congratulate General Grant on his success. He died May 29, 1866, at the age of 80 years. All the honors that the country could bestow were paid to his memory, and, amid the sorrow of the nation, his body was interred in the cemetery at West Point.

to give no one an excuse for not attending the celebration of mass he had an immense tent of good material manufactured specially for the use of the regiment. On Sunday mornings, particularly, it was a refreshing sight to the chaplain and others to see our stalwart soldiers on their knees in divine worship,— kneeling as only men kneel whose faith in their knowledge of God comes through the teachings of our Saviour and the Catholic church. Catholic soldiers from all parts of the army, far and near, were likewise present on that and other days of the week. The men were much better after it. They were more cheerful, more contented, better in a moral sense, quick to obey, ready and willing for any and all duty, if called on, either day or night. The writer can declare from his experience as an officer that, comparatively speaking, but few men were derelict in their duty, and that he very seldom had occasion to reprimand his men, or to administer punishment. Under arms, night or day, they were model soldiers, prompt to respond to the " long roll," and eager to have a dash at the enemy.

Much interest was always shown by the men in our regular Sunday morning inspections. On one of these inspections the colonel offered a prize to be awarded to the cleanest man in the regiment. The prize consisted of a ten days' furlough. During the week the companies were all notified of the colonel's offer. It created a great deal of interest and produced many competitors. On this particular Sunday the colonel and staff went through the inspection very carefully, scrutinizing each man and his equipments, etc., in a most thorough manner. The cleanest men selected from each company were then assembled, after the regimental inspection, and again carefully examined, and as flaws were detected in one way and another, they were gradually dropped, one by one, until finally the competition stood between two men. Both of these men were fine specimens of physical manhood; soldierly in their bearing, and the pink of neatness. The colonel was now in a quandary as to which one of these two men should be selected. It was at last suggested that the man having the cleanest feet be awarded the prize. The suggestion was acted on, and all interested retired to the adjutant's office, where the question was quickly decided by awarding the cleanest-footed man the ten days' furlough.

At daily guard mounting the cleanest and neatest men were selected for orderlies, positions of routine duty that were considered among the men as " soft snaps," as they were then relieved from doing guard duty and night work. It was surprising to see how neat and clean some men could be when one takes into consideration their close quarters and other drawbacks on the tented field. Men who had the best facilities at home for presenting a clean personal appearance in dress and toilet were in many instances just the reverse in cleanliness during camp life, while those who had to put up with poor advantages at home were at their very best as soldiers in the field, presenting, as they did, a clean and neat appearance at all inspections.

At this camp great interest was manifested in an order for a grand review of the army. After thorough preparation and inspection the regiments of the brigade assembled in light marching order, without overcoats, on the morning of Wednesday, Nov. 20, 1861, and took up the line of march for Bailey's Cross Roads. Our brigade was then known as Morell's 2d brigade, and consisted of the Ninth Massachusetts Volunteers, 62d Pennsylvania Volunteers, 4th Michigan Volunteers and 14th New York Volunteers. The great field at the Cross Roads was likewise near Monson's Hill, the latter place being a few miles or more to the left of our camp. This ground was the scene of the greatest review of troops, up to that date, which had ever occurred on this continent. When it was announced to take place it created universal interest in the city of Washington, and, in fact, throughout the whole country, including the Southern army and Confederacy. Since Bull Run General McClellan had been working assiduously in organizing the Army of the Potomac. His labors were not as yet fully accomplished, owing to a lack of equipments. The following list represents the strength of the army of the Potomac on that day,— aggregate present for duty, equipped : —

Infantry	. . . . . .	114,742
Artillery	. . . . . .	6,859
Cavalry	. . . . . .	10,764
Total	. . . .	132,365
Miscellaneous troops, unequipped	.	36,929
Total strength	. . .	169,294

Out of this number all that could be spared from duty without detriment to the service, assembled on the field at the Cross Roads, and numbered about 60,000 ; that is, about 50,000 infantry and 10,000 artillery and cavalry. The army was promptly on time and each arm of the service was drawn up *en masse* in their respective positions. In their great numbers and full equipment they presented a magnificent sight. On our front and centre, handsomely mounted, appeared President Lincoln, with his cabinet, U.S. senators, congressmen, and other distinguished citizens, together with General McClellan and his brilliant staff.

At the call of the bugle the consolidated brass bands struck up their martial music. The President and friends, escorted by General McClellan and staff, rode up and down the lines of the assembled troops. The drums rolled, the trumpets flourished and the bands played as the President and staff and General McClellan and staff passed rapidly along on their tour of inspection. The infantry, brigaded *en masse*, in blue uniforms, with arms and equipments brightened and polished until they glittered in the light of a clouded sun, filled the beholders with pride and confidence. The artillery, with its solid appearance in men, horses, guns, caissons, etc., all in fine condition and good order, ready, as it were, to fire death and destruction at the foe, won the admiration of the cavalcade. The cavalry presented to the official inspectors an arm of the service, which in warlike appearance promised effective work in active service in the near future.

The tour of inspection being ended, the President and General McClellan, with their escorts, were once more in their places on the centre ready to review the army. The order was sent down the line to pass the reviewing officer in "double-quick time." This order suited the men of the Ninth Massachusetts, for, thanks to the incessant drill of the colonel, they were veterans at double-quick movements, and felt confident that they could do it to the satisfaction of themselves and their reviewers. Not so, however, with those who had not practised the double-quick step, fully armed and equipped, for it would go hard with them on that damp and slippery ground such as we were going to double-quick over. The review commenced by the right of the infantry taking distance from *en masse*, and wheeling into column on the way to the reviewing officers. At about thirty yards from the left of the cavalcade the troops took the step from the band, then playing a double-quick strain near the reviewing officer, and passed along in company front as best they could. Very soon our turn came and every man was determined to do his best. Having wheeled to the left in quick time we went forward with steady ranks and caught the double step. Tramp! tramp! tramp! we went, our company lines well dressed both front and rear ranks. Our companies were larger, both in size and numbers, than the average regiment of the same strength, because none were on detached duty and none were sick in camp. The colonel insisted on every man turning out, barring only company cooks and a small camp guard. Every man held his head well up, showing lines of tanned and determined Irish faces. The left forearm was against the left hip;

the right hand firmly grasped the butt stock of the musket as it sloped firmly over the right shoulder. Steady we went, preserving a perfect alignment in every company. Tramp! tramp! tramp! until the cadenced step of the regiment made it appear like one great piece of united moving machinery. The colonel could be excused for feeling proud of his regiment, for it did nobly and won honors as it passed the reviewing stand, and shortly took a left turn in a new direction. As the last of the infantry passed in review the artillery then came forward at a trot. In all its solidity and full equipment it presented to the eyes of the beholders that warlike appearance which only trained and disciplined artillery on the field can show. As the long line of guns passed briskly in review they created a most satisfactory and lasting impression as to their future service in the terrible work that was before them. As the last battery passed, the brilliant squadrons of cavalry were moving forward in quick time. Arriving at the proper distance they advanced toward the reviewing stand at a trot, fully meeting all expectations as a great body of warlike horsemen, whose future service in their country's cause would be crowned with success.

The grand review of our new army was, at last, at an end, and it is needless to say that the President, General McClellan, and all others who saw or participated in it, were duly impressed with its importance. It strengthened the Union cause. It inspired the President and the government behind him with greater hope and fuller confidence than they had ever felt before. It brought new and deserved honors to its organizer, and inspired the Army of the Potomac itself with a strength and confidence in its own powers and invincibility which the darkest hours of subsequent defeats and misfortunes could never deprive them of. As we marched back to camp congratulations on the brilliant success of the grand review were heard on every hand. Every one, from the general to the private, was imbued with the feeling that the Army of the Potomac would be soon ready for active warfare. With this prospect in view, the rigid discipline under which the army had grown to such large proportions was continued, so that when tattoo was nightly sounded every one who could was glad enough to retire to rest in order to resume, with freshened vigor, the arduous duties of the following day.

Christmas was now fast approaching, and, as is customary with Catholics, great preparations were under way to celebrate the event in the Ninth Massachusetts Volunteers. The whole camp was decorated with arches of evergreen and ivy, and adorned with appropriate mottoes. The regiment attended the celebration of mass, Father Scully celebrant, after which the holiday was devoted to innocent enjoyment.

5

In the evening the officers had a banquet in the large tent, the latter kindly loaned them by the chaplain. Many distinguished officers of the division were present as invited guests. The festivities were also graced by the presence of several ladies — the wives of officers — who were on a visit to the camp. A caterer from the city of Washington furnished the banquet, which, on the whole, proved to be a most enjoyable occasion. Music, speeches, poetry and song filled up the closing hours, much to the enjoyment of all present. Boxes of good things from home had arrived early in the day, and were distributed through the regiment to their several owners. Our winter quarters, with all its monotonous routine, was greatly enlivened by this celebration. It was as refreshing to our soldiers in camp as the sight of an oasis in the desert is to the weary traveller. While it was the first of the kind that we had enjoyed since entering the army, it was also the last one for many of our brave fellows, who subsequently laid down their lives for the Union and the Flag. As a reminder of our Northern homes in Massachusetts the snow began to fall that night, and it continued to silently cover our camp until several inches in depth whitened the ground like a white soft carpet. In the mild weather which followed it quickly disappeared the next morning under a warm Southern sun.

Lieut.-Col. Robert Peard, who had been sick with liver trouble for several months, died on the 27th day of January, 1862, greatly regretted by the regiment. A military funeral, led by our band playing the "Dead March in Saul," escorted his remains to the railroad station. A military escort of officers went with the body to the city of Washington. From thence it was sent to Milford, Mass., for final interment. Lieutenant-Colonel Peard was an earnest and patriotic soldier and an indefatigable worker. As a field officer he was always prompt and reliable in the performance of his duty. It can be truly said of him that through unswerving devotion to duty he sacrificed his life on the altar of his adopted country. This was the first death among the officers since the formation of the regiment, and it cast a feeling of gloom and sorrow among us which words cannot describe. His widow and family in their bereavement received the heartfelt sympathy of the regiment.

Our army, although lying snugly in its winter quarters, was not allowed to forget that a large army of the enemy was likewise encamped in winter quarters at Centreville and Manassas. Cavalry raids were of frequent occurrence on both sides. The intermediate ground between the picket lines was the scene of light skirmishes between bodies of cavalry, which occasionally called out infantry support. At such times the drummers' " long roll " would call out a regiment or two in a great hurry. When the Ninth was ordered out it took the double-quick step and would hurry to the scene of action to find that the scare was all over and the enemy had disappeared. Sometimes in the open country one would get a distant view of the discreet foe on some far away hills, as it alternately appeared and disappeared on its homeward journey to some distant wooded camp. Random shots from cavalry raiders would sometimes hit an exposed picket. Cavalry videttes were sometimes surrounded, surprised and captured by some of the more daring raiders. Instances occurred where some of our reserve pickets with strong nomadic instincts would wander off between the lines to some distant plantation residence and, falling into the hands of the unexpected enemy, were made prisoners and sent to Richmond. It was suspected that signals from these dwellings accounted for the sudden appearance of cavalry who captured the unwary Union soldiers.

On the 14th of February, 1862, the Ninth Massachusetts went on a reconnoissance to Vienna and found about half a mile of the railroad, which connects Alexandria and Leesburg, destroyed. A part of the road was thrown down the embankment; other portions of it were destroyed by fire. To accomplish this the sleepers were piled up together, and the rails, previously removed, placed on top of the pile. The ties were then set on fire; as the wood burned the rails in time became red-hot at about the centre, which received all the heat. In this red-hot condition they were then given a turn or two around telegraph poles and trees in the vicinity. More of them were doubled up and bent out of all shape, and entirely ruined for all practicable purposes. The regiment by main strength hauled back that portion of the track which was thrown down the embankment, and replaced it on the roadbed again. After many hours spent in the vicinity of Vienna we failed to hear or see anything of the enemy, and late in the afternoon returned to camp much exhilarated by our labor and reconnoissance. As our cavalry had a brush with the enemy's cavalry, we, as supporting infantry, felt that we were engaged in the skirmish in a moral sense. Feb. 20, 1862, we went to Dranesville, looking for an encounter, but the swift-footed enemy was not disposed to gratify our wishes, except to the extent of a skirmish with our cavalry. As the affair was of short duration, and of the runaway kind, we were forced to put up with our disappointment in not getting a shot at the enemy. In this way we were often called out, only to return to camp disappointed in not having a good skirmish. It appeared evident to us then that the cavalry on both sides were amply satisfied, after chasing each other back and forth, in not coming within range of the infantry fire.

The warm southern spring of 1862 was fast approaching.   A large Southern army was in our front.   The Army of the Potomac was fully organized and eager for an advance on the enemy.   The following figures will show the strength of the Army of the Potomac, which was under the command of Maj.-Gen. George B. McClellan, on the 28th of February, 1862.

Number present for duty . . .	185,420
Aggregate, present and absent . .	222,018
Number of pieces of field artillery . .	465
Number of pieces of heavy artillery . .	69

CHAPTER V.

SIEGE OF YORKTOWN.

GENERAL McCLELLAN RETURNS TO DUTY — THE CONFEDERATE ARMY MOVES SOUTH — THE SPY SYSTEM — BAD ROADS AND LABORIOUS MARCHING — STRENGTH OF THE SOUTHERN FORCES — GENERAL McCLELLAN'S COMMAND REDUCED — FAIRFAX COURTHOUSE — OUR MARCH TO ALEXANDRIA — STEAMER " STATE OF MAINE "— IN CAMP NEAR HAMPTON — RECONNOISSANCE — SIEGE OF YORKTOWN — EVACUATION BY THE ENEMY — BATTLE OF WILLIAMSBURG — THE ARMY PUT INTO FIVE CORPS — EXPLOITS OF THE FOURTH MICHIGAN — CAMP OF THE NINTH AT GAINES' MILL — RICHMOND IN SIGHT — OBSERVATIONS FROM THE BALLOON " INTREPID."

"BEFORE THE BATTLE."

THOMAS MOORE.

" By the hope within us springing,
Herald of tomorrow's strife;
By that sun, whose light is bringing
Chains or freedom, death or life — .
Oh! remember life can be
No charm for him who lives not free!
Like the day-star in the wave,
Sinks a hero in his grave,
' Midst the dew-fall of a nation's tears."

*　　*　　*　　*　　*

ABOUT the middle of January, 1862, General McClellan had recovered from a severe illness. On his return to duty he found that the administration was excessively anxious for an immediate movement of the United States forces.

The Secretary of War, Edwin M. Stanton, had been recently appointed a member of the President's Cabinet. General McClellan, therefore, laid before him his plan of attack on Richmond by the Lower Chesapeake. By direction of the Secretary of War he submitted the plan to the President. The result was that the President disapproved of it. Without consulting the major-general commanding, the President then issued War Order No. 1, January 27, appointing Feb. 22, 1862,

as the day for a general movement of the land and naval forces of the
United States against the insurgent forces.

In this order it was specially mentioned that the army at and
about Fortress Munroe; the Army of the Potomac; the Army of Western Virginia; the army near Mumfordville, Ky.; the army and flotilla
at Cairo, and a naval force in the Gulf of Mexico be ready to move
that day.   A few days following — January 31 — a supplemental
special War Order was issued to the effect that all the disposable force
of the Army of the Potomac, after providing safely for the defense of
Washington, be formed into an expedition to seize and occupy Manassas Junction on or before Feb. 22, 1862.

General McClellan objected to the President's orders as imprac-
ticable, and, with permission, forwarded his reasons in writing in a
letter to Hon. E. M. Stanton, Secretary of War, dated Feb. 3, 1862.
Immediately after submitting this letter several verbal conferences
ensued between the administration and General McClellan.   One of
the results of these conferences was that the orders of the President
were never formally revoked or referred to in any shape afterwards.
But on the 27th day of February, 1862, by authority of the President,
the war department proceeded to procure the necessary steamers and
vessels to transport the Army of the Potomac, to the Peninsula.

The appearance of the *Merrimac* off Old Point Comfort on the 8th
day of March, 1862, and its attacks on our wooden war vessels, was
the object of great solicitude to our government.   But the engagement
of the *Merrimac* with our gunboat *Monitor*, on the following day,
March 9, demonstrated conclusively that the Union sea forces were
then masters of the situation.

On Sunday, the 9th day of March, 1862, positive information
reached General McClellan that the enemy's forces were evacuating
Centreville and Manassas, and moving south towards Richmond.   This
sudden movement of the Confederate army, which lay all winter in
front of Washington, was the natural consequence of the commencement of the Peninsula campaign; and a result that was predicted by
General McClellan in his late letter to the Secretary of War, previously
referred to.

The city of Washington was, at that time, and in fact all during
the war, the hot-bed of rebel spies and correspondent informers of the
Confederacy; so that absolutely nothing which the administration collectively attempted to do could be kept secret.   Male and female spies,
inside and outside of the departments, many of them actual salaried
employees in the civil service of the government, were active and vigi-

lant, night and day, in gathering information from official and other sources for transmittal to the government of the Southern Confederacy. Spies, ostensibly in the service of the Union, were in many instances actually engaged in aiding and abetting the Southern cause, particularly at this early date. Thus, the sudden movements of the Southern army were readily accounted for.

The roads between Washington and Richmond, at this early season of the year, were almost impassable for an army of large dimensions, and fully prepared for aggressive battle. While it was a bad movement for the Confederate forces, stuck fast in the mud as they were, it was likewise a savior for them also, for it was impossible to pursue them owing to the horrible condition of the roads and the country generally. Except on turnpike roads field artillery and wagons generally would sink to their axles in mud and mire. This condition of the ground in the early spring, if nothing else, would hinder the Union forces from pursuing or overtaking the enemy. General McClellan, however, deemed it a proper measure to set his army in motion preparatory to entering on the Peninsula campaign. On the night of the 9th of March orders were accordingly issued for a general movement towards Centreville. The Ninth regiment broke camp early on Monday morning of the 10th of March, 1862.

At this camp for the first time we were made acquainted with the "poncho" tent. The quartermaster had one set up for the individual inspection of ·the regiment. It consisted simply of a rubber blanket, the new issue, two yards long, by one wide, with buttons and buttonholes. One blanket for each man. Two of them buttoned together lengthwise and set on a ridge pole, so as to give a slanting roof, with each end supported by a slender upright and the four corners fastened to the ground until it stood up like the letter A, were sufficient covering for two men when lying down. It served admirably to protect them from the rain and heavy dew. In cold weather four men would sometimes get together and stop up both ends of their little tent and sleep warm if not comfortably. When first issued to the soldiers it was the occasion of much curiosity, fun and wit. When its usefulness was rightly understood it was so much appreciated that no soldier would be without one. They were afterwards made of a light tough material which would readily shed heavy rain, and during a campaign were a great comfort to the troops.

With three days' rations in haversacks, and in heavy marching order, the regiment joined in with the brigade, Monday morning, *en route* for Fairfax Court House, a distance of twelve miles. As the road was heavy with mud the marching was very laborious. The artillery, cavalry and wagon trains which preceded us left the roads in bad condition for the infantry. We had passed about five months in winter quarters and during all that time accumulated a large quantity of clothing and personal effects which were hard to part with, so that most of the knapsacks which our men carried when they started out of camp looked like small-sized black leather trunks well packed. Add to this blankets, overcoats and equipments, etc., and one can readily imagine that many of them soon discovered that they were heavily handicapped. The whole army in fact started out in about the same condition. To drop a blanket or an overcoat, or both, in the road, as a means of relief was a very easy thing to do; other extra superfluous clothing sometimes followed until the line of march was strewn with soldiers' effects for several miles. Nearly every man had reduced his knapsack more or less until it assumed a lighter weight, before he had passed over half his journey.

Two regiments of cavalry were in the advance, and reached the enemy's lines at Centreville by noon of that day. The camps and works in every direction were evacuated, and military stores and valuable army property were set on fire in heaps and still burning. On reaching Manassas the same destructive state of affairs was discovered. The Southern army was miles in advance making its way with great difficulty through the mud towards the south. The information which General McClellan had received on the 9th of March, about the evacuation of Centreville and Manassas, was now verified by this reconnoissance. The evidence elicited from spies, deserters, prisoners, refugees and slaves, who came from the enemy's lines, both before and after the evacuation, aided General McClellan in making a close estimate of the strength of the Confederate works and the numbers of its army. The Secret Service Corps, at this time, likewise contributed much valuable information, obtained through various sources, among which were some of the enemy's intelligent railroad employees. From all these sources of information it was estimated that the army in our front and vicinity numbered at the lowest figure one hundred and fifteen thousand men. The fortifications at both Centreville and Manassas proved to be of a formidable character, with a capacity for three hundred field guns, and about thirty siege guns. The flanks of these long lines of earthworks were protected by impassable swamps, streams, woods and broken ground. The skill of the Southern engineers was so complete that every available approach was directly under the sweep of their guns and intrenchments.

This reconnoissance of our army in force exploded the reports about " Quaker Guns," — a ruse, by the way, easily and quickly set up at the last moment by an army contemplating a retreat — and an inferior enemy. It furthermore conclusively proved that an aggressive movement and assault in that quarter, under all the developed circumstances, would have resulted in a doubtful issue. On that account credit is due to General McClellan for his military wisdom and foresight in opposing a proposed movement in that direction, and in selecting the Peninsula for his campaign against Richmond. Events have proved that if the latter movement had been faithfully supported by the administration, as originally agreed upon, it would have been successful.

As this reconnoissance was led by General McClellan in person he obtained much valuable and reliable information of the enemy's movements which he communicated to the administration.

The Confederate army having entirely evacuated their formidable works at Centreville and Manassas, were falling back behind the Rappahannock river, on Fredericksburg and Gordonsville. Owing to their sudden movement south and the horrible condition of the roads — excepting the turnpikes — they were obliged to abandon many wagons, military stores, etc. That they suffered great hardships by their forced mud march, and the abandonment of comfortable winter quarters, is beyond question.

While General McClellan was engaged in this movement he was — unexpected by him — relieved of the command of the United States army on March 11, 1862, by the President's War Order No. 3, and his command was thereby reduced to the " Department of the Potomac."

A council of war was held at this time, March 13, 1862, by Generals McDowell, Sumner, Heintzelman and Keyes, at army headquarters, Fairfax Court House, which resulted in the endorsement, under certain conditions, of the proposed Peninsula campaign. It was assented to by General McClellan and forwarded to the President. No objection was made to it by the President, provided Manassas Junction was held by a sufficient force, and the city of Washington left entirely secure.

It was shortly after noonday when we halted near Fairfax Court House, the shire town of Fairfax county. In time of peace the place contained about six hundred inhabitants. At this period of the war the grown male population was absent with the Confederate army, which was somewhere between us and Richmond struggling to extricate itself from the mud and mire of its early spring movement. As the capital of the Confederacy was one hundred and twenty miles further south of us it was somewhat difficult then to exactly locate the position of the enemy except in a general way. We remained in the vicinity of Fairfax until the 15th of March. In the meantime a large part of our army had arrived and some of the infantry were bivouacked under " shelter tents," a name which by general consent the men had given to the original " poncho."

On Saturday the 15th we took up the line of march for Alexandria. To say that it rained is putting it mildly. It poured most of the march in torrents until the troops were wading at times through water knee deep. After going about twelve miles in the drenching rain over a turnpike road we went into camp at Camp California, near the ancient city of Alexandria on the Potomac. This camp had a number of tents already pitched and was lately occupied by some regiments of the " Irish brigade." The latter were still at the front somewhere on the plains of Manassas. Stumps of trees recently felled were standing here and there over the campground as evidence of the thick woods which but a few months before covered the hillside. Like all deserted camps it had a cheerless and forlorn appearance which mud and rain did not relieve it of. It was dubbed " Camp Stump " by some of the men and " Camp Misery " by others. At night the weather cleared and Sunday morning opened up bright and pleasant. By noontime our clothing, etc., was well dried, and our condition was somewhat improved by changing camp a few hundreds yards back, in front of Fort Worth.

Monday, March 17, 1862, was our first St. Patrick's day in the army. Owing to recent events no arrangements were made to celebrate the day. The routine discipline of camp life such as we followed during the winter at Miner's Hill, was now a thing of the past. Enough however was adhered to to keep our men busy. Camp rumors on the situation of affairs were numerous at all times of the day, most of them being pure inventions for fun by those with a comic side to their character. The fact that we were in daily expectation of going by water to the Peninsula was verified on the 21st by orders to break camp and proceed to Alexandria for transportation. A short march brought us to the steamer *State of Maine*, Captain Cauldon, bound for Fortress Monroe. Our quarters on board this fine large steamboat, under its genial captain, were a great change from the hardships which we had endured on land since leaving winter quarters. It not only afforded the regiment a fine opportunity to " gather itself together," as it were, but it likewise gave a dry, warm place to sleep and rest; a comfort which we greatly needed and appreciated. Much enthusiasm was created in the Ninth regiment the next day when the captain of the steamboat had our green flag hauled up to the main truck. Cheers from hundreds of Irish throats greeted the green flag of Erin as it fluttered and snapped its folds in the strong breeze like a thing of life suddenly set free. For the time being many Irish hearts were swelling with pride and pleasure at such an unusual sight. Those who witnessed the scene remembered it vividly through life. As a flag raising it was emblematic of the lifelong desire of their hearts, *i.e.*, " freedom for Ireland."

After a short and agreeable passage the regiment debarked at the wharf, near Fortress Monroe, on Sunday morning, the 23d of March, 1862, and marched off to the plains in the vicinity of Hampton. We found that this once picturesque town was now in ashes. The place was ruthlessly destroyed by the enemy some months previous when it was driven from the vicinity. There was an abundant supply of wood obtained from the adjacent forest, and that night particularly, the regiment enjoyed the luxury of many big campfires. Colonel Cass had a great liking for a large campfire of logs. In the evenings at his headquarters the regimental band would give a concert for several hours. At such times large numbers would congregate in the vicinity of the great bright blazing campfire, to smoke, talk and enjoy the musical scene until late in the evening. This particular campfire was so attractive that the writer, with others, would take a blanket and picking out a green spot of earth, repose there all night. The colonel, not being a well man, was a poor sleeper, and occupied some of the time in horse taming, after the style of the famous Rarey. When the band concert was over, he would, with great skill, put the harness on a horse and throw the animal to the ground, and in a short time be complete master of him. The roll of a drum, the firing of a revolver, the drawing of a sword, or any other ordinary device for startling a horse, would have little or no effect on his newly tamed steed. While it was entertaining to the lookers on, for he carried the pastime far into the night, it likewise helped to pass the time pleasantly to the sleepless, and in some instances it was a benefit to the horse.

On the third day after our arrival we changed camp to a place near New Market Bridge, about two miles off, in order to give more room to the troops which were now arriving daily in large numbers.

An order for a reconnoissance to Big Bethel was sent to our colonel on the afternoon of the 26th; on receiving the order he notified his adjutant to see that every man was supplied with forty rounds of " buck and ball " ammunition, and ready to move in light marching order at daylight in the morning. The captains of companies were duly notified to prepare for the movement. On applying to the quartermaster for the cartridges it was all at once discovered that he had in his possession only rifle ammunition of 59 calibre, and no " buck and ball " such as the regiment required. It appeared that our venerable quartermaster — through no fault of his — had delivered to him by the ordnance officer, sometime previous, 59 calibre rifle, instead of 69 calibre " buck and ball " ammunition. As the boxes of both were much alike the difference was not observed until occasion called for its use. The colonel was soon informed that the ammunition on hand was of no use, and he immediately sent for the acting quartermaster-sergeant. The colonel inquired of him about the ammunition. On being told that it was 59 calibre rifle cartridge, he asked the sergeant if he could not take it down to Fortress Monroe and exchange it for the same quantity of buck and ball. The acting quartermaster-sergeant replied that he thought it could be done. He was then ordered to go about it at once. It was then 3 o'clock P.M. It took some time to go on foot to the division corral and obtain a six mule army wagon team, one of a large lot which had lately arrived and were but newly broken to harness. In fact it was the army's first experience with mules as it had been all along using horses. To return to camp again and load up forty boxes of ammunition and then take the road to Fortress Monroe consumed much valuable time, particularly as the sergeant was alone in this matter, no detail being made or asked for. The sergeant with his team and driver had been on the road but a short time when he saw in the distance a solitary horseman galloping at full speed towards him. As he came nearer it proved to be Colonel Cass. On reaching the team he pulled up his horse, after nearly running the sergeant down in his impetuous course, and cried out: " Where in thunder have you been?" The sergeant mildly replied — thinking there was some trouble in store — that he had been obeying orders, that he had the ammunition now in the team, and was on the way to Fortress Monroe to exchange it. " Well," said the colonel, " I thought you were fool enough to go off without it "; without waiting for a reply he continued, " look at my horse!" On looking the horse over — a fine bay " hammer " headed animal — he presented the appearance of hard driving, being covered with foam, sweat and dust, for the afternoon was intensely hot; the horse besides was panting quite freely. On remarking that his horse was much heated the colonel then said to the sergeant: " I've been down the road about five miles after you thinking that you went off without that ammunition !" Everything appearing satisfactory the colonel moved off towards camp while the sergeant continued on in the direction of Fortress Monroe. The road was hot, dusty and deserted, save by the sergeant and his team. It was after sundown when they reached the fortress, and for fear of being denied admission, the driver whipped up his team and went over the bridge to, and through the sally-port on the gallop. The guards let them pass without a word thinking no doubt they were on some important business. So they were as far as the sergeant was concerned. Arriving inside the fortress, which appeared then like a quaint, small-sized village, the sergeant after inquiry found the ordnance officer and delivered his errand, presenting at the same time receipts and invoices, which he had taken the precaution to prepare before leaving camp. The ordnance officer was a regular 1st lieutenant and a very gentlemanly man. He refused to sign receipts, or exchange vouchers in any event, and owing to the fact that it was growing dark, likewise refused to deliver the required ammunition, as he considered it a dangerous undertaking to enter the great magazine with lanterns. Here was a dilemma! The sergeant had firmly made up his mind, hours before, not to go back to camp and face Colonel Cass without that " buck and ball." The meeting with the colonel on the road a few hours ago only served to strengthen that resolution. The sergeant was then in appearance, tall, slender and boyish looking, and no doubt, to the mature looking lieutenant, who wore a mustache and goatee, appeared as green as a leek, and a " no account " volunteer, who did not know exactly what he did want. The sergeant on hearing the ordnance officer's decision was not greatly surprised, and mentally, did not blame him for not entering the magazine after dark. It was a dangerous thing to do, if it were to be done with lighted lanterns. The uppermost thought, however, in his mind was that the regiment must have buck and ball cartridges for that reconnoissance at daylight tomorrow; and so the sergeant told the lieutenant as quietly and firmly as he knew how, and then submitted this proposition : that he would, if allowed, remain where he was with his team all night, and at the first dawn of the morning receive from his hands the required ammunition, and then move forward until he would overtake his regiment, perhaps before they met the enemy; that to go back the long distance to camp without it that night was not to be thought of. The lieutenant listened to these remarks very quietly and appeared in deep thought but made no reply. The sergeant likewise held his peace, thinking he had given him enough to " chew " over. In a few moments the lieutenant began to write on the back of the papers the sergeant had previously handed him, then passing them back said : " Go to the magazine and inquire for Ordnance Sergeant ———— and hand him this." Before the team could be brought to the spot and the order obeyed, the lieutenant was on the ground himself, having no doubt, on second thought, concluded to superintend the job for fear of accident. In a few moments a dozen men, besides those holding lighted lanterns in line far into the magazine, were rapidly engaged in unloading the team and filling it up with the much sought for " buck and ball " ammunition, every box of which the sergeant inspected so as to be sure of no mistake. It was a great relief that evening when all was completed and they were on the road back to camp. They were in no great hurry now, and barring accident, would arrive at camp by taps or shortly after. They met with an accident however. The driver must have been tired and sleepy, or his mules were contrary, or both, for going over a short bridge near camp, he stalled one side of his wagon in the ditch. To unload and get the wagon out and then reload was quite a job and it consumed time, but they finally struck the camp of the Ninth shortly after taps were sounded. It was late when the sergeant reported results briefly to the colonel. He was evidently pleased to know that the ammunition was on hand, but he didn't say so in the sergeant's presence. The colonel was not given to compliments or flattery. Getting a blanket, and after eating a couple of hard-tack by the colonel's big campfire, and gazing at the stars for a while, the tired sergeant was soon fast asleep.

This episode is related to show the reader the anxiety and restlessness of Colonel Cass in performing military duty. This lack of ammunition, when discovered, worried him so that it drove all ideas of rest or sleep from his mind. He would have watched and waited all night for the acting quartermaster-sergeant's return in order to feel sure of its arrival. It is out of the question to say what the result would have been if the " buck and ball " had not been obtained.

Our orders for a reconnoissance to Big Bethel found us on the road, in light marching order, on the early morning of Thursday, March 27, 1862. The weather was fine, and the infantry were in high spirits ; that is if the disposition of the soldiers of the Ninth was any criterion to go by, for they were as happy as larks at the prospect of a skirmish, as it was reported that Big Bethel was full of " Johnnies." After marching till about noontime the regiment struck Big Bethel on the double-quick, as our skirmishers reported the enemy in front on the retreat — "skedaddling," in Southern parlance — at a rapid pace. The enemy in the vicinity — said to have been about five hundred in advance of its reserves — on our unexpected approach made no resistance, but on the contrary, left in a hurry as was shown by the apparent preparations for dinner which were left behind. We followed them some distance beyond Big Bethel but to no purpose as they were moving rapidly and had too much the start of us. After a short rest and refreshments from our rations and the enemy's dinner, we returned and reached camp by dark, having marched in all some twenty odd miles without firing a gun. Routine duty continued until Friday, April 4, 1862, when with three days cooked rations in haversacks, in heavy marching order, we left camp and started on the advance march for historic Yorktown.

General McClellan's command by this time had been so far reduced by the orders of the administration that on reaching Yorktown it covered only that portion of the Army of the Potomac which was engaged in attacking the enemy at that place. In reducing Yorktown General McClellan had originally planned to commence the work with 155,000 men. Besides this number 42,000 soldiers were held around Washington for the protection of that city. In the Shenandoah Valley to meet any emergency which might arise in that district there were 35,000 more. Later on General McClellan was informed by the administration that General Blenker's division of 10,000 men would be withheld from his command. The 10,000 soldiers under General Wool at Fortress Monroe which McClellan expected would join his army at Yorktown, were also denied him at the discretion of General Wool. Another reduction of 43,000 men of the First Corps under General McDowell was made on the day of our advance towards Yorktown. So that the whole number of troops under the command of General McClellan in his movement up the Peninsula was reduced in all to 92,000 soldiers. Out of this army actually available for battle were only about 68,000 soldiers, according to General McClellan's estimate. The United States army, east and west, was, at this period, divided into four independent commands. All were under the direction of the President and his advisers at Washington.

Since the 8th day of March, 1862, the Army of the Potomac had been by orders from Washington organized into army corps as follows : —

The First Corps — 4 divisions — Gen. I. McDowell; the Second Corps — 3 divisions — Gen. E. V. Sumner; the Third Corps — 3 divisions — Gen. S. P. Heintzelman; the Fourth Corps — 3 divisions — Gen. E. D. Keyes. The reserve artillery, the regular infantry and cavalry, and the Engineer troops were attached to General McClellan's headquarters. General Hooker's Division of the Third Corps, General

Casey's Division of the Fourth Corps, and General Richardson's Division of the Second Corps, were still encamped in the rear awaiting army wagons and means of transportation. On that account they were unable to join the main body of the army at Yorktown until the 10th, 16th and 17th of April, respectively. In the meantime sickness and other casualties were making sad havoc with some of our troops.

The Ninth Massachusetts Volunteers was now attached to the 2d Brigade, General Morell; 1st Division, Gen. Fitz John Porter; Third Corps, General Heintzelman.

On the 4th day of April our division led the advance of the army towards Yorktown. When in sight of Big Bethel the enemy fired a few shells at our skirmish line — of which Companies I and F of the Ninth formed a part — and then they left in a hurry for Yorktown. We passed Harwood's Bridge, and through Cockletown, near which we bivouacked that night. The 5th day of April found us about one o'clock, P.M., skirmishing within four hundred yards of the fortifications of Yorktown. The batteries shelled our lines quite furiously, throwing some very large shell apparently from their greatest guns. Our brigade took shelter in a ravine, protected by a hilly elevation, under the fire of the enemy's batteries. Many of their shells dropped and exploded very close to us, killing and wounding at one time several men in the 62d Pennsylvania of our brigade, and in line next to the Ninth. The fact that the enemy could neither see nor locate our position saved us many lives. On Monday night the Ninth was detailed to throw up a small redoubt for one of our field batteries. The men proceeded quite close to the works in their front and finished the job before dawn of the next day. At daylight the enemy caught sight of the little redoubt and began to shell it as our field-pieces opened fire. The enemy succeeded in making it too hot for our battery. Under such terrific shelling it was deemed futile to continue, and the little redoubt was quickly abandoned without any casualties. The rain began to fall very heavily and it steadily continued for over two days.

On Thursday the 10th day of April we fell back with the division and took a position to our right in line before Yorktown. Our camp was situated in a large and well defined peach orchard over which the shells of the enemy were continually passing both day and night. The shells could be traced at night by their burning fuses as they passed overhead. The noise they made on their deadly journey sounded very much like the quick puff! puff! puff! of an engine passing out of a railroad station. During the siege several shells burst along our line of battle with fatal effect, but as a general thing they passed far to our rear doing comparatively little damage to life or limb.

Yorktown was said to have for its defense at this time some 15,000 troops. At Norfolk and vicinity some 15,000 more of the enemy were at hand, and at Gordonsville the bulk of the Confederate army was concentrated ready, when the emergency required, to reinforce their Yorktown troops. Our line of battle reached from the York river on our right to the Warwick river on our left. General Heintzelman's Third Corps (ours) held the right of the line. Our division was on the right of the corps near the York river and in view of Gloucester Point, which is on the opposite bank of the river. Gloucester Point was also in the possession of the enemy and strongly fortified. Wormley's creek was in our front. General Keyes' Fourth Corps held the left of our line at the Warwick river and environments, with Lees' Mills in front. General Sumner's Second Corps occupied and held our centre. Having established this line of battle it was the intention of the original plan to use McDowell's First Corps as a flanking column to capture Gloucester Point from the rear, and with the assistance of our war vessels, ascend the York river and surround the enemy in Yorktown by a counter-flank movement on our left with Keyes' Corps. But as before stated, McDowell's Corps of four divisions of 43,000 men was detached from the Army of the Potomac on the day of our advance, by the administration, for the additional defense of Washington. General McDowell's army was then made an independent command. Owing to the great reduction in his command General McClellan deemed it necessary to lay siege to the fortifications at Yorktown.

One day during the siege an exciting incident occurred. The military balloon was in use by McClellan, and it went up in the air about a thousand feet almost daily for observation. On the day referred to it broke from the single guy rope which held it, and the occupant, General Porter, was carried over the enemy's lines at Yorktown for quite a distance. As the balloon continued to rise and sail away it fortunately struck an opposite current of air which carried it back to our lines, where it quickly descended in safety much to the relief of the Union army which was watching it intently. It is safe to say that the enemy were disappointed on seeing it return to our lines. It was a fortunate escape from capture as the balloon was a valuable one. Ever after this event four cables were attached to the balloon to insure its safety.

The military maps of the topography of the country, in that particular part of the peninsula, at that time, were incorrect and misleading. In the vicinity of the Warwick river the swamps and lowlands were flooded to the depth of four and five feet by a system of dams constructed by the enemy. The distant fortifications were found to be more numerous and formidable than previously reported. These works, which were considered easy of capture by assault, proved on the several attempts to surprise and take them, to be anything but weak. The Fourth Corps did some hard fighting here, and lost many brave men in their assaults on the enemy's works. Passing as they did through long stretches of mud and water, waist deep and over, under the galling fire of the intensely active infantry and artillery behind the fortifications in their front, their lack of success is not to be wondered at. During the siege our sharpshooters were a great annoyance to the enemy; their aim was so deadly that it was at times difficult for the Confederates to work their heavy guns. The enemy's sharpshooters retaliated continually upon our men whenever opportunity offered.

After repeated requests for reinforcements, to turn and capture Gloucester Point, General Franklin's division of General McDowell's Corps was sent to the Peninsula where it arrived about April 22, 1862. Up to this time the enemy had likewise greatly increased its forces in our front. The Confederate army at Yorktown now consisted of Generals Magruder's, Longstreet's and D. H. Hill's Army Corps, all under the command of General Johnston, and in line from their right to left in the order above named.

The month of April was now drawing to a close. Nearly a hundred siege guns and mortars were mounted on our batteries at ranges of fifteen hundred to two thousand yards. Preparations were in progress to land General Franklin's division in the rear of Gloucester Point. The gunboats and war vessels in the river were waiting to take some part in the general attack.

On the evening of the 3d of May, we were somewhat astonished at the vigorous and continued fire from the enemy's big guns, not even guessing its purport. It was as it shortly proved the farewell shots of the foe. General Johnston with his army was evacuating Yorktown. The last shell fired dropped close by our camp, wounding several men in the next regiment. At 9 o'clock P.M. all the guns of the enemy were silent. As the night passed along the unusual silence in our front was noticed all along our lines, and floating rumors of evacuation began to circulate from camp to camp. Early Sunday morning, May 4, 1862, we first heard the definite news that the enemy had gone from our front and were rapidly retreating to their line of earthworks at Williamsburg. Our brass bands, which had been silent for about a month, now began to play their familiar airs to celebrate the great event. The day was bright and pleasant. During the forenoon one division after another moved forward in pursuit of the enemy. Two divisions, General Franklin's and Porter's, remained in camp. Our regiment received orders to move. At 1 o'clock P.M. we left camp in light marching order, which was a sign that we would soon return.

On reaching the forts at Yorktown we were warned to look out for buried and concealed shells with sensitive fuses, which, being kicked or trodden on, would explode with murderous effect. Some prisoners of war were captured at Yorktown and beyond that point. These men were set to work searching the ground along the road and under the trees after the buried shells and made to mark the spots where they lay. The writer saw many places that were marked with upright sticks, which were said to contain buried shells. It was reported at the time that some of our men were killed and wounded by stepping on them, or otherwise coming in contact with them, previous to this precaution being taken. This mode of warfare was severely condemned by everyone at that time, and many execrations delivered on the heads of the enemy who were murderous enough to perpetrate so foul a scheme for taking life needlessly. That same evening our regiment was relieved from guard duty and returned to camp, where our division impatiently awaited orders to move.

A rainy morning greeted us on the 5th of May, and the sounds of heavy and continuous artillery firing in our front, in the direction of Williamsburg, could be distinctly heard. As it subsequently proved, a part of our army under the command of Gen. Edwin V. Sumner had attacked the enemy in its last line of works near Williamsburg. General Longstreet's corps and D. H. Hill's corps had made a stand for the purpose of saving their wagon trains which were slowly forging on towards Richmond over bad roads heavy with mud and rain.

The battle of Williamsburg on our part was carried on by Hooker's and Kearney's divisions of the Third Corps, and Couch's, Smith's and Casey's divisions of the Fourth Corps. General Hooker's division held the brunt of the battle. About one-third of Kearney's, Couch's and Smith's divisions were actually engaged.

Near the close of the day the fighting had ceased, and in the rain and gloom which followed, General Longstreet with his army moved on through the night towards Richmond. At 7 o'clock P.M. our division was for a short time on the road when it was ordered back to camp for the night.

The battle of Williamsburg was over, and for an engagement with the so-called rear guard of the enemy the losses were quite heavy on both sides, and were as follows: Union forces: 468 killed, 1,442 wounded, 373 missing or captured. Total, 2,283. About two-thirds of these losses were in General Hooker's division. Confederate losses: 288 killed, 975 wounded, 297 missing or captured. Total, 1,560.

The next morning, May 6, our troops found the enemy's works abandoned and took possession of them, and likewise entered the historic town of Williamsburg, where they found several hundred of the enemy's wounded. Our cavalry went in pursuit of the retreating foe, but outside of capturing some stragglers the chase was fruitless. Our troopers reported the roads in a terribly bad condition, deep with mud and greatly cut up by the enemy's retreating trains and artillery. General Franklin's division was transported up the York river, and debarked at Eltham Landing near West Point at 1 o'clock P.M., May 6.

On the morning of the 7th the enemy discovered Franklin's presence and opened an immediate attack. This assault continued for more than six hours, and although the enemy had a superior force, it withdrew at 3 P.M. and resumed its retreat up the Peninsula. Had the enemy known the exact situation of our forces on that day it is more than likely that it would, with its superior numbers, have attacked Franklin in full force and virtually annihilated his whole division. Part of our army was then at Yorktown awaiting transports; part at Williamsburg, and a part (Franklin's division) near West Point. Efforts were being made to concentrate the divided forces, but not until the 10th of May could it be said that they were in supporting distance of each other. Our division left its old camp at night on the 7th, entered Yorktown about midnight and bivouacked to wait for transports. At 3.30 P.M. the next day we went on board our steamer in the York river and reached West Point that night.

By Friday of the 9th our regiment was comfortably encamped in a piece of woods. We were now enjoying fine weather for nearly four days, but in the sun it was extremely hot. Our camp in the woods was a relief from the heat on account of the shade it afforded our shelter tents. The drying power of the southern sun was something surprising. The roads so lately deep with mud were now growing hard, and in a few more days of such hot weather they would become dusty.

Here in our vicinity were to be seen the newly-made graves of those who fell in the late battle. Soldiers who were fighting for the preservation of the Union and men who were fighting against it had lately given up all that they could give for the cause they espoused. Friends and foes were sleeping their last sleep side by side.

On Sunday, May 11, General McClellan and staff passed along the road. " Little Mac," as the soldiers loved to call him, was vociferously cheered as he rode rapidly by. The enthusiasm for McClellan, by his soldiers, seemed to increase every day. Whenever and wherever he appeared it was always the same. Caps were thrown up, and cheers from thousands of throats rent the air throughout the army. A general knowledge of affairs, which one always finds throughout an intelligent army of men such as the Army of the Potomac was composed of, had long since entered the minds of nearly every man and through this knowledge the army realized that great obstacles were in his path hourly and daily, and that on his young shoulders rested great responsibilities. As their gallant leader in their march " on to Richmond " his soldiers gave him their fullest confidence and their minds and hearts went out to him as their beloved commander. Thus it was that the occasions to cheer him and encourage him were never allowed to pass without doing so to their utmost. None of the commanders of the Army of the Potomac, who came after him during those terrible years of warfare, ever aroused in the hearts of their soldiers such love and admiration as he received and held to the end of his brilliant career.

Early Tuesday morning, May 13, we were again on the march. The weather proved to be very hot, and the road which was but lately deep with mud and rain was now thick with dust kicked high in the air by the moving army. The reflecting rays of the hot southern sun on the dusty road severely affected the soldiers, causing straggling, or falling out of the ranks, and obliging numbers to relieve themselves of knapsacks and clothing, which at the time proved a burden too great to carry. The inventive genius of some produced what was termed the " horse collar." An army blanket was spread on the ground and a few necessary articles of clothing selected from the discarded knapsack and spread thereon; then the blanket and its contents were carefully and tightly rolled up, the ends brought together and firmly tied. This circular roll was put on over the head and rested on one shoulder and against the opposite side under the arm; in this manner it was easily and lightly carried. When tired of carrying it on one shoulder it would be shifted over to the other. At a halt for a few minutes it was used as a cushion to sit on. It was found to be, on fatiguing marches, a great relief from the much despised knapsack with its cutting straps and awkward, heavy back burden. Ever after thousands of our army would carry their luggage of personal effects in no other way; so that the " horse collar " was a success from the start. When once settled in winter quarters new knapsacks were easily procured from the quartermaster. After the day's fatiguing march we bivouacked at Columbia Landing for the night. Another move forward in a few days found us at White House Landing. In the meantime a heavy fall of rain brought our dust-laden roads again to the condition of "mud to the ankles," and our artillery and wagon trains were laboring along in mud and slush to their axles; while at the same time the mules and horses were struggling to haul their heavy wheels knee and belly deep, through the rutted cradle holes and miry places for which Virginia country roads were noted during the war. The wagon trains and the army being dependent on each other in a hostile country, were now more or less inseparable, so that the slowness of one retarded the progress of the other.

On the 18th of May, 1862, the Army of the Potomac was concentrated partly in the vicinity of Cumberland Landing, partly at New Kent Court House, Eltham, and White House Landing. At the latter landing on the Pamunkey river, a permanent depot for army supplies of all kinds was established.

The Army of the Potomac was now newly reorganized into five army corps as follows : —

The SECOND CORPS, under General Sumner, had two divisions commanded by Generals Sedgwick and Richardson.

The THIRD CORPS, under General Heintzelman, had two divisions commanded by Generals Kearney and Hooker.

The FOURTH CORPS, under General Keyes, had two divisions commanded by Generals Couch and Casey.

The FIFTH CORPS, under Gen. Fitz John Porter, had two divisions commanded by Generals Morrell and Sykes. The RESERVE ARTILLERY was attached to the Fifth Corps, General Hunt commanding.

The SIXTH CORPS, under General Franklin, had two divisions commanded by Generals Smith and Slocum.

On the 11th day of May the James river was opened to our forces. This result was brought about by the *Monitor* when she defeated the *Merrimac*.

The success of the campaign against Richmond would have been assured if the Army of the Potomac had been transferred to the James river. The available protection of our gunboats would have secured rapid transportation at all times, both in supplies and reinforcements. Fate, and the administration, directed otherwise. It was planned that General McDowell's army would advance from Fredericksburg to the north of Richmond, and form a junction with the Army of the Potomac when in front of the Confederate capital. If this plan even had been adhered to the fall of Richmond would have been a question of only a short time. As McDowell's advance was at the last moment abandoned, only disaster and failure finally resulted to our devoted army.

While lingering in the vicinity of White House one could not help but admire the surrounding country. At this time of the year nature was at her best. The fields, the woods and the streams were delightful to the eye in all their natural beauty. In time of peace the inhabitants of this section of Virginia must have indeed enjoyed their country life. Now its inhabitants had fled leaving everything in the face of two contending armies, which were destined for several years to come and go leaving unmistakable signs of death and destruction in their ruthless pathways.

In moving forward again the regiment left behind two companies — I and A — which were detailed for fatigue duty, in unloading a vessel lately arrived at the landing with supplies for the army. Having performed the task assigned them they proceeded to join the regiment which was now encamped some six miles ahead at Tunstall's Station and about eighteen miles from Richmond. Short marches during the following three days brought our division within ten miles of Richmond.

Heavy showers of rain kept the roads in wretched condition much to the detriment of both man and beast. The slaves who lived on the plantations throughout the surrounding country, and received news of the approach of the Union army — "Massa Linkum's sojers" — were now coming in from all quarters. Camps were organized where they had to be taken care of, and fed with army rations. These dark-skinned wanderers included men, women and children of all ages and sizes. They were well received and treated kindly by the soldiers. Some of the young fellows attached themselves to the officers of the different regiments and became faithful servants. Most of the slaves appeared happy and contented with their new-found freedom, and were ready to go anywhere except back to their old servitude. The confidence which the poor innocent blacks placed in the Union soldiers was quite touching. That they knew and felt they were among friends and on the road to freedom, was freely expressed and sincerely shown.

On the 24th of May the 4th Michigan regiment of our brigade was ordered out on a reconnoissance in connection with the cavalry. This aggressive party forded the Chickahominy river — which was but a few miles from our camp — about a mile above New Bridge and attacked the camp of the enemy. The 4th Michigan after several hours fighting drove a superior force of the enemy. The latter lost ten killed, and twenty-three wounded and thirty-seven captured. The 4th Michigan lost two killed and six wounded. On the return of the 4th Michigan to camp the news of their gallant exploits created a breeze of excitement throughout the brigade. The next day, Sunday, the 25th of May, many of us attended the funeral of the slain of the 4th Michigan.

The following day, the 26th, we changed our camp a few miles further to the front near Gaines' Mill. The mill was the property of the Gaines family which lived near. It was a building of several stories in height and was at that time said to be the finest grist mill in that part of Virginia. It stood on elevated ground particularly from the Cold Harbor side. The water from the mill-pond which drove the wheel ran down into Powhite creek thence to the Chickahominy river. During, the exceedingly hot days of June, 1862, the mill pond was a favorite resort for those who liked the water for a good swim. In some parts the pond was quite deep, and although it had a dark and treacherous look, we greatly enjoyed our bathing.

Our camp at Gaines' Mill was composed of shelter tents only, for the men; one wall tent for the officers of each company, and four wall tents for the field and staff officers. The transportation for the regiment consisted of five army wagons — six mule teams — three of which were to carry three days' rations of hard-tack, coffee, sugar and pork. One wagon carried the baggage for the field and staff officers, and one the baggage for the line officers.

Richmond in a bee line was about eight miles distant. From the lookout, which was established near our camp, the steeples of the churches, and houses on the hill in Richmond could be plainly seen on a clear day with the naked eye. Through a glass they could be seen distinctly.

Professor Low's military balloon, the "Intrepid," was in constant use nearly every day at army headquarters. It was attached to four guy ropes, each held by eight men and allowed to rise to the height of one thousand feet. From this elevation the works around Richmond, the Confederate army in our front, and the surrounding country were surveyed through powerful glasses. General Porter, principally, was the one who went up in the balloon. When it was rising or descending, and reached a distance of 250 or 350 feet, the enemy would fire solid shot and shell at it hoping to hit the gas bag and burst it, or perhaps knock the occupant out of the basket. Although continually firing at it when in use the missiles never came anywhere near hitting it. At such times the exploding shells were intently watched by the soldiers of both armies. The occupant of the basket seemed to be entirely innocent of the attention which he, at such times, attracted.

CHAPTER VI.

BATTLE OF HANOVER COURT HOUSE.

ORDERS TO MARCH — MEETING THE ENEMY — CLEARING THE WAY FOR
GENERAL McDOWELL — THE BATTLE — THE NINTH MASSACHUSETTS
IN ACTION — GENERAL McCLELLAN ARRIVES — "THE FIGHTING
NINTH" — OUR LOSSES — COLONEL CASS' REPORT OF THE NINTH IN
ACTION — LIST OF CASUALTIES — BURYING THE SLAIN — COMPANY E
CAPTURES A FLAG — GENERAL McDOWELL'S ARMY HELD BACK —
SUCCESS OF GENERAL JACKSON'S "SCARE" IN THE VALLEY — BATTLE
OF FAIR OAKS — CASUALTIES — BAD CONDITION OF THE CHICKA-
HOMINY RIVER — TWO MEN OF THE NINTH SWIM THE RIVER —
GENERAL PRIM OF SPAIN — GENERAL STUART'S CAVALRY RAID —
THE POSITION OF THE UNION ARMY — GENERAL LEE'S AND JACKSON'S
PLANS.

BEFORE THE BATTLE.

* * * * * *

"Many a heart that now beats high,
In slumber cold at night shall lie;
  Nor waken even at victory's sound.
But oh! how bless'd that hero's sleep,
O'er whom a wondering world shall weep!"

* * * * * *

THOMAS MOORE.

ON the first day of our encampment at Gaines' Mill, orders were
received to hold the regiment in readiness to move forward, at
a moment's notice, in heavy marching order on the following
day; that is the 27th day of May, 1862. Company inspections were
held and every man was supplied with buck and ball ammunition to
the number of eighty rounds each. Two days' extra rations were likewise issued. The colonel cautioned and ordered the company commanders to see that every available man was present for duty, as it
was his purpose to have the full effective force of the regiment in line of
march in the morning. A long march was in view, and a battle was
in prospect. The colonel's instructions were carried out to the letter,

and the regiment was in fine fettle at the prospect of a spirited engagement on the morrow.

Early on the morning of the 27th, the Ninth Massachusetts was in line, about nine hundred strong, and presented a fine appearance. The rain commenced to drizzle steadily, much to our discomfort and disappointment, and it continued so until 12 o'clock M., when the sun came out clear and hot.

On the march the roads were found to be heavy with mud, which was very soggy and slippery, a condition of things which always adds to the fatigue of long and steady marching. Wagons from the regiment, with extra rations and ammunition, were to follow, which only proved that several days would be spent on this expedition.

Lieutenant-Colonel Guiney was in command of the regiment when it left camp. Colonel Cass, who was suffering from serious illness and exposure, was ordered by the surgeon to remain in camp. But the prospect of clearing weather and the expectation of an engagement with the enemy was too much for the war spirit within him, and although a seriously sick man from internal troubles, he in a few hours later was on his horse dashing over the road to join his regiment. Everyone was surprised to see him when he overtook the Ninth. But, on his appearance, a general satisfaction was felt that he was to be present; for his regiment had full confidence in him as a brave and able soldier, and a discreet and trusted commander.

Our objective point was from eighteen to twenty-three miles distant, and about twelve miles to the north of Richmond, in the vicinity of Hanover Court House. The Confederate General, L. O'Brien Branch, with his North Carolina brigade, and the 45th Georgia regiment, were encamped at Hanover Court House. General Anderson's Confederate brigade had reached Hanover Junction on the 25th instant, from in front of the anticipated forward movement of General McDowell's army at Fredericksburg. These troops of the enemy numbered in all about 12,000 men.

General McClellan deemed it advisable to clear the way for General McDowell's army, and to protect as far as possible the right flank of the Army of the Potomac and adjacent territory; to destroy the Virginia Central railroad, telegraph wires, etc., and to drive out besides all of the enemy to be found in that section of Virginia. All of this work was successfully accomplished, and the country was opened and cleared of the enemy so that General McDowell's army was free to join General McClellan in his contemplated assault for the capture of the Confederate capital.

This expedition was under the direction of Gen. Fitz John Porter, the Fifth Corps commander, and was composed of the 1st division, commanded by General Morell. Our whole force numbered twelve thousand men. The infantry consisted of three brigades. The 1st brigade was commanded by Gen. J. H. Martindale and was made up as follows: 2d Maine, present; 13th New York, absent on detached duty; 18th Massachusetts, absent on picket duty; 22d Massachusetts, present; 25th New York and Berdan's Sharpshooters in the advance column.

The 2d brigade was commanded by Col. James McQuade of the 14th New York, senior colonel and acting brigadier-general of General Morell's old brigade, and made up as follows: 14th New York, 9th Massachusetts and 62d Pennsylvania, present for duty; 4th Michigan, present in reserve.

The 3d brigade was commanded by Brig.-Gen. Daniel Butterfield and made up as follows: 12th New York, 44th New York, 17th New York, 83d Pennsylvania and 16th Michigan, all present for duty.

The artillery present in action consisted of Massachusetts Battery C, Capt. A. P. Martin; 5th U.S. Battery D, Capt. Charles Griffin; and Captain Benson's Horse Battery, 2d U.S. Artillery.

On the march there was, far in advance of the main body of the 1st division, the 5th and 6th U.S. Cavalry; Benson's Horse Battery of the 2d U.S. Artillery; the 25th New York Infantry, and Berdan's Sharpshooters. About noon the cavalry reached the vicinity of the junction of the Ashland and Hanover Court House roads. Here they encountered the enemy, a part of General Branch's brigade in position, holding the road to the Court House. The 25th New York and the Sharpshooters supporting Benson's battery, immediately engaged the enemy. It was soon discovered that superior numbers were in their front and on their flank. After a long fight, during which several of the 25th New York were surprised and captured, our troops succeeded, with the assistance of the cavalry, in holding Branch's forces in check until the arrival of our main body. The sounds of battle hastened our division forward. General Porter rapidly advanced with the 3d brigade and ordered General Butterfield to charge his command on the enemy's line of battle, which he did in a most gallant manner, driving the foe towards Hanover Court House, capturing one piece of artillery and many prisoners. The pursuit was continued by the cavalry. The 2d (our) brigade followed after the 3d, in close supporting distance. On information received from the 5th U.S. cavalry, that a body of the enemy was in the vicinity of Peak's Station and had attacked our detachments, which had been subsequently sent in that direction to destroy the railroad and telegraph lines, the 1st brigade, having only two regiments present — the 2d Maine and 22d Massachusetts — under General Martindale, was, on arrival, sent forward to reinforce them, and was under the direction of General Morell, the division commander. They found the 44th New York with a section of Martin's battery in charge of a lieutenant, furiously assailed by the enemy, who appeared in large numbers. The guns were captured and the 44th driven back.

The 1st brigade's two regiments now engaged in the fight and were assisted by the 25th New York. The attacking force proved to be the principal part of General Branch's brigade which came upon us as it was moving south towards Ashland from the direction of the woods on the left of Hanover Court House, thus striking our detachments in the rear while they were carrying on the work of railroad and telegraph destruction. Unless support arrived General Morell's defeat was certainly only a question of time. Information was slow in reaching General Porter as to the critical condition of the detachments in his rear. The difficulty of conveying information on this battlefield may be realized by the reader if he will picture to his imagination several square miles of country intersected by country roads, large belts of thick tangled woods, wheatfields, fences, swamps and railroads. In the meantime the forces are constantly changing direction and the general commanding is moving hither and thither, as the emergency demands, so that aids and orderlies find it very difficult to deliver their messages until after a long and diligent search, going as they do through great danger, and sometimes to their death or capture. On receiving information that the enemy was in force in his rear, General Porter at once ordered the 2d and 3d brigades to the " right about." With the 2d brigade in front they went on the double-quick in the direction of the battleground. The 2d brigade had arrived on the field about 3 o'clock P.M., owing to the fact that they were the left and rear of the marching column. It was now nearly 5 P.M.

The Ninth regiment, after their long march, unslung their knapsacks and threw them on the ground and then double-quicked in column of companies in the direction of the heavy firing, through a wheatfield, to the edge of the woods, where the regiment formed in line of battle. Under direction of the brigade commander, Colonel Cass ordered his regiment to charge into the dense woods, which they did with an Irish cheer, long and loud. Onward they went, over fallen trees, ditches and fences, under a galling fire from a slowly retreating enemy, capturing large numbers of the foe that they had overtaken, only to pass them by in their eager pursuit of the main body which had now broken and were in full retreat across the railroad, making through the open spaces for the protection of the houses, fences and woods in their front and on their flank.   In emerging from the woods, from which the enemy had so lately beaten a flying retreat, the left wing of the Ninth struck another wheatfield and, in their hot pursuit of the foe, got far ahead of the right wing which still continued to move forward in the tangled brush of the dense woods.   Lieutenant-Colonel Guiney in command, on discovering the sudden disappearance of the left companies, halted his men to investigate.   It was soon learned that the left of the regiment, in command of Major Hanley, had reached an opening and were rapidly advancing through the wheatfield.   First Sergeant J. W. Macnamara, comprehending the situation, quickly volunteered to take Company I and make a connection.   Acting under orders from Colonel Guiney, he commenced deploying his men at speaking distance, by the flank; he dashed along on the double-quick until he overtook the left wing where it had partially halted, vainly looking for the appearance of the missing companies.   To report to Colonel Cass the condition of affairs and pass the word along the connecting line of his " living telegraph," was only the work of a few moments.   Very quickly the right wing came in sight on the double-quick, and, as it assumed its place in line of battle, cheers went up from the regiment, long and loud, which made the enemy believe that reinforcements had arrived.   Once again the battle-line of the Ninth advanced on the foe, with the right and left companies, I and F, deployed as flankers.

Under a heavy fire from the enemy, which fortunately went high over head, the line charged forward down the bank, across the railroad and up the opposite bank.   On gaining the level field the colonel reformed his line quickly and charged again under a rapid and random fire in his front, which did but little damage to the men.   The determined pursuit and formidable appearance of the long battle-line of blue-coats of the Ninth, as they charged on the foe, seemed to strike them with dismay, and, as they broke and ran towards Richmond, a derisive cheer from the men of the Ninth went up as they followed in hot pursuit.   Many more prisoners were captured besides retaking the two pieces of Martin's battery which the enemy had vainly endeavored to take with them.   Many of their wounded were found in the houses in the vicinity.   Quantities of their knapsacks, clothing, guns and equipments were scattered over the field, belonging to those who were killed, wounded, fled and taken prisoners.

Colonel Cass was highly pleased with the entire action of his regiment during the battle. General McClellan, who came up late in the afternoon, and General Porter, the Fifth Corps commander, both complimented the regiment for the quick and gallant work which they had accomplished in their share of the battle. General Porter gave the regiment then and there the sobriquet of "the Fighting Ninth," by which title they were known ever after. At the close of the day the casualties proved to be one man mortally wounded and eleven men seriously and slightly wounded in the Ninth regiment. The enemy were so actively engaged in getting away from us that they had little opportunity to do much execution. Their firing was too high. Captain Martin's Massachusetts Battery; Captain Griffin's U.S. Battery, and Benson's Horse Battery spread great destruction amongst the enemy during the day. All the troops of the 1st division, Fifth Corps, which were actively engaged, did gallant service during the battle. The ambulance corps carried our wounded to the transports on the Pamunkey river.

Our total losses in the division, were 4 officers and 58 men killed; 12 officers and 211 men wounded; 2 officers and 68 men missing and captured; total, 355.

The enemy (estimated) lost some 200 killed, 200 wounded, and 730 prisoners captured. Large quantities of cars, military stores, telegraph wires and railroad lines were destroyed.

The writer in conversing with some of the prisoners, who were North Carolina men, was surprised to hear them declare " that they were glad they were captured; that they were Union men at heart and didn't believe in the secession war." These expressions were freely made by them. Our men were very friendly and the prisoners appreciated the kindly spirit shown them. During the years that followed in our terrible struggle, this spirit of manly kindness towards prisoners of war continued till the close amongst the *fighting men* of both armies.

An official report of the part taken by the Ninth in the battle of Hanover Court House was made by Col. Thomas Cass, commanding Ninth Massachusetts Volunteers, as follows : —

FIFTH PROVISIONAL ARMY CORPS, PORTER'S DIVISION, SECOND BRIGADE. }
HEADQUARTERS NINTH MASS. VOLS., June 4, 1862. }

WM. SCHOULER, *Adjutant-General, State of Massachusetts.*

General : The Ninth started on the morning of the 27th with the brigade, under command of Lieutenant-Colonel Guiney, as the poor state of my own health prevented me from accompanying it whilst it rained so heavily as it did at the beginning of the march. So soon as the weather promised to be tolerably fair, although very faint and weak from an illness of three weeks, at times more or less severe, I joined my command on the way to the Virginia Central Railroad, passing the scene of the struggle that had taken place but a short time before our arrival, between the 25th New York and a party of rebels, and down the Hanover road where the brigade halted. For a brief period no firing was heard; soon, however, it was evident that the enemy intended a demonstration on our rear, he making a detour from our front around to the left. "About face!" "Forward!" were the commands, and the troops retraced their steps. The Vincent House passed, now on our left, a little way on the road the regiment moved into a field on the right into column of companies through a wheatfield to near the verge of a wood in which the fight seemed to rage heavily. Everything indicated a fierce contest in the front. Colonel McQuade, our brigade commander, accompanied by some artillery officers, rode up to us, and, rising to full height in his saddle, with full emphasis said, "Colonel Cass, the enemy has taken two pieces of Martin's battery, and I want the Ninth Massachusetts to retake them, which I know they can and will do." A line of battle was formed, I repeated to my men the wish of their brigade commander. "Forward, Ninth!" A loud and vigorous cheer was given, and a bold dash made into and through the woods by my command. For some time not a shot was fired by them. Every eye seemed distended to catch a glimpse of the retiring foe in some force. Prisoners of war were captured in fives, tens and twenties. Onward heroically and determinedly the boys of the Ninth pushed their way notwithstanding a long and fatiguing march from early in the morning (it then being about 5 o'clock P.M.). Our charge was over felled trees, through brush and tangled brambles, swamps such as Virginia produces, over a ditch and fence from behind which the enemy poured a hot fire, but which was charged upon with redoubled energy, he scattering in every direction. All the obstacles that could be thrown in the way of an advancing force in a close wood by a resisting foe were surmounted. Six companies got out to the road and into the fields and small orchard on the left, where the enemy still held ground behind and in the vicinity of four or five houses and huts. At the further house Captain O'Leary's company (F) captured seventeen prisoners and an ambulance at the nearest one, leaving several wounded Confederates in the houses. The woods were cleared by both wings. The line was reformed as it moved along in a wheatfield in the teeth of an incessant fire, miraculously doing us little hurt. Companies I and F were deployed out on the right and left flanks with a view to engage the attention of the enemy who had now, after leaving the two pieces of artillery of Martin's battery in rear of the houses in the orchard, taken up a position behind a fence and two houses on its left, extending across the field to the verge of a wood running at right angles to the one from which we had issued. They poured at us then a scorching and heavy fire, flying over and around us in a perfect torrent. Down and up the steep banks of the cut made for the railroad I moved my regiment by the right flank. Having cleared the railroad a solid front was again presented to the enemy. Another dash at right shoulder shift arms was made towards him when he precipitately fled closely pursued by the companies deployed as skirmishers. During the fight we had one mortally wounded (since dead) and nine seriously and slightly.

The starry banner of the Union, side by side with our green flag through the fight, came out of it unscathed, while the latter was pierced by eight buck and ball shots and the lower tie torn away. I am well pleased with the bearing of both my officers and men, all endeavoring for victory in the contest.

Respectfully submitted,

(Signed)   THOMAS CASS,

Colonel Commanding Ninth Mass. Vols.

KILLED OR DIED OF WOUNDS.

Sergeant Daniel J. Regan, Co. G.

WOUNDED.

Privates Michael O'Brien, Co. B, in shoulder, slightly; John Leonard, Co. C, in face, seriously; John D. McGuire, Co. C, in right breast, seriously; Samuel Smith, Co. E, in leg, slightly; James McLaughlin, Co. F, in thigh, slightly; Corporal William Armstrong, Co. G, in breast, slightly; Private William McGrath, Co. H, in calf of leg, slightly; Sergeant Lawrence Conlin, Co. I, in thigh, slightly; Private John Spillane, Co. I, in groin, dangerously.

The following additional were reported wounded at Hanover Court House, May 27, 1862, in a subsequent report of Company C, viz. : —

Privates John Harvey, George Williams.

Total casualties in regiment: 1 killed, 11 wounded.

At an early hour on the following morning, Wednesday, May 28, 1862, the Ninth took part in the closing scenes of the battle. Details from the regiment were made to assist in burying the dead, both friends and foes. Long pits or graves were dug or scooped out, to the depth of three or four feet, and the bodies of the slain were laid in them in groups as they were found, as many as twenty-five being placed in one pit, without ceremony and without blanket, shroud or coffin. Space was economized by placing the dead soldiers heads and feet alternately, until all were laid out and covered over with a few feet — or less — of earth. About two hundred of the enemy were thus buried by details from the division and the places marked by board slabs for future identity. Our own dead were buried and their graves marked in a similar manner. The principal part of the regiment was, in the meantime, engaged in destroying the railroad and in capturing more prisoners, weary stragglers who failed to keep pace with their retreating comrades. Company E brought in a flag captured from a North Carolina company. By nightfall the division had succeeded pretty thoroughly in the destruction of everything that would be useful or serviceable to the enemy, including miles of telegraph and railroad. On information that McDowell's army was not coming, the bridges on the South Anna and Pamunkey rivers, which yet remained, were destroyed. All was now accomplished to the satisfaction of our victorious troops.

Recent information was received by General Porter that the order to General McDowell's army to make connection with the right of the Army of the Potomac for a general assault on the city of Richmond had been countermanded, and McDowell's army, which had been several hours on the march, was returning back to Fredericksburg. We had fought the battle of Hanover Court House on the preceding day and cleared the way for a rapid and uninterrupted march of McDowell's army, only to learn later that the administration at Washington had hurriedly ordered it back to defend the capital from a threatened attack.

In the light of subsequent events it appears that the much dreaded Confederate general, " Stonewall " Jackson, who for several weeks had been attacking and whipping our troops in detail in the Shenandoah valley, had again lately attacked General Banks' army with an inferior force and defeated and driven him to the Potomac river, producing thereby terror and consternation in the city of Washington, so much so that it had the effect of causing the authorities to recall General McDowell in great haste from his march in the direction south to Hanover Court House and thereby destroying the great opportunity of making the contemplated junction with the Army of the Potomac and capturing Richmond. The great opportunity was lost and " Stonewall " Jackson, in the Shenandoah valley, had gained his point and accomplished all that his heart desired, which was the recall of McDowell's army. The city of Washington, surrounded by strong fortifications and an army or armies of — including McDowell's — nearly 80,000 men, was held in dread of an attack and capture by Stonewall Jackson, with a force of less than 15,000 men ! Having successfully accomplished his designs and hoodwinked the authorities in Washington, Jackson immediately set to work to join Lee's army in front of Richmond in the latter part of June.

In the face of the general disappointment that occurred regarding the army of 43,000 men under General McDowell, preparations to return to camp were made on the 29th of May. The Ninth received orders at noon to be in readiness to move. The right wing of the regiment was on picket during the day and was relieved and joined the left wing at 1 o'clock. At 3 o'clock P.M. they started with the brigade for

Gaines' Mill, and after a tiresome night march, reached camp at 2 o'clock A.M. of the 30th.

The failure of McDowell's army to make connection with the right of the Army of the Potomac rendered it imperative for the Fifth Corps to abandon its isolated ground at Hanover Court House, and on that account it was obliged, for its own safety, to return to its old position on the right of the army, at Gaines' Mill and vicinity.

A few historical facts in reference to these movements it is hoped will not be deemed out of place.

During the month of May and part of June General " Stonewall " Jackson, with an army of some 9000 men, which was subsequently increased to about 15,000 soldiers, caused dismay and uneasiness in Washington by his unparalleled strategic movements throughout the Shenandoah valley. Up to the 17th day of June he had fought and won four desperate battles, defeating in detail the separate commands of Banks, Fremont, Schenck and Milroy, in the valley, one after another. General Shields' army which he fought at Kernstown was the only instance where he suffered defeat. The successes that Jackson met with by his characteristic generalship seemed to paralyze with dread and consternation the government at Washington and to demoralize the various generals and their armies in its vicinity. By the 27th of May General Jackson had to such an extent affected the government of the United States that they revoked the order to McDowell to act in conjunction with McClellan's army in its assault on Richmond. That a fatal mistake was made in withholding McDowell's army from joining the Army of the Potomac at that time, is believed by all sides familiar with the subject.

Both of these Union armies — McClellan's and McDowell's — were in fine condition, fresh, thoroughly equipped, and having, besides, the best furnished corps of field artillery possible. Their combined attack in the latter part of the month of May and the first of June, 1862, would have captured the city of Richmond, destroyed General Johnston's army and ended the rebellion in Virginia.

General McClellan, before the McDowell court of inquiry in December, 1862, is quoted as follows: " I have no doubt said, for it has ever been my opinion, that the Army of the Potomac would have taken Richmond had not the corps of General McDowell been separated from it. It is also my opinion that had the command of General McDowell joined the Army of the Potomac in the month of May by way of Hanover Court House from Fredericksburg, we would have had Richmond within a week after the junction. I do not hold General

McDowell responsible in my own mind for the failure to join me on either occasion."

Regarding " Stonewall " Jackson's generalship, Confederate General Imboden says : " Jackson moved all his troops southeast and on the 25th (June, 1862) arrived at Ashland, seventeen miles from Richmond. This withdrawal from the valley was so skilfully managed that his absence from the scene of his late triumphs was unsuspected at Washington. On the contrary, something like a panic prevailed there, and the government was afraid to permit McDowell to unite his forces with McClellan's lest it should uncover and expose the capital to Jackson's supposed movement on it." " Jackson's military operations were always unexpected and mysterious. In my personal intercourse with him in the early part of the war, before he had become famous, he often said there were two things never to be lost sight of by a military commander : ' Always mystify, mislead and surprise the enemy, if possible, and when you strike and overcome him, never let up in the pursuit so long as your men have strength to follow; for an army routed, if hotly pursued, becomes panic-stricken and can then be destroyed by half their number. The other rule is, never fight against heavy odds, if by any possible manœuvring you can hurl your own force on only a part, and that the weakest part of your enemy and crush it. Such tactics will win every time and a small army may thus destroy a large one in detail and repeated victory will make it invincible.' His celerity of movement was a simple matter. He never broke down his men by too long continued marching. He rested the whole column very often, but only for a few moments. He would order his men to lie full length on the grass, saying to them, ' One rests all over when he lies flat on the ground.' "

In the meantime the Army of the Potomac was drawing nearer to Richmond. By the 25th of May the Third and Fourth Corps had crossed the Chickahominy river at Bottom's Bridge and were in position to intrench near Seven Pines, a place situated at the junction of the Williamsburg and Nine-Mile roads and about one mile from Fair Oaks, a station on the Richmond and York River Railroad. The distance to Richmond is about five miles. The Second, Fifth and Sixth Corps were still on the left bank of the Chickahominy river. General Johnston had at this time under his command a large Southern army in front of Richmond and was awaiting reinforcements preparatory to giving battle. It was his intention to bring on a general engagement before McDowell's army could reach the right wing of the Army of the Potomac. He was confident that, with the reinforcements he himself was receiving, he could readily overcome the army under McClellan, and by securing a permanent victory relieve the city of Richmond from threatened capture.

The fears of our government regarding an assault on the city of Washington were well known to the Richmond officials. It was to their advantage to extend these forebodings by every means in their power; hence the ceaseless activity of Jackson in the valley. The Confederate government at Richmond was in the same fearful predicament, but for them the situation was a stern reality and as rigid almost as it could be. An immense army had settled down on their front for the purpose of taking their capital. It now required all of their energies and resources to muster an army superior to it in order to save themselves from destruction. When the battle of Hanover Court House took place on the 27th of May, their fears were increased; and at no time after that would they have been greatly surprised if the Union army, with its promised additional forces, had succeeded in its plans. To relieve their city of the besiegers at the earliest possible day and before additional forces arrived was now uppermost in their minds; hence their preparations for a desperate battle. The welcome intelligence, to them, of McDowell's return to Fredericksburg, caused General Johnston to change his plans for an extensive assault and to commence an immediate attack on our left wing and to annihilate, as he anticipated, the Third and Fourth Corps. The enemy's army consisted of six large divisions or corps, composed of twenty-seven brigades. These corps were commanded by Gens. D. H. Hill, Longstreet, Huger, G. W. Smith, Magruder and A. P. Hlll.

Both of the opposing forces were daily feeling each other's positions by the customary scouting, skirmishing, picket attacks and reconnoissances, until the 31st of May. On the afternoon of the 30th a heavy thunder storm broke over both armies. The thunder and lightning which for hours was incessant might be termed terrific. To the knowledge of the writer one man in the 44th New York was killed by lightning and several others were knocked senseless or prostrated. The fall of rain was unusually heavy and continued during the night. It is, perhaps, superfluous to say that both armies were soaking wet all night and tramping ankle and knee deep in mud and water the next morning.

The battle of Fair Oaks (or Seven Pines) commenced on the following day — May 31, Saturday, which was fine but cloudy — at 1 o'clock, by a savage attack on the part of the Confederates on General Casey's division. In the afternoon General Sumner's corps was ordered across the river in support of our troops who were being slowly forced back by the fierce attacks of the superior numbers of the enemy. The Second Corps (Sumner's) experienced great difficulty in crossing the Grapevine bridge owing to flooded meadows, swamps and roads, and a swollen river from the rain of the preceding day and night. A part of the Second Corps reached the battlefield at 4.30 P.M. One division was delayed until dark. The batteries of artillery had great difficulty in crossing. Nightfall closed the battle of the first day. A large part of our lines were weak and were driven back about a mile, owing, principally, to the superior numbers opposing them. Gen. J. E. Johnston, commander-in-chief of the Confederates, was severely wounded late in the afternoon and carried from the field.

The engagement was renewed on the following morning — Sunday, June 1. The weather fine but hot. The Southern army was commanded by Gen. G. W. Smith, as Johnston was dangerously wounded. Our forces, now increased to three corps, drove the enemy back and re-established their old original lines of battle. At the close of the day's fighting our victorious troops held the field while the enemy, having met with an unexpected and serious repulse, fell back in the direction of Richmond.

The total casualties of the two days' battle were : —

Union losses : Killed, 790 ; wounded, 3594 ; missing, 647 ; total, 5031.

Confederate losses : Killed, 980 ; wounded, 4749 ; missing, 405 ; total, 6134.

The Fifth and Sixth Corps remained on the left side of the Chickahominy to protect our right and to repel any advance over the river that the left wing of the enemy might make ; also to act as a reserve force in case of need. General McClellan's headquarters were near Gaines' Mill, a point where the firing could be heard and the cloud of battle smoke seen as it arose over the field of action. On the 1st of June, 1862, the Ninth Massachusetts Volunteers with the brigade, moved under orders from camp at 7 o'clock A.M., fully prepared for battle and marched to the Chickahominy, but could not cross on account of the flooded condition of the defective bridges and the adjacent banks and shores of the river. Were it not that the elements were against us, it is very evident that our regiment would have had the opportunity of inscribing on its banners the battle of " Fair Oaks." After being thoroughly convinced of the impossibility of crossing the " booming Chickahominy " that day, we slowly returned to camp, listening to the heavy and constant firing of a desperate battle and praying in our hearts that victory might perch upon the banners of our brave comrades.

The Chickahominy river in its normal condition is, where our army lay, a sluggish stream. The natural water-bed is of unequal width; in some places forty feet, in others eighty feet or more. It is bordered by swampy, spongy, low or bottom lands, and covered with dense woods and undergrowth. The large trees grow right through the bed of the river as well as along its banks of mud and slimy shores. When its rank foliage is in full bloom it is impossible to see the land on the other side, or in fact the water of the river itself. Along both banks of this stream the ground rises very gradually into plains, hills and bluffs, ranging in height from ten to one hundred feet or more. During rainy weather these highlands act as a water-shed, which, in twenty-four hours, increases the depth of the river from three or four feet to eight, ten or twelve feet, and spreads out over the lowlands along its shores for hundreds of yards on each side. An army bridge of logs to span so treacherous a stream must cover ground from one-third to half a mile or more. During a big freshet it will run at the rate of four or five miles an hour, and after flooding a bridge will sweep parts of it away like straw. Were it not for the great trees in the river our bridges would last no time. In the early morning, even in the hottest season, the damp fog that hangs over this forest river and the chill air which comes from it enters the bones and marrow of those who are unfortunate enough to come under its deadly blighting influence, like a shiver of death. That the whole Army of the Potomac was not stricken down with malignant chills and fever from the effects of the atmosphere of the Chickahominy was no doubt owing to the fact that youthful years and its adjunct of strong rude health were in their favor. Even then many lives were lost by it, and those who escaped it carried the chills and fever as a souvenir during the rest of their lives. As the Chickahominy approaches the James river, where it empties, it becomes quite a respectable body of fresh water.

The isolated condition of the Army of the Potomac on the 31st day of May, divided as it was by that incubus, the Chickahominy river, and the unprepared and untrenched condition of our corps on the south side of the stream, were great obstructions to success when they came in contact with the concentrated attacks of General Johnston's army of superior numbers. These several drawbacks, added to our inferior force moving in mud and water, assisted in our temporary defeat on that day. When victory came to our banners on the second day's battle and the enemy was driven from our front back onto their own original ground, it proved conclusively that the deprivation of long-promised reinforcements in sufficient numbers was the principal reason from which the Union cause suffered.

That the Confederate army was disappointed in the final results of this battle is sufficiently evident from the fact that it failed to renew the assault on the 2d of June. No doubt the loss of their commander in being seriously wounded on the evening of the first day, had a depressing effect upon them. On the 2d of June, 1862, Gen. Robert E. Lee permanently superseded General Johnston and relieved the acting commander, General Smith. A change of commanders is incidental to a change of plans. The reverse of the crushing defeat of the left wing of our army was an event which the enemy had not looked forward to and it taught them the lesson that great reinforcements must likewise come to them before they could successfully free their capital from the assaults of the determined army which continued to hem them in. That in the course of less than a month they succeeded in relieving Richmond was due not so much to them as it was to our administration in depriving the Army of the Potomac of the long-promised assistance of General McDowell's troops. It would seem from the situation of affairs that a sufficient force could have been gathered together from various sources since April 4 to relieve McDowell's army and then send forward his trained corps to the Chickahominy.

To our left and front the city of Richmond lay on the James river. Seven Pines was again in possession of our forces, a point that is only five miles from Richmond. This was the nearest to the Southern capital that the Union troops under General McClellan had thus far reached.

Artillery firing and heavy skirmishing on our left, on the south side of the river, occupied both armies on the 3d of June, Tuesday. In the early morning of the following day it rained heavily and continued so during the day, flooding the Chickahominy to such an extent that it was impassable for troops. Two men were called for from the Ninth Massachusetts Volunteers to volunteer to cross the river with despatches. Matthew Lynn of Company E and John Hernon of Company B offered their services and performed the duty by wading and swimming the now booming Chickahominy and returning, in like manner, in safety. Great praise — only — was awarded these men for successfully performing this arduous and dangerous feat. They never had anything to show for their gallant act afterwards. As opportunity offered, the various bridges crossing the river were being rebuilt by the engineer corps, assisted by details from the different regiments.

From the 5th of June till the 12th, the Ninth regiment performed guard duty along the river and fatigue duty in bridge building and corduroy road building. While performing this laborious work the men were at times knee-deep and waist-deep in mire and water. At noontime each day a ration of one gill of whiskey was served out to each man to brace him up and keep off the chills. No doubt as a medicine, under the wet circumstances, it effected a good purpose in keeping the blood in circulation and stimulating the laboring capacity of the toilers.

On the 12th of June the 22d Massachusetts Volunteers appeared on the ground and relieved the Ninth about 2 o'clock P.M. As we started back to camp at Gaines' Mill, which was about three miles distant from Woodbury's bridge, the scene of our labors, we noticed that the 22d Massachusetts buckled down to their work like veterans, and, as we were never called on again, we concluded that they finished the job by the next day. We venture to say that they will agree with us when we affirm that it was hard work all through, more particularly the digging in the ditches.

At this season General Prim of Spain was on a visit to the Army of the Potomac. He was the guest of General McClellan and occupied the time in an extensive inspection of the army, and in reviewing the various branches of the service, more particularly the infantry. From time to time the various corps were reviewed by him. On the 9th of June, under the escort of General McClellan and General Porter and their brilliant staffs, he paid a visit to the Fifth Corps, which turned out for review in his honor. General Prim, who was a soldierly looking officer on horseback, complimented the corps on its veteran-like appearance as they passed in review, presenting as they did steady lines of blue and superior marching.

On the 13th day of June considerable commotion was caused by a cavalry raid of the enemy under Gen. J. E. B. Stuart at the head of twelve hundred mounted men and one section of horse artillery. The raiders started from Ashland, thence to Hanover Court House, thence to Old Church, and thence pursuing a course some six to eight miles on the right flank of the Fifth Corps, to Tunstall's Station, across New Kent county to Sycamore Ford on the Chickahominy river, in our far rear; thence through Charles City county to the James river on our left flank, thence onward twenty-five miles to Richmond, on the

James river road. On this two days' raid they travelled rapidly. Their unexpected appearance generally scattered our detachments of cavalry found on duty in isolated places. By their rapid movements they likewise surprised our infantry guards and pickets, capturing, according to their own reports, one hundred and sixty-five prisoners, including teamsters and other non-combatants; a couple of hundred horses and mules, with more or less harness, and a quantity of small arms. The raiders lost one man killed and several wounded. Our losses were equally small in killed and wounded. When the raid was successfully consummated the Southern press teemed with glowing and exaggerated accounts of Stuart's raid around the "Yankee army." It filled the secession people with inflated courage for many a day. The opinion grew upon them that all that was now necessary to be done was for General Lee and his army to go forth and annihilate all the "Yanks" in front of Richmond. It was undoubtedly this popular pressure that hastened the great battles which shortly followed. The non-combatants of the South were as impatient and as unreasonable in their clamor for battle as were those of the North in regard to the advance of the Union army. The appalling slaughter that shortly occurred between both armies in their desperate conflicts after this raid, satiated for a time the appetites of the non-combatants of both sides for bloody war.

The successful ending of Stuart's raid was due to a lack of prompt and proper information from our cavalry commanders and our scouts. Had the course of the raiders been trailed and information as to their movements promptly furnished to army headquarters, a sufficient force could have been thrown out on our left flank to the James river to intercept and capture them. In their fatigued and jaded condition after so long a ride across the country, they would have had to succumb to superior numbers, such as the Army of the Potomac could then furnish. At the first information of this raid our division was ordered out and on taking the field formed into line of battle and threw out skirmishers. Companies I and F from the Ninth went forward over the country in front and flank some three miles and not meeting anything in the shape of an enemy, returned. Had the division rapidly advanced with a force of cavalry in front, by our rear flank some five or six miles, they would have either struck the raiders or got on their trail. But as the information received at division headquarters was meagre and indefinite as to who and what the enemy were, the matter was at first looked upon as a big scare. Still later in the day all kinds of rumors and reports were chasing each other throughout the entire army.

The raid was simply a hurried ride by Stuart's command through the rear country partially occupied by the Union army, without any direct purpose of fighting unless actually compelled to do so in self-defence, and then to escape and continue onward. When unmolested they intended to hurriedly destroy things generally, and then continue their flight. The fear of momentarily meeting a superior force of our cavalry and infantry hung over them, and helped to accelerate their headlong movements. The raiders in a jaded condition were more than glad when they reached their own lines near Richmond at early dawn on Sunday morning of the 15th and dispersed to their respective camps. General Sheridan's raid about two years afterwards more than balanced the account, a raid in which the same General Stuart was mortally wounded.

On June 19 the Sixth Corps moved from camp on the north side of the Chickahominy, and took up a new position in line with the other three corps on the south side of the river, that is, the Second, Third and Fourth Corps. The Fifth Corps, which had been joined by recent reinforcements, composed of General McCall's division (the Pennsylvania reserves) from McDowell's army at Fredericksburg, the 10th New York and the 1st Michigan, together with Generals Cooke and Stoneman's cavalry, was now the only large force on the north side of the river, and all under the command of General Porter of the Fifth Corps.

The great opportunity, which had passed, for a final trial of strength between the two armies was only deferred. The fruits of the victory of the 1st of June were lost by the apparent impossibility of reinforcing our left and centre. The impassable Chickahominy river was now the best ally that the enemy could have, for it prevented details of the Fifth and Sixth Corps from joining our army on the south side and continuing the battle of Fair Oaks, thereby reaping the benefits achieved by the great successes of June 1. But it seems it was not to be.

In the meantime the enemy, under its new and vigilant leader, was drawing around it all the available forces of the Confederacy from far and near. Even the fighting corps of the mysterious " Stonewall " Jackson, which had long paralyzed Washington city and the numerous forces around it, was on its way, by forced marches, from the distant valley, to join General Lee's army in front of Richmond in order to participate in the great battle which was only a few days off. That the reader may better understand the activity and secret methods of the enemy the following letter is offered for perusal : —

HEADQUARTERS NEAR RICHMOND, VA., June 16, 1862.

MAJ.-GEN. T. J. JACKSON, *Commanding Valley District.*

General: I have received your letter by the Hon. Mr. Boteler. I hope you will be able to recruit and refresh your troops sufficiently for the movement proposed in my letter of the 11th. You have only acknowledged my letter of the 8th. I am therefore ignorant whether that of the 11th has reached you. From your account of the position of the enemy, I think it would be difficult for you to engage him in time to unite with this army in the battle for Richmond. Fremont and Shields are apparently retrograding, their troops shaken and disorganized, and some time will be required to set them again in the field. If this is so, the sooner you unite with this army the better.

McClellan is being strengthened, Burnside is with him, and some of McDowell's troops are also reported to have joined him. There is much sickness in his ranks, but his reinforcements by far exceed his losses. The present, therefore, seems favorable for a junction of your army and this. If you agree with me, the sooner you can make arrangements to do so the better. In moving your troops, you could let it be understood that it was to pursue the enemy in your front. Dispose those to hold the valley, so as to deceive the enemy, keeping your cavalry well in their front, and at the proper time suddenly descending upon the Pamunkey. To be efficacious, the movement must be secret. Let me know the force you can bring, and be careful to guard from friends and foes your purpose and your intentions of personally leaving the valley. The country is full of spies, and our plans are immediately carried to the enemy.

Please inform me what arrangements you can make for subsisting your troops. Beef cattle could at least be driven, and, if necessary, we can subsist on meat alone.

Unless McClellan can be driven out of his intrenchments, he will move by positions, under cover of his heavy guns, within shelling distance of Richmond. I know of no surer way of thwarting him than that proposed. I should like to have the advantage of your views and be able to confer with you. Will meet you at some point on your approach to the Chickahominy. I enclose a copy of my letter of the 11th, lest the original should not have reached you. I am, with great respect, Your obedient servant,

R. E. LEE,
General.

By the 25th of June Jackson's corps from the valley had reached Ashland station, twelve miles north of Richmond. He had previously also met Lee in person and between them plans were arranged for an immediate and combined attack of the Southern army upon the right wing of the Union forces on the north side of the river. In the meantime the authorities at Washington and the generals in that environment were all at sea as to Jackson's whereabouts or the position in which his corps was located. McClellan was engaged in continuing his plans by advancing the left of his forces towards Richmond, on the south side of the river, and as yet had not given up hope of being joined by the ever promised army of reinforcements. His first positive news· of Jackson's whereabouts was received when his pickets were driven in by Jackson's men in front of Mechanicsville, on the 26th of June. Thus it was that in the midst of his offensive movements towards Richmond he was suddenly thrown on the defensive by Jackson's secret and brilliant movement in joining Lee's army, and, by consultation with his chief, in seconding his plans for an offensive attack in great force on McClellan's weakened right flank. For information regarding the Confederate army in front of Richmond, General McClellan had to depend principally upon the reports furnished by the " Secret Service," a body employed by our government, with Chief Allen at its head. From the day that the Peninsula campaign commenced and until it ended, the information furnished by the Secret Service division was continually greatly over-estimated ; so much so that, in the light of the present day, their reports look like deliberate and gross exaggerations. If they intended to assist the Southern cause at that time they succeeded in doing so. May 3 Chief Allen reported 120,000 of the enemy in Yorktown, when there were not over 53,000 effective men there. On June 26 the enemy was reported in front of Richmond at 180,000 and again at 200,000 men. It turned out that at that time they did not have one-half that number. This is only a sample of the information (?) concerning the enemy which the headquarters of the Army of the Potomac had to depend on. Add to this, an inefficient staff and the opposition at Washington to properly or promptly furnish aid; and furthermore, when it is considered that a large part of the supplies for the troops had to be transported in army wagons over seventeen miles of bad roads from the military station at White House landing, one only wonders, in reviewing the situation at this late day, that, with these and other innumerable petty drawbacks, the army did not meet with greater disaster than it did in the seven days' battles.

CHAPTER VII.

THE BATTLE OF GAINES' MILL.

THE UNION FORCES — THE CONFEDERATE FORCES — BATTLE OF OAK
GROVE — BATTLE OF MECHANICSVILLE — UNION FORCE WITHDRAWN
— BATTLE OF GAINES' MILL — DESCRIPTION OF THE FIELD — COLO-
NEL CASS ORDERED TO HOLD THE BRIDGE — GENERAL McCALL'S
DIVISION — MAJOR HANLEY IN COMMAND OF THE SKIRMISH LINE —
A THRILLING INCIDENT — GENERAL PORTER'S REFERENCE TO THE
NINTH — UNION AND CONFEDERATE LINES OF BATTLE — THE MAIN
BATTLE — DESPERATE FIGHTING — GENERAL SLOCUM'S REINFORCE-
MENTS — FINAL CHARGE OF THE CONFEDERATES — UNION LINES OVER-
WHELMED — GALLANT ACTION OF THE NINTH — SECOND LINE OF
ARTILLERY — REINFORCEMENTS ARRIVE — THE ENEMY FALLS BACK
— UNION FORCES CROSS THE RIVER — LIST OF HEAVY CASUALTIES
IN NINTH MASSACHUSETTS.

THE BATTLE.

* * * * * *

" They kneel as one man from flank to flank,
The fire comes sharp from the foremost rank;
Many a soldier to the earth is sent;
Many a gap by balls is rent;
O'er the corpse before springs the hinder man,
That the line may not fail to the fearless van;
To the right, to the left, and around and around,
Death whirls in its dance on the bloody ground."

* * * * * *

SCHILLER.

ON the 25th of June, 1862, Gen. Fitz John Porter's Fifth Corps
of the Army of the Potomac, with detached reinforcements,
was on the extreme right of the line, on the north of the
Chickahominy river, left bank. His command was composed of General Morell's 1st division; General Sykes' 2d division of regulars and
two volunteer regiments; General McCall's division of Pennsylvania
Reserves; four companies 1st U.S. Cavalry; five companies 5th U.S.
Cavalry; six companies 6th Pennsylvania Cavalry; and 8th Illinois
Cavalry, each cavalry company averaging forty men.

On the south side of the Chickahominy — right bank — continuing the position of the army line of battle to the left, was General Franklin's Sixth Corps, composed of the divisions of Generals Smith and Slocum. Next in line was General Sumner's Second Corps, composed of Generals Richardson's and Sedgwick's divisions. Next in line was General Heintzelman's Third Corps, composed of the divisions of Generals Kearney and Hooker; then came lastly General Keyes' Fourth Corps, composed of the divisions of Generals Couch and Peck.

The forces of the Army of the Potomac consisted of 150 regiments of infantry, 2 regiments and 1 battalion of engineers, 1 regiment of heavy or siege artillery, 58 batteries and 10 regiments of cavalry.

The Confederate army under command of Gen. Robert E. Lee was composed of General Longstreet's division of six brigades; Gen. A. P. Hill's division of six brigades; Gen. D. H. Hill's division of five brigades; General Magruder's division of six brigades; General Hugar's division of three brigades; General Whitney's division of two brigades; General Jackson's division of four brigades; General Ewell's division of three brigades; General Holmes' division of four brigades.

The Confederate army consisted of 173 regiments and 12 battalions of infantry; 71 batteries; and 12 regiments of cavalry.

The first battle of the " seven days " is reckoned to include the 25th day of June. On that day General McClellan advanced his left line to Oak Grove in front of Seven Pines. The Second and Third Corps found the enemy in great force, but succeeded in pushing it back under strong opposition and in establishing a heavy picket line. This movement was made for the purpose of gaining a good position in order to support Franklin's Sixth Corps the next day in a contemplated attack on Old Tavern. Our lines on the left were now within four miles of Richmond. McClellan thus made good his promise to reach the vicinity of the enemy's capital.

The Union losses at Oak Grove on the 25th were 67 killed; 504 wounded; 55 missing; total, 626.

The Confederate losses in killed, wounded and missing were a total of 441.

BATTLE OF MECHANICSVILLE.

Mechanicsville, on the Mechanicsville turnpike, is on the road to Richmond, which is some six miles distant. It is likewise situated on or near the Chickahominy river on high ground, midway from Beaver Dam creek. The creek is wide and deep; its banks are steep and altogether impassable for an army without the aid of substantial bridges.

On the east side of Beaver Dam creek, which empties into the Chickahominy river, strong earthworks and log fortifications had been built, particularly in front of Mechanicsville and at Ellison's Mill. These works were greatly concealed from the view of the enemy by the trees and foliage along the creek, while at the same time the troops behind these fortifications had an almost uninterrupted view of the plains and rising grounds as far back as, and in some places beyond, the town of Mechanicsville.

The clear warm morning of the 26th of June, 1862, found Gen. Geo. A. McCall's division of Pennsylvania reserves behind the works at Beaver Dam creek. The commanders of the brigades of this division were Brig.-Gens. John F. Reynolds, Geo. G. Meade and Truman Seymour. A strong Union picket line covered the ground in front, from Mechanicsville bridge to Meadow bridge, on the Chickahominy river. The flanks and rear of Beaver Dam creek were amply protected from surprise and attack by infantry and cavalry pickets and outposts.

General Martindale's brigade of General Morell's 1st division, with Capt. A. P. Martin's battery, were sent to the right of McCall's line. General Butterfield's brigade, with Allen's battery, were sent off to Old Church, to the north, to support the cavalry. Our 2d brigade, now under command of Charles Griffin, recently promoted to a brigadier-general, was held in reserve in camp at Gaines' Mill with Weeden's battery in camp likewise. General Griffin was, since the beginning of the war, the captain of Griffin's 5th U.S. Battery D. No braver or better fighter as an artillerist held rank in the regular army than General Griffin. His promotion to that of brigadier-general was won by honest merit and hard work. During the whole war his brilliant career proved the wisdom of his selection.

On the opposite side of the Chickahominy river the Southern forces were quietly concentrating; a part of them were moved from the right of their line, opposite our left, at Oak Grove and vicinity. General " Stonewall " Jackson's army was moving down from the north — from the valley — and expected to arrive in the vicinity of Mechanicsville, off on the right flank of Beaver Dam creek. Generals Longstreet, D. H. Hill and A. P. Hill, in command of large divisions, lay on the right bank of the river watching for the signal of Jackson's arrival. The signal was never given.

Up to 2 o'clock P.M. of the 26th, the Southern forces were seen to be in motion. At 3 o'clock their columns arrived at the bridges. Gen. A. P. Hill's division was the first to cross the river at Meadow bridge. Generals Longstreet and D. H. Hill, with their forces, crossed at Mechanicsville bridge. On the appearance of these heavy columns of troops our pickets and outposts along the river bank gradually fell back to their main line on the east side of Beaver Dam creek. Our batteries swept all the approaches from Mechanicsville.

As the enemy poured into the valley and across the hills and plains, by front and flank, in their thousands, they presented a fine display. When about half way down the plains our magnificent batteries opened on them suddenly with shot and shell, followed by a terrific and well directed fire from the infantry. Round after round from our batteries and volley after volley from our infantry, followed in rapid succession, caused at first great surprise; then consternation seized them as they witnessed the great slaughter all along their line. Flesh and blood could not stand it, and the disheartened enemy fell back as rapidly as the situation would admit of, their men falling at every step taken. The incessant fire from our infantry and artillery drove them into Mechanicsville and beyond, in great confusion, when they would rally and reform and again advance with lesser numbers and greater caution. The assaults on Ellison's Mill, on the left of our line, were long and desperate and repeatedly made by fresh regiments in superior numbers. Our intrenchments were strong and they were gallantly defended by the Pennsylvania reserves, for they repulsed the enemy at every fresh assault with heavy losses. At 5 o'clock P.M. our brigade arrived on the battlefield. As the right of our line, under General Reynolds, who was supported by General Martindale's brigade, was severely pressed by superior numbers, the 14th New York and 4th Michigan got a chance for immediate engagement between Reynolds and Martindale. The Ninth Massachusetts and the 62d Pennsylvania, with Weeden's battery, were in the open field and lay in reserve, patiently waiting under fire for the call to battle. The fighting along the whole line was kept up till dark.

The more severely the enemy's lines were repulsed and beaten, the more bloodthirsty and desperate they became. The bravery of their repeated assaults upon our lines was something to be admired; but the slaughter they received from the fire of our troops was deplorable as an afterthought. Our strong position along Beaver Dam creek was a revelation to them. The next day when they had a chance to examine the works, no doubt they saw the foolhardiness of their desperate and frequent charges. The works, against even numbers, were simply invincible. The right flank was the only vulnerable point in the whole line.

Our troops lay under arms that night. After caring for our wounded we commenced to withdraw from the battleground before daylight. Shortly after daylight the Ninth Massachusetts was preparing breakfast in their old camp at Gaines' Mill.

The Ninth lost one man killed and two wounded at Mechanicsville. Killed, Company B, Joseph Gordon; wounded, Company B, John B. Burke; wounded, Company K, Joseph Flynn. The Union forces engaged were 11 regiments and 6 batteries. The Confederate forces engaged were 21 regiments and 8 batteries. The Union losses in killed and wounded were 361.

The Confederate losses in killed and wounded were 2000. Other authorities (Confederate) put the Southern losses at an estimate from 3000 to 4000. The 44th Georgia regiment alone lost in killed and wounded 335 men, nearly as many as all the Union losses together.

General Longstreet in the *Century Magazine*, writes as follows: " We had attacked at Beaver Dam and had failed to make an impression at that point, losing several thousand men and officers. This demonstrated that the position was safe * * * * ; so that the Federals in withdrawing not only abandoned a strong position, but gave up the *morale* of their success and transferred it to our somewhat disheartened forces; for, next to Malvern Hill, the sacrifice at Beaver Dam was unequalled in demoralization during the entire summer."

Positive information from our pickets and outposts in the direction of Hanover Court House reported " Stonewall " Jackson's army forcing its way towards Mechanicsville on the 25th and 26th of June. His march was obstructed in every possible manner by our forces. That they succeeded in delaying his army is evident from the fact that he did not reach Mechanicsville at all on the 26th. He had made his calculations to be there in the early morning of that day in order to take part in the attack on Beaver Dam creek. It can only be surmised what the result would have been had Jackson's forces reached the rear of Mechanicsville on the morning of the 26th and attempted, as he intended, to flank our works on the right. Our reserves, in that event, would have been massed at this point, and that battle would have been more desperate and of doubtful issue that night. General Jackson's absence from the battlefield on that day was deemed unfortunate by the Confederate generals; particularly when they realized how terribly they were beaten, and the dispiriting effect which their heavy losses had on their rank and file.

General McClellan, who was on the field that afternoon and night, ordered the withdrawal of his troops in view of information that the enemy was concentrating in great force in that vicinity. Although in itself a strong post it was too far to the front and flank to be of any strategic benefit to the main line at Gaines' Mill.

BATTLE OF GAINES' MILL.

The immediate country over which this battle was fought on Friday, the 27th day of June, 1862, covers on estimation about nine square miles. The extreme northern and western part of the field is heavily wooded. In the northwestern section stood Gaines' Mill. To the west of Gaines' Mill, bearing partially south, at a distance of about two miles, is Old Cold Harbor. About a mile southwest of Gaines' Mill is New Cold Harbor. The millpond on the upland, back of the mill, empties into Powhite creek, a small stream that drains the ravines and swamps on the west side of the battlefield, as it runs down to the Chickahominy river for a distance of two miles to the south. About north of the centre of the battleground is Boatswain's swamp, which is drained by Boatswain's creek, several branches of which form and run from east to west until they meet as a main stream running through a ravine-like valley, lined with brush and trees; after an irregular course it finally turns south and empties into the Chickahominy river. Running in a downward course in the direction of the Chickahominy there are, on this field, many small creeks, ravines and gullies, which are, for the greater part of the year, "dry runs," but which, in the rainy season, become respectable sized feeders to the creeks and river.

Several farms are to be found on the high land and throughout the hills and undulating valleys and table-lands, fenced and ditched. Among the few houses are McGhee's, Adams' and Watts'. Belts and clumps of woods cover several portions of the field and along the river border which includes, likewise, much swamp land. A few common roads intersect the country from the towns to the mills and the fords on the river. The Chickahominy has an irregular southeasterly course at this point and is crossed by bridges commencing near Powhite creek on the northeast. They were named, respectively, Duane's, Woodbury's, Alexander's, Grapevine and Sumner's bridges. They were built by our engineers and troops. Taking this piece of country altogether, it is a most undesirable place for a battlefield.

Up to the 27th day of June, the day of the battle, this field was without any kind of earthworks or breastworks, as the writer can testify from personal knowledge of the situation. General Porter intended that his men should fell trees for the purpose of building log breastworks and obstructing the roads, etc., with abatis during the morning and forenoon of that day. He mentioned the need of axes to General Barnard of General McClellan's staff, who agreed to attend to the matter. The army was abundantly supplied with these useful tools within easy carting reach from the other side of the river. The axes, however, were not delivered until late in the afternoon and, as a matter of course, when the greatest portion of the field was in the hands of the enemy, they were of no use to the corps. It was a great mistake in not furnishing the soldiers with axes in the morning. They would have been of immense benefit in forcing up works and obstructions for defence, and would have been the means of saving many valuable lives of our brave men and officers whose only breastworks, that day, were their own bodies. Besides, it would have put a different phase on the results of the day, and all in our favor. It would likewise have inspired the troops with more courage and confidence and increased their discipline and *morale*. It is evident that some one had grievously blundered.

The temporary breastworks and rifle pits constructed in the forenoon were done with axes and implements borrowed from the artillery companies on the field. The tools were, comparatively speaking, few in number, but fortunately there were many artillery companies and greater results were finally produced than the corps had reason to expect. Whatever works the enemy encountered during that day were only those hurriedly and imperfectly erected by our corps that forenoon with the tools obtained from our artillery as before mentioned.

On the morning of that eventful day the Ninth Massachusetts Volunteers, recently returned from Mechanicsville, remained at its old camp at Gaines' Mill long enough to eat an army breakfast and to be supplied with three days' cooked rations. Buck and ball ammunition to the amount of eighty rounds per man was also distributed. The wagons of the regiment, laden with the baggage of the officers and three days' rations for the men, left camp at an early hour and moved to the right and rear in the direction of the Chickahominy swamp, showing conclusively that the army was about to change its base to the James river. The road to White House Landing was in our rear, bearing partly to the left, and appeared wholly deserted. The great chapel tent belonging to our chaplain, Father Scully, was abandoned for lack of transportation and said to have been later destroyed by fire to prevent it from falling into the hands of the enemy.

The Ninth, having recovered somewhat from the fatigue of the previous day and night at Mechanicsville, formed line in heavy marching order and moved at a route step down the road, past the grist mill, gazing for the last time on the old building, with its great motionless water-wheel; and, casting a farewell look at the deserted mill-pond, in which we would swim no more, continued onward in the direction of New Cold Harbor. Passing to the east of the few houses that formed the place, at a mile or so from Gaines' Mill, the regiment halted in line of battle with the brigade, which was composed of the Ninth Massachusetts, 62d Pennsylvania, 4th Michigan, and 14th New York, commanded by our new brigadier-general, Charles Griffin.

In the course of the forenoon Colonel Cass received orders from General Griffin to advance his regiment in the direction of Gaines' Mill, and hold the bridge crossing over the mill creek. This was the bridge — a small affair — over which we had passed a short time ago after leaving camp. The southern road leading to this bridge descended from the highlands, on which the mill stood, until it gradually reached the open plain, across the bridge, in the vicinity of both Cold Harbors, and near where the regiment was to make a stand. General Griffin informed Colonel Cass at the same time, that two more regiments from the division would be sent forward to support him. It subsequently proved that, for some unknown reason, those two regiments never put in an appearance in support of the Ninth regiment, much to the surprise of General Griffin afterward.

It goes without saying that in their detached position the Ninth would have gladly welcomed the assistance of the promised regiments ; yet, nevertheless, their failure to appear at Gaines' Mill did not deter, in the least, the colonel of the Ninth regiment and his officers from undertaking and performing to their utmost ability the dangerous, not to say desperate task assigned them. In their isolated position of holding a short bridge against the head of an advancing army they were about as near to a " forlorn hope " as one solitary unsupported regiment could be under all the circumstances.

General McCall's division had not moved far from the vicinity of Beaver Dam creek until the morning of the 27th, and not until they had destroyed, the night before, the bridges and obstructed every available crossing over the creek. Having accomplished all that could be done to retard the advance of the enemy they fell back on the road that leads to Gaines' Mill. In the morning they were pursued by a part of the Confederate army which had succeeded in effecting an early crossing on improvised bridges.

A large part of " Stonewall " Jackson's force still continued to move to the southeast on our right, in the direction of the Pamunkey river, with the intention of keeping on our flank, believing all the time that the movements of our army would tend down the Peninsula in the direction of White House Landing. This strategic (?) movement of

Jackson was the cause of his delay in reaching the battlefield of Gaines' Mill on the 27th.

General Seymour's brigade of McCall's division was the rear guard from Mechanicsville, and they were rapidly falling back on Gaines' Mill under cover of the fire from Captain Tidball's and Captain Robertson's horse artillery. These troops of McCall's having successfully retreated and joined Porter's army, late in the forenoon, the Ninth Massachusetts found, on nearing Gaines' Mill about noon, a section of Tidball's battery unsupported and throwing shells in the direction of the enemy. As the section of the battery retired Colonel Cass sent forward, as skirmishers, the right flank company (I), Captain McCafferty, and the left flank company (F), Captain O'Leary. These two companies deployed on the double quick. As the enemy's skirmishers came down the road by Gaines' Mill they rallied at the bridge and were met by rapid and deadly irregular volleys of buck and ball from Company I in their front, and by a persistent enfilading fire on their right flank, from Company F, which drove them back in confusion onto their main column.

Fresh from the memories of the field of slaughter of the day before, on their army at Beaver Dam creek, and Ellison's Mill, the enemy hesitated ere they again took to the bridge over which the bullets of the Ninth's skirmishers continued to rain with unrelenting fury. Again and again did General Gregg's brave South Carolinians seek to advance over that short and narrow defile, in order to drive the Ninth's skirmishers back from their advantageous field, but without avail. Reinforced by two more companies of the Ninth, A and D, with Maj. P. T. Hanley at their head, our gallant band of heroes continued to pour their increased leaden hail into the daring and devoted ranks of the foe. Maddened by the destructive opposition with which they were received the enemy now sought to force the passage by large bodies in column of companies, which were in turn pushed forward by larger bodies in their rear, coming down the incline, until they gained a crossing, over their dead and wounded, and reached the open field in our front. The utter impossibility of holding their ground against the fierce onset of these advancing columns of the enemy forced the Ninth skirmishers to fall back, firing rapidly as they retired to a new line.

Four companies from the Ninth, under the direction of Major Hanley, with renewed vigor now poured into the foe a withering fire which held them in temporary check. Regiment after regiment of the South Carolina infantry deployed over the field to their left flank until the whole of Gregg's brigade were in our front. Major Hanley and his subordinate officers held their line of fire with most persistent bravery, and not until several more large bodies of Gregg's infantry advanced, and opened a terrific fire upon them would they give way.

As the Ninth skirmishers slowly fell back in the vicinity of New Cold Harbor, heavy columns of the enemy from Gaines' Mill were marching rapidly onto the field and extending over towards Old Cold Harbor. Our skirmishers then received orders to fall back on the main line. Major Hanley thereupon rallied his command on the east side of a creek, in the vicinity of an abandoned wagon laden with stockings and other goods. (By the way, some of our men appropriated a few pairs of stockings for future use, without considering, in the meantime, their chances of getting killed.) "Now, boys," cried the Major, " let us give them one more shot, and then fall back as fast as we can." The last shot was fired, as directed by the major, and our skirmishers retreated for their own lines in the face of Gen. A. P. Hill's corps, composed of six brigades and nine batteries of General Lee's advancing army.

An incident occurred at this particular time, on the skirmish line, the relating of which will be of undoubted interest to the reader.

Second Lieut. Frank O'Dowd was in command of Company I, which was on the right flank, and the last in retreat, the captain (McCafferty) and the 1st lieutenant (Nugent) having been killed in the skirmish. As the line commenced to retire a shell struck and exploded near Lieutenant O'Dowd breaking his leg above the ankle. He fell and was unable to rise, and cried out to 1st Sergt. J. W. Macnamara, "For God's sake, Jim, don't leave me." The two men had been sergeants—color-bearers—and tentmates, and a strong friendship existed between them. Macnamara quickly responded to O'Dowd's request, and, with two of his men, Jerry Cronin and William Winn, rushed to assist him. Shells and bullets were now flying and bursting thick and fast about them, at the same time the columns of the enemy were rapidly approaching.

Lieutenant O'Dowd was taken up and placed on Winn's back, and, with a man supporting them on each side, they moved along toward their lines as fast as the circumstances of their perilous situation would admit. But a few minutes had passed, as they hurried forward, before a bullet went clear through the lieutenant's body at the back, and passed out of Winn's chest. At the same time the 1st sergeant received another bullet in the calf of the leg, striking the bone and remaining there. O'Dowd was killed, Winn was mortally wounded, and Macnamara was dangerously wounded and disabled. The sergeant then ordered Cronin to make for the regiment and save himself from capture.

In a few minutes the enemy was upon them. One of their skirmishers charged bayonets on Sergeant Macnamara,* as he sat on the ground examining his wound, and yelled out, "Get up, Yank!" The sergeant pointed at his leg and said he was wounded and couldn't move, at the same time asking for a drink of water. Wonderful to tell the kind-hearted Confederate, without a moment's hesitation, or a word, unslung his canteen of water and threw it to him, and passed on. In moments such as these, water was worth its weight in gold.

For weeks Sergeant Macnamara — as did all the rest of our wounded who fell into the hands of the enemy — suffered terribly, more particularly from a flyblown wound, being obliged to pour turpentine into it to drive out the maggots. It was the only remedy that saved his leg and kept off gangrene. There was no attendance, no hospital, very little to eat, and all the time exposed in the open air. Poor Winn, the brave fellow, died in a short time. Cronin reached the regiment in safety.

Under the fire of the enemy's shells and advancing infantry, the Ninth very quickly reached the brigade line. They fell into position with the 62d Pennsylvania and supported Captain Martin's 3d Massachusetts battery. The Napoleon guns of this battery were bravely and gallantly served under the direction of Captain Martin and his subordinate officers. Their fire was rapid, frequent, and terribly destructive, so much so that the columns of the approaching enemy on the New Cold Harbor road were driven back with great slaughter. As their disordered lines rallied and charged forward to capture the guns, they were gallantly met by the Ninth and the 62d, and driven back. Our troops then quickly unmasked the battery, which was only waiting for a clear front to deal death and destruction on the determined but baffled foe.

Referring to this affair General Fitz John Porter writes as follows in the *Century Magazine*: —

"At Gaines' Mill Col. Thomas Cass' gallant Ninth Massachusetts Volunteers, of Griffin's brigade, obstinately resisted A. P. Hill's crossing, and were so successful in delaying his advance, after crossing, as to compel him to employ large bodies to force the regiment back to the main line. This brought on a contest which extended to Morell's centre and over Martin's front — on his right — and lasted from 12.30 to near 2 o'clock, Cass and his immediate supports falling back south of the swamps. This persistent and prolonged resistance gave to this battle one of its well known names" (*i.e.* Gaines' Mill).

---

* Afterwards captain, killed at the Wilderness.

It was about 2 o'clock P.M. when the Ninth, under command of Colonel Cass, reached its position in the main line of battle south of the swamps, after having passed through an ordeal of skirmish fighting, while holding the bridge at Gaines' Mill, alone and unaided, then fighting and falling back to the main line, which the corps, generally, knew little or nothing about.

Each command, from the highest to the lowest, was so taken up with its own internal affairs during these exciting hours, that it was hardly possible, at that time, to tell what others were doing or where they were stationed. Outside of the commanding general and our division and brigade commanders, the great gallantry displayed by the Ninth Massachusetts Volunteers in the immediate vicinity of Gaines' Mill for nearly two hours, on that day, was scarcely known, or, if known, little thought of by the Fifth Corps generally, for the reasons, as before stated, that other duties of momentous importance engrossed the minds of nearly all with their immediate surroundings. So it was with the Ninth when they arrived at their position. They found, to their great surprise, that the corps had intrenched here and there behind crude and hurriedly built works of logs, earth, rails, knapsacks, stumps, slashed timber, etc., much of which proved a comparatively useless and flimsy construction when the battle raged.

The line of battle was held by General Morell's first division from the centre away to the extreme left, and by General Sykes' second division from the centre away to the extreme right. General Griffin's 2d brigade of four regiments held position on the right of the first division, the Ninth on the right of the brigade at the centre of the line of battle ; the 62d Pennsylvania in the second line in reserve. Next in line on our left stood General Martindale's 1st brigade of four regiments, with the 22d Massachusetts in the second line in reserve. Next to them in line, on the extreme left, was General Butterfield's 3d brigade of four regiments, two of which, the 12th New York and 16th Michigan, were in the second line in reserve. The extreme right and left flanks of our line of battle were heavily supported and protected by batteries of artillery and by cavalry. Each interval, between the brigades and divisions along the whole line, was held by our best artillery on commanding ground. Captain A. P. Martin's 3d Massachusetts battery held the centre interval between the two divisions and covered the road from New Cold Harbor. The Ninth was on Martin's immediate left. The line of battle to our right swept up the hill, and was held by General Sykes' 2d division of regular troops and two volunteer regiments. Their lines were held in a somewhat similar manner as those on the left but on higher ground. His brigades were commanded by Colonel Warren, Major Lovell and Colonel Buchanan, all of whom were regular officers and acting brigadier-generals. General McCall's division of Pennsylvania Reserves was held in rear of the line in reserve and in support of the centre.

Two regiments of General Morell's division, that is, the 18th Massachusetts Volunteers, Col. James Barnes, and the 17th New York, Colonel Lansing, were detailed to perform duty at White House Landing, and subsequently join the Army of the Potomac at Harrison's Landing after the seven days' battle. This left General Porter with 18,000 infantry. In front of General Porter's line of battle, on the north side of Boatswain's creek, on high ground near New Cold Harbor, the Confederate General, A. P. Hill, had deployed his brigades in line of battle, covering nearly directly the field opposite our centre. A little later General Longstreet's corps deployed on A. P. Hill's right, where he was sheltered by the woods, and in front of our left wing. Gen. D. H. Hill had previously occupied, with his brigades, a strong position for his line of battle, in front of General Sykes, and fully covering the right wing of the regulars. About an hour later, Gen. " Stonewall " Jackson's corps came hurriedly into line, between the commands of the two Hills, on ground near Old Cold Harbor, and well in front of Sykes. Jackson's delay in getting into action was caused by a long march and detour through the woods to the north of Old Cold Harbor, where he had " reckoned " to intercept the Fifth Corps when it was driven (?) in the direction of White House Landing. As the " Yankees " failed to fulfil his expectations, after a long wait, he concluded to go and meet them. His appearance finally on the battlefield was a great relief to General Lee's anxiety, as Gen. A. P. Hill's engagement was somewhat premature, and at the time of Jackson's coming his (Hill's) corps was jaded and looking for reinforcements. The strategic position of the Union lines, forming, as they did, an irregular semi-circle, with its arc to the front, obliged the Confederate army to take up more ground than we occupied in order to properly deploy their large forces, and to gain good positions to assail us from, with any show of success. The enemy's army which wholly confronted us that day numbered fully from sixty to sixty-five thousand men. This number has been contradicted from Southern sources as too large, but never authentically disproved. These four corps of the Southern army were all, comparatively speaking, fresh troops, with their full complement of men, barring their losses since the commencement of the campaign, and in the valley.

The fact that General Magruder had command of the balance of the Army of Northern Virginia, a force that consisted of twenty-five thousand men, at the most, and confronted four corps of the Army of the Potomac on the morning of the 27th of June, is good evidence that the bulk of the Army of Northern Virginia was in front of the Fifth Corps, and their number was fully up to sixty or sixty-five thousand.

At no time during that day's battle did General Porter's combined forces, reinforcements and all, amount to more than thirty thousand men, and rather under that figure than over it. Generals French and Meagher's brigades of four small regiments each, arrived at the close of the day, and were not actively engaged in fighting. Two regiments as before stated were absent from Morell's division. Four Union divisions of three brigades each against four Confederate corps cannot, as regards numbers, be very well equalized.

On the south side of the river on that day we had four Union corps, the bulk of our army. From it was drawn one division — of three brigades — (Slocum's) engaged, and two brigades of four regiments each, not engaged.

Half an hour — or more properly speaking, at 2.30 P.M.— after Gen. A. P. Hill's advanced brigades drove the Ninth regiment back from Gaines' Mill ground to the main body, what may be termed the beginning of the general engagement all along our lines was commenced by Hill's brigades fiercely assailing our centre. Captain Martin's magnificent battery had the sweep of the New Cold Harbor road and adjacent field. It was ably supported by the Ninth Massachusetts Volunteers, and later by the 62d Pennsylvania. General Branch's brigade — the same that the Ninth had assisted in defeating and driving from the field at the battle of Hanover Court House, a month previous to the day — supported by Pender's brigade, made many desperate assaults on Martin's battery. These repeated charges were met and successfully repulsed by the Ninth Massachusetts Volunteers and 62d Pennsylvania, bravely supported by the 1st U.S. Sharpshooters and the 14th New York. Every time our infantry returned to their places, after checking the onsets of the enemy, and unmasked our battery, its guns were ready to belch forth through wreathing smoke a double discharge of grape and canister which dealt awful slaughter in the ranks of the baffled foe, as it fell back in confusion to reform and renew its ineffectual attacks. In one of these charges the gallant commander of the 62d Pennsylvania, Colonel Black, while leading his regiment against the enemy, fell among the killed. All the efforts put forth by the enemy to capture and silence Martin's superb battery were bravely made and bravely repulsed by us to their utter confusion and defeat.

At 3 o'clock P.M. General Longstreet's brigades opened up with a united and desperate assault, under cover of the woods, on the left and centre of General Morell's lines. They met with a terrific battery and infantry fire from that part of our division, which brought their lines to a halt, and then caused them to fall hurriedly back to the cover of the woods in great confusion, over their dead and fallen men, to reform their broken ranks and continue their assaults. Gen. D. H. Hill had likewise, in the meantime, engaged General Sykes' gallant regulars, only to meet with the same disaster and defeat that the enemy were now receiving all along the line. In the midst of the hard fighting on every side General " Stonewall " Jackson's veteran corps of Valley fame arrived on the field, after their fruitless march previously referred to, and took position on Gen. D. H. Hill's right, where his brigades sought for immediate engagement, and where they met " foemen worthy of their steel." It was soon demonstrated to their grim satisfaction that the present scene of their labors was to be the reverse of the " picnic " which they had so long enjoyed as " sprinters " in the Shenandoah Valley. Fighting, and not foot racing, was to win on the field of Gaines' Mill. The " foot-cavalry " of " Stonewall " Jackson's corps had now a chance to rest their feet for a day and work their hands. The only cause of regret to us was that the advantage of numbers which were against them in the Valley, were now greatly in their favor, on their side at this battle.

The superior numbers now brought into action by the enemy pressed our lines so severely that our second line and reserves were pushed forward to strengthen our forces, and to hold our position by giving energetic battle all along our whole front.

The deadly contest now fiercely raged through woods and swamps, and over hills and plains, and ravines, with all the determined strength that fighting men could force from infantry lines, and from batteries belching forth, through dense battle smoke, a deadly hail of bullets, shot, shell and canister. The opposing lines of infantry charged fiercely, with cheers and yells against Union batteries, to be driven back by infantry, with responding and prolonged yells and cheers, again and again. Men fell dead and wounded on both sides like grain before the reaper's sickle. Guns were captured and retaken by desperate charges and counter-charges. Confederate regimental colors were snatched and taken from their bearers in hand-to-hand encounters. Prisoners were captured in the dense smoke of battle as they became lost and bewildered and separated from their broken and defeated battalions. For one long hour the fiercest fighting of the war prevailed on the right, the left and the centre, and still our little army was full of patriotic courage and fought desperately against the fierce assaults of superior and sometimes almost overwhelming numbers of fresh troops that dashed forward with unrelenting fury.

McCall's Pennsylvania reserves had relieved some of our decimated ranks, and filled the gaps in Morell's and Sykes' weakened lines. As the battle was pushed with renewed vigor over every foot of ground contested, it seemed only to increase the enemy's repeated and headlong charges. On our left a desperate conflict was going on to drive back our forces from the woods along the river in the vicinity of the Adams House. Several times the enemy charged up to the woods but at each fresh assault they were driven back with great slaughter.

General Porter had frequently sent for assistance but his calls were not responded to until 4 o'clock P.M. At that hour General Slocum's 1st division, consisting of three brigades, from Franklin's Sixth Corps, arrived on the field from across the Chickahominy river. General Newton's brigade, of this division, went to the centre on the right of Griffin. The four regiments of General Taylor's brigade filled weakened points in Morell's division. The brigade commanded by Colonel Bartlett went finally to aid General Sykes' stalwart regulars on the right.

Up to this time there had been no remarkable sign of wavering along our lines, although at times hard pressed by the masses of fresh troops thrown against them. The bravery of the continued charges of the enemy against our lines in the face of a terrific fusilade of shot and shell was most remarkable, plunging forward as they did, through their own disordered lines, over their own dead and wounded, with unrelenting strides seeking for victory or death.

General Newton's brigade brought renewed vigor to General Griffin's men, and again the battle in the centre continued in our favor under the steady fire of our infantry and Martin's gallant battery. At 5 o'clock P.M., General Porter sent word to General McClellan that he was sorely in need of reinforcements and that his lines were in a critical condition. Our brave troops had now withstood the shock of battle against the best efforts of the enemy without breaking for three long hours. The determined resistance that the enemy had met with since the commencement of the battle seemed to confirm Generals Lee and Jackson and their subordinates in their opinions, first formed, that they had in their front the " bulk of McClellan's army." In the light of present history it is to be regretted, for our sake, that such was not the fact.

Shortly after 5 o'clock a lull gradually came over the contending forces. Like one of nature's raging storms, the desperate fierceness of the elements engaged had become partially spent. Our little army was well nigh exhausted. Reinforcements from any of the four corps on the other side of the Chickahominy were few and far between. If they failed to respond then we looked forward to the night as our best and only ally. The lull in the fight on the part of the enemy boded evil. The humblest private then present, and living, knew by experience and intuition, if not by report, that the forces of the foe in our front far outnumbered our own, which was now reduced in strength by the thousands of killed, wounded, sick and exhausted, after the day's terrible work. The activity of the enemy warned us that they were concentrating on our flanks. Their unsuccessful and herculean attempts to pierce our centre had thus far signally failed. Our lines were strengthened with the forces now at hand in the best possible manner that the condition of our regiments would admit of. Two brigades of the Pennsylvania reserves, and some of the New Jersey regiments, that were engaged at 4 o'clock, reinforced the centre of Morell's division. Active preparations were made in supplying the lines with ammunition. The expectations of a renewed attack began to materialize.

At about 5.30 the enemy was discovered advancing from the woods and over the plains along their whole line. Longstreet's division, with Whiting's heavy reinforcements, in double column of regiments in line of battle, crossed the incline and with rapid strides rushed down the open descent through the fire of shot and shell that our batteries and infantry poured into them from General Morell's centre and left. As the enemy's lines recoiled under the terrific fire that tore great gaps in their brave ranks, others pushed forward from their rear and filled the spaces made vacant by the dead and wounded until they reached the ravine, and rushed on to a terrific fire of musketry. The enemy now returned the fire and charged across the ravine with prolonged yells, in double ranks and lines, in great numbers, forcing and following our troops with such rapidity as to reach the vicinity of our battery lines in time to receive and repel a charge of five companies of the 5th U.S. Cavalry as they broke, pell mell, through our now terribly disordered line of batteries and infantry. As our cavalry reached the space in front of the foe they were thrown into confusion, and back on to their own lines, by a terrific fire of musketry under which many officers, men and horses fell indiscriminately. This diversion of our cavalry was at once taken advantage of by General Longstreet's troops, who were now covering the ground in all directions. With a vigorous charge and yell they once more rushed forward and captured fourteen guns as the most of our forces rapidly retreated to the hill and grounds overlooking the bridges on the Chickahominy. As the left of our lines swept back from the field taken and now held by the enemy, the right wing gave way, likewise, under the desperate attacks of the divisions of Generals D. H. Hill, Ewell and Jackson and they fell back in as good order as the confused circumstances would admit of. This desperate state of affairs on both flanks threw the centre line into confusion thus bringing on a general retreat.

The action of the Ninth Massachusetts Volunteers at this critical period of our defeat is described in the following extract from the military correspondent of the New York *Herald.*

" The Ninth Massachusetts regiment was the rear of the retreating column which had just passed over a hill into a large open plain. . . . . To break and run was not for the men who had covered themselves with glory during the entire day. Col. P. R. Guiney (now in command) decided to form a line of battle on his colors, and resist the approach of the enemy until the advance of the retreat should have been far enough to leave ground sufficient to enable him to commence his retreat in good order. Colonel Guiney with his standard-bearers, advanced upon the rebels with the words, " Men, follow your colors ! " It was enough. Before that small band of jaded heroes waved the Stars and Stripes and the green flag of Erin, and with loud huzzas, they rushed upon the rebels, driving them up the hill. Nine times did the remnant of the Ninth drive, with ball and buckshot, the advance of the rebel army before they could make good their retreat, the rebels being often within sixty yards of them."

The critical position of the Ninth was brought about from the fact that they did not become in any manner panic-stricken. As they and their supports had held the enemy at bay since the commencement of the battle, it never entered their minds but what they would continue to do so to the end ; or at least, until the reinforcements that were called for should arrive. Furthermore they were not aware of the successes of the enemy on their left, neither did they know that the centre and left of their division had given way under the desperate attacks of Longstreet's troops. As these points in the division had been strengthened with some of Generals Slocum's and McCall's infantry it was considered strong enough to resist all attacks.

As our lines on the left flank and those on the right flank gave way the centre followed until the Ninth suddenly found itself, as it were, without warning, last in the line of retreat. To them it was an unexpected situation of affairs. As the enemy came rushing towards them they fought with buck and ball, and charged upon their yelling and attacking advance with responding cheers and prolonged yells, through the dense battle smoke, that now hung over the ground, and drove them back in confusion.

To break and run was not the nature of the men of the Ninth; but to retreat in good order, before the enemy could surround them, was now their only alternative. This they did under the direction of Lieutenant-Colonel Guiney and Major Hanley and their brave subordinates. Colonel Cass — who, to his great credit be it said, had fought with his regiment until he was overpowered from physical exhaustion superinduced by his long sickness — was obliged to retire, as he was unable longer to stand upon his feet. Previous to leaving the field he sat resting wearily upon an adjacent stump, thoroughly exhausted but full of pluck, and turning to some of his men, who stood ready to assist him in any and every emergency, he exclaimed, "Boys, go back and do your duty like men; God knows I would be with you if I was able." Truer words were never spoken. The brave and patriotic Colonel Cass, sick and all as he was, received his mortal wound five days later at Malvern Hill, while again bravely fighting for his adopted country at the head of his gallant regiment.

The smoke of battle that now hung over the field and enveloped the regiment prevented them from obtaining a clear view of the advancing lines of Lee's army. The terrific hail of whistling bullets in front, and the enfilading fire on both flanks, was creating sad havoc in the ranks of the Ninth as it continued to fall back. To halt and rally and fire a volley or two, and then charge the enemy's line with a prolonged Irish yell from time to time until nine successive attacks were repulsed, was the only desperate method of preserving the Ninth from capture or annihilation. As the regiment drew nearer to its own lines in the rear, the atmosphere became somewhat clearer, and support rallied to our assistance from the remnants of survivors of other gallant regiments which like the Ninth had been fighting all day in the hot sun.

The siege guns and field artillery that were planted on the south side of the Chickahominy, and were continually worked during the day, rendered great assistance now in shelling the lines of the enemy under the direction of our Signal Corps. Precautions had been taken to plant extra batteries of field artillery in our rear during the early part of the day, to meet just such an emergency as the Fifth Corps now found itself in, and as they now opened on the enemy a check was put upon their further advance. Twilight had set in as the Ninth, after losing two hundred and forty-nine of their number in killed and wounded, reached the main line in retreat.

Loud cheering from our rear in the direction of Alexander's bridge on the Chickahominy now broke upon the air. Louder and louder it arose as the long-looked-for reinforcements came in sight and marched upon the field, and into the midst of our jaded troops. The brigades of Generals French and Meagher (Irish brigade) from General Sumner's Second Corps, composed of eight gallant regiments, were the welcomed reinforcements that rapidly advanced to the front and took position in the front line of battle. The enemy heard the " slogan " from the " Yankee " lines, and fearing an attack from fresh forces quickly withdrew their batteries that had rapidly assumed position on the high ground in our front. Darkness began to fall suddenly upon us. All firing had ceased. The hardest fought battle of the war had ended. The battered but still gallant Fifth Corps — or what was left of it — now felt that its eight hours of terrible conflict were not in vain.

That great incubus, the Chickahominy river, by which our movements at the close of the day were held, as it were, in a pocket against great odds, would ere tomorrow's sun be a bulwark of defence against the baffled enemy; for on its southern side were to be found rest, security and the united Army of the Potomac. Under the direction of General Griffin our brigade was reformed and placed in position in line. At about 2 o'clock A.M. of June 28, we marched across the Chickahominy bridge and went into bivouac. The troops of the Fifth Corps having all withdrawn to the right bank by daylight, or a little after, the bridges were all destroyed that same morning.

CASUALTIES IN THE NINTH MASS. VOLUNTEERS AT GAINES' MILL, VA.,
FRIDAY, JUNE 27, 1862.

List of Killed and Mortally Wounded.

OFFICERS.

Capt. William Madigan, Co. C; Capt John Carey, Co. G; Capt. Jeremiah O'Neil, Co H; Capt. James E. McCafferty, Co. I; 1st Lieut. Richard P. Nugent, Co. I; 2d Lieut. Frank O'Dowd, Co. I.

COMPANY A

William Adams, James Doherty, James Foley, John Gleason, Patrick Keating, Maurice Lynch, John Manning, James McGuire, Peter McIntire, Paul Melanfry, Roger Pope, Hugh Tiernan.

COMPANY B.

Andrew Conlon, John Cullinan 1st, Daniel Doherty, Thomas Hogan, Dennis Hyde, Michael Keenan, Patrick McGaffany (or McGaffigan), John McQuade, John O'Brien.

COMPANY C.

Sergeant George Grier, Corporal Patrick McGee, Corporal James Hughes, Corporal Daniel Leary, Charles Greaney, John Hyde, Michael Slattery.

COMPANY D.

First Sergeant Patrick Collins, John Flynn, Neil McConologue, James F. McDonough, William McFeeley, Terrence McGrade, died of wounds received, Francis McKenna, John Cartwright, died of wounds received (Co. I).

COMPANY E.

Timothy Cahill, James Condon, Michael Fitzgerald, Joseph Lambert, Thomas Marrin (misspelled Marvin), Joseph (F.) Smyth (or Smith). Died of wounds June 29, 1862. Michael Sullivan, died of wounds June 29, 1862. Michael Horan, died of wounds June 29, 1862.

COMPANY F.

Robert Farrell, John F. Finney, died of wounds July 6, 1862, Peter McNamara, Patrick Meagher, James Reagan.

COMPANY G.

Patrick Clark, John Crowley, Bartholemew Finnerty, Cornelius Long, Charles Quinn, Patrick Scolland.

COMPANY H.

Thomas Cummings, Simon Curley, Samuel Day, William McBrian (or McBrine), James McGovern, died of wounds Aug. 7, 1862, Jeremiah Murphy, John O'Neil, John Haggerty, died of wounds June 27, 1862.

COMPANY I.

Corporal Maurice Cotter, Patrick Curran, Corporal Charles Kearney, John Fitzgibbon, John Garrity, Patrick Nagle, William Winn, mortally wounded.

COMPANY K.

Corporal Hugh O'Hare, John Butler, Patrick Dennison, Daniel Riordan 1st, Daniel Riordan 2d, Bartlett Tully.

SUMMARY.

Commissioned Officers killed	6
Non-Commissioned Officers killed	8
Privates killed	68
Total killed and mortally wounded at Gaines' Mill . . .	82

List of Wounded.

COMPANY A.

Sergeant Michael McDermott, Corporals Bartholemew Taylor, John Dwyer, Patrick Walsh, Privates Vassal P. Boynton, John Ennis, Charles McGlone, John McLaughlin, James Moore, Thomas O'Reilly, John Thornton, John Moakler, Bartholemew Corkery.

COMPANY B.

Captain Michael Scanlan, Corporals Dennis McCarthy, Michael C. Creighton, Thomas Quinlan, Private William Smith; Sergeant John W. Cullinan, Privates Joseph Scanlan, Patrick McLaughlin, James Riley, John Burns 2d, John Curran, Michael Gleason, John Griffin, John Hernon, William Harney, Thomas Newton, George Greany, John Kelleher, Charles Lyons.

COMPANY C .

Corporal Wm. Pyne, Privates Martin Burke, John Clancy, William Craig, Patrick Gilday, James Gosling, Maurice O'Donnell, Michael O'Toole, John Ring, John Ryan 3d, Daniel J. Sheehan, Alexander Somerville, Henry Walder, Thomas Murphy, James McCarthy, William Mullen, Charles Murray.

COMPANY D.

First Lieutenant Michael W. Phalen, Privates John E. Jameson, Patrick Burns, Dennis Brown, Peter Dowd, Patrick Doyle, Bernard Duffy, Edward Hegan, George Lynch, James McLaughlin, Thomas Mallahan, William Maloney, Edward O'Brien.

COMPANY E.

Sergeant Daniel Ford, Corporals Owen Crahan, Thomas Sullivan, Privates Daniel Buckley, Peter Boyle, Jeremiah Coffey, Terrence Connor, John Danahy (or Donavan), John Denny, Timothy Horrigan, John Halloran, Bernard Monaghan, Thomas McGavisk, William A Palmer, Timothy Reagan, Edward Walsh, John Spellman, John Sullivan.

COMPANY F.

Lieutenant John Doherty, Sergeant Thomas Fallon, Corporal John Clynes, Privates Martin Kennedy, John Morrissey, Cornelius Reagan, Daniel Sweeney, John Walsh, Maurice Hurlihy, Patrick Cusick, John Hynes, James H. Jenkins, Patrick O'Hara.

COMPANY G.

Privates Thomas B. Brigham, John Buckley, Cornelius Cotter, Felix Daly, Richard Furfey, William Lavery, Michael McCann, John McCurdy, Thomas McGuire, Daniel Sullivan.

COMPANY H.

Captain Timothy Burke, Sergeant James W. Tobin, Corporal Malachi Curley, Privates Daniel Callahan, John Clifford, Patrick Flynn, Edward Fitzpatrick, James Keenan, Patrick Houran, Patrick Lynch, James McNeal, John Murray, John O'Grady, James Rowe, Dolty Sweeney, Thomas Slattery, Patrick White, Michael M. Warren, Daniel Sweeney, Hugh Gilbride prisoner, John O'Keefe.

COMPANY I.

First Sergeant James W. Macnamara, Sergeants Bernard Hayes, William Gillis, Corporals Andrew Doran, William Phelan (or Phalon), Privates Stephen Blake, James Buckley, Michael Buckley, William Burns, William Connell, Peter Donnelly, Michael Duffy, Thomas Early, Patrick Garvey, Michael Garrity, Michael Hayes, Patrick Lane, Daniel McCarron, John McGarrity, James McKeever, Michael McGuire, Hugh McLaughlin, Francis Murphy, Patrick O'Neil, John Quinn, Andrew Reagan, James Sullivan, John P. Sullivan, Cornelius Sullivan, Edward Sliney.

COMPANY K.

Lieutenant William R. Burke, Sergeant John B. Rice, Privates Michael Clark, Thomas Clifford, Michael Connelly, John Dooley, John Gartland, Sergeant William Linahan (or Linnehan), Privates Michael Martin, Neil Murray, James Rice, Roger Cunningham, Joseph Flynn.

TAKEN PRISONERS.

Lieutenants Michael F. O'Hara and Patrick W. Black. These officers were taken by the enemy as the regiment retired from skirmishing at Gaines' Mill. Chaplain Rev. Thomas Scully. Father Scully was taken prisoner while bravely attending to the spiritual welfare and comfort of the wounded and dying. He escaped from the enemy that night, and was again taken at Savage Station. A full account of his hardships is given in Chapter IX.

WHOLE NUMBER.

Prisoners	3
Officers killed	6
Officers wounded	5
Non-Commissioned Officers killed	8
" " " wounded	23
Privates killed	68
Privates wounded	139
Total Casualties at Gaines' Mill	252

CHAPTER VIII.

THE SEVEN DAYS' BATTLES CONTINUED.

TRIBUTES OF PRAISE TO THE NINTH MASSACHUSETTS — THE " GREEN FLAG " OF THE NINTH — GENERAL JACKSON AND THE FIFTH CORPS — GENERAL MAGRUDER'S TACTICS — HEROIC EFFORTS OF THE FIFTH CORPS — THE NINTH MASSACHUSETTS ON TRENT FARM — ON THE MOVE — THE MARCH TO MALVERN HILL — BATTLE AT GOLDING'S FARM — BATTLE AT ALLEN'S FARM, OR PEACH ORCHARD — BATTLE AT SAVAGE'S STATION — GENERAL JACKSON'S ARRIVAL AND ARTILLERY ATTACK — WHITE OAK STREAM AND SWAMP — BATTLE AT GLENDALE — THE AFFAIR AT TURKEY BRIDGE.

> " Prepare you, generals :
> The enemy comes on in gallant show ;
> Their bloody sign of battle is hung out ;
> And something to be done immediately "
>
> JULIUS CÆSAR, *Act* V., *Scene* I.

GEN. FITZ JOHN PORTER, the corps commander, under whose immediate command the battle of Gaines' Mill was fought throughout the day; Gen. George W. Morell, the 1st division commander; Gen. Charles Griffin, the commander of the 2d brigade, to which the Ninth Massachusetts Volunteers belonged, and other general officers on the field, who were cognizant of the courage displayed by the Ninth regiment in its masterly retreat at the close of the battle on the 27th of June, expressed themselves in strong terms of praise, at that time, on the valor and bravery of the regiment in repelling the attacks of the foe, and thereby holding the advance of the enemy in check. The writer feels it a duty that is due to the Ninth regiment to quote from the " History of the Irish Brigade," written by Capt. D. P. Conyngham, A.D.C., in reference to this particular affair. (Page 186.)

" During the charge of the brigade an incident occurred too thrilling to be omitted. The first regiment thrown into the fight to stem Jackson's force of over twenty thousand men was the Ninth Massachusetts, an Irish regiment, then commanded by the brave Colonel Cass. This noble regiment dashed on the enemy, hurling back their advance lines. The enemy, seeing the green flag, thought it was the advance of the Irish brigade, and Jackson ordered up his reserves to sweep away, ' that d —— brigade.' This brave little regiment stood the shock of the whole of Jackson's force, but being fearfully mowed down, they had to fall back to some temporary entrenchment, still fighting like so many tigers at bay. Just then the Irish brigade was gallantly dashing in, as the *Times* correspondent said, ' breathing fire and dirt.' Colonel Cass, seeing himself reinforced, sallied forth again with his handful of men. General Meagher was at the head of his brigade; when he saw the colonel in his shirt all covered with blood and dirt, he called out, ' Colonel Cass, is this you?' ' Hello, General Meagher, is this the Irish Brigade? Thank God, we are saved.' "

As mentioned in the previous chapter, Colonel Cass was obliged to retire, and at the hour referred to by the historian of the Irish brigade, Lieutenant-Colonel Guiney was in command of the Ninth; a mistake in commanders easily accounted for at that exciting hour in the evening twilight, when it was scarcely possible to distinguish faces. At that time Colonel Guiney was known to be in his shirt sleeves.

There is every reason to believe from what has been written, coming from Southern sources, that the enemy in our front, when they beheld the green flag of the Ninth Massachusetts Volunteers, jumped at the conclusion that General Meagher's Irish brigade, composed of four regiments, was then fighting against them. In fact articles by Southern writers have been published in the past relating how bravely and persistently the Irish brigade had fought them all that day to the very last. Of course all these accounts are very flattering to the Ninth Massachusetts Volunteers, and they feel honored to think that they and their fighting qualities were so fierce and furious as to be mistaken for the gallant old Irish brigade.

In the light of this claim by Southern history — which has been dropped since they discovered the error — at the battle of Gaines' Mill, the query naturally arises that if they mistook the Ninth Massachusetts Volunteers — carrying a green flag — for four regiments of the Irish brigade, and fought it as such, is it then to be wondered at that they " reckoned " all through the day's terrible battle that they were opposed by the bulk of McClellan's army?

The fact was at that time, most, if not all, of the Southern generals had underestimated the fighting qualities of the Northern soldiers — such as were then to be found in the Army of the Potomac

— and none more so than " Stonewall " Jackson, who was, at that time, fresh from the Shenandoah Valley, where he had, with an inferior force, driven and pursued General Bank's demoralized army to the Potomac river, much to the terror of the authorities at Washington. Jackson had likewise been playing " fox and geese " with the little armies of Fremont, Milroy, and the rest of them,· even to holding McDowell's army of 43,000 in check.

Whipping, or paralyzing as it were, nearly every force of Union troops that he came in contact with, Jackson's fight with the Fifth Corps was a revelation to him. On the night of the 27th of June there did not exist a more incredulous and astonished man than Jackson, when he learned, for the first time, that the bulk of the Southern army had been all day fighting against the Fifth Corps.

It has been a matter of regret, by the survivors, since that day, that the bulk of our army on the Richmond side of the river did not send sufficient reinforcements when they were so urgently demanded by General Porter.

General Magruder, with his division and auxiliaries of twenty-five thousand men between our army and Richmond, made a great success, by his rapid manœuvres all day, in throwing dust into the eyes of his " Yankee " enemy, through which he made it appear that he then commanded three or four times more troops than the number which he actually had.

It appears that the " calculations " of our generals of the strength of the opposing forces on the south side of the river, about balanced the " reckoning " of numbers in front of them by the enemy on the north side. There was this difference, though : Lee's army had the courage of its convictions, and fought the best they knew how ; while our generals were all day looking for a battle that never materialized, and they feared to bring on, unless the affair at Golding's farm, by General Hancock's brigade about sundown, can be termed one. At that time the enemy made an attack on the right of General Smith's division, when the gallant Hancock drove them back and silenced their artillery.

It cannot be gainsaid but that there were grave misunderstandings as to numbers and positions of troops on both sides at that period. It further goes to show that the reports of " secret service men," " scouts," " spies," " prisoners of war," etc., were greatly exaggerated, and sadly misleading to the generals commanding in both armies. In order to approach success and to achieve victory, the strategy of war, as a science, must be based on as perfect a knowledge as possible of the opposing forces as to numbers and intended movements. Without this knowledge of the enemy one is in doubt and darkness, a condition that leads to disaster.

Subsequent histories of the battle of Gaines' Mill — while they show superb fighting on both sides; bravery even to confront slaughter at the cannon's mouth; repeated instances of an utter contempt of death; closeness of contact in bloody battle seldom equalled — have conclusively proved that the science of war was greatly at fault with both army commanders. If the Fifth Corps, on this particular day, was to act as a " stopper " for the advance of Lee's army for a certain period of time, then its subordinate commander succeeded on that point and saved the army. Great lack of knowledge of the situation was displayed in not sending forward the reinforcements, when so urgently called for, in sufficient numbers. The result of the day's battle was a failure for General Lee; inasmuch as his plans, for a flank movement and the destruction of McClellan's army, were subverted. This failure in the plans of the enemy occurred principally through the heroic efforts of the Fifth Corps, supported by the divisions of Generals McCall and Slocum during eight hours' battle.

The arrival of the gallant brigades of Generals French and Meagher, just before dark, was most opportune, and they deserve great praise for the brave and dashing manner in which they assumed the offensive and thereby cheered the hearts of our jaded troops. It will always be a matter of regret that they did not appear on the field three hours before; a time of our sorest need for assistance in repelling the united charge of the enemy when they finally pierced our left centre. But all regrets are useless, for it is an utter impossibility to carry out human plans, particularly on the battlefield, without falling into more or less miscalculations. It is enough to make one shudder though, to contemplate the huge blunders through which the Union army staggered, like a drunken man, before it achieved final victory.

The Ninth Massachusetts Volunteers remained in bivouac, as did all the rest of the Fifth Corps, on Trent Farm, until two o'clock P.M. of the 28th of June. The destroyed bridge crossings on the Chickahominy river were well guarded by our infantry and artillery, while our troops were taking a much needed rest. All was quiet with the enemy on the other side of the river.

Colonel Cass was with his regiment reclining in an ambulance that was placed at his disposal that day. Although he was a very sick man he could not be prevailed upon by any one to leave his regiment for a much needed rest, and for medical attendance. His ambition was to continue with his command until the fighting was over, and an opportunity offered to take a leave of absence for home, where he could procure proper medical aid, and recuperate his failing health and strength. The terrible work through which the corps had passed during the past few days had its effect on him, and the regiment generally.

An unusual quietness reigned in all the regiments and batteries. If one were to shut his eyes, at this particular time, he never would imagine, by any sounds that struck his ear, that he was surrounded by many thousands of soldiers, so quiet did every one appear. Yet they were busy in refitting, and preparing their arms and clothing, and receiving ammunition for the move that was soon to come.

The men of the Ninth Massachusetts would talk in quiet tones of those who were gone, telling where they saw such a one fall; how another one was hit, and fell dead or wounded by shot or shell; or what such another one said as the stretcher bearers carried him, weak and wounded, off the field. Speaking about stretcher bearers; much praise is due to the men of the Ninth who composed Bandmaster O'Connor's Ninth Regiment Band. These musicians, some twenty-four of them, exposed themselves to the fire of the enemy while acting as stretcher bearers in carring off our wounded. Many disabled officers and men of the regiment are indebted to the musicians for taking them from the field, where they would have been otherwise left to die, or been captured by the enemy.

At 2 o'clock P.M. the 1st division (ours) was on the move; it marched by way of Savage's Station to White Oak Swamp, which it crossed to the south side, and went into bivouac. The U.S. Engineer Corps was engaged in constructing a bridge and road across the swamp in order to make a safe and quick passage for wagon trains, artillery, infantry, etc. In this work they were assisted by fatigue parties from the Ninth and other regiments. Morell's 1st division was in the advance of the Fifth Corps. Three hours later the 2d division (Sykes') followed, and at 9 o'clock P.M., McCall's division moved after us.

The wagon trains, numbering about 5000 wagons, were on the roads heading for the James river, accompanied by herds of cattle, "fresh beef on the hoof." The trains carried hospital stores, ammunition, officers' baggage, quartermasters' stores, and commissary rations. The army headquarters wagons led the train. But little rest was given these trains as it was a matter of urgent necessity to get them beyond the reach of the enemy as quick as possible. As the roads became terribly cut up it was hard work to keep them moving.

All surplus commissary supplies were at a discount and were destroyed by fire to prevent them falling into the hands of the enemy. The army was supposed to carry enough of rations in their haversacks, and in their knapsacks, etc., to supply their wants until they arrived at the James river. The Ninth had received eight days' marching rations on the 25th of June, consisting of hard tack, coffee, sugar, and pork or salt beef. Five days of this supply was carried in their knapsacks. As their knapsacks and effects were unslung and piled on the ground at Gaines' Mill battlefield, and were never seen afterwards, it is safe to predict that the enemy appropriated the rations. In the meantime the Ninth were living on the contents of their haversacks, and any chance supplies found on the march. Ammunition of all kinds, that was not needed for present use, was likewise set fire to and exploded. The result was that immense fires were burning in the vicinity of McClellan's headquarters, and at other places on the line of march.

On the 29th we moved to the junction of Charles City and Quaker roads and remained all day in supporting distance of General Keyes' corps. When night approached we were again on the move forward. The nights were dark and somewhat dismal, with light rains and heavy dews. The narrow roads through the woods and over the plains and farming country were cut up into ridges and hollows of mud and slush, and, in many places, blocked with trains, artillery and herds of cattle, to an immovable extent. Owing to the blocked condition of affairs, and the heaviness of the roads, the Ninth did not get into bivouac again until late the next forenoon, although the entire distance marched did not exceed ten miles. In the afternoon we received orders to march to Malvern Hill without loss of time. Again we encountered the difficulties of a night march through an unknown territory. The head of our division column was misled by the guide, and after long halts and counter-marching we finally reached our destination about nine o'clock A.M. on the 30th of June. The distance in a bee-line from where we started the night before was about five miles.

To go back to the afternoon of the 28th when we left the banks of the Chickahominy; the enemy under Magruder made another attack on Smith's division of the Sixth Corps. It resulted in a loss on our side of 150 men, killed, wounded and captured. This affair was called the battle of Golding's (or Garnett's) Farm. After repairing the bridges—New bridge and Grapevine bridge—the enemy commenced to cross the Chickahominy early on the 29th of June. Our Second and Third Corps, which were in front of Magruder's army, fell back on Allen's Farm between Orchard and Savage's Stations. On the morning of the 29th Magruder followed them up and commenced an attack about 9 o'clock. He was three times severely repulsed with heavy loss by Sumner's corps, and finally driven from the field. This affair is known as the battle of Allen's Farm, or Peach Orchard.

Heintzelman's corps, after destroying the military stores along the line of the railroad, crossed White Oak Swamp at Bracket's Ford, and proceeded by the Charles City road to Glendale, which it reached that night, the 29th, and went into bivouac.

BATTLE OF SAVAGE'S STATION.

That same day—Sunday, June 29—was hot and sultry; genuine enervating Southern weather, and hard to bear by a full-blooded Northern man. The Sixth Corps (Franklin's) moved into position before daylight in the vicinity of the Richmond and York River Railroad near Savage's Station. The Second Corps (Sumner's), fresh from its battle in the morning at Peach Orchard, approached and extended the line of battle to the left of Franklin between the railroad and the Williamsburg road. By order of McClellan, Slocum's division had withdrawn from Franklin and moved beyond White Oak Swamp. It was the intention of General Sumner, who was in command, to await the attack of the enemy. General Keyes', Porter's and Heintzelman's troops had already crossed White Oak Swamp, as before stated, and these other two corps were under orders to follow that night.

During the day, and while our troops were on the lookout for an attack from Magruder, great quantities of army stores were burning near them at the railroad station and vicinity. Considerable ammunition was among the flames, and shells were bursting in the pile, at intervals through the day. The Union soldiers were weary and in need of rest. Those who had the opportunity were denied it by these exploding shells. As they were expecting an attack at any moment it was hard to tell whether the exploding shells came from the fire, or from the direction of the enemy. It was a further reminder that they must be on the alert and not caught napping. The great volumes of smoke which ascended to the sky throughout that hot sultry day told the enemy that immense supplies belonging to the "Yankee" army were slipping from their grasp, and that their enemy was only waiting for their destruction in order to follow the troops which preceded them.

Just before five o'clock in the afternoon the outposts and signal officers reported that the enemy were in sight, approaching from the direction of Richmond. They were accompanied by a railroad car with a thirty two pounder rifled cannon on it, protected by iron plates. The car stopped at a cut in the railroad, and the gun commenced to throw shell into our lines on both sides of the road. One battery after another, from our lines, opened a rapid fire on it, and in a short time silenced the " railroad iron-clad, " and compelled it to pull back out of range. Several advances of the enemy's infantry were met by our troops charging upon them with a prolonged cheer. At each fresh assault the enemy broke and fell back in disorder under a galling infantry fire with great loss. The battle was continued all along our line until near dark, when the enemy fell back altogether behind their batteries and into the woods, where they remained.

After the first few onsets it was noticed that the enemy was not over anxious for close range attacks. The willingness with which they finally fell back to the woods excited some surprise. General Sumner declared that his command had won a decided victory, and that if he had 20,000 more men he would crush the rebellion. The old veteran was elated at the ease with which he had whipped the enemy, and was loathe to leave a victorious field. It subsequently appeared that General Magruder was the only attacking party with 13,000 men.

General McClellan's orders to Franklin were peremptory. All the Union troops were to move across White Oak Swamp that night and then destroy the bridge. Jackson's three divisions, with D. H. Hill's division, were on the march to the swamps from Grapevine bridge on the Chickahominy, and it was desirable to put the swamps between the Union army and Jackson's troops. By ten o'clock the next day — June 30th — all our forces had crossed and then destroyed the bridge. This movement of the last of the Union forces, from Savage's Station to the south side of White Oak Swamp, left that section of the country in the hands of the enemy.

At the commencement of hostilities on the 27th of June our wounded were carried to Savage's Station on account of its close proximity to the railroad. It was likewise in the line of our movement to the James river. Our medical directors and surgeons concentrated all their work at this point. Scenes were enacted daily, which when once beheld, left impressions on the mind never to be effaced. Many thousands of wounded Union soldiers were transported to this place. Those who could walk, and, in a measure, take some care of themselves, after being attended to, were sent north. The wounded who were helpless, — that is, unable to travel, were operated on as soon as possible, and then placed in tents in charge of attendants.

Surgeons in their shirt sleeves, exposed to the hot sun and weather, worked hard and continually extracting bullets, binding up wounds, and cutting off arms and legs. It was considered safer to take off a wounded and shattered limb, and then let nature do the healing on a clear cut, than to take chances on a ragged wound, with broken bones, and run the risk of gangrene setting in, which was very liable, and generally fatal to the one attacked by it. Very many of our brave fellows died before being attended to; and many of those who underwent amputation died under the operation, or shortly after it.

Their systems were run down by hardships and for the want of proper nourishment, not to mention the nervous strains through which they had passed on the battlefield. Exhausted both physically and mentally they, in many instances, easily succumbed to the surgeon's knife and saw.

Temporary hospital tents were erected, in the best selected spots, for the wounded to lie in. Mother earth was the best bed that they all had. Negro huts, barns, and the like, were utilized for the accommodation of the medical department. Our surgeons and their assistants worked nobly to relieve their patients, and did all that they possibly could do, under the circumstances, for our brave wounded men. If any neglect occurred it was due to a lack of supplies and skilled nurses. The pyramids of arms and legs that had been lopped off were a gruesome sight to behold.

Fatigue parties were employed in digging burial trenches, for burying the dead, and, as occasion required, covering them in. It is needless to say that for several days they were kept quite busy. When the place fell into the hands of the enemy acres of ground were literally covered with wounded men in all kinds of conditions and positions. The enemy's wounded were mostly sent to Richmond, but many of them were first taken to the station. Their surgeons acted in friendly concert with ours in carrying on the Good Samaritan work. When the place fell into the hands of the enemy some 2500 of our wounded were there, with about 500 surgeons and assistants and other attendants. All of course were accounted for as prisoners of war by the enemy.

On the morning of June 30, about three o'clock, "Stonewall" Jackson's army arrived at Savage's Station. Here they had a view of our hospital, and a chance to see the battlefield of the previous day's action. It was a fortunate occurrence for us, and the small number that were there, that this large force of the enemy arrived the day after that battle. Jackson, since his arrival in front of Richmond, failed to exhibit that alacrity of movement in his marches for which he had become so famous some weeks previous in the Shenandoah Valley. The fierce opposition that he met with when he ran up against the Fifth Corps, without doubt, accounted for the slowness of his movements later. His ardor in "defeating and capturing the Army of the Potomac, or driving it into the river," had evidently somewhat abated.

After spending the 28th and 29th days of June on the Gaines' Mill battlefield in burying the dead and disposing of the wounded, and in repairing Grapevine bridge, Jackson's forces proceeded to cross the Chickahominy river. While engaged in the charitable work of burying the Union dead they first stripped them of their clothing and appropriated it to their own use; for General Jackson's men were very ragged and sadly deficient in wearing apparel. On first thought it seemed to be a sacrilegious act, but when the living were suffering for raiment to cover their nakedness it appeared to them to be a useless waste of good clothes to bury them in the soil with the dead. At any rate this was a sufficient argument for the enemy to despoil our dead, and it was done, no doubt, without any compunction of conscience. To men of finer feelings it would seem to be a revolting practice; but, as "necessity knows no law," they continued to appropriate the uniforms of our dead on every battlefield, afterwards, when opportunity offered.

About noonday of the 30th Jackson's men arrived in the vicinity of White Oak Swamp. His troops were all deployed under cover of the woods, and their presence was unknown and unsuspected by our forces on the opposite side of the swamp. It seems hardly probable that so large a force of infantry and artillery could take possession of a field within rifle shot of their opponents without immediate discovery, but such was the fact. Jackson, however, was not long in announcing his presence.

He massed about thirty pieces of artillery under cover of the woods and then opened fire upon our troops, wagon trains and artillery, which were on the other side of the swamp, in the open field in full view of the enemy in the woods. Consternation and confusion prevailed at this unexpected assault. The infantry hastened to get under cover of the woods. Our batteries after a while got into position and returned the fire, which in time silenced some of the enemy's guns and slackened their firing. At first the bombardment was rapid and furious and lasted about half an hour without ceasing. After that it slackened, but during the day it continued fiercely at intervals.

The wagon train managed to get away during the day after being considerably smashed up by shell. Our artillery, after it got into good working order, did much damage to the enemy, and silenced many of their guns during the rest of the day. General Franklin's infantry and our sharpshooters, by their fire, controlled the crossings at White Oak Swamp so that all attempts made by Jackson's men to press forward that day were fruitless, and not until the Union troops retired was he enabled to cross the swamp by rebuilding the bridge that our forces had partially destroyed.

The source of White Oak Stream is about a mile from Seven Pines, and about six miles from Richmond. The waters flow through the swampy land for a distance of about twelve miles into the Chickahominy swamps and river. It runs irregularly east by south, and turns, when about three miles from the Chickahominy, and runs east by north, and strikes the river about two miles below Bottom bridge. The swamp covers some fifty irregular square miles, and is prolific in woods and undergrowth with spots of hard ground here and there. There are several small ford crossings ; Brackett's being the largest. The roads from Savage's Station and Bottom bridge are the only main roads that cross the swamp by a bridge. This bridge from the opposite side leads to the roads to Richmond and to Malvern Hill, etc.

On the north side of the swamp, where Jackson planted his batteries, the country was thickly wooded. On the opposite side (south) the ground was clear and gradually ascended to a hill on which was an old farmhouse. Some rifle-pits and entrenchments covered the ground, with abatis well to the front. A part of the Second Corps were the recipients of Jackson's bombarding, and being unexpected, it was quite a surprise to them. The casualties were light. Savage's Station on the York River Railroad is about seven miles from White Oak Swamp bridge.

BATTLE OF GLENDALE, OR NELSON'S FARM.

Generals Longstreet and A. P. Hill's forces crossed the Chickahominy river over New Bridge on the 29th of June, and after a march of fourteen miles reached the intersection of the Darbytown and New Market roads, and that night went into bivouac about three miles southwest of Frayser's farm. On the 30th they moved out on the Long bridge road about two miles, near Charles City road, where they struck McCall's picket line and went into line of battle. General Lee at this time intended to form a circular line of battle with General Holmes at Malvern, Magruder next, Longstreet and A. P. Hill next,

Hugar next and Jackson and D. H. Hill swinging across White Oak Swamp. As General Longstreet put it, "Thus we were to envelop the Federal rear, and make the destruction of that part of McClellan's army sure."

Longstreet's and Hill's line of battle encountered McCall's, Kearney's, Slocum's, Hooker's and Sedgwick's divisions in position. Hugar's division was far to the left of Longstreet, near White Oak Swamp, and was engaged about 2.30 P.M. in an artillery fight with Slocum. At 4 P.M. the general engagement commenced and continued until dark. As darkness set in the gallant General McCall fell into the hands of the enemy, having run into the enemy's lines while endeavoring to bring up some of his forces.

The battle in its severest parts was against McCall's and Kearney's divisions. The Confederates made a most determined fight, and continued their desperate charges on our well defended batteries with persistent bravery, and suffered thereby heavy losses in killed and wounded. It was expected by Longstreet that Jackson would come to his assistance after defeating and driving the enemy from his front. But the fact that Jackson's army was held at White Oak Swamp by Franklin and his supporters never occurred to Longstreet's mind, for he little knew at that time the position that Jackson was in. General Lee sent Magruder to Longstreet's aid but he lost the way and never found it. Longstreet was keenly disappointed by the lack of heavy reinforcements. He did intend to "bag" (?) all the Union troops in his front long before dark. But somehow or other Lee's plans didn't turn out as originally intended.

As night closed in on the field our forces at Glendale and White Oak Swamp marched off in the direction of Malvern Hill, where they mostly arrived that night and the next morning. The next morning the enemy discovered that the "destruction of McClellan's army was, as yet, not accomplished," and that the Army of the Potomac was rapidly getting into position at Malvern Hill and vicinity.

THE AFFAIR AT TURKEY BRIDGE.

About 9 A.M. on the 30th of June (Monday), the Fifth Corps arrived at Malvern Hill, and the divisions and brigades were assigned positions by General Porter. When the troops arrived the farms were resplendent in tall growing wheat which, from military necessity, was trampled under foot. Our soldiers were tired and hungry; rations had become exhausted, and none were likely to be issued until the

fighting was over. The new wheat was a change of diet, and by rolling out the kernels into the palm of the hand they furnished sweet suc-
culent morsels which the troops eat as long as the cereals were to be
had. Much of it was cut down and used for bedding that night on
Malvern Hill. The next morning, the day of the battle, little or nothing was to be seen of the hundreds of acres of wheat; it was all
trampled into the ploughed ground which in time became a flat surface
under thousands of tramping feet of men and horses.

About 3 o'clock P.M., on the 30th of June, the enemy was seen
approaching, off on the left flank, along the River road from the direction of Richmond. This road runs in view of the James river from
Richmond. It proved to be the Confederate General Holmes, in command of 6000 infantry, 6 batteries of artillery, and 2 regiments of
cavalry. He was told that the Federal army was passing over Malvern Hill in a demoralized condition. The Fifth Corps, being at rest
around the hill, no doubt presented, to the casual observer, the
appearance of troops in a disorganized state. In fact at that time crowds
of them were passing verbal observations on Holmes' army.

The reports that General Holmes received about the Federal
army fleeing over Malvern Hill coincided with all that he had been led
to believe regarding the present condition of the Army of the Potomac.

The continual boasting of some of the Southern generals that they
had McClellan's army " whipped," and that it was only a question of
a few days before they would be all " captured," was, at that time,
believed to be true in Richmond, and had, likewise, gained great cre-
dence in the rank and file of Lee's army. Without doubt much of this
boasting was said in the hearing of the Southern soldiers to encourage
them from day to day. It was a sugar-coated pill easy to swallow,
but its drastic properties opened the eyes of the credulous Confederates when they fairly encountered that " demoralized Yankee army "
at Malvern Hill.

General Holmes being, as it were, the first victim of this credul-
ity, opened on us from across the meadow lands, on our left at Malvern Hill, about 4 P.M., with his artillery. General Hunt, our chief
of artillery, had thirty-six pieces of cannon, some of heavy siege calibre, in position in that direction, which was less than a mile to the
left and rear of the Crew house. Having nothing better to do at that
particular hour all of this artillery opened fire on Holmes' force ; at
the same time from the river our gunboats began to throw their
immense shells in the same direction.

Holmes' troops, it is said, had never been under fire of this or any other kind before, and to be greeted with such a terrific bombardment from a lot of " demoralized Yankees " was more than they could stand under. One of their batteries was smashed to pieces in a few minutes, and the rest silenced and driven from the field. Their cavalry was the first to break and fly. Some of the artillery men cut their traces and mounted in hot haste after the cavalry. The infantry, as a matter of course, being the last to seek safety in flight, were soon out of harm's way. The quick doubling up of this force of the enemy was viewed at a safe distance by thousands of the Fifth Corps with grim satisfaction. Their losses were slight, two killed and forty-nine wounded, and a few prisoners that we captured. Also two guns and six caissons, which were afterwards abandoned by us. On July 1 — the next day — Holmes' force took no active part in the battle of Malvern Hill. He gave as a reason that it was out of the question to attack so strong a position with his inadequate force. In the judgment of many the old veteran was right in his opinion.

It is related of General Holmes — who was almost totally deaf — that in the midst of the heaviest cannonading, he stepped outside of his headquarters, and putting his hand behind his right ear, said to those about him, " I thought I heard some artillery firing! " His cavalry, flying up the road a mile or two, had also, " thought they had heard firing." It did not take long however to convince the old general that the place he was in was too hot for his little army; and those that remained soon sought safety in a hasty retreat to the rear. Without doubt in after years of the war these raw troops of the enemy rendered a good account of themselves. No farther attempt was made by the enemy to occupy the meadows and fields on our left and rear, between Malvern Hill and the James river.

In following the fortunes of the Army of the Potomac in its change of base to the James river only the briefest outlines of its engagements with the enemy have been given. To portray all the military movements of the army as it approached the James river from day to day would, if entered into, fill a volume in itself. The history of these movements is minutely written by those in command on both sides, and has been published to such an extent that the students of history can, without much loss of time, obtain it from the libraries.

The history of the Ninth Massachusetts Volunteers is so closely connected with that of the brigade, division, corps and army to which it belonged that the writer has deemed it necessary to mention in a briefly connected form the line or skeleton movements of the whole body as it were, in, it is hoped, as accurate a way as possible. The Ninth regiment moved with the corps to which it belonged, at all times of day and night, ready to bravely and patriotically act its part in any and all emergencies. At Malvern Hill it once more became engaged in a terrible battle for the Union, second only to that of Gaines' Mill, a battle where the brave Fifth Corps again acted a most prominent part, but with this encouraging difference, it was in conjunction with the Army of the Potomac.

CHAPTER IX.

THE BATTLE OF MALVERN HILL.

GENERAL LEE'S AGGRESSIVE PLANS — GENERAL McCLELLAN'S CHANGE OF
BASE — NO MATERIAL SUCCESS IN GENERAL LEE'S ASSAULTS — DE-
SCRIPTION OF MALVERN HILL — LINE OF BATTLE OF THE ARMY OF
THE POTOMAC — ARTILLERY FIRING — SKIRMISHING AND SHARPSHOOT-
ING — INFANTRY LYING UNDER FIRE — THE ENEMY'S POSITION —
OUR RESERVE ARTILLERY — WATCHING THE. ENEMY — THE CONFED-
ERATES' CHARGE — REPEATED AND DESPERATE CHARGES — GREAT
SLAUGHTER — COLONEL CASS MORTALLY WOUNDED — MAJOR HANLEY
IN COMMAND AND WOUNDED — CAPTAIN O'LEARY IN COMMAND —
THE BATTLE ENDED — LIST OF CASUALTIES IN THE NINTH — EXTRACT
FROM GENERAL PORTER'S RECENT LETTER — ACCOUNT OF LOSSES —
OUR COLOR BEARERS — FATHER SCULLY'S THRILLING EXPERIENCE.

* * * *

" Hand to hand, and foot to foot;
Nothing there, save death, was mute :
Stroke, and thrust, and flash, and cry
For quarter, or for victory,
Mingle there with the volleying thunder."

BYRON.

* * * *

THE success of " Stonewall " Jackson, in the Shenandoah Valley,
in preventing McDowell's army from reinforcing McClellan's in
front of Richmond, and then joining his forces, from that point,
with those of Lee's Army of Northern Virginia by rapid and successful marches, in order to become the aggressor, culminated in a united
attack of the Southern forces on the right flank of the Army of the
Potomac on the 26th and 27th of June, 1862.

The unfortunate division of the Union army by the Chickahominy
river placed it, under these circumstances, in a most perilous position.
The Southern generals had now united on a plan to relieve Richmond
of the hostile attitude of the Union army at any cost, and it was
believed that, by the aggressive force of their large army, they could
defeat and drive the Union troops down the peninsula, cutting them to

pieces by desperate battles as they fell back in detail in the direction of the York river.

When McClellan gave up all hope of further reinforcements to aid him in his assault on Richmond, he still deemed his present army inadequate for the task, yet he continued his advancive movements up to the 25th of June at Oak Grove, where his picket line reached within four miles of Richmond.   In the meantime the aggressive plans of Lee culminated in the attack on the following day — the 26th — at Mechanicsville, Beaver Dam Creek and Ellison's Mill.

The news of Jackson's arrival, and the active hostilities of Lee's army, determined McClellan to act on his well considered change of base to the James river — a position for army operations that he was always partial to.   The fact that he did not move down the peninsula, onto the line of the York river, was a disappointment to Lee and Jackson, as they had planned to battle against the Union forces in that direction.   Their subsequent slowness in solving the problem of McClellan's real movements was sufficient evidence that they did not anticipate his change of base to the James river until it was well nigh accomplished.   The expectations of General McClellan to reach his new base of supplies, and preserve the *morale* and discipline of his army intact, were about to be realized, although in its accomplishment great losses in the destruction of all kinds of war material and soldiers had followed in his daily movements since the commencement of operations.

The strong and aggressive army that had bent all its great energies to drive the Union forces from the investment of their capital, had, likewise, suffered great losses in men and material, thus far, without gaining any success in their boasted " capture and destruction of McClellan's army."

No material successes of this nature could be counted on by the enemy at Oak Grove on the 25th of June; at Mechanicsville, Beaver Dam Creek and Ellison's Mill on the 26th; at Gaines' Mill and the Chickahominy on the 27th; at Garnett's and Golding's Farm on the 28th; at Garnett's Farm, at Allen's Farm or Peach Orchard, and at Savage's Station on the 29th; at White Oak Swamp, at Glendale, or Charles City Cross Roads, and at Turkey Creek on the 30th of June; while at Malvern Hill the foe met with defeat and disaster, in men and material, which obliged them to seek the shelter of their fortifications around Richmond for the purpose of reorganizing their shattered army.

Malvern Hill is about sixty feet in height from its northern side, where it rises somewhat abruptly.   In all other directions it falls in a sloping formation, exposing to the view, from its plateau-like summit, hundreds of acres of clear farming, or plantation lands. The whole hill is easy of access for man or beast, on any of the roads that cross it. The Western run, or river, flows on the south and east at its base, and is covered by a thick undergrowth of woods, which continue in the distance around to the north and west. The Quaker road runs up the hill from the Willis church to the Crew house, where it divides. Along the base of the western side of the hill is the New Market road.

The slopes of the hill to the north, on the battlefield, are so extensive and so gradual that large bodies of troops would find no difficulty in manœuvring in all directions. To the north or front of our line of battle were dense woods from a half to one mile away. To the right and east of the battle line the forests continue and extend in broken sections. The enemy held possession of this wild country which bounded our front and right.

The morning of July 1, 1862, opened up hot and sultry, and it found the Army of the Potomac encircled in an impregnable line of battle on and around Malvern and Crew hills and environments. The engineering ability and generalship displayed in putting the infantry and artillery in position on this battlefield could not be improved upon. The front and flanks were so admirably arranged that reinforcements of infantry and artillery could be thrown from point to point inside the lines with remarkable quickness.

The Fifth Corps—composed of General Morell's 1st division and General Sykes' 2d division — had been in position since the day before — the 30th — and lain in bivouac on the line of battle all night; seeing, hearing and watching the enemy constantly. General Griffin's 2d brigade occupied the left flank front line of battle in support of the U.S. artillery; the 14th New York on the left, the 4th Michigan next, the Ninth Massachusetts next, and the 62d Pennsylvania next.

The Ninth Massachusetts Volunteers were directly supporting Griffin's old battery of Parrott guns; D, 5th U.S.; Captain Kingsbury commanding. The regiment was lying on the ground, in rear of the guns, near the Quaker road. This road ran through the centre of the field in the direction of the enemy by Willis church to Glendale. The 1st brigade (Martindale's) was in the second line in support. The 3d brigade (Butterfield's) was in the third line in support. In the immediate rear of Martindale's position the Richmond road ran parallel with the line of battle, and was cut, for some distance, west, beginning at the Quaker road, through the hill to the depth of four or five feet. It was used as a temporary hospital for the treatment of the wounded. Here only one brave surgeon held forth. The embankment was his only shelter while stray shells from the enemy dropped on the road or burst overhead. This road ran to the left, down to the meadows, and connected with the River road, that led to the city of Richmond.

A bridle path ran from this road onto the battlefield near the left of the position occupied by the Ninth regiment, and passed along by a barn, or tobacco dryhouse, on the left, in the direction of the Crew dwelling. On this path Colonel Cass had his headquarters, on account of the shade from the barn, as he was still a very sick man. He sought in every available way to reserve his strength for the ordeal of the great battle which was that day hourly expected. The left of his regiment lay within a few yards to the front of where he sat meanwhile watching the lines of the enemy. During the battle many of our wounded, and those of other regiments, were carried hither, and under its roof many a brave man suffered and died of mortal wounds. Its position on the battlefield prevented any possibility of medical attendance in any shape.

Two brigades of Sykes' division, commanded by Buchanan and Lovell, held position on the flank in rear of Morell's division in support of the batteries in that direction. The other brigade of this division, commanded by Warren, was in position farther to the rear in the valley, guarding the River road, and within supporting distance of the artillery reserve. The extension of the front line of battle to the right of Morell and the Quaker road, near the West dwelling, was held by General Couch's division of three brigades, commanded by Palmer, Abercombe and Howe. About 4 o'clock P.M., this line was reinforced with Caldwell's brigade of Richardson's division and Sickles' brigade of Hooker's division, in the second and third lines in support. Heintzelman's Third Corps, composed of Kearney's and Hooker's divisions, was next on the right of Couch; Sumner's Second Corps came next near the Binford house, composed of Sedgwick's and Richardson's divisions. General Franklin's Sixth Corps, composed of Smith's and Slocum's divisions, was next to the Second Corps. General Keyes with his 2d division of the Fourth Corps (the 1st division under General Couch being in the front), with artillery supports, was in the vicinity of Carter's Mill, where several roads converge from the river, protecting the flank and rear towards Haxall's. McCall's division, under General Seymour (General McCall being a prisoner in the hands of the enemy), was held in reserve on the right of the Malvern mansion, in rear of Malvern Hill battleground. This mansion was General Porter's headquarters. General Hunt's artillery reserve of some thirty-six guns of various calibre was in position overlooking the low meadow lands on the left, in full sweep of the roads leading to and from Richmond. In cases of unexpected reverses in the tide of battle, and other unlooked for circumstances that required immediate support, the reserve artillery was so arranged by General Hunt that it could respond to any call without needless loss of time. Between the Crew house and the West house (both houses situated on the field) in front of Morell's division, were placed about five batteries — twenty-six guns. On the left, the centre and the right of Couch's division were four more batteries — about twenty-two guns. This particular artillery was under the direction of Gen. Charles Griffin, commanding the 2d brigade. He was a West Point artillery officer of great skill, bravery and experience. His great activity in placing batteries in position, and his general supervision of the artillery battle-line that day was most conspicuous from the fact that, at times during the early part of the day, he was the only mounted officer to be seen on the field directing operations. He was an officer greatly beloved by all the soldiers that he ever commanded. Our lines on the right flank, composed of three corps, gradually dropped to the rear on account of marshy ground, thick woods and undergrowth, along the confines of the Western river or " run " on the north and east.

The Union army now lay awaiting battle, feeling doubly secure in their position with the gunboats of Commodore Rogers on the James river. That Malvern Hill was a fine selection for our final engagement is shown by the results of that battle, which, as far as fighting on July 1 is concerned, was a most brilliant victory for our arms.

Breakfast (?) on that morning was a go-as-you-please, and " every man for himself." Rations of all kinds were scarce. In fact the personal effects, etc., of every one in the regiment were exceedingly light in weight and measure. When it left Gaines' Mill camp on the morning of the 27th, it was in heavy marching order, but after the battle of that day the regiment found itself in very light marching order, being minus " horse collars," knapsacks and contents. Since then the rations had dwindled away. Tobacco was a great consolation to most of the soldiers of the Ninth, and pipe smoking acted as a substitute for several wants. There were no cases of actual hunger; but cooking rations or making coffee in that vicinity was out of the question. Each man eat and shared what little he had without any complaint.

About 10 o'clock A.M., a desultory artillery fire was begun by the enemy, as a feeler along our front. It was preceded and invited by intervals of skirmish fighting and sharpshooting in the morning, and after it commenced, it was continued, more or less, on both sides till noon. During the forenoon General Griffin was activity itself as he rode in all and every direction over the field occupied by his artillery. As fast as our batteries came galloping up from the right and rear he would ride up swiftly at their head and lead them into good positions. In every instance he personally directed each new arrival while shot and shell flew over the field ; a matter of fact that he treated with cool indifference. The troops of the division, while quietly watching his movements, commented freely on " Black Jack's " (a nickname for General Griffin on account of his swarthy complexion) chances of getting hit, momentarily fearing that the danger he courted would surely end in wounding or killing him ; but he bore a charmed life it seemed. When asked why he didn't dismount, he said it would not do for him, for his legs shook so that he couldn't stand. No braver man than General Griffin was in the army ; notwithstanding his weak legs.

The infantry supports along the front lines were lying close to the ground inactive. The shells from the enemy went over and among them where they exploded, either on the ground or in the air, killing and wounding our brave troops continually. Occasionally some daring spirit would rise and move along the line, although cautioned not. to, at the imminent risk of being blown to pieces.

Sergeant Meany of the Ninth, while acting sergeant-major, was stiuck by a shell while moving about, which carried away his head. Many other brave fellows were. killed or mortally and dangerously wounded under this severe trial of passive inactivity. It is the strongest test of patience and courage that a soldier can be placed under, for it severely tries the nerves and the stamina of the best and bravest.

The wounded were carried to the cut road in the rear of the 1st brigade, and left in the care of the one gallant surgeon who was there, while the bearers quietly returned to their places in front. Several of our brave fellows who were mortally wounded were carried to the shelter of the barn, in rear of the regiment, only to die in a short time of their terrible wounds. Others, able to walk, made the best of their way to the field hospitals several miles in the rear towards Harrison's landing.

At about noontime, during some lively cannonading, General Griffin dashed up to the headquarters of General Martindale, near the cut road, on the bank under the friendly shade and protection of a large tree, and reining up his active bay horse, called out in his characteristic shrill tones, that were plainly heard by the writer : " Martindale, come out here, and I will show you the best artillery fighting that you ever saw." Receiving only a negative shake of the head from General Martindale in reply (who was at the time in command of his brigade near by), General Griffin dashed away to place another newly arrived battery in position where it would do the most good for the Union army. While hastening towards this particular battery his orderly's horse was struck with a piece of an exploding shell on the ear and across the back near the saddle. The orderly quickly dismounted and removed the harness from his disabled animal and then went to the rear for another mount. The poor horse, finding himself free, wandered away bleeding from his wounds and shaking his head to free his ear from the blood that trickled into it. In the meantime General Griffin had gone down the line at a rapid canter, wholly oblivious of the fact that his brave orderly had suddenly disappeared.

The enemy's line of battle in our front had now assumed strong proportions. The division of General Whiting was on the left of the Quaker road; that of Gen. D. H. Hill was on the right of the same road, while General Ewell's division was in their rear in reserve. Gen. " Stonewall " Jackson's forces were back near the Willis Church. Those of Generals Magruder, Hugar and McLaws were to the right of D. H. Hill. Generals Longstreet and A. P. Hill were far to the right and rear of the Confederate line of battle in reserve. The ground occupied by the enemy was interspersed with forests, swamps, creeks and ravines. While their artillery was posted in selected positions and did great execution, many of their batteries were knocked out and disabled by the splendid artillery fire of Griffin's guns. During the afternoon General Hunt's reserve artillery, partly consisting of twenty and thirty-two pounders and ten-pounder Parrott guns, did much damage to the enemy by shelling from the rear of our lines, over our line of battle, from elevated ground near the Malvern mansion. The rapid fire from a number of our batteries about 1 o'clock drove small lines of the advancing enemy back with loss. Generals Armistead and Wright's brigades had taken possession of a ravine in front of their main line, and assisted by the natural inequalities of the ground in their front, attempted to assault and capture some of our guns. At intervals the persistent enemy repeated these charges and were always driven back to cover by our well manned batteries with losses each time. Three or four batteries that were brought forward to aid their movements gained positions on elevated ground, about eight hundred yards off, and opened on our lines only to be knocked to pieces or driven from the field by our resistless guns. As the time sped by our killed and wounded increased all along the lines of Morell and Couch. The enemy continually endeavored to put new batteries into favorable places with the intention of raking our lines and crushing our destructive fire; but General Griffin's artillerists would, literally speaking, knock each battery to pieces as it came into position under his fire. Between the hours of 2 and 3 o'clock the infantry and artillery blazed away on both sides almost incessantly. Small bodies of infantry continued their spasmodic attacks on our lines seemingly without any preconcerted action on the part of the whole. They accomplished nothing by it, unless it was intended to give occupation to troops that would otherwise lie idle under our destructive artillery fire.

After 4 o'clock a remarkable stillness fell upon the lines of the enemy. A large body of the enemy's cavalry now came into view for a while, but the fire from our guns was too hot for them and they soon retired. What their object might have been can only be surmised, for it was never developed further than for them to appear before us and then quickly disappear. Sharpshooting was continually kept up on both sides, much to the detriment of the victims who became exposed to the aim of these hidden, cool, calculating and cold-blooded soldiers.

Comparative silence now hung over the battle-smoked field with its dead lying unmolested in every direction. This silence on the part of the enemy called to mind the battlefield of five days ago at Gaines' Mill, and the heavy assault that succeeded it, and which broke our lines on the left centre into such frightful disorder and panic. General Porter and his subordinates began to make every preparation to guard against the occurrence of a similar disaster. The lines along Morell's and Couch's front were strengthened in their weak points by additional troops and batteries from the right and rear of our lines. In rear of all the lines the artillery in reserve was rearranged and placed in such a manner as to open fire, if necessary, with a terrific and concentrated effect on the points that a pursuing enemy would, in the nature of the roads and ground, be likely and obliged to take.

Ammunition was freely supplied to all the infantry. The artillery, that required it, was relieved and replaced by fresh batteries. Many field glasses in the hands of general officers were closely observing the line of woods where the enemy lay in partial concealment. Much activity in shifting artillery and in moving infantry was seen and speculated on. It was soon the general opinion that the " graybacks " were concentrating in our front and that " the woods were full of them." The comparative quietness on the field had lasted about an hour and a half when that peculiar ringing boom of shotted cannon, so familiar to the veteran's ear, along the enemy's line warned the Union army that " the fight was on once more."

The artillery fire was of short duration; as it ceased long lines of gray colored infantry came forth from the woods with a quick, long, swinging stride onto the open plain. Brigade followed brigade and regiment followed regiment into line of battle as they deployed along our front three-quarters of a mile away. As they manœuvred in their thousands they were watched with intense interest by thousands of eyes from our infantry, lying on the ground, and from our batteries of artillery, every gun of which was loaded with double-shotted canister, grape and shrapnel, and every battery man eager at his post. General Griffin rode up to his brigade, on his spirited bay horse, and, in his clear shrill tones, called on his regimental commanders to " get ready to charge." He likewise warned each brigade commander to be ready. Again, in a short time, he dashed on to the line of the Ninth and cried out " Colonel Cass! Get ready to charge! They are coming! "

Major Hanley, who was now acting lieutenant-colonel in command of the right wing of the regiment, saw General Griffin coming, and was on his feet in an instant ready to assume command, thinking, perhaps, that Colonel Cass would · be unable to go forward in the charge.

Lieutenant-Colonel Guiney, who had been prostrated since the close of the battle of the 27th ult., had previously been taken violently sick on the field, and had to be assisted to an ambulance. From lack of proper food, medicine and rest, he was so weak as to finally be unable to move without assistance. The surgeon pronounced him sick with malarial fever and ordered him home. Colonel Cass ordered Captain O'Leary of Company F in charge of the left wing of the regiment, as acting major. At the same time he placed Sergt.-Maj. P. E. Murphy in command of Captain O'Leary's company, as there was no lieutenant with the company, one being absent wounded, and the other a prisoner in the hands of the enemy since the battle of Gaines' Mill.

Colonel Cass on hearing General Griffin's orders, which the latter supplemented by shouting, " Up Ninth and at them! ". cried out at once, " Attention, battalion! " whereupon every man of the Ninth sprang from the ground like magic, eager for the fray.

In the meanwhile the enemy's long line of gray had steadily advanced up the slope. So far they had not fired a shot. Their guns were trailed and their long swinging march had increased to a rapid

stride. No doubt they expected to be very soon among the guns of
our artillery, which so far had waited for orders. The enemy's line
was within a hundred and fifty yards of our guns. The heavy tramp
of their feet could be heard. The order was then given to our batteries, " Fire ! " The lanyards were pulled, and from the muzzles of
fifty pieces of artillery death and dire destruction were spread amongst
the lines of the gallant foe. Great gaps were instantly seen in the
still advancing lines of gray. But they were as quickly closed without
seeming to check their advance. Again and again our guns poured
their death-dealing missiles into the foe as the brave fellows pressed
forward with the hope of reaching and capturing our batteries, little
heeding that their trail was marked by hundreds of their dead and
wounded comrades. The artillery fire was then held back, and the
orders rung out along our lines " Charge bayonets ! " With a rush like
the wind the Ninth went forward, joined by the 4th Michigan on the
left and the 62d Pennsylvania on the right. With a defiant Irish cheer
that broke into a prolonged yell, loud enough to almost raise the dead
from the field, our blue line of glittering steel went over the ground
with relentless impetuosity for sixty yards or more, to meet and drive
back the now steadily advancing lines of the determined foe.

The solid line of blue, holding with a firm grip their rifles, with
their glittering bayonets at a charge, go forward yelling like demons.
The onset is terrible and resistless. The enemy's line hesitates,
wavers, breaks, turns and flies. Along the Union line the cry rung
out, " Back to your guns ! Quick ! Back to your guns ! " The line
of blue rushed back. The artillery was unmasked. Its deadly fire
was then poured forth in flame and smoke into the backs of the wildly
retreating foe. Our infantry joined in the slaughter with buck and
ball and rifle shot " at will " until the enemy sought shelter in the
ravines and woods and behind the natural protection of the elevated
ground around them. In the meantime the brigades of D. H. Hill
furiously assaulted the lines of Couch on our right and were driven
back with great slaughter.

With a perfect recklessness that is wholly regardless of consequences the enemy's line is reformed and reinforced with fresh troops,
and the charge is renewed. With a steady and rapid stride the long
line of determined men push surely and swiftly up the slope. Soon
they are falling thick and fast from our galling infantry fire and the
heavy shells that burst along their front. Double-shotted canister cut
great swaths in their ranks as they approach ; still they do not hesitate

or seem to waver in their forward movement, or notice the terrible slaughter in their midst; on the other hand, they draw together each moment and shoulder to shoulder increase the rapidity of their steps, hoping to reach and capture our guns, and force back our lines of infantry in confusion. But they are doomed to disappointment. Another wild rush and cheer, with furious yells, and our solid lines of blue are upon them driving them back in wild disorder and capturing many prisoners. " Back to your guns! " is the cry, and as soon as our batteries are unmasked the demoralized lines of the enemy are raked with canister, shell and rifle shot. Again and again Magruder and D. H. Hill charge their brave and resolute lines against the resistless fire of our splendid guns without avail. Our reserves are pushed forward to the front line and relieve our tired and war-worn men, who retire only to replenish their ammunition boxes and reform for another charge.

The enemy try desperately to pierce our lines. In vain they press forward in their thousands against Morell's front only to be repulsed with great slaughter. Fresh lines rush forward against Couch's and Kearney's front where they meet only death and disaster.

Near sunset our gunboats opened fire from the river at Turkey Bend but their great shells burst in our own lines near Tyler's siege battery, at the Malvern house, killing and wounding a few of his men. The promptness with which our Signal Corps sent orders to cease firing was instantly obeyed by the gunboats and that saved us from further accidents.

General Hunt's thirty-two pounders and Tyler's siege guns continued to throw their heavy ordnance into the enemy's lines till dark. This fire was mistaken by the enemy as coming from the gunboats.

General Porter sent to Sumner for some reinforcements and about 7 o'clock Meagher's gallant Irish Brigade crossed our lines going towards our left front. As they passed the survivors of the Ninth they were warmly welcomed and greeted with hearty cheers.

The Irish Brigade took position well to the left and front of Morell, and opened on the enemy with a most gallant charge and ringing cheer and yell, driving them back with loss and in great disorder. Their charge was succeeded by a rapid rifle fire, and shot and shell from our batteries. For over an hour the Irish Brigade was engaged in supporting our line on the left, in a severe struggle with a superior force of the enemy, when they finally drove them back to the cover of the woods with great loss. In their last charge they came in close and bloody conflict with the enemy and brought off many prisoners.

General Meagher's brigade lost many brave officers and men before darkness closed upon them and ended their fighting.

As the regiments of the Irish Brigade, with General Meagher at their head, left their places in the Second Corps to respond to the call of General Porter for assistance, they came forward on the " double-quick," and were greeted by the cheers of our troops as they passed along. The survivors of the Ninth Massachusetts Volunteers gave them a hearty greeting as they went to the left and front. This was the second time during the " seven days' battles " that the gallant Irish Brigade rendered assistance to the 1st division of the Fifth Corps. It is needless to say that ever after the old Fifth Corps held them in kindly remembrance, and that the Ninth Massachusetts was proud of their brave and patriotic countrymen.

Whenever the Irish Brigade was called upon to reinforce the weak places on the battle-line their coming brought renewed courage and confidence to the jaded troops. " Here comes the Irish Brigade ! " " Don't you see the green flags ! " " Three cheers for the Irish Brigade ! " was heard on all sides, and the cheers that filled the air followed them into the post of danger and death, where they were sure to turn the tide of battle in favor of the Union and victory. To have been in the Army of the Potomac and not know and hear of the valor of Meagher's Irish Brigade was among the impossibilities. Their renown will live forever in the pages of American history. Song and story will ever recite their sacrifices on the altar of freedom for their adopted country.

In the woods, to the extreme right of our lines, the enemy had placed their sharpshooters and expert rifle infantry. From this quarter a deadly fire was kept up on our lines as they charged forward during the afternoon. Owing to this enfilading and oblique fire large numbers of officers and men were killed and wounded. General Kearney's division had opened fire on these woods and partially succeeded in clearing them, but it was impossible to effectually clear this forest and swamp, and all through the battle our lines suffered terribly from the unerring aim of these hidden sharpshooters. It was from these woods that Colonel Cass, while charging at the head of his regiment, received that terrible wound in his face and mouth that cost him his life. When Colonel Cass fell and was carried from the field, Acting Lieutenant-Colonel Hanley assumed command of the regiment. In the next charge that followed he too received a bullet from the same quarter in his right arm, which proved to be a most dangerous wound, followed by an immediate swelling of his whole arm which obliged him to relinquish the command of the regiment to the Acting Major, Captain O'Leary. He escaped injury and fought the regiment till dark, and that night marched it off the field. He continued as the commander of the regiment until he was relieved in August following by our new commander, Colonel Guiney.

Several of our line officers and a great many of our men were killed and wounded from the deadly fire on our flank, which ceased only with the coming of night. It was about 9 o'clock that night when the last parting shell was fired in the direction of the enemy's lines. While our army rested on their arms in the vicinity of the battlefield the rain commenced to fall.

The Ninth Massachusetts bivouacked a short distance from the field, comparatively few in number, war-worn and weary, but neither dejected nor disheartened. Nearly one-half of their number had been killed and wounded, which, added to the sick, exhausted and disabled, left but the skeleton of a once gallant regiment. After lying on the ground without any covering in the rain, the regiment was ordered to " fall in." The few hours' sleep somewhat refreshed them, and as the rain continued to fall upon their already wet clothes they moved forward with other troops through the darkness of early morning in the mud and slush on a weary tramp of seven miles to Harrison's Landing.

The following incident is related by Lieut. M. W. Phalen: At the battle of Malvern Hill, the right wing separated from the left, taking the colors with them, and went forward joining the left of the 44th New York. After advancing a considerable distance, and when we were about ready to retire, Acting Lieut. John F. Doherty was wounded in the leg. On retiring with the colors, we were under an oblique fire from the enemy. Lieutenant Flaherty was on Doherty's left and I was on his right, all facing to the rear. This brought me on the danger side of Doherty which he immediately recognized and refused to go a step farther until I had taken a position on the left; thus exposing himself to the fire and shielding us, claiming, in his most vehement manner, that as he was wounded and therefore useless for further service, the best use he could make of himself was as a bulwark or protection to us who were not wounded. Bearing in mind the surroundings and the fact that there was great uncertainty whether any of us would safely reach the rear, and that there was no one to applaud his speech or his conduct, this incident has always held a prominent place in my memory as one of the rare instances of true bravery.

CASUALTIES IN THE NINTH MASSACHUSETTS VOLUNTEERS AT THE
BATTLE OF MALVERN HILL, JULY 1, 1862.

List of Killed and Mortally Wounded.

OFFICERS.

Colonel Thomas Cass, mortally wounded; 1st Lieut. John H. Rafferty, killed; 1st Lieut. Edward McSweeney, killed.

COMPANY A.

Sergeant Patrick Early, Privates Hugh McGlone, William Davis, Daniel Kennedy, died of wounds July 14, 1862, John Nickerson.

COMPANY B.

Sergeant Thomas Meany, Acting Sergeant-Major, Privates Charles Thompson, Mathew Smith.

COMPANY C.

Privates Charles Duncan, John Waters, died of wouuds Nov. 5, 1862, James Shehan.

COMPANY D.

Privates John McLaughlin, died of wounds, Wm. J. Teate, died of wounds, Mitchel Provost, Michael Conway.

COMPANY E.

Corporal Owen Gallagher, Corporal Henry Roas, died of wounds Aug. 18, 1862, Private Patrick Boylan, died of wounds July 13, 1862.

COMPANY F.

Privates John H. Ganley, Edmund Regan, died of wounds Aug. 22, 1862, at Philadelphia.

COMPANY G.

First Sergeant Robert Daley, Privates John Mahoney, Cornelius Furfey.

COMPANY H.

Corporal Thomas Hubon, died of wounds, Private Patrick Holien.

COMPANY I.

Private David Mulcahey, died of wounds.

COMPANY K.

Privates Patrick Dermody, John Scannell, John Twoomey, died of wounds Jan. 1, 1863 (as James), Simon Howard, died of wounds Sept. 14, 1862, James McLaughlin, died of wounds Nov. 12, 1863.

List of Wounded.

OFFICERS.

Major Patrick T. Hanley, Acting Lieut -Col., Captain Geo. W. Dutton, Captain John W. Mahan, 1st Lieut. James F. McGunnigle, Acting Lieut. Patrick E. Murphy, Sergt.-Major, Acting Lieut. John F. Doherty, Q.-M. Sergt., Hospital Steward Nathan D. Parker, Band Musician John Leitch, Stretcher Bearer.

COMPANY A.

First Sergeant John B. O'Hara, Sergeant James Hickey, Privates Jeremiah Coughlin, James Deboa, Austin Durkin, John Donavan, John Kanery, Thomas Lewellen, Charles Lovett, John McCarthy, Wm. F O'Callahan, Peter O'Brien, Bernard Sheridan, Daniel Sullivan, Robert Phillips.

COMPANY B.

First Sergeant Robert A. Miller, Sergt. Patrick Brickley, Privates Thomas Powers, Dennis Collins, Michael Griffin, Charles ⸢Lyons, Michael McGurn, Philip McGovern, William Sullivan, John Martin, Martin Cummings.

COMPANY C.

First Sergeant John P. Murphy, Sergeant Michael Lyons, Corporal Thomas McMahan, Corporal James Gillis, Privates John Lynch, Michael Moynahan, Jeremiah Murphy, Thomas McAuliff, Michael T. McNamara, William Mullen, John Ryan.

COMPANY D.

First Sergeant Nathaniel ⸢Carnes, ⸢Corporal Edward C. Scott, Corporal James Cavanagh, Privates James Murray, James Carr 1st, Michael Clancey, John P. Good, James McCann, John D. Doherty, Andrew Reddy, Thomas Collins.

COMPANY E.

Corporal Charles Hayes, Privates William Bloomis, John Denny, Edward Denny, Francis Kelly, Patrick O'Connor, Matthew Regan, Francis Spencer, Dennis Rourke.

COMPANY F.

Sergeant Edward Geigle, Corporal Patrick Tierney, Privates John Carey, Richard Carney, John Daley 2d, Thomas Darcy, Wm. Densmore, John Clynes, James Connor, Morgan Sweeney, James Connelly, John Hennessy, John Coogan, Patrick Dolan, Humphrey Moynihan, Bernard Fillnan, William Graham, William Rogan, Edward Neil.

COMPANY G.

Corporal Timothy Quinn, Privates Wm. Murnane, Martin Fahey, Martin Lyndon, John McCurdy, Wm. McEnery, Owen Fullard, Michael Farley, Lawrence Kelly.

COMPANY H.

Corporal James W. McGowen, Corporal John F. Donovan, Corporal David Slattery, Privates Michael Coakley, Maurice Cahill, Cornelius Carmody (Co. A), John Cain, John O'Keefe, Wm. Broderick, James Connors, Patrick Houren, David Burke, Michael Burke, Michael M. Warren, Edward Fitzpatrick, James McNeal, Patrick Roach.

COMPANY I.

Sergeant Patrick Rabbit, Sergeant Thomas Flynn, Corporal Joseph Barry, Privates Henry Boylan, John Cullen, Cornelius Dacey, Michael H. Kirty, John Kiernan, John Morris, Peter Shields.

COMPANY K.

Sergeant Michael Downey, Privates James Butler, Patrick Cunningham, Joseph Ford, Alexander Ford, Richard Kelly, Robert Lee, Philip McKenna, James Mahoney, James O'Sullivan, Edward Riordan, William Verriker.

CASUALTIES, SEVEN DAYS' BATTLES

FROM JUNE 25, 1862, TO JULY 1, 1862, INCLUSIVE,

NINTH MASSACHUSETTS VOLUNTEERS.

WHOLE NUMBER AT MALVERN HILL.

Officers killed and mortally wounded	3
Officers wounded	4
Non-Commissioned Officers killed or mortally wounded	6
Non-Commissioned Officers wounded	28
Band wounded	1
Privates killed and mortally wounded	25
Privates wounded	99
Total, Battle of Malvern Hill	166
Total, Battle of Gaines' Mill	252
Total, Battle of Mechanicsville	3
Total, killed and wounded, including three officers taken prisoners	421

FINAL NUMBER SEVEN DAYS' BATTLES.

Total, officers and men killed and mortally wounded	117
Total, officers and men wounded	301
Total, officers prisoners	3
Total	421

General Porter, in a late personal correspondence with Captain O'Leary, Ninth Massachusetts Volunteers, uses the following complimentary expressions concerning the Ninth Regiment in the "seven days' battles."

119 West 47th Street,
Capt. Timothy O'Leary,   New York, May 1, 1896.
610 E. 7th St., Boston, Mass.

Dear Captain : * * * * * The services of the regiment, Ninth Massachusetts Volunteers, during the seven days' fight were extraordinary and unsurpassed by gallantry and stubborn fighting, and the surviving members of those days might well claim a medal of honor for them.

*   *   *   *   *   *   *   *.   *   *

Yours truly,

(Signed) FITZ JOHN PORTER.

This brief encomium being unexpected and unsolicited by any one is all the more valued as coming from the general commanding under whose eye the regiment fought. The writer has read the autograph letter above referred to, and publishes this extract copy with the knowledge and consent of its recipient.

Losses in the 1st Brigade (Martindale's) were : —
Killed, 114 ; wounded, 443 ; missing 329   886
Losses in the 2d Brigade (Griffin's) were : —
Killed, 182 ; wounded, 772 ; missing, 199 .   .   . 1,153
Losses in the 3d Brigade (Butterfield's) : —
Killed, 166 ; wounded, 546 ; missing, 269 981
Losses in staff, cavalry, artillery, sharpshooters : —
Killed, 21 ; wounded, 82 ; missing, 25   128

Total in 1st Division, 5th Corps   .   .   . 3,148

SEVEN DAYS' BATTLES.

Total losses of the Army of the Potomac : — *

Killed	.	.	.	.	.	.	.	1,734
Wounded	.	.	.	.	.	.	.	8,062
Captured and missing		.	.	.	.	.		6,053
Total loss	.	.	.	.	.	.		15,849

The number present for duty and equipped in the Army of the Potomac on June 20, 1862, as per official records XI., part II., page 238, were : —

Engineers	.	.	.	.	.	.	.	1,511
Cavalry	.	.	.	.	.	.	.	6,513
Artillery	.	.	.	.	.	.	.	6,446
Infantry	.	.	.	.	.	.	.	90,975
Total force	.	.	.	.	.	.		105,445

Total losses of the Confederate Army is approximated at : —

Killed	3,286
Wounded	15,909
Captured or missing	940
Total loss	20,135

The total strength of the Confederate Army in the seven days' battles is not especially given, but it probably ranged from 80,000 to 90,000 in effective force.

At Gaines' Mill, June 27, 1862, the Union losses were : —

Killed	894
Wounded	3,107
Captured and missing	2,836
Total loss, Gaines' Mill	6,837

Confederate losses not given, but are estimated to be between 8000 and 9000, at Gaines' Mill.

The reader will notice that the whole force of the Army of the Potomac was 105,445 men, and that the Confederate army was estimated between 80,000 and 90,000.

In accounting for the number of soldiers in the Union army the " Morning Reports " included every man " present and absent." Owing to the great number of men on detached and detailed service throughout the army, and in the various departments in Washington, and other cities and places, the reported strength of the army was thus reduced about thirty per cent. At that rate the number actually present for field service and battle would be, say in round numbers, 74,000 men.

With the Confederate army in this regard it was entirely different. Detached and detailed men were not accounted for in their field reports. Every man that was reported in their army was present for duty, and carried a gun, a carbine or worked at a cannon. When they said they had 80,000 or 90,000 men they meant that those were the number present for battle. Every able-bodied man was sent to the front and kept there to fight. Their " home guard " was composed of old men and boys and they were obliged to attend to all detached and detailed services. The negro slaves with them were utilized for every duty under the sun in the way of manual labor, except carrying " weepons." The Southern cry was : " Never trust a nigger with a gun."

With our National army it was far different. The detachments taken from the main bodies of our fighting forces were extraordinary and to a great extent unnecessary. During the first year or so of the war, most of our detachments throughout isolated places in the South were simply having a " picnic," and of no earthly use in putting down the rebellion. Wherever the opposing armies of the South were, our armies should have been there in front of them *to fight*, and not off hundreds of miles away holding useless territory. Political influence in the beginning, and lack of knowledge in military affairs, by congressmen and those in authority, were the prime factors in scattering our army into detachments under so many independent commanders.

Our regular color-bearers were Sergt. Thomas Fallon of Company F, who carried the National flag (Old Glory), and Sergt. " Jack " Barry of Company B, who was the bearer of the " Green flag of Ireland "; emblematic of the place of birth and descent of the men who composed the Ninth, and dear to every Irish heart. No regiment was allowed, by orders, to carry more than two stands of colors, and as the Ninth would be lonesome without the green flag they were, with great regret, obliged to discard the ensign of the old Bay State. Under the Stars and Stripes, on the 27th of June, ten of our bearers fell, either killed or wounded; while Sergeant Barry was fortunate enough to carry the Irish flag throughout the whole battle of eight hours without being hit.

The Irish standard was very heavy, and the physical strain on the brave sergeant brought on varicose veins in both legs which permanently injured him for life. Sergeant Barry was the victim of much official injustice up to within a short time of his death, which occurred April 19, 1890. All the facts were laid before that great true friend of the Union soldiers, U.S. Senator George F. Hoar, in Washington. He was the means of having the sergeant's case rectified before the brave fellow died.

Sergt. Thomas Fallon was the first color-bearer to fall on that day. He was shot with a rifle bullet through the left lung, and was carried on a stretcher from the field. He recovered in time from the terrible wound to a certain extent, but never was the same again physically in health. He continued on duty in the regiment, and was mustered out on the expiration of its term of service. His life was shortened by his wound and he died at his home in Salem, Mass., on Sept. 7, 1888, greatly respected and beloved by kindred and friends.

Sergt. John F. Donovan, Company H, was one of the brave color-bearers of the Stars and Stripes at Gaines' Mill and the Chickahominy, after eight or nine gallant soldiers fell under its folds. He was promoted sergeant on the field. At the battle of Malvern Hill he was badly wounded and was succeeded as color-bearer by Sergt. Malachi Curley, Company H. The difficulty of obtaining the names of other color-bearers renders it impossible to mention their names here.

Our beloved chaplain, Father Scully, had a remarkable and thrilling experience during the seven days' battles. He was a Roman Catholic priest who, everywhere on the battlefield, wholly regardless of its dangers and liable at any moment to be killed or wounded, administered to the spiritual and personal welfare of the wounded and dying. At the battle of Hanover Court House, at Mechanicsville, at Gaines' Mill and the Chickahominy, he diligently followed his priestly office unobtrusively and unmolested, until he was discovered by the enemy inside their lines on the 27th. Our forces had fallen back so suddenly that Father Scully was unaware of his exact position until he was taken prisoner. He declared to his captors who and what he was, and being unarmed and a non-combatant, expected to be allowed to attend to the wounded; but, strange to relate, he was arrested and placed under a guard of soldiers. This unaccountable proceeding of arresting a Catholic chaplain while in the discharge of his office amongst hundreds of wounded men of the same faith, and placing a guard directly over him, can only be accounted for from the fact that it was instigated through narrow-minded Southern prejudice or from a lack of Christian education on the part of his captors. Had they been barbarians one might furnish the excuse that they knew no better.

The argument might be used that he was a spy, and would escape and give information to the enemy. Admitting the points of the argument; thousands of our soldiers were in the hands of the enemy, many of them dying, many of them wounded; among them were to be found Catholics looking and wishing for the consolation of their spiritual guide and father. In that case he should have been allowed freedom, under surveillance if necessary, to exercise the functions of his priestly office among the wounded and dying captives. But no; he was closely guarded like any ordinary prisoner not wounded, and treated no better.

Finding no mercy at the hands of his enemies, Father Scully resolved to gain his freedom at the first opportunity or perish in the attempt. As night wore along the guards became negligent and sleepy. As the sentinel soon fell asleep the chaplain suggested to a few of the prisoners near him that they quietly crawl away and make their escape. His suggestion was acted upon, and they were not long in reaching the shadows of the woods in the swamps of the Chickahominy. They had barely entered the cover of the woods when they were missed, and the alarm given; at once the sentinels went in pursuit of them.

As Father Scully and his companions broke through the woods they made considerable noise; this brought on the fire of the pursuers, and the bullets whistled quite freely over the heads of the fleeing prisoners. In order to gain time and baffle the enemy, Father Scully resorted to strategy; he directed the men to gather up handsful of mud, for the swamps were full of it, and together they would throw it off on their flank; as it rattled through the trees and branches it drew the force and fire of the guards off in that direction. In the meantime they rapidly gained headway, until finally everything in their rear became silent. In wading through the river, which was quite low at this time, they lost their boots and shoes in the mud, and of course, were obliged to continue in their stocking feet. They were fortunate in not running up against the enemy, and in coming up with the Union army, where they were soon enabled to join their regiments.

At Savage Station, Father Scully had the misfortune to fall into the enemy's clutches a second time. His capture was somewhat similar to his first experience, that is, he was attending to the wounded, and unaware of his proximity to the foe. He was, if anything, treated more harshly than when first taken. While in their hands he witnessed some brutal treatment of our wounded men by the Southern guard, and at once remonstrated against it in a vigorous manner. A Confederate officer present ordered him away, and in an angry manner told him it was none of his business, but Father Scully insisted that it was his affair, and that he would not stand by and see wounded Union soldiers brutally treated without attempting to prevent it. This courageous and manly attitude on the part of our chaplain stirred the bile in the gentleman (?) who represented Southern chivalry on horseback. In shrill, excited tones and with a strong Southern accent he cried: " Yer —— Yank, if I had a rope here I'd hang you up to one of these yere trees." As this gallant (?) officer had no rope handy, the hanging of Father Scully did not take place. Again the same rough treatment was used, and he was hurried off to Richmond with other prisoners under guard.

At Richmond the Provost Marshal — to whom Father Scully was taken — treated him with the kind forbearance of a Christain officer and gentleman. He allowed him the freedom of the city, only requiring of him to report to him once each day. After the great excitement through which he had passed for several days was over, he was stricken with a terrible fever and lay at death's door in a brother priest's house, unconscious and delirious for three weeks. When sufficiently recovered in health and strength to move about once more, he was unconditionally released and sent north.   The malarial fever that had taken hold of his whole system continued to keep him in poor health, so much so that his physician would not allow him to go south again, and he was obliged to resign his commission as chaplain of the Ninth Massachusetts Volunteers on account of disability.   He never fully recovered in health and strength from the hardships and dangers through which he passed in the Army of the Potomac.   At the present writing he is the permanent rector of St. Mary's of the Annunciation Catholic Church, Cambridgeport.

CHAPTER X.

HARRISON'S LANDING.

THE MORNING AFTER THE BATTLE — ARRIVAL OF THE 32D MASSACHU-
SETTS — REVIEW OF THE ARMY — PRESIDENT LINCOLN AT HARRISON'S
LANDING — GENERAL McCLELLAN'S ADDRESS TO HIS SOLDIERS —
MALARIA AND SICKNESS — DEATH OF COLONEL CASS — REVIEW OF
THE FIFTH CORPS — GENERAL HALLECK APPOINTED COMMANDER U.S.
ARMY — BOMBARDING HARRISON'S LANDING — COMMUNICATIONS FROM
GOVERNOR ANDREW AND GENERAL PORTER — COLONEL GUINEY AND
LIEUTENANT-COLONEL HANLEY ARRIVE — GENERAL McCLELLAN
ORDERED TO ABANDON THE PENINSULA — REGIMENTAL BANDS MUS-
TERED OUT OF SERVICE — ORDERS TO MARCH — MARCHING THROUGH
WILLIAMSBURG — PASSING BY YORKTOWN — AT HAMPTON — AT NEW-
PORT NEWS — ON BOARD THE "JOHN BROOKS" — SAIL FOR AQUIA
CREEK, VA. — BIOGRAPHICAL SKETCH OF COLONEL CASS.

> " Decide not rashly. The decision made
> Can never be recalled. The gods implore not,
> Plead not, solicit not; they only offer
> Choice and occasion, which once being passed
> Return no more."
>
> LONGFELLOW.

ON the morning of the 2d day of July, 1862, the scenes for miles
between Malvern Hill, Shirley, Westover and Harrison's
Landing, which met the gaze of the survivors of the Ninth
Massachusetts Volunteers as they marched from the late battleground
with the Fifth Corps, were pictures of lively misery filled with woe-
begone appearances. The scattered lines of our war-worn troops, wet
to the skin, and covered with spattered mud, seeking for a fitting place
to rest and reorganize, was anything but an edifying sight in the
drenching, drizzling rain. Besides being in light marching order —
owing to the fact that the men had nothing heavy to carry but their
guns — many of the officers and soldiers were in their stocking feet.
This latter state of affairs was brought about by halting in the soft
muddy soil for a few minutes, long enough for their feet to disappear;
the adhesive quality of the soil was so great, and the suction so strong,

that on attempting to move forward many of them found, to their
dismay, that their shoes were left in the mire and out of sight, for the
top slush gently oozed over the hole from which they had drawn their
stocking feet, leaving no trace of the spot where their shoes were
buried; they were lost to the wearer as if they were in the bottom of
the river.

On approaching Harrison's Landing the James river itself presented a lively appearance; gunboats, steamers, schooners, barges and
small boats in great numbers were moving about or floating at anchor
on the broad expanse of the river, which at this landing is unusually
wide. Along the bank was piled in some confusion the new stores of
the quartermaster's and the commissary's departments for the use of
the approaching army. Ambulances, with their loads of wounded
from the late battle, were seeking opportunities to put their helpless
living freight on board the transports. Large numbers of sick and
wounded were still on foot, likewise awaiting means of transportation
down the river. Negro laborers in great numbers were at work carrying goods on shore and loading up army wagons. Wall tents, A tents,
Bell tents, etc., were erected in great numbers for the use of " Uncle
Sam's " non-combatants, who were now moving about in all directions
working to make the army comfortable — by and by.

But the army in the meantime, fresh from the field of slaughter,
was now without tents, quarters, or food of any kind. The sight of
these scenes along the river, however, put some animation into the
marching column, for they could now see their way to better times.

General Griffin's 2d brigade of the 1st division, Fifth Corps, were
not long in finding sufficient space of — comparatively speaking — good
soil on which to bivouac.

The Ninth were soon assigned a campground and when the rain
ceased they fell to work trying to make themselves " at home."
Rations were issued and the camp, under the direction of the commander of the regiment, Captain O'Leary, was soon laid out, so that
everyone had a comfortable place to sleep and rest under covering of
some kind. With our camp guard once more posted we felt comparatively secure.

The morning of July 3 was clear and pleasant, a circumstance
that added greatly to the cheerfulness of the whole army. Although
the day was full of sunshine and pleasant weather, yet beyond our
camp towards the river, mud was king. No man moved in that direction on foot unless he was obliged to. Those who did go to the river
went in mud for a long way up to their ankles at least.

The principal excitement which occurred in the course of the day was the arrival and assignment to our brigade of six companies of the 32d Massachusetts Volunteers, Col. Francis J. Parker, commanding. As they landed from their transport, marched up the wharf and arrived on the bank of the river, they were, to the eyes of the beholders, resplendent in their apparently new uniforms and bright equipments, presenting as they did the appearance of a fine body of infantry. Our tanned, begrimed and war-worn veterans, who turned out to see them, were now more or less merry at the expense of the newcomers. As they eyed the polished shoes and the clean trowsers of the 32d they grinned all over to think that they would soon be baptized in slush and mud clear to the knees with the " sacred soil " of " ole Virginny." As the 32d took to the broad road of liquefied soil without flinching and marched forward in a gallant manner, seemingly regardless of their pedal extremities, or the mire that bespattered their clean blue uniforms, they captured the hearts of the " old fellows." Their soldierly bearing soon won the respect of the army veterans, and a friendship sprung up between the 32d and the Ninth that continues till this day. In their subsequent years of patriotic service in the Army of the Potomac they proved themselves a brave and gallant regiment. When the recruits and re-enlisted men of the Ninth were to be transferred on the expiration of its three years' service, they were unanimous in their wishes to be turned over to the 32d Massachusetts Volunteers. General Griffin allowed it, and they received them with kindness and pleasure; thereby cementing, as it were, more firmly together the friendship of both regiments. Six more companies finally joined the 32d, making a large regiment of twelve companies, which served by re-enlistment till the close of the war, recording to their credit three years and seven months of the hardest kind of service, most of it at the front.

The " Glorious Fourth " found the army preparing for review. The reviewing officer was General McClellan. What his thoughts were as his depleted battalions marched by, many of them under the command of a line officer, acting colonel, may be better imagined than described. He was personally acquainted, so to speak, with every colonel and every regiment under his command, and he knew the value of each. To one of his kindly nature the late losses throughout his army must have been keenly felt. National salutes for Independence Day were given at the different corps headquarters and the brass bands played patriotic airs. In the evening O'Connor's Ninth Regiment Band gave a concert at regimental headquarters. In a word the day was marked with salutes, music and an unusual display of patriotic good-feeling throughout the army.

Since their arrival at Harrison's Landing the army was in receipt of daily rumors of sudden attacks to come by Lee's army in force. As the days went by orders to be ready to move at a moment's notice and to be constantly on the alert night and day were less frequent. They were occasioned by the active movements of the enemy on the other side of the river. Reconnoissances were made from time to time; picket duty was performed, and all other necessary precautions taken to obtain information of the enemy, and ascertain their movements and intentions. Food, clothing, tents, etc., were now plentifully supplied to the troops, and they were also getting a good share of much needed rest. Companies were busy preparing muster and payrolls, and in posting up the company books on losses and casualties.

A sad and regrettable affair occurred at this camp on the 6th day of July. It appears that James Burns of Company I became demented and hovered on the skirts of the camp, among the trees, with a musket and fixed bayonet in his hands. When approached by any one he would charge bayonets upon him, or them, in a furious and excited manner without uttering a word. The officer of the day ordered the camp guard to arrest him. All were in doubt as to whether the musket he was using with so much dexterity was loaded or not. At any rate the guard took the benefit of the doubt, and failed in their futile attempts to capture the crazy fellow, who, all the while, charged bayonets on all comers. The commander of the regiment after witnessing the trifling action of the guard ordered the officer of the day to " take that man, dead or alive." The officer thereupon drew his revolver and fired on Burns, who dropped to the ground mortally wounded. The demented victim died in hospital July 13, 1862.

President Lincoln arrived at the landing on the 8th inst., and made a general visit to the camps. Late in the afternoon he reviewed the army. The moon was shining over the river, which gave to its waters the appearance of glittering silver, when our regiments marched past the reviewing officer. As the Ninth had been, in the past, reviewed several times by the President they could recognize his tall form, and " stove-pipe " hat, as he sat mounted in the moonlight some distance away, although partly surrounded by General McClellan and staff. A cool, chilly, miasmatic air swept up from the river as the moon arose, which, added to the late and unusual hour for reveiw, threw a damper over the troops, and a noticeable stillness prevailed, that was impossible to shake off.

The President returned to Fortress Monroe the next morning. No doubt his mind was in great trouble and perplexity in trying to determine what action was best to take regarding the next movement of the Army of the Potomac.

After the above events transpired the following address was read on dress parade.

HEADQUARTERS ARMY OF THE POTOMAC, ⎱
CAMP NEAR HARRISON'S LANDING, VA , July 4, 1862. ⎰

Soldiers of the Army of the Potomac: Your achievements of the last ten days have illustrated the valor and endurance of the American soldier. Attacked by vastly superior forces, and without hope of reinforcements, you have succeeded in changing your base of operations by a flank movement, always regarded as the most hazardous of military expedients. You have saved all your material, all your trains and all your guns, except a few lost in battle; taking in return guns and colors from the enemy. Upon your march you have been assailed, day after day, with desperate fury by men of the same race and nation, skilfully massed and led; and, under every disadvantage of numbers, and necessarily of position also, you have, in every conflict, beaten back your foes with enormous slaughter. Your conduct ranks you among the celebrated armies of history. No one will now question that each of you may always say with pride, "I belonged to the Army of the Potomac!" You have reached this new base complete in organization and unimpaired in spirit. The enemy may at any moment attack you. We are prepared to receive them. I have personally established your lines. Let them come, and we will convert their repulse into a final defeat. Your government is strengthening you with the resources of a great people.

On this, our Nation's birthday, we declare to our foes, who are rebels against the best interests of mankind, that this army shall enter the capital of their so-called Confederacy; that our National Constitution shall prevail, and that the Union which can alone insure internal peace and external security to each State, must and shall be preserved, cost what it may in time, treasure and blood.

GEO. B. McCLELLAN,
Major-General Commanding.

The sentiments of this patriotic address to the army found a responsive echo in the hearts of the soldiers of the Ninth Massachusetts Volunteers, and undoubtedly throughout our entire army; but more particularly do we mention our own old Fifth Corps, whose losses in the late seven days' battles counted up to over one-half of that of the whole army. They had borne the brunt of their engagements successfully and unflinchingly, and were now ready to follow their leader into the conflict again. It can be said with truth, of the Army of the Potomac, that misfortune of any and all kinds could not daunt their matchless courage. Their faith in ultimate victory, while indefinable, was likewise ineradicable.

The intolerable hot weather, with its countless myriads of army flies, began to tell upon the troops, particularly on the late arrivals from the north. The malaria from the river and swamps, together with the use of bad drinking water, was getting in its deadly work, and increasing very rapidly the length of the sick list. The Ninth was pretty well acclimated and stood it much better than the average. No doubt this part of Virginia was, to the native element, a very fine country, with a very fine climate and a very productive soil to the planters: it agreed with the negro slaves who once flourished and labored here bringing wealth and prosperity to their masters. But during July and August, 1862, it was a tough place for Northern soldiers and freemen to live in. The writer never heard any loud expressions of regret when our army was called to leave this "garden spot" of the "Old Dominion." Rain, mud and malaria were exchanged while here for dust, drouth, debility and sickness, and vice versa. When the orders came the army was glad to move.

The regiment learned at this time with heartfelt sorrow of the death of Colonel Cass, from wounds received at Malvern Hill, July 1, 1862. He passed away at his home in Boston on the 12th day of July. His funeral was attended by Lieutenant-Colonel Guiney, Major Hanley, and others of the Ninth who were home, sick and wounded, together with a large concourse of relatives, friends and citizens. His widow and children were the chief mourners. He was buried with military honors at Mount Auburn Cemetery.

Exchanged prisoners of war and those who were absent sick and wounded were now joining the army from day to day. In the meantime large numbers of sick were leaving the army for the hospitals north. The poor fellows who were victims of the malarial fever were suddenly reduced in strength, and, unless they were promptly sent to a more northern climate, they were, in nine cases out of ten, sure to die. Sympathy and assistance from hardened soldiers was very poor stock for a sick man to depend on. If the surgeons, stewards and nurses did not befriend him, then he was friendless indeed.

A review of the Fifth Corps by General McClellan on the 25th of July, started new rumors of a forward movement, which seemed to be verified by a visit to army headquarters from General Halleck, who was appointed commander-in-chief of the Army of the United States on the 14th of July, 1862.

The most exciting incident that occurred at this time at Harrison's Landing, to the writer's knowledge, was the bombardment of our camp by the enemy, from the opposite side of the James river, in line with our division, about midnight of July 31.   It was subsequently ascertained that one Gen. L. G. French left Petersburg, Va., which the enemy then occupied, with two brigades of infantry, and arrived at the James river accompanied by one Gen. W. N. Pendleton, with a force of six or eight batteries of artillery.   The guns, to the number of forty or more, were placed in position along the bank, and opened a rapid — not to say terrific, — fire of shell into and over our lines.   This unexpected assault on our camp, at midnight, when all but the guards were buried in sleep, aroused the greatest astonishment imaginable. The panic-stricken were soon fleeing in every direction from the vicinity of the river where most of the non-combatants were quartered.

None of the shells fell into the camp of the Ninth, but in the next regiment, the 62d Pennsylvania, one man was killed.   Most of the missiles burst or fell beyond our line, killing in all ten men, and wounding fifteen others.   This fusilade of shells lasted fully forty minutes, and during that time about one thousand shots were fired. Some of our batteries returned the fire, and our gunboats likewise opened on them from the river.   The assailants lost one killed and seven wounded.   When they began to get a dose of what they were sending us the poltroons ceased firing and ran away.   This cowardly style of warfare did not coincide with vaunted Southern chivalry.   It was on a par with the dastards who planted shells with sensitive fuses in the roads and works at Yorktown when it was evacuated a few months previous.   Men may forget such baseness, but the history of it will never die.

To effectually guard against a future crazy attack of this kind our forces took possession of the place the next day.   The woods were felled and the houses in that vicinity destroyed.   The native owners were the final losers.   The enemy gained nothing but a smirched reputation.

It is surprising to relate, but it is nevertheless true, that many officers and men slept soundly through all the booming of cannon and the consternation going on at that hour of night.   All that they — the sleepers — ever knew about it was what they heard related by their comrades the next morning.

Some soldiers who were sensitive to every alarm in the early days of their service became hardened after passing through the hardships and excitement of actual warfare, and would sleep anywhere in the midst of danger, or near the firing of guns.   Others were always on the alert and wakeful, and ever would be, even if all their lives were spent in active campaigning.   In the first instance the mental and physical capacities of the soldiers in time became blunted or hardened, to a careless, and even reckless, sense of danger, through which their strong selfish instincts predominated.　In the second instance we find that the mental and physical elements of the men were those of a superior quality to the first; they were trained by long service to the nature of their calling; they were unselfish and watchful not only on their own account, but for the good of all those around them.　They possessed the material that make brave and efficient officers and soldiers.　The hardened sleepers became good campaigners under the direction of others.

Just after the close of the month of July the following communication was received by the commander of the regiment, and read on dress parade.

COMMONWEALTH OF MASSACHUSETTS,
HEADQUARTERS, BOSTON, July 30, 1862.

SPECIAL ORDER, No. 568.

The Governor directs that the following letter of Brig.-Gen. Fitz John Porter, commanding the Fifth Army Corps, in the Army of the Potomac, with the nominations attached thereto, be published and promulgated in a Special Order from these Headquarters as a fitting tribute to many brave officers and men, and as an honorable incentive to future patriotic effort and daring.

The commissions recommended will be issued immediately.

Copies of the order will be transmitted to General Porter, and through him to the commanders of the Corps of Massachusetts volunteers he has so honorably mentioned.

By command of His Excellency,

JOHN A. ANDREW,
Governor and Commander-in-Chief.

WILLIAM SCHOULER,
Adjutant-General.

GENERAL PORTER'S LETTER.

HEADQUARTERS OF FIFTH ARMY CORPS,
HARRISON'S LANDING, VA., July 26, 1862.

TO HIS EXCELLENCY, JOHN A. ANDREW, GOVERNOR OF MASSACHUSETTS, Boston, Mass.

Governor: — I have the honor to present for your consideration an order appointing, subject to your approval, field officers for the Ninth Massachusetts Volunteers.

I take pleasure in bearing testimony to the admirable conduct of these officers in action, especially at the battle of the Chickahominy, and to sustain thereby the recommendation of their brigade commander and the choice of the regiment.　It affords me great gratification to express to you my admiration for the noble conduct of the troops from your State under my command in the late action before Richmond.

No troops could have behaved better than did the Ninth and 22d regiments and Martin's battery and portions of Allen's, or done more to add to our successes. Their thinned ranks tell of their trials, the brave men lost, their heroic dead, and gallant conduct and devotion to their country.

Their discipline was never excelled, and now, with undaunted hearts, they await, with confidence of success, the order to advance. I hope you will be able to send on men to fill their depleted ranks, even in parties of ten, as fast as recruited. A few men joining us now gives great heart to all the men, and adds to our strength nearly five times the same number in new regiments. I am, Governor, with high respect,

Your obedient servant,

F. J. PORTER,

Brigadier-General, Commanding

NOMINATIONS

HEADQUARTERS, FIFTH CORPS, ⎱
CAMP NEAR HARRISON'S LANDING, VA., July 26, 1862. ⎰

SPECIAL ORDERS No. 92.

* * * * * * * * * * * * * *

2. The following named officers are hereby appointed to fill the vacancies occurring in the Ninth Regiment Massachusetts Volunteers of * * * losses in action. These appointments are made for gallant conduct on the field of battle, and are subject to the approval of the Governor of Massachusetts.

Lieut.-Col. Patrick R. Guiney, to be Colonel, *vice* Colonel Cass, deceased; Major Patrick T. Hanley to be Lieutenant-Colonel, *vice* Guiney, promoted.

These officers will be obeyed and respected accordingly.

By command of

BRIG.-GEN. F. J. PORTER.

F. T. LOCKE,

Assistant Adjutant-General.

On the 4th of August, 1862, our late Lieutenant-Colonel, P. R., Guiney, joined his regiment at Harrison's Landing as its commander, having been commissioned colonel by Governor Andrew, in accordance with the foregoing recommendation, July 26, 1862.

He at once took charge of the regiment, relieving Capt. Timothy O'Leary, who had ably performed all the duties of commander during the absence of Colonel Guiney and Major Hanley.

About August 11, our late Major, P. T. Hanley, likewise joined the regiment, having been commissioned Lieutenant-Colonel by Governor Andrew, July 26, 1862, in accordance with the special order above referred to. He was fully recovered from his wound and ready for immediate duty. The arrival of our new field officers added vigor to the regiment which was gradually recovering in numbers and strength from its late battles.

A number of sergeants in the regiment, of which the writer was one, were appointed at this camp to fill existing vacancies of 2d lieutenants in the different companies. After performing the duties of that office faithfully they finally received their commissions from Governor Andrew *dated September 26, 1862.* By this official negligence they lost the pay and emoluments of that rank as far back as July 2, 1862. The injustice occasioned by this blunder was never rectified. At that time the parties interested were the victims of considerable disappointment and chagrin.

After the visit of the President, and also the one that followed from General Halleck, it was continually rumored that the Army of the Potomac would be largely reinforced, and another advance then made for the capture of Richmond. These and all other rumors and reports, with which the army was kept in lively suspense, were rudely set aside by a telegram from General Halleck, on the 4th of August, to General McClellan, ordering him to abandon the Peninsula and move his army to Aquia Creek. The key to the situation, for the capture of the city of Richmond, that the army now held firmly in its grasp, was to be thrown away. The communication from the north, to this point, which had cost the country so much blood and treasure to achieve, was to be incautiously abandoned.

The soldiers of the Ninth Massachusetts Volunteers little thought then that less than two years hence, when their term of three years' service expired, they would take their farewell from the army at Bottom bridge on the Chickahominy river, and march from thence, over their old stamping ground, to White House Landing on the Pamunkey river, for water transportation, on the 10th day of June, 1864, for home and muster out. Or that the army, after desperate fighting and great losses for nearly two years, would still be hovering along the swamps of the old Chickahominy (at the old stand), striving to capture Richmond, and end the rebellion. But, alas! such was the fact.

General McClellan was a disappointed man. He was likewise grieved at what he considered a suicidal act by the administration or by General Halleck's order. His firm belief in holding his ground and in fighting the enemy from that line was clearly portrayed in his letter in response to the telegram.* (*Vide* Records of the Rebellion, Series I.,

---

* Generals Dix, Burnside and Sumner, likewise protested against this movement. Halleck said he would risk his reputation on it. He lost it!

Vol. XI., page 81.) In reply General Halleck only reiterated his order, in obedience to which preparations were at once commenced. The wounded and sick, and those unable to march, went north by water transportation. Surplus army supplies were likewise shipped down the James river.

A few days before the regiment moved an order was received to discharge and muster out of service all regimental brass bands. We don't know how other regiments felt over the order, but we can say that the men of the Ninth were sorry to part with their " wind jammers." No more homesick men would sob themselves to sleep under the musical strains of " Home, Sweet Home," and other dear familiar airs, that carried the minds of the listening soldiers back to their homes and firesides ; or cause as it did in many instances, to the sleepless, a depression of spirits that could not be shaken off for some time. Henceforth we were to have only the soul-stirring sounds of the bugle and the drum, to call us forth to glory and to battle.

Some few brass bands were retained in the army at various divisions or corps headquarters. The far-off strains of music were pleasant to hear as they rose and fell on the distant air, but they lost the charm that clustered around the band in camp, as one loitered near the evening camp-fire, listening to its soothing, dreamy, strains. On the 10th of August the regiment bid farewell to Bandmaster Michael O'Connor and his corps of musicians, as they left camp to take transportation on the river for home. The charm of all future dress parades had now departed forever. The resonant voice of the bandmaster as he gave the order on parade : " One ! Two ! Three ! Play ! " would now be heard no more.

Orders to march from Harrison's Landing down the Peninsula were now received beyond a doubt. Late in the afternoon of the 14th day of August the Fifth Corps commenced to move forward, little dreaming what bad fortune was before them. Good and bad, such as it was, the brave old Army of the Potomac proved itself able to bear it to the bitter end. About 5 o'clock that day the Ninth Massachusetts broke camp and after marching a few miles came to a halt and found the road blocked up with artillery, wagon trains, cavalry and infantry. Resting on the greensward of slightly elevated ground we quietly waited for a chance to take the road. Darkness fell upon us, and as there was no sign of a forward movement, we lay on the turf through the warm night till daylight, when, without breakfast, on the 15th we moved forward at a rapid march, passing through Charles City Court House, which was kept up till 1 o'clock. The early part of

the day was slightly cloudy, warm and pleasant, and the road dusty;
the heat was intense at noonday. A short halt about 1 o'clock was
made for refreshments, which lasted about twenty minutes. We again
moved forward like a lot of "sprinters." The orders were to keep
well closed up. At the gait our division was going they soon became
"thickly scattered." The march was continued with very short intervals of rest until 11 o'clock that night. At that hour the Ninth reached
the broad waters of the flowing Chickahominy and bivouacked for the
night with a long list of stragglers to account for, many of the poor
fellows throughout the corps being pretty well played out. Many of
the men halted and bivouacked on their own account in small groups
for the purpose of cooking the chickens and fresh pork which they
bought (?) or that were kindly given (?) to them by the natives.
Foraging was against orders; but, in a reasonable way, on the march,
it was winked at by the officers generally, especially when hunger was
rampant, and they received a share of the plunder.

This first day's march, after lying in camp for several weeks, was
conducted with poor judgment, and after the veterans came to that
conclusion they moved along at their own gait, regardless of repeated
orders to "close up lively." When the nagging was continued it
created friction, and made men ugly, so much so that in order to get
rid of it, they quietly dropped behind after each halt in ones and twos;
then got together again; exhilarated by the freedom thus obtained
they went foraging. When the food was captured the next thing in
order was to stop in a good place where water was handy and cook it.
As for catching up with the marching column that was an after consideration. Generally speaking this class of men were good soldiers, but,
under irritating circumstances, and what they deemed a lack of consideration on the part of officers in command in forcing them to march
long into the night unnecessarily, a general "kick" was arranged
among themselves and quietly adopted when opportunity offered.

Our brigade had rested during the night near the mouth of the
Chickahominy river. It proved to be quite a respectable navigable
stream, a quarter of a mile wide, as it flowed into the James river in
the distance. It was spanned at this point by a well laid pontoon
bridge twelve hundred feet long.

After a good breakfast, and a bath in the river, the Ninth Massachusetts crossed the bridge with full ranks. After the experience of
the thirty-mile march of the day before Colonel Guiney decided to pay
no attention to the column in his front. He adopted a systematic
route step which kept his companies in good order, and after an under-

standing with General Griffin, a regular short rest was taken at hourly intervals, so that no more straggling took place in the Ninth. Late in the afternoon we passed through the ancient and historic city of Williamsburg, the seat of William and Mary College, next to Harvard, the oldest in the United States. It was here that Virginia, "the mother of Presidents," educated her sons. Williamsburg was the capitol of Virginia from 1698 till 1779, when the seat of government was transferred to Richmond. After that event it gradually lost its population and importance. For a small place it contains many fine old (once public) buildings and private residences, all built of English brick and material. It stands today an interesting relic of "Old Colonial times when we were under a king." Duke of Gloucester street is the centre and main avenue. The names of other streets are reminders of Tory days.

Washington, Lafayette, Rochambeau and other revolutionary heroes had headquarters here. It is fifty-eight miles from Richmond and twelve miles from Yorktown. The peculiar sickening malaria, which at certain seasons of the year surrounds the place, had no doubt everything to do with its desertion. As we passed through its silent streets we saw none of the few inhabitants who then lived there. It has no suburbs.

With a sense of relief the column marched out onto the plains, and bivouacked near Fort Magruder, one of the numerous earthworks that were held by the enemy in May last.

This was our first time to march through this section of Virginia, for in May last we sailed up the York river, after the evacuation of Yorktown, and landed at West Point. It was with feelings of much interest, mixed with curiosity, that we looked upon the enemy's fortifications, which were about three miles outside the city, and which were the scenes of our first engagement after the evacuation. Vegetation and solitude now reigned over these fields that once resounded with the terrible noise of bloody battle.

On the 17th we moved forward with all the men of the Ninth "present and accounted for" at an easier gait and in better spirits than when we first started. We were evidently receiving through our systems that invigorating tone that is promised to all soldiers who enlist in Uncle Sam's service, and which is derived from much "travel" and "scenery," not to mention the care taken to provide "good medical attendance, food and clothing" (?). As for sleeping apartments, we were like the birds of the air in freedom, for we could roost wherever night overtook us, unless otherwise ordered.

During the afternoon we were marching by and gazing about the familiar works at Yorktown, and as we moved along the road of that quiet but eventful place, a youthful group of the "Lost Children," with three rows of brass buttons on the front of their jackets, stood silently gazing at us from the ramparts. What their thoughts were of the travel-stained and — to them — dirty looking, dust-covered veterans of the Army of the Potomac we never knew, for they were as mum and distant as infants when gazing into strange faces for the first time. They made no response to the friendly salutations from our ranks, and as we tramped briskly along the road they were soon lost sight off.

After a good long rest that night, the 18th of August found us passing Big Bethel, and with full ranks, we reached Hampton a few hours before dark. As soon as the regiment bivouacked the writer started for Chesapeake hospital, a few miles in our front, and found his wounded brother, James, who had been exchanged, and was now slowly recovering his locomotion, with a slug of a bullet still in his leg. Rather than risk destroying the tendons the bullet was allowed to remain where it lodged and became securely embedded. The healing process proved to be very slow.

The following day — the 19th — we moved forward to Newport News, greatly refreshed and invigorated by the salt air from the bay. Here we had the pleasure of welcoming to our ranks a large batch of recruits lately from Boston under the charge of Acting Lieut. P. E. Murphy, who had also returned to duty fully recovered from a wound received at Malvern Hill.

The fresh white complexions, and the new clean uniforms of the recruits were a great contrast to those of the tanned faces and begrimed and broken uniforms of the Ninth Massachusetts. We knew in our hearts, though, that it would not take long to alter their appearance for the worse.

After comfortably boarding the steamer *John Brooks* we immediately steamed away for Aquia Creek. The trip up Chesapeake Bay and the Potomac river was very enjoyable, and it gave us an opportunity to clean up and look respectable.

Colonel Thomas Cass.

In writing a short sketch of Colonel Cass it cannot be expected that full justice can be done to one possessing his strong traits of character and bravery as an officer and soldier. The work of recruiting and organizing the Ninth Massachusetts Volunteers, of which he was the head and leading spirit, was in itself an undertaking at that time, which proved him to be a man of strong personal soldierly qualifications far above the ordinary run of men. He was at that period in the meridian of life and possessed of the military experience which only a captain in the Massachusetts militia could boast of. Added to these few brief years of service, however, were the natural instincts, ability and confidence which he innately possessed as a disciplinarian and a leader of men.

To say that he was in a degree arbitrary in his manner, and severe in his decisions and discipline as a commanding officer, is only another way of declaring that he was human; for who can point out a military man of any note who did not, in a more or less degree, display similar traits of character? The iron rule of military discipline enforces impartial severity in time of war more particularly. It is tempered, however, by implicit obedience.

That Colonel Cass was ambitious to lead a regiment which would prove an honor to his countrymen and a credit to the State of Massachusetts, no unbiased mind can deny. That his labors in this direction were eminently successful the history of his regiment amply testifies. Smarting, as he and his subordinate officers then were, under the arbitrary acts of Governor Gardner, it was his patriotic ambition to lead an Irish-American regiment against the enemies of the Union and his adopted country, as a living proof that he and they loved the flag and country of their adoption to such a degree as to lay down their lives in its defence.

He and his subordinate officers and the rank and file of his regiment were, as a whole, a class of men of superior standing and reputation in the community of our adopted citizens whose loyalty to the flag and the Union during three years' arduous service at the front, must stand henceforth in the history of the republic unchallenged and undisputed till the end of time. When he fell in honorable battle at the head of his regiment after four hundred and more of his brave officers and men were killed and wounded, he and they sealed their devotion to the republic.

Colonel Cass was born in Farmly, Queens County, Ireland, in 1821. In his boyhood he left his native land with his parents and emigrated to Boston. He resided at the old North End where he attended the public schools and subsequently learned the currier's trade. At a later period in life he joined his father in commercial pursuits and keeping store. In the meantime he became an active member of the Columbian artillery, Company B, 5th regiment artillery, M.V.M. As an ardent soldier of the militia he developed much talent as a bright and active military man, advancing through all the grades in his company to that of captain. In the course of time as a business man in the North End he became very successful and was acknowledged by his kinsmen and friends as a leader in their military and political affairs.

Previous to the breaking out of the rebellion he was elected and served on the school committee. In the organization of the Ninth regiment he displayed remarkable energy and activity, and, as its commander in the field, proved himself to be an able disciplinarian and tactician.

At the battle of Malvern Hill, on the 1st day of July, 1862, he went into action at the head of his regiment. When charging the enemy he received a terrible wound in the face and head from a rifle bullet. The responsibilities and hardships of the previous thirteen months' campaigning had weakened his system so that, in addition to the terrible wound from which he suffered, he was unable to rally. In the meantime his journey in the hot weather from the battlefield to his home in Boston aided greatly in debilitating his already worn and weakened system. His inability to swallow sufficient nourishment from the wounded condition of his mouth continued to add to his weak state. Death finally released him from his sufferings on the 12th day of July, 1862, just one day over thirteen months since his muster into the United States Volunteer service. His loss was deeply regretted by his regiment and by all his friends in Boston and elsewhere. He likewise left a widow and grown-up sons and daughters to mourn his decease.

At the instance of Governor Andrew, Adjutant-General Schouler addressed the following letter to the widow of Colonel Cass :—

BOSTON, July 12, 1862.

Mrs. THOMAS CASS :

Madam : — The death of your brave and gallant husband, Col. Thomas Cass, has just come to the knowledge of His Excellency, the Governor, and he has directed me to assure you of the deep sympathy he feels for you in this moment of sad bereavement, and of his regret of the great loss which the Commonwealth and the nation sustains in the death of one who so bravely did his duty, and who has fallen a martyr to the cause of liberty and Union As a token of His Excellency's respect for the character and his high appreciation of the services of Colonel Cass, I am directed to tender, in behalf of the Commonwealth, the 2d Regiment, M.V.M , as a military funeral escort. I will confer with any gentleman you may designate in regard to the arrangements necessary to be made. With great respect, madam, I have the honor to be,

Your obedient servant,

WM. SCHOULER,

Adjutant-General.

His funeral was an imposing one and a heartfelt tribute of respect from the State of Massachusetts, and likewise from his friends and fellow-countrymen in Boston to one of their kinsmen who gave his life and all he held dear in this world in defence of the flag of his adopted country.

CHAPTER XI.

THE SECOND BATTLE OF BULL RUN.

GENERAL POPE'S ARMY — GENERAL JACKSON'S FORCE — FORCES ENGAGED
AT CEDAR MOUNTAIN — GENERAL LEE AT GORDONSVILLE — THE
ENEMY'S RAID — GENERAL POPE'S ARMY ON THE MARCH — GENERAL
LONGSTREET FOLLOWS JACKSON — FIGHTING NEAR SUDLEY'S SPRINGS
— THE NINTH MASSACHUSETTS ON DETACHED DUTY — THE FIFTH CORPS
COMES TOGETHER — GENERALS PORTER AND McDOWELL — OUR
BRIGADE NEAR CENTREVILLE — SECOND BATTLE OF BULL RUN —
SECOND BRIGADE AND MARTIN'S BATTERY — THE FIFTH CORPS LOSSES
— CHANTILLY AND GENERAL KEARNEY — GENERAL LONGSTREET ON
GENERAL PORTER'S FIFTH CORPS — UNION FORCES OUT-GENERALLED
— THE PRESIDENT AND GENERAL McCLELLAN — THE FORCES ENGAGED
IN BATTLE — LOSSES ON BOTH SIDES — THE NINTH MASSACHUSETTS
AT MINER'S HILL ON THE OLD CAMP-GROUND — THE EFFECT OF
GENERAL McCLELLAN'S ARRIVAL.

*　　*　　*　　*

"The primal truth neither dies nor slumbers,
But lives as the test of the common right,
That the laws proclaimed by the sworded numbers
May stand arraigned in the people's sight.
The Word is great, and no Deed is greater,
When both are of God, to follow or lead;
But, alas, for the truth when the Word comes later,
With questioned steps, to sustain the Deed."

*　　*　　*　　*

JOHN BOYLE O'REILLY.

INASMUCH as the Army of the Potomac was on the 14th day of August, 1862, ordered from the Peninsula to Aquia Creek and Alexandria and to the vicinity of the Rappahannock river, it is deemed requisite to make a brief reference to some of the events which took place in that section of Virginia while the Army of the Potomac was on the Peninsula, and on its journey therefrom.

During the first part of June, 1862, Secretary of War Stanton, under the direction of the President, had undertaken to consolidate the armies of Generals McDowell, Banks, Fremont, etc., under one head, and had sent to the far west for Gen. John Pope in order to place him in command, although he was the junior officer of all the rest. On the 27th day of June (the day that the desperate battle of Gaines' Mill was fought) General Pope assumed command of the new army in front of Washington which was to be known as the " Army of Virginia." General Pope's army, with his subordinate commanders, consisted of General Sigel's (in place of Fremont) First Corps of 13,2(0 men; General Banks' Second Corps of 12,100 men; General McDowell's Third Corps of 19,300 men; besides 5,800 cavalry, and 200 men at headquarters; total, 50,600 men. General Halleck's lack of foresight was fully demonstrated when he sent General Pope and his inexperienced little army so far to the front as the Rapidan river in the direction of Gordonsville, with immense supplies in his rear at the stations on the Orange and Alexandria railroad; notably at Bristoe's Station and Manassas Junction.

" Stonewall " Jackson, imbued with the old spirit that gained him so much renown in the early days of spring of 1862, in the Shenandoah Valley, left the James river, on Lee's order, with his own division and reached Gordonsville on the 19th day of July, to resist the advance of Pope's army then in his front near the Rapidan. Jackson, finding that his command was too small to successfully cope with Pope's army, remained inactive, quietly awaiting the coming of Gen. A. P. Hill's division which arrived about the first week of August. By this additional force his command was increased to about 20,000 men. After being allowed to remain, with his small force, unmolested for a couple of weeks in front of Pope's army, Jackson was thankless enough to attack Banks and McDowell at Cedar mountain on the 9th of August. After a fierce battle from 3 p.m. until dark, Jackson won a doubtful victory, otherwise he would have continued his battle the next day, and never let up until he had driven his opponents to destruction. The forces engaged on each side were about equal.

That night the Union troops crossed over to the north side of Cedar run. Jackson fell back behind the Rapidan there to await the arrival of Longstreet's army and General Lee. About the middle of August that portion of the Confederate army under Jackson and Longstreet, composed of 49,000 men, was at Gordonsville with Lee in command. The rest of Lee's forces were still in front of Richmond watching McClellan and the Army of the Potomac, which, it will be remembered, was already moving to evacuate the Peninsula. Pope soon realized his weakness in the face of such generals as Lee, Jackson and Longstreet, and fell back behind the Rappahannock at Rappahannock Station.

In the meantime Stuart and his horsemen were raiding from day to day on anything and everything belonging to the Union army from Pope's headquarters to an army mule. Jackson left Lee and Longstreet at Gordonsville on the 25th of August and marched up along the Blue Ridge, through Thoroughfare Gap, and fell upon Bristoe's Station and Manassas Junction where his division was well supplied with Union rations, etc. Everything then in sight was destroyed by fire. Generals Jackson and Stuart continued their raid between General Pope and Washington to the delight and profit of their half-starved army. General Pope learning of Jackson's raid, and having received information of the arrival of the Army of the Potomac, moved to Warrenton Junction, August 26. He had, in the meantime, several skirmishes with Longstreet, who feigned attack along the Rappahannock. When Pope moved, Longstreet took Jackson's route along the Blue Ridge for Thoroughfare Gap where he arrived on the 28th. On finding the gap held by Union troops (Rickett's division) he went over the mountain with a part of his army and drove out his opponents. His troops then passed through the gap and went forward with the intention of joining Jackson on the 29th who was then on his left near Sudley Springs doing battle with our forces under Hooker, Kearney and Reno.

Our steamer arrived at the wharf at Aquia Creek in the forenoon of August 20, and to our surprise and pleasure, the regiment was ordered to board the cars in waiting, and take a railroad excursion to Falmouth, nearly opposite Fredericksburg on the Rappahannock river. Arriving here quite refreshed we bivouacked under marching orders, until the 22d inst., without seeing or hearing anything definite of the enemy or of General Pope. The regiment then marched to Ellis' Ford up the river where we remained in peaceful seclusion until the 27th of August.

While soldiering here we crossed over the ford on a visit and made the acquaintance of the natives. One Mr. Ellis, after whom the ford was named, occupied quite a mansion surrounded by out-buildings and slave quarters. Judging from general appearances a northern man would " calculate " that the old man was quite wealthy at one time in slaves and plantations. How his wealth would be counted at the close of the war was then an unsolved problem.

While here Colonel Guiney, with a few of his officers, visited one afternoon some Southern ladies at their residence, a short distance from camp, and over which he had placed a safeguard for their protection. On arriving they were received with distant but lady-like politeness, and invited to seats on the broad piazza. In front of the house several large shade trees added beauty and coolness to the surroundings. In the course of conversation one of the ladies was quite an outspoken champion for the Southern cause. After giving the " northern invaders " a polite but forceful dressing down, she declared that before she would surrender she would starve, and, pointing to the shade trees, said, " until obliged to eat the bark off those trees." While not agreeing with her sentiments at all, the party had to admire her frankness, her courage and her determined spirit. Her sparkling eyes and emphatic words made an impression that was often mentioned afterwards. On leaving she smilingly invited the party to call again, assuring them a welcome. Virginia was full of these determined women. In most instances their sacrifices were greater than the men's. Is it little to be wondered at that the war was a death struggle to the bitter end with such determined foes to combat?

General Pope's army having been finally located, we took up the line of march once more, on the 27th, and struck the Orange & Alexandria railroad, near Bealton, and moved along parallel with the railroad until we reached Warrenton Junction, well fatigued after a long and dusty march in hot weather. We bivouacked in the woods till early morning of the 28th, about 3 o'clock, when we were aroused and again moved forward, picking our way in the cimmerean darkness through the artillery and wagon trains that blocked the road and woods, greatly impeding our march; alternately moving slowly forward, then halting a short time to feel our way. As daylight broke upon us we moved along with more freedom; we passed Catlett's Station and continued on to Bristoe's Station where we arrived about 8 o'clock A.M. Far to our left on the march and well out to the front, we heard heavy artillery firing, sure signs that a desperate battle was now going on.

We viewed with some concern, not unmixed with curiosity, the dire destruction wrought by the enemy in this vicinity. Engines and cars were burnt up and smashed. Rails were twisted when red hot into all conceivable shapes, leaving this part of the road in a pitiful condition. The dead and wounded which we saw here told in forcible but mute words of the recent battle at this place between General Hooker's division and General Ewell's division. The prisoners of war guarded by Union soldiers reminded us that our forces had made a success of it in driving the enemy; this fact was confirmed by their dead and wounded which were left in our hands. Columns of our infantry passed and repassed, some going in the direction of the battle-line and others the reverse. Wagon trains and artillery were continually on the move.

The movements of our brigade were irregular, and the appearance of things looked to us somewhat undecided. The Fifth Corps, for the first time since leaving the Peninsula, was now all together again, and we finally went into bivouac at about sunset on the plains near Bristoe's Station and Broad Run. At this hour artillery and heavy musketry firing could be plainly heard in the distant front which called vividly to our minds the fact that many brave fellows were getting killed and wounded. Meanwhile we prayed that success would crown the efforts of our arms.

The next morning — Friday, August 29 — we learned that some of Jackson's troops had a bloody encounter with King's division near Groveton. Early in the morning of the 29th we moved off in the direction of Manassas Junction where we arrived about 9 o'clock A.M. We halted long enough to view with some disgust the smouldering ruins of our baggage cars so lately laden with supplies for our army. The general destruction, including tracks and bridges, proved to our satisfaction that as modern vandals, Lee's army were adepts in the business. Countermarching from here the column moved in the direction of Gainesville, our line of march being parallel with the Manassas Gap railroad. This road ran at about right angles with the Orange & Alexandria railroad.

We had been up and down the destroyed road so often in the past day or two that it was a standing joke, oft repeated among the men of the Ninth, that we were "guarding the railroad." At this time the report reached us that Longstreet's command had succeeded in passing through Thoroughfare Gap, our forces, which were holding the pass in Bull Run mountain, having fallen back. General King's division had joined our column at Manassas; Generals Porter and McDowell had come together. In the meantime we were changing our position from time to time, marching back and forth and consuming much time without any apparent definite purpose, until about 6 o'clock P.M., our brigade moved forward until we struck a dirt road which led uphill through the woods and onto a large open piece of hilly country. In the front of our regiment was a valley which was thickly wooded in that part, which one would say from observation was the foot of the hill. Over these woods the hills could be seen rising up abruptly in the distance. Far to the front against the sky immense clouds of dust seemed to rise and fall as though large bodies of troops or cavalry were on the march in that quarter. Our regiment went into line of battle on the brow of the hill with the rest of the brigade to our right. Between half past 6 and 7 o'clock a shell or solid shot was fired from one of the hill ranges in our left front. It was followed by another and another at intervals; they passed over to the right of the Ninth. The shots seemed to be " feelers," inviting a reply. Very soon one of our batteries opened and the firing from the enemy ceased, only to be renewed a short time afterwards more to our right which cleared the Ninth of all danger from that source. Far to our right the sounds of a heavy battle could be heard with now and then heavy and repeated volleys of musketry.

Our regiment remained standing all this time in the same place in line of battle. Darkness fell upon us, and a surprising stillness appeared to surround us, owing no doubt to the wooded surroundings of our elevated position. We got orders to stack arms and lay down where we stood. Our pickets were out. One of the regiments doing picket duty that night was the 22d Massachusetts Volunteers of the 1st brigade. The Ninth was entirely out of rations of all kinds; even crumbs of hard tack were at a premium. If we had had coffee or anything to cook, we could not do so as no fires were allowed.

The night was not over warm; so tired and hungry as we were, we lay silently down upon the grass — not very thick grass either — and the regiment, one and all, were soon asleep, and as still as dead men. Just before daylight on the 30th whispered orders were given— with a gentle kick on the soles of the sleeper's shoes — to fall in. In a few moments the regiment stood in line — our toilet consisted in rubbing our eyes and stretching our limbs — and, quietly breaking their stacks, shouldered their muskets and marched by the " right face; file right," down the dirt road in the direction of the plain from whence we came the night before. On the way down daylight revealed to our gladdened sight Quartermaster Mooney with several wagons of hardtack, coffee and sugar. As we came upon him he cried out, " Help yourselves"; " Fill your haversacks with all you want"; and we did.

A short time after receiving rations the brigade went into bivouac and were soon drinking a " delicious " mixture of hot coffee and chicory juice and munching hard tack. There was something about a pint dipper of black hot coffee to a hungry soldier in the morning that seemed to cheer and exhilarate in a way that it is impossible to explain. Every one who has seen active service in the field will admit that this particular army coffee, which was drank on all occasions, was the soldiers' panacea. It is well to say, however, that food and drink which would be looked upon with hungry eyes and a moist mouth in the service and voraciously devoured on the march, would in civilized life, at home, find no customers.

Our brigade was the rear one of the division, and as the other two moved before we did, our orders were to follow them to Centreville. In the course of the day we reached the plains near Centreville but failed to find the rest of the division. Our division commander, General Morell, was with us, and he was as much in the dark as any one else as to the whereabouts of his other two brigades. It was subsequently learned that on the march the destination was ordered changed from Centreville to the front near Groveton. The 1st and 3d brigades got the order all right and proceeded to the front. Our brigade, being in the rear of the column, and out of sight, owing to long lines of wagon trains, artillery, infantry, etc., on the road and vicinity, failed to get the order. Whoever was negligent in this, the blame cannot, surely, be laid on our brigade. Its commander, General Griffin, who was noted as a brave and persistent fighter, would have obeyed the order on its receipt, if he lost his life and those under him the next minute. Under the circumstances nothing could be done in good judgment but to wait at Centreville for orders; and as we waited, orders were expected and looked for every minute while there.

The 22d Massachusetts Volunteers overtook our brigade on the march, having but recently returned from their tour of picket duty the night before. They were hungry and entirely out of rations, and thus far were unable to procure any. They were in search of their brigade on the road to Centreville when they overtook us. General Morell told them to continue with the 2d brigade until we should come up with the rest of the division, which he expected to do shortly. We passed rapidly through the "burnt district" known as Manassas Junction. It was a desolate reminder of Jackson's mysterious movements. Thence we moved over Bull Run bridge, onto the old battleground of 1861, and arrived at Centreville. Not finding the division, Generals Morell and Griffin moved the brigade and the 22d Massachusetts back into the country and halted to await information and orders. Late in the afternoon General Griffin received orders to proceed to Groveton on the line of battle now in progress some six miles distant. General Morell, on receipt of this order, left personally in great haste to take command of his division as soon as he found out where it was.

As the brigade moved forward many wounded men on foot were going towards Centreville, followed by ambulances loaded with more wounded. The brigade had not moved far before it was completely surrounded by thousands of men in a disorganized mass who appeared to cover the country as far as the eye could reach in the direction of the battlefield. From the language and conversation of this retreating army, and from information given us by many of them, we learned that our lines of battle on the right had been turned and driven and the whole force rapidly driven back. The fords and bridge across Bull Run were blocked by surging masses of armed and unarmed and retreating men, which together with artillery and ambulances, rendered it utterly impossible for any body of organized troops to pass through and go forward, so that General Griffin did the only thing that could be done at that time in that situation. He halted his brigade and formed it in line of battle and thus it stood at order arms, awaiting the turn of events.

The 22d regiment Massachusetts Volunteers had, on the receipt of orders, left our brigade and struck out for itself, hoping to reach the line of battle, but they had no better luck than we did, for they found it impossible to move forward any great distance against the tide of demoralized humanity coming across Bull Run from the battlefield. Much cursing and swearing was indulged in at the known and unknown causes of defeat by these incensed and retreating masses as they moved along in twos, fours and large groups towards Centreville. No one gave them orders; no one attempted to control them. They would not then have obeyed if any one had.

For miles across the country they moved along at a route step — routed indeed. When those in our vicinity reached our brigade and found it standing intact, in line of battle, many of them halted seemingly reassured, on sight of us, that all was not lost. Several of them gave up their guns and equipments at the request of our line officers, to our unarmed recruits, as we had been unable ever since leaving Newport News to obtain guns, etc., for them. We laughed to think that Pope's men were so willing to give away their guns on asking. They knew at all events that there were plenty more where those came from. Besides, there were hundreds of men in that demoralized mass who had thrown away guns and equipments in order that they might be free to move faster if necessity demanded it.

It afforded much amusement to see several barouches and covered carriages drive up within earshot of our line, fresh from the city of Washington, in which were seated " statesmen " from the Capitol which we were defending under the leadership of incompetent generals whom they had forced upon the volunteer army. Allowing these citizens to come to the front, in time of battle and panic, was on a par with other distracting and incompetent measures carried on in the city of Washington. The way the soldiers in the mob that surrounded these carriages " ballyragged " and bamboozled the occupants was, to men in our situation, most amusing to all of us. Even General Griffin, grim and statuesque as he appeared on his horse, had to give way to a little of the hilarity in which the brigade, that had been standing in line like statues for two hours, was forced to join in joke and laughter, all at the expense of the carriages and their occupants, who very soon found that they were out of place and not wanted, and showed that they had some sense left by turning around and driving rapidly away through Centreville.

Just before dark Captain Martin's 3d Massachusetts artillery was sent further to the front and his guns put in battery. Our brigade took a position in rear, in support of Martin's battery, where we lay all night. It rained quite hard during the night. The morning found us wet as drowned rats, but we were unmolested by the enemy.

The 22d Massachusetts Volunteers informed us that on the night of the 29th of August, when they were doing picket duty in front of our division, Longstreet's army was in our front fresh from Thoroughfare Gap, and that during the night a part of his forces were on the move towards General Jackson on their left (our right). They could hear the orders of the Southern officers to their men as they marched along to " close up! " " close up! " and could plainly hear, in the stillness of night, the rattle of their canteens and equipments as they were forced along the road to reinforce General Jackson. General Longstreet's command, all told, numbered 30,000 men. On the 29th when McDowell withdrew, taking with him King's division, he left Porter with his own corps of 8500 men.

On the morning of the 30th General Longstreet discovered that the Union troops in his front had disappeared. He thereupon marched the rest of his men over in support of General Jackson. All the orders issued that day (30th) by General Pope declared that Lee's army was retreating. The defeat of the Union troops in the afternoon only shows how egregiously mistaken General Pope was as to Lee's movements.

If General McDowell, who was senior to General Porter, had remained with the Fifth Corps where he was on the 29th, and attacked Longstreet on the morning of the 30th, Jackson could not have been reinforced; and in all probability his force would have been insufficient to turn our right. Hence the result would have been in our favor. Many people are under the impression, on account of the subsequent court-martial and sentence of General Porter, that the Fifth Corps did no fighting at Bull Run under General Pope. The following statement from Colonel Powell's history of the Fifth Corps will disabuse that impression : —

" The Fifth Corps was heavily engaged on the 30th — excepting the 2d brigade in the 1st division — and they lost altogether 30 officers killed, 68 wounded, and 8 captured; 301 men killed, 1294 wounded, and 450 captured; being a total of 2121. This was a large list of casualties out of a total of 6500 men of the corps engaged, and it was greater than any of the other corps in the fight."

Any one reading Gen. John Pope's subsequent animadversions on the movements and actions of the Fifth Corps will at once see the injustice of his statements, especially the one sent to General Halleck September 1 at 8.50 A.M. by telegraph from Centreville. By reading it — in his report elsewhere — the reader will see that through chagrin and malice he intended that the Fifth Corps should become the scapegoat of all his mistakes and bad generalship.

The following morning — Sunday, August 31 — the rain continued to fall and it found the 1st division of the Fifth Corps very wet — particularly the 2d brigade — somewhat dejected, but well organized. Our division was in the field on the south side of Centreville. The 2d division of regulars were bivouacked in the works at Centreville.

While lingering here our active enemy had swung around our right and rear and were gaining ground with the intention of putting themselves between our army and Washington. It was a daring movement when we consider their small, though active army in the face of more than double their number in front of Washington and in the vicinity of Centreville. When Lee's army was located the troops of Generals Sumner, Heintzelman and others were sent to check it. This brought on the battle of Chantilly on the afternoon of September 1. The enemy were routed at all points.

At Chantilly the gallant soldier, " Fighting General Kearney," received his death wound. His loss was greatly regretted by every soldier in the Army of the Potomac; his bravery and patriotism had long since won their love and respect. The Republic could ill afford to lose, at this time, so able a soldier and general.

The writer feels justified here in showing that the true history of the 2d Bull Run battle has proved that the animadversions cast by Generals Pope and Halleck upon General Porter and the Fifth Corps were wholly groundless. The defeat of General Pope's army would have occurred on the afternoon of the 29th of August were it not for the fact that General Longstreet hesitated to reinforce Jackson that day when he found Porter's Fifth Corps in his front. An extract from the report in the Century Magazine of that battle, by Gen. James Longstreet, will give the reader a partial idea of the Confederate position in front of the Fifth Corps on the 29th.

General Longstreet goes on to say : —

" General Pope, sanguine by nature, was not careful enough to keep himself informed about the movements of his enemy. At half past four on the afternoon of the 29th (August, 1862), he issued an order for Porter to attack Jackson's right, supposing I was at Thoroughfare Gap, when in fact I had been in position since noon and was anxiously awaiting attack. It has been said that General Stuart, by raising a dust in front of Porter, so impressed him that he did not offer battle. I know nothing of the truth of the story and never heard of it till after the war. If from any such cause Porter was prevented from attacking me it was to our disadvantage and delayed our victory twenty-four hours. Porter knew I was in his front; he had captured one or two of my men, which gave him information of my position before he actually saw me. If Porter had not appeared when he did I would have attacked by our right early in the afternoon. In that event Porter would have a fine opportunity to take me on the wing and strike a fearful blow. As it was he was a check upon my move against Pope's main position. If I had advanced upon Pope I would have been under an enfilade fire from Porter's batteries, and if I had advanced upon Porter I would have been under a fire from the batteries on Pope's front, as severe as the raking fire from my batteries the next day when Pope was massed against Jackson. Had Porter attacked me between noon and night on the 29th, I should have received his nine thousand with about double that number. I would have held my line to receive the attack and as soon as his line developed his strength, I would have thrown three brigades forward beyond his extreme left. When my line of battle had broken up the attack, as it certainly would have done, these three brigades would have been thrown forward at the flank and at the same time my main line would have pushed on in the pursuit. The result would have been Porter's retreat in confusion, and I might possibly have reached Pope's left and rear in time to cut him off. When his army was well concentrated on the 30th he was badly cut up and defeated. It does not seem unreasonable to conclude that attack on the 29th in his disjointed condition would have been attended with more disastrous results to him. If I had been attacked under the 4.30 order the result might have been less damaging, as Porter would have had the night to cover his retreat and the Federal army could have availed itself of the darkness to screen its move across Bull Run. But Porter's attack at night, if not followed by the back retreat of the army, would have drawn me around the Federal left and put me in position for striking the next day.

" Col. Charles Marshall of General Lee's staff, in his evidence before the Fitz John Porter Board, puts my forces on the 29th at 30,000. It is difficult to see how Porter with 9000 men was to march over 30,000 of the best soldiers the world ever knew. Any move that would have precipitated battle would have been to our advantage, as we were ready at all points and waiting for an opportunity to fight. The situation will be better understood when we reflect that the armies were too evenly balanced to admit mistakes on either side. I was waiting for an opportunity to get into the Federal lines close upon the heels of their own troops. The opportunity came on the 30th, but the Federal army was then concentrated; had it come on the 29th I would have been greatly pleased."

Lee, Jackson and Longstreet outgeneraled Halleck, Pope and McDowell. From the commencement of the campaign to the finish it was a losing fight to the Union army. The subsequent arraignment of Fitz John Porter was the means of making him a scapegoat to cover over the glaring blunders and bad generalship of Halleck, Pope and McDowell.

Defeat met Pope at every turn before Porter and the Fifth Corps arrived, and it continued after their arrival. The Fifth Corps marched and countermarched until the 29th of August when McDowell and Porter were ordered to attack Jackson's right flank. McDowell withdrew all the forces he had and went to the right front, leaving Porter with only his own corps and no reserves with orders to " go in here." When Porter with 8500 men went " in " he found on his flank and front, instead of a clear country on Jackson's right, some 14,000 to 20,000 of Longstreet's army lately arrived by way of Thoroughfare Gap, protecting Jackson's right and rear. Instead of being reinforced by Pope with more troops to enable Porter to fight and hold Longstreet from aiding Jackson, he was ordered to leave the ground before daylight of the 30th and take position in front of Jackson. The latter, after being heavily reinforced by Longstreet, attacked Reno, Kearney, Hooker and others on his left, and McDowell, Porter and others on the right and centre and drove them by desperate assaults and good generalship in confusion from the field.

General Halleck sat in his office in Washington and wrote General Pope his " God bless your noble army " order, in the midst of its greatest misfortunes, instead of sending the veteran corps of the Army of the Potomac to the front, with orders to attack Lee wherever found, under a general who knew how to successfully command them. Why an army of 70,000 men, with a reserve force of 50,000 more, was ingloriously defeated by an opposing army of 49,000 men is a problem worth pondering over.

An army of brave Union soldiers and willing fighters were scattered over the country beween Bull Run and Washington, and wandering about like frightened sheep without a fold or a shepherd. A general with brains, ability and courage to command them, was all that was needed.

The 20,000 men — demoralized men — which straggled in from Bull Run to Washington created intense excitement in the capital, so much so that the government had gone so far as to get ready to leave and to abandon the city to the victorious enemy which they thought was upon them, but which never came. Four brave army corps were in front of Washington. It was utterly impossible for Lee to capture the Union capital after the panic or before.

Sumner, Heintzelman, Porter and Franklin, in command of their respective corps, were calmly awaiting orders. That night, when McClellan was known to be with the army, joy beyond measure was carried to the hearts of all of his old soldiers. The blood in their tired bodies leaped through their veins with accelerated vigor on receipt of the news, until they forgot defeat and hardship and were once more ready to follow him utterly regardless of any higher authority. They believed in his unselfish loyalty to the Union cause. They knew he would not hesitate to go into battle, and that once in he would carry his army through with honor. Whatever his shortcomings were as a dashing fighter or field marshal, they felt that in all other respects he was a giant in intellect and experience and a trained general of undoubted courage. The charge of inferiors as to his slow movements was ill-timed from the fact that a large army with a purpose is necessarily slow when compared to the movements of a smaller one, without trains and supplies, looking for food and plunder.

The President and General Halleck, in what they considered their trying hour, called on General McClellan and told him that they considered that all was lost, that the city would be taken by Lee, and that they were preparing to evacuate. McClellan assured them both in unmistakable language that he could save Washington and that all was not lost. With the command of the army he would bring order out of confusion and protect the capital. He was ordered verbally to take command, but not to interfere with Pope unless his army came inside McClellan's lines. In that event he was to command them. It is needless to say that they got there.

Toward morning of the 2d of September we quietly withdrew in the darkness from our position and passed through the earthworks on the left of Centreville at daylight and continued on our march, with Chantilly on our left, to Fairfax. We met large bodies of infantry, mostly the Sixth Corps, under Franklin. The only part of the Sixth Corps engaged was Taylor's brigade of Slocum's division, on the 27th of August, at the railroad bridge over Bull Run. They lost their gallant general and many men.

The following troops were engaged on the Union side at the second battle of Bull Run, viz.: General Pope's army, composed of the First, Second and Third Corps, commanded respectively by Generals Sigel, Banks (not engaged on the 30th) and McDowell. General Sturgis' Reserve Corps. From the Army of the Potomac, General Heintzelman's Third Corps, composed of Kearney's and Hooker's divisions. General Porter's Fifth Corps, composed of General Morell's division (2d brigade, not engaged on 30th), and General Sykes' division. Ninth Corps, General Reno. Total force, 70,000. Total losses in the campaign: killed, 1747; wounded, 8452; missing and captured, 4263; total, 14,462.

Southern forces, Gen. Robert E. Lee commander: General Longstreet's Corps, right wing, composed of five divisions, commanded respectively by Generals Anderson, Jones, Wilcox, Hood and Kemper. General Jackson's Corps, left wing, composed of three divisions, commanded respectively by Generals Taliaferro, A. P. Hill and Ewell. General Stuart's Cavalry. Total, 49,000. Estimated losses in the campaign: killed, 1553; wounded, 7812; missing, 109; total, 9474. (Considered a low estimate.)

After leaving Fairfax Court House on the 2d of September we marched by way of Vienna to Miner's Hill. As we reached the old camp-ground where we had lived six months previous to March 10, 1862, and from which we had now been absent for six months lacking a few days, it presented to our eyes that afternoon, for the last time, a sad sight to contemplate. Along the ground where the tents of the field, staff and line officers stood, were strewn relics and utensils of their former camp life still undisturbed; reminders to us now of the well-known and remembered occupants in former days,— officers full of young life and manly years, many of whom had since given up their lives for their country. A short ways off, in the direction of the parade ground, ten streets, with ten rows of " cellars," containing rude bunks and rude, broken-down chimneys and fireplaces, stared us in the face and seemed to inquire of us in mute surprise, " Where are the men who lived here? why are they not with you? " Where once stood ten rows of " A " tents, twenty-five in each street and from three to four stalwart soldiers in a tent, there now remained nothing to show for it but the dilapidated " cellars " and the rubbish that was scattered in and around them. The rank weeds had grown up in irregular patches all over the place, which added to the loneliness of the forsaken camp. Into this desolate camp and into these streets we marched, silently and slowly. Our companies were small now and reached about one-third way down, where, a few months ago, there stood about one hundred brave men in each to answer roll-call, and who daily made the air resound with life, laughter and merry songs. Many were dead — killed in battle — many were absent from wounds, sickness and disability. As our men had broken ranks and were looking about, one cried out: "Hello! that looks like one of my old shoes"; and such it proved to be as he picked it up in one of the tent cellars. Another said, "Here is an old canteen," as he picked it up and scrutinized it. "That belonged to Mike Murphy; I know it by the mark of the bayonet when Joe Smith punched a hole in it. How mad Murphy was when he found his canteen ruined. Well, the brave fellow has gone where canteens don't count. God be good to him." Thus the men talked as they discovered relics here and there. After awhile a group got sitting together and one opened the conversation by saying: "I hope they will move us out of this place, I don't wish to camp here tonight. It makes me feel lonesome-like when I see so many dumb acquaintances scattered around that belonged to our poor boys that's dead and gone, God rest their souls." "I know every cellar in this street," said another, "and I could tell the names of those who messed together; I never realized what a horrible thing this bloody war is until now. It's just awful, so it is, when I think of the brave young chaps that have been killed. More luck to us, it's not through yet, by a long shot. I'm thinking there won't be many of us on top of the earth this time twelve month. Lee and his ' secesh ' army are hard to beat. Do you mind the way he walloped Pope with only half the number of men? It's lucky for Pope that Bob Lee didn't have his whole army with him." At the close of this long-winded speech, which was quietly listened to by the crowd that clustered around the speaker, a comical chap broke out with, "Oh!, whist! don't be talking nonsense. Don't you know, sure, that if Lee had his whole army in the fight *we* would have been called in? Then what show would the ' Johnnies ' have with ' Black Jack ' and his old Second brigade and Martin's battery filling their bellies with grape and canister?" This rebuke, spoken in a jocose manner, drew forth shouts and laughter from the crowd and changed the conversation. "Here comes ' Mac ' with a box," said one; "I understand that Quartermaster Mooney has got some packages from home for some of the boys." Mac arrived and opened his box. The chickens, cake and oranges, etc., were found to be all dried up for the reason that they had been some months on the road. The little jug in the box, however, was heavy and corked tight. It was soon uncorked, smelt of, then some of it poured out and tasted. " Good cherry brandy, as I'm a sinner," exclaimed Mac. Then he was generous enough to give all his comrades a " drop " as far as it went. After partaking of this good cheer the bugler sounded the assembly. " Fall in ! Fall in ! " now resounded through the camp. " Good," cried the men, " we are going some place else to camp." The general desire to leave the " old campground," with all its sad memories, was pleasing to all and the orders to march were obeyed with alacrity. It was just before sunset. The regiment went to Upton's hill, a short distance off, and into bivouac for the night.

The same evening another batch of recruits arrived for the regiment. Among them were four of the original commissioned officers of the regiment who had gone out of service under Colonel Cass. They enlisted as privates under Colonel Guiney and expected in time to be promoted. Two of these ex-officers received lieutenant's commissions and two more were grievously disappointed at not being finally commissioned; this was due principally to the rapid reduction, from casualties and lack of recruits, in the numerical strength of the regiment.

When the Army of the Potomac lay in bivouac after its march from the battlefield of the second Bull Run, to the defences of the city of Washington, the effect of the report that " General McClellan is here " was electrical. It roused the tired and sleeping soldiers from their slumbers. The welcome news spread from man to man, company to company, regiment to regiment, brigade to brigade, division to division, and corps to corps with wonderful rapidity. Cheers filled the air in the silent night and rolled along the lines until it swelled into volume after volume from one end of the army to the other and died away in the distance. At this supreme moment the hardships of the past were forgotten. The effects of the defeat of General Pope sank into insignificance. It was enough for them to know that their beloved general had arrived on the field — as they believed — to take command. The " pleasures of hope " entered the minds and hearts of the soldiers of the Army of the Potomac until the good news found vent in wild cheers and pleasant congratulations on all sides. The spontaneous warmth of this greeting from " the army which never treated their young chieftain with coldness " must have filled the heart of McClellan with pride and pleasure. Which were right in their estimation of the man? Those who marched, fought and died under his leadership, or those who dwelt in security, giving him half-hearted support and secretly plotting his downfall? Impartial history has yet to decide this question.

CHAPTER XII.

THE BATTLE OF ANTIETAM.

THE CONFEDERATE ARMY IN MARYLAND — GENERAL McCLELLAN IN COM-
MAND — THE NINTH MASSACHUSETTS VOLUNTEERS MARCHES INTO
MARYLAND — CONFEDERATE PLANS DISCOVERED — BATTLE OF SOUTH
MOUNTAIN — THE FORCES ENGAGED — THE SURRENDER OF HARPER'S
FERRY — LOSSES AT SOUTH MOUNTAIN — THE CONFEDERATE ARMY AT
SHARPSBURG — THE ARMY OF THE POTOMAC AT ANTIETAM — THE
BATTLE OF ANTIETAM — THE NIGHT AFTER THE BATTLE — DESPATCHES
SENT TO GENERAL McCLELLAN — MARCHING THROUGH SHARPSBURG
— UNDER FIRE ON THE POTOMAC RIVER — OUR TROOPS FORD THE
RIVER — A SUCCESSFUL ASSAULT — GENERAL GRIFFIN'S OLD BATTERY
— PICKET DUTY ON THE POTOMAC — UNION LOSSES — CONFEDERATE
LOSSES.

" The waves
Of the mysterious death river moaned;
The tramp, the shout, the fearful thunder-roar
Of red-breathed cannon, and the wailing cry
Of myriad victims, filled the air."
                                        PRENTICE.

THE success which attended General Lee since he first assumed
command of the Southern Army of Virginia, in the spring of
1862, was most remarkable. Every movement of his restless
army ended in opening up greater territory to him for continued operations against the Union forces. By his superhuman efforts he relieved
Richmond and the Peninsula, the latter movement having been accomplished by the misdirected aid and order of the new commander-in-
chief (Halleck) of the U.S. armies. Through Confederate successes
which followed, General Lee was also partially enabled to beleaguer
the Union capital and bring consternation on the United States government for a brief period at least. His plans at this time evidently were
to continue in waging an aggressive warfare and thereby hold the
Confederate capital free from future assaults if possible, a stratagem
which he successfully accomplished up to within a short time before his
final surrender. It was apparent that he intended to subsist his army,

as much as possible, on the country and likewise at the expense of the enemy whenever and wherever opportunity offered.

Maryland was too tempting a field to pass over, at this time, with all her coming harvest ready for the reaper. An adjacent State, said to be in a great measure friendly to the cause of secession, which was overflowing with milk and honey, fat cattle and " roasting ears " of green corn, was not likely to be slighted by a general whose troops were always familiar with " short rations." Elated with recent successes he lost no time in marching his soldiers into the "land of promise."

The news of his rapid movements across the upper Potomac, near Leesburg, into Maryland, brought dismay, not only to the Union authorities in Washington, but likewise to the hearts of the loyal inhabitants of that rich and happy border State. The excitement attending the disasters of the Pope campaign was still at fever heat. The retirement of General Pope and his subordinates brought once more into prominence General McClellan, whose star seemed brighter at this period, coming as it did from its brief obscurity. Again his aid and counsel were sought for by the President and the Commander-in-chief, General Halleck, in this dark hour of affliction. The result of which was, to state it briefly, that McClellan was ordered, on the 3d day of September, 1862, to assume command of the army and pursue the invaders and give them battle until they were driven back to the " sacred soil " of Virginia, or destroyed and captured. His orders were verbal and therefore easily controverted by General Halleck afterwards. With what alacrity General McClellan obeyed the orders of his superiors in office is better told in his own brief words : " Being honored with the charge of this campaign I entered at once upon the additional duties imposed on me with cheerfulness and trust." (Union and Rebellion Records, Vol. XIX., p. 25.)

After arranging sufficient troops for the defence of Washington, General McClellan sent forward into Maryland on the 5th of September, under command of General Burnside, the First and Ninth Corps, commanded, respectively, by Generals Hooker and Reno. They were followed on the 6th of September by the Second Corps, General Sumner ; the Sixth Corps, General Franklin ; the Twelfth Corps, General Williams ; and also by the detached divisions of General Couch (Fourth Corps), and General Sykes (Fifth Corps). These troops moved forward in three separate marching columns, in supporting distance of each other.

When the authorities at Washington were thoroughly convinced that *all* of General Lee's army was in Maryland and that the city was safe from attack by General Longstreet and the rest, the scattered brigades of our first division were ordered to march. On the morning of September 12 our 2d brigade was on the move.

The colonel of the Ninth Massachusetts cautioned his regiment to prepare for a long and toilsome march in the hot weather by abandoning at once all extra clothing and superfluous baggage. The experience of most of the men had taught them that a soldier on a campaign must, for his own comfort and convenience, carry as light a load as possible. Nearly every man was without a knapsack, which, outside of winter quarters, was now considered a worse than useless article on account of the liability to cast it aside when going into action, and lose all. The rolled blanket held all the soldier required. Trinkets, keepsakes and the like were carried in the pockets and around the person, so that when worst came to worst they were not lost while the soldier lived. It was 6 o'clock A.M. when the Ninth left Upton's hill. In a few hours the regiment crossed the Aqueduct bridge into Georgetown and passed through rapidly into Washington. We found the heat of the city intolerable and its streets full of people. To our eyes it had lost much of its Southern aspect and many of the people looked and acted more like Northern folks. The ladies offered us fruit, mostly peaches, as we hurried by them, a kindness we didn't expect. On reaching Pennsylvania avenue we took to the shady side of the street and scudded along on the sidewalk through the crowd, and were soon again on the road to the open country by way of 7th street. The sun was now high and hot and the air warm and debilitating. The usual amount of dust was kicked up and, friendly like, travelled along with us. The particles of dust which alighted and accumulated on our sweaty faces were cut by miniature rivulets as the perspiration trickled down. When one's face was rubbed with the back of the hand to throw off the tickling sensation produced by the perspiration, it looked, in time, like an old war map of Sebastopol, with the Black Sea fully illustrated. Many a laugh we had at each other's comical phiz as we tramped along the hot and dusty road. In the afternoon we struck a huge pile of clothing which had been dumped in a field by the side of the road. It contained quilts, sheets, night-gowns, cotton underwear, "biled" shirts, etc. Much fun was made of it for awhile, but none of our men had any use for it. It was said that the Sanitary Commission had left it there for the soldiers (?). It might do in a hospital, but the campaigners of our brigade had no use for any of it. We passed many men resting by the roadside with their huge knapsacks on the ground alongside of them. They were evidently much exhausted by their long march in the hot sun over a hard and dusty road. It brought to our minds some of our own first experiences in the spring of '62, and, thinking of that, we sympathized with them accordingly. If they could be induced to part with the bulk of their pack they would be happier, not to say wiser men. Experience was one of the methods which would eventually drive them to it. Examination of one's effects is the first step in that direction. Then one comes across so many familiar things which are useful that he can't at first sight part with any of them. So with a heavy heart he will rest awhile and again trudge along with a load that is breaking him down. When he becomes extremely exhausted and finds that he is still far in the rear of his regiment he will begin to part first with one thing and then another; but he does it grudgingly and with sighs of regret. Even then it takes him days sometimes to reduce his pack to a decent sized carrying load. On this account and knowing how hard it is for men generally to part with any of this world's goods, some wise colonels would halt their commands at a convenient barn and order every man to leave his knapsack there, taking from it only just such needful things for actual present use; and he would promise to have a wagon sent back after them from the next permanent camp. Thus instructed the credulous but tired soldiers would do as ordered, not without some misgivings, and with a long, lingering look at the cause of much of their troubles, they would go on their march rejoicing at having been relieved of a tiresome cutting load. In a few days they get " weaned " and do not feel the want of a knapsack. Unless they are mentioned they will rarely think of them; if they do it is only to wonder what became of them, for, if on a long march, they will never see them again. After this step and their first battle, they very soon become veterans in the service. When they in turn met with a new regiment with big knapsacks, they remembered their own experience and realized that the recruits must live and learn.

We passed through Silver Springs to Leesboro and went into bivouac late that afternoon. Many of the Ninth had supper under a friendly roof that evening. The natives appeared kindly disposed and ready to entertain all they could accommodate at half a dollar a plate. It was a long time since we had the pleasure of eating a good meal at a table indoors, and it is needless to say that it was very enjoyable. After a refreshing night's sleep on mother earth we were again on the road, marching through Rockville, Middlebrook and Nealsville. In the afternoon we arrived at Clarksburg and went into bivouac. Once more the knowing ones enjoyed a good supper with the friendly people of this place at a reasonable expense, and at night slept as only the weary soldier can sleep in the open field under a calm summer sky.

An event occurred on this day that was of great significance to General McClellan. The Twelfth Army Corps arrived at Frederick, Md., about noon on the 13th of September. The 27th Indiana volunteers of that corps bivouacked on the same ground which the Confederate General D. H. Hill's troops had occupied the night before. Private B. W. Mitchell of Company F, of that regiment, picked up an order which was wrapped around three cigars. It was taken to the corps headquarters and from there to General McClellan. After a thorough examination it proved beyond a doubt to be genuine. It was a General Order, giving directions for the movements of General Lee's entire army. Were it not for the finding of this order it is probable that the battles of South Mountain and Antietam would never have been fought; for it is believed that Lee intended, after carrying out his plans, to recross the Potomac and avoid battle if possible. The following is a copy of that famous order : —

HEADQUARTERS ARMY OF NORTHERN VIRGINIA,
SPECIAL ORDERS,
No. 191.
Sept. 9, 1862.

The army will resume its march tomorrow, taking the Hagerstown road. General Jackson's command will form the advance, and after passing Middletown, with such portions as he may select, take the route toward Sharpsburg, cross the Potomac at the most convenient point, and by Friday night take possession of the Baltimore & Ohio railroad, capture such of the enemy as may be at Martinsburg, and intercept such as may attempt to escape from Harper's Ferry.

General Longstreet's command will pursue the same road as far as Boonsboro,* where it will halt with the reserve, supply and baggage trains of the army.

General McLaws, with his own division and that of Gen. R. H. Anderson, will follow General Longstreet; on reaching Middletown he will take the route to Harper's Ferry, and by Friday morning possess himself of the Maryland Heights, and endeavor to capture the enemy at Harper's Ferry and vicinity.

General Walker with his division, after accomplishing the object in which he is now engaged, will cross the Potomac at Cheek's ford, ascend its right bank to Lovettsville, take possession of Loudoun Heights, if practicable, by Friday morning. Keye's ford on his left, and the road between the end of the mountain and the Potomac on his right. He will as far as practicable co-operate with General McLaws and General Jackson in intercepting the retreat of the enemy.

Gen. D. H. Hill's division will form the rear guard of the army, pursuing the road taken by the main body. The reserve artillery, ordnance and supply trains, etc., will precede General Hill.

* Changed by Lee to Hagerstown afterwards.

General Stuart will detach a squadron of cavalry to accompany the commands of Generals Longstreet, Jackson and McLaws, and with the main body of the cavalry will cover the route of the army, and bring up all stragglers that may have been left behind. The commands of Generals Jackson, McLaws and Walker, after accomplishing the objects for which they have been detached, will join the main body of the army at Boonsboro or Hagerstown.

Each regiment on the march will habitually carry its axes in the regimental ordnance-wagons, for use of the men at their encampments, to procure wood, etc.

By command of

GENERAL R. E. LEE

R. H. CHILTON, *Assistant Adjutant-General.*

MAJOR-GENERAL D. H. HILL, *Commanding Division.*

General Hill, to whom this order was sent, denied ever having received it. Who it was that lost it has never been publicly divulged.

Within an hour after finding the order McClellan's army was on the move and the enemy was overtaken the next day at South Mountain.

The next morning, the 14th, the regiment joined in the line of march for Hyattstown, thence to Urbana, and, on arriving at Monocacy Station, halted for the day. On the following morning our march was continued to Frederick city, through which we passed as quickly as possible in order to keep the men on the move and out of temptation. On reaching Middletown we went into bivouac. The air and atmosphere at this camp was quite bracing compared to the hot and dusty roads over which we had passed in the last three days. The inhabitants who were on the streets in Frederick, appeared friendly enough, and, as they noted the contrast in appearance between the Union soldiers and the Confederate army which had passed through there a few days before, they were nothing loath to express their admiration for "Uncle Sam's" well kept and well dressed soldiers. Their opinion of the appearance of the Southern men was not at all complimentary, but they "reckoned they'd fight." The latter statement was accepted without a dissenting voice, and in a few days it was fully verified on the field of Antietam.

On the 16th we went forward to South Mountain, passing through Turner's Gap. This section was the scene of the late battle between Burnside's troops, which occurred on Sunday, September 14. The Union forces engaged were composed of General Hooker's First Corps and Reno's Ninth Corps. They encountered Gen. D. H. Hill's division and a part of Longstreet's Corps. In the early morning the fighting took place at Fox's Gap, about a mile from Turner's. At the latter place the battle raged fiercely from 3 o'clock P.M. until dark. General Reno of the Ninth Corps was killed about dark.

General McClellan was present during the engagement. The battle proved a victory to the Union troops. The enemy fell back rapidly during the night, in the direction of Sharpsburg, leaving 600 prisoners and their dead and wounded in our hands.

General Lee's object in fighting at South Mountain was to hold McClellan's advance in check until Jackson should capture Harper's Ferry and rejoin the rest of the Southern army. It was evident that Lee was surprised at the appearance of the Union forces and was forced by their arrival to give battle.

Colonel Miles, with 12,000 Union soldiers, was in command at Harper's Ferry at that time   The Southern forces commenced the attack on the 14th at Loudoun heights. It was followed up on the morning of the 15th from the surrounding heights (Bolivar and Maryland), when Colonel Miles surrendered to " Stonewall " Jackson, and about the same time Miles was mortally wounded by a fragment of a shell from the enemy, and died the next day. Some 2500 Union troops at Martinsburg fell back on Harper's Ferry and were among the forces surrendered.

It appears that General McClellan advised the withdrawal of the garrison from Harper's Ferry from the first and predicted its capture, if left there. This was before he left Washington. General Halleck treated his advice with disdain.

General Franklin's corps attacked the enemy at Crampton's Pass, South Mountain, at midday on the 14th and, by dark, drove them over the mountain into Pleasant Valley. The next day was too late for him — Franklin — to relieve Harper's Ferry, as it had surrendered.

Two of our regiments of cavalry escaped from Harper's Ferry on the night of the 14th and on their way to join McClellan captured a Confederate ammunition train of 97 wagons and its guard of 600 men. The attempt to destroy the Baltimore & Ohio railroad bridge was a dismal failure, as the enemy found all the masonry construction too strong for them to injure.

South Mountain was a hard and difficult battlefield for the Union troops. The passes run through wild and rocky declivities, heavily wooded on both flanks, with here and there open spaces at irregular intervals. Every advantage was taken by the enemy, as they had the choice of positions for concealment behind woods, rocks and boulders and fallen trees — improvised barricades as it were — to pour their deadly fire into the Union lines as they charged up the steep acclivities. A flank movement at Turner's Gap aided our forces greatly in gaining the top of the mountain and driving the foe from his stronghold.

Losses at South Mountain, Sept. 14, 1862.   Union: killed, 443; wounded, 1806; missing, 76.   Confederate: killed, 500; wounded, 2343; missing, 1500.

The effect of the defeat of General Lee's forces at South Mountain caused great rejoicing, particularly amongst the Union people of Maryland.   As his army retreated towards Sharpsburg it was believed that he would continue on across the Potomac, at that place, into Virginia, and leave Maryland to enjoy once more peace and prosperity.   Without doubt if Lee had twenty-four hours more of headway he would have crossed the river, but, as it was, McClellan's army was now in full pursuit and too close on his heels to undertake the movement.

As we marched over the mountain and gained the opposite declivity our eyes were gladdened by the beauties of Pleasant Valley and its environments, arrayed as it was in all the gorgeous splendor of a plentiful harvest.   This beautiful garden spot of Maryland had, indeed, all the appearance of prosperity and happiness, even marred as it was by the ravages of contending armies.   As we marched through Boonsboro and Keedysville we were met with welcome by the inhabitants, who were delighted at their happy deliverance, for they began to feel now that they had seen the last of the Confederate forces.

The wagon trains, artillery and cavalry which we passed on our line of march to Antietam, were the precursors which told us of our approach to the field of battle and that Lee's army was concentrating in our front.   About sunset we took our place in the temporary line of battle, surrounded in all directions by McClellan's army, the majority of which had now gone into bivouac, if we except that portion situated two miles, more or less, to our right, which appeared from their rapid artillery fire to be engaged with the enemy.   General Hooker, with the First Corps on the right of our line, had crossed the creek at bridge No. 1 and at the ford, in order to get into position, and ran up against the Confederate left, on the high ground, and engaged Hood's division. A severe fight was the consequence in that part of the field, which continued long after dark.   General Mansfield's Twelfth Corps likewise crossed the creek during the night of the 16th and went into position in rear of the First Corps.

When the 1st division (ours) of the Fifth Corps arrived on the field of Antietam they began at once to imitate their neighbors by lighting camp-fires and preparing for supper.   As a general thing the army was in excellent spirits and confident of success.   An indefinable feeling prevailed that, thus far, McClellan had everything pretty much his own way and, having overhauled Lee, he was now forcing him to stand and give battle. As the Ninth stood around their camp-fires smoking, talking and cooking, many amusing comments were passed on the situation. At one of the fires a Ninth man exclaimed suddenly : "Where are we now, anyway?" "You're in Maryland," was the reply. "Yes, smarty, why didn't you say we were in the United States? Tell me, if you can, what particular part of 'My Maryland' this is."

"Well, listen to me and you will know more in a few minutes. Do you see that steeple over yonder against the sky?"

"I do."

"Well, that is in Sharpsburg where the 'Johnnies' are now. Beyond Sharpsburg a mile or two, more or less, is the Potomac river with Virginia on the other side."

"Are you sure of that?"

"I am. In a few days, after we have helped 'Little Mac' to wallop Lee, you will be going down that way and can then see it all for yourself."

"Very good. I suppose we have got to chase them 'secesh' devils back to Bull Run or somewhere else, bad luck to them!"

"It's more like to my mind you'll find yourself back to the Rappahannock, in front of Fredericksburg, for winter quarters, doing picket duty, with the 'Johnnies' for neighbors, on the other side of the river."

"Hear him!" broke in a new voice, "planning. It's on McClellan's staff you ought to be, to give advice, and not here in obscurity in the ranks, my fine fellow."

At this sally the many attentive listeners broke out into loud laughter. Just then several tin dippers of coffee on the fire commenced to boil over and they were quickly grabbed up and the group scattered to eat supper.

With darkness the picket lines were established on fronts and flanks. All night long, each side watched the other, to see that no advantage was taken while the armies lay buried in slumber. As the hour arrived for tattoo a medley of bugles, drums and fifes rang out on the quiet autumn night air with musical distinctness. On this particular night of the 16th of September, 1862, it was only a useless perfunctory military observance, for long before the hour of 9 o'clock P.M., the rank and file, not for duty, were deep in slumber, resting their tired bodies on mother earth, dreaming perchance of home and kindred. It was the last night of life for many thousands in both armies, for their young and manly forms tomorrow night would lie dead and scattered over the great field of slaughter in victory for one side, and defeat for the other.

At daylight on the 17th of September, 1862, both armies were in position for the approaching battle, subject, of course, to subsequent changes during the progress of the conflict.

General McClellan's headquarters were at the Pry house, within five hundred yards of the Sharpsburg and Boonsboro turnpike, in his rear, and situated on high ground, overlooking Antietam creek in the valley, his own and the enemy's positions.

General Lee's headquarters were at the farther end, or Potomac river side of Sharpsburg. The hill on the enemy's line of battle, which is now called the National Cemetery, was his field headquarters. The hill in front of the line of battle of the Fifth Corps, and opposite Morell's division, was used by General McClellan for his field head-quarters. These two commanders-in-chief were about one mile and a quarter apart, and partially under fire of the batteries when directing their forces.

The battlefield was about four miles long and four miles wide, that is, it covered about sixteen square miles of finely cultivated farm-ing country. The Potomac river was in General Lee's rear, and its winding course was from, say, one to three miles from his battle front.

The right of the Union battle-line was on the west of Antietam creek; but from General McClellan's headquarters to his extreme left the Union army was on the east side of the creek. Antietam creek runs south through that whole section at the foot of the hills, bearing westerly until it runs due west into the Potomac river.

The enemy's line of battle was nearly straight, holding a strong position on high ground; on the extreme left it was thrown back to the rear to meet our line on our right and was about four miles long. The Union battle-line was also about four miles in length and occupied ground that formed it into two irregular sides of a triangle; the enemy's line completing the irregular third side of the triangle.

Maj.-Gen. Joseph Hooker's First Corps was composed of three divisions, as follows: General King's division had four brigades; General Rickett's division had three brigades; General Meade's divi-sion had three brigades. They occupied the right of our line on the west side of Antietam creek.

Maj.-Gen. Ambrose E. Burnside's Ninth Corps was composed of four divisions, as follows: General Wilcox's division had two brigades; General Sturgis' division had two brigades; General Rodman's division had two brigades; General Cox's division had two brigades. They held the left of our line near bridge No. 3, " Burnside's bridge," on the east side. This bridge is built of three arches of mason work and wide enough for an army wagon to cross with a few feet to spare on each side; or for about eight files front of soldiers to march across, and is perhaps about one hundred yards long. At this point the contending forces were within easy speaking distance of each other.

In the centre of our line of battle, and held in reserve, was posted Maj.-Gen. Fitz John Porter's Fifth Corps of two divisions as follows : Maj.-Gen. Geo. W. Morell's 1st division of three brigades. The Ninth Massachusetts belonged to the 2d brigade of this division. General Sykes' 2d division of three brigades, mostly regular army soldiers. (The new 3d division, General Humphrey's, was at Frederick City.) They were on the east side of the creek in rear of the hill which Generals McClellan and Porter used for field observations.

On the right of the line and in rear of General Hooker's First Corps, on the west side of the creek, Major-General Mansfield's Twelfth Corps held its position, composed of two divisions as follows : Gen. A. S. Williams' division of two brigades; Gen. Geo. S. Greene's division of three brigades.

Between Porter and Hooker, and on the right of McClellan's head-quarters at the Pry house, on the east side of the creek, Maj.-Gen. Edwin V. Sumner's Second Corps was massed. It was composed of three divisions as follows : General Richardson's division of three brigades — among them was General Meagher's Irish Brigade — General Sedgwick's division of three brigades; General French's division of three brigades. The cavalry division was likewise massed at McClellan's headquarters.

General Franklin's Sixth Corps bivouacked at Rohrersville, on the night of the 16th of September, and left there at 5.30 A.M. of the 17th for Antietam, which they reached about 10 o'clock of that forenoon. The Sixth Corps went into position on the reserve between Hooker and Sumner. Major-General Couch's division of the Fourth Corps was ordered to occupy Maryland Heights; before reaching there he was ordered to Antietam but did not arrive until the 18th. General Humphrey's new division of the Fifth Army Corps did not arrive at Antietam until the morning of the 18th. The Union army had forty-four batteries.

CONFEDERATE FORCES.

The battle-line of the Confederate army was divided into the right and left wings, commanded respectively by Generals Longstreet and

Jackson, both under command of General Lee as Commander-in-Chief. The right wing was composed of General Walker's division of two brigades and General Jones' division of eight brigades.

The left wing was composed of General Ewell's division of four brigades; General Jackson's (old) division of four brigades; Gen. D. H. Hill's division of five brigades and General Hood's division of two brigades; the cavalry division of three brigades under General Stuart.

General McLaw's division of four brigades and General Anderson's division of six brigades were not present when the battle opened, but were crossing the Potomac river at Boteler's ford and reached the vicinity of Sharpsburg about sunrise. Gen. A. P. Hill's division, of five brigades and six batteries, was at Harper's Ferry, and left there at 7 o'clock A.M. of the 17th, reaching Sharpsburg at 2.30 P.M. of that day, and went into line of battle in front of Burnside.

The Confederate army had forty batteries.

Antietam creek is crossed by four substantial bridges, and is likewise fordable at several points, along our line of battle. The upper bridge on our right is at the Keedysville and Williamsport turnpike. Two and one-half miles below is another on the Sharpsburg and Keedysville turnpike. The third one is about a mile further to our left at the Rohrersville and Sharpsburg road, and is known as the " Burnside bridge." The fourth bridge is on the road from Harper's Ferry to Sharpsburg. During the rainy season the stream is a rushing torrent. At the time of the battle its waters were slow moving and sluggish in appearance. It looked somewhat like a huge sewer system exposed to view rather than a living stream of fresh water.

The success met with by " Stonewall " Jackson, in the fall and capture of Harper's Ferry, undoubtedly decided General Lee to make a stand at Sharpsburg. The chances of defeating the Union forces there opened up to his vision the capture of the city of Washington, which would follow, and thereby gain the desired recognition of the Confederacy as a nation from the British government.

That Lee was the man for the hour cannot be gainsaid, for, like the successful gambler, he was ever ready to take great chances at desperate odds. His line of battle was on high ground, and in many ways admirably fitted for defensive purposes. Backed as he was by the broad Potomac river with only one ford for his army to cross over to the other side, it must be admitted that he took desperate chances in case of complete defeat.

At daylight of the 17th of September, 1862, " Fighting Joe Hooker " proceeded to advance his First Corps towards higher ground in his front, passing through cultivated farms and orchards as his well formed lines pressed onward. General Doubleday's 1st division was on the right, and General Rickett's 2d division was on the left. General Meade's 3d division followed in the second line in reserve covering the centre of the first line, and ready to go in where the weak places were apparent during the battle.

They soon discovered the enemy in force in a thirty-acre cornfield in their front. On these lines of infantry he opened his batteries with canister, driving the enemy through the cornfield with great slaughter. As they fell back in confusion he followed them with his charging lines until the opposition became stronger as it reached the woods. Here the retreating enemy found support from a fresh line of their infantry and artillery about northeast of Dunkard church. Finding his advanced lines thus suddenly checked by the fresh and fierce fighting of Jackson's supports, Hooker ordered in General Mansfield's Twelfth Corps. Mansfield deployed Williams' division on the left of Hooker and Greene's division on the left of Williams.

While thus engaged under a terrific fire from the enemy General Mansfield fell, mortally wounded, and was carried from the field. General Williams then took command of the Twelfth Corps and General Crawford took charge of the 1st division.

The opposing forces at this point were mostly composed of Generals D. H. Hill's and Hood's divisions. Later they were reinforced by troops from Longstreet's right.

For several hours in this part of the field the infantry and artillery fought with varying success bravely and desperately on both sides amid great slaughter. At the first the battle was most favorable to General Hooker as he had forced back Jackson's left flank by his gallant attacks. If he had been strong enough to continue them he would have turned the enemy and driven him to the river, but reinforcements from Longstreet's right came to Jackson's assistance and by concentrated charges in large numbers he recovered partially his lost ground and his flank line.

General Hooker was badly wounded and loathe to leave his command, but he became weak from loss of blood and was obliged to retire from the field, which at that time was a great loss to our army. General Hooker was a brave and persistent fighter and his presence alone was worth a legion. In command of a corps of troops under his individual direction he never met defeat, and was known in the army as " Fighting Joe Hooker." Brig.-Gen. Geo. G. Meade then took command of the First Corps as Hooker retired.

At 7.30 A.M. General Sumner was ordered to move across the creek with the Second Corps. After crossing, it advanced on the enemy in the following order. General Sedgwick's 2d division went forward in three columns with skirmishers on front and flanks. They met and drove in the enemy's skirmish line through the cornfield with but little resistance. On they went in massive lines up the rising ground. Their columns marched in quick time with as much discipline as though on drill. Suddenly from their concealment the enemy's batteries belched forth flame, smoke and canister that mowed them down like grass. French's 3d division which followed advanced into the jaws of death only to be mowed down in a similar manner. Amid the derisive yells of the foe the brigades rallied and their regiments opened up in reply with volleys of musketry. Lacking the support of artillery they were obliged to take ground to the right and rear to avoid as much as possible the terrific fire of the enemy's batteries. Being somewhat sheltered by the low ground from the death-dealing missiles they continued to pour into the enemy a rattling musketry fire which tended in a measure to slacken the fire from the enemy's guns. A determined charge was made on Sumner's left but it was handsomely repulsed after some hard fighting. About 10 o'clock General Richardson's division of Sumner's corps arrived on the field and formed line of battle by brigades in a ravine near the Roullette house.

The brigades of Meagher, Hancock and Caldwell, by superb charging and fighting, drove the enemy from the sunken road or "bloody lane" over beyond Hagerstown turnpike. During the heavy firing on both sides General Richardson was mortally wounded by a spherical case shot and carried from the field.

General Franklin's Sixth Corps arrived on the field about 10 o'clock A.M. and went into the battle in support of the Twelfth and Second Corps. His corps met the enemy at the opening on the flanks of these two corps and charged them in a gallant manner; thus turning what appeared to be a successful movement of the enemy into a disastrous rout as they broke and fled under Franklin's irresistible onset. With cheers and yells the Union lines followed up this turn of the tide of battle by pouring a terrific fire of musketry into the panic-stricken foe as they fled from the field to the protection of their artillery and supports.

Up to this time General Burnside's Ninth Corps, on the left of our line at bridge No. 3, in the valley, had actually accomplished nothing. The enemy, taking full advantage of this inactivity on his part, sent all the troops they could spare, and more, to assist Jackson on the left who was so desperately pressed by Hooker at one time as to be on the verge of breaking and retreating.

General McClellan sent aid after aid during the morning and fore-noon to General Burnside with orders to cross the bridge and attack the enemy's right. Colonel Key, the senior aid, finally went with imperative orders to Burnside to capture the bridge, take the heights and push on to Sharpsburg. This order was partially accomplished at *1 o'clock P.M.* The bridge and the bluff in front of it were gallantly carried and then Burnside made a stand.

At 2.30 P.M. Gen. A. P. Hill, with his division of five brigades and six batteries of artillery, arrived from Harper's Ferry, having marched seventeen miles since 7.30 A.M. that day, and passed within a mile of General Burnside's corps at bridge No. 4, on to the right of the Confederate position. There he deployed his forces into line of battle and met and checked all advances of the Union troops against Sharpsburg. By Hill's arrival all of Burnside's chances for a fruitful victory were lost for the day.

On the morning of the 17th of September, our 1st division, com-posed of three brigades, relieved Richardson's division, Second Corps, on the right of Sykes' division, covering the army trains and reserve artillery and supporting the batteries which crowned the high ridge in the vicinity of bridge No. 2. Our 1st division occupied a shallow basin-like valley, long and narrow, along the road that led to Sharpsburg. In our front was a hill or ridge, that rose to the height of thirty feet. On top of the hill several field batteries were in position. General McClellan's headquarters were at the Pry house, to our right and rear, but most of the day he was on these heights in our front. General Porter and other officers were likewise in the vicinity. From this elevation we had a splendid and comparatively safe view of the battle-field, as the hill was situated about the centre from right to left. The right of the line being about two miles off required field glasses to clearly distinguish what was going on, as in fact, most parts of the field did. The artillery during the most of the day kept up an incessant roar, and cheers and yells in the distance would occasionally reach the ear. The day continued clear, cloudless, pleasant and very warm. About 4 P.M. the 2d brigade (ours) under General Griffin and the 3d brigade, Colonel Stockton, received orders to march to the support of General Sumner. After moving on the road about half a mile the order was countermanded and we returned again to our old spot in the valley. Several times during the day, before and after this incident, we were cautioned to be ready to move at a moment's notice.

When the Ninth Massachusetts Volunteers was moving forward on the road, as above mentioned, along came the 10th Massachusetts Volunteers from the opposite direction. The regiments with consecutive numbers while passing each other were quite amused at the coincidence. They were close enough to shake hands if they could stop to do so. As the men caught on to the numbers on their caps they began cheering each other, and crying out, " Hello Ninth!" " Hello Tenth!" and one droll fellow of the Ninth cried out, "I say, Tenth, as you're the last out, have you any letters for us?" This witty inquiry amused the 10th boys very much. While both regiments were enjoying the fun the rest of the troops in hearing distance were wondering what so much cheering and laughing was about, " anyway."

While lying in this valley the recruits in the Ninth were supplied with equipments, muskets and ammunition (buck and ball) and were as full of confidence and as eager for the fray — in fact more so — as the veterans of the regiment. The discipline of our army was impaired by the addition of undrilled and inexperienced new regiments; while on the other hand it would have been strengthened and improved if recruits had been promptly supplied from time to time, as they were required, to the veteran regiments, thereby keeping up the pluck and vigor of our fighting men. The confidence which the recruits received, and the rapidity with which they learned their various duties when thrown among the veterans was remarkable. Their innate pride stimulated them to become as keen, expert and brave as their older comrades in the art of war. While the old regiments were suffering for recruits new regiments were organized, it would appear, solely for the purpose of giving politicians and their friends commissions.

As the afternoon advanced the fighting on both sides came to a standstill from sheer exhaustion until about 5 o'clock. This hour of the day seemed to be a favorite one with the Confederates to open with artillery for about thirty minutes and then to charge with lines of infantry for a last grand stroke for victory. The Union army was " on to their game," and after the cannonading ceased it was ready for any and all surprises and emergencies. About 5 P.M. the enemy's batteries opened on our lines from right to left. The Union guns promptly responded until the ringing discharges filled the air with the thunder of hundreds of field pieces, and with flying bursting shells and solid shot. This tremendous artillery duel lasted as long as the guns could bear it when they gradually ceased. The Union forces looked forward in vain for the charging lines of the enemy to advance. The contemplated order to charge on our lines was reconsidered by Jackson.

Caution was beginning to crop out as a new auxiliary in "Stonewall's" character.   The wily old general did not care to take desperate chances with even numbers for, as he says in his report: " I found his numerous artillery so judiciously established in his front and extending so near to the Potomac, which here makes a remarkable bend . . . . as to render it inexpedient to hazard the attempt." Thus the battle of Antietam ended.   That night the army remained as it was at the close of the battle, each organization in its place resting on its arms, while the pickets and outposts watched the enemy to give timely warning in case of danger from attack.   All that night, on six-teen square miles of battleground, the living and the dead of both armies remained unmolested except by the small and noiseless parties which were looking for, and bringing into the hospitals the helpless wounded who could not be succored during the fight.

General McClellan did not continue the battle on the morning of the 18th.   The army expected that he would, but there was no move made in that direction.   General Lee crossed his forces over the river, below Sheppardstown at Boteler's ford, on the night of the 18th; a movement which must have taken many hours to accomplish, and one in which he was left in great danger by having his army more or less divided by a wide and deep river such as the Potomac was at this point excepting at the ford — where the water was dammed up for the use of Boteler's Mill — which made a wide and shallow way for man and beast to cross over in safety.   Perhaps McClellan was satisfied with all that had been accomplished with the force at his command.   Lee was defeated in his purpose to raid the Northern States and attempt the capture of the city of Washington.   He was also checked in the endeavor to supply his ragged and shoeless soldiers with large sup-plies of raiment and rations.   He was driven back to Virginia poorer than when he came, with his army greatly reduced by heavy losses in killed, wounded, prisoners and deserters.   The loyal country was greatly relieved by the results of this battle, and it was rejoiced to learn that the Confederate army was not the invincible body which their previous successes had led the people to believe, and all rebeldom north and south to rejoice over.

If General Humphrey's new 3d division of the Fifth Corps had not been delayed or held at Frederick City by General Halleck's orders, it would have made a great material difference which cannot now be fully estimated.   By its presence on the field, however, with the Fifth Corps, it now appears that our 1st division (Morell's) could have been spared from the reserve force in the centre, and sent to the support or assistance of the left. We would have captured the bridge, over which Burnside dallied so long, taken the bluff in front of it by assault and driven the right of Lee's army flying through Sharpsburg. This action would have turned Lee's right and forced a final surrender as there was no possible escape for the enemy; as for fighting on his part it would only lead to the slaughter of his men and capture afterwards. It was not known to us then but it was reported at a later period that General Lee's army of 90,000 men was terribly decimated by their previous losses in battle and by desertions and straggling. At that rate the condition of affairs was to our advantage. According to General Lee's own report we greatly outnumbered him (in the aggregate). He claimed afterwards that he fought General McClellan with but 43,000 men. By that low estimate his army invisibly dwindled away. A few days afterwards in Virginia he evidently must have obtained a large reinforcement.

The boast that was industriously circulated with untiring persistency north and south by sympathetic writers that one Southerner could whip five " Yankees " was, as we battled with the enemy, being gradually dispelled, particularly amongst the Southerners who were running up against our " Yankee " lines on the various battlefields.

During the war thus far it was our experience to meet the enemy with the odds of two and three to one against us; it was so at Hanover Court House, at Gaines' Mill, through the " seven days' battles " to Malvern Hill and at the second Bull Run. The enemy often took desperate chances by boldly concentrating their forces in carrying out their design to charge our lines in great numbers. They sent many men to slaughter in their fruitless efforts. The same accusation can be laid at the door of Union generals without fear of contradiction. The generalship is stupid indeed that will throw solid lines of infantry charging against battery lines of field pieces which are belching forth flame, smoke and double-shotted canister; or against infantry in overwhelming numbers when sheltered by stone walls and backed by batteries. The Union army has cause to remember Fredericksburg, Chancellorsville, Wilderness and Cold Harbor. The Confederates will not forget Beaver Dam Creek, Gaines' Mill or Chickahominy, Malvern Hill and Gettysburg.

General McClellan was in daily and hourly receipt of despatches from General Halleck in Washington, warning him to be cautious, etc., that the enemy might draw him off, and suddenly move on Washington, etc. The following extracts are taken from some of Halleck's despatches :—

September 9. " I think we must be very cautious about stripping too much the forts on the Virginia side. It may be the enemy's object to draw off the mass of our forces, and then attempt to attack from the Virginia side of the Potomac."

September 11. " I think the main force of the enemy is in your front; more troops can be spared from here."

September 13. " I am of opinion that the enemy will send a small column toward Pennsylvania, so as to draw your forces in that direction, then suddenly move on Washington with the forces south of the Potomac, and those he may cross over."

September 14. " Scouts report a large force on Virginia side of the Potomac, near Leesburg. If so, I fear you are exposing your left flank, and that the enemy can cross in your rear."

September 16. " I fear now more than ever that they (the enemy) will recross at Harper's Ferry, or below, and turn your left, thus cutting you off from Washington."

President Lincoln despatched to McClellan, September 12, that he believed the enemy was recrossing the Potomac river and added: " Please do not let him get off without being hurt."

The following extract is taken from the posthumous notes by General McClellan: " I was afterwards accused of assuming command without authority, for nefarious purposes, and in fact I fought the battles of South Mountain and Antietam with a halter around my neck, for if the Army of the Potomac had been defeated and I had survived, I would, no doubt, have been tried for assuming authority without orders; and in the state of feeling which so unjustly condemned the innocent and most meritorious Gen. F. J. Porter, I would probably have been condemned to death. I was fully aware of the risk I ran, but the path of duty was clear and I tried to follow it. It was absolutely necessary that Lee's army should be met, and in the state of affairs I have briefly described there could be no hesitation on my part as to doing it promptly. Very few in the Army of the Potomac doubted the favorable result of the next collision with the Confederate army, but in other quarters not a little doubt prevailed, and the desire for very rapid movements so loudly expressed after the result was gained, did not make itself heard during the movements preceding the battles; quite the contrary was the case, as I was more than once cautioned that I was moving too rashly, and exposing the capital to an attack from the Virginia side." The foregoing quotations are made for the benefit of the reader who may, after their perusal, become interested enough to follow the matter further, and ascertain all the historical facts of General McClellan's career in the Army of the Potomac from first to last.

In the light of subsequent defeats such as the lamentable failure and heavy losses under Burnside at the battle of Fredericksburg ; of Hooker's defeat and losses at Chancellorsville, and the continuous failure " to capture and destroy Lee's army," — these events must be remembered and considered before blame is thoughtlessly laid at McClellan's door in not following up Lee's army by giving battle on the 18th of September. That it would increase the list of casualties on both sides if we had fought on the 18th cannot be denied, but that Lee, Jackson and Longstreet with their army would have been defeated and destroyed is hardly probable. The opportunity to accomplish that result was thrown away by Burnside the day before.

Under Grant's unlimited resources, with supreme control, it took nearly a year's desperate fighting with unusual heavy losses in two campaigns to accomplish the defeat and surrender of Lee. This was *two and a half years* after Antietam, when the Confederate army was in bad form and had lost many able officers, foremost among them being " Stonewall " Jackson and J. E. B. Stuart.

The day and night of the 18th of September were occupied by the medical department and their auxiliaries, in caring for the wounded and in burying the dead. The latter duty occupied about three weeks' time. Those whose duty it was to carry it out to the end for friend and foe had a task to perform that could never be forgotten. The dead of both sides were gathered in rows near where they fell and were buried in shallow pits, each army by itself. The work was hurriedly performed with the view to reinterment. In years subsequent the bodies of the Confederates were taken up and sent South. The Union dead were removed and placed in the beautiful National Cemetery now on the field near Sharpsburg. Many besides were sent north.

On the 18th our 1st division of the Fifth Corps relieved Burnside's men and held the front line waiting for orders to advance. On the morning of the 19th we moved forward with our brigade into Sharpsburg on the double quick. As the Ninth went into the town and turned to the left a man was standing in the door of a house cursing the " d— rebels " for a parcel of robbers, with the energy of a madman. We stopped long enough to hear him tell his listeners that they had torn the carpets off his floor, and taken the quilts and blankets off his beds as they were passing through that morning down to the Potomac. He expressed a strongly qualified wish that we might overtake them and " blow them to h—." As we went by his house in a hurry he no doubt expected that we would carry out his wishes, and at once annihilate the enemy that had despoiled him of his property. As the nights were getting cool and the fall was fast approaching, Lee's vandals were evidently taking all they could reach to keep their half clothed bodies warm during the chilly nights with their malaria-searching winds and fogs.

On reaching the vicinity of the ford at Boteler's Mill on the Potomac river — which is about three miles from Sharpsburg by the road — the troops of the Fifth Corps formed line of battle along the river, near the Chesapeake and Ohio canal which here follows close to the course of the Potomac. We were soon under the artillery and rifle fire of the enemy from the opposite bank. Our batteries, having gained good positions, returned the fire with shell which somewhat cooled the ardor of the enemy. Our artillery sharpshooters evidently dropped their shells where they did the most good. About 5 o'clock P.M., the 1st United States Sharpshooters were ordered to cross the ford and " feel " the enemy. They were supported by the 4th Michigan of our brigade which immediately followed. These troops took to the water in gallant style and rapidly crossed the ford. Under a brisk fire they gained the opposite bank and dashed into the enemy with cheers and yells, quickly driving the foe from the river bank and capturing their cannon. It proved to be a Confederate force under General Lawton supporting Pendleton's artillery. After dark our troops recrossed the river. The 4th Michigan lost one killed and six wounded; the U.S. Sharpshooters lost two killed and five wounded.

The next morning — September 20 — early, the 4th Michigan and the 62d Pennsylvania with battery horses, crossed the ford and returned with three captured guns and several caissons. The enemy did not appear on the scene. General Griffin, who had been the captain of Company D, 5th U.S. artillery, lost his battery at the first Bull Run in July, 1861. Among the guns captured by the 4th Michigan was one or two of his old lost battery. When General Griffin recognized one of his old pieces he was delighted and to every one he met he would cry out in his characteristic shrill tones, " I've recaptured one of my old guns that was taken at Bull Run." His joy was contagious, and all who heard him were highly pleased at the fortunate capture. General Griffin was seldom known to be very demonstrative or hilarious on anything. He was well liked and respected throughout the corps as a brave and able officer, and it pleased everyone to hear him tell of his prize. On this same day, the 20th, two small brigades of regulars of General Sykes' division, numbering about one thousand men, and the 1st brigade of General Morell's division, composed of one thousand eight hundred men, crossed the river on a reconnoissance. The rest of the Fifth Corps remained in camp. It was soon ascertained that the enemy was in their front in large force. As it afterwards proved there were nine brigades of infantry under Generals Early and Hill.

Our regulars, on receiving this information, discreetly retired in good order across the river. They were soon followed by the 1st brigade (commanded by Col. James Barnes) who received and returned the fire of the advancing enemy as they prepared to recross the ford. The 118th Pennsylvania of the 1st brigade was the last regiment to return, and as the enemy rapidly advanced upon them, firing, they suffered heavily in killed and wounded in their defenceless retreat to and across the Potomac. They were armed with defective Enfield (English) rifles. The attacking forces fell upon the 118th when it was in an unfortunate predicament, caused, as they declared, through a miscarriage of orders — or a lack of orders — from the brigade commander. As the regiment made for the river it failed to find the ford, and it was thrown into great confusion both by the terrific fire of the enemy — which was not returned — and the hilly conformation of the cliffs on the bank of the river, over which they were flying in disorder. They unfortunately struck deep water above and between the dam and the ford where quite a number of their wounded were said to have been drowned. The 118th Pennsylvania lost in this affair about 269 men in killed, wounded and missing out of a total of 737 effectives. The losses in the rest of the brigade were, comparatively speaking, light; about 92 in killed and wounded.

Gen. A. P. Hill, who was in command of the Confederate forces, made a most exaggerated report of his part of the affair, so much so that were it not for the disaster to the 118th Pennsylvania it would be a most laughable piece of composition. He evidently imagined that the 2800 men who composed the Union force were the " bulk of the Army of the Potomac." The unfortunate 118th regiment was known as the " Corn Exchange," and but recently mustered into service, which accounts for its large number of men for duty, and no doubt in a great measure for the unfortunate situation in which it was caught.

During the next few days we were engaged in bringing over several of the captured guns, caissons and forges to our side of the river. On the 27th the brigade (ours) crossed over as a guard to a train of wagons foraging for hay which was " found " in great abundance. We returned to camp unmolested. After this event we quietly settled down to camp life. Both armies now picketed the Potomac, the men soon became friendly and swam the river daily to make exchanges in tobacco, coffee and sugar and newspapers. As there were no positive orders against being friendly the officers of the picket usually turned their backs on all such affairs.

At this camp near Sharpsburg the long-looked-for commissions for the " non-coms " arrived, and although nearly three months' pay was lost by their late arrival, those who received them were well pleased to be able to don shoulder-straps. Visits were made to the hospitals around Sharpsburg. Many hundreds of Southerners were left in our hands, and in addition to our own we had a formidable lot of cripples " manufactured." Men with arms and legs off were in great numbers. Wounds of every conceivable nature were to be met with among the brave fellows. Most of them recovered rapidly in the tents and open air, and as fast as able to bear the journey, were sent away as convalescents.

UNION LOSSES.

	Killed.	Wounded.	Missing and Captured.	Total.
At South Mountain . .	325	1,403	85 . . .	1,813
" Crampton's Pass . .	113	418	2 . . .	533
" Antietam	2,108	9,549	753 . . .	12,410
" Skirmishes	83	213	151 . . .	447
Total	2,629	11,583	991 . . .	15,203

Confederate losses are estimated to be at the battle of Antietam (Sharpsburg), in killed, 1512; wounded, 7816; captured and missing, 1844; total, 11,172, being a low estimate.

General McClellan's report in the official records, Vol. XIX., part I, page 67, says that about 2700 of the enemy's dead were counted and buried upon the battlefield of Antietam, and that a portion of their dead were also previously buried by the Confederates themselves.

According to General McClellan's official reports his army numbered 87,164 and the number engaged in action about 60,000 men. General Lee reports his army at about 40,000 men. With losses estimated from 15,000 to 25,000 men during the Maryland campaign, it is marvelous what recuperative powers the Confederates were possessed of, when it is shown that less than three months afterwards, at Fredericksburg, these same forces had increased to 65,000 men. It is evident that at all times the official reports of the Confederates were purposely misleading.

CHAPTER XIII.

GENERAL McCLELLAN SUPERSEDED BY GENERAL BURNSIDE

IN CAMP IN MARYLAND — PICKET DUTY ON THE POTOMAC — PRESIDENT
LINCOLN VISITS AND INSPECTS THE ARMY — RAID BY GENERAL STUART'S
CAVALRY — ON A RECONNOISSANCE — GENERAL MORELL ASSIGNED TO
ANOTHER COMMAND — THE ARMY MOVES INTO VIRGINIA — GENERAL
SYKES' DIVISION FEELS THE ENEMY — ARRIVAL AT SNICKERS GAP —
GENERAL McCLELLAN AND GENERAL FITZ JOHN PORTER RELIEVED
FROM COMMAND — GENERAL McCLELLAN LEAVES THE ARMY — GEN-
ERAL PORTER'S DEPARTURE — GENERAL BURNSIDE TAKES COMMAND
— THE ARMY REORGANIZED INTO THREE "GRAND DIVISIONS" —
SPIES AND DESERTERS — THE ARMY IN CAMP ALONG THE RAPPAHAN-
NOCK — A COLD WINTER — MEN DIE FROM EXPOSURE AND DISEASE
— PREPARING TO MOVE ON THE ENEMY AT FREDERICKSBURG.

> " Who steals my purse, steals trash; 'tis something, nothing;
> 'Twas mine, 'tis his, and has been slave to thousands;
> But he that filches from me my good name,
> Robs me of that which not enriches him,
> And makes me poor indeed."
> OTHELLO, ACT III., SCENE III.

THUS far, in the late campaign, the Ninth Regiment, although
always under fire on the battlefield, and ready for action at all
times, escaped serious casualties, barring one wounded, Patrick
McLaughlin, of Company D, at Antietam.

On the 20th of September our camp was permanently fixed on
high ground. A short distance off stood a belt of woods between us
and the Potomac river. Although lacking in proper camp equipage,
clothing, shoes, etc., our men were not disposed to grumble, more
particularly when they learned about the dilapidated condition of General Lee's Confederate soldiers. The stories told by the wounded
Southern prisoners of their privations, not only in clothing and camp
equipage, but in lack of food and rest during their long and continued
marching and fighting for several months past, bordered so near on
pure misery that one could hardly believe it. As the tales of hardships endured by them were repeated by many different tongues each

15

day when interviewed at the hospitals, and borne out by the tattered raiment and poor physical condition of the narrators themselves, it could not be doubted. By comparison we concluded that the condition of the Union army in its worst days was far better than that of the Confederate army in its best days. Our privations were due principally to incompetent managers, while theirs were brought about by a lack of supplies which their government was unable to produce. At any rate the soldiers of the Ninth Massachusetts Volunteers were always remarkably patient under the worst of circumstances, and their wants when not supplied — though keenly felt — were passed over with a good deal of philosophy mingled with Irish wit. As they stood loitering around their camp-fires smoking their pipes many odd conversations, like the following, could be heard.

"It will be time enough to grumble," said one, "when we are compelled to rob the slain for clothes and shoes to wear as the 'Johnnies' do when opportunity offers, and to eat hardtack from a dead man's haversack as they are only too glad to do when the chance of getting at our fellows comes in their way."

"No sir, I'm no grumbler from this out. I'll take what I get and say nothing."

"I believe you, man," chimed in a listener, "for I haven't heard you say anything about that chicken you captured and carried into your tent last night."

"Never you mind," replied our philosophical soldier, as his comrades, standing around, began to laugh at his expense, "about that little bird, he's gone where I hope to put many another." This was said as he gently patted his umbilical region with the palm of his right hand, and the satisfied unction with which he did it, as he rolled his eyeballs about in recollection of his chicken feast, caused many a soldier around the fire to laugh heartily.

Stories heard and retailed, with more or less additions, about the ragged and hungry condition of "Stonewall" Jackson's "foot cavalry," and "sprinters," and of their endurance and patience while going long distances without rations of any kind, only looking forward and longing for the promised capture of a "Yankee commissary train," had a salutary effect on our men, whose wants and privations in comparison seemed trifling to that of the suffering Southerners.

The Army of the Potomac, in corps, divisions, brigades, and in regimental formations now lay in camp for a distance of fifteen miles, or so, along the Maryland country of the Potomac river. The routine duties of guard, drill, picket and fatigue were resumed with regularity. The pickets of both armies were posted along the banks of the river as friendly as the most gossiping soldier could wish. Each side talked, traded, and killed time during the day, and watched each other during the night with that trustful ease and friendly confidence born of many hardships. As it was chilly and damp through the night the coal that lay along the Chesapeake canal in abundance was utilized along our part of the picket line by keeping live fires in sheltered places gently burning after the manner of a coal fire in a blacksmith's forge; the cold night breeze acting as the bellows. Our neighbors, the "Johnnies," on the opposite bank, were very quiet during the night, and, without doubt, found a way of keeping their bodies warm. Each morning they were chipper enough and made no complaint. As time passed the enemy drew away from us, and their picket line disappeared inland.

Occasionally our cavalry crossed by the ford as if to reconnoitre the enemy, and always returned with as full ranks, and as much mystery, as they used to be shrouded in when in front of Washington during our early days of inexperienced soldiering.

What with our peninsula experience and that of the last two campaigns, our cavalry had lost caste altogether with the infantry. Their reported skirmishes with the enemy, and "driving in the rebel pickets," were received with incredulous smiles and jeers until they became as mum as oysters. When hailed for information, on their return, about the "Johnnies" and their reported movements, they would gaze at the infantry in stupid wonder at such questions, then laugh among themselves at some remark of one of theirs about "dough boys": the laugh would then change to sullen anger as some shrill-voiced infantry veteran would inquire, loud enough to be heard a mile away, "Did you see any dead cavalry men out there?" This pertinent question had the effect of making every rider drive spurs into his horse and move briskly forward, while the sounds of laughter and jeers long and loud of their tormentors, the "dough boys"! followed them. After Phil Sheridan took command of them these questions were never asked, for the bravery and gallantry of our cavalry was as conspicuous under him as it was inglorious at the beginning and during the first half of the war. All they needed was a brave and gallant leader to bring out the fighting stock that was in them all the while. Their glorious deeds under General Sheridan's leadership proved them to be superior to the once dreaded Confederate "Black Horse" and other cavalry of Generals Stuart and Lee of the early days of the war.

On the 1st of October, 1862, our army was enlivened with the presence of President Lincoln. A visit from "Old Abe" was generally considered as the precursor of a movement, or change of some kind. The conflict of opinion that was going on between General McClellan and the Washington officials, for some time past, had evidently induced the President to come amongst us and see for himself how things looked. On the 3d of October he reviewed, or rather inspected the Fifth Corps. In the morning we turned out brigaded *en masse*. The usual presidential salute of 21 guns was fired by Captain Martin's battery. The President rode up and down the front and rear ranks of each regiment, evidently intending to give us a sharp scrutinizing; after that he dispensed with our passing in review. He wished to satisfy himself on our general condition under arms, and as the soldiers on such occasions turned out the cleanest and best that they knew how he evidently concluded that we were in good marching form as the sequel will show.

After inspecting the army in this manner, and visiting the recent scenes of the great conflict at South Mountain and Antietam, the President and party returned to Washington.

On the 5th of October, by orders from Washington, General Cox's division of 5000 men was detached from the army and sent off to West Virginia. This did not look like reinforcing McClellan. On the 7th of October, 1862, General McClellan received an order by telegraph from the General-in-Chief, H. W. Halleck, directing him to cross the Potomac and give battle to the enemy, or drive him South; that the army must move now while the roads were good. That the Army of the Potomac was waiting for supplies of clothing, shoes, etc., at this time, was well known to the General-in-Chief. Why the requisitions made on the quartermaster's department were so long delayed, it would seem, ought to be inquired into by those in authority in Washington. It was a well-known fact that General McClellan was not one to neglect the wants of his army. The supplies were finally furnished.

This order then was the sequel to the visit of the President three days ago. Notwithstanding the long pending requisitions for necessary supplies of clothing, shoes, etc., we must move without them and give battle to the enemy. After the battle the number wanting shoes, etc., would be greatly reduced. Besides, new clothes and shoes on the slain would be an indirect way of supplying the enemy in case of defeat. It will be noticed that this was accomplished by General McClellan's successor a few months subsequently. It follows, therefore, that in such an event it were better to fight the enemy ragged and shoeless in order to prevent giving him aid and comfort, *i. e.*, clothes and shoes.

The monotony of camp life was enlivened by the news that on October 10 General Stuart with two thousand Confederate cavalry made a raid into Maryland and Pennsylvania, but before our forces of slow moving horsemen could either intercept or overtake them they were back again into Virginia loaded with plunder. This pursuit, fruitless though it was, used up many hundreds of our cavalry men and horses.

The Ninth Massachusetts hailed with delight an opportunity for a little excitement on the 16th of October. Our brigade was ordered on a reconnoissance with other troops, under command of General Humphrey.

Our 2d brigade was now composed as follows, Brig.-Gen. Charles Griffin commanding : —

2d District of Columbia . . . . . Colonel Alexander.
9th Massachusetts Volunteers . . . Colonel Guiney.
32d Massachusetts Volunteers . . . Colonel Parker.
4th Michigan Volunteers . . . . . Colonel Childs.
14th New York Volunteers . . . . Colonel McQuade.
62d Pennsylvania Volunteers . . . . Colonel Sweitzer.

We crossed the ford at Boteler's Mill in the morning, and found the water-way in bad condition. It was anywhere from two to five feet deep at irregular intervals from right to left. This irregular rocky bottom was caused by the excessive use which the ford had been put to during the past five or six weeks by the infantry, artillery, cavalry and wagon trains of both armies. No attempt had been made by any one to keep the ford crossing in any kind of level condition, so that our soldiers found it difficult to avoid " cradle " holes and deep water. When one's trousers were rolled up as high as possible it was very unpleasant to stumble over a rock and into a hole up to one's waist, wetting everything thoroughly, and then to be laughed at besides. The greatest anxiety under these circumstances was to prevent guns and equipments, etc., from getting wet. Many of the men took off shoes, stockings and trousers, and marched over regardless of every danger under foot, and then dressed themselves on the other bank. Others marched boldly and recklessly through the water as though they were going over a dry road. On reaching the other side of the river they would drain off what water they could and let their clothes dry on the march. The point was to get over the river, and as there were no particular orders about it, everyone took the journey as he saw fit.

After a short march we arrived at Sheppardstown. The inhabitants who were on the street were "secesh" clear through and apparently, at this late day, not at all alarmed at our arrival. They were composed mostly of women and boys, both white and black, in full view, on the sidewalks and doorsteps, and quite talkative. Many of the enemy's wounded, on parole, were still here, otherwise the scarcity of the male portion of the population was remarkable. One could not help but notice that thrift, business and cleanliness were abandoned and that war had left its indelible mark on the whole town and its partially denuded and deserted female and juvenile dwellers. The general appearance of everything in the place, at this time, was sad to contemplate. The serious and troubled expressions on the countenances of a few ladies who kept aloof from the crowd excited one's sympathy as they gazed, in seemingly mute despair, on our soldiers.

After a long halt we continued our march into the open country. Flankers and skirmishers were now deployed to prevent surprises as we penetrated some ten miles inland. Our advanced troops and batteries found the enemy, and, after a brisk fire and skirmish, succeeded in driving them in the direction of Charlestown, Va. Shells from the enemy reached our regiment and did little damage, but made a good deal of noise for a short time. Thomas Mullen of Company H was severely wounded in the head by a piece of an exploding shell that burst overhead that company. It rained and thundered heavily in the afternoon, wetting us completely. A large part of our force went into bivouac near Kearneysville for the night. The Ninth, as well as the other regiments, was given the choice to bivouac or go to camp that afternoon; we chose the latter course and after a weary march reached and crossed the ford without much ceremony and arrived at our old camp that night, where we had a good opportunity to dry ourselves before a roaring camp-fire, and to refresh ourselves with hot coffee and hardtack.

Maj.-Gen. George W. Morell was detached from the command of our division on the 27th of October, the day that General McClellan commenced to cross his army into Virginia. He was assigned to the command of all the Union troops which remained on the upper Potomac and vicinity. General Morell had been our brigade commander in the past and subsequently commanded the division. He had thus far shared the dangers and privations of all our campaigns, and like the brave and accomplished officer that he always proved himself to be, had endeared himself alike to the officers and men of his old division. It was with feelings of great regret that we parted with him. General

Butterfield succeeded him as division commander. October 30, the Fifth Corps was on the move into Virginia.

The Ninth Massachusetts Volunteers joined the line of march about seven o'clock P.M. The grounds lately occupied by the troops were all ablaze, more or less, with fires built from the wood and "furniture" around the camps. These fires served to show up the now deserted camps in all their desolation, for a more gloomy and uninviting place to look at cannot well be imagined. When the orders came to move the soldiers hated to leave, but when once it was settled that they were going away forever, then the work of destruction began in earnest. The demon of mischief seemed to possess the lively spirits, here and there, and into the fires throughout the camps everything went that would burn. Every movable article that was to be left behind was kicked and tossed about until it finally landed onto the fire. Thus it was, as one might say, that we left our camps in a blaze of glory.

As we marched along the road the camps were soon forgotten while we looked forward to a new life and strange scenes. It was a moonlight night and the road was good marching for the whole distance, which was about ten miles. Tall cliffs and hills towered above us as we tramped over the road in its winding formations where it was built to flank heights that were impossible to climb. By midnight we halted in the fields, in the chill autumn air, and rolling ourselves in our blankets dropped off to sleep. In the morning we found that we were within three miles of Harper's Ferry. About ten o'clock A.M. we crossed the pontoon bridge, over the Shenandoah river, into the historic town. As the principal street through the town caught the eye it presented a miserable, dirty appearance; what with dilapidated houses, shanties and tents it looked like the sutler's paradise, for goods of that sort were everywhere for sale at most exorbitant prices. As it was several months since the army was paid off the great majority of the men were " dead broke " so that business with the sutlers was dull. Now and then some thrifty soldier would be seen sneaking up to a shop where he could get in out of sight and make a purchase of some eatables, for that was about all the average soldier ever cared to buy. The provost marshal's headquarters, and the various guards scattered about the place, no doubt prevented the boys from " rallying " on the sutler.

The wrecked bridges and railroads — with their engines and cars tumbled into the river half submerged as they rested on angles of great rocks in the bed of the river, and the dismantled buildings together with the general dilapidated appearance of everything visible — greatly marred the grand natural scenery of this part of the country. The hills and heights of Maryland and Virginia, in sight of the rushing waters of the Shenandoah, hastening on and into the broad Potomac in the distance, are most picturesque scenes of natural beauty.

The late surrender of General Miles and his command to Gen. " Stonewall " Jackson was brought to mind as we passed along, or rested, in the vicinity. We were likewise reminded that we were passing over the historic ground of the unparalleled raid of the immortal John Brown. Here was the scene of his efforts to effect a rising of the slaves, to strike for liberty, with his following of twenty men.

In the meantime we continued to pursue our march until we went into bivouac some four miles beyond Harper's Ferry. This halt was necessary in order to straighten out the army lines of infantry, artillery, cavalry and wagon trains, which were now rapidly covering this section of Virginia. The 2d division of the Fifth Corps under General Sykes went forward on a reconnoissance and engaged the enemy the next day, November 3. The Confederates were found to be in great force on the opposite side of the river. We moved forward to Snickers Gap in the Blue Ridge on the 2d of November. The day was pleasant enough but towards night the cold wind that swept across the country was very searching, reminding a Bostonian of the raw east winds in the month of March in the vicinity of Boston Harbor. On such nights as these the poncho tents were fully appreciated as they broke the cold piercing winds from the soldiers as they slept on the ground in their blankets.

That night at Snickers Gap four unfortunate line officers of the Ninth Massachusetts were deprived of blankets, overcoats and " grub," by an unlucky incident. The man in charge of the mess failed to turn up, after the march, with his horse and mess kit, etc. It seems that in order to avoid a raid, which was contemplated and put in force by the provost marshal-general of the army, on all pack horses and mules belonging to infantry regiments, our man, in order to protect himself, took to the woods and flanked the enemy which was after him — that is, the myrmidons of the aforesaid provost marshal-general of the army. By this adroit strategy our man, with horse and pack, escaped capture. Army headquarters had miles of wagons to carry their luxurious household and personal effects in order that they might bivouac with ease and pleasure. Their servants fared and slept with comfort that was a stranger to the ordinary line officer of an infantry regiment. It was attempted on several occasions to deny infantry officers the right or privilege to transport their mess kits and belongings on pack mules and horses. This premeditated raid on them was on a large scale, so that our man was obliged to go many weary miles out of his march to avoid being taken and did not therefore get around until late the next day. This particular night at Snickers Gap these four officers waited several hours after the regiment went into bivouac, alongside of a single log fire, for their man to put in an appearance. After giving up all hope of his coming two of them at dusk went foraging for their supper and a place to sleep. The other two remained by the little fire, too proud to attempt to " sponge " on those who had barely enough for themselves, although they were hungry men after their day's march. The wind was quite piercing as it blew over the mountain range and through the gap. Becoming sleepy one officer lay in front of the diminutive fire and was soon in deep slumber. After awhile the other officer tried the outside berth, but being debarred by his comrade from the heat he soon got chilled through and was obliged to get up. He sat cogitating for awhile over his hard luck, with hunger, assisted by a lack of sleep, gnawing at his vitals ; and now to be deprived of sleep on account of the cold was something he had not bargained for. Having compassion on his companion and fellow-sufferer, he allowed him a reasonable amount of time to sleep, then he gently rolled him over and lay down in his warm place and fell into a deep sleep himself. Suddenly he awoke chilled through and very cold, and found, to his disgust, that his brother officer had, on awaking in a similar plight, returned the compliment by rolling him over and again dropping asleep in his old place. After a little time standing around sleep became so needful and overpowering that he, the second victim, must have it, and, as the only way to get it was to lay in front of the fire, he once more rolled his friend over and dropped into his warm place, and was asleep as soon as he touched the hard ground. Soon, however, he again awoke, cold and shivering in the freezing night wind, only to find that his companion in misery had performed once more the same rolling trick on him. It was now mutually recognized, without any consultation, as absolutely necessary that this kind of relief must be kept up in order to get much-needed sleep. It was an awful tedious way to keep from freezing, particularly after the midnight hour ; for, as morning began to approach, the cold wind was intensely cutting, not to say freezing, as it penetrated their now weakened systems. When daylight broke this pair of lieutenants were a sorry sight to behold as they stamped their feet to limber their stiffened limbs and send the blood circulating through their chilled hearts. That night of hardship they never forgot and never cared to experience the like

again.   Pride did not stand much in their way ever after.   " Ask and
you shall receive; knock and it shall be opened unto you," was an
admonition which they ever after practised when luck and circumstances
were against them.

We remained at Snickers Gap until the 6th of November, then
moved by way of Snickersville to Middlebury and bivouacked three
miles outside the town.   The next day we marched to White Plains.
It snowed all the afternoon and the weather generally did not improve
our wretched surroundings, for it was cold, wet and intensely disagreeable to those who dwelt in shelter tents.   On the 8th we marched to
New Baltimore; the following day found us at the town of Warrenton
where we remained till the 17th of November.

Many surprising changes occurred in the meantime by orders from
Washington.   General McClellan's headquarters were at Warrenton.
His whole army was now in position confronting Lee's forces which
lay in detachments west of the Blue Ridge.

The Army of the Potomac was in excellent condition and spirits
and looking forward to another general engagement.   The good spirits
of the army at large can be accounted for from the fact that the general
who commanded them was looked up to as their trusted leader and,
under his direction, they were confident that they could win victory.
Under McClellan's generalship the tide of battle had turned in their
favor, " which, taken at the flood, leads on to fortune."   Nothing now
seemed to dampen their ardor.   It was felt and firmly believed that
the next battle would be the beginning of the end, and that the end
would be the destruction of General Lee's army and the capture of
Richmond in the near future.   But the exalted aspirations of the grand
old Army of the Potomac were again doomed to bitter disappointment.
Their high spirits and great hopes were suddenly blighted and dashed
to the ground by peremptory orders from the President, through his
Commander-in-Chief, Halleck, on Nov. 5, 1862, relieving General
McClellan from the command of the Army of the Potomac and assign-
ing Major-General Burnside to the command of the army.   Major-
General Hunter was likewise by the same order appointed to the
command of General Burnside's corps.   Maj.-Gen. Fitz John Porter
was also relieved, by the same order, from the command of the Fifth
Corps, and Major-General Hooker was designated as his successor.

The orders to General McClellan were to immediately turn over
his command to General Burnside and repair to Trenton, N.J., his
home, and to report on his arrival by telegraph for further orders.
General McClellan received these orders on the 7th of November,

1862. He thereupon turned over his command to General Burnside, and, as it afterwards proved, this terminated his active military career in the United States army.

With universal regret the various organizations of the Army of the Potomac listened to the reading of a heartfelt and patriotic address from their beloved commander. On the 10th of November General McClellan rode down the lines of the army which had turned out under arms for a parting farewell. None regretted his leave-taking more than the Ninth Massachusetts Volunteers, for on several occasions in the past the regiment had been the recipient of his personal kindly remembrance. The fortunes of war had relieved him before and it likewise returned him again to command. At this time the thought occurred that perhaps once again he might be at an early day restored to the army for good. His loyalty to his country, his ability, which was undoubtedly great, and his bravery were never more firmly established in the minds and hearts of his soldiers than they were at the last moment of parting with him at this time and place.

As " Little Mac " rode down the lines of the " army which had grown up under his care and in which he had never found doubt or coldness," the pent-up feelings of his veteran troops found vent — regardless of discipline — in a great roar of wild and enthusiastic cheering which rose higher and higher as it rolled along with him until he finally passed 'from our view forever. The *esprit de corps* of that noble army alone prevented it from breaking from the ranks that they might express more fully the unbounded love and admiration they had for a general whom they looked upon as the victim of unjust and harsh treatment. When the future historian weighs and measures the great events of the past he will undoubtedly find that the Army of the Potomac estimated General McClellan at his true standard, for with them he was never found wanting.

Gen. Fitz John Porter was, likewise, as mentioned, relieved of his command. On the 12th of November he received his final orders, and at 12 o'clock the same day General Hooker assumed command of the corps. At 4 o'clock P.M. following, General Porter took his farewell of the brave old Fifth Corps.

Our gallant commander at the battles of Hanover Court House, Mechanicsville, Beaver Dam Creek, and through the " bloody battles of the seven days' fighting," particularly at Gaines' Mill, departed that day with the sincere regrets of all of his soldiers, little thinking then that they were to see him no more, or that his connections with the Union army were to be ruthlessly severed forever. Amid loud cheers and regrets he passed from our view never to return. His subsequent court-martial was a mortal blow to his brilliant military career, and after suffering under an unjust sentence for twenty years he was finally restored to his rank in the regular army. He was vindicated at last, but who and what will repay him for his wounded honor of twenty years' standing? The persistent fight which General Porter made against his political and military enemies for so many long years is fully reviewed in the " History of the Fifth Army Corps," and is the sublime vindication of an officer and soldier who suffered contumely most unjustly for many weary years.

The innate honesty of purpose that governed all the movements of President Lincoln in directing the affairs of the nation and in guiding the helm of state, rendered him unable to cope with the designing politicians and ambitious military magnates who surrounded him. The eagerness of these classes of men to forward the personal interests of their friends and favorites and to place them in positions of trust and power, wholly regardless of their lack of fitness and abilities, was truly appalling to the minds of honest and patriotic public men and private citizens of the republic of that day. At this period of the war, history alleges, the seat of government at Washington was permeated with civil and military intrigue, seemingly regardless of all patriotic impulses. The changes now wrought in the Army of the Potomac doomed it to the blackest period of its existence. False arguments and pernicious influences had forced the President to violate that homely but trite expression of his, namely, " Never swap horses when crossing a stream." These changes proved to be among the greatest mistakes of the war, and they fell like a horrid nightmare on the high-spirited and recently victorious Army of the Potomac. The black clouds of disaster appeared at once on their horizon and for seven long weary months they were doomed to pass through dire defeat and incompetent generalship unequalled in the history of civilized warfare. But even then, veterans that they were, they remained intact as an army, and achieved a glorious victory in the near future.

General McClellan's matured plan of campaign against the enemy in our front disappeared when he bade farewell to the great army that he had fostered and loved and led to victory.

On the 17th of November, 1862, General Burnside proceeded to lead the Army of the Potomac on to their trials.

The recent appointment of General Hooker as commander of the Fifth Corps was changed in a few days by the selection of General Butterfield in his stead.

We marched to Warrenton Junction and bivouacked till the 20th; from there we continued on to Hartwood Church. On the 22d we reached Stoneman's Switch, near Falmouth, with the city of Fredericksburg on the other side of the Rappahannock river, three miles in our front. The active pursuit of General Lee's forces was evidently abandoned and our anticipated opportunity of attacking his divided army with every chance of victory in our favor was now lost.

The Confederate forces were wholly ignored, as though they had no existence, in order, as it appeared, to establish a " base of supplies " at Aquia Creek; doing exactly what McClellan had been, time and again, condemned for by his critics.

McClellan's contemplated engagement with Lee at Culpepper and Gordonsville, and prospective movement on Richmond without delay, was still urged by the administration, but Burnside opposed the plan and was finally allowed to settle down in front of Fredericksburg and reorganize the Army of the Potomac. The result of our reorganization was as follows : —

Right Grand Division : composed of the Second and Ninth Corps, under the command of Maj.-Gen. Edwin V. Sumner.

Centre Grand Division : composed of the Third and Fifth Corps, under the command of Maj.-Gen. Joseph Hooker.

Left Grand Division : composed of the First and Sixth Corps, under the command of Maj.-Gen. William B. Franklin.

Practically the Army of the Potomac was now divided into three separate armies, each on a small scale, unwieldy for quick or concentrated movements, and, altogether, of doubtful utility.

Our Fifth Corps was organized as follows, under command of Brig.-Gen. Daniel Butterfield : —

The 1st division was commanded by Brig.-Gen. Charles Griffin and composed of three brigades, four batteries and 1st U.S. Sharpshooters.

The 1st brigade, under Col. James Barnes (18th Massachusetts Volunteers), was composed of the 2d Maine, 18th Massachusetts, 22d Massachusetts, 1st Michigan, 13th New York, 25th New York, 118th Pennsylvania, 2d company Massachusetts Sharpshooters.

The 2d brigade, under Col. Jacob B. Sweitzer (62d Pennsylvania), was composed of the Ninth Massachusetts Volunteers, Colonel Guiney; 32d Massachusetts Volunteers, Colonel Parker; 4th Michigan, Lieutenant-Colonel Lombard; 14th New York, Lieutenant-Colonel Davies; 62d Pennsylvania Volunteers, Lieutenant-Colonel Hull.

The 3d brigade, under Col. T. W. B. Stockton (16th Michigan), was composed of the 20th Maine, 16th Michigan, 12th New York, 17th

New York, 44th New York, 83d Pennsylvania, Brady's company Michigan Sharpshooters.

ARTILLERY.

Massachusetts 3d Light Battery (C) . Capt. A. P. Martin.
Massachusetts 5th Light Battery (E) . Captain Phillips.
1st Rhode Island Light Battery (C) . Captain Waterman
5th United States Battery (D) . . . Lieutenant Hazlett.
1st United States Sharpshooters . . . Lieutenant-Colonel Trepp.

The 2d division was commanded by Brig.-Gen. George Sykes, and composed of three brigades and two batteries.

The 1st brigade, under Lieut.-Col. R. C. Buchanan, was composed of the 3d, 4th, 12th and 14th U.S. Infantry.

The 2d brigade, under Maj. C. S. Lovell, was composed of the 1st and 2d Battalions, 6th, 7th, 10th, 11th, 17th and 19th U.S. Infantry.

The 3d brigade, under Brig.-Gen. G. K. Warren, was composed of the 5th, 140th and 146th New York Volunteers.

ARTILLERY.

1st Ohio Light Battery (L) . . . . Lieutenant Dorries.
5th United States Light Battery (I) . Lieutenant Watson.

The 3d division was commanded by Brig.-Gen. Andrew A. Humphreys, and was composed of two brigades and three batteries.

The 1st brigade, under Brig.-Gen. E. B. Tyler, was composed of the 91st, 126th, 129th and 134th Pennsylvania Volunteers.

The 2d brigade, under Col. P. H. Allabach, was composed of the 123d, 131st, 133d and 155th Pennsylvania Volunteers.

ARTILLERY.

1st New York Light Battery (C) . . Lieutenant Phillips.
1st United States Batteries (E and G) . Captain Randol.

General Lee was kept well informed on nearly all matters of what might be termed general information pertaining to and occurring in the " Yankee army." This information was received not only through his regular native spies and scouts, but it was likewise carried into his lines by deserters from our army. Many of our best fighting regiments are pointed at on account of the seemingly large percentage of desertion on their rolls. By looking into the matter it will be seen that nearly fifty per cent of the desertions were by unprincipled recruits, men without a country, who received bounties for enlisting. Many of these men were undoubtedly Southern spies who had made their way north for the express purpose of enlisting, deserting, and carrying information into the enemy's lines. In this connection it will be observed that regiments in our volunteer service which had what the old veterans called a " soft snap," and short terms, were exempt from harboring the " deserting " and " bounty jumping " recruits. They all went to the front where they had the range of the open country into the enemy's lines. Others of them were professional bounty jumpers and substitutes, who had been through the " mill " a score of times without being detected. They were a curse to the volunteer service and they brought unjust odium on the regiments which they joined. Their bad example was imitated by some weak-minded soldiers who would otherwise have continued to be good men.

Deserters in the interest of the enemy, after reaching the front, seized the first opportunity to gain the enemy's lines; most of these desertions occurred during the night. So quick was the time between their arrival and departure that they were barely acquainted with any of the men of the regiments they disgraced.

General Lee knew of the changes in our army commander and his subordinates twenty-four hours after the order was issued. At his headquarters at Culpepper Court House he was in receipt of daily and hourly information concerning the movements of our whole army. Working on the knowledge derived from General Burnside's daily movements, General Lee proceeded to secure the hills and heights south of Fredericksburg. General Lee's army was organized into two corps. The First Corps was under the command of General Longstreet. The Second Corps was under command of General " Stonewall " Jackson, who was on the south side of the Rapidan river. Two of Longstreet's divisions arrived on the hills south of Fredericksburg about 3 o'clock on the afternoon of the 21st of November.

Sumner's grand division had previously arrived at Stafford Heights overlooking the city. General Patrick, provost marshal of the army, crossed the river under a flag of truce and delivered a letter, dated the same day, Nov. 21, 1862, to the mayor, demanding the surrender by the civil authorities of the city of Fredericksburg, threatening in case of refusal to bombard the town the next day. The threat in this instance was never carried out. General Sumner had previously asked for orders to occupy the city, but General Burnside decided against it.

The demand for the surrender of the city created much excitement therein, and the inhabitants began at once to leave for a safer place, most of them going by rail to Richmond.

General Jackson's corps had now joined General Longstreet on the right, thus completing the line of battle of the Confederate army of 65,000 men under command of General Lee. The city of Fredericksburg was now forced to occupy a part of the battleground between both armies.

The Rappahannock river in our front, while being a great detriment to us, was a line of protection to the enemy. It was an immovable obstacle to the approach of our magnificent batteries against the enemy's strong positions on the heights. It obliged our infantry columns to assault the enemy's stronghold without the valuable assistance of this strong arm of the service. In fact the army fought this battle with, as it were, one arm tied behind it. Taking these and many other disadvantages into consideration the battle should not have been fought at all. The city, without the formality of surrender by its mayor, was, through the fortunes of war, the property of the army that could take and hold it. It fell into the hands of first one side and then the other, much to its immediate destruction.

The pontoon bridges which General Burnside had been waiting for arrived on the 25th of November. No attempt was made to bridge the river until December 9.

On the early morning of the 28th of November, our cavalry pickets, under the command of Captain Johnson, at Yellow Chapel, a place about eight miles from Falmouth, were surprised and raided on by about two hundred of General Hampton's Confederate cavalry who crossed the river at Kelly's Mill the day before. The great success of the enemy was evidently due to a complete surprise of our troopers, for they captured eighty-seven of our men, five officers and two colors, with all their horses and equipments. For this gross neglect of duty and lack of discipline, the commanding officer was, on investigation, summarily dismissed the service.

December 1 the 1st brigade of our division (the 1st), under the command of Colonel Barnes (18th Massachusetts), was ordered on a reconnoissance to the place where our cavalry-men were so ignominiously captured. The expedition, by the seven regiments which composed the brigade, was wholly fruitless in its results, and after suffering great hardships they returned to camp on the second day, feeling that they were the victims of a badly managed affair.

Although the army held their camps in this part of Virginia for six months it was always a matter of uncertainty how long we should remain. December was now close upon us and we were enjoying (?) alternately the weather of the four seasons. The rain of spring, the sunshine of summer, the wet dreary days of a cheerless fall and the snows and blasts of winter were chasing each other in a circle in rapid succession. The nights, however, seemed to be all of one mind, that is, cold to freezing and uncomfortable in quarters. We hugged the camp-fires during parts of the night, warm on one side and cold on the other.

In the tents and huts the cold and dampness were at times unbearable. By lying close together in pairs and threes it was possible to sleep with some show of warmth. During the day the routine of camp duty was rigidly followed, which together with chopping and gathering wood, and transporting it, chiefly on their shoulders, building huts, and making their quarters as comfortable as circumstances would allow, our men had enough to occupy their minds and to keep them out of mischief. Never before were we any worse off for supplies. Rations particularly were short. As soon as the railroad to Aquia Creek —'our base of supplies — was in running order we were promised " full and plenty." As a bridge of formidable dimensions had to be built before rails could be laid it caused no end of delay. In the meantime our army wagons were doing their best over the wretched roads which they were obliged to transport rations, but their best efforts were unequal to the demands of the great hungry army which now lay along the Rappahannock. " Thanksgiving day " was turned into one of involuntary fasting, but no praying of a general public nature took place. These hardships began to tell upon the army. Our casualties from sudden sickness, disease and death were on the increase. On the night of the 6th and 7th of December four inches of snow fell. The storm was accompanied by cold freezing weather. Two men of the 20th Maine were reported as having been frozen to death. The men of the Ninth Massachusetts, however, were still holding their own remarkably well, in fact better than the average, and looking forward to better days.

The report that ovens were about to be built for baking " soft bread " for the army was received with much fun and incredulity. Around the camp-fires it was continually prognosticated that we would soon settle down into " winter quarters " and then live like " fighting cocks." These and a thousand other rumors of the most absurd kind were manufactured and indulged in chiefly for the sake of talk, and to create inquiry and a laugh.

Very soon however the camp prophets were all at fault. By the 9th and 10th of December decided reports of a forward movement in

some direction were in circulation.   The inevitable.preparation of supplying abundant marching rations, together with ammunition, etc., which
followed after company and regimental inspections, pointed to an early
movement, and " no mistake."   All of the camp prophets in the Ninth
were effectually squelched by orders from regimental headquarters to
be ready to move in heavy marching order, with three days' cooked
rations, at daylight on the morning of the 11th inst.   It is unnecessary to say that at the appointed time the veterans of the Ninth were
all ready.

CHAPTER XIV.

THE BATTLE OF FREDERICKSBURG.

OUR ARMY IN LINE ON THE RAPPAHANNOCK — THE ENEMY IN FREDERICKS-
BURG — PONTOON BRIDGES — BOMBARDING THE CITY — THE CITY
CAPTURED — OUR ARMY CROSSES THE RIVER — POSITION OF THE
CONFEDERATE ARMY — THE LEFT GRAND DIVISION PARTLY ENGAGED
— LOSSES — THE RIGHT GRAND DIVISION IN BATTLE — THE IRISH
BRIGADE — LOSSES — GENERAL GRIFFIN'S DIVISION CROSSES THE RIVER
— THE NINTH MASSACHUSETTS UNDER FIRE — A NIGHT ON THE
BATTLEFIELD — RELIEVED SUNDAY NIGHT — TOTAL LOSSES IN BOTH
ARMIES — LIST OF CASUALTIES IN THE NINTH MASSACHUSETTS —
IN THE CITY — PREPARED FOR AN ATTACK — PRESENTATION OF GREEN
FLAGS IN THE IRISH BRIGADE — LEAVING THE CITY — RETURN TO
THE OLD CAMP — LOSSES — BURYING UNION DEAD.

> " And there was mounting in hot haste : the steed,
> The mustering squadron, and the clattering car,
> Went pouring forward with impetuous speed,
> And swiftly forming in the ranks of war;
> And the deep thunder peal on peal afar;
> And near, the beat of the alarming drum
> Roused up the soldier, ere the morning star;
> While throng'd the citizens with terror dumb,
> Or whispering, with white lips — ' The foe!
> They come! they come! ' "
>
> BYRON.

AT DAYLIGHT, Thursday, Dec. 11, 1862, the Ninth Massachusetts Volunteers, in heavy marching order, moved out from
their camp near Stoneman's Switch, by the flank at a route step,
four deep, and joined the 2d brigade on its march to the banks of the
Rappahannock river, — opposite the little city of Fredericksburg — a
distance of about three miles. We moved along the road in a still,
but foggy atmosphere. The winter chill of the early morning ceased to
be disagreeably felt when the blood coursed quickly through our veins,
and warmed us up, as we marched over the hard road.

Our corps went forward in three division columns, each body of
infantry under its regular commander. General Sykes' (2d division)
moved on the right by the Stafford road. General Griffin's (1st divi-

sion) went by a route to the left. General Humphreys' (3d division) marched by a route to the right of Griffin.

The right grand division, General Sumner, was directed to concentrate near the location of the. upper and middle pontoon bridges; the left grand division, General Franklin, to concentrate in the vicinity of the pontoons below the city. The centre grand division, General Hooker, to mass near to and in rear of General Sumner, and after crossing the river to hold his command in readiness to support either Sumner or Franklin.

The Army of the Potomac was one of great general intelligence, composed of thinking men who were bound by the " iron rule of military discipline " to trust their fate, as soldiers, with patriotic devotion to the direction of one master mind. It can be said of them that they were true soldiers of the Republic in this as in all other respects. On this momentous morning they remembered the absence of their late commander — General McClellan — with regret. The ability of General Burnside to direct the movements of our great army of one hundred thousand men, and cope successfully with the veteran commander, General Lee, and his tried, trusted and able lieutenants, Generals Jackson and Longstreet, was yet to be severely tested.

Confidence is a plant of slow growth, as yet it had hardly taken root with the army in this direction. The man who held it had gone from them forever. This lack of confidence in their present leader was not of their own creation. As the commander of a great army he was new to the situation, and acknowledged a lack of confidence in himself ; this, added to his recent reorganization of the Army of the Potomac, complicated matters. In his new formation of the army there was a disposition made of corps commanders which engendered much dissatisfaction. Besides, his subordinate generals were not in accord with their commander in his plans — or lack of plans — in attacking the enemy. Taking everything together as it appeared on that morning the campaign opened under circumstances which were anything but encouraging to the army. In spite of this lack of harmony the rank and file were determined to do the best they could at all times. This was afterwards proved by the way they sacrificed their lives in a hopeless assault; the casualties on that field were mostly confined to them.

The movements of our divisions were slow and solemn. The moving columns of men were quiet and serious as they marched and listened to the action of the artillery duel and the irregular musketry firing which was heard going on in our front, and recognized as the forerunner of the bloody battle which was now anticipated by all. As the sun shone out clear and bright that morning the fog gradually disappeared under its warm rays, and a light pleasant breeze began to blow, giving every indication of an unusually fine day for the terrible work before us.

We soon reached the vicinity of army headquarters at the Phillips house — a large brick mansion — on the heights in front of the river, and in full view of the little city of Fredericksburg on the opposite shore. It likewise held a sweeping survey of the country and hills beyond the river. The troops of our corps were massed at this point on a level tract of land. Our brigade rested in an open field near the road which led to the river. Many of our field batteries and our reserve artillery were in position along the north bank of the river to the number of 147 guns, covering our whole line from right to left, that is, from Falmouth town on the right, to the Massaponax river on the left, a distance of about five miles.

Fredericksburg is built of substantial brick and frame buildings on the right bank of the Rappahannock river down close to the stream. About six streets run parallel with the river, and a dozen or more streets run crosswise down to the water's edge in full sight of the opposite bank; showing altogether a compact mass of buildings of all sizes which compose the town. The city was in possession of the enemy, a small force composed of the 17th and 18th Mississippi regiments of General Barksdale's brigade of Longstreet's corps, supported by the 8th Florida of Anderson's division. These troops held the water front. The rest of the brigade, the 13th and 21st Mississippi, supported by the 3d Georgia regiment, were in the heart of the city in reserve.

At daylight on the 11th of December, 1862, the engineer brigade commenced to lay the pontoon bridges under the protection of two infantry regiments from Hancock's division, and the artillery on the bank. Three bridges were partially floated when the fire from Barksdale's regiments obliged the engineers to retire as the incessant sharpshooting from windows and rifle-pits on the opposite side riddled both boats and planks, and became too hot and fatal for regular bridge building on pontoon boats. The work was not given up by the engineers until several attempts to renew it were frustrated by the persistent force of 3000 men who lay concealed along the river in warehouses, dwellings, streets, barricades and rifle-pits, picking our men off without dangerously exposing themselves in the least. This situation of affairs away up to 1 o'clock P.M. had become irritating to the commander of the engineers, and it provoked exciting comments among the troops in that vicinity. Many of the regiments were clamoring to be sent across the river in pontoon boats in order to land and attack the enemy on equal ground, and thus put an end to their cold-blooded tactics.

At this juncture of affairs orders were given to the artillery along the city front to open on the enemy with their batteries and see what effect it would have on the well-concealed foe. The fire from the batteries made things lively and exciting and drove the riflemen out of their pits and hiding-places up into the heart and rear of the town. The exploding shells caused several fires to break out in different parts of the city, shrouding the place in volumes of smoke, besides riddling the houses, in and around the side streets, pretty thoroughly. After two hours of artillery firing our pontoon boats loaded with gallant volunteers, in the meantime, pulled across the stream as the batteries gradually ceased, and, before the enemy could fully recover from their surprise, they landed along the bank, charged up the streets in gallant style, and drove the now fleeing Mississippians and Floridians through the city, and out onto the plain, capturing numbers of them and killing and wounding many more.

Our brave troops suffered some in killed and wounded from detachments of the enemy still concealed in houses along the line of pursuit. They fired from cellars and roofs, and from behind closed blinds in the upper stories of dwellings, wounding some of our men in a most unusual and unexpected manner as their bullets went up or down and obliquely from their hiding-places. The assault was quickly and gallantly accomplished and created much favorable comment throughout the Army of the Potomac. The regiments engaged were from Hall's brigade, Howard's division, Second Corps, the 19th Massachusetts, under the command of Captain (afterwards Major) H. G. O. Weymouth; and the 7th Michigan, commanded by Lieutenant-Colonel Baxter. After these two regiments landed and attacked the enemy they were reinforced by the 20th Massachusetts, commanded by Capt. George N. Macy. The latter regiment led a charge up into the heart of the city where they met with severe opposition. The enemy could not withstand their determined onset however, and fled to the plains in disorder. The prisoners captured were mostly men who concealed themselves in houses to shoot down our soldiers unseen; but the "Yankees" showed them a trick worth two of theirs by charging into these houses and capturing them like rats in a trap. The order that General Longstreet sent to General Barksdale to retire from the city after this little affair began was wholly unnecessary, for they did not wait for the order of going but went at once when our infantry came in sight.

The bravery displayed by our soldiers in this assault is all the more commendable from the fact that the enemy's troops consisted of six regiments, numbering in the neighborhood of 3000 men. Our assaulting regiments were less than one-half that number.

The bombardment of the city — if it might be termed so — by the Union batteries would not have taken place if it were not for the worse than useless attempt made by the enemy to prevent us from laying our pontoon bridges. Further destruction of the town was wrought by the enemy's batteries, particularly on the 13th, as our forces debouched from its narrow streets onto the plain.

As soon as a pontoon bridge was laid —about 4.30 o'clock P.M. — the other two regiments of Hall's brigade crossed. The rest of Howard's division soon followed and held possession of the city that night. Three bridges in all were laid that afternoon and night. Two more bridges — making five in all — were laid a mile and a half below the city — where Deep Run creek empties into the Rappahannock — that same morning; and at 11 o'clock A.M. were all ready for the left grand division (General Franklin) to cross. The efforts of the enemy to prevent the floating of these two bridges were held in check by canister and shell from two of our batteries. It was a comparatively easy matter to keep the enemy at a respectful distance here as they lacked the facilities for concealment offered up the river by the houses of the city. When a brigade crossed over the attacking party quickly retired to their main line on the hill.

At daylight on the 12th of December, General Franklin's command commenced to cross. This movement occupied all the time till 1 o'clock P.M. By 4 o'clock P.M. the left grand division was in position to make the attack on Jackson's right wing. The same day (the 12th) in the morning, the right grand division (General Sumner) proceeded to cross over to the city and join General Howard's division which had taken possession of the town the night before. The Ninth Corps occupied the left of the city, and the Second Corps, at the same time, held the right. General French of the Second Corps was ordered by General Couch to prepare his division for the advance. Orders at the same time were given to General Hancock to be prepared to follow with his division. On the night of the 11th General Hooker — in compliance with orders — sent Generals Sickles' and Birney's divisions, of General Stoneman's Third Corps, to the support of General Franklin on the left front, and General Whipple's remaining division of the same corps to relieve General Howard's division of the Second Corps in Fredericksburg in order that he might be enabled to join his corps at the right of the line.

During the last twenty odd days General Lee was engaged in watching Burnside's army and in keeping himself informed by his scouts and spies of all his movements. His army was for many days in position on the heights, and working day and night fortifying his vulnerable points and strengthening his position by earthworks and batteries. The right wing of his army, under General " Stonewall " Jackson, along the hilly elevation at Hamilton's Crossing, was composed of some 30,000 or more effectives. His extreme right was protected by General Stuart's cavalry and horse artillery. Gen. D. H. Hill's division held the right in reserve with General Early's division next in the front line; General Taliaferro's division next and Gen. A. P. Hill's division next. General Longstreet's corps of 35,000 or more effectives was the left wing. General Hood's division continued the line to the left, next to A. P. Hill, in vicinity of Deep Run creek. General Pickett's division next covered the base of Telegraph hill (now Lee's hill). The base of Marye's hill, the next in range, and more to the front, was held by Generals McLaw's and Ransom's divisions behind the stone wall — a mile or so in length. This wall protected the sunken Telegraph road. This latter road was well filled, and reinforced with infantry. The stone wall was " shoulder high," and banked with earth. From its commanding position it was the strongest kind of defence for infantry, backed as they were by batteries. The road was twenty-five feet wide. Gen. R. H. Anderson's division, at the base of Taylor's hill, continued the line to its conclusion on the left down to the Rappahannock river, Falmouth being on the opposite bank. The Washington artillery occupied Marye's heights. General Lee's line of battle — for defensive purposes — was about three miles long.

General Lee considered Anderson's position at Taylor's hill unassailable. He considered Marye's heights, which was of gradual ascent, and the nearest towards the town, and lowest of the range, the most assailable point, and placed his troops accordingly. Telegraph hill was the highest of all and farthest back, and looked upon as comparatively safe from attack. The enemy's batteries occupied all the commanding positions along Lee's line to his front, and swept the plains beyond, and held complete range of every outlet from the city onto the plains.

In volume X., page 617, *Century Magazine*, General Longstreet writes as follows : —

" An idea of how well Marye's heights was protected may be obtained from the following incident. Gen. E. P. Alexander, my engineer and superintendent of artillery, had been placing the guns, and in going over the field with him before the battle, I noticed an idle cannon. I suggested that he place it so as to aid in covering the plain in front of Marye's hill. He answered, ' General, we cover that ground now so well that we will comb it as if with a fine tooth comb. A chicken could not live on that field when we open on it.' "

General Franklin, on our left, ordered General Reynolds, commander of the First Corps, to commence the attack on General Jackson's lines. He thereupon sent forward General Meade, whose division marched forward, in a foggy atmosphere, and made a desperate assault at 8.30 o'clock A.M. (on the 13th) at a charge. He was supported by General Gibbon's division on the right, and next in line to the Sixth Corps. General Meade's infantry broke through the woods in gallant style; drove the enemy's line back, crossed the railroad, and carried the hill from base to summit. His troops captured two flags and two hundred prisoners. General Gibbon went forward with his division in like manner and captured a number of prisoners after driving back the enemy's front line by close and hard fighting. The battle continued in Reynolds' favor until reinforcements in the shape of two fresh Confederate divisions under Generals Early and Taliaferro came forward with great vehemence, driving General Meade's infantry back, who, all the while, made a stubborn resistance. General Gibbon's troops were shortly after assailed, likewise, by these fresh brigades of the enemy and repulsed. General Birney of the Third Corps was sent in with his division to Meade's relief, and by gallant fighting they held the woods after driving the Confederates back to their former line. General Sickles' division (Third Corps) was ordered in, and, after relieving General Gibbon's division, continued to occupy the ground held by his troops. The enemy thereupon made no advance or offensive movement, his tactics being evidently on the defensive.

No further attack in force was made on Jackson's lines. Generals Birney and Sickles commanded the two divisions sent from the centre grand division to relieve a like force of the First Corps who were to make a contemplated movement on Jackson's right flank, but which, from unforeseen delay, was finally abandoned. It was afterwards looked upon as somewhat singular that Birney and Sickles should be sent into battle when only two divisions of the two army corps on the right were the first engaged.

General Franklin's line of battle of 35,000 or 40,000 men was re-established that afternoon and they continued comparatively inactive as long as they remained on the south side of the river; that is, till the night of the 15th of December. A large square stone mansion, occupied by one Mr. Bernard — who became troublesome when the fight opened and was sent to the rear out of harm's way — was used as a hospital for our wounded. General Franklin established his field headquarters near this building.

The losses in the left grand division were 401 killed; 2761 wounded; 625 captured and missing; total, 3787.

Preparations for an attack by General Sumner's right grand division were carried out in the meantime. Both of his corps — the Second, General Couch, and the Ninth, General Willcox — bivouacked on the night of the 12th (Friday) in the city. On the morning of the 13th (Saturday) written instructions were sent to General Couch by General Sumner from the north side of the river, to form a column of a division and push out in the direction of the Plank and Telegraph roads and seize the heights; this column to be instructed to advance in three lines and to be covered by skirmishers on front and flanks. Also another division at the same time to be held in readiness to advance to its support and to go forward in the same order as the first. On receipt of these instructions General Couch directed General French (Second Corps) to prepare his division in three brigade lines for the attack. General Hancock was ordered to follow with his division in the same manner. The distance between the brigade lines to be two hundred yards as they advanced over the plain.

The fog that clung to and hung over the city all the morning lifted about 10 o'clock. At 11 o'clock A.M. General French's division moved rapidly forward out of the city by two parallel streets onto the Plank and Telegraph roads and vicinity, which led to the hills, direct for Marye's heights. The brigades encountered the wide canal, or ditch, which crossed their track and was impassable here except by bridges, stringers and planks, more or less broken and torn up by the enemy. On passing this obstruction the brigades deployed one after another for the advance and charge. They passed here and there houses and fences in their path over the ascending plain. A group of houses, fences and gardens, etc., were met at a fork of the Telegraph road. On a parallel road to the south of this locality stood a large square brick house. To the front, right and left, was the stone wall, about one hundred and fifty yards off, behind which waited thousands of hostile infantry, eager to greet our charging lines with volleys of cold lead. A short distance in front of the houses mentioned there was an abrupt rise in the formation of the surface of the ground; from this rise a plateau formation began which led, prairie-like, up to the enemy's works. This abrupt rise of ground served as a slight protection to our men from the incessant infantry fire of the well-protected enemy, but not from the discharge of their artillery. Behind the few houses shelter could be had from the terrific fire which fell against them. They were used as a rallying point and served to cover many of our badly wounded.

Shortly after 12 o'clock — noon — French's division charged for the first time on the stone wall at the foot of Marye's heights. As they went across the plateau the converging fire of the enemy's artillery met them with death and destruction every inch of the way; the dead and wounded fell at every step. To this terrific fire from the batteries the infantry, behind the " stone wall shoulder high," almost immediately added their sheets of flame and lead. Only a few moments of this terrible work was necessary to convince the living, as their ranks thinned out, that it was impossible to capture or even reach the works by assault. The bursting, hurtling shot and shell and myriads of whistling bullets, soon demonstrated to our troops that while it was sure death to go forward there was a living chance in retreat, and they went back, some more rapidly than when they went forward, to obtain shelter and rest behind the rising ground, if such a thing could be found there while deadly missiles were flying and exploding around, about and overhead.

General Hancock followed General French, with his division, and they immediately joined in the first assault, meeting with the same terrific fire that came across the level plain for one hundred and fifty yards, until human endurance, weakened by its losses in dead and wounded, had to give way while bravely and vainly endeavoring to push forward into the jaws of defeat and death.

Gen. Thomas Francis Meagher's brave Irish Brigade was in General Hancock's division. It was composed of the following renowned regiments which charged across that fatal field : —

> 69th New York Volunteers.
> 88th New York Volunteers.
> 63d New York Volunteers.
> 116th Pennsylvania Volunteers.
> 28th Massachusetts Volunteers.

The gallant 28th Massachusetts was composed mostly of Irishmen or their immediate descendants, and was assigned to the Irish Brigade from the Ninth Corps, about Nov. 23, 1862. A synopsis of their brilliant record can be found in the history of the Irish Brigade, by Capt. D. P. Conyngham, A.D.C. The following extract is taken from that history, page 341. It refers, in part, to the brigade's action on the morning of the 13th of December, 1862, at Fredericksburg: —

" Early in the morning the Irish Brigade was drawn up in line of battle at ' order arms ' and a ' parade rest.' A green sprig was ordered by General Meagher to be placed in the caps of both officers and men, himself first setting the example. At about half past nine o'clock they were marched up to the centre of the city, nearer the enemy, and formed in line of battle on a street running east and west. Here brigade and regimental hospitals were established. General Meagher, accompanied by General Hancock and the members of his staff, now addressed his ' little brigade,' each regiment separately, briefly in his eloquent style and in words of real inspiration. Each man was made aware of the great and terrible work before him and each man measured in his mind the part he had to perform. The general's remarks were responded to by the men with great spirit and accla- mation. Colonel Nugent gave instruction to his boys in his usual calm and earnest manner, when every man stood in his place, with set lip and flashing eye, awaiting the word to advance. French's division was first to attack the enemy, supported by Zooke, Meagher and Cald- well's brigades of Richardson's (Hancock's) division in succession. General French made the attack about 12 o'clock M., when the battle became general. Zooke's brigade moved up, followed by Meagher's. The aspect was already terrible. Noonday was turned to dusk by the smoke and storm of battle. A ravine in rear of the town, through the centre of which runs a mill-stream seven or eight feet wide, over which we were obliged to cross on a rude bridge, was swept by a raking fire from the enemy's batteries. Having crossed this the brigade halted in line of battle. They relieved themselves of their blankets and haversacks and awaited the order to advance.

" French's division fire, fall, lie down, scatter, rally ; but in vain — it is already placed *hors de combat*. Zooke's brigade advanced in fine style, but rapidly fell ; and though its ranks were thinned, still on they went ! ' Irish Brigade, advance ! ' is heard in bold, distinct accents above the clamor of battle — ' Forward, double-quick, guide centre ' ; and on it dashes through the conflict, in the face of the most invulnerable point of the enemy's works. They are greeted by a murderous fire of grape and canister and minie balls. Gaps are opened in the ranks, but they close again and move still forward. The first fence is gained and passed. The enemy now falls back from his first behind his second line of breastworks. They gain the second fence, within sixty yards of the enemy's batteries, and are met by a most disastrous enfilade and direct fire from the rebel artillery and infantry. They had not a single piece of artillery to support them, and yet they stood against shot and shell, grape and canister, minie and conical balls, to fight a formidable enemy, artillery and infantry, posted behind stone walls and fortifications. The rebel position was unassailable; it was a perfect slaughter-pen, and column after column was broken against it. Our artillery did so little injury to the enemy that they were able to concentrate all their fire on the advancing columns of troops. Besides, an oblique flank fire swept us, so that whole regiments melted away before it. Some broke for the rear, others lay down among the dead. The advance of the brigade was actually impeded by the bodies piled upon one another. Brave fellows! their own bodies were soon to be added to the number. But foremost in the ranks of the honored dead were the boys with the green sprigs in their caps."

At 1 o'clock P.M. Generals Hancock and French were again ordered to carry the Confederate works by storm. In the face of the terrific and galling fire which was kept up by the enemy, the three separate assaults on this first line of works which were made by this part of Sumner's command were without effect, and again fruitful of great slaughter to the assailants. Generals Hancock and French called for support and General Sturgis' division of the Ninth Corps on the left sent two brigades to the forlorn encounter, only to meet the fate of their predecessors. General Howard's division, having passed through the fire of shot and shell on leaving the city, after being relieved from duty there, was ordered in on the right of French and Hancock and sent forward to storm the right flank of the stone wall. It was protected with artillery and infantry on the flank doubly stronger than in front, and, as the division charged, they met with an oblique and direct fire which decimated their ranks in the twinkle of an eye. Having added to the dead and wounded on the field without a possibility of success, they fell back to the shelter of the house and rising ground in their rear, to await further orders and take their chances under the enemy's fire. Generals Humphreys' and Sykes' divisions (Fifth Corps) of Hooker's command, were sent to the support of the right grand division. General Humphreys' division, led in person by their gallant commander, charged over very nearly the same ground that the divisions of French and Hancock had so gallantly and repeatedly fought over, but they failed, like the rest, to reach the stone wall, and only added more brave men to the rows of dead and wounded which covered the field in every direction. General Getty's division of the Ninth Corps was ordered in and charged over the fatal field by the unfinished railroad, his gallant soldiers dropping at every step forward and falling in like manner as they fell back for shelter. Hazard's and Frank's batteries were brought forward, but could not live in the rain of lead and shells that came upon them. Their efforts were short-lived and a tragic close of the battle in their vicinity.

The losses of the right grand division were: 523 killed, 4281 wounded, 640 captured and missing; total, 5444.

The 2d division (Sykes') and the 3d division (Humphreys') of the Fifth Corps went forward to reinforce the right as the 1st division (ours), under Gen. Charles Griffin, commenced to cross the pontoon bridge between 2 and 3 o'clock P.M. The march was slow across the river and up the bank into the city. As the Ninth Massachusetts was moving leisurely along they met some of the wounded of the Irish Brigade; many of them belonged to the 28th Massachusetts and were old friends. They shook their heads in a rueful and not assuring manner. One wounded veteran captain of the 28th remarked that it was the toughest place he had ever been into and that he was sorry to see us going in. At this particular moment we were grouped on the river bank, when a shell burst close to us; a piece of it struck a Ninth officer's colored servant boy, knocking him over. The little fellow was quickly picked up by willing hands and found to be unhurt. The iron had fortunately struck a " horse collar " roll of blankets, which hung over his shoulder and across his body, which saved him from injury and perhaps death. The tears that it brought to the pretty mulatto boy's eyes were quickly dried by the sympathy and praise showered upon him by those around him. As it was a shell from one of our own batteries on the other side of the river, much strong indignation was expressed at the recklessness of such a premature explosion. It was said to be a defective shell which ought not to have been used. On the remark that the shell came from the German battery, one of our men created a laugh by saying, " This going to the *front* to be shot in the *rear* by one of our own ' Dutchmen,' is d —— poor generalship, I say."

Shortly after this incident we marched rapidly into the city and beheld chaos let loose. It looked as if " Pandora's box " had been opened in Fredericksburg. The streets were full of straggling soldiers; some were wounded, but most of them were not. Mounted officers and officers on foot were numerous, some apparently on duty, others not particularly engaged. Whole and broken furniture and broken pianos were strewn in every direction. Small fires were burning in the streets, made of pieces of furniture, to cook coffee and rations. Shells were bursting occasionally over different parts of the city and smashing into the houses. Houses and stores were opened up and soldiers were going in and coming out, some carrying plunder, others empty handed.

While taking these things in at a glance we were moving off to a street that led out to the open plain. Each company of the Ninth threw their luggage onto the sidewalk against a fence and then jumped across a stream or ditch and went rapidly over the field by the right flank. As quick as the enemy sighted us coming out of the street they dropped their shells over and about us with a precision and rapidity that we did not admire in the least. The faster we " double-quicked," the faster they seemed to explode. The explosion of a shell is generally the first notice given of its arrival; if you are not hit *then*, you are all right till the next one comes along. A stray bullet has relieved many a brave fellow of all anxiety about shot or shell. We soon struck marshy ground and got our feet very wet with very cold slush. Having gone in this direction for several minutes Colonel Guiney gave the order, " By the left flank, march! " The movement brought the regiment into line of battle facing Marye's heights. We went forward without changing step on the double-quick until, in addition to the shells we were getting, our ears were greeted with the constant sound of zip! zip! zip! of the enemy's bullets. This hissing sound each man faintly hears only as the bullets come in close proximity to his head and ears as they pass swiftly along on their deadly errand. Having reached the place where the rise of ground occurs, which marks the beginning of the plateau, we were ordered to halt. Just then the scattered remnant of a late charging regiment was making a remarkable run in our direction to the rear. We stopped the color bearer — who begged to be let go — just long enough to find out the State he hailed from. The number of his regiment was beyond the hundred. When let loose he resumed his course and gait, and it is safe to say that he could hold his own with the best of our Shenandoah Valley sprinters of early memory.

As we stood in line of battle, with the Stars and Stripes and the Irish flag fluttering in the December breeze, in full view of the enemy, the bullets went singing by our ears like so many bees, wounding our men frequently. It can hardly be credited, but we were waiting for orders from our brigade commander. Fifty yards to our left thousands of our troops were lying close to the ground.

While standing here General Humphreys attracted our attention as he rode some twenty yards to the front off on our right flank. He was finely mounted on a light-stepping bay horse and was accompanied by two or three aides who quickly turned to the rear and rode away, leaving the general conspicuous and alone. Several voices now cried out at once, like one mind, " Three cheers for General Humphreys " — for he was well-known by the Ninth men. The cheers by the Ninth were given with a will. General Humphreys turned towards us as though on review, and, like the brave cavalier which he then appeared, doffed his McClellan cap with a smile and bow of acknowledgment to the men of the Ninth and then leisurely rode away. The bullets were all the time flying and shells were bursting in air.

Under circumstances such as we were then laboring under, that is, inactive and standing in line of battle under a heavy fire, many of our men stood as though they were breasting a storm of rain and sleet, their faces and bodies being only half turned to the storm, with their shoulders shrugged. We could only account for General Humphreys' presence at that time and place by thinking that he had in contemplation another charge by his division against the stone wall in our front, and that he was selecting with his engineering knowledge the best starting point for a successful attack. Nothing, however, came of it as far as we ever heard. Perhaps he prevented a charge across that ill-fated field which he knew would only end in failure and slaughter. For at that late hour the troops on the plain had lost all confidence in General Burnside's plans and generalship. Attacking General Lee's army, wholly in front, by assault at his strongest point, on such a wide field in broad daylight, without strong artillery support, struck the army as the height of folly. Next in line behind us was the gallant 62d Pennsylvania Volunteers, breasting the storm of bullets and shells, and, like ourselves, waiting for orders. Capt. Christopher Plunket, a lieutenant of the Ninth at this time, was an aide on Colonel Sweitzer's staff, and as he came dashing up to our regiment on horseback we asked him if he had any orders and where our brigade commander was. He replied, " No, but wait till I return; General Sweitzer is over at that house." His bay horse soon carried him off on our left flank. The infantry of the enemy in our front was under cover. From their defences one could occasionally be barely distinguished as a head appeared and as quickly disappeared, so that the regiment did not as a whole indulge in a useless expenditure of buck and ball. Captain Plunket soon returned on his spirited charger and gave Colonel Guiney instructions to move by the left flank. The order was given by the colonel to his regiment. It was misunderstood by four companies of the right wing and they began to move off by the right flank. They were soon called back by the order to " right about," passed along by willing voices. In the meantime the " color company," commanded by Capt. James W. Macnamara, was halted and dressed on the colors by its captain as calmly as if on parade. On this the colonel dressed the regiment and then moved it in perfect order by the left flank, as originally intended. In a few moments we passed through a piece of fencework, and, as we again changed direction to the front, struck more fences; having cleared all our obstructions, the regiment was ordered to " lie down." Several other regiments of our division were already lying in our immediate vicinity. The 22d Massachusetts was off on our left getting in their work on the stone wall in front of the Telegraph road, which was now filled with hostile infantry. The 62d Pennsylvania had likewise taken cover under the rising ground. All our troops now joined in firing at the stone wall. No doubt for every " Johnny " hit a ton of lead was expended, as the enemy kept closely concealed behind their defences. At intervals the enemy's sharpshooters would climb up the roof of a story and a half house to our left front and while resting their pieces on the ridge-pole fire down on our men as they lay on the ground. Many of our soldiers were wounded by these means. Our sharpshooters would soon drive them off. Just as the regiment arrived at its last position a shell burst directly over the centre, in rear of the colors, where the colonel and a group of officers and men were. For a few seconds the pieces of iron whistled and shrieked as they flew to the ground and scattered the dirt over us. The next moment some one asked the colonel where his scabbard was. Holding his sword in his right hand he quickly caught up with his left a piece of scabbard about a foot long which still hung at his side. A piece of the lately exploded shell had cut the steel scabbard smoothly in two without the knowledge of Colonel Guiney. It was a narrow escape from what might otherwise have been a bad wound in his thigh.

Our division was fortunate in having as its general a trained and experienced regular soldier of Gen. Charles Griffin's shrewd discernment. He could see the folly and futility of any further advance against the strong position occupied by Lee's army. Only under the severest pressure would he make a move that would end, in his judgment, in the sure defeat and slaughter of his soldiers. While a brave and able general like Griffin was willing to fight and take the chances of losing life, yet he wanted to see some living show of success.

17

Before us there was none and General Griffin knew it, and his brother officer of the same corps, General Humphreys, knew it, for he had tried it with his own division.   Were it not for their wisdom our division would that afternoon have added large numbers more to the list of the slain, for their order could have sent us forward on the fatal charge.

Many spent bullets dropped among us ; sometimes they would strike one with great severity, cutting through the clothes and leaving black-and-blue marks ; a number of our men were slightly wounded by them. Evidently some of the pieces used by the enemy were defective, or else the force of the bullets was partially spent as they passed through the boards, slats and rails of the fences in our front.   Much of the shelling of the enemy was directed to a house on our left and rear.   It appeared to be a target for their artillery.   While this relieved our line from many of the shells it was doing injury to the infantry in front of the house.

The 32d Massachusetts Volunteers of our brigade, on coming up to the rising ground, took position on our right and rear.   They evidently were not satisfied with the firing " at will," which was going on along the line, for we could continually hear the orders from them :   " Company ! "   " Ready ! "   " At stone wall ! "   " Aim ! " ' Fire ! " " Load ! "   When the Ninth first heard these orders some of our men would sing out : " Bully for the 32d ! "   " Give it to 'em ! " " More power to your elbow ! "   If the volleys they fired went where they intended that they should go, then many a foe bit the dust that afternoon.

Towards the hour of sunset an incident occurred which is worth relating, as it goes to show what ideas of war some of our volunteer generals had.   Colonel Guiney and his officers on duty near the centre of the regiment were talking about one thing and another, when an officer, who appeared to be an aide, rode along on horseback and inquired for Colonel Guiney of the Ninth.   Being directed to where the colonel stood, he said : " Colonel, General ———— (his name is forgotten) wants you to take your regiment and charge on the enemy's works."   Several of the Ninth officers were listening to this order (?), doubting its truthfulness, or whether they heard aright.   Colonel Guiney promptly replied : " You go and tell your general that I take my orders from my immediate superiors."   The mounted officer turned without a word and rode off to our left.   That was the last we ever heard or saw of him or his general.   An indignant officer of the Ninth who had heard the whole conversation, could not suppress his wrath any longer and exclaimed: " The man, or general, who sent such a message as that, must be either drunk, crazy, or a confounded ass — or all three put together. The idea of thinking that one little regiment could live long enough to reach that stone wall with the concentrated fire of the infantry and artillery of the whole Southern army behind it, eager for Yankee blood, is too preposterous to dwell upon for a moment." Others commented on the incident with many emphatic expressions, wondering all the while why the aforesaid general didn't take his own troops and dash over to the stone wall.

In despite of the shooting and shelling going on around and over us both ways, there was much conversation kept up. A soldier's contempt for danger grows as he becomes familiar with it. One of the Ninth men who had been busy quietly selecting victims behind the stone wall for his musket shots, remarked, as he reclined on his elbow, loading his gun with buck and ball: " I wish we were a little nearer to that stone wall."

" And what the deuce do you wish that for? " inquired a comrade in a surprised vein.

" Well," replied the first speaker, " I've been firing in that direction now for the last hour or more, and I don't know whether I've killed or hit a ' Johnny Reb ' or not; if we were about as near again as we are now, I could tell better. There is great satisfaction to me in knowing that I hit a victim once in awhile, and am not wasting all my ammunition ; as it is now, there is nothing to brag about."

" Why, man," exclaimed his listener, " you talk like a cold-blooded assassin; it's among the sharpshooters you ought to be ; those fellows with telescope rifles who can count the buttons on one's blouse and see every man fall that they hit. In the excitement of battle I don't care how many men I wound or kill — the more the better; but I don't wish to know anything about it. Your idea of coolly and deliberately aiming and shooting men down is too much like murder to suit me."

" Murder, you say," queried the first speaker. " Look out yonder along that plateau, and all around us, for that matter, and see the rows of slaughtered dead, heaped one upon the other, many a one mortally wounded and still alive and suffering painfully. If it wasn't for the grand cause which we are fighting for the title of manslaughter would fill the bill; but, my friend, brave men who fight and fall in honorable warfare for a grand cause like ours are heroes in the eyes of their patriotic countrymen. Your harsh term -is misplaced. We, who are here today, know what war is, and when I term it a horrible piece of business you will agree with me; but all honorable warfare cannot be stigmatized as murder. No, no! If it was not for a few ambitious Southerners, who are backed by British interests to destroy our republic, the Union of States would be all right and you and I, and all the rest, would be living in peace with our families and friends around us in the good old State of Massachusetts."

As this conversation was going on a lull had taken place in the firing on both sides, for it was about sunset. Only a stray bullet whistled by now and then and men began to move about carelessly, when the last speaker cried, " Ah! I'm hit! "

" Hold on," said a comrade alongside of him, " I guess you aint hurt much," and with that remark pulled off his cap and picked out a musket ball. " We were both hit by that spent ball, but not hurt much; just enough to say you were wounded. My head feels as though it was hit with a stone. How do you feel? All right? They must be short of ammunition over yonder, for these spent shots have hit quite a number. It looks like a 69 calibre smooth-bore bullet. This paper of buckshot dropped down here a few moments ago." The speaker exhibited a brown paper package, as long as a finger, with a dozen buckshot wrapped up in it and tied with a string.

One man who sat with his profile to the enemy, enjoying a smoke, was greatly astonished at having his pipe knocked out of his mouth by a spent ball. After he recovered from his surprise and repaired damages, he was pulling away as hard as ever at a lower elevation of his head, at the same time ejaculating: " It's sundown! The day's work is done! Why don't those —— ' Johnnies ' quit their —— shooting? "

A recruit who had joined the regiment a few months previous was the object of much merriment in the heat of the firing, by his emphatic and serious ejaculations and the difficulty he experienced in cutting tobacco to fill his pipe. As the bullets came, zip, zip, zip, he would drop pipe, knife and tobacco, and flatten out, face down, on mother earth, as mum and quiet as an oyster, until reassured by those around him that the firing had ceased. As he sat up his pipe-filling would commence again and his loquacity return to enliven the listeners. Among many odd exclamations he said, in a rapid manner, " It's awful! awful! awful! Just think of it! To come to a place like this! See these brave men all killed! killed! All round us, dead! dead! dead! If I get out of this with a whole skin I'll never, never, never go into another battle! This is my first! With the help of God it will be my last! It's awful! awful to be called into the presence of your Maker without a moment's warning!" Zip, zip, zip, came the bullets again, and as a shell burst overhead and scattered many of us with dirt, it was impossible to refrain from laughing to see the agility of our recruit in flattening out, face downward, on the ground, to escape being hit after the danger had passed, all the while muttering, "My God! My God! It's awful! awful! awful!" The serious quickness with which he uttered his words was remarkable for its distinctness. When darkness fell upon us and all firing ceased, our recruit became calm and more resigned to the situation. As he was a man past middle life, of a nervous and excitable temperament, his mental suffering must have been intense under the enemy's fire. It is needless to say that he was not long in the service afterwards.

Our friend and ally at last arrived, a welcome guest to all the living now on the battle-line. It was the darkness of a starry night which came to our relief. We all began to move about as if a great load had been lifted from our hearts and a chance was now offered to straighten out our cramped and chilled limbs and once more create a normal circulation of the blood. It was a long time before we recovered from the effects in our feet and legs produced by the confined position which we were obliged to occupy during daylight. As we meandered through the dead, which thickly strewed the ground in our vicinity, and approached the fences beyond our lines in our front, we could hear with great distinctness the picks and shovels of the enemy as they continued to strengthen their fortifications. It was remarked by one of our deep-thinking lieutenants that the enemy gave evidence by this labor of pick and shovel work which was going on, that they still feared that on the morrow we might succeed in breaking through their line of works. We listened for the sound of Southern voices, but could hear none. Instead, the groans and faint cries of some of the wounded in the distance greeted our ears with painful distinctness. They held our sympathy, but we were powerless to give them succor.

The December weather was fortunately mild all day; at night it was cold enough to border on freezing. As the hours wore away we rested along our line of battle, on rails and boards, that were picked up for temporary protection from the mud and cold ground. Through the night we talked and joked on various subjects and made conundrums about the stars which shone clear and bright in the peaceful firmament above us. Sleep was a stranger to most of our eyes that night, but to the indifferent, who could and would sleep under any and all circumstances, slumber was no stranger, for many of the officers and men slept sound. During the early part of the night our different companies took advantage of the darkness to secure ammunition, fresh water and hardtack. During the day it was all a man's life was worth to attempt to go for a canteen of water. The risks were taken, however, all along the line, and those who returned to their places with a whole skin were deemed lucky mortals. The enemy's sharpshooters always kept their eyes on the springs and water course so as to shoot a " Yankee " before he could quench his thirst. The limping wounded and their companions lugging the helpless wounded to the rear, were always ".' plugged " at with bullets when opportunity offered. The ordinary sharpshooter considered everything on two legs legitimate warfare, in his line, which came under his eye. Many a brave fellow, wounded at the front, bit the dust from a sharpshooter's cowardly bullet while limping faint and weary to the hospital in the rear, when he least expected it.

Sunday morning broke forth clear and pleasant. Imperative orders were received to cease all firing on our part. The elevated ground and hills and heights in our front were alive with men who looked, in the distance, like moving pygmies. They opened on us with infantry and artillery, but, as they did not draw our fire, they soon ceased. At intervals during the day they would blaze away, but, no doubt puzzled at our stillness, would soon cease. The sharpshooters on both sides continued to exchange compliments all day. They were privileged to kill each other and anybody else they could get a bead on, without question. As the enemy were thirsting for blood all day Sunday, we were confined to the ground. We could view the city far in the rear for awhile, then change our position and gaze on " our friends," the enemy, for a time. Between our line and the city, over the whole plain from right to left, the ground was covered by the enemy's guns so thoroughly that it was wounds and death, or both, to any daring soldier who attempted to cross it in broad daylight.

The night before (Saturday) at 11 o'clock General Sykes' 2d division, Fifth Corps, relieved the troops of the Second Corps on the right. On being relieved the Second Corps moved into the city and bivouacked.

Sunday night, an hour or two before midnight, the three divisions of our corps (the Fifth) were relieved by troops from the Ninth Corps, and we then gladly turned our faces to the city. On reaching its streets we stacked arms, established a regimental guard, cooked a square meal, and, with a dipper of boiling hot coffee, refreshed our weary frames and then turned in to sleep after thirty-two hours of mental and physical torture on the battle-line.

General Hooker's centre grand division lost 352 killed; 2501 wounded; 502 captured and missing; total, 3355.

The aggregate in the three grand divisions numbered 1284 killed; 9600 wounded; 1769 captured and missing; grand total, 12,653.

Our engineers lost 8 killed; 49 wounded; 2 captured or missing; artillery reserve lost 8 wounded; total, 67, included in the above grand total.

Confederate army lost in General Longstreet's corps: killed, 251; wounded, 1516; captured and missing, 127. General Jackson's corps: killed, 344; wounded, 2545; captured and missing, 526. Stuart's cavalry: wounded, 13; grand total, 5322.

Although the Ninth Massachusetts had been under the fire of the enemy for thirty-two consecutive hours, it appeared miraculous that none of our officers were killed, or even seriously wounded, particularly those at and in the vicinity of the colors, a position which is always under severe exposure to the enemy's fire. Many officers and men were slightly wounded and still continued on duty and were not desirous of being mentioned in the official list of the regiment. In fact, bullets and spent balls had hit or gone into and through the clothing and hats and caps of at least somewhere near thirty men and officers of the regiment. They were matters to be talked over for days afterwards somewhat as follows : " Look at that hole in my blouse; it went close to the skin. Wasn't I lucky? "

" See that hat (or cap) ; one inch lower and I was a goner."

" I was struck in the shoulder, hard; but in feeling for a wound I couldn't find any blood; it left a black and blue mark, but that's nothing."

It was generally acknowledged that, taking everything into consideration, the regiment was very fortunate with only the following list of casualties at Fredericksburg, Dec. 13, 1862 : 1 killed, 4 mortally wounded, and 29 wounded, viz. : —

List of Killed and Wounded.

COMPANY A.

Sergt. James Burke, Corp. Daniel J. Kenney, Privates Robert Semple, Wm. B. Odey, Patrick Hagan, Cornelius Carmody.

COMPANY B.

Privates Dennis Driscoll, Michael Fallon, Michael O'Brien.

COMPANY C.

Privates Daniel J. Sheehan, Alexander Somerville, James Kelly, Michael Boylston, Michael Ford, Michael Sullivan, Daniel Donovan.

COMPANY D.
None mentioned.

COMPANY E.
Privates Michael Lynch, died of wounds Dec. 31, 1862, at Washington; Martin Lynch, died of wounds Dec. 31, 1862, at Washington; Thomas L. White, wounded.

COMPANY F.
Private John Morrissey died of wounds, March 2, 1863.

COMPANY G.
Privates Daniel Sullivan, Lewis Stone.

COMPANY H.
Privates Jeremiah Ring, killed; James Dooley, died of wounds, Dec. 20, 1862; Michael Coakley, James Corcoran.

COMPANY I.
Corporals Michael Roach and Thomas Lavin; Privates Edmund Flynn, Edward Slyney, John Walsh.

COMPANY K.
Corporal Michael Martin, Privates John Lawless, David Smith.

In order to be prepared for the possible, but not probable, aggressiveness of the enemy, General Burnside so ordered the divisions and corps in Fredericksburg that an attack, if contemplated by General Lee, would be met and severely repulsed, at least.

The rear of the town, that side of it facing the heights, was accordingly quietly fortified for infantry defence on the 15th, and the different brigades and divisions of the Second, Third, Fifth and Ninth Corps were prepared to assume the defensive, and when, by the chances of battle, opportunity offered, they would again become the aggressors. It was surmised rightly by our ablest generals that General Lee was too astute and experienced a soldier in the art of war to fall into the error of attacking the Union forces under the present condition of affairs. Longstreet's corps on the open plain, on even terms, would act in a different manner than it did from its position behind unassailable fortifications; for a successful assault on the city either by artillery or infantry, or both, would, indeed, be doubtful. General Jackson had plenty of chances, if he so desired, to cross swords with General Franklin, on the 13th, 14th or 15th of December. And, however much it was reported that he contemplated doing so, the fact remains that he did not put his troops to the test of a battle in the open field before him. As it was, it will be noticed that Franklin's attack on his intrenched position on the hills on the 13th resulted in very nearly equal losses in killed, wounded, etc., the difference being slightly in Jackson's favor.

On paper, that is, in our morning reports, the Army of the Potomac is credited with 120,000 men in round numbers. Allow thirty per cent of that number for stragglers, detached men, absent sick, etc., and it will leave 84,000 men. Deduct from the latter estimate the number lately killed, wounded, captured, missing and sick, say, 14,000, and it leaves 70,000 effectives or reliable fighting men under Burnside on the 15th of December.

The Confederate army reported 65,000 effective men. Their daily reports were based on men who carried guns and were present in the ranks for duty. Deduct from that their losses in killed, wounded, captured, missing and sick, say 6500; that would leave them 58,500 men for battle on December 15. How, as some writers claim, Generals Lee, Jackson and Longstreet were going to drive the flower of the Army of the Potomac out of Fredericksburg and into the river, backed as it was by its superb artillery, has yet to be explained. The army which went through the Peninsula campaign, the seven days' battles, Pope's campaign, the Antietam and South Mountain campaign, and now stood with 70,000 seasoned veterans under the heights of Fredericksburg, could not be driven by any such means.

General Lee and his able lieutenants took great chances in battle all through the war. They knew our condition as well as they did their own, notwithstanding statements to the contrary. *If there was a ghost of a chance for success* in attacking our army at Fredericksburg on the 14th, 15th or 16th days of December, 1862, General Lee and his lieutenants would have taken the venture.

The apparent chaos in the city and the general appearance of a lack of discipline among the divisions was, to the inexperienced eye, a sign of demoralization. Yet, had occasion called for it, the army there would have astonished the inexperienced observer at its prompt response to a call for battle. Witness, for instance, the prompt evacuation of the city on the dark morning of Tuesday, the 16th, in rain and mud. Not a bugle sound or a drum beat was given to call the troops to arms. The great majority, officers and men, did not know whether they were going to the front or rear — to fight or retreat; even the few orders given were short, sharp and decisive, not loud or boisterous, to fall in and march. Yet the veteran army moved in the best of order, like the great living machine that it was. Every officer and man knew his place and was ready for any emergency.

Monday morning, Dec. 15, 1862, the streets of Fredericksburg exhibited a living panorama of warfare which never occurred there before or since, or ever will again. The perforated walls of its bombarded houses, by the artillery of both armies, were, to the contemplative mind, a sad loss to their owners and former inhabitants. All of the latter, with a few rare exceptions, were now absent, and could have only a faint idea of the great destruction of property and household effects that had taken place in a few days only. Its streets were now occupied with infantry which had been to the front since the morning of the 13th; their decimated ranks having been relieved by fresh troops who were now simply holding a thin line of battle under the shadow of the heights occupied by Lee's army. The enemy's shell could still be heard and seen bursting in the air. At intervals one would strike a building in the city as a reminder, as it were, that the battle was still lingering in our midst. Long and irregular stacks of muskets and rifles stood in the streets marking the lines of regiments which had arrived from the front in the night, and who were now more or less scattered about the streets of the little city. A sentry here and there marked the headquarters of a brigadier or major-general who had taken possession of some home-like house which its former occupants had deserted without disturbing its furniture and furnishings. Groups of soldiers were clustered about small fires, cooking rations and coffee. Officers of nearly every rank, mounted and on foot, were moving in all directions or lingering about the doors of deserted dwellings. Each one of the thousands who were now scattered throughout the city had something to talk about or to occupy his attention. Written documents and papers from the archives of the town, that were of value to their owners, were scattered about the sidewalks and street, and trampled under foot as worse than useless; this was the work of the " Goths and vandals " — or in modern parlance the bummers and stragglers — in our army, who had strewn the streets of the place with all kinds of small articles which they had plundered from stores, offices and dwellings, and looked upon afterwards as of useless value and then thrown away. Some soldiers were indoors quietly resting themselves at the open windows, taking in the scenes going on before their eyes. At times the notes from a piano would strike the ear from some house, showing that the musically inclined were bent on enjoying, while they might, an hour of music and song, and, under its soothing strains, banish for a time at least all thoughts of war, danger and hardship. All this time the provost marshal and his assistants were patrolling the streets, doing their best to suppress rank disorder and riotous conduct.

Colonel Guiney and his officers received an invitation from General Meagher to attend a banquet to be held at the Theatre building in Fredericksburg on the afternoon of the 15th, in honor of the distri- bution of three beautiful Irish silk flags to the New York regiments of the Irish Brigade, *i.e.*, the 69th, 88th and 83d regiments. To say that Colonel Guiney and his subalterns were surprised on receiving an invi- tation of this nature, at this time and place, is putting it mildly. On reaching the theatre, a short way down the street from where the Ninth regiment was bivouacked, we entered and moved up stairs and found a large hall set with ordinary board refreshment tables, over which were scattered large quantities of cold turkeys and chickens, etc., with num- bers of bottles of champagne. On the stage, at the further end of the theatre, we noticed General Meagher and several other general officers of the gallant Second Corps. The floor that we occupied was well filled with field, staff and line officers of the Irish Brigade, the Ninth Massa- chusetts Volunteers, and other invited guests, all standing. Without ceremony we obeyed with hungry alacrity the order to " fall in " to the good things before us, and it is needless to say that every one enjoyed the cold birds and liquid refreshments immensely. It was something that we did not run across every day, for flag presentations were infre- quent. General Meagher presented the flags to his gallant regiments, in the name of their lady donors of New York city, in one of his char- acteristic eloquent speeches, and was followed by other speakers, whom he happily introduced. Many of the audience began to grow enthusi- astic over the speeches, and at intervals would give three cheers for the speaker and his sentiments. As the cheering was heard outside the building, at army headquarters, word was sent to suppress it, as it was feared that it would attract the attention of the enemy, and perhaps draw their fire on the building. For a time this order had its effect, but the enthusiasm over the orations could not be subdued, so that orders were sent by General Burnside to end the meeting, which was obeyed at once. Every one retired from the building quite pleased with the unique flag presentations and entertainment held under the batteries of the distant enemy. All agreed that only an " Irish Brigade " could carry out such a jolly affair at such a time and place.

The rumors, since the night of the 13th, of another assault, in force, on Marye's heights, by the Ninth Corps, to be led by the commanding general in person, were — happily for the Ninth Corps — not verified, as no movement in that direction took place. Monday night many and various rumors were in circulation, most of them pure inventions of those in our army given to romance.

As far as our brigade was concerned we were without orders and night found us once again bivouacked in the street of the city at the old stand. The night was very dark and the enemy was closely watched by our pickets. After midnight a mist settled on the town, and this was followed by a drizzling rain and a strong wind. About an hour before daylight our regiment fell into line, as did all the troops in our vicinity.

All doubts were set at rest as to our objective point when the line of march led towards the river and we crossed the pontoons. As the gray of the rainy morning began to break we were climbing the muddy and slippery ascent from the river bridge up the bank and onto the road that led to Stoneman's Switch.

As we marched along we could hear the cries of men, in the semi-darkness, who fell into the ditches, that were some twelve to eighteen feet deep, along the road, and could not find their way out on account of being blind — moon blind. No particular attention was paid to their cries for assistance, except to find out who they were, as it was well known that with daylight they would climb out all right and overtake their different regiments. This moon blindness was an affliction that occurred to some men in the army which prevented them from seeing at night. During the day they had no trouble, but as soon as it became dark they were stone blind. It was termed "moon blindness," as the blame for the affliction was laid to that orb shining in their faces as they slept on the ground without a tent.

After a disagreeable tramp of three miles we entered our old camp-ground. In a few hours we transformed its dilapidated aspect into something like its former comfortable appearance.

Our 2d brigade (1st division, Fifth Corps) lost in killed, 4 officers, 19 men; wounded, 17 officers, 176 men; captured and missing, 6 men; aggregate, 222 in the brigade. Our Fifth Corps lost in killed, 21 officers, 185 men; wounded, 125 officers, 1544 men; captured or missing, 300 men. Casualties in the aggregate, 2175. By noonday of the 16th of December our army had all arrived in camp; the pontoon bridges were taken up without opposition, in fact without the knowledge of the enemy. In the afternoon the enemy had possession of the city. The Union dead on the field of battle were not buried until the following Saturday, the 20th of December. In the meantime they were stripped of all their belongings by the needy enemy.

CHAPTER XV.

GENERAL HOOKER SUPERSEDES GENERAL BURNSIDE.

ONE VIEW OF THE SOUTHERN CAUSE — STRATEGY OF GENERAL LEE —
GENERAL MEADE COMMANDS THE FIFTH CORPS — ON A RECONNOIS-
SANCE — REVIEW OF THE FIFTH CORPS — THE "MUD MARCH" —
GENERAL BURNSIDE COMMUNICATES WITH THE PRESIDENT AND IS
RELIEVED — GENERAL HOOKER PLACED IN COMMAND OF THE ARMY
— THE PRESIDENT'S LETTER TO GENERAL HOOKER — THE ARMY
REORGANIZED — THE NINTH MASSACHUSETTS CELEBRATES ST. PAT-
RICK'S DAY — HORSE RACING AND OTHER SPORTS — QUARTERMASTER
MOONEY'S FATAL ACCIDENT — CORPS BADGES — THE PRESIDENT
REVIEWS THE ARMY — FATHER TISSOT ACTING CHAPLAIN OF THE
NINTH REGIMENT — GENERAL MEAGHER PRESENTS A GREEN FLAG TO
THE NINTH MASSACHUSETTS VOLUNTEERS — BIOGRAPHICAL SKETCH
OF MAJ. GEO. W. DUTTON.

"Thy father's merit sets thee up to view,
And shows thee in the fairest point of light,
To make thy virtues, or thy faults conspicuous."

ADDISON.

CHRISTMAS time in 1862 was a gloomy period, not only in the
Army of the Potomac but throughout the homes of the Union
States. The disasters through which our army had passed
were causes for rejoicing in the Confederacy. The monarchical friends
of the "Southern Cause" across the Atlantic, particularly in England,
likewise rejoiced with them as they learned with composure of the heavy
blows that they believed were leading to the looked-for downfall of
Democracy and of Republican institutions in America.

The prestige gained by the Confederacy in defeating a so-called
large army of the Union was a moral influence in their favor. It confirmed in the minds of their friends everywhere the belief of the final
triumph of the Confederacy. It never occurred to their biased judg-
ments that both armies, as to numbers, were fighting on very nearly
equal terms. It was not taken into consideration then that the drudgery
of army life, in all its avenues of labor, was performed in the Union
army by enlisted men detailed from the ranks for that purpose, thereby
reducing, by a large percentage, the effective fighting force which was

reported on paper, or that the same kind of work in the Southern army was performed by negro labor almost wholly; and by this auxiliary force exempting from army drudgery the rank and file of the Confederate army.

The Southron claimed to be a cavalier — a gay soldier — with all its romantic life. It was his idea to fight, march, and enjoy the fruits of victory. The drudgery must be performed by a million of negro slaves — substitutes for the white soldiers — who were at the beck and call of men who were their masters through generations of vassalage.

General Lee knew the situation on both sides, at that time, better than any other living Southerner. He defeated General Burnside by strategy — a style of warfare which the latter failed to comprehend. In the beginning he chose his ground, fortified it, and remained there waiting for the assault which he knew would be made; for he knew his man. Subsequent events proved the correctness of his judgment. With his great strategic ability he was fighting against the commanding general, not against his army. The latter affair was a secondary consideration. If he succeeded in the first he knew that the defeat of the latter was a foregone conclusion. He defeated Hooker subsequently in the same manner but on a grander scale. Fredericksburg was only the beginning of the hard trials through which the Army of the Potomac must pass. The days that came and went, however, were not all shadows, there was some sunshine which the army enjoyed in its own way while it lasted. Christmas day was remembered and quietly observed in the Ninth regiment. The great American turkey was conspicuous by his absence from our dinner tables; it served to remind us of the homes " so far away " where many vacant chairs stood — chairs that were never to be filled again by many of the absent ones — around the family tables on which the majestic birds reposed after their release from a hot oven. The soldier could not afford to dwell on thoughts of home and all its creature comforts long at a time, and they generally took wings and went up with the smoke that he contentedly puffed from his pipe.

On the 26th of December the Fifth Corps was fortunate in having assigned to it, as its new commander, Maj.-Gen. George G. Meade. His reputation as a brigade and division commander was well known throughout the Army of the Potomac. The appointment of this brave and able officer to our corps was received by both officers and men with great satisfaction.

About 1 o'clock, Tuesday, December 30, the Ninth Massachusetts moved out of camp and joined the brigade and division on a reconnois-

sance.   It was a " cavalry expedition " under General Averill, planned
at army headquarters, and, as usual, had to be reinforced by the
infantry.   The night of the 30th, after a very tiresome tramp, we bivouacked in a ploughed field.   The usual pickets were posted, and, after
our long march, we received peremptory orders that no fires of any
kind should be lighted.   After a miserable night's rest on the cold,
ploughed ground we went forward at daylight to within five miles of a
place called Morrisville.   While halted on a sunken road we heard
artillery firing in our front.   In the meantime fires were started by the
Ninth and coffee and hardtack, with partially cooked pork, were
devoured as a standing and unsatisfactory breakfast.   In the course of
an hour — about 11 o'clock A.M.— we countermarched and headed for
camp some twenty-five miles away.   Late in the afternoon we reached
Hartwood Church, and were given the choice of going into bivouac or
to continue our tramp to camp.   The Ninth chose the latter alternative.
The cold had become intense and the air raw.   Being free from the
marching column the Ninth moved along the road through the obscure
woods and quiet clearings at a fairly rapid gait.   All was silent save
the sound of tramping feet and the clinking of the canteen against the
bayonet.   Without a halt we sighted camp about 8 o'clock P.M. of the
31st; then we slackened our pace as we moved along the familiar
road — for we were cold, tired and half starved — into our old camp.
A gill of whiskey, that was issued to each man without much delay,
revived our drooping spirits.   After a good (?) supper and hot coffee
we were soon sound asleep.   The latter favor was nature's reward
of merit to those who endured hardship and fatigue.

Some of the regiments of our division — the 22d Massachusetts
among them — had crossed and recrossed the river.   As the water was
deep and cold to freezing, the brave fellows must have suffered much from
cold and wet afterwards.   A few of the enemy's pickets were captured
across the river.   The expedition, as such, proved a failure.   The details
of it can be found in the Union records of that period (December, 1862).
The next day we intended to have the laugh on some of the regiments
which bivouacked near Hartwood Church the night before, instead of
continuing on to camp as we did.   They were obliged to pass our camp
on their homeward march.   As they came in sight they drew forth our
sympathy instead of our mirth, for they looked, what they felt, tired
and wretched after their cold night's exposure.   Many of the gallant
fellows tried to look like " gay soldiers " when they approached our
camp, but we knew by their forced smiles and straggling ranks how
painfully tired they felt.   The only real smile they evinced was when

we mentioned that " a whiskey ration was waiting for them in camp and it would warm the cockles of their hearts." Considering that 55 to 60 miles had been tramped over in about a day and a half, it was little wonder that the infantry were tired. An order for the review of the corps set the rumors going again among the regiments. A review was generally the forerunner of a campaign, but being in the depths of winter it was doubtful now as to what was meant by it. On the 8th of January the regiments, etc., of the Fifth Corps passed in review before General Burnside. It created much interest all around, for it was a long time since we had a corps review ; in fact, to several regiments which had joined the corps recently it was a new and imposing affair. As day after day passed company and regimental inspections were held with much scrutiny, and deficiencies in guns, equipments, clothing, etc., were being supplied. All the sick were ordered away to Aquia Creek. This activity kept the rumors flying until the 16th of January, when orders were received about " marching rations," cooked and uncooked, and to be ready to move in heavy marching order on the 18th of January, 1863. The latter order was countermanded and the

MUD MARCH

did not take place until the 20th of January. Profiting by past experience the colonel (Guiney) of the Ninth cautioned company commanders not to destroy any of their comfortable quarters, as it was more than possible, if not probable, that we would return again and occupy the same ground. The men of the regiment were quick to see the point, and, with a few light exceptions, refrained from indulging in the usual bonfires afforded by camp " furniture." Quartermaster Mooney was instructed to look after the vacant camp as long as he could. As it afterward proved he had ample opportunity to do so, for he hardly lost sight of the place while the regiment was away. During his daily visits to the regiment, while it was stuck in the mud, he assured us that everything would be in apple-pie order when we got back. The quartermaster was certain that we were going back to our old camp in a few days, for he had the opportunity of obtaining much valuable information as he journeyed back and forth through the army. He had a " nose for news " and could give " points " to some of our general officers on army movements at times.

After patiently waiting over half the day (on the 20th) the Ninth Massachusetts took its place in the 2d brigade, and in line with the Fifth Corps, moved forward on the road in a northwesterly direction for the fords on the river to " surprise the enemy." (?) Our progress was exceedingly slow on account of the way being blocked by troops, artillery and wagons on our line of march. After going about *two miles* the Ninth was ordered into bivouac. The threatening weather turned into rain, and it fell very steadily all night. The attempted movement of the army the next day in the falling rain proved disastrous. The soft country roads became utterly impassable for man or beast. After laboring through the mud and rain for hours the Ninth Massachusetts halted in a piece of woods about three miles from Hartwood Church, and were instructed to remain there until further orders. Fires were made and as night approached we endeavored to make the situation as comfortable as the rain would allow. It is needless to say that we were very wet, and that our overcoats, blankets, etc., were greatly increased in weight on that account. At intervals along the road, on a line with our bivouac, artillery and wagons were fast in the mud to their axles. It puzzled us somewhat to know how they got along so far and became stuck so deep and fast. The drivers of the horses and mules had given up all idea of pulling out. The animals were up to their bellies in slush and mud and could hardly move. The regiments of the different brigades of our corps were scattered about while seeking decent places to bivouac along their line of march. A supply of axes having arrived the Ninth Massachusetts was one of the many regiments which went into the woods to fell trees and corduroy the road. With logs for fulcrums and limbs of trees for levers the Ninth raised a caisson and several other wheeled vehicles out of the mud and built the road with corduroy under them before the animals would or could pull them along. In many instances the horses and mules became so weak and discouraged that they would not pull the teams until the wheels were started by the soldiers. Friday was reasonably pleasant and we worked all day, chopping, carrying and corduroying, until we had the pleasure of seeing our road cleared of stalled teams and artillery. The Ninth received some hard tack and a whiskey ration on Friday and, all things considered, concluded that they fared as well as the average. On Saturday the weather was pleasant and we found no difficulty in getting back on our own corduroy road to our old camp. Once there we resumed the old order of camp life.

It was somewhat mortifying to learn that the enemy across the river knew as much about our condition as we did ourselves. Along their picket line at the fords they placed signboards marked with charcoal: " Stuck in the Mud "; and " Road to Richmond." They had many an amusing (to them) joke at our expense, as they bantered our pickets on the river bank. Our boys took it all in good part.

The " mud march," as its title indicates, proved from beginning to end a most lamentable failure, and it capped the climax of General Burnside's career as the commander of the Army of the Potomac. As the closing act in this military drama General Burnside wrote a General Order, No. 8, on Jan. 23, 1863, in which he expressed disparaging views of the actions of some of his subordinate generals during his term as commander. By this order the following officers were recommended to the President for dismissal from the United States service, namely: General Hooker, Gen. W. T. H. Brooks, Gen. John Newton and Gen. John Cochrane. The following named he ordered to be relieved from duty and to report without delay to the adjutant-general of the U.S. Army: Generals Franklin, Smith, Sturgis, Ferrero, and Lieut.-Col. J. H. Taylor. The President on receiving the order from General Burnside disapproved of it. It was therefore never officially issued. General Burnside thereupon requested to be relieved from his position as the commander of the Army of the Potomac.

On the 25th of January, 1863, the following changes were made by order of the President, through the regular official channels, and thus the following named officers were relieved from further duty in the Army of the Potomac: Major-Generals A. E. Burnside, E. V. Sumner and W. B. Franklin. By the same order Maj.-Gen. Joseph Hooker was assigned to the command of the Army of the Potomac. He assumed command of it on the 26th of January, 1863. This appointment of General Hooker was made by the President against the wishes of many of his advisers, including General Halleck and Secretary Stanton. The same day the President sent the following unique, not to say characteristic, letter to General Hooker. The document is marvellous for its directness, its honesty of purpose, and its brave, determined spirit. If the subject of it had made a practice of reading it every night before he retired to his army bed it would very likely have kept him close to his line of duty, and the downfall that he brought upon himself and his noble army would have been averted.

EXECUTIVE MANSION, WASHINGTON, D.C., }
Jan. 26, 1863. }

MAJOR-GENERAL HOOKER.

General: I have placed you at the head of the Army of the Potomac. Of course I have done this upon what appears to me to be sufficient reasons, and yet I think it best for you to know that there are some things in regard to which I am not quite satisfied with you. I believe you to be a brave and skilful soldier, which of course I like. I also believe you do not mix politics with your profession, in which you are right. You have confidence in yourself, which is a valuable, if not an indispensable quality. You are ambitious, which, within reasonable bounds, does good rather than harm; but I think that during General Burnside's command of the army you have taken counsel of your ambition, and thwarted him as much as you could, in which you did a great wrong to the country, and to a most meritorious and honorable brother officer. I have heard in such a way as to believe it, of your recently saying that both the army and the Government needed a dictator. Of course it was not for this, but in spite of it, that I have given you the command. Only those generals who gain successes can set up as dictators. What I now ask of you is military success, and I will risk the dictatorship. The Government will support you to the utmost of its ability, which is neither more nor less than it has done and will do for all commanders.

I much fear that the spirit you have aided to infuse into the army, of criticising their commander and withholding confidence from him, will now turn upon you. I shall assist you as far as I can to put it down. Neither you nor Napoleon, if he were alive again, could get any good out of an army while such a spirit prevails in it. And now beware of rashness, but with energy and sleepless vigilance go forward and give us victories.

Yours very truly,

A. LINCOLN.

It is no discredit to the Army of the Potomac itself to say that General Burnside left it in disorder. It suffered from men absent without leave, desertion, sickness, and demoralization in the quartermaster's and commissary's departments. It could not be otherwise after his disastrous generalship and lack of direction and discipline from the day he assumed command until the day he left it. On the other hand great credit is due to General Hooker for his promptness and marked ability in reorganizing the Army of the Potomac and bringing it back to that high plane of discipline and good spirits which it had reached under General McClellan when he was removed for the last time. General Hooker returned from the " Grand Divisions " of General Burnside's day to the old corps formations. On Feb. 5, 1863, the army was reorganized as follows : —

First Corps	Major-General John F. Reynolds.
Second Corps	Major-General D. N. Couch.
Third Corps	Brigadier-General D. E. Sickles.
Fifth Corps	Major-General Geo. G. Meade.
Sixth Corps	Major-General John Sedgwick.
Eleventh Corps . .	{ After General Sigel, Major-General O. O. Howard.
Twelfth Corps . . .	Major-General H. W. Slocum.
Artillery Corps . . .	
Cavalry Corps . . .	Brigadier-General Stoneman.

The Ninth Corps was sent to General Dix, Fortress Monroe. The Pennsylvania Reserves were sent from the First Corps to Alexandria, Va. The United States Regulars, 2d division, Fifth Corps, were reorganized by consolidation. Brig.-Gen. Charles Griffin continued in command of our first division of the Fifth Corps. Our 2d brigade was commanded alternately by (1) Col. James McQuade, 14th New York, and (2) Col. Jacob B. Sweitzer, 62d Pennsylvania. The brigade was now composed of the

9th Massachusetts .	Colonel P. R. Guiney.
32d Massachusetts .	Lieutenant-Colonel Luther Stephenson.
4th Michigan . . .	Colonel H. H. Jeffords.
14th New York . . .	Lieutenant-Colonel T. M. Davis.
62d Pennsylvania .	{ Lieutenant-Colonel J. C. Hull, or Colonel Sweitzer.

The 2d division of the Fifth Corps was in command of Maj.-Gen. George Sykes. The 3d division of the Fifth Corps was in command of Brig.-Gen. A. A. Humphreys.

General Hooker proved a veritable Santa Claus to the army under his command. The peculating commissary department was brought to a sense of its duty ; so that rations, particularly vegetables, that belonged to the regiments were sent forward to their proper destination instead of, as heretofore, being disposed of to cash customers and itinerant purchasers. The money received in this way went into the commissary's private purse, and the regiments of the different brigades were charged with having received *a full supply of rations* on the false and final monthly returns, or accounts, sent to the head of that department in Washington, D.C. No authentic vouchers were required with these monthly accounts. It was a system of single (not to say singular) entry that enriched many a captain and " assistant commissary of subsistence " for the rest of his life.

The quartermaster-general's department was aroused from its lethargy, and the supplies of clothing, shoes, and camp equipage, etc., came forward in large invoices to meet army requisitions of months' standing. Purveyors, sutlers, bakers and paymasters followed in quick succession until the army was abundantly supplied with full rations, including " soft bread," also cash to spend with the purveyors and sutlers, and to send home to their families, friends and dependent people. Company, regiment, brigade, division and corps inspections and reviews were in order until in a short space of time the whole army was on the high road to health and good spirits. Our turn for picket duty came about once a month. The tour of duty lasted three days and the regiment, as a whole, went to the picket line, which was about four or five miles out from camp, in the direction of Stafford Court House, between there and the river. The fine weather of February was modified by a couple of snow and rain storms. These storms left the roads and camps in bad condition for days at a time.

Leave of absence for ten days was now allowed to officers of the army. Two from each regiment were to go and return, then two more, until all had enjoyed the benefit of a short visit to their families and friends. The officers of the Ninth had a very unfortunate, not to say disgusting experience on account of the action of the first pair who went from the regiment under this arrangement. Having arrived home they remained there for several months. On their failure to return to the regiment at the proper time, indignation meetings were held by the officers of the regiment in the field, petitions were signed, and every honorable means was adopted by the colonel to bring the delinquents to a sense of duty, justice and honor without avail. The manner of operating to overstay their time was to secure from a surgeon in Boston, or elsewhere (by means best known to themselves and to others who " played the same game "), what was called a " sick leave " certificate, and then follow it up (at any cost) by repeated extensions. Our two healthy officers — who were never known before that time to have ever seen a sick day — worked the " game " in this way until the order allowing a leave of absence was revoked, and all absentees were ordered to return to their commands under pain of dismissal from the service. The action of these two officers engendered much ill will which redounded to their discredit; and, although they did not seem to realize it, there was hardly an officer in the Ninth who would not have moved for their dismissal from the service on account of their selfish and ungentlemanly behavior. They deprived all the rest from visiting their families and friends, and in some instances from ever seeing them. The enlisted men were likewise allowed furloughs of ten days, two to go at a time from each company. With the exception of a few desertions and " stay-overs " the honorable action of the men was an example that would put to shame the above-mentioned commissioned officers. In a few instances the men overstayed their time and were reported " absent without leave." On their return to the regiment proper military punishment was inflicted, which every one saw they deserved, except the victims of it themselves.

The early part of the month of March moved along with alternate days of snow, rain, thunder and pleasant weather. The 17th of

March was drawing near, and the men of the Ninth Massachusetts, true to their Irish instincts, were looking forward to a jolly celebration of St. Patrick's day. Having passed through the defeats and misfortunes of the battle of Fredericksburg, the " mud march," and abortive reconnoissances, the long winter had been, to say the least, a gloomy one for the Army of the Potomac. As one wag expressed it, " Our misfortunes were enough to drive all the officers in the army to drink ! particularly the generals !" It is feared that it did affect some of them in that manner. It required no effort for a veteran in the service, when wet, cold and hungry, to drink commissary whiskey — when he could get it. The writer has known officers and men to refuse it the first year of their service, but the second year generally brought them to it. After that it required a great effort to use the spirits with moderation on the part of many who became addicted to its use.

The anticipation of the coming sport on the 17th acted as a leaven to the lethargy that permeated the soldiers of the army to a more or less extent. The light-heartedness that was now visible throughout the Ninth Massachusetts was contagious and very soon affected the rank and file of the 62d Pennsylvania, who were in winter quarters near us. They, too, looked forward to a jolly time with their old friends of the Ninth. Adjutant M. W. Phalen and Quartermaster Mooney were given full charge of the entertainments. About a week before the eventful celebration they announced the following program : A sack race ; race for a greased pig ; climbing a greased pole ; jumping matches ; refreshments ; horse racing in the afternoon ; mock dress parade. Prizes of small amounts of money were to be given to the winners, and the pig to the one who caught it. The successful climber of the greased pole would be entitled to a ten days' furlough, which was pinned on top of the fifteen-foot pole. A general invitation was extended to the whole division, and General Griffin and staff promised to be present. March 17 opened up with pleasant, sunny weather. After guard mounting the fun began. The main road from army headquarters ran by the front of our camp, and beyond it was vacant land in all directions, so that a fine opportunity was given for games and races. The spectators were numerous and enjoyed the fun of the sack races, greased pig, etc. Climbing the greased pole was, as one man expressed it who had tried, " a corker." The one who applied the grease did a thorough job, for it was thick with it from base to apex. After several failures, the man who claimed to know said that a clear space ought to have been left for at least six feet from the ground up. After several hours' repeated efforts for the coveted prize it was reluctantly given up, and the furlough continued to flutter in the breeze in sight of longing eyes until noon, when it was declared off. At 11 o'clock A.M. a gill of whiskey was issued to each man of the Ninth; this they shared with their comrades of the 62d Pennsylvania, and had a jolly time. After dinner the horse racing took place. At the close of the regular races it was " go-as-you-please," and several running matches by officers of the division, who largely attended, took place. Before the afternoon was half over a sad and unexpected accident occurred. The track was half a mile down to the stake and return. Two horses had gone off down the track, under daring riders with loose reins, at a break-neck pace. Before they reached the half-mile stake two more riders followed and went flying down the track in like manner. Quartermaster Mooney was one of the latter riders; he met one of the returning horsemen and they approached each other at full speed, and quick as a flash the horses struck full abreast with a dull sound that could be heard half a mile away. Both horses dropped dead in their tracks. The riders went up in the air and down to the ground heavily. Quartermaster Mooney struck on his head and was carried off unconscious. He died from his injuries a few days afterwards. Dr. Faxon, surgeon of the 32d Massachusetts, who rode the other horse, escaped with a dislocated shoulder and slight bruises. This sad affair put a damper on the races, which were shortly after discontinued.

The mock dress parade of the regiment late in the afternoon had a large attendance, for it was wholly in charge of the enlisted men. The parody on the manual of arms, and the clever imitation of Colonel Guiney's voice and manner by " Napoleon " of Company F; who acted the part of commander, was highly amusing to the spectators and to the regiment generally. As a day of recreation for the troops it was productive of much good, both mentally and physically. Great regret was expressed among the officers and men of the regiment at the sad accident that befell Lieutenant Mooney. We were all sorry to lose the companionship of our genial old quartermaster, for he had become a great favorite in the regiment.

The writer at this time being first lieutenant in the line was, on the 20th of March, 1863, appointed by the colonel quartermaster of the Ninth Massachusetts, in place of Quartermaster Mooney, deceased. The non-military reader may wish to know something of the duties of that office in an infantry regiment *in time of war*. The quartermaster holds the rank of first lieutenant and is a member of the colonel's mounted staff. It is his duty to keep the regiment properly supplied — when possible — with wearing apparel, camp equipage, rifles,

military equipments, ammunition, rations, wagons, etc.   In fact to procure and take charge of everything that pertains to the personal and
general welfare of his regiment.   He is assisted in his duties by a quartermaster-sergeant and a commissary sergeant, with such other men
as the emergency calls for.   Monthly accounts of all property received,
distributed and expended, are made up and sent to the department in
Washington.

Horse racing was pronounced by our army surgeons as a good
" constitutional," in the way of exercise and recreation, not only for
those actually engaged in it, but likewise for the benefit it gave to the
soldiers in our own camp and to soldiers of other regiments who came to
see it.   It served to break up in a way that lethargic monotony that
fell upon our army when long confined in camp in the winter months,
more particularly so when we could get a lot of innocent sport out of
a race like the following.   Assistant-Surgeon Ryan of " ours " was a
great lover of horseflesh.   It made no difference to him whether it
was " blooded stock " or ordinary " common horse," so long as there
was a chance to have a race.   At this camp he became possessed of a
" buckskin " colored animal, which stood about fourteen hands high.
It was short, thin, wiry and skittish, and had a habit of kicking out
sideways its hind leg in a vicious manner when touched with a spur.
The doctor was as full of mischief as usually falls to the lot of one man.
His greatest fun was to get an interested crowd of men around him and
talked race and horse, and to offer all kinds of fabulous amounts on
the " Cat."   This was the name he had given to his "buckskin."   To
his interested listeners, officers and men, he would say, " I'll run the
' Cat' against any horse in the regiment or in the brigade.   No! I
won't bar the division ! bring on your horse.   Here's a hundred dollars
that I win best two out of three, one mile — down and back — to each
heat."   In the meantime the crowd had increased in numbers, all on a
broad grin at the doctor's remarks.   Many of them, partaking of his
exuberant spirits, would interject comical expressions, and make game of
the owner and his horse, to the amusement of the crowd.   When the
doctor considered that the fun had gone far enough he would carelessly
throw himself into the saddle and then the real sport would commence.
Pulling his " Cat " up smartly by the reins and touching him with the
whip — without appearing to — and giving him a gentle feeler of the
spur, all in the same movement, the " Cat " would kick out his hind
leg continually at the crowd, and rapidly swing around in a circle by
the rear, holding his ground all the while with his forefeet under his
rider's secret guidance.   The doctor, acting as though the horse was

almost unmanageable, would repeatedly cry, " Whoa! whoa! whoa there!" " What are you about?" and to the crowd that he was knocking in every direction, " Get out of the way there, if you don't want to get hurt!" " I can't hold him still!" " Whoa! whoa!" As the circle enlarged, and some of the wounded limped away, and all chances for further damage to the crowd vanished, the doctor would leap from his saddle, and with great rapidity rush for his horse's head and grab him fiercely by the bridle. This would give the horse a scare and he would back so suddenly — apparently pulling the doctor with him — that he would be into a part of the crowd again; there would be another rush of the men tumbling into each other, to get out of the way of the " Cat's " heels. After a while the animal would become quiet and the doctor would gently pat him on the neck, and while laughing quietly all the while would say to those in hearing, " He's a wonderful horse! Just a little skittish, but I'll break him of that! Did you notice how dexterously I handled him that time? I was greatly afraid (?) at one time that he would take the snaffle in his teeth and dash down the road! "

" It's a —— pity he didn't," said one man limping about.

" Hello!" said the doctor, " did he hurt you — is your foot hurt much? Go over to my tent and I'll fix it all right for you."

As the doctor walked off leading the " Cat " across the road the crowd would follow him with their eyes, and remark something funny when out of earshot, as one of them did: " He's as foxy as any horse jockey that I ever saw in the old country, and that's saying a great deal, for the devil himself couldn't get the best of some of them, and I saw many a shrewd one in my day."

The race referred to was made up at one of our camp symposiums — the doctor to ride the " Cat," and Lieutenant Dacey was allowed to ride any horse he chose. The stakes were one hundred dollars a side, and the judges and stakeholder duly appointed. The heats to be the best two out of three, down the half mile track and return, one mile each. It took place the next day, no postponement on account of the weather. The next morning the ground was covered with snow to the depth of several inches. At the appointed hour of 10 A.M the surgeon was on hand with the " Cat." In a short time Dacey appeared on a splendid stepping bay horse sixteen or seventeen hands high, which looked every inch the racer that he was. As the crowd gathered around one man remarked, as he eyed the contrast between the two animals: " Doctor, you're bet." " Fifty dollars I aint," said the surgeon, pulling out a wad of " greenbacks," and looking at the one who spoke, and then on the crowd with a smile of confidence, but no one offered to cover it. " The little doctor has great courage," quietly remarked the first speaker as the riders commenced to prepare for the first heat. Very soon the word " Go " was given. With whip and spur the doctor laid it onto the " buckskin " as Dacey's horse flew past him like the wind. Everybody then held their breath and watched the flyer as he went by the half mile stake without a sign of turning until he was far beyond it; gradually the lieutenant pulled his racer around to the left making a large circle, and running at great speed, headed for the return. In the meantime the " Cat " was handsomely and closely turned by his rider at the stake, and was half way home as Dacey's horse came flying back. The excitement was intense as it was no one's race yet. The doctor was laying on whip and spur within a hundred yards of the goal as Dacey reached the lower half mile pole, his horse coming up at two-minute speed. The sympathy of the spectators went with the " Cat," and as the doctor neared the winning pole the cheers and yells that went up for his success were terrific, but ten yards more and he would be the winner; the bay horse was coming up like the wind. One length further and the " Cat " went by the winning pole as the lieutenant's racer lapped his flank and ran a half mile beyond the pole before his rider could pull him in. The doctor received the cheers and congratulations of his friends with his usual modesty (?) and at once offer to bet money that he would likewise win the next heat. The game little " buckskin " seemed to realize the situation and calmly received the patting and petting of his numerous admirers. He was wet with sweat but his wind was all right. Once more the horses came to the scratch, and at the word " Go," were off again as before. The lieutenant and his bay went down the track at the same breakneck pace as before, and he appeared unable to turn his horse until far beyond the stake. This time he took a sweeping circle, in his frantic efforts to guide his horse, away to the right, and horse and rider suddenly disappeared from view. It looked as though the ground had opened and swallowed them. The doctor turned the stake in fine style and was on the home stretch as his opponent disappeared into the ground, and as he saw nothing of it continued to ply whip and spur to the " Cat " until he passed the winning pole amid the cheers of the crowd. On the sudden disappearance of Dacey and his horse several horsemen present rode over to ascertain what became of him. As they approached the spot they found both rider and horse stalled in a cellar of a deserted camp; owing to the snow that covered the vicinity he failed to see the hole until it was too late. In a short time the lieutenant was again on his steed, neither of them the worse for the tumble. The doctor won the stakes but magnanimously offered to run the last heat again if Dacey was dissatisfied at the decision. The lieutenant said he had all of that kind of horse-racing that he wanted. If the doctor would run a straight race he was ready for him. The surgeon replied to this proposition as follows : " Tim, I would like to accommodate you very much, but you see the ' Cat ' *isn't a straight heat horse.*" This was said with a chuckle peculiar to the doctor and it produced a broad grin on all who heard it. As for Dacey he dashed off at a canter somewhat disgusted with his defeat.

The Irish Brigade, which was encamped about two miles from the Ninth, entered into the celebration of St. Patrick's day on a grand scale. Their sports consisted of a steeple chase and hurdle races with various athletic games. In the evening theatricals and recitations were furnished by the talent in the various regiments. Songs and poetry were also a part of their program. General Hooker and staff enjoyed their hospitalities during the celebration.

March 21, 1863, an order was issued from the Headquarters of the Army of the Potomac, obliging each officer and soldier to wear on the top and centre of his cap a corps badge, in order that the corps and division of the wearer could be, on sight, recognized. It would likewise serve the purpose of showing the corps and division of those slain in battle, etc. They were designed as follows : A circular piece of cloth or leatherette, one and a half inches in diameter, was the badge of the First Corps ; a trefoil or shamrock was the badge of the Second Corps ; a diamond shape was that of the Third Corps ; a maltese cross represented the Fifth Corps ; a Greek cross was for the Sixth Corps ; a crescent shape badge was for the Eleventh Corps ; a five-pointed star marked the Twelfth Corps. The 1st division was red, the 2d division was white, and the 3d division was blue. These were for the Army of the Potomac as organized under General Hooker at this time.

The corps and division reviews in the month of March were followed by the grand review of the army by the President on the 8th of April, 1863. The soldiers were always interested in Abraham Lincoln. He was the guiding star of the Union. He was to them like the North star, always in the same place. Changes were constantly going on, but to the army " Honest Old Abe " never changed. He was loved and revered by every one from the highest general to the lowest private. It was enough for them to know that he was true to the cause for which all were ready to die. It was a great satisfaction for the army to stand and look at the President. They would gaze without a murmur as long as Abraham Lincoln remained in view. As the troops passed in review every eye was kindly, lovingly turned towards him. His tall form and silk hat as he sat on horseback were ever in their mind's eye. His face was engraved on their hearts. The news that the President was with us, and going to review the army, was enough to make every one feel pleasant, and with great alacrity every man prepared himself by a thorough and general cleaning up of uniforms and equipments, etc., as if each, individually, was going to be inspected by the President. So on the 8th of April when the army turned out on parade they looked magnificent. God only knows what was passing through the brain of our sad-faced President as he sat on his horse almost motionless gazing on those splendid columns of divisions of veteran infantry with their guns and equipments glittering in the sun as they marched past him with the step of one man until all that vast army of 100,000 men had disappeared in their camps. " Will the next engagement be a victory ! or will it be another disastrous defeat of this grand army?" A question such as this may have passed through the mind of the President as he offered up a prayer to the God of the Christians for the success of the army and the Union. After this noted review every soldier knew that the campaign would soon open and that another general engagement was near at hand.

The men of the Ninth were blessed and fortified, while in this camp, by hearing Mass celebrated by Father Tissot, chaplain of the 37th New York (Irish Rifles). Every opportunity was given to our men to attend to their religious duties by Father Tissot, whose kindly smile, and pleasant words and instructions, won the love and respect of all. Since Father Scully was obliged to retire from the service as chaplain of the Ninth on account of disability incurred while a prisoner of war, we had not as yet been favored with another in his stead. On that account Father Tissot's voluntary attention and services were greatly appreciated by us. The opportunity to attend to their religious duties at this time and place was of great spiritual benefit and consolation to the regiment.

The Ninth had the honor of being presented with a beautiful green silk flag, at this camp, by Gen. Thomas Francis Meagher, commanding the Irish Brigade. It was somewhat of a surprise to the regiment at large, although Colonel Guiney knew that it was coming. In the afternoon General Meagher, and part of his staff, arrived at the Ninth headquarters with the flag, and immediately the regiment was turned out and formed into " hollow " square, with General Meagher and Colonel Guiney and staffs inside. General Meagher made a neat speech of presentation, which was replied to by Colonel Guiney in acceptance. The regiment was then dismissed. The history of this particular green flag is this : It was originally intended for the 29th Massachusetts volunteers, a regiment which was attached to the Irish Brigade about six months. As General Meagher wished to have each regiment of his brigade carry an Irish flag, this one for the 29th Massachusetts was made at the time the three others were for his three New York regiments. When Lieut-Col. J. H. Barnes, who commanded the 29th Massachusetts, learned of the green flag for his regiment he refused to carry it, as he claimed his regiment was not an Irish regiment. (Irishmen by birth and descent were members of it, to a certain extent, as they were, more or less, in all Massachusetts regiments.) Under these circumstances the flag was withheld from the 29th and afterwards transformed — by taking out the silk threads which made the figure 2 — into a Ninth Massachusetts flag. As everything else about it was suitable it was turned over, as described, to Colonel Guiney's " Irish Ninth " regiment. The regiment carried it until it was tattered and torn by shot and shell in the storms of many battles. It now stands in Doric Hall, State House, Boston, Mass., with our other battleflags.

At this camp Maj. George W. Dutton resigned on account of wounds received and left the regiment, much to the regret of officers and men. He subsequently served with distinction, with the rank of Major, in the Veteran Reserve Corps.

MAJOR GEORGE W. DUTTON.

Major Dutton was born in Cambridge, Mass., Dec. 7, 1839. His father, William P. Dutton, was a native of Boston where the Dutton families for past generations belong. When he was two years of age his parents removed to Boston. There he received his education in the public schools. At the breaking out of the rebellion he was elected captain of Company K, Ninth Massachusetts Volunteers. He participated in all the battles of the Peninsula campaign, and was severely wounded at the battle of Malvern Hill, July 1, 1862, being shot by a minie ball through the left thigh. Upon his return to the regiment in the following December he was promoted major. After Fredericksburg and the " mud march " his wound broke out and disabled him to such an extent that he felt obliged to retire from active field service and he resigned March 29, 1863. He was reappointed as major in the Veteran Reserve Corps where he served till mustered out in July, 1866.

Major Dutton was in command of the old Capitol Prison in Washington, D.C.   He had many noted prisoners in his charge.   Among them were Henry Wirz, the Andersonville prison-keeper, who was hanged there; Mrs. Mary E. Surratt, and those implicated in the assassination of President Lincoln.   He was in command of the detachment which had charge of four of the assassins when they were taken to the Dry Tortugas.

During Major Dutton's service in the Ninth Massachusetts Volunteers he proved himself to be an intelligent and brave officer under every trial, and when he left the regiment he carried with him the respect and esteem of all its officers and men.   At the present day he still retains these kindly feelings among the survivors of the regiment. He has always been active at the reunions of the Ninth Massachusetts, and at the present time (1898) is the honored president of the association.

CHAPTER XVI.

THE BATTLE OF CHANCELLORSVILLE.

THE STRENGTH OF BOTH ARMIES — OUR FIRST AGGRESSIVE MOVEMENT —
OUR ARMY ON THE MOVE — PROFESSOR LOWE'S BALLOON — JACKSON'S
FLANK MOVEMENT — THE ELEVENTH CORPS ROUTED — THE MIDNIGHT
BATTLE — DEATH OF "STONEWALL" JACKSON — THE ASSAULT AT
HAZEL GROVE — GENERAL HOOKER INJURED — THE ARMY FALLS
BACK — CHANCELLORSVILLE HOUSE ON FIRE — THE SIXTH CORPS
MOVEMENTS — THE FIFTH CORPS — CROSSING ELY'S FORD — GENERAL
GRIFFIN'S DIVISION WAITING FOR ORDERS — HEARING DISTANT BATTLES
— LEE'S ARMY DIVIDED AND GIVING BATTLE — CONSULTATIONS OF
GENERALS — GENERAL COUCH IN COMMAND — RECROSSING THE RIVER
— FIFTH CORPS REAR GUARD — LIST OF CASUALTIES AND LOSSES —
WORDS OF PRAISE FOR THE FIFTH CORPS — OFFICERS AND MEN OF
THE NINTH COMMENDED BY THEIR COLONEL.

> " What though the field be lost!
> All is not lost — the unconquerable will,
> And study of revenge, immortal hate,
> And courage never to submit or yield :
> And what is else not to be overcome."
>
> MILTON.

PRESIDENT LINCOLN found the Army of the Potomac after his late review to be in splendid condition. The commander of the army — General Hooker — received great credit for the work that he and his subordinate generals had accomplished in this direction. The " morning report " at army headquarters showed an aggregate of 130,000 men, covering all branches of the service. The *effective men* represented in this aggregate report were far below this number, particularly in the infantry branch of the service, *present for duty and carrying guns.* The non-effectives would cover at least twenty-five per cent of the aggregate.

Without going into the details of our daily routine life it will be sufficient to say that the usual camp, picket and fatigue duties — with which the non-military reader is now somewhat familiar — were performed from day to day, in the month of April, with army regularity. Unmistakable signs in the various departments of the army, daily pointed to preparations for the movement which occurred on the 27th of that month. When the order came to march every officer and soldier present was prepared for it.

General Lee's Confederate army still occupied their old grounds along the heights in front of Fredericksburg. He was credited with 60,000 effective men (estimated). It would seem that the wily old general was patiently waiting and watching for the opening of the spring campaign by the Union forces. General Hooker had submitted his plans of attack, on the 11th of April, to the President and they had received his approval. The first aggressive movement was to be made by the cavalry corps (10,000 men), under command of General Stoneman. He commenced to move forward, as directed, on Monday, April 13, 1863. On account of heavy rain and swollen river, etc., the bulk of his command — he claimed — was obliged to remain in the vicinity of Warrenton Junction, on the Orange & Alexandria railroad, until the 29th of April. He then crossed the Rappahannock river at Kelly's Ford, sixteen days after his orders to march.

The President and General Hooker, who were in constant correspondence, were much annoyed at the delay of General Stoneman. According to General Hooker's plans the cavalry was expected to proceed some eighty-five miles south and keep between General Lee's army and the city of Richmond, destroying, in the meantime, the railroad and other communications. He was expected to cross the Rappahannock above the railroad bridge on the 13th; proceed thence to Culpepper and Gordonsville and across the Richmond & Fredericksburg railroad in the vicinity of Hanover Court House. This latter move would place him within a few miles of Richmond. On the 8th of May the President telegraphed to General Hooker that Richmond might have been taken. There were no organized bodies of troops in the city. Had General Stoneman known it while on this raid, he could have captured the city and President Davis, and destroyed everything of value.

April 15, the President wrote General Hooker in regard to General Stoneman's delay saying, among other things, "I do not know that any better can be done but I greatly fear it is another failure already. Write me often, I am very anxious."

Notwithstanding this disappointment by the cavalry, General Hooker, without regard to it, moved his infantry, artillery, etc., on the 27th of April.

The details of the movements of the Army of the Potomac, from April 27 to May 6, from hour to hour and day to day, in all their minutiæ, including the same by the Confederate army, would fill a volume, and be of little interest only to those of military training. The latter, when they desire it, can refer to the official reports. What follows here is a *résumé* of many of the principal events that occurred, from day to day, until the end of a disastrous movement, which, at the start, presaged a glorious close of the war in Virginia.

The Fifth, Eleventh and Twelfth Corps on reaching Kelly's ford were to move across the river on pontoons — General Slocum in command — and concentrate at Chancellorsville — ten miles west of Fredericksburg. After exhaustive marches and wet and muddy bivouacs, this large body of infantry arrived in the vicinity of Chancellorsville on the 30th of April (Thursday). The First, Third and Sixth Corps were to act as the left wing, under command of General Sedgwick of the Sixth Corps. He was instructed to cross the river below Fredericksburg, in the vicinity of General Franklin's old pontoon bridge landing, and form in front of General Lee's army, which was still in its old camp, and hold it there under orders by all the strategy at his command. The Second Corps held a temporary position at Banks' ford, while one division of it remained, also temporary, at Falmouth. These troops were in easy supporting distance of General Sedgwick. General Hooker intended by a simultaneous movement of his right and left wings to engage General Lee on the flank and rear from Chancellorsville, and on his front from Fredericksburg, and by rapid fighting and tactics crush the enemy at once, or drive him south and take Richmond. General Sedgwick didn't succeed in holding the enemy at the heights. On the contrary General Lee, having gained information of Hooker's movements on his left and rear, on the 30th, withdrew General Jackson's corps from the heights, leaving General Early's division and General Barksdale's brigade to hold the hills of Fredericksburg. About 11 o'clock A.M., Friday, May 1, his army reached General Anderson's position, confronting Hooker's advanced lines, near the Tabernacle church on the plank road. General Lee had here two divisions of Longstreet's corps (General Longstreet was absent at, or below, Petersburg with the rest of his corps) and Jackson's corps of four divisions — Early's division and Barksdale's brigade still remaining at the heights — and one hundred and seventy pieces of artillery. Friday afternoon, May 1, General Jackson threw out a strong skirmish line and advanced slowly and steadily until nightfall without bringing on an engagement. His object was to learn, as near as possible, the exact direction and position of Hooker's line of battle. General Sykes' division of the Fifth Corps was in position on the old Turnpike road, about two miles east of the Chancellorsville house, when the enemy were advancing. In order to avoid being flanked Sykes' division fell back to Chancellorsville onto the main line while skirmishing with the enemy in his front.

General Sedgwick's command at Fredericksburg remained, comparatively speaking, inactive. General Couch's Second Corps was ordered from Banks' ford on Thursday, the 30th of April; it crossed at United States ford, and joined the right wing on the afternoon of the 1st of May. On the night of the 30th, General Sickles' Third Corps was ordered up, and crossed the United States ford early on the morning of the 1st, and was in position on the Plank road near Chancellorsville that afternoon. General Sedgwick's command was still inactive; the First Corps was ordered around to the right wing, and arrived there on the night of the 2d. This left only the Sixth Corps — the largest corps in the army, about 22,000 men — under the command of General Sedgwick. The main body of General Lee's army was now in position to the south of Hooker. General Hooker's line of battle, May 2, Saturday, was facing south. The right and left flanks were resting across the Plank road. The Eleventh Corps held the right flank, the Twelfth Corps was next; the Fifth Corps next; the Second Corps next. The two last mentioned corps lay across, and in vicinity of the Plank road, facing mostly to the left flank and west of the Chancellorsville house, with the Third Corps in support. General Lee's position was a mile or more south of our line.

Saturday morning, May 2, General Jackson with three divisions — Generals A. P. Hill's, Colston's and Rhodes' — moved out from his line of battle on one of the most daring — not to say reckless — manœuvres that only men who considered themselves in desperate straits would think of undertaking. He moved by a circuitous route by the Brock road, on a parallel with and three miles from our line, and reached the Plank road late in the afternoon.

At noontime General Birney's division, which had held a portion of the line of battle between the left flank of the Eleventh Corps and the right flank of the Twelfth Corps since early morning, was ordered to the front to reconnoitre the movement of Jackson's corps as it went off to the west and south towards the Brock road. As Birney's division went forward a gap was left between the Eleventh and Twelfth Corps. General Birney's command took up its new position northwest of Catharpian road, near the Furnace, in front of the enemy's (General Anderson's) right. Excepting an artillery fire of shells on Jackson's moving columns he was allowed to continue his march unmolested. At this time Professor Low's balloon was up a thousand feet in the air at Fredericksburg, north side of the river, with two individuals in it taking observations through powerful field glasses. The occupants of the balloon were Professor Low, and Sergt. Edward S. Dewey of Company G, 10th Massachusetts Volunteers (afterward a lieutenant in the 57th Massachusetts Volunteers), who had been permanently detailed for that service. He was an artist in sketching, and all that he saw in his daily observations worthy of note was taken down and sent to army headquarters. On this particular day — Saturday, May 2, 1863 — he wrote several messages dictated by Professor Low relative to the long column of· the enemy making a detour to the south and west towards the right flank of the army. These communications he dropped, with a stone for a weight wrapped up in them, to the officer in command of the detail below who had charge of the cables that held the balloon in position. These messages were sent to General Hooker's headquarters. How much further this information went Lieutenant Dewey never knew; but it is his opinion that it was the first knowledge that General Hooker received of the enemy's flank movement. If, as it has been asserted, General Hooker came to the conclusion that General Lee's army was in retreat to Gordonsville, it is a sad reflection to say that he was egregiously mistaken. By this desperate movement of Jackson, General Lee's army of 60,000 men was, on that day, scattered many miles apart.

Halting on a line with our right flank, in the vicinity of the junction of the Brock and Plank roads, General Jackson deployed his position of attack in three division lines — Rhodes first, Colston second, A. P. Hill third — within a mile of the right flank of the Eleventh Corps. General Howard, with three divisions in his corps in line of battle before the enemy, had few or no pickets out in this direction. His troops had virtually gone into bivouac; arms were stacked, equipments off, cooking going on, cattle being butchered, and his command in that sort of disorder incidental to complete rest under expected orders to move with plenty of time to prepare for it. General Jackson accompanied by other officers rode forward on the Plank road in front of his own lines, and calmly surveyed the scene before him, with great satisfaction, unmolested. About 5 o'clock P.M. he gave the order to charge on thousands of temporarily unarmed and unsuspecting victims who composed the Eleventh Corps. Forward the enemy marched! Forward they double-quicked! Forward they rushed to the charge! through clearings and woods in solid lines, giving their high pitched "rebel yell" as on they went into Howard's 1st division. Under shot and bayonet Howard's unarmed soldiers scattered, fell and ran in wild disorder, carrying the 3d division with them as they rushed on and into it, pell mell towards Chancellorsville and adjacent territory. The 2d and last division attempted to form line and check the wildly fleeing troops of their own corps but in vain; they, too, were swept onward and away by the headlong flight of thousands, closely followed by the pursuing columns of Jackson's yelling "foot cavalry." General Sickles, on surveying the scene at a distance, realized the situation at once, and promptly brought forward the Third Corps to check the rout. General Pleasanton joined in with cavalry and artillery, as did General Williams with the Twelfth Corps, meeting and repulsing the enemy until the panic in the Eleventh Corps gradually died out. The enemy continued to hold the temporary earthworks lately occupied by the Eleventh Corps, and for several hours after dark kept up a heavy fire into our lines. This was answered by our artillery shelling the woods and clearings occupied by the enemy until late in the night.

General Sickles gained the consent of Generals Slocum and Hooker to form his lines for an attack on the enemy at 11 o'clock P.M. Under a bright moon and a clear night his brigades charged forward on the enemy now massed in the open space about Dowdall's Tavern. Our troops were met with a terrific fire from infantry and artillery as they charged successfully forward and gained the house and Plank road and captured the breastworks. The enemy was brave and persistent and made a daring counter-assault, but they were met by men equally as brave and determined and were wholly repulsed and driven back into the woods, and held there by our magnificent artillery. This midnight attack by General Sickles was successfully accomplished by 2 o'clock A.M.

After General Jackson's assault on the Eleventh Corps, he went forward with Gen. A. P. Hill's division to relieve Generals Rhodes' and Colston's divisions. Proceeding down the Plank road towards our lines he and his escort were fired upon. He and his party then turned back and as they rode towards their own lines, it is claimed, they were fired upon by their own men. The first volley killed two of his escort. On the second volley General Jackson was wounded in both hands and in his left arm. Under an artillery fire from our guns he was, with much difficulty in the darkness, carried to the rear. General Jackson's arm was amputated. He gradually sank under his wounds and died the following Sunday, May 10, 1863. His death was greatly mourned by General Lee and his whole army.

Gen. A. P. Hill succeeded to the command of Jackson's corps, and was wounded in the midnight battle which followed; Hill was succeeded by Gen. J. E. B. Stuart.

Two divisions of the Third Corps, and Barlow's brigade of the Eleventh Corps, now held the high ground at Hazel Grove after the midnight battle. At sunrise the next morning — Sunday the 3d of May — Hazel Grove was abandoned by orders from General Hooker. General Stuart, now commanding Jackson's old corps, was on the alert, and advanced on our retiring troops with his three divisions. His fierce assaults and charges were handsomely repulsed by our forces as they fell back on the new line of battle and intrenchments along the skirt of the woods at Fairview near the Plank road and to the west of Chancellorsville.

The First Corps held the right; the Fifth Corps was next; the Third Corps next; the Twelfth Corps next; the Second Corps next and the Eleventh Corps next on the left near the bend of the Rappahannock river. The right and left flank lines were thrown back thus leaving the convex centre in front at Fairview. The Third, Twelfth and Second Corps bore the brunt of the battle and the heavy assaults of General Lee's army.

General Stuart was quick to take possession of Hazel Grove, an elevated position, and, as it proved, the key to the situation. Here he planted his batteries which did great execution. General Stuart assumed the aggressive, with the assistance of Generals McLaws and Anderson, and his assaults and charges on our lines were fierce and fearful with much slaughter. General Hooker lay for a long time that morning, inert and insensible, at the Chancellorsville house from an injury received from a cannon shot that struck a pillar of the house where he was standing. No one was directed to take command of the army all this time and the attacks of the enemy were met and repulsed, in a sort of random way, by those generals receiving the assaults. To add to this discomfiture our lines, in many places, were short of ammunition. The troops fell back at the centre and vicinity by default of proper generalship. Through this neglect, likewise, the First, Fifth and Eleventh Corps were all this time comparatively out of the fight. Reinforcements were sadly needed, and loudly called for, by those in action, but there was no response to these demands. None were sent. There appeared to be no responsible head to order them forward to save the day. It is claimed that General Couch, the senior general on the field, was uninformed of General Hooker's disability, or in any way ordered to assume command of the forces during this direful necessity. After several hours spent in gaining a recovery General Hooker again took command, but his injuries were more severe than were supposed; so much so, in fact, that he was in no condition to properly direct so great a charge as that of commander of the gallant army which was being defeated in detail before his eyes for lack of proper generalship by one able man. When General Hooker appeared, portions of his army had been for hours without reinforcements, stemming the fierce and well directed assaults of Lee's well-nigh exhausted brigades, and he now found his line of battle in a dreadful state of chaotic disorder and uncertainty.

General Hooker ordered all his army corps to fall back north of the Chancellorsville house and formed a new position towards the river which extended over and covered the ground from Ely's and United States fords. This movement took place between 1 and 2 o'clock P.M., Sunday. The change of position left the Chancellorsville House and adjacent territory between both armies. The house, tents, and grounds and outlying woods, were filled with wounded in the thousands when the building took fire from the shells that struck it. The woods caught fire likewise and a large number of the helpless wounded were burned to death; some few were rescued, and many escaped by their individual exertions. The fire burned with terrible force, sending up great volumes of smoke, and the crash of timbers amid the loud roar of the flames, that spread all over the great house, drowned the shrieks and cries of those who perished helpless with their painful wounds in the flames. The fire spread into the forest for miles and caught in a death trap hundreds of wounded soldiers who were unable to move from where they lay. This terrible scene added new horrors to the battlefield and forced a truce on the contending lines that would otherwise have fought until darkness closed the battle.

GENERAL SEDGWICK'S SIXTH CORPS.

About 11 o'clock on the night of the 2d of May (Saturday) General Sedgwick moved up the river to Fredericksburg, by orders from General Hooker, to take the line of march to Chancellorsville, on the road from the city, and to destroy any forces he might meet. At daylight he reached Fredericksburg, after a tedious night's march.

The Sixth Corps now numbered about 22,000 men. General Early held the heights, Lee's old position, with 8500 men. At 11 o'clock Sunday morning, in beautiful weather, the Sixth Corps assaulted the heights on flank and front and carried them handsomely.

The enemy broke and ran in great disorder. Sedgwick having no cavalry, pursuit was out of the question; 1000 prisoners, several battle-flags and pieces of artillery were captured. The Sixth Corps lost in this assault about 1000 men in killed and wounded. Advancing his corps four miles to Salem church — a two-story brick building — he met the enemy in position — a part of Lee's troops withdrawn from Hooker's front to reinforce Early — and became immediately engaged; the battle lasted till dark. The Sixth Corps lost about 1500 men in killed and wounded in this fight.

That night, May 3, General Lee withdrew McLaws' and Anderson's divisions from General Hooker's left front to reinforce Early. The next morning they opened on the Sixth Corps with all their available strength and drove it towards the river in the vicinity of Banks' Ford. General Lee had evidently determined that, at all costs, Sedgwick's force should be prevented from joining Hooker.

While vainly expecting aid from Hooker, Sedgwick received, instead, orders to cross the river. Falling back to the river under cover of the night he crossed Banks' ford at 2 o'clock A.M. of the 5th of May, after repulsing several assaults of the enemy, who had in the meantime about completely surrounded his troops to the river front. The total loss in the Sixth Corps were 4610 in killed, wounded and captured.

MOVEMENTS OF THE FIFTH CORPS.

When the troops of the Fifth Corps left their camps on the 27th day of April, 1863, to engage in the Chancellorsville movement they were instructed by General Orders No. 15, to move in the following order: General Sykes' division at 10 o'clock A.M.; General Griffin's division at 11 A.M., and General Humphreys' division at 12 M. Each division to be supplied with eight days' rations in haversacks and knapsacks and to be accompanied by only one battery and two ambulances and a packtrain of small arm ammunition. In order to conceal the movements of the troops from the enemy the usual duty calls by drum and bugle were suspended. Only small fires for cooking purposes were allowed.

The Ninth Massachusetts under command of Colonel Guiney left camp about 11 o'clock A.M. on the 27th of April, 1863, in heavy marching order and joined the 2d brigade, 1st division, Fifth Corps, on the route to Chancellorsville. That night the regiment bivouacked in the vicinity of Hartwood Church after a nine miles' tramp from our old camp at Stoneman's Switch.

After a toilsome march of eighteen miles in rain and mud we went into bivouac near Kelly's ford on the Rappahannock river on the night of the 28th and early the next morning crossed the river on a pontoon bridge; continuing the march for sixteen miles we reached Ely's ford on the Rapidan river in the latter part of the afternoon (the 29th). Two squadrons of our cavalry, which were in the advance, crossed the ford and drove off the enemy's cavalry, a small force that was reconnoitring in that section of the country. General Humphreys' (3d) division of our corps was left at Kelly's ford on detached duty with the ammunition and ambulance trains, and pontoon bridges. His division joined the corps a few days later.

The Rapidan river is a feeder to the Rappahannock and runs easterly into it from the Blue Ridge mountains, where it has its source.

Kelly's ford on the Rappahannock is about twenty-five miles northwest from Fredericksburg. After crossing this ford we returned south to the Rapidan, to Ely's ford, which is near the famous but detestable Wilderness through which we had to march before reaching the Chancellorsville house.

General Hooker intended that Stoneman's cavalry should sweep the enemy's cavalry from this quarter, that is, from Culpepper to Gordonsville and beyond, and prevent it from communicating with General Lee at Fredericksburg. As it was, General Lee did not get any definite reports that General Hooker's *infantry* was northwest of Fredericksburg until the 30th of April.

At Ely's ford the water was three to four feet or more deep, and had to be waded by the infantry. On arriving at the ford the order to cross this swift, narrow and deep-running stream set the tongues of a thousand men wagging, all in good nature. As it was " go as you please," every one on foot in the regiment stripped off their lower garments, and, raising their personal effects, guns, equipments, etc., high in air, waded, splashed and stumbled through the icy cold water of the Rapidan as it came clear and swift from the mountain springs of the Blue Ridge in the distance. The scene at the ford was one of great hilarity. Hundreds of men were scattered on the bank, in the water, and on the other side of the stream, laughing, talking and shouting, as they entered the cold water or landed on the opposite side. Having successfully passed through the water ordeal each man dropped his personal effects on the ground preparatory to a reorganization of his scattered habiliments.

Cavalry " life savers " were posted a short way down the stream to catch any short or tall man who got carried away by the swift current; before the two divisions had passed over there were several luckless fellows went down all over to be quietly fished up by the horsemen, who did their duty kindly and promptly, and thereby gained friendship with the "dough boys." "I'll never say a hard word against a cavalry man again, in the army or out of it," said one of our men as a horseman deftly fished up a garment which was floating rapidly down stream, and passed it to the above-mentioned infantry-man, who, while he stood waist-deep in the river, was more than pleased to receive his clothing, dripping wet as it was.

That night two divisions of our corps, the 1st and 2d, crossed the ford, made their camp-fires, and remained in bivouac till morning. The rain poured during the night and the rivulets that ran in all directions wet the skin of many a veteran as he slept, unconscious of the elements.

General Meade, the Fifth Corps commander, sent out at early dawn of the 30th of April one squadron of cavalry in the direction of Chancellorsville, and one squadron to take the road to United States ford. The latter place was to be a position of great importance to our army, as it was the key to the river crossing nearest to Chancellors-ville. The cavalry was instructed to drive the enemy, when found, out of these sections. A few hours after daylight the infantry were pre-pared to follow in the same direction.

General Griffin, commanding our 1st division, was ordered to push on his infantry and artillery to Chancellorsville, where we arrived, after a long tramp through the woods, at 11 o'clock A.M. General Sykes, commanding the 2d division, in accordance with orders marched to United States ford and found the communications with our forces under General Couch, on the other side of the river, all clear. He then turned his column towards Chancellorsville and joined General Griffin at that place. Chancellorsville was simply a large brick and wood dwelling, or country mansion, situated in a clearing of a hundred acres, surrounded by woods, thickets and forests. The Wilderness borders on the north and east of it. Our division went into bivouac on the southeast side of the house. During the afternoon the 1st brigade of our division — to which the 18th and 22d Massachusetts belonged — was ordered out to support the cavalry in an affair to open the road to Banks' ford. On the old turnpike road in the direction of Fredericksburg, about two miles from Chancellorsville, they struck two brigades of the enemy on high ground, posted with artillery com-manding the road and vicinity. After a light skirmish the brigade was ordered to withdraw without forcing the enemy; it returned through the woods and joined the division now in line of battle.

The Eleventh and Twelfth Corps had crossed the Rapidan river by way of Germanna ford and arrived at Chancellorsville about 2 o'clock P.M. on the 30th and were assigned to their position in the line of battle on the right of the Fifth Corps, by General Slocum.

General Hooker arrived at Chancellorsville from his late head-quarters at Falmouth on the evening of the 30th. Early on the morning of May 1 General Humphreys, with his 3d division, arrived and took his place in line with the Fifth Corps.

On the morning of May 1 in a general movement of the Fifth and Twelfth Corps to uncover Banks' ford, which is about three miles and a half from Fredericksburg, General Griffin's division, followed by General Humphreys', proceeded on the river road and had reached Decker's house, within view of Banks' ford, without meeting any of the enemy, when they were recalled by orders from the commanding general. On its return march Griffin's division was ordered to halt and form line of battle through the woods on the right of Hancock's division of the Second Corps, lately arrived to support Sykes' division, the sound of whose artillery and infantry fire could be now heard engaged with the enemy on the old turnpike road in advance of every-thing.

General Meade's corps was ordered to occupy a line from Chancellorsville to the river. About 6 o'clock P.M. Sykes' division, in order to avoid being flanked completely by Lee's approaching army, fell back to the main line near Chancellorsville. The Twelfth Corps advanced on the Plank road to the right and rear of Sykes and felt the enemy's lines as it fell back further south.

Hancock's division had followed Sykes' when it fell back. Humphreys' 3d division had likewise returned to the main line. General Griffin, with our 1st division, by some mischance failed to receive any orders. He soon discovered, while in line of battle in the woods, that the troops which he was supposed to be connected with could not be felt on either flank. From the sounds that reached his ear he knew that the enemy was in force off on his flank and front. It was a moonlight night and not as dark in the woods as it otherwise might have been. We marched cautiously and counter-marched between long halts, standing in line and listening to the noise of the enemy to the south and west of us. General Griffin, who was a trained and brave officer, was evidently waiting and expecting positive orders to fall back. About midnight he concluded to move west in the direction of Chancellorsville. The division marched with as little noise as possible and reached the line of the Fifth Corps early in the gray of the morning, much to the surprise and pleasure of the rest of the Fifth Corps, which was on the anxious seat as to our actual whereabouts all that night. May 2, Saturday, was mostly occupied in throwing up earthworks, fortified with logs and abatis, on our line of battle on the left, facing south-southeast. Towards sunset, between 5 and 6 o'clock, the general stillness that prevailed was suddenly broken by the sound of the distant shrill " rebel yell," so familiar to the veteran's ear. The time was recognized as " Stonewall " Jackson's favorite hour for a charge in force. Musketry firing was followed by an incessant heavy fire of artillery which was kept up for several hours. The latter proved to be the repulse of General Jackson's flank attack on the Eleventh Corps. The Fifth Corps was ready for any emergency, but the gradual dying out of the artillery fire was evidence that the battle was about over and our assistance not required. The music of the band of the regulars at this time of night allayed all apprehension of any suspected disastrous attack on our right flank. Between the hours of 11 o'clock and midnight a terrific musketry and artillery fire from the same quarter as the battle in the early evening greeted our astonished ears. We were quickly under arms awaiting the unexpected. The fight that we heard lasted till 2 o'clock A.M. It proved to be General Sickles' gallant attack for the rescue of Berry's division, and the recovery of the ground lost by the Eleventh Corps. It turned out to be a brilliant success ; besides retaking all our guns and caissons and a portion of Whipple's mule train, two pieces of the enemy's artillery and three caissons were captured. The night of the 2d and early morning of the 3d of May, the Fifth Corps fell back on the new line of battle and occupied a position from Chandler's house, along the road that led to Ely's ford,→ Sykes' division on the right; Griffin's next, and Humphreys' in rear of Sykes' on the reserve; the First Corps on the right of the Fifth. This line was strengthened by throwing up earthworks.

At daybreak Sunday, 3d, a heavy battle opened on our right and front at Fairview in front of the Third Corps, supported by the Twelfth and Second Corps. General Stuart, with Jackson's old corps (General Jackson having been dangerously wounded on the night of the 2d), had gained possession of Hazel Grove and opened on the Third Corps with aggressive fierceness. General Sickles called for reinforcements ; none were sent, although the First, Fifth and Eleventh Corps were comparatively idle. General Hooker was wounded, sick, out of condition. There was no head to direct. General Couch was next in command by seniority, but did not receive any official information of

Hooker's disability. On that account, for several hours of the conflict, the army was without an active commander. Generals Sickles and Slocum fell back, reformed and fought again and again, persistently followed by the much exhausted enemy. Between 1 and 2 o'clock P.M. General Hooker, having partially recovered, ordered all the corps back to a new line of battle covering United States ford, with both flanks on the river; a position that could neither be enfiladed nor flanked. This rear movement was a surprise to everyone and looked upon as a disastrous affair. It placed the Chancellorsville house between both armies. The house took fire from the shells thrown into it and burned to the ground. It set fire to the woods and thickets and burned hundreds of our helpless wounded.

General Stuart in command of Jackson's old corps was about the only force in front of our army of five corps. His line of battle was concealed for safety in the woods. Our batteries opened on it. Our brigades went forward to draw the enemy out of the forest. Stuart's troops would appear in sight and at once fall back into the woods again. Late in the afternoon our 2d brigade went forward to draw the enemy out of their cover. They came forward a short ways pretending to meet our advance, then broke as they were charged upon and disappeared into the depths of the woods. The brigade fell back to avoid the artillery fire of the enemy and did it in such fine style as to draw cheers from the whole line as they quickly resumed their position. Owing to the low sweep of the field in this direction the fire from the enemy passed high overhead, thus letting our brigade off with slight injury.

While Lee with a part of his army, six miles away, was driving the Sixth Corps to the river, we lay supinely idle, with only Jackson's corps in our right front. The night was clear and bright with moonlight. During the night, at intervals, the enemy continued his ruse of threatened assaults by heavy picket firing.

General Hooker, in the meantime, maintained his long line of battle at the fords comparatively inactive and unmolested by any general assault. Late in the afternoon of the 5th of May rain followed the foggy weather and at night it fell in torrents. The trenches and low surface in the fields and roads were flooded. The poorly sheltered army during the night was in a wretchedly wet and sleepless condition, but still undismayed. Properly commanded they could, at that time, have been led to victory, defeated Lee's army, gone to Richmond, and ended the war in Virginia. General Hooker, sick and suffering from his injuries, had consulted his corps generals individually and collectively, without arriving at any decision satisfactory to himself or them. Evidently laboring under a heavy depression of spirits he sent for General Couch and ordered him to take command of the army and direct its movements across the river. Then General Hooker at once proceeded across the pontoon bridge to seek much-needed rest and medical treatment at his old headquarters at Falmouth. At dark on the night of the 5th the army commenced to move at a snail's pace, through rain and mud, towards the two pontoon bridges at United States ford. All night long corps followed corps in the steady downpour over the swift-running and flooded river. The river torrent threatened at times to sweep the pontoons from their fastenings. Only the skill and hard work of our engineers saved the bridges from destruction.

The morning of the 6th of May dawned on the Fifth Corps as it moved forward from its line of battle as the rear guard of the slowly retreating army. About 8 o'clock A.M. we reached the northern bank of the river and were ordered to push on to our old camp. This we did with much labor over the wretched muddy roads for about eight miles, arriving in camp near Stoneman's Switch about noon. That night the Army of the Potomac slept in their old camps, and for the first time since the 27th of April they secured a good night's rest and a square army supper.

CASUALTIES AT CHANCELLORSVILLE IN THE NINTH REGIMENT MASSACHUSETTS VOLUNTEERS, APRIL 27, 1863, TO MAY 6, 1863.

List of Wounded.

COMPANY A.

Privates James McCabe, Angus McDonald.

COMPANY C.

Private John Fleming.

COMPANY E.

Second Lieutenant Philip E. Redmond, died Sept. 17, 1863; Private Louis Webber.

COMPANY F.

Corporal James McLaughlin, Privates David Cashin, Cornelius Creeden, Thomas Gorman.

COMPANY H.

Private John Donnelly.

COMPANY I.

Privates Wm. Burns, Daniel McCarron, Patrick McAuliffe.

COMPANY K.

Private Thomas Clifford.

Total casualties, 14 men wounded.

CASUALTIES AT CHANCELLORSVILLE, VA., IN THE ARMY OF THE POTOMAC, APRIL 27, 1863, TO MAY 6, 1863.

Killed	1606
Wounded	9762
Captured and missing	5919
Total	17,287

CASUALTIES IN THE CONFEDERATE ARMY AT CHANCELLORSVILLE, VA.

Killed	1649
Wounded	9106
Captured and missing	1708
Total	12,463

Our 2d brigade lost 9 men killed, 2 officers and 44 men wounded, 7 missing and captured; aggregate, 62.

Our 1st division lost 1 officer and 16 men killed, 4 officers and 104 men wounded, 13 missing and captured; aggregate, 138.

The losses in the Fifth Corps were 6 officers and 63 men killed, 19 officers and 453 men wounded, 5 officers and 154 men captured and missing; aggregate, 700, which includes the 2d brigade and 1st division above mentioned.

This light list of casualties is accounted for, owing to the reason that the Fifth Corps was not regularly engaged.

Chancellorsville, like Fredericksburg, ended on the Union side in a dismal failure. Both of these defeats were brought about principally by a *lack of decisive generalship.* The Confederate generals won victory on the latter field (Chancellorsville) by skilful strategy, daring manœuvres and sleepless activity. Generals Lee and Jackson lived on the battlefield in the midst of their men. They ignored houses and mansions during their hours of danger. Neither did they linger around permanent headquarters miles in rear of their battle-lines. Wherever the advantage was to be gained during the hardest and the thickest of the battle they were to be found there, directing and encouraging their brave battalions. They were quick to see an advantage and to use their military skill in gaining the victory. With consummate strategy and tactics they fought their artillery and pushed forward their infantry by flank and front, regardless of the enemy's lines or numbers. Every knoll, every hill, every piece of rising ground, was seized and held with the tenacity of a bulldog. They stopped neither to eat, drink nor sleep, until the point they had in view was gained, and having won it they bent all their skill and strength to hold it against all comers. Their aggressive assaults and successes astounded General Hooker and seemed to paralyze whatever fighting qualities he possessed. He evidently looked for the immediate retreat of Lee's army to Gordonsville or further south towards Richmond. Hence the conclusion jumped at when Jackson's columns were reported on the move, apparently in that direction. He was undoubtedly as much surprised as General Howard or any of his subordinates, at the unlooked for assault on the right flank of his army and the Eleventh Corps. The President told General Hooker in emphatic words: "The next time you go into battle, *put in all your men.*"

Lee and Jackson fought with every man they had of 60,000, night and day, front, rear and flank, without rest.

Out of seven corps Hooker fought only four and some of the latter only partially. He was defeated in detail by generals abler than himself and whose persistent aggressiveness was wholly unlooked for. When he realized the situation he became despondent after his unfortunate injuries, and determined to recross the river before other failures overtook him. Without doubt General Hooker was physically exhausted by his labors and injuries and mentally overburdened with a task too great for his abilities as the commander of so large a body as the Army of the Potomac. Who knows but his retreat, under all the circumstances, was the best part of his judgment?

The Fifth Corps commander, General Meade, in his report on Chancellorsville, writes as follows: —

"To my division commanders, Major-General Sykes and Brigadier-Generals Humphreys and Griffin, I have to return my thanks for their prompt and hearty support throughout the ten days' campaign. To the men under their command I cannot adequately express the satisfaction with which I witnessed their ready and cheerful obedience to all orders, their submission to every privation and exposure, night marches in mud and rain, fording deep streams, using the axe and spade more than the musket, and ready at all times to go forward and meet the enemy. It is such service as this that tries and makes the real soldier.

* * * * * * * * * * *

"Finally, the conduct of the brigades of Griffin, the one advanced on the 30th and the other on the 4th, proved by their steadiness and coolness that this division only wanted a fair opportunity to show that the laurels acquired in so many previous fields were still fresh and undimmed."

On the 10th day of May, 1863, the following General Orders No. 3 was read to the Ninth Regiment at dress parade : —

HEADQUARTERS NINTH MASSACHUSETTS VOLUNTEERS, }
May 10, 1863. }

GENERAL ORDERS, }
No. 3. }

In the recent marches and in the subsequent battles which took place in the vicinity of Chancellorsville, the Colonel commanding expresses his profound gratification at the conduct of and disposition manifested by his command. It is true that the regiment was at no time engaged in any of the more serious conflicts from which this brigade was to a degree exempt by assignment to no less important but less hazardous duties in occupation of positions supporting and defending batteries that were showering death upon the foe. Still those qualities which made an undying name for the regiment during the ordeal of the Peninsula were perceptible in the alacrity, energy and intelligence with which every duty was performed. The Colonel commanding tenders his thanks to the following named officers for meritorious services : Lieutenant-Colonel Hanley, Adjutant Phalen, Captains Mahan, O'Hara, Roche, Tobin and Phelan. Also to the non-commissioned officers and men of Companies E, G and H, who, under their respective officers, gallantly repulsed a superior force of the enemy while on outpost duty.

By command of

COL. P. R. GUINEY.

(Signed)　M. W. PHALEN,
Adjutant.

CHAPTER XVII.

THE BATTLE OF GETTYSBURG.

THE ARMY OF THE POTOMAC NOT DESPONDENT — EXPIRATION OF SERVICE
IN SOME REGIMENTS — THE NINTH ON DUTY AT THE FORDS — CON-
FEDERATE ARMY REORGANIZED — CONFEDERATES MARCH INTO MARY-
LAND — THE UNION ARMY FOLLOWS — THE NINTH ON THE MARCH —
LOCATION OF OUR ARMY CORPS — GENERAL HOOKER RELIEVED AND
GENERAL MEADE IN COMMAND — ON THE MARCH TO GETTYSBURG —
THE FIRST DAY'S BATTLE — THE FIFTH CORPS AT GETTYSBURG —
THE NINTH MASSACHUSETTS AT BIG ROUND TOP — THE SECOND DAY'S
BATTLE — GENERAL LEE'S UNSUCCESSFUL ATTACKS — THE BATTLE ON
THE THIRD DAY — GENERAL PICKETT'S CONFEDERATE CHARGE —
GENERAL LEE'S RETREAT ACROSS THE POTOMAC RIVER — LOSSES IN
BATTLE ON BOTH SIDES.

* * * * * *

"But by her soldiers' graves Columbia proves
How fast toward morn the night of manhood moves.
Those low white lines at Gettysburg remain
The sacred record of her humblest slain,
Whose children's children in their time shall come
To view with pride their hero-father's tomb,
While down the ages runs the patriot line,
Till rich tradition makes each tomb a shrine.

* * * * * *

JOHN BOYLE O'REILLY. — "America."

THE rapidity with which the Army of the Potomac regained its
wonted spirits was not only marvellous but highly creditable to
its history as a brave and intelligent body of citizen soldiery.
Its infantry, artillery and cavalry, of one hundred thousand men,
never lost sight of the Union cause or experienced for a moment that
feeling of despondency which prevailed throughout the North after the
failure of the Chancellorsville campaign. The army looked forward to
the administration for the appointment of an able general to command
it; a general who would receive the respect and unqualified assistance
and obedience of his immediate subordinates. Without these indispensable requisites success was impossible for our army, when pitted

20

against the veteran leader of the Confederate forces and his brave supporters. While the army generally was confident of the retirement of General Hooker, they asked themselves with much concern, will the next commander of the Army of the Potomac be the right man in the right place? If so, one brilliant victory will repay us and our country for all that we have gone through with during the last six months. President Lincoln was a just man and slow to condemn another without ample reasons. Profiting by his past vast experience with military men and civilians in public life, he thoroughly investigated in his own way the inside history of the late disaster under General Hooker. He satisfied himself that a change of commanders must be made, and that his successor should come, for the good of the service, from among those generals on active duty in the Army of the Potomac.

Subsequent events proved that the selection made was the best that could be done to satisfy his advisers and to preserve the admirable loyalty and discipline that existed at that time in the grand Army of the Potomac. The active campaign of 1863, which augured so well at the commencement, had thus far only produced bitter fruit. The activity of the Confederate leader warned the administration that there was no time to be lost. Although the President didn't believe in " swapping horses when crossing a stream," yet of the two horns of the dilemma he must now choose the least. Under all the existing circumstances a new commander was imperatively necessary.

The delay in making the change was almost fatal. Luckily, the man selected was fitted for the hour; and nobly did he respond to every duty. Would that his subordinates, in every emergency, had met the issue as ably, bravely and faithfully as did General Meade on the field of Gettysburg.

The army, as one man, was now preparing to continue the summer campaign. Everyone was looking for an early forward movement. Where to? and in what direction? were questions not easily answered. Rumors of great activity in General Lee's army led us to surmise that he held the key to the above questions. At this time the Army of the Potomac had no occasion to find fault with rations or supplies; everything that an army needed and more, too, was on hand for the use of the troops. General Hooker's ability in organizing and supplying his army was proved beyond question, and his soldiers always held a warm spot in their hearts for him on that account, and they deeply regretted the misfortunes that fell to his lot.

In the meantime the three years' regiments were enjoying the pleasure (?) of noting the departure of the nine months' and two years' troops for home and muster out of service. General Humphreys' 3d division, composed of two brigades of Pennsylvania nine months' troops, left for home in a body, excepting two regiments.

General Humphreys was assigned to a command in the Third Corps. The soldiers of the Fifth Corps were sorry to lose such a brave and gallant general officer. By expiration of term of service the 1st brigade lost the 2d Maine and 13th New York. Our 2d brigade lost the 14th New York. The 3d brigade lost the 12th and 17th New York. The 3d brigade, 2d division, lost the 5th New York. The other corps lost some of their regiments for a like reason. Owing to a misunderstanding in regard to the date of " expiration of term of service," several of the New York regiments in our division showed a disposition to leave for home without proper orders; but they found that army discipline must be maintained, and, with sullen reluctance, they were obliged to wait for the orders to move on their homeward journey.

The pleasant days of the month of May, 1863, were rapidly passing when the regiment received orders to move in heavy marching order on the 28th. Our 1st division was ordered to hold the fords on the Rappahannock river, and prevent the enemy from crossing. The division was furnished with a supply train and intrenching implements, and it was accompanied by two batteries of artillery under command of Capt. A. P. Martin. The regiment bivouacked at Hartwood Church on the night of the 28th, and near the Rappahannock on the night of the 29th. On the 30th we encamped in a belt of woods on the bank of the river, in the vicinity of Ellis' ford. Our pickets were posted along the river. We found the enemy's pickets on duty on the opposite bank. Our fatigue party dug rifle-pits and threw up intrenchments. On the night of June 2, while engaged in work on a rifle-pit near the ford, the enemy opened fire from a piece of artillery with grapeshot. They fortunately fired too high to kill, and our men escaped injury. Orders to suspend work caused the enemy to cease firing. We remained on duty here until the 5th of June. The pickets on both sides were inclined to be friendly, but not over-communicative. When asked " Why they fired on us last night?" they replied, " Stop intrenching and we won't fire."

On the morning of June 5 we were ordered up the river to Kelly's ford. Here we found the rest of the 2d brigade encamped. On the 8th our brigade crossed the river at Kelly's ford with orders to report to General Gregg, commanding a division of cavalry, and support him in a reconnoissance. That night the brigade bivouacked near Mountain Run.

On the afternoon of the following day, June 9, General Gregg's division went forward in pursuit of the enemy's cavalry, and found it engaged with General Buford's division in the vicinity of Brandy Station. General Pleasanton says in his report of this cavalry battle: " We captured Stuart's camp, with his orders, letters, etc. He was to move to Maryland with 12,000 cavalry and 25 guns (artillery), and he was camped at the ford we crossed (Beverly's) — a perfect hornet's nest — but we drove them over two miles before Gregg came up."

Late that afternoon our brigade returned to camp on the north side of the Rappahannock, without a skirmish. At Beverly ford, near where the cavalry were for some hours engaged, they had other infantry supports. The Fifth Corps continued to perform picket duty from day to day at Banks', United States and Kelly's fords, with peaceful regularity.

The Confederate army in the meantime had been largely reinforced and reorganized into three large corps, as follows : —

General Longstreet's First Corps, 25,000 men, consisting of General Pickett's division, General Hood's division and General McLaws' division.

Gen. Benj. Ewell's Second Corps (Jackson's old corps), 25,000 men, consisting of General Early's division, General Johnson's division and General Rodes' division.

Gen. A. P. Hill's Third Corps, 25,000 men, consisting of General Heth's division, General Pender's division and General Anderson's division.

General Stuart's cavalry corps of 10,000 men.

Total (estimated) cavalry and infantry forces, 85,000 men.

About June 5 General Lee commenced to concentrate a part of his army at Culpepper, while one corps, Gen. A. P. Hill's, continued to remain at Fredericksburg in sight.

General Hooker submitted plans for another attack on General Lee to President Lincoln, and among other correspondence the President replied to General Hooker as follows : —

June 5 the President wrote: " If you find Lee coming to the north of the Rappahannock, I would by no means cross to the south of it . . . . In one word, I would not take any risk of being entangled upon the *river like an ox jumped half over a fence, liable to be torn by dogs, front and rear, without a fair chance to gore one way or kick the other.*" Later, on June 10, the President wrote : " Lee's army and not Richmond is your true objective point. If he comes toward the upper Potomac, follow on his flank on the inside track, shortening your lines while he lengthens his. Fight him when opportunity offers. If he stays where he is, *fret him and fret him.*"

On the 10th of June General Ewell's corps left Culpepper for the Shenandoah Valley, and, in conjunction with the Confederate cavalry, attacked the Union forces at Berryville and Winchester, which were under the command of General Milroy, on the 14th of June, and cleared them from the valley. This successful manœuvre on the part of the enemy opened up the road to the north for Lee's advancing army. Ewell continued his march into Maryland, crossing the Potomac river on the 22d of June at Williamsport. Longstreet's forces followed on the same road on the 24th, and Hill's corps crossed the Potomac at Sheppardstown on the same day. These corps united at Hagerstown on the 25th. Ewell's corps marched to and reached Carlisle on the 27th; Longstreet and Hill reached Chambersburg on the 27th. Words are inadequate to express the consternation and agitation that prevailed at this time throughout the country at the news of the recent movements of General Lee's army.

In accordance with Lee's order of the 28th, his army proceeded to concentrate at Gettysburg. On their march to the north the Confederate army destroyed all the important bridges on the Baltimore & Ohio railroad, from Martinsburg to Cumberland, Md., likewise doing great damage to the Chesapeake & Ohio canal; at the same time collecting vast quantities of supplies of all kinds and live stock for their army, out of the great abundance to be found in the towns, cities and farms on their routes through Maryland and Pennsylvania.

While General Lee's army covered the ground from Fredericksburg for over a hundred miles north, protected by the Blue Ridge mountains, General Hooker marched the Second, Sixth and Twelfth Corps along the Potomac river, northward, covering the city of Washington at the same time; and the Third, Fifth and Eleventh Corps he moved along the line of the Orange & Alexandria railroad, thence forward on the eastern side of the Blue Ridge. Moving thus he learned daily more definitely the designs of the enemy.

Since the cavalry fight at Brandy Station on the 9th of June, the regiment was under marching orders. On the night of the 13th of June, after a long wait, we moved out of camp about midnight, leaving our camp-fires to go forward in the darkness of a very dark night on the march to Morrisville. On the 14th, at 11.30 A.M., we marched to Beaversville, in the vicinity of Warrenton Junction, on the Orange & Alexandria railroad. On the 15th we left camp at 5 A.M. and marched to Manassas Junction. This section of Bull Run country was, at this time, a dreary scene of uncultivated and uninhabited desolation.

On the 17th we marched to Gum Springs, passing through Centreville, and went into bivouac at 6 P.M. The day was very hot, the roads clouded with dust raised by tramping feet, and drinking-water was very scarce. Every one suffered with the heat throughout our marching columns. Many were severely exhausted and several men throughout the division died from the effects of heat and sunstroke. The sound of distant artillery firing to the north of our line of march could be heard during the day.

On the 19th we marched to Aldie, which was only four miles distant. It had every appearance of being a thriving little town, with country surroundings highly gratifying to the eye. After our short march we were pleased to be ordered into bivouac near Aldie. A day's rest in this delightful country, breathing the pure fresh air from the mountains and drinking its clear spring water, greatly refreshed and invigorated our men. Early on the morning of the 21st of June, the regiment joined the brigade and division and went forward to report to General Pleasanton for orders. In obedience to the instructions then received, which were to support his cavalry during the day in an anticipated fight with Stuart's cavalry, we went forward on good hard roads through the towns of Dover and Middleburgh.

We noticed with pleasure the many handsome dwelling places on the turnpike road leading to Middleburgh. In fact, they surpassed anything we had seen in the residential line in Virginia. This northern part of Virginia had known but little, if any, of the ravages of war, and no doubt its inhabitants dreaded its coming.

But, to tell the truth, it seemed to put new life into our troops and to stimulate their spirits, as they suddenly found themselves in a country that was teeming with milk and honey. One can imagine by this criterion what a stimulating, not to say joyous effect it must have had on General Lee's soldiers as they went north to the land of plenty, after so many months' acquaintance with lack of food and decent raiment on the war-worn hills, valleys and plains of their past campaigns.

After reaching the beautiful open country beyond Middleburgh the Ninth Massachusetts deployed as skirmishers and remained so under orders. The brigade itself was held in reserve, as it were, to meet any repulse that might possibly happen while General Pleasanton's cavalry went forward to engage the enemy — General Stuart's Confederate cavalry — near Upperville, on the Ashby Gap road.

The 1st brigade of our division went forward in advance of us, in active support of our cavalry, and advanced with them as they drove the enemy's cavalry across Crummer's Run to Goose creek and into and beyond Upperville toward Ashby Gap. The affair proved a success for our cavalry and their infantry supports. A number of the enemy were captured and taken prisoners by them.

The orders against foraging, that is, individual wandering in search of food and plunder, were generally observed by our men. But, as the Ninth was on picket, as it were, and not actively engaged in skirmishing or other duty, and having several companies on the reserve, they could not help noticing that in the vicinity of their lines in the woods a great many little pigs were rooting and roaming about in a very familiar way. Metaphorically speaking, these little porklings had a knife and fork on each of their backs, as they ran about and through the legs of the men, begging to be eaten. Our soldiers could not refrain from accepting these pressing invitations and it is needless to say that for dinner, that day, fresh pork was the principal dish served to the Ninth boys. Hunger was good sauce and fresh young pork being an unusual ration, the meal was enjoyed with great relish.

Much care was used in the process of pig killing, so that the natives would not become aware of it. If caught in the act and complained of, it might lead to disagreeable consequences. It was a transgression that no good (?) soldier would be detected in if he could possibly avoid it! Hence the care observed in capturing little porklings.

At 9 o'clock A.M. of the following day, the 22d, we gradually fell back to Dover, under a threatened advance of the enemy, and eventually bivouacked there for the night. The cavalry affair assumed no new developments the next day. In the morning our division returned and joined the corps in bivouac near Aldie.

The Fifth Corps now remained in camp awaiting orders until the morning of the 26th. It was feared at Washington that the enemy would suddenly turn and move on the capital and by this strategy take General Hooker unawares and capture the city. The information obtained from day to day as to General Lee's actual intentions was so meagre that the authorities in Washington required General Hooker to watch the rear as well as the front of both armies. As long as the Confederate forces hovered around their old stamping ground and west of the Blue Ridge, just so long was Washington city considered in jeopardy. Hence the great anxiety of the administration and the required watching of Lee's northerly march and his rear movements, at one and the same time. It was a tacit acknowledgment of fear, on the part of our officials, of General Lee's daring strategic ability, and, at

the same time, it proved a lack of confidence in General Hooker's skill
to cope successfully against the rapid movements of his wily antagonist.

In the meantime General Lee's Confederate columns were rapidly
marching with terrible earnestness into the rich towns and cities of
Pennsylvania, spreading terror and dismay among the farmers and
landowners on their line of march. All doubts as to General Lee's
intentions were now pretty well solved by the most obtuse intellects in
Washington and outside of it. In a word, his army must be fed,
clothed and supplied at the expense of the great State of Pennsylvania;
the Army of the Potomac must be met in battle and defeated; the
cities of Philadelphia and Baltimore occupied, and the city of Washington captured. Then General Lee would dictate terms of peace from
the steps of the Capitol. "Man proposes and God disposes." The
providential defeat of General Lee at Gettysburg, while it saved the
Union, sealed forever the fate of the Confederacy.

On the 26th of June, 1863, the Fifth Corps left Aldie and, passing through Leesburg, crossed the Potomac river at Edwards Ferry
and were once again on Maryland soil.

Having been under marching orders since early morn, and on the
road from 8 A.M. till 8 P.M., we were glad to go into bivouac and
rest our tired limbs. The next morning, 27th, at 7 o'clock, we
moved forward to Poolsville, Beallsville, Barnesville, and crossed the
Monocacy river to Buckeystown and went into bivouac at Ballinger's
creek and remained in camp until the 29th.

We were now in the Monocacy valley, through which the Monocacy river meandered and watered the earth in all directions through
its branches and feeders from its source among the hills of Gettysburg.
For miles in every direction this beautiful country was replete with
cereal and vegetable products. Vast fields of wheat, oats, barley, etc.,
flourished and grew under the hands of the husbandman, and delighted
the eyes of a hurrying, tramping army of men who had just left the
barren fields of war-stricken Virginia. The picturesque farmhouses
and granaries appeared, under the bright sunlight, as white as driven
snow. The undulating farming lands were covered with their rich
nodding plumes of yellow grain which rose and fell in the breeze,
before the approaching eye, on plateaux, valleys and hills, with pleasing effect. The scenery of it all in its greatness, when viewed from
advantage ground, was a magnificent spectacle. The distant immense
mountain heights, glittering and glistening in the morning sun, were
the grand border frame to all the natural beauty with which this part
of Maryland is so richly endowed.

The Army of the Potomac was now, 28th of June, in Maryland, and situated about as follows : The First Corps was at Frederick; the Second Corps was at Monocacy Junction; the Third Corps was near Woodsborough; the Fifth Corps was at Ballinger's creek; the Sixth Corps was at Hyattstown; the Eleventh Corps was near Frederick; the Twelfth Corps was at Frederick; General Buford's cavalry division was at Middletown; General Gregg's division was at New Market and Ridgeville.

General Hooker, in his correspondence with Washington, had requested authority to abandon Harper's Ferry, and add the garrison of 10,000 men to his army. (During the month of June as previously mentioned a number of regiments had left our army for home and muster-out, as their terms of service had expired.) Not receiving the requested authority regarding Harper's Ferry he sent the following dispatch : —

" My original instructions require me to cover Harper's Ferry and Washington. I have now imposed on me, in addition, an enemy in my front of more than my number. I beg to be understood, respectfully, but firmly, that I am unable to comply with this condition with the means at my disposal, and earnestly request that I may at once be relieved from the position I occupy."

The above dispatch was received by General Halleck, Washington, D.C., at 3 o'clock P.M., 27th of June, 1863. On the same day an order from the Secretary of War of even date — General Order No. 194 — was issued relieving General Hooker from the command of the Army of the Potomac, and at the same time appointing Gen. George G. Meade of the Fifth Corps to the command of that army. This order was delivered in person by General Hardie — the bearer of the order — to General Hooker during the night of June 27. He also notified General Meade, officially, of his appointment at 2 o'clock A.M. of the 28th of June, at his headquarters.

Gen. George Sykes was immediately placed in command of the Fifth Corps, which contained three divisions now commanded as follows : 1st division of three brigades — the 2d being ours — Brig.-Gen. James Barnes; 2d division of three brigades — two of regulars and one of volunteers — Brig.-Gen. Romeyn B. Ayres; 3d division of two brigades of Pennsylvania Reserves arrived June 28, the other brigade was left in Washington, Brig.-Gen. Samuel W. Crawford. The artillery brigade, under the command of Capt. Augustus P. Martin, was composed of five batteries of artillery — three volunteers and two U.S. regulars — as follows : 3d Massachusetts (C), 1st New York (C), 1st Ohio (L), 5th U.S. (D), 5th U.S. (I).

June 30, 1863, the Army of the Potomac, Gen. George G. Meade, commanding, had present for duty as follows : —

First	Army Corps, Infantry	.	.	.	9,403
Second	Army Corps, Infantry	.	.	.	12,363
Third	Army Corps, Infantry	.	.	.	11,247
Fifth	Army Corps, Infantry	.	.	.	11,954
Sixth	Army Corps, Infantry	.	.	.	14,516
Eleventh	Army Corps, Infantry	.	.	.	9,197
Twelfth	Army Corps, Infantry	.	.	.	8,193

Total Infantry	.	.	.	.	76,873
Cavalry Corps	.	.	.	.	17,697
Artillery Reserve (guns 110)	.	.	.	2,211
Artillery with the Army Corps (guns 252)	.	.	4,481
Aggregate	.	.	.	.	101,262

On the morning of the 29th the regiment left Ballinger's creek and marched in column with the brigade and division through Frederick, with its 60,000 inhabitants, many of whom were overjoyed to see us in the thousands going for Lee's army. We passed through Mount Pleasant and Liberty and went into camp near Johnsville; moved next morning at 7 A.M., and passed through Union, Union Mills, Frizzleburg, Devilbiss, and bivouacked near Milesville; July 1, 1863, crossed Mason and Dixon line into the State of Pennsylvania. The farmers and countrymen hanging on the fences along our line of march gazed at our ranks in open-mouthed silence. Here and there we received a word of welcome, and grins of satisfaction were visible as they viewed our seemingly interminable columns of infantry. The feeling no doubt entered the souls of these good-natured non-combatants, as they gazed on our tanned and dusty veterans, that the country was safe, and in a short time it would be " all up " with " Lee's invaders." In the afternoon we marched into Hanover, a borough of about 2000 inhabitants, the people receiving us with many welcomes. News from the inhabitants — verified by the dead horses lying about — informed us of the lively cavalry skirmishes that had taken place in this section of the country, between Kilpatrick and Stuart on the 29th. The latter was severely punished, and forced to retire after a short and sharp encounter. During our march to this place we could hear at times the booming of cannon indistinctly. As we halted outside Hanover it was uncertain how long we should rest. The detonations from rapid-firing artillery could be plainly heard; to our practiced ears it told of a desperate battle going on a dozen miles away. The effect of the sounds of battle on our men was almost magical. All thoughts of their long marches seemed to vanish; they were lively and talkative and conjecturing on the sounds and rumors of the distant engagement. The excitement of it set the young, hot blood coursing through their hearts with a livelier beat than usual. That tired feeling was all gone, and each man seemed possessed of sleepless activity. We were under orders to be ready to move at a moment's notice. Eight o'clock P.M. found us on the road to the battlefield. On the march the report reached us, in fact it was in everybody's mouth, that General McClellan was now in command of the army.

" Do you believe that? " said one of the Ninth to another, as they jogged along in the moonlight and heard the rumor.

" No, I don't, not a bit of it," was the reply.

" And why not? " was the next query.

" I'll tell you why, and it's as plain to me as the nose on your face. ' Fighting Joe ' has been relieved and we have a good man in his place; a general that ' Bob ' Lee will find hard to beat. But the ' Johnnies ' are in a desperate way and they will fight for all they are worth, for they are in a hole. Now listen. If we get licked — now, mind you, I don't say we will; but if we do — and may God save us from it — and have to fall back onto Washington, the same as Pope did at Bull Run, then you will see ' little Mac ' in command of a new army from around Washington, marching on to save his country in her hour of peril, and to vindicate his reputation."

" Well, supposing we don't get licked, how then? " chimed in a listener.

" Then, my boy, you will never see ' little Mac ' in command of this army again. No, never! Meade will be the cock of the walk."

This group of philosophers was suddenly startled into activity by the captain of their company crying out close to them, " Close up here! What's the cause of this gap in the ranks? "

" We were talking about General McClellan, sir," said one of the stragglers.

" Oh! is that all? " mildly remarked the captain as he went to the right of his company.

Silence now reigned along the line of march, barring the " clinketty-clink " of the dippers and the bayonet shanks as the Ninth hastened forward to close up the gaps in the line of march.

About midnight the column came to a halt at Bonaughtown. The different regiments filed into the adjoining fields and bivouacked. Fires blazed, coffee was cooked, and the tired stragglers on this weary night march continued to arrive long after most of the men were sound asleep. Gettysburg was only five miles distant.

General Meade, on the receipt of orders, instructions, etc., from Washington on the morning of the 28th of June, at the hands of Gen. J. Hardie, visited and relieved General Hooker at his headquarters without loss of time, and at once assumed active command of the Army of the Potomac. He promptly acquainted himself with the position of his forces and took active measures to prepare to meet the enemy by concentrating his army, contracting his lines, and protecting his flanks with all of his available cavalry. He likewise bent his energies to obtain all possible information of the exact situation of the Confederate troops and to learn all he could of their precise movements. General Buford, in protecting the front and flank of our marching columns with his division of cavalry, had reached Gettysburg town on the 30th of June, and located the advancing lines of a part of the Confederate forces at Cashtown, eight miles distant. That night he posted a strong picket line covering the approaches from Cashtown and Hunterstown, supported with heavy reserves.

The First Day's Battle, July 1, 1863.

Early on the morning of July 1, General Buford's cavalry pickets fell back on their reserves and reported that a large force of the enemy was advancing on the Cashtown road. On the strength of this information General Buford deployed a heavy skirmish line of dismounted cavalry about two miles north and west of the town, extending from Millerstown road, on Willoughby run, across Chambersburg, Mummasburg, Carlisle and Harrisburg roads, etc., supported by his light batteries. The approaching columns of the enemy were two divisions of Gen. A. P. Hill's corps. They were led by Gen. Henry Heth's division of four brigades. These latter troops became cautiously engaged with Buford's dismounted cavalry at 9 o'clock A.M., in a brisk skirmish fight for about half an hour. Under cover of his artillery fire, at this time, General Heth advanced his battle-line against General Buford's skirmishers, forcing them steadily back. With the aid of a battery of light artillery our cavalry were enabled to keep up a stubborn resistance for two hours, when reinforcements came to their relief.

The First and Eleventh Corps were on the march to Gettysburg since early morning and were under the command of General Reynolds, who had preceded his own corps after placing General Doubleday in command of it. General Reynolds arrived at Gettysburg in the morning and after meeting General Buford surveyed the field, and sent back word to hasten along the First Corps.

General Wadsworth's 1st division of the First Corps arrived on the ground about 11 o'clock, and deployed into line of battle under the direction of General Reynolds, relieving General Buford's cavalry. It was at this hour that General Reynolds was shot through the head by a sharpshooter and fell dead from his horse. His loss was deeply deplored for he was looked upon as the ablest of our rising young generals. He was one of General Meade's trusted officers.

General Doubleday, commanding the First Corps, had hastened forward with the 1st division, and now assumed command of the battle. The other divisions of his corps — the 2d under General Robinson and the 3d under General Rowley — now arrived and were deployed into line of battle on the easterly side of Willoughby run. General Wadsworth's division had been heavily engaged up to this time with General Heth's troops. General Pender's division (Hill's corps) arrived and deployed on the field and at once engaged the newly arrived troops of the First Corps on the ridge north of Gettysburg.

The Eleventh Corps came up from Emmetsburg about 11.30 A.M. One division with artillery marched to Cemetery ridge, south of the town, and remained there in reserve. The other two divisions deployed into line of battle near the Mammasburg road. General Howard, commanding the Eleventh Corps, being the senior-general on the field, then assumed command of the battle.

About 1.30 P.M., two divisions of General Ewell's Confederate corps swept onto the battlefield down from the Middleburg and Heidlersburg roads fresh for a general advance. The Confederate line of battle and their reserve forces were now composed of four divisions, under Generals Heth, Pender, Rodes and Early; which according to the estimated strength of General Lee's army would number 32,000 men. The opposing Union forces were the First Corps of 9403 men, and two divisions of the Eleventh Corps of 6130 men. Total in line 15,533 men.

Previous to Ewell's arrival our forces were successful in every encounter besides capturing many prisoners. At 4 o'clock P.M., the enemy's lines pressed forward with unflinching determination, overlapping and outflanking General Howard's battle-lines, forcing his jaded brigades back onto Cemetery ridge after passing through a part of the town of Gettysburg. In the confusion and retreat through some of the streets of the town, our troops were closely pressed by the enemy's artillery and infantry and many hundreds were taken prisoners. One division of the Eleventh Corps was holding a good position on Cemetery ridge in reserve. Our retreating columns, as fast as they arrived, rapidly established their lines here. General Hancock arrived on the ground, and representing General Meade, inspired confidence in the troops, and directed their disposition in time to successfully repulse General Ewell's attack on the right of the line. The battle up to 2.30 P.M. was in our favor against General Hill's two divisions; after that time, when General Ewell's two divisions arrived on the field, it went against us with terrible effect. It was a fatal coincidence that General Howard, the commander of the Eleventh Corps, who was so disastrously driven from the right flank of our army at Chancellorsville on the first day's battle by Jackson's corps, should meet with almost a like misfortune from part of Jackson's old corps, under General Ewell, while he — General Howard — was in command of the Eleventh and First Corps on the first day at Gettysburg. While it is apparently useless to surmise what the general effects of such defeats have on the result of a battle or campaign, it is safe to say that it does not tend to increase the morale of an army — particularly the defeated fraction — or inspire confidence in the leadership of a general who, however brave in defeat, meets disaster at vital points and periods. It must blight, in a great measure, the discipline of a corps, twice defeated, no matter what the conditions were when disaster overtook it.

About 6 o'clock P.M., a part of the Third Corps and all of the Twelfth Corps arrived. General Slocum, commanding the Twelfth Corps, being senior officer, was left in command of the troops while General Hancock returned to report to General Meade at Taneytown. Having issued orders covering all arrangements to concentrate the Army of the Potomac at Gettysburg, General Meade went forward from Taneytown, twelve miles away, and arrived on the field that night, or the morning of the 2d, at 1 o'clock. From that hour he bent all his energies in surveying the field and in establishing his line of battle, for he expected that General Lee would renew his attack in the morning on his right in the neighborhood of the close of the battle of the day before.

At 3 o'clock A.M. of July 2, the Fifth Corps, after a few hours' rest at Bonaughtown, moved forward to the battleground, where it arrived about 5 o'clock A.M., having crossed Rock creek, and halted in close order near Powers hill, on the left of the Baltimore turnpike, where General Slocum, then in command of the right wing, had his headquarters. Here the corps remained in bivouac until 2 o'clock P.M. of that day. On our arrival the brigade commander received an order to detail one of his regiments for detached duty as skirmishers on our left flank. This little matter goes to show that General Meade had realized the great importance of holding Big Round Top since his arrival on the field early that morning.

By quoting the historian of the 32d Massachusetts Volunteers, it will show the reader how the Ninth Massachusetts was sent off on that duty instead of the gallant 32d as follows : " Here the 32d was detailed to form a skirmish line to protect the extreme flank of the army. Colonel Prescott, however, requested that the regiment be excused from this duty, for the reason that it had had no experience and but little instruction in skirmishing. The Ninth Massachusetts was substituted, fortunately for them, and unfortunately for us, for as matters turned out, they were not engaged, and did not lose a single man during the fight of that day." [Page 165, History 32d Mass.]

Colonel Sweitzer, commanding the brigade, heard the request of Colonel Prescott and briefly ordered his assistant adjutant-general : " Then send the Ninth." The " fighting Ninth " being veterans at everything pertaining to military duty on the battlefield, as well as off of it, moved at once from their position in the brigade, and with Colonel Guiney at their head, marched rapidly forward to Big Round Top on the left of the line of battle. It cannot be denied that we left the brigade with much regret while receiving and giving farewells to our old friends of the 62d Pennsylvania, etc., but, as the sequel will show, we were " fortunate." We were engaged, too, and had several of our men both seriously and slightly wounded, but none killed. That didn't interfere with the Ninth, however, in doing its whole duty, bravely and well, in their important position.

The extreme left of our long line of battle ended for the infantry at Big Round Top, a sugar-loaf shaped hill about 400 feet high, measuring from Plum run, on the battlefield — a small stream flowing sluggishly in the marshland at its western base. On the right, connected by a narrow defile, thinly wooded, and about 550 yards in width, stands Little Round Top, about 300 feet in height above Plum run. It is sugar-loaf shaped, and was bare of trees on the west or battlefield side. These hills were wild, rocky and (particularly Big Round Top) wooded ; scattered over their steep sides were great granite or syenitic stone boulders rising hugely and sharply above the irregular surface among the trees, over caverns and pitfalls, that rendered all movements on foot difficult and dangerous. Opposite, half a mile away, on the further side of Plum run marsh, is the Devil's Den, not near as high but as wild and steep, with few trees. Its great boulders are piled up on each other leaving deep crevasses and " dens." In one of these dens, at the base entrance, is a cool spring of fresh water from which at night many a Confederate soldier slaked his thirst. The Devil's Den, the Wheat Field and the Peach Orchard, are within rifle shot of each other. Between the Round Tops and Devil's Den is quite a valley, now known as the " Valley of the Shadow of Death." Many thousands on both sides fell here in battle on the second day.

On reaching Big Round Top the colonel of the Ninth formed his line of battle on the northeast side, near the base of the hill on the rugged road that leads to the top. The colors of the regiment were planted on a large granite boulder which marked the centre of the regiment. A breastwork of solid rocks, well laid by the masons in the regiment, saved them from the bullets of the enemy's skirmishers during the day. Skirmishers from General Hood's division of Longstreet's corps, on the west side of the hill, assaulted this point at various times during the day intending to capture the hill and flank Little Round Top, but they were always driven back by our rapid infantry fire. The enemy, mostly " Hood's Texans," would creep and crawl and stumble through the thickets and underbrush, that grew wild and tangled among the scrubby trees, until they appeared in sight, when the Ninth boys would open on them at a great advantage from behind their stone breastworks. The rapid fire was too much for the enemy's skirmishers and they would get back from tree to tree and rock to rock, until they were out of range or hidden by the declivity of the west side of the hill. Their object was to get possession of this neck of ground, held by the Ninth, some 800 yards from Little Round Top, in order to flank our forces which had taken and were holding Little Round Top. But the activity and fighting qualities of the Ninth that day held the " fort." The regiment would have lost heavily were it not for their breastworks of stone, and their freedom from artillery fire. Their services and position could only be appreciated by military men who understood the advantage of that strategical point which the Ninth occupied and held so gallantly all day against the determined assaults of Hood's skirmishers. If the enemy in any great numbers had gained a permanent hold on the north side of Big Round Top they could have, under the natural protection of the woods and boulders there, poured in a deadly fire onto the south side of Little Round Top that would have made it too hot for our troops to hold for any length of time. There seems to be a dearth of information by some military writers about Big Round Top at this period of the second day. That General Meade realized its importance is shown by sending troops there in the early morning of the 2d, and later in the day when he sent the Fifth Corps to that point on the left long before he knew that the gallant Third Corps was so far advanced from his intended line of defence. The other regiments of our brigade knew little or nothing of where we were or what we were doing, outside of the fact that we were detached and sent off to the left flank on skirmish duty. During the day our brigade of three regiments was engaged and suffered severely while supporting the Third Corps when flanked right and left by Longstreet's divisions, under Hood and McLaws, and Anderson's division of Hill's corps.

THE SECOND DAY'S BATTLE, JULY 2, 1863.

General Meade's line of battle when completed Thursday, July 2, 1863, south of the town of Gettysburg, resembled, as near as possible, from a bird's-eye view, a mammoth fish-hook in its contour. At the barb of the hook lay Culp's hill, a quarter of a mile southeast of Cemetery hill, the latter hill covering and sweeping with the bend and following the shank of the hook, in a partially convex line, to Little Round Top. On the latter's other side, south, connected by a narrow defile, thinly wooded for 550 yards, arose Big Round Top. Beyond Big Round Top our cavalry were protecting the left flank further south. The infantry and artillery line of battle covered about three miles. From our cavalry on the right flank to our cavalry on the left flank the line was about five miles in length. From 1400 yards to a mile, in front of Meade's line, towards the west and northwest, along Seminary ridge and around to the north of the town, and around to the northeast of Culp's hill, lay Lee's line of battle. Willoughby run for a long distance was in rear of his line. In rear of Meade's line was Rock creek. Both streams were very narrow and ran north and south and lay two and one-half to three miles apart.

General Meade's extreme right on Culp's hill was held by the Twelfth Corps; next on the left was the First Corps; the next was the Eleventh Corps; the next was the Second Corps; the next, far to the front near the Emmetsburg road, was the Third Corps. This left the intended position of the Third Corps vacant. The Sixth Corps was in rear of this vacant space massed in reserve. The Fifth Corps was on the left flank, near Little Round Top, its right flank resting on the left of the vacant space in the line.

General Longstreet's corps of two divisions (Pickett's division being far to the rear guarding the Confederate wagon train) held the right of Lee's line in front of the Round Tops. General Hill's corps

21

of three divisions was next on the left, and General Ewell's corps of three divisions next on the left, sweeping around to the north of the town, and ending at the northeast of Culp's hill.

The forenoon of the second day passed along while both great armies watched and waited. General Lee considered that the success of the first day augured well for a great victory on the second. In fact he intended to annihilate the Army of the Potomac. This day's battle was to be, he considered, a fitting close to the brilliant victories of Fredericksburg and Chancellorsville. In his mind's eye victory was already in his grasp. He could see, in his brilliant imagination, his army occupying Baltimore and Philadelphia, and himself the central figure at the Federal capital, surrounded by his gallant officers and his victorious army, all elated beyond measure at the success and recognition of the Confederacy, and the close of the war. In a few hours his whole army was to be thrown with one impact against the enemy in his front. Longstreet was to capture the Round Tops; Hill was to plant his victorious flag on the highest point of Cemetery hill; Ewell was to assault and capture East Cemetery hill and Culp's hill, and all were to' stand exultant victors over the fallen, beaten and disgraced Union army, with Meade and his generals prisoners of war.

"Man proposes and God disposes." Longstreet's attack was a failure. Hill's forward movement came to naught. Ewell was too late and too weak to accomplish anything. At the close of the day Lee's vision of a great victory vanished with the darkness of night. His plans were defeated but the brave old general was still unvanquished. Another day, he thought, would retrieve all.

At 11 o'clock A.M., on July 2, General Longstreet's divisions were discovered by our signal corps moving rapidly through the woods and open spaces to the right flank of their line and getting into position in front of Round Top preparatory to attacking the Third Corps. It took them about four hours to get their line of attack satisfactorily arranged. This gave General Meade ample time for his troops to reach the field and be placed in line. The last to come on the ground was the Sixth Corps, the largest in our army; it arrived about 2 o'clock P.M. It took the reserve position in the centre held since morning by the Fifth Corps. The latter was ordered to the left flank near Round Top. While marching in that direction General Meade went to meet it, and found the Third Corps, much to his surprise and chagrin, far to the front, near the Emmetsburg road, and out of his intended line of battle. During a discussion of the situation between Generals Meade, Sickles and others, the enemy's batteries opened a heavy fire on the Third

Corps. All idea of withdrawing the corps was now abandoned. To hold its position and support it by reinforcements was the only alternative. At 3.30 p.m., Confederate General Hood's division advanced, supported by McLaws' division. On the left of the latter was General Anderson's division of Hill's corps, protecting the left flank of the forward movement. This strong line of infantry came out of the woods in gallant style, and instinctively swinging round from the right, fell upon the Third Corps with tremendous force. Outflanked and doubled up, the gallant Third Corps fought manfully to breast the storm of Longstreet's overpowering assault. While desperately fighting and falling back from the Peach Orchard, the Fifth Corps advanced to its support, led by the 1st division, and opened fire on the exultant forces of Lee, checking for a time their fierce assaults.

The Third and Fifth Corps were reinforced by the 1st division of the Second Corps. The hardest fighting occurred between infantry and artillery, on both sides, at the Wheat Field, Peach Orchard and Devil's Den. As our forces fell back on Round Top and vicinity, the troops from the Sixth and Twelfth Corps were coming to their support. In the tumult of battle, and the constant changing of lines, the Third and Fifth Corps parted, leaving a space of one hundred and fifty yards between their right and left flanks through which the enemy broke and charged forward and were received by our artillery and infantry of part of the Fifth Corps under command of General Warren, on Little Round Top, and at the defile by the Pennsylvania reserves, and gallantly driven back over Plum run. Our forces on the exposed front and summit of Little Round Top suffered severely in officers and men from the enemy's sharpshooters and artillery fire. General Sickles and many others of our gallant generals were either killed or wounded. General Hancock, with the rest of the Second Corps, being now in command of the left wing, followed up with the reinforcements the advantages gained by the dashing charge of the Pennsylvania reserves and by charges and counter-charges drove the baffled enemy back to the Emmetsburg road. The closing struggle was fierce and bloody on both sides, and added many more brave men to the thousands of dead and wounded already lying between the lines. Darkness closed the fighting on our left with the Third Corps in the line of battle near Round Top on Cemetery hill.

General Lee's plans for this battle of the 2d of July were to attack simultaneously both flanks of the Union lines; intending and expecting to turn one or both and then force General Meade's centre back from his formidable position. General Longstreet's attack on our left

was to be the signal for Ewell's advance on Meade's right at East
Cemetery and Culp's hill. Ewell failed, for some reason, to catch any
signal of Longstreet's attack until after 5 o'clock P.M. At that hour
our troops on Culp's hill had been withdrawn to the extent of five brigades from the Twelfth Corps to reinforce our left in front of Longstreet. General Ewell opened with a fierce and rapid artillery fire
which was returned by our splendid batteries so effectually as to
silence his guns in the course of an hour. His infantry then advanced
to the assault and suffered heavy losses when they encountered the
grape and canister from our gallant batteries, and their charges were
repulsed at Cemetery hill by the troops of the Eleventh Corps who
were strongly intrenched behind breastworks.

On Culp's hill which was defended only by General Greene's brigade of the Twelfth Corps, they were more fortunate, for Ewell's brigades under General Johnson gained a position in the vicinity of Culp's
hill, near Rock creek, which they continued to hold. That night the
brigades of the Twelfth Corps returned from our left to Culp's hill.

The Third Day's Battle, July 3, 1863.

The dawn of Friday, July 3, was ushered in by heavy cannonading at Culp's hill and vicinity. Gen. Edw. Johnson's division of
Ewell's corps, from their position of the night before, opened fire on
the right of the Union lines, and was simultaneously met, in reply, by
the well-established artillery of the Twelfth Corps. For an hour the
guns on both sides kept up a rapid and vigorous fire on each other, the
results of which were greatly in favor of the Union batteries. General
Johnson's division had been reinforced by three or four brigades from
Ewell's corps, and after strenous but ineffectual assaults and charges
to capture Culp's hill, his forces were compelled to retire from the position which they held during the night by the successful assaults of the
Twelfth Corps and their supports under General Williams. Dislodged
and driven back, after hours of hard fighting, General Johnson gave
up the contest, as our forces had regained and held successfully all of
their own ground.

At the close of this affair on the right, which lasted till 11 o'clock
A.M., everything along the lines of both armies was comparatively
quiet for the next two hours.

Under General Meade's direction his subordinate commanders had
strengthened their positions at all points by temporary earthworks,
and other additional means of defence at hand which would stop a
bullet or shell and save their men from injury and death. His line of

battle was, in the meantime, made as strong and compact as the nature of the ground would allow. The Twelfth Corps now held a strong position on the curved right at Culp's hill. On its left, in respective order, lay the First, Eleventh, Second, Third and Fifth Corps. The latter corps held a strong position on and between Big and Little Round Tops and was reinforced on its left by one division of the Sixth Corps. The other two divisions of the Sixth Corps were in their old position at the centre in reserve.

During the forenoon a heavy force of our cavalry continued to threaten the right of General Lee's line. Not knowing the exact nature of this demonstration, and fearing an attack to turn his flank, he reinforced the right and rear of Hood's and McLaws' divisions of Longstreet's corps. Our artillery on Little Round Top continued to throw shells into their lines from time to time. The enemy's movements were carefully watched by our signal corps on Round Top, through powerful field glasses, and by the general officers along our lines. Great activity was noticed on the part of the enemy. Their artillery was hurriedly massed and planted opposite our front and centre in great numbers. As a precautionary measure on our part Gen. H. J. Hunt, chief of artillery, rapidly placed in position on Cemetery hill, as far as the nature of the ground would admit, for effective purposes, artillery to the number of eighty pieces.

While it was evident to General Meade that General Lee was preparing for a desperate attack on his lines, still it was impossible to determine what his exact plan of attack would be. He therefore continued to secure his line of battle from right to left with all the artillery and infantry at his disposal; trusting, as the attack developed itself, to reinforce his weak points in a rapid manner from the inside and rear of his position.

Owing to the hard and desperate fighting on the second day the regiments, generally speaking, on both sides, were fearfully decimated. The losses in killed, wounded, captured and missing, amounted to all of 20,000 men in each army. The regiments were further reduced by the exceedingly hot weather of July, and by their great exertions in action, through sickness and exhaustion, to the number of several thousands.

At 1 o'clock P.M., in quick response to their signal guns, the Confederate batteries, numbering one hundred and fifty pieces, belched forth their fire and flame with astonishing noise and rapidity, dropping into and through the Union lines on Cemetery hill and vicinity deathdealing missiles with such frequent accuracy and destructiveness as to astonish the veterans of the Army of the Potomac. With human instinct, sharpened by the flying messengers of danger and death, every inactive man on the field sought the little shelter afforded by his surroundings during the two hours of incessant roar created by this human storm of iron hail. During this killing and intimidating artillery assault the Union batteries were for a time silent, then followed a deliberate and steady fire only to be again followed by almost absolute silence. General Meade looked forward to the hour when clean guns actively served by fresh men with canister on the serried ranks of an approaching column would repay him with compound interest for the injury his army was receiving. The slaughter subsequently poured into the ranks of the enemy by our brave artillerymen, proved the wisdom of his discretion. The enemy's batteries gradually ceased their fire thinking that they had silenced our guns, and that our ammunition was temporarily exhausted. With active speculation and expectation our army looked forward for the next move of the enemy. They had not long to wait. Out from their concealment in the woods the enemy burst forth to view in their thousands. General Pickett, at the head of three brigades of his division — fresh from Chambersburg where they had been on detached duty guarding their wagon train — marshalled his forces for the coming assault assisted by his veteran brigade commanders, Generals Armistead, Garnett and Kemper. General Heth's division, commanded by General Pettigrew, formed on Pickett's left. General Trimble's division held the second line, and General Anderson's division the third line in support, with also two brigades on each flank; thus presenting to the view of the Union lines an assaulting column to the number of 15,000 men (some accounts say 18,000). General Pickett's three brigades were fresh and vigorous, not having been as yet engaged in action on this field. The other divisions had fought or been under fire on the 1st or 2d and were not so active and eager as Pickett's men who now longed to add new laurels to their brows by whipping the " Yankee army " in their front.

This massive column of infantry was commanded and led by Gen. George E. Pickett. His own division was entirely composed of Virginia regiments, which were looked upon by General Lee as the flower of his army, whose valor he believed was invincible. The division under Pettigrew was mainly composed of North Carolina regiments; he had also — as did Anderson and Trimble — regiments from Alabama, Tennessee, Mississippi, Georgia, Florida and Virginia.

When all were ready their long deep'lines moved forward over the crest of Seminary ridge with the cadenced tread of veterans and began to descend the slope. General Longstreet in writing of General Pickett says : —

" As he passed me he rode gracefully, with his jaunty cap raked well over on his right ear and his long auburn locks nicely dressed hanging almost to his shoulders. He seemed rather a holiday soldier than a general at the head of a column which was about to make one of the grandest, most desperate assaults recorded in the annals of war. Armistead and Garnett, two of his brigadiers, were veterans of nearly a quarter of a century's service. Their minds seemed absorbed in the men behind, and in the bloody work before them. Kemper, the other brigadier, was younger but had experienced many severe battles."

The distance between the Union and Confederate lines of battle was about fourteen hundred yards. Scarcely half of it had been crossed by the approaching enemy before shells from our guns at Round Top and Cemetery hill began to fall into their ranks. Those that burst among them would knock over six or eight men every time. Under this fire the veteran columns moved forward with as much precision and steadiness as when they started. When fully half way across the field eighty pieces of Union artillery opened on them with double-shotted canister (each canister held about sixty bullets or pieces of iron and lead ; as they left the muzzles of the guns they spread for several yards on each side and did terrible execution). As our rapid fire tore through their ranks, repeatedly, they closed their lines and passed steadily forward over their dead and wounded visibly shaken but still undismayed. At a distance of three hundred yards from Cemetery hill our infantry sprang from the ground all along the line and a converging fire from thousands of veteran marksmen poured deadly bullets into their ranks like hail. Under this combined assault of infantry and artillery for several minutes the brave Southerners fell by hundreds. Pickett's objective point of direction in charging across the plain was a clump of trees which loomed up behind the position occupied by the Second Corps. It stood in an oblique direction to the left from where they started.

At this point on Cemetery hill, in front of the Second Corps, the hardest fighting was made to pierce our centre. On reaching the sloping ascent to the crest of Cemetery hill the enemy's ranks were wofully broken in many places, and their brigade and regimental formations were lost in a confused mass of men, over whom many Confederate flags defiantly waved, on whom rained infantry and artillery fire front and ·flank with terrible effect, causing many to fall and fly. The supporting divisions were soon beaten and demoralized. Panic stricken they threw down their arms and held up their hands in token of surrender, or fell flat on the ground to escape slaughter. Hundreds rushed back over the ground they had passed a moment ago with so much confidence of victory. Thousands were killed, wounded and captured; while many thousands still continued the fight. Pickett's division was, at the close, the only one which held any semblance of aggressive formation. They were driven back from the hill which they tried to hold, even at the cannon's mouth where they and their brave leaders fell, dead or wounded, to the ground, victims of their own rash bravery. As they pressed on and up, in vain, a destructive fire of infantry assailed both of their flanks, and our reinforced lines poured a deadly fire into their front until their broken ranks melted away under an awful pressure of deadly missiles from every side. The dead and wounded were intermingled with the defeated living who threw down their arms and fell flat themselves in token of surrender. Many fled in the direction from whence they came, under a fusilade of bullets which swept across that fatal field and still carried death and destruction among the fragments of that dismembered column of brave men, swept away finally in less than an hour. Forty-five hundred were prisoners in our hands, and fully one-half that number were amongst the killed and wounded.

Our artillery and infantry ceased firing, while a heavy skirmish line dashed over the field in pursuit of the flying foe; as the pursuers reached the vicinity of Longstreet's lines his artillery was brought to bear on them and our skirmishers retired to their own lines and the battle was ended at Cemetery hill. During and after Pickett's charge, Pleasanton's cavalry divisions were engaged with Stuart's cavalry on our far-off left flank and Longstreet's right flank. Both sides were supported by several brigades of infantry and batteries of artillery. The battle closed at dark, with the results greatly in our favor. It is a noted coincidence that as Gettysburg commenced on the 1st of July on our right, with our cavalry, it ended on the 3d day with a cavalry battle on our left.

The battle of Gettysburg holds such an important place in the history of the rebellion, that in closing this chapter, the writer will be pardoned for quoting from the writings, in the *Century*, of Gen. Henry J. Hunt, Chief of Artillery of the Army of the Potomac, on General Meade's staff. (Vol. XI., page 461.) General Hunt, besides being an able, brave and gallant officer, is a most impartial and truthful authority.

"General Lee now abandoned the attempt to dislodge Meade, intrenched a line from Oak Hill to Peach Orchard; started all his *impedimenta* to the Potomac in advance, and followed with his army on the night of July 4, *via* Fairfield. This compelled Meade to take the circuitous routes through the lower passes, and the strategic advantage to Lee and disadvantage to Meade of Gettysburg were made manifest.

"General Meade has been accused of slowness in pursuit. The charge is not well founded; he lost no time in commencing nor vigor in pushing it. On the morning of the 4th he ordered French at Frederick to seize and hold the lower passes, and put all the cavalry, except Gregg's and McIntosh's brigades, in motion to harass the enemy's anticipated retreat, and to destroy his trains and bridges at Williamsport. It stormed heavily that day, and the care of the wounded and burial of the dead proceeded, whilst the enemy's line was being reconnoitred. So soon on the 5th as it was certain that Lee was retreating, Gregg was started in pursuit on the Chambersburg pike, and the infantry — now reduced to a little over 47,000 effectives, short of ammunition and supplies — by the lower passes. The Sixth Corps taking the Hagerstown road, Sedgwick reported the Fairfield pass fortified, a large force present, and that a fight could be had; upon which, on the 6th, Meade halted the rest of the infantry and ordered two corps to his support; but soon learning that although the pass could be carried it would cause too much delay, he resumed the march, leaving McIntosh and a brigade of the Sixth Corps to follow the enemy through Fairfield Pass. On the evening of the 4th Kilpatrick had a sharp encounter with the enemy in Monterey pass, and this was followed by daily cavalry combats on the different routes, in which much damage was done to trains and many captures of wagons, caissons and prisoners effected. On the 5th French destroyed the pontoon bridge at Falling Waters.

"On the 6th Buford attacked at Williamsport, and Kilpatrick toward Hagerstown on his right; but as Imboden's train guard was strong, Stuart was up, and Longstreet close by, they had to withdraw. The enemy proceeded to construct a new bridge and intrench a strong line covering Williamsport and Falling Waters. There were heavy rains on the 7th and 8th but the infantry corps reached Middletown on the morning of the 9th, received supplies, crossed the mountains that day, and at its close the right was at Boonsboro, and the left at Rohrersville, on the roads to Hagerstown and Williamsport.

"The river was now greatly swollen and unfordable, and Halleck on the 10th advised Meade to postpone a general battle until his army was concentrated and his reinforcements up; but Meade, fully alive to the importance of striking Lee before he could cross the Potomac, advanced on that day and the 11th, and on the 12th pushed forward reconnoissances to feel the enemy. After a partial examination made by himself, and his chief of staff and of engineers, which showed that its flanks could not be turned, and that the line so far as seen by them, presented no vulnerable points, he determined to make a demonstration in force on the next morning, the 13th, supported by his whole army, and to attack if a prospect of success offered. On assembling his corps commanders, however, he found their opinion so adverse that he postponed it for further examination, after which he issued the order for the next day, the 14th. On advancing that morning it was found that the enemy had abandoned his line and crossed the river, partly by fording, partly by a new bridge. A careful survey of the enemy's intrenched line, after it was abandoned, justified the opinion of the corps commanders against an attack, as it showed that an assault would have been disastrous to us. It proved also that Meade, in overriding that opinion, did not shrink from a great responsibility, notwithstanding his own experience at Gettysburg, where all the enemy's attacks on even partially intrenched lines had failed. If he erred on this occasion it was on the side of temerity.

"But the hopes and expectations excited by the victory of Gettysburg were as unreasonable as the fears that had preceded it, and great was the disappointment that followed the ' escape ' of Lee's army. It was promptly manifested, too, and in a manner which indicates how harshly and unjustly the Army of the Potomac and its commanders were usually judged and treated; and what trials the latter had to undergo whilst subjected to the meddling and hectoring of a distant superior, himself but too often the mere mouthpiece of an irresponsible clique, and from which they were not freed until the general-in-chief accompanied it in the field."

That same day, before it was possible that all the circumstances could be known, three telegraphic despatches passed between the respective headquarters.

First. Halleck to Meade: "I need hardly say to you that the escape of Lee's army without another battle has created great dissatisfaction in the mind of the President, and it will require an active and energetic pursuit on your part to remove the impression that it has not been sufficiently active heretofore."

Second. Meade to Halleck: "Having performed my duty conscientiously and to the best of my ability, the censure of the President (conveyed in your despatch of 1 P.M. this day) is in my judgment so undeserved, that I feel compelled most respectfully to ask to be immediately relieved from the command of this army."

Third. Halleck to Meade: "My telegram of July 14, stating the disappointment of the President at the escape of Lee's army, was not intended as a censure, but as a stimulus to an active pursuit. It is not deemed a sufficient cause for your application to be relieved."

During the 3d day of July the Fifth Corps was in line of battle, as previously mentioned, on and between Big and Little Round Tops. The Ninth regiment held its old position on Big Round Top. Up the hill to our left, and in the defile and beyond to our right, most of the regiments of our 1st division were stationed in line of battle. Our lines were, more or less, under the range of the enemy's sharpshooters concealed at the Devil's Den. Their annoying fire was, however, kept down considerably by our infantry, and by Berdan's sharpshooters in our front who took advantage of the woods, stones and boulders in the vicinity for their own protection in front and rear. The moral effect of our position and the cavalry attack on his right flank in the afternoon, deterred, without a doubt, Longstreet's right wing, under Gen. E. M. Laws, in command of Hood's division, and General McLaws' division with supports from Gen. A. P. Hill's corps, from attempting an attack on our left. Supported, as we were, by a division of the Sixth Corps, Big Round Top was impregnable.

On the morning of the 4th of July about 9 o'clock, the Ninth Massachusetts went forward on the skirmish line supported by a line of battle on the field in front of Round Top. We found the enemy still in position and after a lively skirmish, during which three men of the Ninth were wounded, returned to our old position on Round Top. It commenced to rain heavily in the afternoon so that everyone on the field was drenched to the skin. When the thunder-storm partially ceased the regiment was ordered to join the division and go into bivouac. The new ground we occupied was completely flooded by the rain that fell in great showers during the night, so much so that there was no rest after 3 o'clock A.M. In the rain and the gray light of approaching morning, the men in their shoddy uniforms and shoes, drenched and soaked to the skin, were seeking higher ground to spread their wet tents and blankets.

The reader will readily perceive that the Army of the Potomac was in no condition or position to celebrate the " Glorious Fourth." Fatigue details were burying the dead in the crude army way. The Medical Corps was continuing its herculean task of caring for and curing the wounded. The Ambulance Corps was on the move night and day. The wagon trains were being pulled out of the holes and corners of the woods, valleys and towns, into which irresponsible division and corps assistant-quartermasters had run them for safety (?) during the great battle, whilst the army generally was gathering itself together out of the mud and water of several heavy rainstorms, in expectation of orders to move that were sure to come.

During the night of the 4th, in storm and rain, the Confederate army in our front had "lit out," and was hastening south to the mountain passes, thence to seek further safety beyond the Potomac. By this strategic retreat General Lee gave further evidence of his great ability. If General Halleck had possessed one half of Lee's practical strategy he would have had a large contingent force in Virginia, south of the Potomac, to take advantage of just such a movement as this on the part of the enemy. On the morning of the 5th the Sixth Corps was in pursuit on the road to Fairfield. They found the mountain pass held by the enemy. Under the circumstances, to attack and follow the enemy in force was a waste of valuable time and of doubtful utility. General Meade therefore moved by the left flank.

The Fifth Corps left Gettysburg about 5 o'clock P.M. of the 5th. We marched and floundered through the mud and slush till 10 o'clock P.M. and bivouacked at Rock or Marsh creek near Emmetsburg. The night was dark as pitch, which, added to mud anywhere from ankle to knee deep, accounted for the slow progress of the troops. On the 6th at 9 A.M. we moved forward a short distance and then went into temporary bivouac in order to relieve the congested road over which artillery and ordnance trains were laboring hard to go ahead. On the 7th we started at 5 A.M. on an open muddy road and marched by Emmetsburg in the drizzling rain through Mechanicstown and camped at Utica. Everything, and everybody on foot, was soaked with rain and covered with mud. Our cavalry and artillery had left the line of march in a horrible condition for foot passengers obliged to travel after them. On the 8th we took the road, in the still falling rain, at 7 o'clock A.M., and waded through the mud of Utica and Creagerstown; marched over Catoctin mountain and stopped at Middletown, under orders to be ready to move at a moment's notice. Although a short march it was unusually fatiguing on the troops, for they passed through oceans of mud and water in the fields and on the roads. Much-needed rations were issued here, and, as no orders were received to march, the tired veterans enjoyed a good night's sleep on the soft damp bosom of dear mother earth. The dampness of the latter was fully in keeping with our blankets and other personal effects. This kind of weather began to show its effects on the army in the way of the appearance of the twin camp scourges, *Terry* and *Diar*. Stock for the manufacture of future rheumatism and other bodily ailments was likewise abundantly supplied to the army.

The 9th day of July opened up with pleasant weather. At 9 o'clock A.M., we crossed South Mountain at Fox's Gap and bivouacked at Mt. Carmel Church. Boonsboro was a short distance off. On the 10th we marched at 9 A.M. The Keedysville road brought us to the historic field of Antietam. We crossed the creek and halted at 1 P.M., near Delaware Mills. The third brigade of our division went out on picket and skirmish and felt the enemy who were now to the north of us at Funkstown, Hagerstown and Williamsport. On the 11th our corps formed in line of battle and advanced in that position half a mile in a northerly direction. The Sixth Corps held the line on our right and advanced likewise in a similar formation. We went into bivouac that afternoon under orders to move at a moment's notice. The next day, the 12th, the army marched forward a short distance in the afternoon across the country in battle array. Each brigade in column of regiments moved in corps front covering a line of six miles from right to left. The battle-flags were flung to the breeze. Tens of thousands of bright guns and equipments glimmered in the sun. Throughout the miles of deep lines it presented a beautiful sight as with the swinging cadenced step of veterans they moved over cultivated fields of grain, over roads, orchards and vineyards, on plain, valley and hill. Obstructions were leveled by the pioneers in advance, and, regardless of damage, the army of blue swept over the ground with heavy tread, leaving in their rear destruction and desolation over which the eyes of the owners and dwellers fell in dumb dismay. The enemy was in our front centered at Williamsport, heavily intrenched and apparently prepared for an attack. General Meade called his corps commanders together to consider his plan of assault which he proposed to make in the morning. Five out of six of the corps commanders were opposed to it. He telegraphed the situation of affairs to Washington, and was ordered in reply to " act on his own judgment and make his generals execute his orders, and not to let the enemy escape." Since the 4th of July, the elements, at opportune times, were playing into General Lee's hands. On the afternoon of the 12th another terrific rain-storm with thunder and lightning, broke over the army, flooding the roads and country. Our shelter tents were the only protection that stood between us and the pouring rain of half an hour. On the 13th we began to intrench. Our picket lines were in sight of each other, and everyone looked forward to a battle the next day. At 9 o'clock A.M., the 14th, General Meade made a reconnoissance in force in view of the enemy's picket line which however rapidly disappeared as our division lines advanced. It was soon discovered that General Lee and his army had crossed the river the night before. The Washington authorities were disappointed at the " escape " of Lee's army. The press of the country generally expressed its inexperienced opinions detrimental to Meade's generalship in not " bagging " the Confederate army!

To the unbiased mind it is food for thought, if not for argument, when one remembers the fact, that it took one year and nine months afterwards, with all the resources of an immense army, under Grant, and his lieutenants, Sheridan and Meade, to " bag " the same General Lee and his fighting veterans. Even then, if it had not been for Sheridan's ceaseless activity, Lee and his army would have escaped and gone to North Carolina and joined Johnston's forces.

LOSSES AT GETTYSBURG IN THE ARMY OF THE POTOMAC.

Officers killed	246
Enlisted men killed	2,900
Officers wounded	1,145
Enlisted men wounded	13,384
Officers captured or missing	183
Enlisted men captured or missing	5,182
Aggregate	23,040

CONFEDERATE LOSESS AT GETTYSBURG.

Officers and men killed	2,592
Officers and men wounded	12,700
Officers and men captured or missing	5,150
Aggregate	20,442

The report of losses in the Confederate army is said to be incomplete, the number being greater than above mentioned. For instance, the United States record of prisoners of war taken at Gettysburg is 12,227. Of this number 6802 were wounded.

Many thousands of men, not accounted for here by either army, were absent sick and disabled from day to day, and when the disappearance of the irrepressible straggler is considered, the reader will notice that the effective fighting forces of both armies were terribly diminished. It is, therefore, safe to estimate that both armies were now reduced to at least one-half of their original number.

Taking into consideration the impaired physical condition of both the victor and the vanquished, after the superhuman ordeals through which, as soldiers, they had passed for so many weeks, the assertion cannot be maintained that Lee's veteran battalions could be trapped, surrounded, captured, or annihilated, by his present pursuers, through a mountainous country interspersed, as it is, with rivers and streams, great and small, by a flank movement, forced upon Meade by Lee's selected line of retreat through mountain passes, or by attacking his temporary fortified forces at Williamsport, etc.

General Meade, after making the greatest effort of his life and achieving a great victory, was justified in resenting the censure put upon him by one holding at the time the rank of a superior officer. Had he acted otherwise it would have marred his spotless record in the service, and been an insult to his brave army.

The losses in the Fifth Corps at Gettysburg were: —

Officers killed	28
Enlisted men killed	337
Officers wounded	129
Enlisted men wounded	1,482
Officers captured or missing	1
Enlisted men captured or missing . . .	210
Total casualties Fifth Corps `. .	2,187

The three regiments of our second brigade, — that is, the 32d Massachusetts, the 4th Michigan and the 62d Pennsylvania — while engaged in action in the second day's battle with the 1st division, Fifth Corps, passed through some heavy fighting. Colonel Jeffers of the 4th Michigan was among the killed, and Lieutenant-Colonel Stephenson of the 32d Massachusetts was among the wounded.

The casualties are given as follows: —

32d Massachusetts:

Officers killed	1
Officers wounded	7
Enlisted men killed	12
Enlisted men wounded	55
Enlisted men missing and captured	5
	— 80

4th Michigan :

Officers killed 1
Officers wounded 9
Enlisted men killed 24
Enlisted men wounded 55
Officers missing and captured 1
Enlisted men missing and captured 75
                                        — 165

62d Pennsylvania :

Officers killed 4
Officers wounded 10
Enlisted men killed 24
Enlisted men wounded 97
Enlisted men missing and captured 40
                                        — 175
Ninth Massachusetts   15
                                        ——
Total in 2d brigade at Gettysburg . . .   435

The Ninth Massachusetts lost Joseph Ford, Company K, killed while he was engaged in action July 2, in the Fourth Michigan Volunteers, of our brigade. It seems he lost his own regiment after it went on detached duty, and the brave fellow went into battle with the " Michiganders."

The following men of the Ninth were wounded and missing :

COMPANY B.

James Battesby, Timothy Sullivan; John Quinn missing in action July 2, 1863.

COMPANY C.

William Foye, John Campbell, William Flynn.

COMPANY E.

Francis Kelly.

COMPANY F.

Sergeant John Lorrigan, John Daley 2d, James McMahon.

COMPANY I.

Thomas Lavin, Patrick Gallagher, Sergeant Thomas Flynn, Edmund Flynn. Wounded 13, missing 1, killed 1; total 15.

CHAPTER XVIII.

MINE RUN.

OUR ARMY CROSSES INTO VIRGINIA — AFFAIR AT WAPPING HEIGHTS — IN
CAMP AT BEVERLY FORD — EXECUTION OF DESERTERS — OUR NEW
CHAPLAIN — A FORWARD MOVEMENT — NEAR CULPEPPER — MUSKETS
CHANGED FOR RIFLES — GENERAL LEE'S ARMY REDUCED — GENERAL
MEADE'S ARMY REDUCED — GENERAL LEE ATTEMPTS A FLANK MOVE-
MENT — THE MOVEMENT BAFFLED — THE CONFEDERATE ARMY FALLS
BACK — BATTLE OF RAPPAHANNOCK STATION — AT KELLY'S FORD —
GUARDING THE RAILROAD — AGAIN ON THE MOVE — RAIN AND MUD
— COLD WEATHER — WAGONS CAPTURED — AT MINE RUN — PREPAR-
ING FOR AN ASSAULT — ZERO WEATHER — MINE RUN ABANDONED —
OUR ARMY RECROSSES BOTH RIVERS — AT BEALTON STATION.

* * * * * *

"Friend of the brave! in peril's darkest hour,
Intrepid Virtue looks to thee for power;
To thee the heart its trembling homage yields,
On stormy floods and carnage cover'd fields,
When front to front the banner'd hosts combine,
Halt ere they close, and form the dreadful line.
When all is still on Death's devoted soil,
The march-worn soldier mingles for the toil!
As rings his glittering tube, he lifts on high
The dauntless brow and spirit-speaking eye,
Hails in his heart the triumph yet to come,
And hears thy stormy music in the drum!"
* * * * * *

THOMAS CAMPBELL. — "Pleasures of Hope."

THERE was no time lost by General Meade in pursuing the Confederate army into Virginia. July 15, 1863, we started on the
march at 4.30 A.M. and passed through the town of Keedysville,
Md., on the road to South Mountain over which we had a laborious
tramp, and at 4 o'clock P.M. went into bivouac within a few miles of
the town of Burkittsville. The weather was hot and the roads bad.
Many of the men throughout our marching columns, during this toilsome twenty miles, were obliged to fall out from heat, exhaustion and
sunstroke. On the 16th we marched through Burkittsville and Peters-

22

ville, Md., and went into camp two miles from Berlin. On the 17th we marched through the pleasant little town of Berlin, Md., on the Potomac, and crossed the river on pontoons, at this point, and bivouacked at Lovettsville, Va. The "sacred soil" of Virginia was now under our feet. The "Mother of Presidents" was destined to suffer many months longer under the terrible warfare which, by her act of secession, she had brought upon herself.

By direction of the Medical Department the army was allowed to rest here one day in order to enjoy the benefits derived from the curative medicinal properties of the Virginia blackberry. The open country for miles, at intervals, was covered with the creeping vines of this delicious berry, which, for its medicinal properties, was a perfect blessing to our bilious and feverish soldiers. They enjoyed the fruitful feast by devouring enormous quantities during the whole day. On the 19th we marched to Oakland. On the 20th we moved forward at 5 A.M. and passed through the town of Union and bivouacked at Goose creek; remained in camp on the 21st and indulged in another feast of blackberry "medicine." On the 22d we marched from noontime until 4 o'clock P.M. and bivouacked at Rectortown; moved forward at 6 A.M. of the 23d; after a hard march over bad roads we reached Manassas Gap at 5 P.M. The 3d corps was in our front on this march, and the 5th corps was followed by the 2d corps. At this point we were in close order by brigades and divisions. We advanced through the Gap about two miles when the skirmishers of the Third Corps struck the enemy's outposts and skirmishers and drove them onto their main line which had formed in line of battle to meet us. Both sides were now using artillery to advantage. Shells were thrown into each other's lines with lively precision. The Fifth Corps was pushed forward in support of the Third Corps and the enemy was driven back by the latter corps until it became too dark to see anything in our front. We held our position during the night and at dawn of the day continued the advance intending to assault the enemy when found, but he had disappeared. The object of the enemy in holding the pass the afternoon before was to save their wagon train from capture, which, during our engagement, was passing on the run rapidly south. This affair was called the battle of Wapping Heights.

On the morning of the 24th we marched to Orleans, and camped till the 25th. On the 26th we passed through Orleans and marched to the vicinity of Warrenton. The weather was very hot. On the 27th, at 6 A.M., passed through Warrenton and camped about three miles beyond the town. We remained here until August 3, then moved forward at 5 o'clock in the afternoon, and marched till 11 o'clock P.M. and bivouacked. It was rumored that we would stay here at " Tin Pot " run for some time, and our camp was arranged with some little regularity. On the 8th of August, however, we were ordered on the march again at 4 A.M. W.e arrived at Beverly ford on the Rappahannock river, and remained there until September 16. Both armies had up to this time, " protected their capitals from invasion."

Our camp was laid out in regular order on the east side of the long incline of a hill. Evergreen trees were planted, without the roots, along the streets, and, besides presenting a picturesque scene, it afforded shade from the hot sun. The regiment likewise enjoyed good bedding, plenty of wood close at hand, and good water. The Rappahannock river was about a mile distant, and our tour of picket duty on its banks was made easy and pleasant by the friendly feeling created with our friends, the enemy, on the other bank.

The reader will perhaps remember that early in the war volunteering was stopped by orders from Washington. The country was now reaping the fruits of such a short-sighted policy. On the 13th of August, 1863, two brigades of regulars from the 2d division of our Fifth Corps were, with other troops from the Army of the Potomac, detached and ordered. to New York to assist in quelling the " draft riots." The two years' regiments in our army, having served out their term of service, were long since mustered out. The three years' regiments were, for months past, greatly reduced in numbers. The slaughter of troops at Fredericksburg, Chancellorsville and Gettysburg struck terror into the hearts of many of the Northern people. Thousands of families, not lacking in bravery and patriotism, hesitated about sacrificing their sons to the tender mercy of incompetent generals, who " sniffed the battle from afar," while their subordinates were being slaughtered with their commands like sheep at the shambles. In spite of the victories of Gettysburg and Vicksburg, the " copperheads," and anti-war men, and Southern sympathizers had become blatant, offensive and dangerous. The Canada border, with its English backing, was a den of protection for all disunion men. There they were free to hatch inhuman schemes to destroy our country and its loyal people. Our cities contained elements that would overthrow all law and order, and instigate a reign of terror that would defy all civil authority.

The Army of the Potomac was not only taking care of Lee and his army but it now must look after the Northern copperhead and that ilk ; hence the order sending our regiments away from the front where they were sorely needed. All this trouble was brought upon us originally by the order in the early days of the war to stop volunteering. Congress, at a later period, passed a law that each loyal State of the Union should furnish its quota of men for the army. The men thus enlisted were called conscripts. All conscripts were allowed to send out substitutes. The law when first enforced was not popular, and in New York City it caused a great riot which the civil and military authorities soon suppressed. The city of Boston had some little trouble, of a like nature, for a short time. If volunteering had not been interfered with the old regiments in the field could have been kept filled to the maximum with good soldiers, and to spare. As it was now the old three years' regiments had steadily fallen away by casualties from hard service until they were reduced in numbers to mere skeleton regiments with slow prospects of being recruited. Instead of organizing new regiments to give a few favored individuals commissions, recruits should have been enlisted for three years to fill up the old regiments, and newly promoted officers commissioned and mustered for a like period of time in their old regiments. By this method the veteran regiments would have continued in the field up to the close of the war. Besides, the old members, whose first time had expired, would be apt to re-enlist in their old regiments, sooner or later.

Desertions from our army, by new men principally, became so frequent that measures were adopted to prevent them if possible. We had heard of deserters being led out and shot in other corps, but thus far the Fifth Corps had not passed through that experience. A report was in circulation that five deserters, new men assigned to our division, were to be executed all together in a few days. These substitutes had been court-martialed, found guilty, and sentenced to be shot dead by military execution. They had been assigned to the 118th Pennsylvania Volunteers, but were entire strangers to the regiment, Like many other regiments in the Army of the Potomac, the 118th Pennsylvania has to bear for all time the stigma of these deserters on its rolls, and the disgrace —if one may so term it — of this execution brought on, as it appears, by the desertion of these strangers who were only lately assigned to the regiment. Their names were given as Charles Walter; Gion Reanese; Emil Lai; Gion Folaney and George Kuhn. Some of them, it was said, could barely speak our language.

It was at this camp, on the 29th day of August, 1863, that the Fifth Corps — or that portion of it not on duty — was turned out under arms to witness the execution of these men — terrible examples of just retribution. In the afternoon the different regiments of the Fifth

Corps left their camps, and joined their brigades at the place of execution which was but a short distance away. The brigades of our division were closed in mass in front of the ground; at angles to the front, on our right and left, the brigades of our other two divisions stood likewise, thus forming three sides of a hollow square. Five graves in line, a hundred yards in our front, could be plainly distinguished, with the fresh mounds of earth thrown up on each side. The corps stood at order arms and rest. The general and field officers were mounted in their places and at rest likewise. A gradual silence fell upon the thousands of soldiers thus assembled and waiting, until a painful suspense was felt which made one wish that he could leave the ranks and go back to camp. The longer we waited and pondered over the matter the more solemn it appeared. Veterans present who would kill and take the chances of being killed in the fierce excitement of battle, now dreaded to witness the coming methodical execution. Nothing but a sense of duty, and the stern discipline of a soldier's life, kept them there as spectators of the dismal scene about to be enacted. A further perceptible silence fell upon the assembled troops when the strains of the "Dead March in Saul" reached their ears as the funeral procession came towards them, on the right flank, from where the culprits had been confined. Each strain of slow and solemn music from the brass band rose and fell with great distinctness on the silent air as the procession approached, with measured tread, the place of execution. It was a relief to all when it ceased, and the procession halted before the eyes of the assembled troops. The five doomed men, dressed neatly in blue trousers, white shirts, caps, etc., were easily distinguished from those who surrounded them and the eyes of all present were directed towards them. A Catholic priest, a Protestant minister, and a Jewish rabbi, were present with the men all day, giving them spiritual consolation, and instilling into their hearts courage to pass through the last fearful ordeal of their lives on this earth. Two of the prisoners were Catholics, two were Protestants, and one was a Jew, and all were of foreign birth. The coffins, which the culprits had followed, were placed at the head of the graves, and the men were seated on them. The provost-marshal marched his guard of thirty-two men to their position — about ten paces in front of the doomed deserters — where they stood like statues at carry arms. They were picked sharpshooters.

All of the preliminaries being arranged, the bugle, clear and shrill, sounded "Attention!" At this signal the chaplains and doctors retired to the line of troops, and the condemned prisoners, seated on their coffins, were alone in a row under the gaze of thousands of stern eyes, many of which, however, were now softened with pity for the doomed men. The man who sat on the coffin on the left, facing the provost guard, stood up and walked along the front to the man who sat on the right, likewise facing the guard, and bending down kissed him on the cheek, and then returned to his place. This public expression of love and friendship by this unfortunate man affected some of those who noticed it more than they then would wish to acknowledge. The next act in this tragic drama was to bandage the eyes of the doomed men preparatory to the execution. Although the time occupied in arranging these preliminaries was really very short, yet to us, who were looking on, it seemed a long time. Everything being ready the officer of the guard stepped back to the right and front of his line in full view of all his men and made his signals for " Ready ! " " Aim ! " " Fire ! " suddenly there followed a flash and a volley, loud and sharp, and five men fell over instantly from their seats on their coffins pierced with many bullets. The surgeons hastened to them, felt of their pulses and hearts and pronounced them dead. As one individual expressed himself : " It was the prettiest execution he had ever seen." Meaning of course that the guard had done the work well. Word from the surgeons was passed to the corps commander that the culprits were shot dead. The bodies were at once laid in their coffins and the burial party proceeded to place them in their graves as the bugles, drums and music struck up in all the regiments in the corps and they quickly marched off to camp with impressions and remembrances of the sad scene that will last as long as one lives.

The next morning several desertions were reported in the corps from among the recruits that lately joined. They had been witnesses of the execution of the day before. That same night they crossed the river and deserted to the enemy. The penalty, if captured, for going over to the enemy was hanging. Executions throughout the army for desertion were frequent from this time forth. Whether these executions had the desired effect it is hard to determine, for men throughout our army continued to desert up to the very close of the war. Unprincipled men, greedy of gain, banded together throughout the loyal States, were bought as substitutes by the conscripted to fill the quota called for by the government. When once accepted and rendezvoused they seized the first favorable opportunity to desert. The reckless and the desperate accomplished their object sometimes before leaving the State, sometimes on the way to the front, or after they had reached the regiments to which they were assigned. Some of them were caught and executed, but many more were never captured or detected even after they had repeated the operation a dozen or twenty times. That they were in league with Northern bounty brokers, and other unprincipled characters in the business, for the gain there was in it, is only too apparent, and this fact was afterwards acknowledged at the close of the war when the punishment for the crime attached to the act became obsolete. This accounts in a measure for the increased percentage of desertions in the three years' regiments doing duty at the front.

New recruits, the result of the late draft in Massachusetts, consisting of conscripts and substitutes, were assigned to the Ninth Massachusetts and arrived in camp at Beverly ford on the 6th of September, 1863. The regiment manifested much interest in these new arrivals and the drill masters were kept busy in breaking them into their new duties. In a short time they assimilated with the old soldiers and most of them took to their duties in a satisfactory manner.

Father Egan, who came from Washington to attend two of the men recently executed, having been previously invited by Colonel Guiney to visit the regiment, came to our camp and was heartily welcomed by the officers and men of the regiment. We had been without a permanent chaplain since Father Scully had been obliged to resign from disability contracted in the service. The colonel invited Father Egan to accept the vacancy. This he did, after obtaining the consent of the head of his Order — the Dominicans — and he was commissioned chaplain of the Ninth Massachusetts Sept. 18, 1863. He remained with the regiment until its time expired. Father Egan was a true priest and chaplain and a noble-hearted Christian gentleman, greatly beloved by all the regiment and highly respected throughout the Fifth Corps and the army; for he did not confine all his labors to the regiment. Wherever his priestly duties called him in the army, there he was to be found : in the camps, hospitals and on the battlefield. When the regiment left the army for home General Griffin, who commanded our division at that time, invited Father Egan to join his staff, and had him commissioned army chaplain in the field; for General Griffin averred that his services could not be dispensed with. Father Egan served with General Griffin's division and corps until the close of the war. His presence and priestly service was, indeed, a blessing at all times to the wounded, the dying and the distressed. At the present writing he is still living in Louisville, Ky., at a ripe old age, in good health.

The Rappahannock river continued to be the principal dividing line between both armies, with Washington to the north of one and Richmond to the south of the other, each army being a living wall of defence to their respective capitals. By picket lines, scouting parties, cavalry raids and spies, each army commander was kept informed pretty thoroughly of his adversary's movements. In the meantime the Confederate government at Richmond and General Lee could not agree on a line of defence; and our Washington authorities were looking for and urging active operations on General Meade's part, which they confidently expected would end in defeating Lee's army and close up the war in Virginia. More so at this time, as it was known that General Longstreet's corps had been sent to the southwest, leaving General Lee so much the weaker; that is, with only two corps, Generals Ewell's and Hill's. On the 16th of September General Meade issued orders for a general forward movement. We broke camp at Beverly ford on that day and took to the road at 7 o'clock A.M.; crossed the Rappahannock river to the south and west, and, after a march of a dozen miles in the hot sun, went into bivouac at 3 P.M., within a mile of Culpepper. At 7 o'clock the next morning we passed through Culpepper, and after a short tramp camped three miles beyond it. The once handsome shire town of Culpepper was now pretty well war-stricken and apparently deserted by its owners and dwellers, except in a few instances. The stores in its principal street were closed, excepting here and there a few that were occupied temporarily by our army sutlers and camp followers. Its numerous fine dwelling-houses indicated that in peaceful days, " befo' de wah," it was a pleasant, healthy Southern town to reside in. The town was now under the charge of the provost guard from our division, so that the strictest kind of order was preserved at all times. Soldiers found in its streets without official permission or the usual pass were arrested and returned to their camps under guard. On the 18th of September we had a heavy rainfall during the forenoon. That portion of the army off duty remained quietly under shelter which sometimes leaked badly overhead or was flooded under foot. The Ninth was encamped in a piece of woods, and from day to day improved their surroundings, not knowing, however, but what each day would bring orders to march. Picket, guard and fatigue duty, and company and battalion drills, again occupied our attention, and each day was closed with a dress parade.

Colonel Guiney had made application for a change of arms in his regiment. The old smooth-bore 69-calibre musket had been our weapon of defence and offence since our entry into service. These firearms were now obsolete and worn and hard to replace; besides, it was at times difficult to obtain buck and ball ammunition. The Springfield rifle was now the arm commonly used among the infantry and was as effective a weapon as the troops had at this time, barring, of course, those of the breech-loading pattern. At this camp the division ordnance officer notified the colonel of the arrival of Springfield rifles for his regiment. The colonel ordered his quartermaster to take full charge of the matter. As the rifles came in irregular lots from day to day, the regiment was quite busy and interested in making the exchange. Receipts and invoices for the old guns and their fixings were exchanged with each company commander, and the same was done with the new rifles. This was necessary in order that the colonel and his company commanders could send proper quarterly returns and vouchers to the ordnance department at Washington accounting for the United States property in their charge. It is unnecessary to say that the regiment was well pleased with their new 58-calibre rifles.

During our stay at this camp our brigade was called out one afternoon under arms and formed into square to witness the punishment of a deserter from the 32d Massachusetts Volunteers. The culprit was said to be a half-witted French Canadian — more knave than fool — who disappeared on the march to Gettysburg and had been returned under guard to his regiment, where he was tried as a deserter and, as he was " no good as a soldier," he was sentenced to be " drummed out of the service." The brigade was assembled, therefore, to witness the carrying out of the sentence of the court. The deserter was marched under guard into the centre of the square. The left half of the hair on his head was shaved smooth to the scalp, which, when finished, presented a most comical looking sight. On his bare left shoulder they branded a big letter " D." The brigade was then deployed into line of battle and the ranks placed in open order with the front rank facing inward. To the right of this line the culprit was taken and, with the guard on each side and the drum corps in the rear, they beat off the " Rogues' March " down through the open ranks, then out through the camps onto the main road, followed by the crowd, where he was escorted to the railroad train and " fired out " of the army as unfit for military service. Without doubt the poor wretch felt keenly his miserable fate under the scoffs and jeers of the soldiers. It was considered that the punishment of this deserter had as good an effect on the soldiers generally as though he had been shot for his crime before their eyes.

In the meanwhile Generals Meade and Lee were manœuvring

their armies through the country that lay around the Rappahannock and Rapidan rivers and along the line of the Orange & Alexandria railroad, without gaining any decided advantage of each other. General Lee had evidently met his match while seeking the superiority in position to draw on a general engagement,— with all the advantage in his favor. It was not General Meade's intention to slaughter his army by throwing it against the enemy's earthworks. Neither could General Lee be drawn out into the open country to fight on the several occasions offered by his adversary. A change in General Lee's favor occurred on the 24th of September. The Eleventh and Twelfth Corps were suddenly withdrawn from the Army of the Potomac on that day and sent off to reinforce our army in the southwest. The commander-in-chief's interference with General Grant's army in the west had brought matters there into sixes and sevens, and when General Grant was laid up for several weeks by a dangerous fall from his horse the blunders of General Halleck were followed by defeat and dismay. The enemy sent General Longstreet's corps to take advantage of it; and now assistance was sent from the Army of the Potomac to prevent further disaster. As soon as General Grant returned to duty in the west he brought success to our arms throughout that section.

On ascertaining the fact that the Army of the Potomac had been weakened by the loss of two corps, General Lee commenced a move. ment towards the right flank of our army. This strategy on the part of the enemy was met by General Meade withdrawing his forces to the north of the Rappahannock river October 11. General Lee planned to march his forces around our right flank and get between the Army of the Potomac and Washington, in order to obtain a strong defensive line of battle which would force General Meade to attack him. If victorious he could then threaten Washington by making another raid into Maryland. This would be apt to recall our corps from the southwest and relieve the Confederate forces in that section. In the meantime General Lee hoped to successfully assault Washington. General Lee's past record proved him capable of attempting any daring enterprise with his rapid moving army. A few weeks' sojourn in the land of plenty would have been a vacation for his army and each man would have had a chance to supply himself with shoes and clothing for the long winter months that were before him. Without doubt the daring Southern leader would have wound up his fall campaign in Maryland if a good opportunity offered.

After performing our share of picket, guard, and other duties during alternate wet, cool and pleasant weather, near Culpepper, orders came to move on the 10th of October. In the morning our regiment marched to Raccoon ford on the Rapidan river. We stayed there until 4 o'clock P.M. without seeing or hearing anything of the enemy, and then returned to our old camp under orders to be ready to move in two hours. The orders to march, however, were not received until the next morning, Sunday, October 11, at 7 o'clock. At that hour we marched with the division and corps and passed through Culpepper, crossing the Rappahannock at Jones' ford. We formed line of battle during the day, but the expected enemy did not put in an appearance. The march was continued and at 6 P.M. we went into bivouac to the left of our late camp-ground at Beverly ford. On the 12th we moved out a short distance and formed line of battle and remained in position until 1 o'clock P.M. We then recrossed the Rappahannock river, formed into column of divisions, threw out skirmishers and advanced several miles through the woods and swamps. A lively artillery fire of shells was taking place far to our front. We went into bivouac and continued to hear artillery firing off in the direction of Brandy Station where the Second Corps was in position. At 2 o'clock A.M. of the 13th we marched back over the ground of the day before, crossed the river and halted for breakfast on the spot where we bivouacked on the 11th, near Beverly ford. We then continued our line of march to Catlett's Station, on the Orange & Alexandria railroad, to intercept Lee's attempted flank movement, and at 6 P.M. gladly bivouacked after the long hours and weary march of the day. At 9 A.M. the next day, 14th, we followed the line of railroad to Bristoe's Station and halted for dinner. We were but fairly on the march again when a heavy artillery fire opened far to the rear of our column. Our march was not interrupted, however, until we reached the plains of Manassas. Here we formed line of battle and remained in position till 5 o'clock P.M. At that hour we went into column of fours and marched .on the double-quick back to Bristoe's Station, a distance of four miles, to join and support the Second Corps. The Second Corps were engaged with a part of the Confederate forces. After a brisk engagement the enemy was handsomely repulsed by the Second Corps, which captured five pieces of artillery and about 450 prisoners. That evening at supper we could plainly see the reflection of the camp-fires of the enemy in the distance. No doubt they saw ours in like manner. At 8 o'clock P.M. we resumed our retrograde march and by midnight crossed Bull Run at Blackburn's ford. The stream was about knee-deep. At 3 o'clock A.M., 15th, we went into bivouac after covering about thirty odd miles back and forth. At 9

o'clock A.M. we continued our march through to Centreville and
Chantilly, and halted on the old battleground. We went into camp
for the night and on the next day, 16th, it rained hard most of the
day. Bull Run filled up rapidly and ran like a mill race until it
became unfordable.

The enemy was beaten at its own game and when General Lee
found that his flank movement was frustrated he and his army suddenly
disappeared from sight. At 6 P.M. of the 16th we returned to Centreville and went into bivouac. On the 17th we remained quietly in camp
and occupied our time in cleaning up and resting. At such times as
these, after days of rapid marching and fighting, the soldier busies
himself in repairing his wardrobe and cleaning his gun and equipments
in order to be in good condition for immediate service. On the 18th
we were up early and on the march at 5 o'clock A.M. ; halted at 10
A.M. and finished breakfast. General Meade's cavalry, scouts and
skirmishers were actively engaged in every possible way in locating
the position and force of the enemy. General Lee's army was known
to be rapidly falling back and destroying as it went the bridges over
the " runs " and tearing up the railroad track, burning the ties and
bending the iron rails, in order to block the close pursuit of our forces
and cut off our supplies. They succeeded in destroying the Orange &
Alexandria railroad from Bristoe's to Rappahannock Station, a distance
of about twenty miles. Our energetic railroad builders repaired all the
damages in about ten days' time.

We continued our march at noon of the 18th as far as Fox's Mills
and camped. The following morning we moved forward at 7 o'clock
A.M. and marched through that part of the country known as the second
Bull Run. This battlefield was the scene of Gen. John Pope's disastrous rout during the last day of August, 1862. As we moved over
the desolate country night fell upon us and, as it was cloudy weather,
it was very dark. Shortly after the regiment halted they were sound
asleep. In the early morning there was an unusual stir among the
men of the Ninth. They discovered that they had bivouacked among
the skeleton dead of those who were killed over fourteen months ago.
The slight covering of earth had been washed away from their fleshless
forms by the heavy rain-storms of over a year, until the grinning
skeletons of once brave men lay fully exposed in every direction. The
regiment immediately shifted their camp to more congenial ground.
After breakfast the curious ones went to scrutinize the skeleton grave-
yard. The conclusion was reached that Confederate and Union dead
had fallen, or were carried here, and the burial party had hastily

scooped the earth on each side of where they irregularly lay, and barely covered the bodies over. Now the earth had been washed off and the disjointed skulls and bones lay loosely on the top of the hard sod. Patches of uniforms that still clung in small pieces here and there, told us, in mute language, whether they belonged to the Blue or the Gray. We had no means or implements to bury them. It was understood, however, that a detail would be made that morning to place them all in a common grave. And so we left them as we found them, hundreds of " unknown dead " of both armies, " waiting the judgment day."

Early that morning, the 20th, we moved off of this battlefield and at 8 o'clock halted near the Manassas Gap railroad. At noon we resumed our march and passed Groveton, Gainesville and Buckland — all small places — and crossing Broad run, halted two miles this side of the little village of New Baltimore near Bull Run mountain. We camped here until the 24th, then broke camp at 5 P.M. and marched to Auburn. On this short march we found the road heavy with mud. As we approached the mountains we felt the nights of late quite cold. We remained here for seven days, or until October 30, expecting all the time orders to move. At 8 A.M. we marched to Three Mile Station. While in camp here we were well supplied with rations, shoes, etc.

On the 7th day of November, 1863, the Fifth and Sixth Corps, under command of General Sedgwick, fought and won the

BATTLE OF RAPPAHANNOCK STATION.

At 7 o'clock A.M. of the 7th we left camp at Three Mile Station, on the Orange & Alexandria railroad, and reached the vicinity of Rappahannock Station at 1 o'clock P.M. The corps formed into column of divisions and halted for dinner. Not being allowed to make fires our much-desired dipper of coffee had to be dispensed with and the dinner (?) was rather dry without it. We were soon notified of the unseen enemy's proximity by artillery firing and bursting of shells in our front towards the river. In an hour or so we moved forward through a piece of woods and reached a clearing. We threw out skirmishers and crossed to another belt of woods and halted on the edge of another clearing, in full view of the enemy's breastworks along the north bank of the Rappahannock river on elevated ground. They were held by troops of Early's divisions and others of Ewell's corps. The shells from their guns passed over our heads without injury to us. Two of our batteries came on the field and went into position in our front. A lively artillery duel was the result, which lasted a couple of

hours. With few exceptions the enemy's shell went to our rear, no
doubt doing damage to our troops in that direction. Our lines kept
up an infantry fire in addition to that of our artillery till late in the
afternoon. The Sixth Corps then prepared to advance, supported by
the Fifth Corps. Our artillery ceased firing and the Sixth Corps went
forward with a brilliant charge; as they closed in on the works in the
twilight they let out their usual Northern yell and fell upon the enemy
like demons, gallantly capturing fortifications and artillery, together
with 1600 prisoners. A large body of the enemy escaped to the river
by a rapid retreat. The banks were quite steep and in most places the
water was deep, and many were drowned while struggling to get
across. Those who reached the opposite bank with a whole skin,
under the fire of our infantry, were soon lost to veiw in the approaching darkness. Our sudden appearance at Rappahannock Station was
a complete surprise to the Confederates. They were occupying well-
built breastworks and winter quarters. An attack such as we made
on them was wholly unlooked for. After the affair was over we
moved a short distance to the left of our former position and went
into bivouac. Our orders allowed only two small fires to each company for cooking purposes, as there was some fear of a night attack.
Our pickets, however, passed a quiet night.

   At Kelly's ford on the same day, 7th, the Third Corps crossed the
river and assaulted the works lately thrown up by the enemy, and, as
they took them by surprise, captured them, their artillery and 400
prisoners.

   On the 8th we moved at 7 o'clock A.M. and marched to Kelly's
ford, where we halted for breakfast. At 1 P.M. we crossed the river
and after a short march of about two miles went into bivouac. At 5
P.M. the next day we recrossed the Rappahannock and went on duty,
guarding the railroad between Morrisville and Bealton Station. Some
snow fell and everything looked dreary and wintry. We were on this
duty ten days, or until the 19th, when, at 7 A.M., we crossed the river
at Kelly's ford and marched to within four or five miles of Brandy
Station. At this section of the country we went into a piece of woods
and camped. Here the enemy had built some log huts; as they were
poorly constructed and uninviting we demolished them for firewood.
We remained here on picket duty until the 24th.

   General Lee's army was reported south of the Rapidan river in
the vicinity of Orange Court House, intrenching and going into winter
quarters. General Meade planned to move south and flank his position
and works so as to force him into the open country and give battle.

The Ninth Massachusetts joined the line of march on the 24th at 7 o'clock A.M. We moved slowly forward in a rain-storm over a soft heavy road for about two miles, when the infantry, artillery, cavalry and ammunition wagons began to stall in the mud and mire. The heavy rain made it worse and deeper every minute. Our orders to march were countermanded and we returned to camp. The army was pleased to escape from a repetition of the " mud march " of 1862. After two hours in a cold drenching rain we were likewise glad of the opportunity to dry ourselves before a good blazing log fire. After nearly forty-eight hours of drying weather we made another start on the 26th of November, at 8 A.M., and marched until 9 o'clock P.M. Having crossed the Rapidan river at Culpepper ford and passed through Richardsville, we bivouacked that night near Chancellorsville. On the 27th we marched at 7 A.M. and early in the afternoon reached New Hope Church. We arrived here in time to relieve General Gregg's cavalry, which was engaged in a skirmish with the enemy. The Fifth Corps deployed in line of battle as well as the nature of woods and road would admit of, expecting to meet a threatened attack of the enemy. Our skirmishers advanced rapidly and found the enemy heavily intrenched and waiting. General Meade was obliged to forego his intended attack at this time on account of the Third Corps (which was delayed by a skirmish with the enemy at Raccoon ford) failing to arrive and form a junction with the Second Corps. While in line of battle our adjutant, M. W. Phalen, was hit by an unexploded, rico-chetting, spent spherical shell, on the hip. The shock lamed him con-siderably without any other apparent serious damage. He remained on the field, but was unable to perform any physical duty for a few days. One of the Ninth men declared that " Our adjutant was too good a soldier to leave the field, even if he was hit by a cannon ball!" Another man forcibly remarked: " When Adjutant Phalen was a lieutenant commanding our company at Gaines' Mill fight, he was hit in the forehead and bleeding, and then, bedad! he wouldn't go to the rear. He called it a mere scratch. The wound looked then, for all the world, like a red cross in the centre of his forehead." The men's thoughts were turned in another direction when strict orders were given that matches or fires must not be lighted after dark. At this time more unpleasant orders could not be issued. When night fell upon us we were ordered to lie on our arms and be ready to move at a moment's notice. The orders against lighting matches and fires were given through fear of exposing our position and presence and of drawing the artillery fire of the enemy who were reported in full force in our front.

The night proved to be bitter cold and but few, if any, slept much. Broad daylight next morning found us stealthily cooking coffee to warm our chilled anatomy. These kind of nights were a dreadful strain on our youthful stamina.

During the forenoon of the 27th the enemy's cavalry, in trying to locate General Meade's forces, ran across a part of our wagon train in the woods and made sad havoc, by plunder and fire, of fifteen six-mule teams before the guards and additional troops from the marching column could rally sufficiently and drive them off. After the wretched and scattered management of the detached infantry wagon guards, it is a matter of surprise that the enemy did not destroy more. The crack of a carbine from an unknown source was sufficient notice to the average officers of the quartermaster's and commissary's departments to retire rapidly in the opposite direction from whence the report of firearms came. Of course there were exceptions. As they were well mounted one seldom or ever heard of their being shot or captured when their teams were raided.

At 8 o'clock of the 28th we marched on to Robertson's tavern. Our column moved by the right flank and about 2 o'clock P.M. halted and bivouacked for the day and night. A heavy rain had set in, causing delay all around, particularly to the movements of our artillery. The Second, Sixth, First and Third Corps were now in line in front of General Lee's army. At 5 next morning, the 29th, we moved into position with the corps on the east side of Mine run, relieving the Second Corps on the right of the line. At the foot of the hill or elevation on which we were in line, flowed Mine run, about ten feet wide and three feet of water, not to mention the depth of the mud at its bottom; and beyond, for a thousand yards, the open and wooded country ascended gradually to the brow of the hill about one hundred feet high. General Lee had secured this part of the country for several miles for his line of battle behind strongly-built intrenchments of logs and earth, with abatis and rifle-pits, and there awaited our coming. General Warren with the Second Corps and two divisions of the Third Corps was to open the attack on the enemy's right flank and expressed himself to General Meade as confident of carrying everything before him. The Sixth and Fifth Corps were under orders to charge and carry the Confederate left. One division of the Third Corps and the whole of the First Corps were to charge and carry the enemy's centre. The sound of General Warren's guns on the left at 8 o'clock A.M. on the 30th, was to be the signal for the attack by our forces on the right at 9 A.M. Then the charge on the centre was to follow. At 2 o'clock on the morning of the 30th, in zero weather, the troops of the Fifth Corps were ordered to retire and divest themselves of all superfluous luggage in order to be prepared for the charge down the slope, across the stream and up the hill into the fire of the enemy's batteries, through the abatis and other entanglements, and then to carry the entrenchments at the point of the bayonet. The corps after thus preparing for the charge then moved to the right flank about a mile further and, under cover of the woods, took up their position on the extreme right flank. Our line of battle for the assault was formed by brigades in two lines. The hour of 8 o'clock A.M. arrived, but our anxious and listening lines heard nothing from General Warren's artillery signals. Nearly an hour passed when General Meade, who was as anxious as the rest, received a dispatch from General Warren, saying in effect, that the enemy's position was discovered to be so formidable that he would not advise an assault, for, if undertaken, they could not succeed. The conclusion was corroborated later by General Meade and others of his corps generals, by personal examination of the ground in front of General Warren's command. After realizing that General Lee's position was impregnable, General Meade reluctantly consented to withdraw his army and seek winter quarters.

The wisdom of General Meade's final decision consisted in refusing, with the concurrence of his corps commanders, to assault a position that the enemy had carefully selected and then fortified and intrenched to an impregnable degree on front and flanks. After holding our front line till dark we returned to our former ground and resumed our luggage and bivouacked for the night.

The Army of the Potomac, reduced to five small corps when it settled down in front of the Confederate army at Mine run, met with a series of mishaps impossible for a commander to provide against or avoid. The movements of troops, artillery and ammunition trains were delayed on account of the mud in swampy places on primitive roads through dense woods crusted over at times by the frozen mud of zero weather. The enemy having occupied a chosen position for days in advance made it impregnable by strong fortifications, bristling with cannon, such as Lee's veterans now knew so well how to build and defend. Our army was obliged to resort to every device known in athletic exercise to keep from freezing, as fires were not allowed. This continual exertion, added to loss of sleep and scant rations from day to day, reduced their mental and physical vigor to such an extent that the fighting qualities of the average soldier were greatly impaired. That our men were prepared and expected to charge on Lee's works and do their level best, is self-evident. They took care to carry in their clothing their names and regiments. Letters and hurried farewells were written and placed in the hands of those who would be likely to escape or keep out of the slaughter. All present knew that the death-roll would be large, for, added to the killed would be the wounded, who would freeze to death between the lines. Everything to their advantage or disdavantage was talked over and discussed. How, for instance, they would dash down the hill for momentum to take a flying leap over the run. Once over, then assist each other and form line, sweep up the hill and charge with savage yells on the enemy's works even to victory or death. The reader can gain but a faint idea of the hard condition of matters with the brave old army, when the order came declaring the assault abandoned. Their strained nerves relaxed that day and quietness fell upon the troops as they sought to pass the night in a cold blanket on the frozen ground. Tuesday, Dec. 1, 1863, was spent in front of the enemy in order to cover the movement of the army at dark. At 6 P.M. we left Mine run and marched in a slow and tedious manner through the woods and clearings along the Germanna plank road across the Rapidan river at Germanna ford, and bivouacked about a mile or two beyond it at 3 o'clock on the morning of the 2d. After a few hours' sleep and a light breakfast on very scant fare we moved forward at 8 A.M. and halted about noon at Stevensburg, within four miles of Brandy Station, on the Orange & Alexandria railroad. After a much-needed rest until the morning of the 3d we continued our march at 9 A.M., passing Brandy and Rappahannock Stations, and, crossing the river at this point, reached Bealton Station.

General Lee on discovering our disappearance from his front, sent out, on the 2d, a large force to reconnoitre General Meade's movements. On learning that his army had crossed the Rapidan and were moving across the Rappahannock for winter quarters, he did likewise. In fact, Lee's army was pretty well established in winter quarters already.

The losses in the Fifth Corps during the entire campaign in Virginia since July 17, 1863, were reported as follows: 4 men killed, 1 officer and 18 men wounded, 2 officers and 59 men captured and missing; total, 84.

CHAPTER XIX.

CAMP NEAR BEALTON STATION.

IN WINTER QUARTERS — EXCELLENT DISCIPLINE — BAD MANAGEMENT IN THE BRIGADE COMMISSARY — THE RUSSIAN METHOD — THE QUARTER-MASTER DEPARTMENT — PICKET DUTY — MOUNTED RAIDERS — ATH-LETIC GAMES, ETC. — THE HICKORY CLUB — A CIRCLE OF THE FENIAN BROTHERHOOD — ITS HISTORY IN PART — OFFICERS' WIVES IN CAMP — ORDER ON RE-ENLISTING — THE 32D MASSACHUSETTS RE-ENLIST — CHRISTMAS DAY — GENERAL GRANT COMMANDER OF OUR ARMIES — GENERAL MEADE REAPPOINTED — GENERALS GRANT AND SHERMAN — GRANT'S OPINION OF THE ARMY OF THE POTOMAC — ST. PATRICK'S DAY CELEBRATED — THE ARMY OF THE POTOMAC CONSOLIDATED AND REORGANIZED — THE ORGANIZATION OF THE CONFEDERATE ARMY — ENTERING ON THE SPRING CAMPAIGN — THE NINTH LEAVES CAMP — AGAIN ON THE MARCH WITH THE FIFTH CORPS.

* * * * * *

" We have shared our blankets and tents together,
And have marched and fought in all kinds of weather,
And hungry and full we have been;
Had days of battle, and days of rest:
But this memory I cling to, and love the best, —
We have drunk from the same canteen! "

* * * * * *

MILES O'REILLY. — " The Canteen."

THE Ninth Massachusetts Volunteers was fortunate in its selection of a place to camp for the winter. The ground was slightly elevated above its surroundings and well seasoned with a top dressing of dry, hard, sandy soil. The trees were well spaced, very tall, and their roots interlaced the earth in every direction. This dry surface absorbed in a short time all the rain that fell. The sun shone on every part of the camp at intervals during the day; it penetrated through the wide spaces between the trees and branches, giving a liberal share of light and warmth. On the grassy clearings at the edge of the woods on two sides one could enjoy all the sun and exercise he desired. Timber cut from an adjacent woods furnished material for log huts and firewood for the regiment within easy transportation. The water for drinking and cooking purposes was good and abundant. A clear run near camp gave excellent facilities for washing clothes. Under these circumstances in a short time every one in the regiment occupied comfortable quarters. The Orange & Alexandria railroad ran parallel with our camp on the west side, a hundred yards distant, so that we always had a good view of the military trains as they went back and forth over the road.

Colonel Guiney once more resumed a rigid and necessary camp discipline. Guard mounting, for picket and guard duty, company and battalion drills and dress parade, were of daily occurrence. The colonel commanding held regular Sunday morning inspections of the regiment and quarters. A chapel was erected for Father Egan, who said mass regularly and diligently attended to the spiritual welfare of all. The surgeons — Doctors Sullivan and Ryan — had erected a regimental hospital for the care of the sick and likewise looked sharp after the physical condition of the regiment. Adjutant Phalen, who was second to none in his duties, attended diligently to everything pertaining to his office, aided by the sergeant-major of the non-commissioned staff. The quartermaster's, ordnance and commissary's supplies for the regiment were always abundantly furnished under the direction of Quartermaster Macnamara, assisted by his competent quartermaster and commissary sergeants of the non-commissioned staff.

During the winter Colonel Guiney was called upon to act as brigade commander during the absence of that officer. At such times Lieutenant-Colonel Hanley commanded the regiment and ably seconded his colonel's line of discipline with marked ability.

Major Mahan was busily engaged on courts-martial, a line of duty on which he was frequently detailed; for not only in our division, but throughout the army, some unfortunate officers were generally undergoing trial for misdemeanors. Our company commanders, Captains McGunnigle, J. W. Macnamara, Flynn, Finnerty, O'Brien, O'Leary, O'Hara, Burke, Tobin and Phelan, aided by their lieutenants and 1st sergeants, were kept busy attending to the multifarious duties required to keep their companies in a first-class condition, such as the colonel's discipline required and the good-natured rivalry in the regiment demanded. Everything considered, our winter quarters and duties at Camp Bealton were the best we ever enjoyed. Colonel Guiney was wont to remark that everything went along like clockwork; that his field, staff and line officers were efficient and painstaking in their duties, and that he was particularly fortunate in having an adjutant and quartermaster who understood and performed their duties in a thorough manner. Colonel Hanley to this day corroborates these praiseworthy remarks of Colonel Guiney. Our chaplain, Father Egan, who held the love and respect of all the regiment, was a great factor as a peacemaker; and he had the happy faculty of adjusting to the satisfaction of those concerned, all the disputes and little differences that naturally occurred among so many men constantly together. But few of our officers were on detached service while in the army. At this camp Captain Tobin was appointed acting assistant inspector-general on the staff of Colonel Sweitzer, commanding 2d brigade. Captain Flynn, who was in poor health on sick leave, joined the regiment at this camp and was subsequently ordered on detached duty at Galloupe's Island, Boston Harbor, where he remained until the muster-out of the regiment.

Ten days' leave of absence and ten days' furlough, for officers and men respectively, were allowed during the winter. It gave quite a number the opportunity to pay a short visit to their families and friends.

A little episode occurred at this camp after we were well settled, that pertained to the quartermaster's department, which is considered worthy of relating here. Our regiment had scattered amongst the different companies quite a number of recruits who began to grumble about short rations. The grumbling continued until it was quietly investigated by the quartermaster. His commissary-sergeant reported the fact that Captain Burdett, the brigade commissary, was stinting him on vegetable rations; that his salesmen were selling for cash to all comers the vegetables that should have been issued to the regiments. The brigade commissary, nor his salesmen, did not pay any attention to the remonstrances on the part of Commissary-Sergeant Monaghan of the Ninth in regard to this matter. Under these circumstances the quartermaster of the Ninth sent in to the colonel a monthly statement of the quantity of rations of all kinds allowed the regiment, and the quantity received by it for the same period. The difference that was due the regiment, but which it had not received, was rather startling in the vegetable line. This report, which was of an unusual nature, was neatly drawn up in a tabulated form. The colonel sent it along endorsed, "Respectfully forwarded to Colonel Sweitzer, commanding 2d brigade, 1st division, Fifth Army Corps, Army of the Potomac." Colonel Sweitzer, upon receiving this statement, sent at once for Captain Burdett. The brigade commissary — whose sales and clerical work were all performed by his men — could form no conception, apparently, of the statement submitted, or offer any straightforward reply.   He requested to be allowed to send for his chief clerk, a citizen.   When he arrived he made matters worse for his boss, by attempting to deny everything charged.   Enlisted men, detailed, had charge of the sale and issuing of rations.   The captain and his chief clerk, therefore, paid no attention to the matter.   They only looked after the cash receipts and drawing supplies in bulk.   The brigade commander failing to unravel the difficulty dismissed the commissary and his clerk from his presence, and issued a special order which required quartermasters of regiments to draw their rations in person.   The order was lame from the fact that it did not call on the captain and commissary to issue in person; on that account there was one quartermaster who never obeyed it.   The order itself was, to say the least, a stupid way out of the difficulty.   Commissioned officers could not be compelled to draw rations from enlisted men.   Neither could the captain and commissary of subsistence be obliged to give what he did not have on hand.   However, as far as the Ninth regiment was concerned, the report sent in produced the desired effect.   The affair created quite a breeze in the commissary department.   The other regiments, at that time, were not aware of the cause that called for quartermasters to draw rations, particularly when each had a commissary sergeant to attend solely to the business as well as, if not better than any one else.

When next the commissary sergeant of the Ninth drew rations, after the above mentioned order was issued, he was instructed to wait until the other regiments were supplied.   This he did, and the result was that he was more than pleased at the quantities of various goods received, and during the rest of that winter and spring, there was no cause for complaint on his or the regiment's part.

The fact of the matter was our brigade commissary and his staff of employees, like most of the others throughout the volunteer army, were making money for themselves in large sums, " by indirection." The wagon trains in winter quarters were used as wholesale liquor stores and gambling resorts.   Wagon masters (citizens) and wagoners were in league with the commissary of subsistence, or his agents, and they bought and paid in cash fabulous sums for whiskey by the barrel. After the original whiskey was well watered it was retailed, through runners, to the soldiers by the canteen and bottle for unheard of prices. Some of it was so thoroughly watered that it was impossible for the consumers to get drunk on it without spending a small fortune.   Not having the money to indulge their thirst for whiskey of this brand and price, they kept sober against their will.   Army rations of all sorts were sold far above the regulation prices to any and all cash buyers.

Commissaries in their monthly accounts, or returns, to the department at Washington charged the regiments with full rations, whether they received them or not. There was no check on their returns and no vouchers required. Quartermasters of regiments made no returns to Washington for rations received as they were not called for. They were therefore powerless to check the evil. At the end of each month the surplus cash was divided between the commissary and his staff of employees; the captain, as a matter of course, getting the lion's share. A man named Bayley, of the Ninth — above the average in education and intelligence — was on detached duty in Captain Burdett's commissary department. The colonel of his regiment offered to give him a commission as 2d lieutenant if he would return to duty with his company, where he previously held the rank of sergeant. He chose to remain where he was as he was making more money by it. He told the writer some of the inside history of the commissary department from his experience. He estimated Captain Burdett's share of "savings" when he left the service at $40,000. Captain Burdett himself made no secret of the fact that he had amassed a small fortune. The government was powerless to prevent it except by calling for proper returns from regiments. It's a question, then, if that would fully check the evil. The writer has heard of regimental quartermasters who were acting as assistant commissary of subsistence following in the footsteps of their peculating predecessors.

In the Russian army, it is said that officers found defrauding troops of their legitimate rations in any way are taken out and shot. The system of peculating in the commissary department was so rank in our volunteer army during the civil war, that it is simply a matter of wonder that some drastic measures were not used to prevent it, in a degree, by the department at Washington. If the Russian method was enforced many vacancies would have been opened for the political statesmen in Washington to fill again with their friends and favorites.

At this camp the field and staff horses of the different regiments suffered for the want of grain and hay, particularly the latter article of fodder. The army had an abundant supply by rail of bundle hay. Army and the different corps headquarters used their surplus to thatch their stables and for bedding for their horses. It was claimed that the regiments along the line of the railroad were well supplied from the bundles that fell from the platform cars on their way by the various camps. It was a pity that this was not true, but the reverse of it was the fact. The report was denied, still all complaints went for naught. The red-tape line from regiment to brigade, to division, to corps and to army headquarters, was a long and tedious process to go through with the expectation of rectifying anything that went wrong. What was everybody's business was nobody's business; so that the poor horses in the regiments continued to go hungry and grow thin from lack of hay.

High-graded assistant quartermasters, in many respects, were more ornamental than useful. They would caper about on horseback and appear as full of business as a balloon full of gas when tied down to a stump. They were the protégés of politicians, and their importance swelled with the strength of their "pull." It was amusing to see a little captain and assistant quartermaster bobbing up and down on a big galloping horse — little quartermasters always rode large horses — followed helter-skelter by his six mule teams of the 1st division, looking for a place of safety in the woods where the guerillas couldn't find him. The little man would be an important personage presiding over a ladies' tea party, but in the army he was, like many others of his kind, a misfit. Their trains were always excellent plunder for the raiding cavalry of the enemy. Still, withal, this class — the protégés of politicians and place hunters — was always promoted to positions that were sinecures, or if there happened to be more or less work to the office some one else was sure to be called on to do it. The ornamental figure-head, however, always got the credit of it.

Our picket duty across the country and at the river was very severe during alternate changes of frost, snow, rain and mud. Twenty-four hours' tour of duty by details from each company was required. The regiment itself was on guard against the raids frequently made on railroad and bridges by the daring guerillas. We had a strong outlying camp guard and every night each company was cautioned to be prepared to turn out at a moment's notice by drum or bugle and pursue the enemy through woods and clearings. We turned out on several occasions in pursuit of the mounted raiders, but they were too fleet for infantry to capture. A force of cavalry should have been detailed with each regiment for this purpose.

During the daytime, when off duty, the spare hours of the officers were spent in various ways. Broadsword and foil exercise and pistol practice were indulged in. Athletic games, in which quoits, dumb bells, putting the stone, jumping, etc., figured, were also favorite ways of passing a pleasant hour. In the evenings, in the quartermaster's big log hut, the "Hickory Club," with its badge of silver, held debates and other literary exercises. The orator, the poet and the singer, were given full sway in airing their talents for the delight of others.

Poor Ireland occupied a warm spot in the minds and hearts of her exiled children of the Ninth on the sacred soil of Virginia. Regular meetings by a " Circle of the Fenian Brotherhood," were held at various times. The sinews of war were freely contributed and forwarded to the headquarters of that organization, which was then in great strength throughout the United States. One of its members, Lieut. Timothy Dacey of the Ninth, was destined at a subsequent period to enact a prominent and desperate part across the water on behalf of his native land. After the war he went to Ireland in the patriotic cause, was arrested, and while riding in an English prison van was rescued and escaped to America. Allen, Larkin and O'Brien were arrested and charged with killing a policeman in the van, and suffered a martyr's death by hanging at the hands of the English government. They protested their innocence to the last, and United States Minister Adams failed to save them from their doom. They died as brave men. Their death was as patriotic as though they fell on the battlefield. Their memory will live forever green in the Irish heart. Others of the Ninth " Circle " went to Ireland, and more of them were engaged in the fiasco on Canada. But England, " the dark mother of the penal laws," still holds Ireland in her cruel grasp.

*   *   *   *   *   *

" Oh! weep those days, those penal days —
    Their memory still on Ireland weighs.

They bribed the flock, they bribed the son
    To sell the priest and rob the sire;
Their dogs were taught alike to run
    Upon the scent of wolf and friar.

*   *   *   *   *   *

A stranger held the land and tower
    Of many a noble fugitive;
No ' Popish ' lord had lordly power;
    The peasant scarce had leave to live.
      Above his head
      A ruined shed,
No tenure but a tyrant's will —
      Forbid to plead,
      Forbid to read,
Disarmed, disfranchised, imbecile —
    What wonder if our step betrays
    The freedman, born in penal days? "

*   *   *   *   *   *

THOMAS DAVIS. — " The Penal Days."

While merciless to the weak, she seeks alliance with the stronger nation in order to hold and advance her aggrandizing policy. The United States would, indeed, be recreant to its traditions, history and principles, if at any time it joins Tory England in her covert schemes for conquest, or as her crafty statesmen put it, " for extending civilization to the benighted people of the earth."

During the winter many ladies arrived at the front, on short visits to their husbands, officers in the army. In our camp Colonel Guiney and several of the line officers had their wives on a visit. In our locality, during that time, the ladies had several " scares " from the cavalry raiders. In order to entertain the ladies some of the empty houses were utilized for dancing parties occasionally. Horseback riding was also indulged in, but the fear of being captured by the marauding cavalry of the enemy destroyed much of the pleasure of that exciting and healthy exercise. When the time came for leaving the army it is safe to say that none of the ladies regretted going to their northern homes. Their stay in camp no doubt was cheerful for their husbands, but it must have been, when the novelty wore off, cheerless and monotonous for the wives. The army, in time of war, at any and all seasons of the year, is only fit for savage men, who enjoy rude health and are reckless of life, and always ready for battle. Such as these win victories.

A General Order, No. 191, was received about the middle of December, 1863, inviting all three years' men to re-enlist for three years more. As a reward for so doing they would be allowed thirty days' furlough. The order was pretty thoroughly canvassed in the Ninth and argued pro and con. The general sentiment arrived at was to fully serve out the first three years and go home and get mustered out. Then each man would be free to do as he wished afterwards, and enlist in any arm of the service he saw fit. About thirty or so of the regiment re-enlisted and enjoyed the pleasure of a thirty days' furlough.

The 32d Massachusetts were in quarters a few miles from us at a place called Liberty. Most of that regiment re-enlisted and went home in a body in January, 1864. They received a rousing reception on their arrival in Boston, and had a jolly time at balls, parties, dinners, etc., and promptly returned to their old camp where they arrived Feb. 23, 1864, to be known as the 32d Massachusetts Veteran Volunteers.

Christmas was quietly enjoyed by the regiment. Mass was celebrated by Father Egan. Boxes containing eatables, etc., had previously arrived for many of the regiment, and of course were generously shared with others. Turkeys and chickens, although old and cold, were relished by men with good appetites. There were sufficient wet goods to pass around and make the sad ones merry, and the pleasant fellows jolly.

While the winter was passing at the front it seems that the authorities at Washington had agreed on a plan to close up the rebellion. The project was to simply place the whole United States army in all its branches, and the ramifications into which it was twisted by incompetent generals, politicians and others, under the supreme control of one man.

General Grant's great successes in the west brought his name prominently before the country. The public loyal men of the republic, from the President down, called for his appointment to that responsible position and work. Congress restored the grade of lieutenant-general to the army, Feb. 26, 1864. General Grant was appointed to that rank and confirmed by the U.S. senate, March 2, 1864. He was ordered from the west and received his commission as lieutenant-general at the hands of the President on the 9th of March, 1864. On this occasion President Lincoln made a short address, and General Grant on accepting the honor of Lieutenant-General and Commander of all the Armies of the United States, made a short address in reply.

On the 10th of March, 1864, General Grant visited General Meade at his headquarters at Brandy Station, north of the Rapidan river. He there reappointed General Meade Commander of the Army of the Potomac.

March 11, General Grant returned to Washington, and went west to meet, by appointment, General Sherman at Nashville. On arriving there he placed General Sherman in command of the western army. From the first beginning of hostilities these two great generals had been firm friends. Being both stubborn and aggressive characters they had bitter personal enemies. When first appointed to command in the west General Sherman made the statement, in the course of other remarks, that he ought to have two hundred thousand men to hold his lines and accomplish his purpose against the enemy. Simon Cameron, then Secretary of War, who was holding a personal interview with Sherman, and on a visit to that section in his official capacity, afterward in reference to the interview, said in the hearing of others that General Sherman was crazy or insane. This remark, coming from so high an official as the Secretary of War, was taken up by the public press and sent broadcast over the country. This base slander worked much injury, at that time, against General Sherman, and was harped upon so long that it caused him great personal annoyance. It was only by his daring and wonderful achievements that he outlived the injury to his character.   General Grant was no less annoyed during his early career by the slanders circulated about him as a hard whiskey drinker, and that on occasions he got drunk.   These stories proved to be all lies out of whole cloth.   In the course of time the story about Grant getting drunk reached the ears of President Lincoln, at a time when Grant was immensely successful in his western operations.   The President said "that he would like to know what brand of whiskey it was that General Grant drank; if he could find out he would send some of it to his other generals and see if it wouldn't bring them success, too."

At a later day in war times a sycophant thought to flatter General Sherman by disparaging General Grant.   The blunt old veteran stopped him quite suddenly by exclaiming: "Don't talk to me, sir, about Grant in that manner.   It won't do!   I know all about him; he is a great general.   He stood by me when I was crazy and I stood by him when he was drunk!   And now, sir, we both stand by each other!" Exit sycophant, with a flea in his ear.

On the 26th of March, General Grant, having returned to the Army of the Potomac, established his headquarters at Culpepper Court House, a few miles south of General Meade's headquarters.   Here he continued his preparations for an early aggressive campaign in Virginia.

When General Grant was on his way to establish his headquarters at Culpepper, several of the Ninth officers went to Bealton Station to "get a look at him," and, if possible, to "shake hands and speak to him."   When the slow going military train stopped General Grant got off at the station and received the quiet greeting of those present — who approached him — in his usual democratic way.   After a few words of welcome, some one asked him what he thought of the Army of the Potomac.   He replied, "It's a good army, but it has never been fought long enough!"   Those who heard the remark then, and about it afterwards, were somewhat puzzled at its real meaning.   Very little talk was indulged in.   Everyone was looking at the stocky little general; and Grant, apparently unconcerned, was quietly looking around him.   When the whistle blew he stepped onto the train.   It moved away from the station over the ungraded military railroad like a loose jointed sea serpent, rolling over the waves, up and down, over to one side, and then to the other, twisting and dragging its slow length along, in a way that would try the patience of a more phlegmatic temperament than General Grant's.   Before many weeks passed, in the subsequent campaign of May, June and July, 1864, everyone knew what General Grant meant by his reply above mentioned.   The Army of the Potomac had been, indeed, "fought long enough" then, to lose 62,000 men out of the army of 122,000 with which it started on the campaign.

SAINT PATRICK'S DAY.

All praise to Saint Patrick, who brought to our mountains
The gift of God's faith, the sweet light of His love!
All praise to the shepherd who showed us the fountains
That rise in the heart of the Saviour above!
For hundreds of years,
In smiles and in tears,
Our saint hath been with us, our shield and our stay;
All else may have gone,
Saint Patrick alone,
He hath been to us light when earth's lights were all set,
For the glories of faith they can never decay;
And the best of our glories is bright with us yet
In the faith and the feast of Saint Patrick's Day.

Rev. F. W. Faber.

The life and deeds of the noble Apostle St. Patrick, who, by peaceful means, established Catholic Christianity throughout all pagan Ireland over fourteen hundred years ago, and immortalized " the dear little shamrock of Ireland " in his sermon on the Trinity at Tara, is so dear to all true Irishmen that their hearts swell with emotion as they annually celebrate, the world over, the day of his birth. It is a tribute of love paid to the memory of one of the early followers of the cross of Christ for his blessed work in redeeming the Irish from the sins of paganism, and leading them forth into the light of Christianity and the worship of the true God. March 17, 1864, was therefore looked forward to with pleasure as a day of great rejoicing by the Ninth regiment. In our camp at Bealton woods the birthday of Ireland's patron saint was celebrated by her expatriated sons with deep religious faith at Mass, at an early hour, Chaplain Father Egan, celebrant.

The forenoon was rationally enjoyed in viewing and taking part in several athletic games. In the afternoon the exciting sport of horse racing was freely indulged in, and passed off without friction or accident of any kind. Visitors from brigade and division headquarters, the 62d Pennsylvania, 32d Massachusetts Volunteers and other regiments at a distance, were warmly welcomed and cheerfully entertained. Under cover a social and literary entertainment took place in the evening, Colonel Guiney presiding. After the good things, brought previously from Washington by our quartermaster, were indulged in and disposed of, the home talent of the Ninth entertained the party with poetry, oratory and song, in a highly pleasing manner. The evening was remarkable for that easy good-fellowship which only soldiers know how to enjoy, and the pleasant occasion was one long to be remembered. It was the second and last entertainment, on St. Patrick's day, of the regiment while in the service. The different companies enjoyed themselves, and during the evening behaved splendidly. It is sad to say that for many of our brave officers and men, it was their last social gathering on earth, as they were called upon to lay down their lives for their country in the early subsequent campaign that followed.

During the latter part of March, about the 23d, the Army of the Potomac was consolidated and reorganized. The First Corps was merged into the Fifth Corps. The Third Corps was merged into the Second Corps. This new formation of the army did not take place without creating great dissatisfaction in the First and Third Corps on losing their hard-earned identity. Neither did it enhance the *esprit de corps* of the army itself.

The Army of the Potomac was now constituted as follows, Maj.-Gen. George G. Meade, commanding : —

SECOND CORPS (4 Divisions).
Maj.-Gen. W. S. Hancock, Commanding.

First Division	(4 Brigades)	.	Brig.-Gen. F. C. Barlow, Commanding.
Second Division	(3 Brigades)	.	Brig.-Gen. John Gibbon, Commanding.
Third Division	(2 Brigades)	.	Maj.-Gen. D. B. Birney, Commanding.
Fourth Division	(2 Brigades)	.	Brig.-Gen. G. Mott, Commanding.
Artillery Brigade	. . . . .	.	Col. John C. Tidball, Commanding.

FIFTH CORPS (4 Divisions).
Maj.-Gen. G. K. Warren, Commanding.

First Division	(3 Brigades)	.	Brig.-Gen. Chas. Griffin, Commanding.
Second Division	(3 Brigades)	.	Brig.-Gen. John C. Robinson, Commanding.
Third Division { (1 absent) (2 Brigades) }		.	Brig.-Gen. S. W. Crawford, Commanding.
Fourth Division	(3 Brigades)	.	Brig.-Gen. J. S. Wadsworth, Commanding.
Artillery Brigade	. . . . .	.	Col. C. S. Wainwright, Commanding.

SIXTH CORPS (3 Divisions).
Maj.-Gen. John Sedgwick, Commanding.

First Division	(4 Brigades)	.	Brig.-Gen. H. G. Wright, Commanding.
Second Division	(4 Brigades)	.	Brig.-Gen. Geo. W. Getty, Commanding.
Third Division	(2 Brigades)	.	Brig.-Gen. Jas. B. Ricketts, Commanding.
Artillery Brigade	. . . . .	.	Col. C. H. Tompkins, Commanding.

General Burnside was senior to General Meade and his corps was therefore only attached to the Army of the Potomac. He was under the immediate orders of General Grant.

NINTH CORPS (4 Divisions).
Maj.-Gen. A. E. Burnside, Commanding.

First Division (2 Brigades) . Brig.-Gen. T. G. Stevenson, Commanding.
Second Division (2 Brigades) . Brig.-Gen. R. B. Potter, Commanding.
Third Division (2 Brigades) . Brig.-Gen. O. B. Willcox, Commanding.
Fourth Division (2 Brigades) . Brig.-Gen. Edw. Ferrero, Commanding.
Provisional Brigade . . . . . Col. E. G Marshall, Commanding.

CAVALRY CORPS (3 Divisions).
Maj.-Gen. P. H. Sheridan, Commanding.

First Division (3 Brigades) . Brig.-Gen. A. T. A. Torbert, Commanding.
Second Division (2 Brigades) . Brig.-Gen. D. McM. Gregg, Commanding.
Third Division (2 Brigades) . Brig.-Gen. J. H. Wilson, Commanding.
Artillery and Artillery Reserve . Brig.-Gen. H. J. Hunt, Commanding.
Provost Guard . . . . . . Brig.-Gen. M. R. Patrick, Commanding.
Volunteer Engineers . . . . Brig.-Gen. H. W. Benham, Commanding.

In referring to the artillery — over 300 guns — General Grant
says : " This arm was in such abundance that the fourth of it could
not be used to advantage in such a country as we were destined to pass
through."

The Army of the Potomac numbered for duty 122,000 men.

CONFEDERATE ARMY.

Army of Nòrthern Virginia, commanded by Gen. Robert E. Lee.

FIRST ARMY CORPS.
Lieut.-Gen. R. H. Anderson, Commanding.

Maj.-Gen. Geo. E. Pickett's Division of four Brigades.
Maj.-Gen. C. W. Field's Division of three Brigades.
Maj.-Gen. J. B. Kershaw's Division of four Brigades.

SECOND ARMY CORPS.
Maj.-Gen Jubal A. Early, Commanding.

Maj.-Gen. John B. Gordon's Division of four Brigades.
Maj.-Gen. Edward Johnson's Division of four Brigades.
Maj.-Gen. R. E. Rodes' Division of five Brigades.

THIRD ARMY CORPS.
Lieut.-Gen. A. P. Hill, Commanding.

Maj.-Gen. Wm. Mahone's Division of five Brigades.
Maj.-Gen. C. M. Wilcox's Division of four Brigades.
Maj.-Gen. Geo. H. Heth's Division of five Brigades.
Unattached : Fifth Alabama Battalion.

CAVALRY CORPS.
Lieut.-Gen. Wade Hampton, Commanding.
Maj.-Gen. Fitz Hugh Lee's Division of two Brigades.
Maj.-Gen. M. C. Butler's Division of three Brigades.
Maj.-Gen. W. H. F. Lee's Division of two Brigades.

ARTILLERY RESERVE.
Brig -Gen. W. N. Pendleton, Commanding.
Three Divisions, composed of 57 Batteries, Horse Artillery, etc., over 200 guns

The whole number in Lee's army was nearly 70,000 men.

The foregoing represents only the principal formation of General Lee's army. The divisions were known only by the names of their first commanders.

The weather during the month of April, 1864, at Bealton camp was, with the exception of a few days in the middle of the month, remarkably fine and pleasant.

The regiment was in excellent condition as a whole, and carefully preparing for the spring campaign, which was now looked forward to and talked about every day. As baggage transportation was limited Colonel Guiney cautioned his officers to reduce everything in that line to the lowest possible limit. Company commanders were instructed to see that their men reduced their luggage to the lowest possible carrying scale, and to be prepared in every way for long marches and hard fighting. That remark of General Grant, " that the Army of the Potomac was a good army but had not been fought long enough," looked like future business, and was vividly remembered by the Ninth. They were therefore looking forward to a hard campaign and they got it.

We received orders to move April 30, 1864. The regiment broke camp early in the morning of that day. Everyone was busy packing up a few selected things, and discarding the winter's accumulation of useful camp furniture, etc., to be left behind. Like the heartless friendships of selfish humanity they were lightly and thoughtlessly abandoned when they ceased to be of any further use; kicked, as it were, into oblivion, or left behind for other's uses.

It was afternoon of the 30th when the Ninth Massachusetts Volunteers, in good condition and cheerful spirits, went forth on the march, from the old camp at Bealton, to meet the enemy under the direction of General Grant and the leadership of General Meade. After a light march of five miles we bivouacked at Rappahannock station where the regiments of our brigade, division and corps came together again from their winter quarters. The line of railroad that we had watched and guarded so faithfully all winter was now in the hands of the colored division of regiments attached to General Burnside's Ninth Army Corps.

On the morning of May 1, we moved across the Rappahannock river, a rapid winding stream that we had crossed many times under varying circumstances, sometimes in pursuit of the enemy, at other times the enemy were seeking us. The Ninth was now crossing the Rappahannock for the last time. Indeed, the same can be said of our whole army. It was in fact moving west and south to engage in many desperate and bloody battles; herculean encounters, greater than the world had ever witnessed, which finally led up to the close of our fratricidal war, under the direction of a general who never knew or acknowledged defeat.

We passed Brandy Station on our march, and bivouacked within two miles of Culpepper. At midnight, on the 3d, we continued our movements until 8 o'clock the next morning. About that hour we crossed the Rapidan river at Germanna ford and halted for breakfast. After our frugal morning meal a rapid march was undertaken. The sun was hot, and the road was thick with dust. The rapid tramp of thousands kicked the dust high in air, and the column moved swiftly along as though in a hot cloud. The thick floating particles entered our nostrils and settled on our faces and forms with irresistible annoyance. The object was to gain a point at the crossroads on the pike leading to Mine run, fearing all the time that the enemy would secure it before us. We reached the place in time at 2 o'clock P.M., on the 4th, and went into bivouac for the night.

24

CHAPTER XX.

BATTLE OF THE WILDERNESS.

BATTLE OF THE WILDERNESS — DESPERATE FIGHTING — HEAVY LOSSES —
LIST OF CASUALTIES IN THE NINTH MASSACHUSETTS — MOVEMENT
SOUTH BY THE LEFT FLANK — BATTLE OF LAUREL HILL — OUR
INFANTRY AND CAVALRY MOVEMENTS — GENERAL SHERIDAN SUCCEEDS
IN DEFEATING GENERAL STUART — MOVEMENT ON SPOTTSYLVANIA —
ASSAULT AT PO RIVER — BATTLE OF SPOTTSYLVANIA — LOSSES —
MOVEMENT BY THE LEFT FLANK MAY 13 — UNSUCCESSFUL ASSAULT
— CONFEDERATE RAID ON WAGON TRAINS MET AND DEFEATED —
LIST OF CASUALTIES IN THE NINTH MASSACHUSETTS — BIOGRAPHICAL
SKETCH OF GENERAL GUINEY.

*   *   *   *   *   *

See the smoke how the lightning is cleaving asunder!
Hark! the guns, peal on peal, how they boom in their thunder!
From host to host, with kindling sound,
The shouted signal circles round;
Ay, shout it forth to life or death,—
Freer already breathes the breath!
The war is waging, slaughter raging,
And heavy through the reeking pall
            The iron death-dice fall!
Nearer they close,— foes upon foes,—
" Ready!" — from square to square it goes.

*   *   *   *   *   *

SCHILLER.— " The Battle."

THE first battle of General Grant's campaign in Virginia was
fought on the following day, May 5, 1864, and is known in history as the battle of the Wilderness. It was the commencement
of heavy and continued fighting such as the Army of the Potomac had
not engaged in since the days of the desperate seven days' battles,
in front of Richmond, under General McClellan in June and July, 1862.
It was a singular coincidence that General Grant's last battle before
Richmond occurred in the same month of the year, at Cold Harbor, a
village not far from the Chickahominy river, near Gaines' Mill, where
the second day's terrible engagement of the seven days' battles

was fought, under McClellan, by the Fifth Corps and its supports, which was at that time commanded by Gen. Fitz John Porter.

General Grant is authority for saying in his memoirs, that " more desperate fighting has not been witnessed on this continent than that of the 5th and 6th of May, 1864. Our victory consisted in having successfully crossed a formidable stream (the Rapidan river), almost in the face of an enemy, and in getting the army together as a unit. We gained an advantage on the morning of the 6th, which, if it had been followed up, must have proven very decisive. In the evening the enemy gained an advantage but was speedily repulsed. As we stood at the close, the two armies were relatively in about the same condition to meet each other as when the river divided them. But the fact of having safely crossed was a victory."

It is not the province of the writer to enter into the details of the movements of the army in this campaign, or even to follow up those of the Fifth Corps. They are treated in a detailed way by abler pens elsewhere. It is hoped the reader will not be disappointed or critical, if he finds only a brief account of the campaign wherein it is attempted to show in a measure the modest part, in some of the movements, in which the Ninth Massachusetts Volunteers performed its duty in a brave and faithful manner.

Early in the morning of the 5th of May, it was generally reported, or rumored, that the enemy was advancing on our lines. This was hardly expected by Generals Grant or Meade as they believed that the enemy had fallen back from the Wilderness from the fact that no opposition was made to prevent our army from crossing the river a few days previous.

The Fifth Corps was now west of the Wilderness Tavern on the Orange pike. Our brigade being in a dense woods, a mile west of the Orange pike and Germanna plank crossroads, were ordered to build breastworks of logs and earth; a piece of work they accomplished in an incredibly short space of time. It had been well for the Ninth, and the rest, if General Grant had waited for the enemy to advance on these works, but not knowing the intended determination of General Lee to fight him when and wherever found, he moved forward without expecting to meet the enemy in force.

General Ewell's Confederate corps, with Gen. A. P. Hill following, was coming in our direction at as rapid a gait as the dense wilderness would allow. General Longstreet was marching up from the south, but did not arrive until the 6th. In the afternoon our troops left their works and went forward into the Wilderness about half a mile.

Coming under fire of the enemy's skirmishers our line drove them through the dense woods across the pike and suddenly broke into a valley-like clearing of several acres.   The bullets were flying thick and fast from the unseen enemy in the woods beyond.   Under this unexpected heavy fire the officers and men of the Ninth were quickly dropping.   Our gallant Colonel Guiney fell, terribly wounded in the head, losing an eye, and was carried from the field.   The command of the regiment was then taken by Lieutenant-Colonel Hanley.   Two pieces of artillery belonging to Company D, 1st New York, which the enemy had previously captured during the day, were placed together by them on this field and decked out with small flags and bunting to tantalize and draw us on.   These guns the Ninth attempted to recapture.   As the regiment went forward they received a terrific fire from a large body of infantry concealed in the woods on front and flank, under which, if repeated, not a man would have been left.   Colonel Hanley perceiving no supports on either flank, nor in his rear, quickly fell back with his regiment to the shelter of the woods in his immediate rear where his men opened fire on the still unseen enemy in the dense woods beyond the guns in the clearing, and gradually fell back to the original line.

During this advanced attack the Ninth lost twelve officers and one hundred and thirty-eight men in killed and wounded.   The brave and gallant officers, Captains James W. Macnamara and William A. Phelan, Lieutenants Nicholas C. Flaherty and Charles B. McGinniskin, were among the killed and mortally wounded.

When the Ninth retired to the brigade line, Colonel Sweitzer, commanding, rushed up shortly afterwards from the rear and demanded of Colonel Hanley in a loud and insolent tone of voice, " Why don't you take your regiment in ? "   Colonel Hanley replied, " We have been in, and just come out ! "   " Well," said Sweitzer, " take 'em in again."   Colonel Hanley, without a murmur, gave the order to the men of the regiment, who were then resting on the ground talking about the trap they had been caught in, " Fall in, Ninth."   The regiment promptly formed line of battle, and as Colonel Hanley was about to give the order " Forward !" a staff officer came galloping down towards the regiment, and on nearing it, cried out, " General Griffin's orders are not to take the Ninth in again."   Colonel Sweitzer heard the order and moved off to headquarters, in the rear, without a word.   The Ninth resumed its place of rest.   It afterwards proved that when the brigade went forward to the attack that its commander, Colonel Sweitzer, remained in the rear, and was, therefore, ignorant of what his regiments did, or where they went. General Griffin, however, knew all about them, as that gallant officer did of every regiment in his division. He saw the Ninth forming line and surmised correctly that they were ordered in again and sent his aide-de-camp to stop them. The next morning, when the report of casualties was sent to brigade headquarters, Colonel Sweitzer came to Colonel Hanley and apologized, saying, besides that, he did not know that the Ninth had been in and lost so heavily. If Colonel Sweitzer's irrational order had not been countermanded by General Griffin, but few, if any, of the Ninth would have come out of " that hole " again fit for duty. It was known by General Griffin, at that hour, that a large Confederate division of infantry, of Ewell's corps, was in our front.

The historian, Colonel Powell, in the Fifth Army Corps book of a late issue, while mentioning some other regiments, is as dumb as an oyster about the Ninth Massachusetts Volunteers on the 5th of May, 1864 ; in fact the Ninth Massachusetts is conspicuous by its absence from his " Record," except in his tabulated list of casualties, all through his writings from that date up to our return home. The writer merely mentions this omission regarding the Ninth, as something passing strange, and " more in sorrow than in anger."

General Hancock's Second Corps crossed the Rapidan at Ely's ford, and passed Chancellorsville going south, and marched into the Wilderness by the Brock road. At the junction of the Orange plank road he became engaged with A. P. Hill's corps, in line in a southwesterly direction, about 4 o'clock P.M. on the 5th, and fought till dark. Hancock's corps was far to the south and left of the Fifth Corps and their engagements had no connection with each other. The Fifth Corps on its right and left was supported respectively by divisions from the Sixth Corps.

General Lee had a great advantage, for the time being, over General Grant, by his complete knowledge of the Wilderness. He had fought his army successfully against General Hooker a year before over part of the same ground. The country was not only strange to General Grant, but he was more than surprised at General Lee's ability, and the determined fighting qualities of his army. A less determined man than General Grant would have retired from such a jungle as the Wilderness, after the first day's blind fighting and heavy losses ; but the hour required a man with the determined staying qualities that General Grant so strongly possessed. His heart never quailed under the most appalling situations. His merciless military methods accomplished results that could not be produced in any other way. The

successful general on the battlefield is all head and no heart. General
Grant knew that, as his opponent grew weaker under continual blows,
General Lee must in the end succumb to a foe that was superior in
resources. General Grant's hard fighting ended the war and saved the
Union. General Lee's remarkable strategic ability and indomitable
pluck resulted in greater slaughter of Union troops and more terrible
battles than General Grant anticipated at the commencement, until his
severe lesson in terrible losses on his side at Cold Harbor admonished
him to desist in his aggressive " hammering " process at so dear a rate.

On the morning of the 6th of May, following, hostilities were
resumed at 5 o'clock. General Burnside's Ninth Corps reached the
field of action at 6 o'clock A.M. One division was sent to reinforce
Hancock, and one, the colored division, was sent to guard the wagon
trains. General Wadsworth's division of the Fifth Corps was sent,
also, to assist Hancock. Sedgwick's Sixth Corps was on the right of
the line ; Warren's Fifth Corps was next ; Burnside's corps, two divisions, was next ; the Second Corps, with reinforcements, nearly one-
half the army, under General Hancock, was on the left in a southerly
direction. General Ewell's Confederate corps faced our right wing
and centre. Gen. A. P. Hill's corps faced General Hancock. General Longstreet's corps arrived on the field, after a forced march. in
the morning and at once joined General Hill's forces.

At 5 A.M., General Hancock opened on Hill's line with terrific
effect and forced him back about a mile. Longstreet's corps came to
Hill's assistance. Hancock in turn was partly forced back, after hard
and incessant infantry fire and charges on both sides, to his original
lines near the Brock road. Longstreet's assault was sudden and unexpected and made with the intention of turning Hancock's left flank, but
our troops recovered from the onset and repulsed the enemy handsomely. In this assault General Longstreet was wounded and forced to
leave the field. General Anderson succeeded in command of his corps.

The woods and works in front of General Hancock's lines took
fire, and the wind, blowing in his direction, caught many of the helpless
wounded and burned them to death. During this conflagration Lee made
another attack on Hancock in the afternoon and both sides kept fighting through the flames, by infantry fire principally, until dark with no
perceptible advantage on either side. On our right Sedgwick's troops
were attacked late in the afternoon by Early's command. We lost
here by capture two general officers and several hundred men. A withdrawal of troops from the right weakened Sedgwick's lines. After a
vigorous defence he drove the enemy back, but from lack of sufficient

men, at that particular moment, was unable to follow him up except by a terrific fire of musketry in the approaching twilight.

General Sheridan's mounted forces met General Stuart's cavalry at the intersections of the Furnice and Brock roads, and at Todd's Tavern and other places, during the day and was successful in driving them from the field. The Fifth Corps, in line and under fire, was not actively engaged on the 6th and escaped with light losses. The Ninth and in fact the brigade lost none on the 6th. The death-dealing missiles passed harmlessly into their earthworks and over their heads. Our artillery was of little use in the Wilderness on account of the peculiar density of the scrub growth of small trees and entangled underbrush. With a few small clearings and no roads, except the pike and plank roads, manœuvring with either infantry, cavalry or artillery was impossible. Neither side could see each other's lines only for a very short distance in the clearest places, and in some dense localities not at all. The nearness of the enemy was determined only by their line of firing. The fighting was carried on by infantry advances and rifle firing. The continuous roar of musketry nearly all day between both armies, particularly during Hancock's battle, was something terrific, the like of which was never heard before by either army. The dense scrub woods stopped many a bullet, which, with the unevenness and depressions of the ground surface, saved many a life. Directing the troops was done by the points of the compass, the sounds of the firing, and occasional glimpses of the enemy. Surprises were frequent and the opposing lines ran against each other, often and unexpectedly by front and flank, resulting in the capture of prisoners on both sides. By frequent attacking and falling back both sides became inextricably mixed up, and on such occasions for some moments, particularly demoralized. Many mistakes and shortcomings, by some commanders, caused extra losses in troops and position. After two days' blind manœuvring and incessant fighting both sides were exhausted and glad of a chance to rest. As one of the Confederate prisoners expressed it, so it was : " We uns fought hard to beat you uns, but you uns fit like Hell !"

Great difficulty was experienced in reinforcing weak points in the line of battle. Divisions and brigades detached for that purpose, found it almost impossible to break through the dense jungle, and the delays in losing and attempting to find their way in the pathless woods rendered their movements in several instances entirely fruitless. They not only lost their usefulness in the line from whence they started but failed to arrive in time to be of any assistance — if they arrived at all — to those they were sent to reinforce.

Our army lost on the 5th and 6th of May, 17,666 officers and men in killed, wounded, captured and missing. The Fifth Corps' share in this number was 253 officers and 4,897 men. The Ninth Massachusetts Volunteers lost the following named officers and men, May 5, 1864 :—

Killed and Mortally Wounded.

Captain James W. Macnamara, Captain William A. Phelan, 1st Lieutenant Nicholas C. Flaherty, 2d Lieutenant Charles B. McGinniskin.

COMPANY A.

Sergeant Thomas Fitzgerald; Corporal Paul McCluskey, died of wounds July 15, 1864, at Andersonville, Ga.; Privates John Coffee, Timothy Rahilly.

COMPANY B.

Privates Martin Sheehan, John Ferris, John Reagan, James Ward.

COMPANY C.

Privates Michael Dolan, John Flanagan, Edward Pettie, Erasmus D. Marden or Madden.

COMPANY D.

Corporals James I. Healey, James McCann, Private James Walsh.

COMPANY E.

Corporal Richard Condon, Privates James Mullooney, Thomas Murphy; Bernard Conway, died of wounds July 9, 1864, at Philadelphia.

COMPANY F.

Private Patrick Shea, died of wounds May 31, 1864.

COMPANY G.

Privates John Connors, Jedediah Bumpus, Richard Furfey, Peter Hughes, Patrick Mulloy; George L. Green, died of wounds May 12, 1864.

COMPANY H.

Privates Francis Finnerty, William Peachy; James O'Connell, died of wounds in prison Oct. 7, 1864.

COMPANY I.

Corporal Bernard Hayes, Privates Stephen Blake; William Gillis, died of wounds May 5, 1864, Michael Garrity, died of wounds June 17, 1864, Lawrence Mathews, died of wounds May 5, 1864; Thomas Hackett.

COMPANY K.

Sergeant James Hayes, died of wounds May 5, 1864; Privates Michael Connell, Joseph Flynn, Patrick Kelleher, William Schmidt.

List of Wounded.

Colonel Patrick R. Guiney, Captains Timothy O'Leary, Timothy Burke, Lieutenants John F. Doherty, Bernard F. Finan, Patrick E. Murphy, Joseph Murphy, William A. Plunkett.

Company A.

Sergeants Bartholomew Kelleher, Daniel Mullane, Donald Ross, Corporals John McLaughlin, Daniel Kenney, Jr., John Moakler, John O'Donnell, Patrick Gallagher, Wm. C. Gardner, Michael Griffin, James Hickey, Thomas McMahon, Jeremiah Ninan, Peter Smith, David Zeigler, John Weber.

Company B.

Sergeants Patrick Brickley. James Remick, Bernard Lane, Joseph Brown, Joseph Brennan, Henry B. O'Neil, Peter Schofield.

Company C.

Sergeants James McCarthy, Daniel Walsh, Daniel Martin, James Murray, Maurice O'Donnell, Wm. Craig, Henry Flannagan, John Kelleher, Anthony McTighe.

Company D.

Sergeants Edward C. Scott, Thomas Collins, Wm. Cleaveland, John Haggerty, Thomas Keenan or Kerivan, Thomas Kinlan or Kiflan, Wm. McDermott.

Company E.

Corporals John Halloren, Samuel Smith, Daniel Carney, Francis Hewitt, Daniel O'Connor, James Robinson, Timothy Ryan, John Danahy or Donahue, Daniel Buckley, James Butcher.

Company F.

Sergeants Michael W. Boyle, Thomas Fallon, Edward Geigle, Corporals James McLaughlin, Robert Cashin, Wm. Jordan, James Leslie.

Company G.

Sergeants William H. Armstrong, Thomas Hackett, Thomas B. Brigham, Maurice Sullivan, Thomas Conboy, Lawrence Cassidy, James Lanagan, Martin Lydon, Thomas Dineen, Walter Walsh, Peter McQueeny, Oscar Ola.

Company H.

Sergeants Malachi Curley, Thomas Mullen, John Shea, John Melvin, John Holmes, Henry Young, John Foley, James J. Rix, John J. Ford, Michael Finnerty.

Company I.

Sergeant Jeremiah Cronin, Corporals Patrick Carroll, Wm. Carroll, Thomas Green, Patrick Herlihy, John Quinn, Cornelius Dacey, Thomas J. Lewellen, Henry Coy, John Gallagher, John Palmer, Thomas Sheridan, James McNeil, Zenas A. Butterfield.

Company K.

Corporals John J. Breen, Patrick Cunningham, Michael Barry, Justin Eberhardt, John McGowan, Mathias Naphut.

WHOLE NUMBER.

Officers killed	4
Officers wounded	8
Enlisted men killed	40
Enlisted men wounded	98
Total losses Ninth Massachusetts, May 5-7, 1864	150

During the following day, the 7th, both armies held their ground, closely watching each other, without either side being able to boast of having obtained the advantage in the last two days' terrible struggle. General Grant evidently concluded that he had better get out of the Wilderness. General Lee's forces were too crippled to assume the offensive, having lost in all probability from twelve to fourteen thousand men. Comparatively speaking the losses on both sides were about even, that is, about one-seventh of the whole number in each army. At 6.30 A.M., on the 7th of May, General Grant sent to General Meade written orders to move by the left flank as follows: —

HEADQUARTERS ARMIES OF THE U S.⎱
May 7, 1864.   6.30 A.M. ⎰

MAJOR-GENERAL MEADE,
            Commanding Army of the Potomac:

Make all preparations during the day for a night march to take position at Spottsylvania C.H. with one Army Corps, at Todd's Tavern with one, and another near the intersection of the Piney Branch and Spottsylvania road with the road from Alsop's to old Court House. If this move is made the trains should be thrown forward early in the morning to the Ny River.

I think it would be advisable in making the change to leave Hancock where he is until Warren passes him. He could then follow and become the right of the new line. Burnside will move to Piney Branch Church. Sedgwick can move along the pike to Chancellorsville and on to his destination. Burnside will move on the Plank road to the intersection of it with the Orange and Fredericksburg plank road, then follow Sedgwick to his place of destination.

All vehicles should be got out of hearing of the enemy before the troops move, and then move off quietly. It is more than probable that the enemy concentrate for a heavy attack on Hancock this afternoon. In case they do we must be prepared to resist them, and follow up any success we may gain with our whole force. Such a result would necessarily modify these instructions. All the hospitals should be moved today to Chancellorsville.

U. S. GRANT,
Lieutenant-General.

That evening General Grant and his staff, accompanied by General Meade and his staff, with an escort of cavalry, preceded the movement. When they were passing General Hancock's command, going south to flank General Lee, the greatest enthusiasm was aroused. The cheering of the men that broke on the night air was loud and long, so much so that the enemy mistook it for an attack on their lines and opened up with a furious fire of artillery and musketry which lasted for some time without doing any damage. The army was now on the march to Spottsylvania. One object was to get between the enemy and Richmond and draw him into the open country.

The Fifth Corps moved forward with Robinson's 2d division in the lead. Its movements were necessarily slow through the woods in the darkness, each brigade and regiment moving at different times as it came their turn to march. After much halting and tedious marching the head of the column struck the Brock road about midnight. The Fifth Corps was followed by the Sixth Corps. The leading 2d division met the enemy beyond Todd's Tavern and swept them from their front. This secured the road leading to Fredericksburg for the transportation of the wounded to that place and thence to Washington. General Lee was not long in discovering that the Union army was on the move east and south. He jumped at the conclusion that it was going either to Fredericksburg or Spottsylvania. He thereupon ordered General Longstreet's corps, now in command of General Anderson, to occupy Spottsylvania, a town ten miles south and west of Fredericksburg. Through some misunderstanding of orders Confederate General Anderson made a premature march that night, thus, unluckily for us, throwing his forces in advance of the Fifth Corps. At daylight General Robinson's division became engaged near the Alsop house and drove the enemy into their intrenchments; there he met a furious artillery and infantry fire which served to hold his line in check. General Griffin, with our 1st division, came up to the assistance of the 2d division, and charged on the enemy twice but was obliged to fall back as he had no support. The 3d and 4th divisions as they arrived, afterwards, were put into the fight, one after the other, without gaining any advantage. The Sixth Corps failed to arrive till late in the afternoon. Other parts of our army that were looked for failed also to appear. In the meantime the enemy gained and held possession of Spottsylvania. The next day, the 9th, General Lee's army was rapidly at work fortifying its lines.

Were it not for the mishaps in marching, and being blocked on the road by the cavalry, and held in check in detail by the enemy, it was possible, by quick movements, for the Fifth Corps to have reached Spottsylvania and held the place. It was not positively known that Longstreet's corps was marching on Spottsylvania until it was discovered that his troops held the town. The fighting on the 8th of May, 1864, is known to our troops as the battle of Laurel Hill. On that day the Ninth lost eight men killed and eighteen wounded.

Through a lack of unity between Generals Meade and Sheridan regarding the disposition of the divisions of the cavalry corps, the complications of the army movements on the 7th and 8th were still further aggravated, and inadvertently aided, rather than retarded, the enemy in seizing Spottsylvania.

On the 7th General Sheridan directed his division generals, Gregg and Merritt, to move at daylight on the 8th, and gain possession of Snell's bridge on the Po river, and for General Wilson to get possession of Spottsylvania as soon as possible on the 8th. When these movements were accomplished these three division generals were then to act conjointly.

The movements of General Wilson's division was a success as will be seen by the following despatch: —

SPOTTSYLVANIA C.H., May 8, 1864. }
9 o'clock A.M. }

To LIEUTENANT-COLONEL FORSYTH,
 Chief of Staff, C.C.:

Have run the enemy's cavalry a mile from Spottsylvania Court House; have charged them and driven them through the village; am fighting now with a considerable force, supposed to be Lee's (cavalry) division. Everything is all right.

J. H. WILSON,
Brigadier-General Commanding.

During the night of the 7th General Meade, without General Sheridan's knowledge, modified the latter's orders to Generals Gregg and Merritt, thereby breaking up Sheridan's combinations to hold the bridge at Po river, and assist Wilson at Spottsylvania. This interference, unluckily, left the way open for General Anderson's (Longstreet's) corps to cross the Po river and reach Spottsylvania and drive General Wilson's cavalry division from the town.

General Meade's orders holding back the cavalry blocked up General Warren's Fifth Corps. General Sheridan on coming up drew General Merritt's division out of the way. General Robinson's division of the Fifth Corps then advanced about 11 o'clock A.M., and very soon struck Longstreet's corps and was held in check.

About noon of that same day General Meade sent for General Sheridan, and in a fiery manner accused Sheridan and his cavalry of making movements that interfered with the marching of his army, etc., and continued in that strain until, as Sheridan says, one word brought on another, when he told Meade that he could whip Stuart if he (Meade) would only let him; that henceforth General Meade could command the cavalry for he would not give it another order. With that they parted.

General Meade then went to General Grant and repeated his conversation with Sheridan, particularly that part of it where he said he could whip Stuart, etc. On hearing this General Grant remarked: " Did he say so? then let him go out and do it."

Acting on General Grant's suggestion General Meade issued orders to General Sheridan to immediately concentrate his available mounted forces, and with his ammunition trains, and such supply trains as were filled, exclusive of ambulances, to proceed against the enemy's cavalry; that when his supplies were exhausted to proceed, via New Market and Green Bay, to Haxall's landing on the James river and procure supplies and return to the army.

On receipt of these instructions General Sheridan sent for his division commanders, Generals Gregg, Merritt and Wilson, and laid the order and his plans before them. They were astounded at the boldness of the undertaking but unhesitatingly gave it their fullest support. General Sheridan then said : " We are going out to fight Stuart's cavalry in consequence of a suggestion from me ; we will give him a fair, square fight; we are strong, and I know we can beat him, and in view of my recent representations to General Meade I shall expect nothing but success."

On the morning of the 9th of May, 1864, with a cavalry column, horse artillery and train nearly thirteen miles in length, General Sheridan at the head of his bold troopers started out to march around General Lee's right flank and rear, and to whip Stuart's cavalry. The column moved all on one road, and soon crossed the Ny, Po and Ta rivers. General Stuart soon discovered the movement and followed in rear. Several attacks were made on the rear guard without doing much damage. That night Sheridan bivouacked at the North Anna river, after driving off the enemy.

After crossing the river General Custer's brigade went to Beaver Dam station and whipped a small force of the enemy, recaptured four hundred Union prisoners, taken at the Wilderness, destroyed the station, two locomotives, three trains of cars, ninety wagons, ten miles of railroad and telegraph, two hundred thousand pounds of bacon, and a large quantity of medical stores.

On the morning of the 10th Generals Gregg and Wilson whipped the enemy at the North Anna river and moved on to Richmond. General Stuart pulled out in advance in order to get between Sheridan's column and Richmond. This move, on the part of the enemy, gave our troops a chance to feed and rest. After marching about eighteen miles further, unmolested, they bivouacked for the night.

On the morning of the 11th, at 2 o'clock, Davies' brigade destroyed the railroad at Ashland and burned a train of cars and a locomotive, and rejoined the column at Allen's station on the Fredericksburg & Richmond railroad. The column then moved on Yellow Tavern, within six miles of Richmond, Merritt's division leading, followed by Wilson's and Gregg's divisions.

General Sheridan found General Stuart ready to meet him.   Merritt's division at once pressed forward to the attack.   He was followed by Wilson's and Gregg's troops.   A desperate battle now took place in which artillery was freely used.   Brilliant charges were made by Sheridan's brigades at every point.   The Confederate General Stuart fought hard and bravely until he was mortally wounded.   General J. B. Gordon, one of his brigade commanders, was also killed.   The enemy's lines were completely broken and defeated and finally routed, giving our forces complete control of the road to Richmond.   The casualties on both sides were quite severe.   Our troopers captured a number of prisoners.   During this battle intense excitement prevailed in Richmond.   A reconnoitring party went up the Brook turnpike towards the city and drove a small force of the enemy from their outer intrenchments.   After taking care of his wounded and burying his dead, General Sheridan moved on the night of the 11th, at 11 o'clock, and reached Meadow bridge at daylight on the 12th.   After several successful encounters with infantry under command of President Jeff Davis and General Bragg, our cavalry crossed the Chickahominy at Meadow's bridge.   From Gaines' Mill where they bivouacked they went across the country to Haxall's landing on the James river, where they arrived on the 14th.   Here they obtained supplies, left all their wounded to be cared for, and also turned over a number of prisoners and captured field-pieces.   On the evening of the 17th, General Sheridan and his command started on his return trip and reached White House landing on the Pamunkey river.

While waiting for a pontoon bridge from Fortress Monroe a part of his command, Custer's, went to Hanover station and destroyed a railroad bridge over the South Anna river.   Part of his command went to Cold Harbor and Mechanicsville, to make a demonstration in order to cover General Custer's movements.

In the meantime work had been undertaken to repair the railroad bridge over the Pamunkey river which proved highly successful, and on the 22d of May, at noon, our cavalry crossed the river and returned to the army by the 24th of May.

General Sheridan's casualties were 425 in killed, wounded and missing.

Generals Grant and Meade were highly pleased with General Sheridan's success.   His famous raid enabled them to act for more than two weeks without fear of the enemy's cavalry attacks on their flanks and trains. The great raid was likewise a cause of intense alarm to General Lee, not only on account of the destruction wrought in the rear of his army, but because it carried dismay all around him, and more particularly into Richmond, where the excitement during the battle at Yellow Tavern, within a few miles of the Southern capital, was intense. Furthermore, Lee was, for two weeks or more, deprived of the valuable services of his cavalry corps and its commander, while at the same time it was wofully defeated in battle. The death of his intimate brother officer, General Stuart, caused him great sorrow. He is quoted as saying, in regard to him, " I can scarcely think of him without weeping." The human heart will weep at the loss in battle of an intimate friend or brother, when no moisture will dim the eye for thousands of the rank and file who are slain around him. Stuart as a renowned cavalry general was also a great loss to, and regretted by, the whole Confederate army in Virginia.

The moral effect of this raid by General Sheridan cast a gloom over the Confederacy in Richmond and elsewhere that was lasting and looked upon by many as the forerunner of its doom; the shadow, as it were, of the final defeat and downfall that swiftly followed.

General Lee had successfully manœuvred his army out of the Wilderness, to the south of the Army of the Potomac, and on the 9th of May, 1864, taken possession of Spottsylvania, the shire town of Spottsylvania county. It is situated on a fine site of elevated country between two small rivers, the Ny to the north and the Po to the south; a little farther south, in the next county, mostly, is the Ta and the Mat rivers. These four form the source and name of the Mat-ta-po-ny river, which empties into the York river, at the junction of the Pamunkey river, near West Point, Va., to the southeast and which runs by historic Yorktown into the Chesapeake bay, and near the scene of General McClellan's advance up the Peninsula in 1862.

After the misfortunes and delays that beset our Fifth Corps — and the rest of the army — on the 8th in its intended movement from the Wilderness, to take possession of Spottsylvania and get between Lee's army and the city of Richmond, in order to force him onto the open country, the Army of the Potomac found itself confronting the enemy between the Po and Ny rivers and environments. The difficulty of crossing these deep narrow streams and runs without bridges put the troops in great danger and delay when under the range of the enemy's artillery and infantry. It was late in the afternoon of the 9th of May, before the army was all in position. Then General Hancock's corps was on the right, with Warren's, Sedgwick's and Burnside's on his left respectively.

The army learned with great regret of the death of General Sedgwick of the Sixth Corps, who was killed on the morning of the 9th, near his intrenchments, by a sharpshooter. The loss of this brave and unassuming officer was deplored by the whole of our army.

Brig.-Gen. H. G. Wright succeeded to the command of the Sixth Corps. Late in the afternoon part of Hancock's corps crossed the Po river, and made a determined assault on the left of Lee's army, held by Longstreet's corps; darkness coming on made it impossible to further attempt, with any show of success, to turn the enemy's flank.

During the night Hancock's men built three bridges over the Po river. The lines of the Fifth Corps were now within a mile and a half of Spottsylvania Court House behind recently constructed earthworks near Spindler's farm. The Second Corps was on our right and the Sixth Corps on our left in the vicinity of the Brock road. Skirmishers from the Fifth and Sixth Corps occupied our front all day. Our artillery held advantageous positions and planted shot and shell into the lines of the enemy as opportunities offered. Our lines were likewise receiving the enemy's shot and shell. Towards night the Ninth and 32d Massachusetts were on the skirmish line, well to the front, and forced the enemy back. Our fatigue parties then commenced to throw up earthworks and dig rifle-pits after dark, to meet the enemy who were engaged in the same work. Between 9 and 10 o'clock that night the enemy made an unexpected and fierce assault in large force on our working parties which drove them from their labors.

The casualties in the regiment on the 8th and 9th of May were two killed and five wounded. Among them were the following named officers: Lieut. James O'Neil, killed; Lieut. Timothy Dacey, wounded; Capt. John M. Tobin, wounded. The latter officer joined the regiment only a day or two before. He had been previously performing duty on the brigade commander's staff as assistant inspector-general.

The next day at 9 A.M., Tuesday, May 10, the 22d Massachusetts and 4th Michigan of our brigade advanced in a strong skirmish line and recaptured the lost ground and works of the night before, driving the enemy back into the woods. At this point a heavy artillery and infantry fire opened on them from the enemy in the woods as they took refuge in the rifle-pits and earthworks now in their possession. The 22d Massachusetts suffered severely from this sudden firing.

The Second, Sixth and Ninth Corps made several attacks along their lines during the day, which were met by the enemy, resulting in severe losses on both sides. Most of the battlefield was covered with dense woods. Gen. Thos. G. Stevenson, commanding 1st division, Ninth Corps, was killed. About 4 o'clock in the afternoon, Warren's Fifth Corps and Wright's Sixth Corps with Mott's division of the Second Corps, advanced into the woods and engaged the enemy in a fierce battle. A storming party of twelve regiments, in command of Colonel Upton of the 121st New York, went forward and captured the enemy's intrenchments, taking several guns and about one thousand prisoners. He was obliged to fall back on account of his supports — Mott's division — failing to advance in time. Colonel Upton brought his prisoners with him. The guns were abandoned. Colonel Upton was badly wounded and General Grant promoted him a brigadier-general on the field for his gallantry.

General Hancock's Second Corps joined in the last assault with the Fifth and Sixth Corps, and they captured the enemy's works but were unable to hold them, and at night all the troops were withdrawn. The Fifth Corps suffered severely; Gen. James C. Rice of the 2d brigade, 4th division, was among the mortally wounded.

The next day, May 11, both lines were comparatively quiet.

General Grant's letter to the authorities in the city of Washington is so short, concise and full of information, besides being famous for one certain expression, that it is deemed proper to give it to the reader in full. It will be of much interest to those who have never read it before.

NEAR SPOTTSYLVANIA C.H., }
May 11, 1864. 8.30 A.M. {

MAJOR-GENERAL HALLECK,
      Chief of Staff of the Army.
          Washington, D.C.:

We have now ended the sixth day of very hard fighting. The result up to this time is much in our favor, but our losses have been heavy as well as those of the enemy. We have lost to this time eleven general officers killed, wounded and missing, and probably twenty thousand men. I think the loss of the enemy must be greater, we having taken over four thousand prisoners in battle, whilst he has taken from us but few, except a few stragglers. I am now sending back to Belle Plain all my wagons for a fresh supply of provisions and ammunition, and purpose to fight it out on this line if it takes all summer.

The arrival of reinforcements here will be very encouraging to the men, and I hope they will be sent as fast as possible, in as great numbers. My object in having them sent to Belle Plain was to use them as an escort to our supply train. If it is more convenient to send them out by train to march from the railroad to Belle Plain or Fredericksburg, send them so.   I am satisfied the enemy are very shaky, and are only kept up to the mark by the greatest exertions on the part of their officers, and by keeping them intrenched in every position they take.   Up to this time there is no indication of any portion of Lee's army being detached for the defence of Richmond.

U. S GRANT,

Lieutenant-General.

His expression " and purpose to fight it out on this line if it takes all summer," was, at that time, taken up by the press of the country and made famous.   It is also considered that General Lee used the information to his advantage.

The reader will notice that General Halleck, whilom commander of the U.S. army, was at the date of General Grant's letter, occupying a position for which, no doubt, he was well fitted.   Men, like water, if allowed to run long enough will find their level.

Generals Meade and Grant now determined to make a grand assault with the whole army on General Lee's works.   On the 11th of May every preparation was made that was considered necessary for a successful attack.   The Fifth Corps was placed on the right of the line; the Sixth Corps next on its left; the Second Corps next at the centre; the Ninth Corps on the extreme left.   This line of battle extended in a semi-circle from near the Po river on the right, to the vicinity of the Spottsylvania Court House on the left.   Our batteries of artillery, which never seemed to rest, were placed in every advantageous position possible for efficient work.   They opened fire at 5 o'clock A.M. on the 12th, and kept at it all day.

At 4.30 A.M., or as soon as it was light, Hancock's Second Corps, in two assaulting columns, went forward over clear ground, marsh and woods, half way up the hill, then charged on the double-quick, with a united cheer, which was prolonged into a fierce yell, as they went over the enemy's works at the salient, or angle, and vicinity, driving before them General Ewell's corps inside the fortifications where a desperate and bloody struggle took place, with shot, bayonet and clubbed musket, among thousands of fighting men of both sides, who were, for a brief, bloody period, inextricably intermingled in the terrible din and smoke of battle.   After a short and brave resistance, during which the ground was covered with dead and wounded, the enemy's lines broke and fled, resulting in the capture of four thousand men of Major-General Johnson's division of Ewell's corps, including Gen. Edward Johnson himself and Brig.-Gen. George H. Stewart, together with artillery, small arms, thirty colors and other war material.   The enemy,

which fled in disorder, was pursued to a second line of earthworks.
Here they rallied behind their artillery. Further pursuit now ceased
in order to reform our own scattered lines and await reinforcements.
The Sixth Corps moved forward at 6 A.M. to the assistance of the
Second Corps to the right of the " angle." The Confederates had
been reinforced and now made several charges to regain their first line
of works, which had been turned against them, but were quickly
repulsed each time with heavy losses. General Burnside's Ninth Corps
went forward through the woods and, after a long and repeated
struggle, made connections with the Second Corps. General Warren's
Fifth Corps, having now but three divisions, made an unsuccessful
assault from the right on Longstreet's left, at 9 o'clock A.M. The
Fifth Corps went forward on the double-quick in a drenching rain,
through the soft wet mould of ploughed ground, over undulating
surface, to within fifty yards of the enemy's earthworks on the hill,
when the men commenced to fall under a terrific fire of artillery and
infantry. Our wavering lines could not withstand the leaden hail from
Longstreet's infantry and deafening batteries. One break in the line
brought on another, until the disheartened troops fell back in disorder
under the withering fire which followed with an unerring aim. During
this unsuccessful movement the corps lost heavily. Our brigade sustained severe losses in all of their five regiments. The Ninth lost 23
killed, 32 wounded and 2 missing or captured. Among the casualties
Lieut. Archibald Simpson was killed and Capts. James F. McGunnigle
and Martin O'Brien wounded.

In these assaults on Spottsylvania the Army of the Potomac was
laboring under many insurmountable disadvantages. It was obliged
to attack miles of semi-circle fortifications on hilly ground, bristling
with cannon and backed by infantry. Our attacking lines were
required to charge from a distance over a rough country of ploughed
fields, marsh and woodland, on the outside of the circle; while the
enemy, viewing our approaches at their leisure, fought us from behind
the protection of their works on the inside of the circle, with reinforcements quickly at hand to repel our attacks in equal and sometimes
superior numbers. Our whole line required more or less defence at all
times; while the fortified enemy could quickly concentrate in great
numbers on right, left or centre, to meet any assault undertaken
against him at any of the points named.

General Hancock's assault on the centre was admirably managed
and boldly executed. At an early hour in the morning they came
upon the enemy unseen and unexpected, until his brave battalions

were onto their works and in the midst of their lines.   At the " bloody
angle "— the salient — where General Hancock so gallantly sustained
his assault, General Lee made furious attacks to recover.   Five times
during the day he fruitlessly endeavored to drive the Second Corps and
its supports out of their position from behind his own works which
our forces had turned and stubbornly held against all his impetuous
charges.   A tree in range of the musketry fire between both lines,
some eighteen inches in diameter, was literally cut in two by the rifle
bullets fired into it from both sides.   In fact, all the trees in range in
that locality were cut and riddled with artillery and infantry to a most
surprising extent.   This close and desperate fighting continued all
day, although at times it rained heavily, and until 3 o'clock the next
morning, the 13th.   During that time our losses in killed and wounded
numbered 8500 men.   The enemy, being the assailants a good part of
the time, must have suffered far greater casualties outside of the
prisoners we captured.   General Lee was enabled to reinforce his
centre more particularly from the troops on his left, as the assault of
Warren's corps was unsuccessful and not repeated.   General Grant
ordered General Warren, twice, to reinforce Hancock.   His failure to
do so caused General Grant, as he says in his personal memoirs, to
send to General Meade " written orders at 11 o'clock A.M. of the 12th,
to relieve General Warren from his command if he failed to move
promptly."   At a later hour General Warren's corps was temporarily
broken up.   General Cutler's division was sent to General Wright's
Sixth Corps and General Griffin's division was ordered to General
Hancock's Second Corps.   General Humphreys, General Meade's
chief-of-staff, was ordered to remain with General Warren and the
remaining division and instructed to give orders in his (Meade's) name.
The order sending the 1st division (ours) away was countermanded.

On the 13th of May, the following day, there was no fighting
after 3 A.M., and our fatigue parties were occupied in burying the
slain.   Our casualties in the campaign thus far — about two weeks —
was 36,000 men.   The despatch quoted below will show how much
General Grant still underestimated his antagonist.   The " last ditch "
was not found by the enemy until the following spring of 1865.

HEADQUARTERS ARMIES OF THE UNITED STATES, }
May 12, 1864, 6.30 P.M. }

MAJOR-GENERAL HALLECK.
Washington, D.C.

The eighth day of the battle closes, leaving between three and four thousand prisoners in our hands for the day's work, including two general officers

and over thirty pieces of artillery. The enemy are obstinate and seem to have found the last ditch. We have lost no organizations, not even that of a company, whilst we have destroyed and captured one division, Johnson's, one brigade, Dole's, and one entire regiment from the enemy.

U. S. GRANT,
Lieutenant-General.

When night fell upon us on the 13th our corps was ordered to move by the left flank, followed by the Sixth Corps. The troops were wet and the ground was soaked with the falling rain; the march in the deep mud was slow and laborious. The intense darkness added discouragement to our toilsome tramp as we groped our way through the woods and clearings and across the Ny river. It was midnight when we reached our intended point of attack, which was east of Spottsylvania Court House. It was daylight before we gained our position in line to advance on the enemy. Our new line then was facing due west. During the day of the 14th there was comparative rest for us and no fighting. In fact, the movement of the night before had such a demoralizing effect on a part of our troops that time was required to bring up the straggling lines to a proper state of discipline. The rain continued to fall, more or less, all the time. The roads and ground generally were in no condition to move man or beast without a wearisome struggle for both and nothing to be gained in the end. General Burnside's corps had joined our line of battle. This left General Hancock still in his old position. By the 15th General Lee had changed his lines and was facing our front. General Hancock then, having no enemy in his front, marched to our new position and formed in the rear of our centre, on reserve. The weather began to clear on the 17th, until it turned out warm and pleasant. At night our lines advanced several hundred yards towards the enemy and at once commenced to build earthworks. Our brigade and regiment were in the second line. The Second and Sixth Corps, Hancock and Wright, were moved around to their old position on the night of the 17th, to assist in a united assault on Lee's front and rear, which Grant had arranged to take place at 4 o'clock the next morning. But General Lee was not to be caught napping. His troops were in their old works in time and ready to meet all comers. The attack opened in the early morning with a heavy artillery fire, which drew in response a heavy fire from the enemy. The assault which followed by the Second and Sixth Corps proved unsuccessful. Our new lines did not therefore advance. General Grant had, at this time, by this movement, virtually surrounded General Lee, and he hoped to crush him, believing him almost in despair. General Lee, on the contrary, was far from despondent, although General Sheridan's cavalry was going through the country in his rear with a vengeance. His — Lee's — repulse of Generals Hancock's and Wright's corps proved that he was wary and as full of fight as ever. It is evident that General Grant was disappointed at the late turn of affairs. In addition to this he had received bad news of defeats to our forces in other parts of the theatre of war, which, he himself says, was very discouraging and must have been known to the enemy before it was to him. General Grant was also looking for reinforcements which he had called for and some 6000 new troops, under Gen. Robert O. Tyler, had lately arrived and were ordered to join the Second Corps. A comparative rest took place on a part of the 18th and the 19th. In the afternoon of the latter day, about 5 o'clock, General Lee, evidently uneasy at so long a rest, and wishing to get even with General Grant for some of the latter's successful attacks, not to mention the fact that he needed rations badly, moved out two corps on our extreme right. General Ewell's corps first, supported by General Early, advanced rapidly on our rear flank. The new contingent which had arrived under General Tyler had marched from Fredericksburg and were in position, temporarily, off on the extreme right of the Fifth Corps. They were the first to meet the approaching enemy and, as they held their ground, they fought like veterans. General Hancock's troops, then at the rear and centre, hastened, under Hancock's direction, to their assistance. General Birney's division went to Tyler's right and General Crawford's division — late of the Fifth Corps — got on his left, with General Gibbons' division in reserve. They then charged with the new troops on Ewell's corps with such impetuosity as to send him flying back to his own lines in great disorder, carrying General Early's troops along with him, leaving behind them heavy losses in killed and wounded and some two hundred prisoners. General Warren was ordered out to get onto the enemy's retreating rear and flank, but it succeeded in escaping him in the darkness. A detachment of the enemy, as expected, went off toward Fredericksburg to raid on our supply train. Although it was guarded by a division of colored troops under General Ferrero and a body of cavalry, it seems that twenty-five or thirty wagons were captured. Owing, however, to Ewell's complete rout the detachment was driven off and all the wagons retaken.

List of Casualties Ninth Massachusetts Volunteers, at Laurel
Hill, Po River and Spottsylvania,
May 8 to 19, 1864.

List of Killed and Mortally Wounded.

May 9, Lieutenant James O'Neil; May 12, Lieutenant Archibald Simpson.

Company A.

May 12, Corporal Edward Keenan, Edward H. Shahan (or Shanahan),
Thomas J. Glynn, Hugh Slavin, John Lanagan.

Company B.

May 8, Patrick Kelly, John Bresnahan; May 9, William Carney, James
O'Neil; May 12, Sergeant Michael Creighton, Timothy Harrington, Lawrence
Archpool, John Regan.

Company C.

May 9, Sergeant Edward McLaughlin, prisoner, died July 9, 1864, Andersonville, Ga ; May 12, Henry Walder; May 19, John Hurrell.

Company D.

May 8, John O'Hara; May 12, Corporal John Reed, died of wounds May
18, 1864; Michael Roach, died of wounds June 20, 1864, at Arlington, Va.

Company E.

May 8, Charles D. Smith; May 12, Sergeant John B. Newell, James P.
Nole.

Company F.

May 8, James Connor, died June 7, 1864; Wm. Densmore, died Sept. 4,
1864, at Andersonville; Patrick Sullivan, died Sept. 8, 1864, at Andersonville.

Company G.

May 12, Sergeant Michael Clark, died of wounds June 10, 1864; Corporal
John Buckley, died of wounds May 12, 1864; John Foley, Sergeant Richard
Feeley, Silas Walker; Richard Furfey, killed May 12, 1864.

Company H.

May 8, John Mullen, May 12, John R. Goss.

Company I.

May 8, John H. Hale, May 12, Thomas Mangan, May 12, Sergeant Patrick
Rabbitt, died May 12, 1864.

Company K.

May 8, John Cogger; May 12, Thomas J. Murtagh, Patrick Kelleher.

List of Wounded.

May 8, Captain John M. Tobin; May 9, Lieutenant Timothy Dacey; May 12, Captain James F. McGunnigle, Captain Martin O'Brien.

COMPANY A.

May 8, John A. Swinson, Daniel O'Leary (or Leary); May 12, John Lawler, Edwin S. Parker, Thomas Cass.

COMPANY B.

May 8, Michael Gleeson; May 10, James Giblin; May 12, Corporal John Burns, Private Wm. Buchanan, Otto Bush, James Burke.

COMPANY C.

May 8, John Coyne, George H. Elliott, Wm. Jones; May 12, Corporal Edwin Phinney, Corporal Thomas Barnes, Simon Fields, Patrick Jones, Wm. O'Brien, John Ryan.

COMPANY D.

May 12, Corporal John O'Brien, Thomas Conlon

COMPANY E.

May 10, Corporal John Keating, John Breen; May 12, Frank Ash, prisoner, Patrick Barry, Thomas Dady, Geo. F. Doherty.

COMPANY F.

May 8, Patrick Cullinaine, Lawrence Cunningham, Thomas Connor, Corporal Patrick Tierney, Cornelius Creden.

COMPANY G.

May 12, First Sergeant Michael Murphy, John Low, Patrick H. McHugh, Wm. Murnane; May 14, John Murphy.

COMPANY H.

May 8, Francis Murray; May 12, John Tobin, Samuel Burke.

COMPANY I.

May 8, James McKeever, John Flynn, Spencer Church Jr.; May 9, Charles McCarthy, Stephen Perley; May 12, Patrick Griffin, Edmund Flynn.

COMPANY K.

May 8, Wm. Mitchell, James Flynn, Michael Walsh; May 12, John Scannell, John Steward, Corporal John J Breen; May 14, Patrick Kenney; May 18, Dominick Crane.

Losses in Ninth Massachusetts Volunteers from May 5, 1864, to May 19, 1864, inclusive : — Laurel Hill, Po River and Spottsylvania, May 8 to 19, 1864.

Officers killed and mortally wounded	2
Men killed and mortally wounded	39
Officers wounded	4
Men wounded	56
Total	101
Losses May 5, 1864, Wilderness	150
Aggregate May 5–19, 1864	251

Gen. Patrick R. Guiney.

General Guiney was the successor of Colonel Cass in command of the Ninth Massachusetts Volunteers. By education, training and ability he was eminently fitted to command large bodies of men. These traits of character account for his great success as the colonel commanding the Ninth Massachusetts Volunteers. He was born in Ireland, where he first saw the light of day at Parkstown, Tipperary, Jan. 15, 1835. At the early age of seven years he left his native land in company with his father for the freedom of the new world. His boyhood thenceforth was spent in Portland, Me. His ambition to acquire a profession found his early manhood diligently occupied as a student in Holy Cross College, Worcester, Mass. Selecting the law for a profession, he was admitted to the bar in Portland in April, 1856. His ambition for a larger field in his profession induced him to settle in Boston in 1859. Here his career as a rising young lawyer was broken, like that of so many other young men in his profession, by the war spirit within him, and entering into the patriotic ardor of the day, he joined in recruiting the Ninth regiment and went to the front as one of its captains. His active services and abilities in the regiment were rewarded by promotions to major, lieutenant-colonel, colonel, and brevet brigadier-general.

By the fortunes of war, at nearly the close of three years' hard campaigning, he received a terrible wound in the head, losing an eye and almost his life at the battle of the Wilderness, May 5, 1864, where 150 officers and men in the Ninth were killed or wounded. In civil life, after the war, in the city of Boston, his reputation and abilities brought him prominently before the public, more particularly as assistant district attorney of the superior court, and later, when elected to the office of register of probate, etc., for Suffolk county. While holding the latter office his wounds brought on his premature death, which suddenly overtook him in Franklin square, March 21, 1877. His military funeral was large and imposing, attended as it was by his brother officers of the army and prominent citizens. The military escort was the Ninth Massachusetts Militia, a regiment in which he was the first colonel on its organization, shortly after the close of the war. General Guiney's widow and daughter — Louise Imogen Guiney — are left to mourn the loss of one dearly beloved.

On the day of General Guiney's death the officers and men of the Society of the Ninth Massachusetts Volunteers held a meeting of

condolence and unanimously passed by a rising vote the following
resolution : —

* * * * * *

Resolved, That in the death of Gen. P. R. Guiney we suffer the loss of a
true friend and faithful comrade. By his able and patriotic military record
we are reminded that the nation loses a brave, skilled and meritorious commander; and the State a trained and able counselor, and an honored and beloved
citizen. As the Colonel of the Ninth Regiment Massachusetts Volunteers of
the late war of 1861, he won the love and esteem of his command by his skill,
bravery, affability, good sense and honesty and earnestness of purpose. As
a companion he was genial, sympathetic, honorable and high minded.

* * * * * *

General Guiney's remains are buried in Holyhood cemetery,
Brookline. His grave is handsomely marked by a stone of elaborate
workmanship.

CHAPTER XXI.

NORTH ANNA TO COLD HARBOR AND HOME.

MOVE BY THE LEFT FLANK — GENERAL LEE'S ARMY MOVES SOUTH — THE
NINTH AT JERICHO FORD — BATTLE AT NORTH ANNA — GENERAL
LEE'S STRONG POSITION — GENERAL MEADE'S ARMY WITHDRAWN —
A NEW BASE OF SUPPLIES — RECONNOISSANCE IN FORCE — GENERAL
LEE'S LINE OF BATTLE — UNION LINE OF BATTLE — ASSAULT AT COLD
HARBOR — ARRIVAL OF THE EIGHTEENTH CORPS — THE LAST ASSAULT
AT COLD HARBOR — OUR HEAVY LOSSES — LIST OF CASUALTIES IN
THE NINTH — BIOGRAPHICAL SKETCH OF COLONEL HANLEY — DESCRIP-
TION OF THE BATTLEGROUND — CHANGE OF BASE — IN BIVOUAC
NEAR BOTTOM'S BRIDGE — THE NINTH'S TIME EXPIRES — MUSTER OUT.

" And now with shouts the shocking armies clos'd,
To lances lances, shields to shields, oppos'd;
Host against host the shadowy legions drew,
The sounding darts, an iron tempest, flew;
Victors and vanquished join promiscuous cries,
Triumphing shouts and dying groans arise,
With streaming blood the slipp'ry field is dy'd,
And slaughter'd heroes swell the dreadful tide."

AFTER the disaster to his aggressive movement on the 19th of
May, General Lee appeared disposed to wait behind his
intrenchments for General Meade to attack him. He lately
experienced the fact that his present force was too weak or unwilling
to meet its antagonist in the open field, and, while expecting reinforcements, he did not intend to let our army get between him and Richmond; for, in that event, he would be forced to fight the Union forces
on ground of their own selection. On the 20th, Friday, he kept close
to his intrenchments and warily watched for the next move of his
opponent. On the night of the 20th General Hancock was ordered by
General Meade to move south by the left flank. He marched to
Guiney's Station, on the Fredericksburg railroad, thence south to
Bowling Green and Milford, reaching the latter place on the night of
the 21st. A part of General Pickett's division, on the march to join
the Southern army, was attacked and routed at this point and a

hundred or so taken prisoners. Our Fifth Corps followed the Second Corps shortly after 1 o'clock P.M. of the 21st, crossed the Ny river and turned south by way of the railroad; on reaching Guiney's Station we crossed over the bridge to the south bank of the Mattapony river, and bivouacked for the night. The Sixth and Ninth Corps remained in front of General Lee's lines until the night of the 21st, to cover the movement. On the morning of the 22d they arrived at Guiney's Station. The enemy's cavalry was found hovering about their line of march and quickly driven off.

General Lee had early discovered Meade's movement and had left his intrenchments, but without any apparent intention of seeking an engagement. On the contrary, he hastened south to put his army behind breastworks for he evidently did not in future intend to meet General Meade's forces in any other way. It rested his army securely and it saved the lives of his men, while he had the grim satisfaction of slaughtering the " Yankees " to his heart's content when their brave battalions were thrown against his intrenched artillery and infantry.

On Sunday morning of the 22d of May the Fifth Corps continued its march south with our 1st division in the lead, and bivouacked near Harris' store on the road west of Milford. The following morning, the 23d, we marched forward again until we reached the North Anna river. General Lee's army was on the south side of it, having beaten us in the race south. They had not forgotten the lesson in marching taught them by " Stonewall " Jackson. It was always a difficult task for our heavy-weighted Northern men to hold their own with the lank, nimble-footed Southern sprinters. Besides, they were on their own soil, their own homes, as it were, and familiar with the roads and byways across the country. Southern guides could always be found to help them out of a tight place. It seems, further, that Generals Grant and Meade and the rest, were without any proper war maps of this section of Virginia. The army moved south under the direction of engineer and staff officers, who in turn depended on reconnoitring to locate the roads for each army corps. This uncertain method was the cause of losing much valuable time on a flank movement.

About 4 o'clock P.M. our division reached Jericho ford on the North Anna river, our brigade leading. The stream flowed between high, steep banks; the road was rough and rocky and the water all of four feet deep. As the Ninth Massachusetts proceeded to cross the river Colonel Hanley noticed the shortest man in the regiment standing on one side of the road by himself, apparently in deep trepidation. " What's the matter, ' Napoleon '? " demanded the colonel.

"O Colonel, what will I do at all? the water is too deep for me and I can't swim," interrogated "Napoleon" — a nickname by which he was well known throughout the regiment. He was always a jolly, witty little fellow, and a good, brave soldier, withal, and a general favorite. In his present predicament he excited much sympathy and a good deal of mirth. Many comic suggestions of how to cross the running flood were offered by the men as they passed along, all of which "Napoleon" took in good part, but failed to reply to, as the situation was to him a serious matter. The colonel in the meantime was hastening his men over the ford until the last file came along, when he called on a big strapping fellow to give "Napoleon" a lift onto his horse "Dick," a strong, gentle animal, which the colonel rode. As the little man straddled "Dick" behind the colonel, he felt as proud as a peacock and when he landed on the other bank, perfectly dry and clean, he had the laugh on his side. His cleverness and profuse thanks to the colonel for the great favor more than paid his passage. In his warm Irish heart "Napoleon" never forgot the colonel's kindness, and even refers to it to this day at the annual reunions of the survivors of the regiment. On reaching his company in such good condition after crossing the ford, he was greeted with a shout of welcome, and much wit and repartee were indulged in at "Napoleon's" expense, in which he took a lively part himself. After we reached the south side of the North Anna we guarded the ford while the engineers laid a pontoon bridge; our artillery and the rest of our corps then crossed.

General Warren formed his line of battle perpendicular with the course of the river. Cutler's division was on the right, Griffin's division was next and Crawford's on the left towards the river. Our skirmishers along the corps front advanced through the woods and clearings and very soon found the fire of the enemy's skirmishers. In the meantime our line of battle was throwing up temporary earthworks at a rapid rate; before they were completed the enemy appeared coming down on our right. Our brigade held the right of our division line, with Cutler's division on our right. Our skirmishers fell back to the main line, followed by Confederate Gen. A. P. Hill's corps. The latter met with our infantry fire and a heavy artillery fire from our batteries on elevated ground on our left and rear, the latter going over our heads. A charge was made by the enemy on our right with terrific onset. It forced back the brigade on our right, carrying with it the regiment on our right and a part of our own regiment. Cutler's line quickly rallied, with the assistance of our artillery, and our lines rapidly closed up again and opened on the enemy with a heavy fire, driving them back to their intrenchments with a heavy loss in killed and wounded and about 500 prisoners left in our hands.

At nightfall of the 23d the Sixth Corps had arrived at the North Anna and was ready, if necessary, to reinforce the Fifth Corps. The next morning, having crossed at Jericho ford, the Sixth Corps went into position on the right of the Fifth Corps in front of Lee's left wing. Late in the afternoon of the 23d the Second Corps arrived at the wooden bridge near the railroad bridge. The enemy was in force and intrenched at this point and was charged upon by two brigades of the Second Corps with such impetuosity as to drive them over the bridge. Several hundred of the enemy were captured and some who went into the river were drowned. The next morning, the 24th, the Second Corps crossed at Chesterfield ford, and went into line of battle in front of Ewell's corps of Lee's right wing. On the night of the 23d the Ninth Corps arrived in front of Ox ford. In the morning they found Longstreet's corps in their front on the south bank, holding the centre of Lee's lines, both wings of which were thrown back, the right resting on an impassable swamp and the left resting on Little river, in the shape of an acute angle — the salient resting on the south bank of the North Anna. General Lee had been reinforced by some 15,000 veteran troops. The disposition of his forces rendered his lines unassailable to such an extent that if an attack was made it would have been of doubtful issue and accompanied by great slaughter on our assaulting columns. In case of attack General Lee could readily reinforce his weak points from the inside of his lines; whereas General Meade's troops would be obliged to cross the river bridges twice to reinforce from wing to wing, and once each way to reinforce the centre; not to mention the fact that at the latter point the river was between both contending lines. Under these disadvantages it would be only foolhardiness and a great sacrifice of men to be the aggressor on Meade's part. Lee was playing a waiting game and had no intention of attacking the Union forces. He desired to kill and not be killed in return.

On the 25th General Meade was instructed by written orders from General Grant to withdraw his army on the 26th and move by forced march and turn the enemy's right by a detour to the east, and to cross the Pamunkey river below the junction of the North and South Annas at or near Hanover town, which lay to the southeast of his present position and about twenty miles north of Richmond. In executing this flank movement another attempt would be made to get between Lee's army and Richmond. General Lee had the inside track and unless he could be caught asleep it could not be accomplished. Judging by his experience thus far in trying to flank his wily opponent, General Grant himself did not expect success in that quarter. That, however, did not deter him from trying. Hanover Court House, seven miles from Hanover town, is on the Virginia Central railroad, south of the Pamunkey river, and was the scene of our battle with Gen. L. O'Brien Branch May 27, 1862 — two years previous — when General McClellan was promised McDowall's army of 40,000 from Fredericksburg to enable him to take Richmond. It will be remembered that the promised army was not sent as intended, on account of " Stonewall " Jackson's ruse in the Shenandoah Valley, when, with a small force, he drove Banks' army to the Potomac river and scared all our great officials in Washington nearly out of their wits.

The reader can perhaps better understand General Grant's idea of the situation now by reading the following extract from a communication sent by him to Washington May 26, 1864 : —

" Lee's army is really whipped; the prisoners we now take show it, and the action of his army shows it unmistakably. A battle with them outside of intrenchments cannot be had. Our men feel that they have gained the *morale* over the enemy and attack him with confidence. I may be mistaken, but I feel that our success over Lee's army is already assured. The promptness and rapidity with which you have forwarded reinforcements has contributed largely to the feeling of confidence inspired in our men and to break down that of the enemy."

On the 25th our corps assisted in tearing up, burning and destroying many miles of the rails and ties of the Virginia Central railroad in our vicinity. This road connects Gordonsville with Richmond. We were visited by a heavy thunder-storm on the afternoon of the 26th. During the day General Wilson's cavalry division was making demonstrations against Lee's left in order to deceive him as to our approaching night movement. Under Sheridan's active management two divisions of cavalry, with one division of the Sixth Corps, moved towards Hanover town with artillery and trains, on the afternoon of the 26th. At dark our right wing withdrew to the north side of the North Anna. Our corps crossed at Quarles' ford and moved by the rear of Burnside's and Hancock's troops. Wright's Sixth Corps was followed by Hancock's Second Corps. Our Fifth Corps was followed by the Ninth Corps on a road further north of the one taken by the Sixth and Second Corps. The latter corps acted as rear guard of the army.

After the Wilderness battles our base of supplies was at Fredericksburg. On moving south to the North Anna river the base was changed to Port Royal, further down the Rappahannock river. This last move to the Pamunkey river called for a change of base of supplies to White House Landing, on the Pamunkey, by way of the York river. It was the old site of supplies for McClellan's army in 1862. The head of our army column reached the Pamunkey and secured a crossing on the morning of May 27. That same morning General Lee had discovered our movements or had been informed of them by the numerous spies that lurked around our army, and telegraphed the information to Richmond.

We marched with but few stops until we arrived in sight of the Pamunkey river at 6 o'clock P.M. of the 27th, having marched about thirty-five miles. The country we passed through was new to us and well supplied with sheep, pigs, poultry, etc. Our marching columns " travelled on their bellies," for there was much foraging and cooking indulged in to the great chagrin of the natives and owners of the aforesaid live stock. At the end of the journey, however, the troops were all together again, as the foraging and cooking did not interfere with the rapidity of the march. On the 28th strict orders were issued against foraging and straggling. Officers were authorized to shoot, if necessary, to enforce obedience to the orders. By drawing these stringent lines the desired effect was produced on that small fraction of our army which was always skirmishing for luxuries. At daylight on the morning of the 28th we again moved forward and towards noon crossed the river on pontoons at Dabney's ford to the south side near Hanover. Having recently left the late terrible battlefields of 1862, 1863 and 1864, we were now drawing near to the old Peninsula battleground of 1862, there to renew and pass through scenes of warfare as horrible as any that had yet occurred.

General Lee's army was reported to be somewhere in our front, between us and Richmond. There was much marching, manœuvring, reconnoitring and skirmishing on the 28th, 29th and 30th, by both armies. At Hawes' shop, on the Richmond road, General Sheridan had a successful fight with the enemy's cavalry on the 28th, as the result of a reconnoissance. On the 29th a reconnoissance in force was made to ascertain and locate the position of the enemy. The Fifth Corps moved forward on the Shady Grove Church road, crossed the Totopotomy, and met the enemy's outposts. Not being over-curious as to who we were, they soon retired from view. The Second and Sixth Corps pushed out and felt the enemy. The Ninth Corps was in reserve.

This movement advanced our lines from one to three miles. On the morning of the 30th the reconnoissance was again pushed with great vigor in order to exactly define the enemy's position. The Fifth, Ninth, Second and Sixth Corps were more or less successful during the day and night in feeling and driving the enemy from their front back onto their line of fortifications, some of which had been built two weeks previous; so that it was evident that General Lee was drawing our army on to the line of defence which he had deliberately selected weeks before. Our Fifth Corps went forward in column of divisions, our 1st division leading in column of brigades, under General Griffin. The 22d Massachusetts was in our front on the skirmish line, and gallantly led the way over the rough ground of fallen trees, swamps, ravines and underbrush, through clearings and woods, for several miles, driving the enemy's skirmishers at intervals from their defences, where at times they made a stubborn resistance. Our skirmish line, being exposed to sharpshooters, suffered severely in killed and wounded. In the afternoon our corps was attacked by General Early's Confederates with great vigor. At the first onset our lines were forced back by a movement to turn our left flank. With the assistance of a battery posted on the cross-roads from Bethesda Church, the enemy was repulsed and driven from our front. After being reinforced and relieved by a division of the Ninth Corps we fell back at night and went into bivouac.

That night, May 30, General Lee's lines extended from his left at · Atlee's Station, on the Virginia Central railroad, to Old Cold Harbor on his right; covering six or seven miles of ground and taking in Mechanicsville, Beaver Dam creek, and Gaines' Mill vicinity. The city of Richmond was some six miles southwest of the centre and rear of his lines. The latter ran southeast from left to right. On the night of the 30th the Union lines ran southeast and nearly parallel with the Pamunkey river, some distance in our rear; the left of the Fifth Corps was on Shady Grove Church road and extended to the Mechanicsville road. On its right was the Ninth Corps, next the Second Corps, and next, on the extreme right, in a northwesterly direction, the Sixth Corps. General Sheridan with two divisions of cavalry was near Cold Harbor. General Wilson's division of cavalry destroyed a part of the Virginia Central railroad and, after a skirmish with Young's Confederate cavalry, seized Hanover Court House, some seven miles on our right flank.

The heat and dust at this time of the year was intense. On the 31st General Sheridan made an assault on Old Cold Harbor; after a

hard fight his cavalry gained possession of the works.   A large force
of the enemy was sent to recapture the place.   General Wright's Sixth
Corps was ordered to move to Sheridan's relief.   On the 1st of June
two assaults were made on him and were repulsed.   The Sixth Corps
coming up on the morning of the 1st of June deterred the enemy from
making any further attack.

General Smith's reinforcements, the Eighteenth Corps of 15,000
men, were on their way up from White House Landing, but through
some mistake in his orders did not arrive at Cold Harbor until 3
o'clock P.M. of the 1st of June.   He left one division at White House
Landing temporarily.   On the morning of the 1st the enemy advanced
in our front under fire of our artillery and became strongly intrenched.
It was intended to prevent this movement towards our line on the part
of the enemy, but General Meade's combinations were slow to act.
The Sixth and Eighteenth Corps were now at Cold Harbor and about
6 P.M. of the 1st charged across an open space and into the woods,
capturing the enemy's rifle-pits and some seven or eight hundred
prisoners.   At the same hour three assaults were made on our Fifth
Corps lines which were successfully repulsed with heavy loss to the
enemy.   Hancock's and Burnside's lines were likewise attacked without
any advantage being gained on either side.   Frequent assaults were
made in the course of the night which our troops promptly met and
defeated every time.   The Second Corps moved down to the left of the
Sixth Corps; after a long and laborious march in the heat and darkness it got into position at 7.30 o'clock A.M. of June 2.   Unsuccessful
preparations were made to attack Lee's lines in force on the afternoon
of the 2d.   Warren was sent to Smith's left and Burnside moved to
Bethesda Church in reserve.   They were fiercely attacked while making
these changes and, although the enemy was repulsed, he captured
several hundred of our troops.   During the night Lee changed his lines
of battle to cover his antagonist.   They now extended from the Totopotomy creek to New Cold Harbor.   The Union lines were from
Bethesda Church by Old Cold Harbor to the Chickahominy river, with
one division of cavalry guarding the right flank.   Hancock, Wright
and Smith were ordered to prepare to assault the enemy's works on the
3d of June.   Warren and Burnside were to support this movement by
threatening to assault Lee's left if he withdrew troops from that point.
The assault was opened by Hancock's troops at 4.30 A.M. of the 3d by
charging his lines through thickets, swamps and deep ravines, under a
heavy artillery and musketry fire.   Being unable to carry the enemy's

works they held their ground with as much safety to themselves, under the galling fire poured into them, as they could, by throwing up hurried earthworks along their lines. They captured two hundred or more prisoners and three pieces of artillery. The latter were used against the enemy. Wright's corps moved forward on the charge in two lines and only reached the enemy's rifle-pits under a severe fire. Smith's corps charged over the most exposed ground of any, and met with a heavy direct and cross fire which brought his lines to a halt under the cover of a ravine and other natural protection along his front. Warren's and Burnside's corps advanced and held the ground gained. The army now being all in line, close to the enemy, the time was occupied in strengthening their lines with earthworks. This brief assault cost us some 6000 men in killed and wounded. The Confederate losses were comparatively light. The fighting was all over at 7.30 A.M.

Our brigade captured and occupied an outer-work of the enemy which it held and turned against them under fire and continued to exchange shots all day. We were expecting orders to go forward during the forenoon on another charge against the uncaptured formidable works still occupied by Lee's army. General Grant consulted with all the corps commanders on the feasibility of another assault on the enemy's works " all along the line," on the strength of which he sent instructions as follows to General Meade June 3, 1864, 12.30 P.M. : —

" The opinion of corps commanders not being sanguine of success in case an assault is ordered, you may direct a suspension of farther advance for the present . . . . To aid the expedition under General Hunter it is necessary that we should detain all the army now with Lee until the former gets well on his way to Lynchburg (Virginia) . . . ."

During the night, the 3d, the enemy moved away altogether from our right front. Some of their wounded fell into our hands and their dead they left unburied. On June 5 General Grant wrote to General Lee a proposition by which the wounded between both army lines might be cared for and the dead buried. Most of them were ours and the helpless wounded were suffering terribly in the hot sun and weather, and dying rapidly. General Lee's reply called for another letter from Grant on the 6th. Again Lee procrastinated by failing to agree or offering anything definite. On the 6th Grant again wrote a strong letter about the suffering wounded and urged Lee to agree to something. On the 7th he received a reply from Lee, acceding to his proposition ;

but in the meantime all but two of our wounded died on the field. General Grant closed his last note to Lee as follows : —

. . . . "Regretting that all my efforts for alleviating the sufferings of wounded men left upon the battlefield have been rendered nugatory,

I remain, etc.,   "U. S. GRANT,
Lieut.-General."

The following quotation from General Grant's memoirs will be of interest to those who have not read it : —

" I have always regretted that the last assault at Cold Harbor was ever made . . . . No advantage whatever was gained to compensate for the heavy loss we sustained. Indeed, the advantages, other than those of relative losses, were on the Confederate side. Before that the Army of Northern Virginia seemed to have acquired a wholesome regard for the courage, endurance and soldierly qualities generally of the Army of the Potomac. They no longer wanted to fight them ' one Confederate to five Yanks.' Indeed, they seemed to have given up any idea of gaining any advantage of their antagonist in the open field. They had come to much prefer breastworks in their front to the Army of the Potomac. This charge seemed to revive their hopes temporarily, but it was of short duration. When we reached the James river, however, all effects of the battle of Cold Harbor seemed to have disappeared."

The section of country in which both armies were recently engaged in deadly contest was, for miles in every direction, in its wild natural state and covered in part with the swamps of the Chickahominy, Totopotomy and Pamunkey streams and feeders. It abounded in woods, thickets, briars, brambles and clearings, which at intervals were filled with stumps, fallen trees, fences and ravines. Along the enemy's lines were formidable log and earthworks, rifle-pits, redoubts, abatis, slashed trees, swamps and runs, and every possible obstacle which could impede an attacking force. The artillery and infantry fire which swept from the enemy's works played sad havoc with our advancing lines of infantry and cavalry as they attempted to pass, for long distances, through and over these innumerable obstacles. All this gave General Lee's army a most decided advantage over his opponent that even ten times the number in his front could not overcome. He could neither be flanked nor driven from a position that, for the time being, man and nature had made impregnable. The only key to the situation was for a separate army, properly directed, to strike the enemy's left flank and rear from the north of Richmond. The success of this movement would lead at once to the reduction of

Lee's army and the fall of the Confederate capital. Such an army from Fredericksburg, led by General Sheridan, while General Grant held General Lee in his grasp along the swamps of the Chickahominy, would, to the writer's mind, judging by past events, have settled the war in Virginia in a week or ten days. This was General McClellan's plan when he fought the battle of Hanover Court House May 27, 1862. It was frustrated, as history will show, by the authorities in Washington, even when the new army was on its march for that purpose from Fredericksburg. Generals Lee and " Stonewall " Jackson, with their wonderful foresight, saw the doom of the Confederate cause if McClellan carried out his now exposed plan; and, by stratagem, concentrated, in an incredibly short space of time, in front of Richmond, June, 1862, the largest and strongest Confederate army that was ever mustered on that field. The result was, on the part of the Confederates, the aggressive seven days' battles, from the vicinity of Gaines' Mill, over to the James river, ending at Malvern Hill. It, unfortunately for us, relieved Richmond from a siege under which it would have eventually fallen had the Army of the Potomac been reinforced as required at that time. It is true that McClellan's plans in that direction, through no fault of his, were never tested by actual trial, and it is equally true that every general who followed him — Pope to Grant — dismally failed to capture Richmond. General Grant " hammered " the Confederate army all around Richmond until it was finally hammered to death and General Lee in despair was compelled to surrender the skeleton of his army at Appomattox, a town *seventy miles* west of the Confederate capital. The latter place then virtually fell. The writer does not by any means wish to pluck as much as a leaf from the laurels around General Grant's brow, for to him is due the great honor of saving the Union. That he made mistakes is only another way of saying that he was human. It was his methods as a whole that won the final victory. At the close he proved himself as generous and humane as he was brave and persistent.

General Grant having satisfied himself that the country around the Chickahominy swamps was only a death-trap for his aggressive army, and that General Lee's forces had a wholesome dread of engaging in battle outside of anything but strong fortifications, determined to change his base to the James river. He was further satisfied, also, that the Army of the Potomac was confident of moving in any direction and defeating the enemy in battle whenever and wherever it could be met with, outside of fortifications. He was likewise convinced that the backbone of the rebellion was broken and that the end of the war was only a question of a comparatively short time. Under these conditions of things he moved his army by the left flank, without loss of time, towards the James river. On the morning of the 7th of June, 1864, the 1st division of the Fifth Corps, having marched from the late battle-line at Cold Harbor, a few miles away, went into bivouac near Bottom bridge, on the banks of the Chickahominy, about a mile from the Richmond & York River railroad. Our brigade occupied this line with other troops of the corps for several days.

The Ninth, with the rest, had the pleasure of receiving a plentiful supply of clothing, etc., and rations at this point. The term of three years' service of the regiment was drawing to a close and they improved the opportunity of putting themselves in good condition and appearance to leave the field.

On the 9th of June the enemy on the other side of the forest that covered the river which ran between us amused themselves by running an " iron-clad " car down the Richmond & York River railroad, and throwing from it a sixty-pound shell every hour or so, over the forest and onto the field which we occupied. Little notice was taken of this random firing until about noontime, when a breeze of excitement was caused as one of these large shells dropped into a mess of the 5th Massachusetts Battery as they were eating dinner. It exploded and killed three of the brave fellows and wounded five others. Their camp was in a piece of woods about twenty yards from where the Ninth lay. For blind firing it was a terrible shot and it reminded us of the fact that in the field a soldier's life is always uncertain. At a previous hour one of these shells struck the ground, without exploding, near division headquarters, a hundred yards or more away. General Griffin had it boxed up and presented to Colonel Hanley for transportation to Boston. The shell now occupies a place in the armory of the Columbian Guards of the Ninth Massachusetts Militia, as a souvenir of the war from the old " Ninth."

In the afternoon the adjutant assembled the recruits and re-enlisted men of the Ninth regiment whose terms of service were as yet unexpired, and, with the assistance of the quartermaster, transferred them — 209 men, present and absent — to the 32d Massachusetts Veteran Volunteers of our brigade, by whom they were kindly and cheerfully received, to serve out their unexpired term of service. Their names are in the roster attached to this book and can also be found on the roster of the 32d regiment.

On Friday morning of the 10th of June, 1864, Colonel Hanley and his officers, some half dozen now present, called on General Griffin to bid him farewell. The general in saying good-bye complimented the Ninth regiment very highly on its long and faithful service, and referred particularly to its good qualities as a fighting regiment, and hoped that after Colonel Hanley got rested he would see him out again to reorganize the Ninth, for, the general said, he would transfer all the Ninth men over to him again. After saying farewell to many officers and men of the 32d and 22d Massachusetts, 62d Pennsylvania and 4th Michigan, etc., the regiment took up the line of march, with light hearts and a good send-off, for White House Landing, on the Pamunkey river. After a pleasant sail down the York river, over Chesapeake Bay and up the Potomac, we arrived in Washington Sunday morning of the 12th. On Monday, the 13th, we took the cars for home. We stopped at Baltimore, Philadelphia and New York for refreshments. The regiment was bountifully supplied free of cost by the patriotic ladies of each city and our entertainment was most hospitable.

We reached Boston on the morning of the 15th of June at the Boston & Albany station, and were met by thousands of relatives and friends, some of whom, alas! for the first time learned that the loved ones they were looking for were but lately slain or died of wounds, or were absent in some hospital, wounded or sick, or missing, never to be heard from. Many others were there to meet us who had seen the regiment off to the war three years before and came now to welcome back the survivors, missing in their inquiries many friends who died for their country during that time. Colonel Guiney and many others of our lately wounded officers and men were there to give us affectionate greeting. The day had its sad and pleasant memories intermingled, more of the former than the latter, so much so that once in a lifetime was enough to witness, as a member, the return of a war regiment after three years' heavy losses in killed, wounded, missing, disabled, etc.

THE REGIMENT'S RETURN.

* * * * * *

"Men are shouting all around me, women weep and laugh for joy;
Wives behold again their husbands and the mother clasps her boy.
All the city throbs with passion: 'tis a day of jubilee;
But the happiness of thousands brings not happiness to me.
I remember, I remember, when the soldiers went away,
There was one among the noblest who is not returned today.
Oh, I loved him, how I loved him! and I never can forget
That he kissed me as we parted, for that kiss is burning yet!

* * * * * *

Oh, they say he died a hero — but I knew how that would be;
And they say the cause has triumphed — will that bring him back to me?"

E. J. CUTLER.

After breakfast we soon formed column for a parade through some of the principal streets of Boston, escorted by military and civic organizations, the latter in large numbers. Patriotic greetings and decorations met us on every side of the line of march. On the Common we were honored with a salute by Cummings' Battery. We then passed up Beacon street and down to Faneuil Hall. Adjutant-General Schouler received us there with a patriotic address. The governor being absent he acted in his behalf. A bountiful collation was served in the hall, after which the regiment was dismissed to again assemble on the 21st of June, 1864, on the parade ground on Boston Common for muster-out.

In the afternoon and evening of the 15th the Columbian Association kept open house and entertained both officers and men. The out-of-town companies went to their respective homes and were happily received. On the 21st of June, 1864, the survivors of the regiment assembled on Boston Common and were properly mustered out of the United States Volunteer service and once more became peaceful citizens. During the subsequent months of summer and fall many of the survivors of the Ninth re-enlisted in other war regiments and in the navy. Numbers of them went again into battle and were killed or wounded, or remained until the close of the war, to be again mustered out after following the fortunes of the Army of the Potomac in front of Petersburg and up to the surrender of General Lee at Appomattox, April 9, 1865.

CASUALTIES IN THE NINTH MASS. VOLUNTEERS AT NORTH ANNA RIVER, SHADY OAK GROVE, TOTOPOTOMY SWAMP, BETHESDA CHURCH AND COLD HARBOR, MAY 23 TO JUNE 3, 1864, INCLUSIVE.

List of Killed.

COMPANY D.

May 30, Sergeant John D. Doherty.

COMPANY F.

June 3, Corporal James Powers.

List of Wounded.

May 23, Lieutenant Christopher Plunket, right arm off.

COMPANY A.

May 23, Simon J. Riley; June 3, John A. Reynolds; June 3, John O'Brien June 3, Charles Sweeney; June 3, Geo. I. Tirrell.

COMPANY B.

May 23, Sergeant John W. Cullinan; June 3, Corporal Michael Brannon; May 23, John McCurran.

COMPANY C.

No record.

COMPANY D.

May 23, Thomas Mallahan; May 30, James Fleming; June 3, James Cavanagh.

COMPANY E.

June 3, Thomas Carter; June 3, John Brenn; June 3, John Breen; June 3, Daniel Buckley; June 3, Francis Kelly.

COMPANY F.

June 3, Timothy O'Shea.

COMPANY G.

No record.

COMPANY H.

June 3, Sergeant Patrick Doherty; June 3, Corporal Daniel Sullivan; June 2, Nehemiah S. Dodd; June 3, John B. Salkins; June 3, Thomas H. Adams; June 3, Michael Finnerty.

COMPANY I.

June 3, Terence O. Loughlin; June 3, John Flynn.

COMPANY K.

June 3, John Scherer; June 3, Thomas Fulton; June 3, Michael McGuire

WHOLE NUMBER.

Men killed	2
Officers wounded . . ·	1
Men wounded	28
Aggregate, May 23 to June 3, 1864· . . .	31

Col. Patrick T. Hanley.

Colonel Hanley was born in Roscommon, Ireland, March 17, 1831. At the age of twelve years his young mind became imbued with the idea of seeking his fortune in the new world. His force of character was, even at that age in life, too strong to be persuaded from taking the course he intended by those interested in his welfare. In company· with a friend of his uncle he left a cheerful home and beloved mother for the long journey — for a long journey it was in those days — to America. In his early infancy he was bereft of a father's care, whose untimely death by fever left him without that paternal guardianship which could have changed the whole course of his life. After an

uneventful passage he arrived, by way of Montreal, in Hamilton, O.
By diligent perseverance and study he pushed his way to prosperity
and his early manhood found him a cooper by trade and the foreman
of the pork-packing establishment of Fisher & Chapin. Many years
of trusted labor and financial responsibilities were spent with his
employers between Hamilton, O., and Boston. In the latter city he
finally continued to remain, winning golden opinions from his employers and meeting prosperity at every step. Among his kinsmen in
Boston he was always a welcomed friend. He freely joined in their
festivities and societies and was particularly active in the Columbian
Artillery and its later association. At the annual drills for two
successive years he carried off the gold-medal prize as a crack rifle-shot
and marksman. On returning from a short vacation to Ireland and his
native place, he found many of his old companions preparing for war.
In his patriotic ardor he joined his old friend, Colonel Cass, and aided
in recruiting two companies of the Ninth regiment and subsequently
went to the front as 1st lieutenant of Company B. His services
during the war in the Ninth Massachusetts were rewarded by advance-
ment to captain, major, lieutenant-colonel and brevet-colonel, as
mentioned in detail in this work. On being mustered out of service in
1864 he entered business on his own account. Subsequently he held
for many years the lucrative position of brewer and foreman in one of
Boston's most successful ale breweries. In recent years he again
entered business on his own account and is president of the successful
corporation of the Hanley & Casey Brewing Company of Roxbury.
His whole career through life has been marked with that prosperity
and financial success which is gained only by strong force of character
and great business ability.

His services in the Ninth Massachusetts Volunteers being frequently mentioned in this work, it is unnecessary to repeat them here.
It is only justice to him to say, however, that his military career of
three years' hard campaigning is one which he may feel justly proud
to hand down to posterity. He was gallant and meritorious at the
battle of Hanover Court House and at the long and hard-fought battle
of Gaines' Mill. Likewise at Malvern Hill, where he gallantly commanded the regiment after Colonel Cass was mortally wounded and
where he was himself seriously wounded, and succeeded in command by
the acting major, Captain O'Leary. At a later period in his service,
when General Guiney fell, terribly wounded, he proved himself an able
and brave commander from May 5, 1864, to June 10, 1864, and on the
return home for muster-out with the survivors of his gallant regiment.

His home in Roxbury is enjoyed with a large and interesting family of grown-up girls and boys. A shadow was cast upon it in recent years by the decease of a beloved wife and mother. Her native wit and brilliant character and charitable disposition not only endeared her to a beloved family, but likewise to a large circle of dear relatives and friends. For the last few years Colonel Hanley has been at intervals confined to his home by an attack of appendicitis. He has been a great sufferer in the past and is now gradually recovering health and strength. It is hoped that he will continue to live long to enjoy his hard-earned prosperity, and once again attend the reunions of his old regiment, where his presence for the last few years has been greatly missed.

Since the above was written Colonel Hanley died of pneumonia, March 31, 1899. His memory was honored by a large and imposing funeral and, amidst a concourse of his sorrowing family, relatives and numerous friends, he was laid to rest in the old Dorchester cemetery. His memory will ever shine as one of the heroes of the war of '61-'65. May he rest in peace.

> " None knew him but to love him,
> None named him but to praise."

ADDENDA.

DIARY.

The writer has in his possession a diary kept by his brother, Capt. James W. Macnamara, when 1st sergeant of Company I. It covers the time from our first advance on Yorktown to the battle of Gaines' Mill, when he was wounded and exchanged.

Friday, April 4, 1862. Left Hampton en route for Yorktown. Out skirmishing during the march. The enemy left their fortifications at our approach after firing a few shells. Camped at Cockletown that night; distance marched eighteen miles.

Saturday, April 5. Took up our line of march and arrived in front of the enemy's works before Yorktown about 1 P.M., when they opened fire on us. Our company thrown out as skirmishers; advanced to within four hundred yards of the works, the enemy firing at us all the time, doing us no harm, although some very large guns threw shell and shot amongst us rather thick, causing us to retire, being ordered to do so. Camped that night in a ravine.

Sunday, April 6. We lay in the ravine all day. Not allowed to pitch our ponchos on account of being so close to the enemy's forts. An occasional shell burst in amongst us. One shell killed and wounded four men in the next regiment (62d Pennsylvania). Our lights are keeping the enemy at work firing. The balloon (ours) is up. We saw General McClellan for the first time on the Peninsula.

Monday, April 7. Our regiment was out last night and dug an intrenchment close to the enemy's works. Towards morning the enemy shelled us, the shots passing close. It is the first intrenchment thrown up.

Tuesday, April 8. Very wet, raining all day; an awful night, having no tents, it is very uncomfortable. Our turn for picket. Fifty men from each company. The firing between our artillery and the enemy's is pretty heavy; some of our party killed.

Wednesday, April 9. Rain still continues. Nothing of interest. Shells bursting close to us, but few hurt. None of our regiment.

Thursday, April 10. Raining still; shifted camp one mile back in the afternoon. Slept very comfortable last night for the first time for a week.

Friday, April 11. Weather fine. The enemy is firing occasionally. Our men are at work in the trenches.

Here nothing is written until

Tuesday, April 29. Nothing of interest. Fine weather. Occasional firing by both parties.

Wednesday, April 30. Our regiment detailed for picket. In the trenches all night, raining nearly all the time. The enemy shelled us towards morning, but doing no damage, although very close at hand.

Thursday, May 1. Relieved from picket. Heavy firing during the night, both infantry and artillery.

Friday, May 2. Fifty of our men from each company (500) are at work in the trenches. Shells are dropping very close but no one hurt. One shell came directly over our camp, bursting near the General's quarters.

Saturday, May 3. Regiment mustered for pay by Colonel Cass. During the day we had some heavy firing at intervals by both sides; 6 P.M. a shell burst overhead. A piece weighing eight pounds dropped ten yards to the right of our company. The last shell dropped close by at 9 P.M.

Sunday, May 4. 7 A.M., Yorktown reported evacuated. 1 P.M. ordered out in light marching order to guard the forts taken. Our army is on the march. 8 P.M. returned back to camp. 9 P.M. orders to have three days' rations cooked. Our division has been left behind.

Monday, May 5. A rainy morning; we expect orders to march at any moment. Heavy firing in the direction of Williamsburg. 7 P.M. our division was on the road, but ordered back until daylight. Still raining 10 P.M.

Tuesday, May 6. A beautiful sunny day but rather cool. All firing has ceased; we are under marching orders; we have just heard that McClellan has had a complete victory, 1000 prisoners, and the rest are surrounded.

Wednesday, May 7. Weather fine; we march shortly; awaiting transports. 8 P.M. struck our tents. 12 M. started for Yorktown: arrived and lay there all night, slept on the bare ground.

Thursday, May 8. Weather fine; visited the forts in the immediate vicinity of Yorktown. Stood on the spot where Lord Cornwallis surrendered his sword, and got a piece of the stone that marks the spot. 3.30 P.M. embarked on *Columbia*. 7.30 P.M. disembarked at West Point, Va., and marched 1½ miles where we camped for the night; slept on the ground, our tent not having arrived.

Friday, May 9. Shifted camp and pitched tents; very hot day. About twenty-eight miles from Richmond.

Saturday, May 10. Weather fine, but warm. Orders to have three days' cooked rations on hand and ready to march in light marching order for Richmond. Had a bath today for the second time this year. Visited the graves of those killed in the late battle here, West Point.

Sunday, May 11. Weather fine; General McClellan passed by to-day, the soldiers cheered him all along the road. Expect to move at any moment.

Monday, May 12. Weather fine; received orders to have three days' rations, one day cooked, in haversacks.

Tuesday, 2 A.M. struck tents, 4.30 A.M. in line, and on the march.

Tuesday, May 13. The division marched at 4.30 o'clock this morning, very hot day. We marched about fourteen miles over very dusty roads, and felt pretty well used up, a great many dropping behind, some leaving knapsacks and everything behind; beautiful country here.

Wednesday, May 14. Camped last night at Columbia Landing. Received orders to hold ourselves ready to march at a moment's notice, two days' cooked rations; a pleasant day.

Thursday, May 15. Struck tents this morning; awaited all day in the rain, which was very heavy, expecting to march but did not. At night pitched our tents again; about 10 P.M. cleared up.

Friday, May 16. Cloudy, but a pleasant day. Struck our tents and was on the road at 6 A.M. The road was very deep with mud. Marched about six miles, our teams not being able to get along on account of the mud. We camped at a place called White House, belonging to General Lee, the rebel. No tent, slept in the open air as usual; heavy dew.

Saturday, May 17. Pleasant weather. At noon shifted camp to get in our proper position in line. A splendid country in this part of Virginia.

Sunday, May 18. Weather fine. In the afternoon Companies I and A were detailed for fatigue duty until Monday morning to discharge some hay from a couple of schooners.

Monday, May 19. Got relieved about 10 today, and came back to our camp. The regiment has marched, leaving us behind. We concluded to rest until tomorrow, and then join them. About 2 P.M. commenced raining; cleared up at 5.

Tuesday, May 20. This morning started to join our regiment. About 6 o'clock left our camp and arrived at the place where our regiment was camped about 9, having marched about six miles. This is called Tunstall Station, about eighteen miles from Richmond.

Wednesday, May 21. Broke up camp and marched about four miles beyond Tunstall Station on the road to Richmond. Contrabands arriving daily. Houses and cultivation are to be met with oftener in this part of Virginia. Hanover County, Va.

Thursday, May 22. Received orders to march at 5 this morning; got ready when the order was countermanded; 1 P.M. struck our tents and marched about five miles, camping in a large field completely surrounded by woods. A heavy shower of rain during the march.

Friday, May 23. Weather fine. Heard some heavy firing during the day. Saw the balloon up about a mile in advance of our camp. We are now about ten and one half miles from Richmond. Our drums and music to be quiet once more.

Saturday, May 24. Raining the greater part of the day. The Michigans (4th regiment) have just come in from a reconnoitring party. They surprised a brigade of rebels; put them to flight; two killed, six wounded.

Sunday, May 25. Weather fine. This afternoon attended the funeral of the men killed belonging to the 4th Michigan regiment; 9 P.M. orders to march tomorrow at 4 A.M.

Monday, May 26. Pleasant day this. Struck our tents and marched a short distance and camped. About eight miles from Richmond; 8.30 P.M., just received orders to start tomorrow in light marching order with two days' rations.

Tuesday, May 27. Camp Gaines' Mill. Started this morning in light marching order, and marched about eighteen miles. The roads very muddy; rain till 12 M. then the sun came out very hot. Met the enemy and commenced fighting about 3 P.M.; at 5 our regiment got engaged and after firing a couple of volleys charged them and routed them completely.

Wednesday, May 28. Everybody much fatigued after yesterday's hard work. Took a look around the roads and woods; saw dead rebels in any quantity; knapsacks and clothing all along the roads that the rebels threw away in their flight. Destroyed the railroad and captured a great many prisoners. Buried Sergeant Regan today; we had about eleven men wounded and dead in the fight; captured a rebel color.

Thursday, May 29. Hanover Court House. The right wing detailed for picket. Cannot walk one hundred yards without coming across a couple of dead horses, and all over the woods are found dead men; found thirty in one pile; the smell is awful here. Got ordered in from picket; 3 P.M. started on our road back.

Friday, May 30. Arrived in camp about 2 o'clock this morning very much fatigued and very hungry, having eat only two meals the last two days, consisting of hard bread and coffee. After getting our breakfast and a glass of whiskey, turned in and took a nap, which was needed by all of us. This afternoon received orders to hold ourselves in readiness to march. Had a very heavy thunder shower this afternoon; the shower lasted about two hours.

Saturday, May 31. Weather fine, but cloudy. Orders to have three days' rations cooked to march tomorrow at daylight for Richmond. They have had some severe fighting across the river.

Sunday, June 1. Started this morning at 7 o'clock and marched to the Chickahominy; but the river was flooded and bridges not being completed we came back. The divisions that are across have been fighting all day.

Monday, June 2. Weather fine, but hot. Things are very quiet today, only an occasional gun heard now and then. No word about marching, though we expect the big battle soon. One of our men died yesterday.

Tuesday, June 3. Weather fine and very warm; heard heavy firing during the day. Got orders to march at a moment's notice, as they are fighting in front.

Wednesday, June 4. It rained heavy during last night and still continues. Heard some firing early this morning, but it did not continue long. A couple of our men swam the river, crossed with despatches from General Martindale. The rain prevents us from crossing the river, as it is overflowed.

Thursday, June 5. Cleared up, but still continues cloudy. We were sent out to relieve the left wing who were guarding a bridge across the river that was almost finished. There was some firing today between the batteries.

Friday, June 6. Pleasant weather. Relieved this morning at 9 o'clock. Everything is quiet this morning. Received our pay this noon up to May, 1862.

Saturday, June 7. Weather fine, everything quiet; slight shower this afternoon. An occasional gun fired now and then.

Sunday, June 8. Weather fine. Received orders this morning to perform four days' fatigue duty about three miles from here, making a road across a swamp.

Monday, June 9. A fine day. Out at work early this morning, three companies at a time, and worked until 10 o'clock; then came in and nothing more to do during the day.

Tuesday, June 10. Commenced raining about 3 A.M ; 11 A.M. cleared off. Went to work at 1. Six o'clock a slight shower of rain   Came in.

Wednesday, June 11. Weather fine. Nothing of interest. At work on the road. All the regiment one year mustered in the service today.

Thursday, June 12. Weather fine   Nothing of interest. Two o'clock relieved by the 22d Massachusetts Volunteers from fatigue. Marched back to our old camp.

Friday, June 13. Weather fine but very warm. Under marching orders. This afternoon we (our division) were ordered out in line of battle as the enemy have attacked our right. Companies I and F went out about three miles but saw nothing. In camp at 10 P.M.

Saturday, June 14. Weather fine; under marching orders.

Nothing further written until

Tuesday, June 24. Weather fine. Ordered out twice last night. Expect the enemy to make an attack soon. Hear firing occasionally. Slight shower this evening.

Wednesday, June 25. Pleasant weather. No orders to march yet.

Thursday, June 26. Blank.

Friday, June 27. Battle of Gaines' Mill. Wounded and taken prisoner. The rebels are very kind. They have very little to eat, hard bread and bacon.

Saturday, June 28. I have eaten nothing since I have been wounded. Nobody to dress our wounds. In the open air, no covering.

Sunday, June 29. We have got six dead bodies lying around us, the smell is horrible. Eat one biscuit today. Brought one of my company here.

Monday, June 30. A secesh doctor dressed our wounds. Can't eat hard bread so I am about starved out. Am very weak.

Tuesday, July 1. A negro girl made me a corn cake; and a cup of tea that we had, put some life in us again. Lying in the open air still.

Wednesday, July 2. One of our doctors came along, dressed our wounds and took our names. These six days have made a living skeleton of me.

Thursday, July 3. As usual.

Friday, July 4. A wagon came and carried us to Gaines' Mill where there were six more of our men. Nice place considering.

Nothing written until

Wednesday, July 16. Started today for Savage's Station.

And again until

Saturday, July 26. Started early this morning for City Point, via Richmond, to be delivered to our own government.

Monday, July 28. Saw General McClellan and had a shake hands.

Wednesday, July 30. Landed at General Hospital, Fortress Monroe.

This diary in its briefness is copied word for word, and is known to the writer to be genuine and reliable in its data.

His wound at Gaines' Mill was by a rifle bullet in his leg, below the calf, and the ball was never extracted. It was slow in curing and affected the nerves of his toes. He was rejoiced at saving his leg from amputation, for he always said he would rather die than lose a limb.

"THE THREE MACNAMARAS."

Their father, Daniel Macnamara, was born on the soil of his ancestors at Thomond, North Munster, Ire., Jan. 4, 1807. After receiving a good education and learning the trade of masonry he emigrated, with his newly wedded wife, to America and reached the city of Boston, Mass., in the spring of 1833. Here in prosperity were born and reared his family of four boys and two girls. Both parents lived peaceful and quiet lives and gave their children, in the meantime, good religious and secular education. When the Rebellion broke forth in April, 1861, and three of their boys went to the war for the Union in the Ninth Regiment Massachusetts Volunteers, they were, as devout Catholics, cheerfully resigned to the will of God, and with their blessing bid them Godspeed and ever prayed for victory for the Union army. The old folks died in recent years highly respected and loved by their children, relatives and friends, at the good old age of eighty odd years, and were tenderly buried by their kindred at Holyhood Cemetery, Brookline. May they rest in peace!

CAPTAIN JAMES WM. MACNAMARA

was the eldest of three brothers who served in the Ninth Massachusetts Volunteers as non-commissioned and commissioned officers. He was by nature possessed of an adventurous disposition, and at the age of seventeen years chose a seafaring life. It was a time when full-rigged ships and barks were the life of our merchant marine. He closely followed the sea for seven years. During that time he became an able seaman and a proficient navigator. In the course of many voyages he sailed into every commercial port of note in the known world.

At the breaking out of the Rebellion in April, 1861, he was in foreign parts. The news of an impending rebellion in the United States created great excitement abroad. He hastened home in order to take an active part on the side of the Union, for he always was a loyal American citizen to the core. His intention was to enter the volunteer cavalry service. On reaching Boston, however, he found his brothers engaged in recruiting Company E for Colonel Cass' new regiment, and was persuaded to join it as its 2d lieutenant, and was duly commissioned by the Governor. On the day of the muster-in of the Ninth Massachusetts Volunteers he was, without any warning, unjustly deprived of his lieutenantcy. To his honest nature it was a piece of political clap-trap and favoritism that opened wide his eyes with surprise and just indignation. At that early day our young soldiers believed that our war would be a short-lived affair. Impressed with the prevailing opinion he joined the regiment at the last moment as a sergeant and color-bearer of the Stars and Stripes. Being tall and muscular he filled the position to perfection.

Desiring more active duty he shortly afterwards accepted the 1st sergeantcy of Company I, much to the pleasure of that company and

27

its commander, Capt. James E. McCafferty.   It is unnecessary to add
that he performed the arduous duties of that position in a methodical
and excellent manner.   Still, he was only one of many excellent 1st
sergeants which the Ninth most fortunately had.   It is unnecessary to
name them for most of them were in time commissioned officers.   To
be brief: at the battle of Gaines' Mill, June 27, 1862, he was seriously
wounded and disabled on the skirmish line and taken prisoner, after
the three commissioned officers of the company were killed during the
skirmish.   After much suffering and starvation he was exchanged July
26, 1862, and arrived at the General Hospital, Fortress Monroe, July
30, 1862, and later at Chesapeake Hospital, Hampton, for treatment.
On his return to the regiment from hospital he received the following
unusual letter from his colonel : —

HEADQUARTERS NINTH MASSACHUSETTS VOLUNTEERS,
Oct. 15, 1862.

First Sergeant JAMES W. MACNAMARA.

 Sergeant: I hereby appoint you acting Second Lieutenant in this regiment,
and as soon as I am officially informed of a vacancy, which no doubt now
exists, I purpose to recommend you for commission.   This opportunity affords
me sincere pleasure.   You were meritorious at Hanover, gallant at Gaines'
Mill and the Chickahominy, and in camp and on parade your conduct and
appearance entitle you to my esteem and to whatever reward I am able to
bestow.   P. R. GUINEY,

Colonel, Commanding Ninth Mass. Vols.

 In time he rose to the rank of captain, and was always prompt,
faithful and brave in the discharge of every duty.   At the battle of the
Wilderness, May 5, 1864, he fell mortally wounded when leading his
company, with the regiment, in a determined attack on the enemy,
which was in large force and concealed in the woods.   Colonel Guiney
and 149 of his officers and men were killed and wounded in that assault.
He was buried on the field in Virginia, but in a few years, subsequent,
his remains were transferred to his former home in Boston.   After a
largely attended military funeral he was interred at Holyhood Cemetery,
Brookline, Mass.

CAPTAIN MICHAEL H. MACNAMARA

was a law student at the breaking out of the Rebellion, and had,
besides, devoted much of his time to literary pursuits.   On the organization of Company E, which he helped to recruit, he was commissioned captain May 3, 1861, but on muster into service in the Ninth
Massachusetts Volunteers he was deprived of that rank and accepted a
1st lieutenantcy.   This latter change was the sequel to the prearranged
plan which so unjustly deprived his elder brother of his rights as a

2d lieutenant. After more or less extended and disagreeable altercations with the colonel commanding the regiment, Lieutenant Macnamara was in a few months' time obliged to leave the service of the regiment through no fault of his own. Under Colonel Guiney he again joined the regiment as a recruit and private in August, 1862. He adopted this method to vindicate his aspersed character when a 1st lieutenant under Colonel Cass.

When highly recommended for a lieutenant's commission by his colonel and General Griffin, the numerical strength of the regiment was reduced to such an extent that under existing orders he, with others, could not be mustered in as commissioned officers. He therefore served as a non-commissioned officer until the expiration of his term of service June 21, 1864.

Subsequently he went to the front as a war correspondent, and was present at the surrender of General Lee. At the close of the war he finished his studies as a law student and was admitted to the Suffolk bar as a lawyer, in 1867. He continued, besides, to engage in literary work, and was a public speaker and lecturer of some note. While in the field with his regiment at Bealton Station in the winter of 1863–64 he wrote a book entitled the "Irish Ninth in Bivouac and Battle." It was published in Boston in 1867.

In late years an estranged domestic married life changed the current of his existence to such an extent that he left his native city of Boston forever. He travelled much in the West and continued to follow literary and newspaper work. After a short illness in May, 1897, he died in Kansas City. He was cared for and buried by a loving younger brother, John F., who has resided in that city for many years.

QUARTERMASTER DANIEL G. MACNAMARA,

the youngest of the three brothers, served for three years in the Ninth Massachusetts Volunteers successively as 1st sergeant, commissary sergeant, acting quartermaster-sergeant, N.C.S., 2d lieutenant, 1st lieutenant and March 26, 1863, was appointed quartermaster of the regiment, to succeed Quartermaster Mooney, deceased. He was mustered out on expiration of term of service, June 21, 1864.

In the city of Washington General Guiney had occasion to present him a letter, of which the following is a true copy : —

WASHINGTON, D.C., Dec. 22, 1864.

This is to certify that Daniel G. Macnamara, late lieutenant and quartermaster in my regiment, served a full term of three years in the army. He was brave, efficient and intelligent in the discharge of all his duties in the line;

and as regimental quartermaster I cannot say more; and it is due to him that I say nothing less than that, in my opinion, his superior was not in the army. He is thoroughly conversant with the duties and responsibilities of that office.

(Signed) P. R. GUINEY,
Late Colonel Ninth Mass. Vols.

Subsequently he was employed in the army in the quartermaster and commissary departments as an accountant, and after the surrender he went to Brownsville, Tex., on the Rio Grande, with the Twenty-Fifth Army Corps in that capacity. He later entered the service as a lieutenant, during the foreign occupation of Mexico, and was finally mustered out in November, 1866. He returned to Boston where he read law nearly a year. The opportunity subsequently offered, and he entered the classified civil service at the Boston Custom House under Collector Thos. Russell, Nov. 1, 1867, where he is still employed. He is the writer of this book.

BATTLEFLAGS.

Our battleflags, the " Stars and Stripes " and the " Green Flag of Erin," which our color-bearers carried in battle and on the march until riddled by shot and shell and tattered and torn by the elements of war and weather, were turned over to the State officials for safe keeping forever. Several sets that saw hard war service are now at the State House.

AMONG THE FLAGS

IN DORIC HALL, MASSACHUSETTS STATE HOUSE.

BY

LOUISE IMOGEN GUINEY.

Dear witnesses, all luminous, eloquent,
Stacked thickly on the tesselated floor!
The soldier-blood stirs in me, as of yore
In sire and grandsire who to battle went:
I seem to know the shaded valley tent;
The armed and bearded men, the thrill of war;
Horses that prance to hear the cannon roar;
Shrill bugle-calls and camp-fire merriment;
And as fair symbols of heroic things,
Not void of tears mine eyes must e'en behold
These banners lovelier as the deeper marred.
A panegyric never writ for kings
On every tarnished staff and tattered fold;
And by them tranquil spirits standing guard.

What follows here is deemed a fitting tribute to the colors. It is an article by the present writer and began with a quotation from the above poem by Miss Guiney. It was first published in the Brookline, Mass., *Chronicle*, March 28, 1885.

THE COLOR-BEARER.

None but those who served on the battlefield have a true conception of the significance of the "colors" of a regiment. "Men, follow your colors,"* was an order frequently heard during the war as a regiment advanced on the enemy. All eyes turned to the colors, the ranks closed up and a surging front of determined men went forward on the charge, or to a new position, bent on victory or death.

The color-sergeants and color-corporals are picked men, and for cool bravery and precision under arms and in marching, are unequalled. They form four files on the left of the right-centre company, known as the "color-company." Through the iron hail of shot and shell the faithful guard march with their precious colors on to the line of battle, into the charge, over the earthworks, or against batteries of artillery, closely aligned by the right and left wings of their regiment. To waver for a moment, to break or retreat, while death itself confronts them, would bring rout and disaster, followed by defeat upon their regiment. If the color-bearer be shot down the flag is seized by the bravest man and again borne aloft, and onward, fluttering triumphantly in the storm and smoke of battle.

The Massachusetts troops carried the National and State flags side by side through the tempest of four years' warfare. There were 62 regiments of infantry, 5 of cavalry, 4 of artillery and 16 batteries, composing a total of 126,236 men. The aggregate casualties from all sources were 49,220.

The color-guard, being a post of honor, was exempt from the ordinary duty of camp-guard, picket and fatigue. Invariably the colors are kept at the colonel's quarters. On all occasions they are received and returned with the honor of an escort and present arms.

The color company is commanded by the third senior captain; and is, when under fire, a most dangerous post to direct. The flags, waving and fluttering in the breeze, are visible to the naked eye at a great distance, and at times the murderous fire of the enemy is concentrated on the colors. More men were shot down during the war while carrying the colors than in any other position known to the service. The brave fellows were almost certain to lose one or more limbs, or receive a mortal wound. If a regiment breaks, retreats or becomes panic-stricken, or, as the veterans used to term it, "demoralized," its commander stands by the flag and every effort is made to "rally on the colors." It is a mark of lasting disgrace to lose the colors of a regiment in action, unless under extraordinary circumstances and brave fighting; even then a cloud is cast upon the battalion that is hard to remove.

On the muster-out of our regiments their colors were turned over to the State authorities, and are now incased in Doric Hall, not to be removed except by special legislation.

---

* Orders of General Guiney at the battle of Gaines' Mill, Va., June 27, 1862.

The memory of the soldier, who visits Doric Hall and views the veteran flags of the late war, will go back to the scenes of long, weary marches, where " his path was rugged and sore "; to the cheerless bivouac and lonely picket; to the bloody battlefields with their startling sounds of cannonade and musketry; its bursting shells; its grape and canister; and its hissing and whistling bullets. He will view in his mind's eye his wounded and dying comrades, and those who fell dead while gallantly fighting in defence of flag and country.

His blood quickens in his veins as he remembers that under those dear old flags he charged with a swelling heart and wild cheers the enemy's batteries, or dashed up or over the earthworks of the foe.

That millions of men marched with their standard bearers through victory and defeat, for four weary years of intestine warfare, some falling by the roadside from hunger and exhaustion, others swept away by wounds and disease, and all suffering more or less, a soldier's hardships, are a few of the thoughts that rapidly pass in the old veteran's brain as he muses — over these flags — on his soldier-life of the dim past.

Could these flags speak of the anguish they have witnessed in the tumult of victory or defeat on the fields of carnage and death, they would tell a tale of sacrifice and danger that would cause the generations of today to stand in silent wonder, awe-stricken at the story of the patriotic devotion of a nation's sons that fought to preserve their glory.

American mothers, like the Spartan matrons, kissed their sons a final parting, with anguish in their hearts and a smile of love in their faces, and bade them to return with a soldier's honorable record, or not at all. They re-echoed the ancient Spartan sentiment, " come back with your shield, or *on your shield*."

The bravest and best young blood of our land went out from hearts that loved the stars and stripes of Old Glory, and when they fell on the field, their first thoughts, in the throes of death, were for its honor and republican renown.

> " But sweeter than the song of Peace, the ringing battle-shout, —
> When Error's thistle-calyx bursts, Truth's purple blossoms out;
> And lovelier than the waving grain, the battleflag unfurled
> Amid the din of trump and drum to lead the onward world!
> Then mothers, sisters, daughters! spare the tears you fain would shed.
> Who seem to die in such a cause, you cannot call them dead!"

Gentle reader, let it never be recorded in future history that Massachusetts left veteran soldiers, in their declining years, " to the cold charities of a heedless world." It rests with you who know their story only on cold pages of history, to now assist in redeeming the pledges made to them in '61-'65, as they hastened to the front, in the strength and vigor of early manhood, to sacrifice life, fortune and health, on the altar of our common country.

While a veteran of the late war — friendless and alone — is in distress from disease and want, the pledges made them in the dark days of the Rebellion remain unfulfilled.

REUNIONS.

The survivors of the Ninth Massachusetts Volunteers held their first annual reunion on June 11, 1867 — anniversary of muster into the United States volunteer service — on their old campground on Long Island, B. H., and organized as The Society of the Ninth Regiment.

These annual reunions were continued each summer until the city of Boston assumed control of Long Island for the use of some of its public institutions. Reunions were also held, by invitation of citizens, at Salem, Milford, Lawrence and Woburn. The survivors were handsomely received, heartily welcomed, and generously entertained on each annual occasion. Since that time the survivors, with thinned ranks, continue to meet annually at different summer resorts such as Nantasket, Oak Island, Point of Pines, Bass Point, etc. At these reunions in recent years the survivors are joined by their families and friends, so that each coming reunion is looked forward to with increased pleasure.

> " There are bonds of all sorts in this world of ours,—
> Fetters of friendship, and ties of flowers,
> And true-lovers' knots, I ween :
> The girl and the boy are bound by a kiss,
> But there's never a bond, old friend, like this,—
> We have drunk from the same canteen ! "

MONUMENTS.

The Society of the Ninth Regiment has erected a monument at Gettysburg on the slope of Big Round Top. It was dedicated through their committee on the 9th day of June, 1885. It marks the centre of the position held by the regiment during that battle. Massachusetts appropriated the sum of five hundred dollars for the purpose, for each organization engaged on the field of Gettysburg.

A monument has been erected by the State of Massachusetts on the battlefield of Antietam in commemoration of the regiments and batteries from Massachusetts which took part in that great battle. It was imposingly dedicated on the 17th day of September, 1898, by Governor Wolcott of Massachusetts, accompanied by a large delegation from the State.

The Society of the Ninth Regiment raised money by subscription for a monument to the memory of Colonel Cass and his regiment. Through the voluntary efforts of Alderman Short, at the time, it was placed on the Public Garden, although not originally intended to go there.   The statue is a life-like figure of Colonel Cass in granite and was dedicated on the 12th day of November, 1889.   In the meantime the city government of Boston has taken measures to replace the granite monument with a more imposing one in bronze of heroic size. The work is in the hands of Richard E. Brooks, sculptor, who has now been engaged on it for several years at his studio in Paris.

DESERTERS.

Every three years' war regiment has its percentage of deserters. The Ninth Massachusetts Volunteers is no exception to the rest.   Since the close of the war, in recent years, the " Irish " regiments and troops of that nationality, have been assailed in an outrageous manner by certain persons in public speech and through the newspaper press, for desertions from their ranks, and, as a class,— being Catholics — charged with a fabulous percentage of desertions, which, in itself, is highly ridiculous to all reasonable minds.

The Ninth Massachusetts was always at the front during its entire three years' service, and under constant labor, danger, battle and hardship, in all its campaigns.   This arduous service was one cause of desertion by men who lost heart — a disease that affects the brain — and could not stand the nervous strain and hard labor which they were continually put to; and, seeing no other way for rest and relief, resorted to desertion.   Furloughs were not allowed.   Another cause was from unprincipled recruits who enlisted for bounties.   Others joined the army during winter quarters, and, being expert gamblers, made their "pile " at card-playing, then deserted at the first favorable oppor- tunity when the spring campaign opened.   Some men were unjustly charged with desertion who were disabled in the service, and on the long, weary march fell to the rear, were picked up by the ambulances and sent to hospital and finally discharged from there on account of permanent disability.   Others who were lying wounded in hospital were eventually discharged from there on account of disability from wounds and sent to their homes, perhaps to die.   Sometimes men disappeared from camp, or on the march, and were murdered and robbed by " bush- whackers " and " guerillas " and never afterward heard from.   Occa- sionally, in winter quarters, a few furloughs were allowed to men, who, having gained their freedom in a measure, were unprincipled enough to seize the advantage and not return to their regiments. In some cases they enlisted in the navy, or some other branch of the service which was more congenial to them than the infantry. Under assumed names they escaped detection. Others were captured by the enemy in close proximity to their own camp, unknown to any one at the time, and their sudden disappearance was charged to desertion. Under the latter head in the Ninth Regiment, for example, were Patrick and Austin Ford of Company A, commanded by Capt. James F. McGunnigle. Written evidence has been furnished to the proper authorities at Washington, D.C., and at the State House, Boston, Mass., that they were reported on the rolls " deserters," through error, when they were prisoners in the hands of the enemy. Patrick Ford's case is particularly mentioned on account of his prominence as the editor and proprietor of the *Irish World*, a weekly paper published in New York city, which is well known on both continents on account of its strong and unqualified adherence to the patriotic cause of Ireland and the Irish race the world over. Patrick Ford's record has been corrected by order of the war department. Application has been made to correct his brother's record. When a man failed to answer to his name at roll-call he was reported a deserter unless otherwise accounted for. If he turned up again, well and good ; if he didn't, the charge remained against his name without further inquiry and was so reported on the next muster-roll. In this way many men suffered from the unjust charge who were murdered, drowned, captured, or died unknown inside the enemy's lines, or were discharged when absent without proper notice being furnished to their regiments. Another case in mind is that of a soldier who disappeared at Bealton when on fatigue duty chopping wood in the forest. He was put down as a deserter. His family never afterwards heard from him.

Without attempting or intending to detract one iota from other regiments in any way, in the volunteer service, it can be said of the Ninth — for a careful examination of its records will prove it — that its three years' service is as good as the best of the fighting regiments which were continually at the front.

When comparisons are made the *number of men, all told*, and the *years served* must be carefully taken into account.

ROSTER

OF THE

OFFICERS AND MEN

OF THE

NINTH REGIMENT INFANTRY

MASSACHUSETTS VOLUNTEERS

———

JUNE 11, 1861

JUNE 21, 1864

ROSTER

OF THE

NINTH REGIMENT

MASSACHUSETTS VOLUNTEERS.

FIELD AND STAFF OFFICERS.

CASS, THOMAS, Colonel, real estate broker, age 39, married, residence Boston, born in Ireland. Mustered in June 11, 1861, term 3 years. Wounded at the battle of Malvern Hill, July 1, 1862. Died of wounds ·July 12, 1862.

ROWELL, CROMWELL G., Lieutenant-Colonel, policeman, age 35, married, residence Boston, born in Corinth, Vt. Mustered in June 11, 1861, term 3 years. Discharged Oct. 23, 1861.

PEARD, ROBERT, Major, manufacturer, age 49, married, residence Milford, born in Waterford, Ire. Mustered in June 11, 1861, term 3 years; promoted Lieutenant-Colonel Oct. 24, 1861. Died of disease Jan. 27, 1862.

PINEO, PETER, Surgeon, age 37, married, residence Boston, born in Cornwallis, N S. Mustered in June 11, 1861, term 3 years. Discharged Aug. 26, 1861. Subsequently Brigade Surgeon and Medical Inspector of the Army of the Potomac.

O'CONNELL, PATRICK A., Assistant Surgeon, age 26, single, residence Boston, born in Ireland. Mustered in June 11, 1861, term 3 years. Discharged Sept. 12, 1861. Subsequently Surgeon 28th Mass Vols., Brigade Surgeon, Medical Director 9th Army Corps.

SCULLY, THOMAS, Chaplain, clergyman, age 28, single, residence Boston, born in Ireland. Mustered in June 17, 1861, term 3 years. Taken prisoner of war during the "Seven Days' Battles." Resigned for disability Oct. 31, 1862.

EGAN, COSTNEY L., Chaplain, clergyman, age 40, residence Washington, D.C., born in Ireland. Mustered in Sept. 18, 1863, term 3 years Mustered out June 21, 1864. Subsequently commissioned Field Chaplain by the War Department, and served on the staff of Gen. Charles Griffin, 5th Corps.

DREW, STEPHEN A., Surgeon, residence Woburn. Mustered in Aug. 27, 1861, term 3 years. Discharged July 28, 1862.

LINCOLN, FRANCIS M., Assistant Surgeon, age 31, residence Boston. Mustered in Sept. 12, 1861, term 3 years. Mustered out July 12, 1862, to accept promotion in 35th Mass. Reg.

SULLIVAN, JAMES F., Assistant Surgeon, age 24, residence Boston. Mustered in July 31, 1862, term 3 years; promoted Surgeon Dec. 13, 1862. Mustered out June 21, 1864.

FITZPATRICK, JAMES W., Assistant Surgeon, age 40, residence Boston. Mustered in Aug. 14, 1862, term 3 years. Discharged March 29, 1863, to accept promotion in Corps of Surgeons, U.S. Vols.

RYAN, JOHN, Assistant Surgeon, age 27, residence Boston. Mustered in Dec. 13, 1862, term 3 years. Mustered out June 21, 1864.

PERKINS, GEORGE W., Adjutant, cooper, age 47, married, residence Boston, born in Newburyport, Mass. Mustered in June 11, 1861, term 3 years. Discharged Aug. 14, 1862.

MORAN, JOHN, Quartermaster, married, residence Boston. Mustered in June 11, 1861, term 3 years. Discharged Nov. 26, 1861.

NON-COMMISSIONED STAFF.

STRACHAN, WILLIAM, Sergeant-Major, enlisted June 11, 1861, last finisher, age 35, married, residence East Boston, born in Edinburg, Scotland. Mustered in June 11, 1861, term 3 years; promoted 1st Lieutenant-Adjutant Aug. 26, 1861. Cashiered Feb. 25, 1862. Rejoined the regiment as a recruit Aug. 18, 1862, in Co. G. Discharged for disability.

MOONEY, THOMAS, Quartermaster-Sergeant, enlisted June 11, 1861, age 46, married, residence Boston, born in Boston, Mass. Mustered in June 11, 1861, term 3 years; promoted Quartermaster Nov. 27, 1861. Died March 27, 1863.

BLACK, PATRICK W., Commissary Sergeant, enlisted June 11, 1861, student, age 26, single, residence Portland, born in Ireland. Mustered in June 11, 1861, term 3 years; promoted 2d Lieut. Aug. 26, 1861, 1st Lieut. March 1, 1862, Capt. Oct. 20, 1862. Discharged Aug. 3, 1863, as Captain Co. B.

O'DOWD, FRANCIS, Commissary Sergeant, enlisted June 11, 1861, residence Boston. Mustered in June 11, 1861, as Color Sergeant, term 3 years; promoted 2d Lieut. Feb. 10, 1862, Co. I., from Color Sergeant. Killed June 27, 1862, Gaines' Mill, Va., in Co. I.

GRANGER, READ B., Hospital Steward, enlisted June 11, 1861, student, age 20, single, residence Boston, born in Eastport, Me. Mustered in June 11, 1861, term 3 years. Unofficially reported discharged 1863.

PARKER, NATHAN D., Hospital Steward, enlisted Feb. 8, 1862, residence Boston. Mustered in Feb. 8, 1862, term 3 years. Discharged as Hospital Steward 9th Inf. Mass. Vols., Nov. 28, 1862, S.C.D.

SULLIVAN, JOSEPH A., Hospital Steward, enlisted July 29, 1863, age 27, residence Boston. Mustered in July 29, 1863, term 3 years; promoted from private July 29, 1863. Mustered out June 21, 1864.

REGIMENTAL BRASS BAND.

O'CONNOR, MICHAEL, Leader, enlisted June 17, 1861, painter, age 28, married, residence Boston, born in Ireland. Mustered in June 17, 1861, term 3 years. Mustered out Aug. 10, 1862.

BURNS, PATRICK, Musician, enlisted June 17, 1861, laborer, age 27, single, residence Biddeford, born in Ireland. Mustered in June 17, 1861, term 3 years. Deserted July, 1861, at Camp Cameron, Massachusetts.

DAMON, FRANK, Musician, enlisted June 17, 1861, musician, age 40, married, residence Lynn, born in Lynn, Mass. Mustered in June 17, 1861, term 3 years. Discharged for disability Jan. 15, 1862.

DUNN, PETER, Musician, enlisted June 17, 1861, musician, age 23, married, residence Biddeford, Me., born in Ireland. Mustered in June 17, 1861, term 3 years. Discharged Dec. 16, 1861, by reason of Order No 91.

DWYER, EDWIN, Musician, enlisted June 17, 1861, musician, age 20, single, residence Lynn, Mass., born in Lynn. Mustered in June 17, 1861, term 3 years Mustered out Aug. 10, 1862, as " Duryea."

FITZGERALD, PATRICK, Musician, enlisted June 17, 1861, musician, age 22, single, residence Lawrence, born in Ireland. Mustered in June 17, 1861, term 3 years. Mustered out Aug. 10, 1862.

FLINT, CHARLES L., Musician, enlisted June 17, 1861, shoemaker, age 20, single, residence Lynn, born in Lynn, Mass. Mustered in June 17, 1861, term 3 years. Mustered out Aug. 10, 1862.

GRAHAM, WILLIAM H., Musician, enlisted June 17, 1863, painter, age 40, married, residence Mattapoisett. Mustered in June 17, 1861, term 3 years. Mustered out Aug. 10, 1862.

GIBSON, VICTOR, Musician, enlisted June 17, 1861, bootmaker, age 29, married, residence Milford, born in St. Johns, N.B. Mustered in June 17, 1861, term 3 years. Mustered out Aug. 10, 1862.

GUSTIN, GEO. A., Musician, enlisted June 17, 1861, bootmaker, age 21, married, residence Weymouth, born in Weymouth, Mass. Mustered in June 17, 1861, term 3 years. Mustered out Aug. 10, 1862.

HIGGINS, JOHN, Musician, enlisted June 17, 1861, carpenter, age 21, single, residence Buffalo, N.Y., born in Ireland. Mustered in June 17, 1861, term 3 years. Mustered out Aug. 10, 1862.

KNIGHT, WILLIAM A., Musician, enlisted June 17, 1861, musician, age 20, single, residence Lynn, born in Lynn, Mass. Mustered in June 17, 1861, term 3 years. Mustered out Aug. 10, 1862.

LEITCH, JOHN, Musician, enlisted June 17, 1861, musician, age 22, single, residence St. Johns, N.B., born in St. Johns, N.B. Mustered in June 17, 1861, term 3 years. Wounded at Malvern Hill, July 1, 1862; wounded absent in hospital, Brooklyn, N.Y.

MAHENE, JOHN, Musician, enlisted June 17, 1861, musician, age 22, single, residence Biddeford, Me., born in Biddeford, Me. Mustered in June 17, 1861, term 3 years. Discharged Dec. 16, 1861, as " Murnane," by reason of Order No. 91.

MAHENE, THOMAS, Musician, enlisted June 17, 1861, musician, age 19, single, residence Biddeford, born in Biddeford, Me. Mustered in June 17, 1861, term 3 years. Discharged Dec. 16, 1861, as "Murnane," by reason of Order No. 91.

MURRAY, JOHN, Musician, enlisted June 17, 1861, musician, age 25, single, residence Lawrence, born in Ireland. Mustered in June 17, 1861, term 3 years. Mustered out Aug. 10, 1862.

McCABE, MARTIN, Musician, enlisted June 17, 1861, musician, age 23, single, residence Winchendon, born in Ireland. Mustered in June 17, 1861, term 3 years. Mustered out Aug. 10, 1862,

RUSSELL, THOMAS, Musician, enlisted June 17, 1861, musician, age 40, married, residence Boston, born in Ireland. Mustered in June 17, 1861, term 3 years. Discharged Dec. 16, 1861, by reason of Order No. 91.

ROUNDS, A. K. P., Musician, enlisted June 17, 1861, musician, age 32, married, residence Lynn, born in Ireland. Mustered in June 17, 1861, term 3 years. Discharged for disability Sept. 16, 1861.

SCANLAN, JAMES, Musician, enlisted June 17, 1861, painter, age 34, married, residence Roxbury, born in Ireland. Mustered in June 17, 1861, term 3 years. Discharged Dec. 16, 1861, by reason of Order No. 91.

TIERNEY, WILLIAM, Musician, enlisted June 17, 1861, musician, age 27, married, residence Biddeford, Me., born in Ireland. Mustered in June 17, 1861, term 3 years. Mustered out Aug. 10, 1862.

WARD, THOMAS E., Musician, enlisted June 17, 1861, shoemaker, age 23, single, residence Lynn, born in Lynn, Mass. Mustered in June 17, 1861, term 3 years. Mustered out Aug. 10, 1862.

WOOD, EARNEST, Musician, enlisted June 17, 1861, spinner, age 27, married, residence Biddeford, born in Manchester, Eng. Mustered in June 17, 1861, term 3 years. Mustered out Aug. 10, 1862.

ZOLLER, LEWIS, Musician, enlisted June 17, 1861, musician, age 31, single, residence Taunton, born in Germany. Mustered in June 17, 1861, term 3 years. Sick in hospital, Baltimore, Md.

OFFICERS AND ENLISTED MEN.

COMPANY A.

Gallagher, James E., Capt., bricklayer, age 33, married, residence Boston, born in Londonderry, Ire. Mustered in June 11, 1861, term 3 years. Resigned July 8, 1862.

Scanlan, Michael, 1st Lieut., trader, age 39, married, residence Boston, born in Clare, Ire. Mustered in June 11, 1861, term 3 years; 1st Lieut. from June 11, 1861, to Jan. 27, 1862, promoted Capt. and transferred to Co. B. Wounded June 27, 1862, Gaines' Mill, Va., as Capt. Co. B. Resigned Oct. 15, 1862.

O'Hara, Michael F., 2d Lieut., safemaker, age 24, single, residence Boston, born in Boston, Mass. Mustered in June 11, 1861, term 3 years; promoted 1st Lieut. Feb. 26, 1862, Capt. June 28, 1862, Co. G. Taken prisoner at Gaines' Mill, Va., June 27, 1862. Mustered out June 21, 1864.

Coughlin, Jeremiah, 1st Sergt., enlisted June 11, 1861, laborer, age 32, married, residence Boston, born in Boston, Mass. Mustered in June 11, 1861, term 3 years; reduced from 1st Sergt. to Private, Sept. 1, 1861. Wounded July 1, 1862, at Malvern Hill, Va. Discharged for disability, Sept. 4, 1862.

O'Hara, John B., Sergt., enlisted June 11, 1861, expressman, age 25, single, residence Boston, born in Boston, Mass. Mustered in June 11, 1861, term 3 years. Wounded July 1, 1862, Malvern Hill, Va. Mustered out June 21, 1864, as Private.

Maloney, William B., Sergt., enlisted June 11, 1861, gasfitter, age 24, single, residence Boston, born in Boston, Mass. Mustered in June 11, 1861, term 3 years; promoted Commissary Sergt., 2d Lieut., March 1, 1862, Co. A, 1st Lieut., Sept. 26, 1862. Resigned March 23, 1863, from Co. E.

Earley, Patrick, Sergt., enlisted June 11, 1861, trunkmaker, age 23, single, residence Boston, born in Tyrone, Ire. Mustered in June 11, 1861, term 3 years. Killed July 1, 1862, Malvern Hill, Va.

Doherty, John F., Sergt., enlisted June 11, 1861, printer, age 22, single, residence Boston, born in Glasgow, Scotland. Mustered in June 11, 1861, term 3 years; promoted 1st Sergt., Commissary Sergt., Q.M. Sergt., Acting Lieut , 2d Lieut. Sept. 26, 1862, 1st Lieut. March 30, 1863, and transferred to Co. H; transferred to Co. A, Oct. 25, 1863. Wounded at Malvern Hill, Va., July 1, 1862, and at Wilderness, Va., May 5, 1864. Mustered out June 21, 1864.

Taylor, Bartholemew, Corp., enlisted June 11, 1861, tailor, age 37, married, residence Boston, born in Cork, Ire. Mustered in June 11, 1861, term 3 years. Wounded June 27, 1862, Gaines' Mill, Va. Discharged disability Nov. 22, 1862, Washington, D.C.

Burke, James, Corp., enlisted June 11, 1861, trunkmaker, age 23, single, residence Boston, born in Kerry, Ire. Mustered in June 11, 1861, term 3 years. Wounded Dec. 13, 1862, Fredericksburg, Va.; transferred to Invalid Corps as Sergt., no date.

Flynn, Thomas, Corp., enlisted June 11, 1861, trunkmaker, age 23, married, residence Boston, born in Boston, Mass. Mustered in June 11, 1861, term 3 years. Deserted as Private June 22, 1861, at Boston, Mass.

Palmer, John M., Corp., enlisted June 11, 1861, wool sorter, age 30, single, residence Lawrence, born in St. Albans, Me. Mustered in June 11, 1861, term 3 years. Transferred to Co. B as Private Aug. 31, 1861. Discharged for disability Jan. 20, 1863, as Private Co. B.

Dwyer, John, Corp., enlisted June 11, 1861, hostler, age 28, single, residence Boston, born in Cork, Ire. Mustered in June 11, 1861, term 3 years. Wounded June 27, 1862, at Gaines' Mill, Va. Discharged for disability Nov. 24, 1862, Philadelphia, Pa.

McDermott, Michael, Corp., enlisted June 11, 1861, laborer, age 24, married, residence Boston, born in Ireland. Mustered in June 11, 1861, term 3 years. Wounded June 27, 1862, Gaines' Mill, Va. Discharged for disability as Sergeant Sept. 6, 1862, Washington, D.C.

O'Reilly, James, Corp., enlisted June 11, 1861, porter, age 21, single, residence Boston, born in Cavan, Ire. Mustered in June 11, 1861, term 3 years. Discharged for disability April 7, 1863, as Sergeant.

Foley, James, Corp., enlisted June 11, 1861, blacksmith, age 26, single, residence South Boston, born in Galway, Ire. Mustered in June 11, 1861, term 3 years. Killed June 27, 1862, Gaines' Mill, Va.

Tracy, William, Wagoner, enlisted June 11, 1861, teamster, age 32, married, residence Roxbury, born in Galway, Ire. Mustered in June 11, 1861, term 3 years. Mustered out June 24, 1864.

Bayley, Ralph, Musician, enlisted June 11, 1861, age 23, single, residence Boston. Mustered in June 11, 1861, term 3 years. Mustered out June 21, 1864.

Kane, Daniel, Musician, enlisted June 11, 1861, age 18, residence South Boston. Mustered in June 11, 1861, term 3 years. Deserted July 15, 1861, Washington, D.C.

Adams, William, enlisted June 11, 1861, printer, age 25, single, residence Cambridgeport, born in Kilkenny, Ire. Mustered in June 11, 1861, term 3 years. Transferred to Co. H. Killed June 2, 1862, at Gaines' Mill, Va., in Co. H.

Aaron, Otis F., enlisted Nov. 9, 1861, age 19, single, residence Boston. Mustered in Nov. 9, 1861, term 3 years. Died of disease March 15, 1862, Brighton, Mass.

Bacheldor, Benjamin, age 40, residence Chatham. Mustered in Aug. 18, 1862, term 3 years Transferred to V.R.C. Sept. 7, 1863.

Bench, Edward, enlisted Aug. 20, 1863, farmer, age 35, single, residence Sidney, N.Y., credited to Westport. Mustered in Aug. 20, 1863, term 3 years. Deserted Sept. 22, 1863, Washington, D.C.

Billows, John, enlisted Aug. 17, 1862, laborer, age 21, single, residence Salem, born in St. John's, N.B. Mustered in Aug. 17, 1862, term 3 years. Mustered out June 21, 1864.

Boynton, Vassel P., enlisted Nov. 9, 1861, laborer, age 21, single, residence Boston. Mustered in Nov. 9, 1861, term 3 years. Wounded June 27, 1862, Gaines' Mill, Va. Discharged for disability March 23, 1863.

Bradley, William, enlisted Dec. 29, 1863, glassblower, age 19, single, residence Brooklyn, N.Y., credited to Charlestown, Wd. 1, born in Canada. Mustered in Dec. 29, 1863, term 3 years. Transferred to 32d Mass. Vols. June 9, 1864.

Brady, Edward, enlisted June 11, 1861, shoemaker, age 31, single, residence Salem, born in Longford, Ire. Mustered in June 11, 1861, term 3 years. Mustered out June 21, 1864.

Brennan, John, enlisted April 17, 1861, ropemaker, age 26, single, residence Roxbury. Mustered in July 7, 1861, term 3 years. Deserted Jan. 21, 1863, Falmouth, Va., from 5th U.S. Art.

Brown, John, enlisted Aug. 12, 1862, farmer, age 40, single, residence Boston. Mustered in Aug. 12, 1862, term 3 years. Died of disease Dec. 6, 1862, Falmouth, Va.

Brown, Jonathan, enlisted Nov. 24, 1863, teamster, age 29, single, residence South Boston, credited to Boston, Wd. 12, born in Liverpool, Eng. Mustered in Nov. 24, 1863, term 3 years. Transferred to 32d Mass. Vols. June 9, 1864.

Buckley, David, enlisted June 11, 1861, age 30, single. Mustered in June 11, 1861, term 3 years. Drowned June 23, 1861, Boston harbor.

Burke, Patrick, enlisted June 11, 1861, laborer, age 30, married, residence Boston, born in Cork, Ire. Mustered in June 11, 1861, term 3 years. Discharged for disability Feb. 2, 1863, as Corporal.

Burke, Alexander A., enlisted April 17, 1861, laborer, age 18, single, residence Boston. Mustered in June 11, 1861, term 3 years. Deserted Sept. 12, 1863, Washington, D.C.

Carroll, Thomas, enlisted June 11, 1861, laborer, age 38, single, residence Boston, born in Ireland. Mustered in June 11, 1861, term 3 years. Discharged for disability Aug. 18, 1861, at Arlington Heights, Va.

Cass, Thomas, enlisted July 18, 1862, gasfitter, age 24, single, residence Boston, born in Ireland. Mustered in July 18, 1862, term 3 years. Wounded May 12, 1864, at Spottsylvania, Va. Mustered out June 21, 1864.

Cass, William, enlisted June 11, 1861, age 27. Mustered in June 11, 1861, term 3 years. Discharged for disability at Long Island, Boston.

Clancy, Patrick J., enlisted Aug. 8, 1862, clerk, age 21, single, residence Boston, born in Ireland. Mustered in Aug. 8, 1862, term 3 years. Discharged for disability Nov. 22, 1862, Harpers Ferry, Va.

Coffee, John, enlisted Dec. 26, 1863, laborer, age 23, single, residence Boston, credited to Boston, Wd. 7, born in Ireland. Mustered in Dec. 26, 1863, term 3 years. Missing in action May 5, 1864, Wilderness, Va.

Comerford, John, enlisted June 11, 1861, shoemaker, age 33, single, residence Boston, born in Kilkenny, Ire. Mustered in June 11, 1861, term 3 years. Discharged Feb. 2, 1865.

Carmody, Cornelius, enlisted June 11, 1861. For record see Co. H roster.

Corkery, Bartholemew, enlisted June 11, 1861, age 20. Mustered in June 11, 1861, term 3 years. Wounded June 27, 1862, at Gaines' Mill, Va. Deserted June 27, 1862, Gaines' Mill, Va.

Cronan, Maurice, enlisted Aug. 5, 1862, laborer, age 44, single, residence Cambridge, born in Ireland. Mustered in Aug. 5, 1862, term 3 years. Mustered out June 21, 1864.

Cryan, Patrick, enlisted July 31, 1862, farmer, age 20, single, residence Tyngsboro, born in Ireland. Mustered in July 31, 1862, term 3 years. Discharged for disability Jan. 30, 1863, Falmouth, Va.

Cummings, James, enlisted June 11, 1861, currier, age 31, single, residence Charlestown, born in Roscommon, Ire. Mustered in June 11, 1861, term 3 years. Mustered out June 21, 1864.

Dacey, Daniel, enlisted Feb. 4, 1862, bootmaker, age 27, married, residence Quincy, born in Ireland. Mustered in Feb. 4, 1862, term 3 years. Deserted April 29, 1863, Falmouth, Va.

Davis, William, enlisted June 11, 1861, moulder, age 26, single, residence Portland, born in London, Eng. Mustered in June 11, 1861, term 3 years. Killed July 1, 1862, Malvern Hill, Va.

Deboa, James, enlisted June 11, 1861, currier, age 26, married, residence Salem, born in Dublin, Ire. Mustered in June 11, 1861, term 3 years. Wounded July 1, 1862, at Malvern Hill, Va. Discharged for disability Oct. 29, 1863, Washington, D.C.

Doherty, James, enlisted June 11, 1861, soldier, age 18, single, residence Roxbury, born in Donegal, Ire. Mustered in June 11, 1861, term 3 years. Killed June 27, 1862, Gaines' Mill, Va.

Dolan, Martin, enlisted June 11, 1861, currier, age 25, single, residence Boston, born in Ireland. Mustered in June 11, 1861, term 3 years. Deserted June 25, 1861, Boston.

Donavan, John, enlisted Feb. 6, 1862, bootmaker, age 18, single, residence Boston, born in Ireland. Mustered in Feb. 6, 1862, term 3 years. Wounded July 1, 1862, at Malvern Hill, Va. Discharged for disability Jan. 19, 1862, Washington, D.C.

Durkin, Austin, enlisted June 11, 1861, porter, age 32, married, residence Boston, born in Sligo, Ire. Mustered in June 11, 1861, term 3 years. Wounded July 1, 1862, Malvern Hill, Va. Deserted Oct. 1, 1863, Washington, D.C.

Edwards, George, enlisted Aug. 20, 1863, sailor, age 36, single, residence Boston, credited to Boston, Wd. 8, mustered in Aug. 20, 1863, term 3 years. Discharged for disability Jan. 6, 1864, Washington, D.C.

Ennis, John, enlisted June 11, 1861, age 20, residence Boston. Mustered in June 11, 1861, term 3 years. Wounded June 27, 1862, Gaines' Mill, Va. Mustered out June 21, 1864.

Felye, Bernard, enlisted Nov. 21, 1863, confectioner, age 21, single, residence Newport. R.I., credited to Boston, Wd. 1, born in Newport, R.I. Mustered in Nov. 21, 1863, term 3 years. Transferred to 32d Mass. Vols., June 10, 1864.

Flaherty, William, enlisted June 11, 1861, currier, age 32, married, residence Woburn, born in Cork, Ire. Mustered in June 11, 1861, term 3 years. Discharged for disability Arlington Heights, Va.

Flood, John H., enlisted June 11, 1861, bootmaker, age 22, single, residence Canton, born in Providence, R.I.   Mustered in June 11, 1861, term 3 years.   Deserted Jan. 21, 1863, Falmouth, Va., from Battery D, 5th U.S. Art.

Flynn, Edward, enlisted May 13, 1862, farmer, age 22, residence North Chelsea, born in Burlington, Vt.   Mustered in May 13, 1862, term 3 years. Mustered out June 21, 1864.

Fitzgerald, James, enlisted June 11, 1861, currier, age 26, married, residence Boston, born in Cork, Ire.   Mustered in June 11, 1861, term 3 years. Discharged for disability Dec. 29, 1862, Washington, D.C.

Fitzgerald, Thomas, enlisted June 11, 1861, painter, age 23, married, residence Boston.   Mustered in June 11, 1861, term 3 years.   Killed May 5, 1864, Wilderness, Va., as Sergt.

Foley, John, enlisted June 11, 1861, tailor, age 23, single, residence Boston, born in Ireland.   Mustered in June 11, 1861, term 3 years.   Deserted as Corp. July 31, 1863, at Frederick, Md.

Ford, Thomas, enlisted Aug. 30, 1862, shoemaker, age 27, married, residence Boston, born in Ireland.   Mustered in Aug. 30, 1862, term 3 years. Mustered out June 21, 1864.

Ford, Austin, enlisted Aug. 13, 1863, printer, age 22, residence Boston, born in Ireland.   Mustered in Aug. 13, 1862, term 3 years.   Application has been made recently to the War Department to read the same as his brother's (Patrick Ford) record, that is: Discharged to date Jan. 21, 1863, by order of the Secretary of War, to complete his military record; consequently all charges of desertion on or subsequent to that date fall.

Ford, Patrick, enlisted Aug. 13, 1862, printer, age 25, residence Boston, born in Ireland.   Mustered in Aug. 13, 1862, term 3 years.   Discharged to date Jan. 21, 1863, by order of the Secretary of War, to complete his military record; consequently all charges of desertion on or subsequent to that date fall.

Gallagher, Patrick, enlisted June 11, 1861, age 22.   Mustered in June 11, 1861, term 3 years.   Wounded May 5, 1864, Wilderness, Va.   Mustered out June 21, 1864, as Corp.

Gardner, William C., enlisted July 28, 1862, cook, age 35, married, residence Boston, born in Portugal.   Mustered in July 28, 1862, term 3 years. Wounded May 5, 1864, Wilderness, Va.   Mustered out June 21, 1864.

Garrity, Michael, enlisted Aug. 21, 1862, laborer, age 25, married, residence Malden, born in England.   Mustered in Aug. 21, 1862, term 3 years. Died of disease Jan. 28, 1863, Washington, D.C.

Gleason, John, enlisted June 11, 1861, currier, age 25, single, born in Kilkenny, Ireland.   Mustered in June 11, 1861, term 3 years.   Killed June 27, 1862, Gaines' Mill, Va.

Glynn, Thomas J., enlisted Jan. 2, 1864, carriage painter, age 37, married, residence Boston, credited to Boston, Wd. 3, born in Ireland.   Mustered in Jan. 2, 1864, term 3 years.   Killed May 12, 1864, at Spottsylvania, Va.

Griffin, Michael, enlisted Jan. 7, 1864, shoemaker, age 21, single, residence Abington, credited to Boston, Wd. 11, born in Ireland.   Mustered in Jan. 7, 1864, term 3 years.   Wounded May 5, 1864, Wilderness, Va. Transferred to 32d Mass. Vols. June 10, 1864.

Hagerty, Bernard, enlisted June 11, 1861, teamster, age 24, married, residence Boston, born in Donegal, Ire.   Mustered in June 11, 1861, term 3 years. Deserted June 22, 1861, Medford, Mass.

Haggerty, Patrick, enlisted Aug. 4, 1862, farmer, age 36, residence Boston, born in Ireland. Mustered in Aug. 4, 1862, term 3 years. Mustered out June 21, 1864.

Hagan, Patrick, enlisted July 23, 1862, laborer, age 28, married, residence Boston, born in Ireland. Mustered in July 23, 1862, term 3 years. Wounded Dec. 13, 1862, Fredericksburg, Va. Mustered out June 21, 1864.

Hentch, Christopher R., enlisted Aug. 1, 1862, currier, age 40, residence Boston, born in England. Mustered in Aug. 1, 1862, term 3 years. Died of disease Nov. 26, 1862, Washington, D.C.

Hennessey, James F., enlisted June 11, 1861, currier, age 30, married, residence Chelsea, born in Cork, Ire. Mustered in June 11, 1861, term 3 years. Discharged for disability Aug. 18, 1861, Arlington Heights, Va.

Hickey, James, enlisted June 11, 1861, age 20. Mustered in June 11, 1861, term 3 years. Wounded July 1, 1862, at Malvern Hill, Va.; wounded May 5, 1864, Wilderness, Va. Mustered out June 21, 1864.

Hurley, Edward, enlisted June 11, 1861, servant, age 39, married, residence Boston. Mustered in June 11, 1861, term 3 years. Discharged for disability Oct. 9, 1862.

Kanary, John, enlisted June 11, 1861, laborer, age 35, married, residence Boston, born in Cork, Ire. Mustered in June 11, 1861, term 3 years. Wounded July 1, 1862, at Malvern Hill, Va. Discharged for disability Nov. 14, 1862, at Washington, D.C.

Keating, Patrick, enlisted June 11, 1861, laborer, age 26, single, residence Salem, born in Dublin, Ire. Mustered in June 11, 1861, term 3 years. Killed June 27, 1862, Gaines' Mill, Va.

Keenan, Edward, enlisted June 11, 1861, trunkmaker, age 25, single, residence Boston, born in Ireland. Mustered in June 11, 1861, term 3 years. Killed May 12, 1864, Spottsylvania, Va., as Corp.

Kelly, John, enlisted June 11, 1861, age 40. Mustered in June 11, 1861, term 3 years; at Boston for duty. Transferred to Battery D, 5th U.S. Art.

Kelleher, Bartholemew, enlisted June 11, 1861, brittania worker, age 20, single, residence Boston. Mustered in June 11, 1861, term 3 years; promoted 1st Sergt. from Sergt. March 21, 1864. Wounded May 5, 1864, Wilderness, Va. Mustered out June 21, 1864.

Kenney, Daniel, Jr., enlisted June 11, 1861, painter, age 23, residence Boston, born in Boston, Mass. Mustered in June 11, 1861, term 3 years. Wounded Dec. 13, 1862, Fredericksburg, Va.; wounded May 5, 1864, Wilderness, Va. Mustered out June 21, 1864.

Kennedy, Daniel, enlisted June 11, 1861, currier, age 25, married, residence Boston, born in Glasgow, Scot. Mustered in June 11, 1861, term 3 years. Wounded at Malvern Hill, Va., July 1, 1862. Died of wounds July.14, 1862.

Kirvan, Thomas, enlisted June 11, 1861, trunkmaker, age 24, single, residence West Quincy, born in Waterford, Ire. Mustered in June 11, 1861, term 3 years. Deserted Aug. 21, 1863, Washington, D.C.

Lalley, Daniel, enlisted Dec. 11, 1863, bootmaker, age 43, married, residence Randolph, credited to Randolph, born in Ireland. Mustered in Dec 3, 1863, term 3 years. Transferred to 32d Mass. Vols. June 10, 1864.

Lanagan, John, enlisted Feb. 10, 1862, bootmaker, age 26, single, residence Boston, born in Ireland. Mustered in Feb. 10, 1862, term 3 years. Killed May 12, 1864, Spottsylvania, Va.

Lawler, John, enlisted Aug. 18, 1862, laborer, age 27, married, residence Boston, born in Ireland. Mustered in Aug. 18, 1862, term 3 years. Wounded May 12, 1864, Laurel Hill, Va. Absent in hospital.

Leary, Daniel, enlisted Dec. 29, 1863, blacksmith, age 44, married, residence South Boston, credited to Boston, Wd. 10, born in Cork, Ire. Mustered in Dec. 29, 1863, term 3 years. Wounded May 8, 1864, at Laurel Hill, Va. Transferred to 32d Mass. Vols. June 10, 1864, as " O'Leary."

Lewellan, Thomas, enlisted June 11, 1861, age 32. Mustered in June 11, 1861, term 3 years; at Boston for duty. Wounded July 1, 1862, Malvern Hill, Va. Discharged for disability Feb. 21, 1863, Washington, D.C.

Lovett, Charles, enlisted June 11, 1861, shoemaker, age 21, married, residence Boston, born in Weymouth, N.S. Mustered in June 11, 1861, term 3 years. Wounded July 1, 1862, at Malvern Hill, Va. Discharged disability Sept. 27, 1862, Fort McHenry, Md.

Lynch, Maurice, enlisted June 11, 1861, printer, age 29, single, residence Chelsea, born in Limerick, Ire. Mustered in June 11, 1861, term 3 years. Killed June 27, 1862, Gaines' Mill, Va.

Lynch, John T., enlisted June 11, 1861, bootmaker, age 20, single, residence East Stoughton, born in East Stoughton. Mustered in June 11, 1861, term 3 years. Mustered out June 21, 1864.

Manning, John, enlisted June 11, 1861, currier, age 25, single, residence South Danvers, born in Ireland. Mustered in June 11, 1861, term 3 years. Killed June 27, 1862, Gaines' Mill, Va.

Mehan, Michael, enlisted July 8, 1862, tailor, age 27, married, residence Boston, born in Dublin, Ire. Mustered in July 8, 1862, term 3 years. Discharged for disability Oct. 29, 1862, Sharpsburg, Md.

Melanfry, Paul, enlisted June 11, 1861, machinist, age 24, single, residence Boston, born in Boston. Mustered in June 11, 1861, term 3 years Killed June 27, 1862, at Gaines' Mill, Va.

Moakler, John, enlisted June 11, 1861, grocer, age 21, single, residence Boston, born in Boston. Mustered in June 11, 1861, term 3 years. Wounded at Gaines' Mill, June 27, 1862; wounded May 5, 1864, Wilderness, Va. Re-enlisted Dec. 31, 1863, credited to Boston, Wd. 1. Transferred to 32d Mass. Vols., June 10, 1864.

Moore, James, enlisted June 11, 1861, age 28, married, residence Boston. Mustered in June 11, 1861, term 3 years. Wounded June 27, 1862. Gaines' Mill, Va. Discharged for disability, no date or place.

Moore, Alexander, enlisted June 11, 1861, marbleworker, age 30, married, residence Boston. Mustered in June 11, 1861, term 3 years. Mustered out June 21, 1864.

Mullins, Jeremiah, enlisted June 11, 1861, bootmaker, age 23, single, residence Randolph, born in Cork, Ire. Mustered in June 11, 1861, term 3 years. Deserted Sept. 12, 1862, Washington, D.C.

Mulligan, Thomas, enlisted June 11, 1861, paper stainer, age 27, single, residence Roxbury, born in Ireland. Mustered in June 11, 1861, term 3 years. Discharged for disability Dec. 18, 1861, Miners' Hill, Va.

Mullane, Daniel, enlisted June 11, 1861, currier, age 23, single, residence South Danvers, born in Cork, Ire. Mustered in June 11, 1861, term 3 years. Wounded May 5, 1864, Wilderness, Va. Mustered out June 21, 1864. Sergt. from Corp. March 21, 1864.

Murray, Lawrence, enlisted June 11, 1861, laborer, age 19, single, residence Boston. Mustered in July 7, 1861, term 3 years. Deserted Sept. 25, 1862, Baltimore, Md.

Murphy, Patrick, enlisted Dec. 22, 1863, laborer, age 40, married, residence Westfield, credited to Westfield, born in Ireland. Mustered in Dec. 22, 1863, term 3 years. Transferred to 32d Mass. Vols. June 10, 1864.

Murphy, Peter, enlisted July 27, 1862, currier, age 27, married, residence Groton, born in Ireland. Mustered in July 27, 1862, term 3 years. Discharged for disability March 1, 1864, Washington, D.C.

Murphy, John, enlisted June 11, 1861, shoemaker, age 26, single, residence South Danvers, born in Cork, Ire. Mustered in June 11, 1861, term 3 years; transferred to Co. E. Deserted June 27, 1862, Gaines' Mill, Va.

McCabe, James, enlisted Aug. 8, 1862, porter, age 27, single, residence Boston, born in Ireland. Mustered in Aug. 9, 1862, term 3 years. Wounded at Chancellorsville, Va. Discharged for disability May 20, 1864, Washington, D.C.

McCarthy, John, enlisted June 11, 1861, age 34. Mustered in June 11, 1861, term 3 years; at Boston for duty. Wounded July 1, 1862, Malvern Hill, Va. Discharged for disability June 16, 1863, Washington, D.C.

McCarthy, Michael, enlisted June 11, 1861, shoemaker, age 23, single, residence Randolph, born in Ireland. Mustered in June 11, 1861, term 3 years. Deserted June 29, 1863, Frederick, Md.

McCarville, Patrick, enlisted July 28, 1862, baker, age 21, married, residence East Cambridge, credited to Cambridgeport, born in East Cambridge Mustered in July 28, 1862, term 3 years. Transferred to 32d Mass. Vols., June 10, 1864, as "McArville." Re-enlisted Feb. 16, 1864.

McCloskey, Paul, enlisted June 11, 1861, laborer, age 35, single, residence Boston, born in Derry, Ire. Mustered in June 11, 1861, term 3 years. Wounded May 5, 1864, at Wilderness, Va. Reported died July 15, 1864, Andersonville, Ga.

McDonald, Angus, enlisted July 17, 1862, carpenter, age 35, married, residence Boston, born in Nova Scotia, Mustered in July 17, 1862, term 3 years. Wounded at Chancellorsville, Va. Died of disease March 25, 1864, Washington, D.C.

McGinniskin, Thomas J., enlisted June 11, 1861, messenger, age 19, single, residence Boston, born in Boston, Mass. Mustered in June 11, 1861, term 3 years. Mustered out June 21, 1864.

McGlone, Charles, enlisted June 11, 1861, glassblower, age 26, single, residence Somerville, born in Donegal, Ire. Mustered in June 11, 1861, term 3 years. Wounded June 27, 1862, Gaines' Mill, Va. Discharged for disability Feb. 24, 1863, as "McGlove."

McGowan, Edward, enlisted July 24, 1862, fireman, age 20, married, residence Boston, born in New York city. Mustered in July 24, 1862, term 3 years. Discharged for disability Oct. 27, 1862, Sharpsburg, Md.

McGlone, Hugh, enlisted June 11, 1861, bootmaker, age 21, single, residence Milford, born in Donegal, Ire. Mustered in June 11, 1861, term 3 years. Killed July 1, 1862, at Malvern Hill, Va.

McGuire, James, enlisted June 11, 1861, glassmaker, age 24, single, residence South Boston, born in Boston. Mustered in June 11, 1861, term 3 years. Killed June 27, 1862, Gaines' Mill, Va.

McIntire, Peter, enlisted June 11, 1861, oyster opener, age 29, married, residence Boston, born in St. John, N.B. Mustered in June 11, 1861, term 3 years. Killed June 27, 1862, Gaines' Mill, Va.

McLaughlin, Terrence, enlisted June 11, 1861, laborer, age 24, single, residence South Boston, born in Tipperary, Ire. Mustered in June 11, 1861, term 3 years. Mustered out June 21, 1864.

McLaughlin, Michael, enlisted June 11, 1861, glasscutter, age 20, single, residence Cambridge, born in Londonderry, Ire. Mustered in June 11, 1861, term 3 years. Mustered out June 21, 1864, as Corp.

McLaughlin, John, enlisted June 11, 1861, painter, age 24, single, residence Boston, born in Derry, Ire. Mustered in June 11, 1861, term 3 years. Wounded June 27, 1862, Gaines' Mill, Va.; wounded May 5, 1864, Wilderness, Va. Mustered out June 21, 1864, as Corp.

McMahon, Thomas, enlisted June 11, 1861, laborer, age 24, single, Chelsea. Mustered in June 11, 1861, term 3 years. Wounded May 5, 1864, Wilderness, Va. Mustered out June 21, 1864.

McNamara, Owen, enlisted Aug. 14, 1862, bootmaker, age 35, married, residence Holliston, born in Ireland   Mustered in Aug. 14, 1862, term 3 years. Discharged for disability Oct. 29, 1862, Sharpsburg, Md.

McNulty, James, enlisted Aug. 19, 1862, laborer, age 24, single, residence Boston, born in Ireland. Mustered in Aug. 19, 1862, term 3 years. Mustered out June 21, 1864.

Nichols, William, enlisted July 30, 1861, painter, age 18, single, residence Boston, born in Boston. Mustered in July 30, 1861, term 3 years. Deserted April 27, 1863, Falmouth, Va.

Nickerson, John, enlisted June 11, 1861, carriagemaker, age 22, single, residence Boston, born in Dublin, Ire. Mustered in June 11, 1861, term 3 years. Killed July 1, 1862, Malvern Hill, Va.

Nihann, Daniel, enlisted Aug. 23, 1862, laborer, age 30, married, residence Boston, born in Ireland. Mustered in Aug. 23, 1862, term 3 years. Mustered out June 21, 1864. Discharged as " Daniel Ninan."

Nihen, Jeremiah, enlisted Jan. 7, 1864, machinist, age 21, single, residence Boston, credited to Boston, Wd. 11, born in Cork, Ire. Mustered in Jan. 7, 1864, term 3 years. Wounded May 5, 1864, Wilderness, Va., as " Ninan." Transferred to 32d Mass. Vols. June 10, 1864. (Proper name is " Ninan.")

Noonan, Edward, enlisted Aug. 13, 1862, printer, age 22, married, residence Boston, born in Ireland. Mustered in Aug. 13, 1862, term 3 years. Discharged for disability March 10, 1864.

Odey, William B., enlisted Aug. 12, 1862, blacksmith, age 30, single, residence Wrentham, born in England. Mustered in Aug. 12, 1862, term 3 years. Wounded Dec. 13, 1862, Fredericksburg, Va. Discharged for disability Oct. 6, 1863, Washington, D.C.

O'Brien, Peter, enlisted June 11, 1861, laborer, age 29, married, residence Boston, born in Cork, Ire. Mustered in June 11, 1861, term 3 years. Wounded July 1, 1862, at Malvern Hill, Va. Discharged for disability Aug. 30, 1862, Annapolis, Md.

O'Brien, John, enlisted Nov. 27, 1863, printer, age 29, married, residence Halifax, N.S., credited to Boston, Wd. 7, born in Halifax, N.S. Mustered in Nov. 27, 1863, term 3 years. Wounded June 3, 1864, at Bethesda Church, Va. Transferred to 32d Mass. Vols. June 10, 1864.

O'Callahan, William F., enlisted June 11, 1861, laborer, age 19, single, residence East Cambridge, born in Cork, Ire. Mustered in June 11, 1861, term 3 years. Wounded July 1, 1862, Malvern Hill, Va. Discharged for disability March 5, 1863.

O'Connor, Patrick, enlisted June 11, 1861, cooper, age 30, married, residence Boston, born in Kerry, Ire. Mustered in June 11, 1861, term 3 years. Transferred to Co. E; transferred to V.R. Co. Sept. 15, 1863.

O'Connell, John, enlisted June 11, 1861, shoemaker, age 19, single, residence South Boston, born in Ireland. Mustered in June 11, 1861, term 3 years. Deserted Sept. 22, 1863, Washington, D.C.

O'Donnell, John, enlisted June 11, 1861, teamster, age 18, single, residence Boston, born in Boston. Mustered in June 11, 1861, term 3 years. Wounded May 5, 1864, Wilderness, Va. Mustered out June 21, 1864.

O'Hare, John P., enlisted June 11, 1861, trunkmaker, age 19, single, residence Boston, born in Kingston, Can. Mustered in June 11, 1861, term 3 years Mustered out June 21, 1864.

O'Keefe, David, enlisted Aug. 12, 1862, cabinetmaker, age 44, married, residence Reading. Mustered in Aug. 12, 1862, term 3 years. Died of disease June 23, 1863, Fairfax Seminary Hospital, Va.

Parker, Edwin S., enlisted July 13, 1863, bootmaker, age 22, single, residence Paxton, credited to Holden. Mustered in July 13, 1863, term 3 years. Wounded May 12, 1864, at Spottsylvania, Va. Transferred to 32d Mass. Vols. June 10, 1864.

Phillips, Robert, enlisted June 11, 1861, laborer, age 27, married, residence Boston. Mustered in June 11, 1861, term 3 years. Wounded July 1, 1862, Malvern Hill, Va. Discharged for disability Aug 25, 1863.

Pope, Roger, enlisted June 11, 1861, shoemaker, age 23, single, residence East Boston, born in Cork, Ire. Mustered in June 11, 1861, term 3 years. Killed June 27, 1862, Gaines' Mill, Va.

Priggs, John, enlisted Aug. 20, 1863, baker, age 38, married, residence Brooklyn, N.Y., credited to Boston, Wd. 11. Mustered in Aug. 20, 1863, term 3 years. Deserted Oct. 28, 1863, Auburn, Va.

Quinn, William, enlisted June 11, 1861, currier, age 38, married, residence Boston, born in Cork, Ire Mustered in June 11, 1861, term 3 years. Discharged for disability Sept 26, 1862.

Rahilly, Timothy, enlisted Dec. 3, 1863, laborer, age 27, single, residence Boston, credited to Boston, Wd. 7, born in Cork, Ire Missing in action May 5, 1864, Wilderness, Va.

Reynolds, John A., enlisted Aug. 18, 1863, farmer, age 20, single, East Haddam, Ct., credited to North Hampton. Mustered in Aug. 18, 1863, term 3 years. Wounded June 3, 1864, at Bethesda Church, Va. Transferred to 32d Mass. Vols. June 10, 1864.

Riley, Simon J., enlisted June 11, 1861, brassfinisher, age 23, single, residence Boston, born in Boston. Mustered in June 11, 1861, term 3 years. Wounded May 23, 1864, at North Anna River, Va. Mustered out June 21, 1864.

Riley, Thomas O., enlisted Feb. 13, 1862, laborer, age 21, single, residence Boston. Mustered in Feb. 13, 1862, term 3 years. Wounded at Gaines' Mill, Va., June 27, 1862. Killed July 1, 1862, at Malvern Hill, Va., as "O'Rielly."

Rodman, William C., enlisted Aug. 18, 1863, operative, age 23, married, residence Moodus, Ct., credited to Hadley. Mustered in Aug. 18, 1863, term 3 years. Transferred to 32d Mass. Vols. June 10, 1864.

Ross, Donald, enlisted June 11, 1861, carpenter, age 24, single, residence Boston, born in Prince Edward Island. Mustered in June 11, 1861, term 3 years. Wounded May 5, 1864, Wilderness, Va. Sergt. from Corp. March 24, 1864. Mustered out June 21, 1864.

Schultz, Edward, enlisted Aug. 20, 1863, hostler, age 27, single, residence Middletown, N.Y , credited to Somerset. Mustered in Aug. 20, 1863, term 3 years. Deserted Oct. 28, 1863, Auburn, Va.

Semple, Robert, enlisted Aug. 8, 1862, painter, age 46, married, residence Boston, born in Halifax, N.S. Mustered in Aug. 8, 1862, term 3 years. Wounded Dec. 13, 1862, at Fredericksburg, Va. Discharged for disability Dec. 24, 1862, Falmouth, Va.

Shahan, Edward H., enlisted June 11, 1861, age 21, single, residence Charlestown, born in New York city. Mustered in June 11, 1861, term 3 years. Mortally wounded in action May 12, 1864, Spottsylvania, Va.

Sheehan, Timothy, enlisted June 11, 1861, currier, age 21, single, residence Boston, born in Cork, Ire. Mustered in June 11, 1861, term 3 years. Mustered out June 21, 1864.

Sheridan, Bernard, enlisted June 11, 1861, glassmaker, age 22, single, residence Baltimore, born in Baltimore, Md. Mustered in June 11, 1861, term 3 years. Wounded July 1, 1862, at Malvern Hill, Va. Discharged for disability Jan. 15, 1863, Washington, D.C.

Slavin, Hugh, enlisted Dec. 31, 1863, laborer, age 22, single, residence Providence, credited to Wellfleet, born in Ireland. Mustered in Dec. 31, 1863, term 3 years. Killed May 12, 1864, Spottsylvania, Va.

Smith, Phillip, enlisted June 11, 1861, currier, age 22, single, residence South Danvers, born in Ireland. Mustered in June 11, 1861, term 3 years. Deserted Sept. 12, 1862, Washington, D.C.

Smith, Peter, enlisted Aug. 18, 1863, farmer, age 20, single, residence Lunenburg, credited to Shirley. Mustered in Aug. 18, 1863, term 3 years. Wounded May 5, 1864, Wilderness, Va. Transferred to 32d Mass. Vols. June 10, 1864.

Smith, Henry, enlisted Aug. 21, 1863, seaman, age 22, single, residence Philadelphia, credited to Weymouth. Mustered in Aug. 21, 1863, term 3 years. Transferred to 32d Mass. Vols. June 10, 1864.

Sparrow, Phillip O., enlisted July 15, 1863, bootmaker, age 25, married, residence Medway, credited to Medway. Mustered in July 15, 1863, term 3 years. Discharged for disability Dec. 16, 1863, Alexandria, Va.

Sweeny, Charles, enlisted Aug. 4, 1862, plasterer, age 39, married, residence Boston, credited to Boston, Wd. 2, born in Ireland. Mustered in Aug. 4, 1862, term 3 years. Wounded June 3, 1864, at Bethesda Church, Va. Transferred to 32d Mass. Vols. June 10, 1864.

Sweeney, Daniel, enlisted June 11, 1861, currier, age 20, single, residence South Danvers, born in Cork, Ire. Mustered in June 11, 1861, term 3 years. Deserted Sept. 12, 1862, Washington, D.C.

Swinson, John A., enlisted Aug. 20, 1863, farmer, age 25, single, residence New York, credited to Boston, Wd. 11. Mustered in Aug. 20, 1863, term 3 years. Wounded May 8, 1864, at Laurel Hill, Va. Transferred to 32d Mass. Vols. June 10, 1864.

Sullivan, Daniel, enlisted June 11, 1861, bootmaker, age 21, single, residence East Stoughton, born in Boston. Mustered in June 11, 1861, term 3 years. Wounded July 1, 1862, at Malvern Hill, Va. Discharged for disability Feb. 15, 1864, Washington, D.C.

Thomas, David, enlisted June 11, 1861, harnessmaker, age 25, single, residence Boston, born in Boston. Mustered in June 11, 1861, term 3 years; at Boston for duty. Deserted Sept. 12, 1862, Washington, D.C.

Thornton, John, enlisted June 11, 1861, cabinetmaker, age 21, single, residence Boston, born in Glasgow, Scotland. Mustered in June 11, 1861, term 3 years. Wounded in groin at Gaines' Mill, Va., June 27, 1862. Discharged for disability Nov. 2, 1862, Fort McHenry, Md.

Tiernon, Hugh, enlisted June 11, 1861, upholsterer, age 28, married, residence Boston, born in Ireland. Mustered in June 11, 1861, term 3 years. Killed June 27, 1862, Gaines' Mill, Va.

Tirrell, George I., enlisted Aug. 19, 1863, farmer, age 21, single, Needham, credited to Marblehead. Mustered in Aug. 19, 1863, term 3 years. Wounded June 3, 1864, at Bethesda Church, Va. Transferred to 32d Mass. Vols. June 10, 1864.

Tracy, Patrick, enlisted July 24, 1862, shoemaker, age 33, married, residence Boston, born in Ireland. Mustered in July 24, 1862, term 3 years. Deserted July 31, 1863, Maryland.

Ulhaas, John, enlisted Aug. 19, 1863, cheesemaker, age 27, single, residence New York, credited to Marblehead. Mustered in Aug. 19, 1863, term 3 years. Transferred to 32d Mass. Vols. June 10, 1864.

Walsh, Patrick, enlisted June 11, 1861, currier, age 22, single, residence Boston, born in Mayo, Ire. Mustered in June 11, 1861, term 3 years. Wounded June 27, 1862, Gaines' Mill, Va. Mustered out June 21, 1864.

Ward, Thomas F., enlisted June 11, 1861, bootmaker, age 20, single, residence Randolph, born in Randolph, Mass. Mustered in June 11, 1861, term 3 years. Mustered out June 21, 1864.

Warring, William H., enlisted Aug. 20, 1863, clerk, age 23, single, residence New York, credited to New Bedford. Mustered in Aug. 20, 1863, term 3 years. Deserted Oct. 28, 1863, Auburn, Va., as "Warren."

Warren, Charles R., enlisted June 11, 1861, mason, age 20, residence Boston. Mustered in June 11, 1861, term 3 years. Discharged, term expired, June 11, 1864, as Sergt.

Weber, John, enlisted Aug. 20, 1863, shoemaker, age 29, single, residence Boston, credited to Boston, Wd. 11. Mustered in Aug. 20, 1863, term 3 years. Wounded May 5, 1864, Wilderness, Va. Transferred to 32d Mass. Vols. June 10, 1864, as "Webber."

Welch, James, enlisted Aug. 9, 1863, bricklayer, age 23, single, residence Albany, N.Y., credited to North Hampton. Mustered in Aug. 19, 1863, term 3 years. Discharged for disability Dec. 15, 1863, Alexandria, Va.

Welch, Patrick, enlisted June 11, 1861, age 25, residence Boston. Mustered in June 11, 1861, term 3 years. Deserted June 16, 1861, Long Island, Boston harbor.

White, William, enlisted June 11, 1861, chairmaker, age 24, married, residence Boston, born in Meath, Ire. Mustered in June 11, 1861, term 3 years. Mustered out June 21, 1864.

Wilson, George, enlisted Aug. 15, 1863, porter, age 21, single, residence Brooklyn, N.Y., credited to Newton. Mustered in Aug. 15, 1863, term 3 years. Transferred to 32d Mass. Vols. June 10, 1864.

Wyman, Henry G., enlisted June 11, 1861, cook, age 19, single, residence Boston. Mustered in June 11, 1861, term 3 years. Mustered out June 21, 1864.

Young, Austin, enlisted July 15, 1863, bootmaker, age 20, single, residence Wrentham, credited to Wrentham. Mustered in July 15, 1863, term 3 years Discharged for disability Dec. 15, 1863, Alexandria, Va.

Zeigler, David, enlisted Aug. 20, 1863, blacksmith, age 26, single, residence New York, credited to Plymouth. Mustered in Aug. 20, 1863, term 3 years. Wounded May 5, 1864, Wilderness, Va. Transferred to 32d Mass. Vols. June 10, 1864.

COMPANY B.

Plunkett, Christopher, Capt., clerk, age 31, married, residence Boston, born in Ireland. Mustered in June 11, 1861, term 3 years. Resigned Aug. 27, 1861. Enlisted as a recruit, see Co. C.

Hanley, Patrick T., 1st Lieut , cooper, age 32, single, residence Boston, born in Ireland. Mustered in June 11, 1861, term 3 years; promoted Capt. Aug 26, 1861; Major Jan. 28, 1862; Lieut.-Col. July 26, 1862; brevetted Col. for gallant and meritorious service. Wounded July 1, 1862, at Malvern Hill, Va. Mustered out June 21, 1864.

Walsh, Patrick, 2d Lieut., clerk, age 23, married, residence Boston, born in Cork, Ire. Mustered in June 11, 1861, term 3 years; promoted 1st Lieut. Aug. 28, 1862. Resigned Jan. 4, 1862, in Co. E. Enlisted as a recruit in Co. E.

Miller, Robert A., 1st Sergt., enlisted June 11, 1861, shoemaker, age 24, married, residence Boston, born in Liverpool, Eng. Mustered in June 11, 1861, term 3 years; promoted 2d Lieut. Aug. 27, 1862, and transferred to Co. F; 1st Lieut. March 21, 1863; transferred to Co. G Aug. 10, 1863. Wounded July 1, 1862, at Malvern Hill as 1st Sergt. Dismissed from Co. G by order War Department, Sept. 14, 1863.

Dacy, Mathew, Sergt., enlisted June 11, 1861, clerk, age 23, single, residence Boston, born in Boston. Mustered in June 11, 1861, term 3 years; promoted 2d Lieut. Jan. 5, 1862; 1st Lieut. Sept. 26, 1862. Resigned Oct. 14, 1862.

King, John, Sergt., enlisted June 11, 1861, stonecutter, age 28, single, residence South Boston, born in Boston. Mustered in June 11, 1861, term 3 years. Deserted Dec. 28, 1862, Falmouth, Va.

Barry, John, Sergt., enlisted June 11, 1861, sawyer, age 39, married, residence Boston, born in Clare, Ire. Mustered in June 11, 1861, term 3 years. Discharged for disability Jan. 28, 1864.

Barker, Thos., Sergt., enlisted June 11, 1861, morocco dresser, age 33, married, residence Lynn, born in Ireland. Mustered in June 11, 1861, term 3 years. Discharged for disability Aug. 10, 1862.

Sullivan, William, Corp., enlisted June 11, 1861, mason, age 23, single, residence Boston, born in Ireland. Mustered in June 11, 1861, term 3 years. Wounded July 1, 1862, at Malvern Hill, Va. Discharged for disability Sept. 20, 1862.

Donovan, John 1st, Corp., enlisted June 11, 1861, teamster, age 25, single, residence Medford, born in Boston. Mustered in June 11, 1861, term 3 years. Deserted April 5, 1862, at Yorktown, Va.

Meaney, Thomas, Corp , enlisted June 11, 1861, bookbinder, age 29, single, residence Boston, born in Co. Clare, Ire. Mustered in June 11, 1861, term 3 years. Killed July 1, 1862, Malvern Hill, Va., Sergt.

Greany, Geo., Corp., enlisted June 11, 1861, harnessmaker, age 22, married, residence Boston, born in Co. Cork, Ire. Mustered in June 11, 1861, term 3 years. Wounded June 27, 1862, Gaines' Mill, Va. Discharged for disability April 16, 1863.

Dobson, William, Corp , enlisted June 11, 1861, printer, age 20, single, residence Boston, born in Ireland. Mustered in June 11, 1861, term 3 years. Discharged June 21, 1864, expiration of service.

Barker, Owen, Corp., enlisted June 11, 1861, morocco dresser, age 29, married, residence Lynn, born in Ireland. Mustered in June 11, 1861, term 3 years; transferred to Invalid Corps Nov. 27, 1863.

Flynn, Edward F., Corp., enlisted June 11, 1861, laborer, age 34, married, residence Boston, born 'in Co. Dublin, Ire. Mustered in June 11, 1864, term 3 years. Deserted Miners' Hill, Va., March 4, 1862.

Farley, John, Corp., enlisted June 11, 1861, brassmoulder, age 25, single, residence Boston, born in Boston, Mass. Mustered in June 11, 1861, term 3 years. Mustered out June 21, 1864, as Private.

Burns, James, Wagoner, enlisted June 11, 1861, teamster, age 21, single, residence Roxbury, born in Roxbury. Mustered in June 11, 1861, term 3 years. Died of disease Sept. 27, 1862, Roxbury, Mass.

Hart, Patrick, Musician, enlisted June 11, 1861, woolen spinner, age 23, single, residence Blackstone, born in New York City. Mustered in June 11, 1861, term 3 years. Re-enlisted March 28, 1864; credited to Blackstone; transferred to 32d Mass. Vols. June 9, 1864.

Boyle, Patrick, Musician, enlisted June 11, 1861, brickmaker, age 26, single, residence Boston, born in Ireland. Mustered in June 11, 1861, term 3 years. Mustered out June 21, 1864, as Private.

Adams, Carl, enlisted Aug. 21, 1863, storekeeper, age 20, single, residence New York, credited to Roxbury. Mustered in Aug. 21, 1863, term 3 years; transferred to 32d Mass. Vols. June 9, 1864.

Adams, George, enlisted June 11, 1861, paper-stainer, age 25, single, residence Boston, born in Cork, Ire Mustered in June 11, 1861, term 3 years. Discharged for disability Aug. 8, 1863.

Alonzo, Peter, enlisted Aug. 19, 1863, seaman, age 26, single, residence Lawrence, credited to Melrose. Mustered in Aug. 19, 1863, term 3 years. Deserted Oct. 19, 1863, as "Pedro."

Archpool, Lawrence, enlisted Aug. 21, 1863, farmer, age 21, single, residence East Bridgewater, credited to Taunton. Mustered in Aug. 21, 1863, term 3 years. Killed May 12, 1864, at Spottsylvania, Va.

Bacon, William F., enlisted July 13, 1863, mechanic, age 24, single, residence Millbury, credited to Boston. Mustered in July 13, 1863, term 3 years; transferred to 32d Mass. Vols. June 9, 1864.

Battesbee, James, enlisted June 11, 1861, blacksmith, age 26, single, residence Lowell, born in Co. Cork, Ire. Mustered in June 11, 1861, term 3 years; promoted Corp. April 9, 1864. Wounded at Gettysburg July 3, 1863. Mustered out June 21, 1864, as "Battesby."

Berg, Herman, enlisted Aug. 20, 1863, jeweller, age 23, single, residence New York, credited to Duxbury. Mustered in Aug. 20, 1863, term 3 years. Deserted Oct. 19, 1863.

Branon, Michael, enlisted June 11, 1861, morocco finisher, age 23, single, residence Lynn, born in Ireland. Mustered in June 11, 1861, term 3 years. Wounded June 3, 1864, at Bethesda Church, Va. Absent wounded as Corp. Discharged Aug. 20, 1864.

Brennan, Joseph, enlisted Aug. 19, 1863, painter, age 20, single, residence New York, credited to North Hampton. Mustered in Aug. 19, 1863, term 3 years. Wounded May 5, 1864, Wilderness, Va. Transferred to 32d Mass. Vols. June 9, 1864

Bresnahan, John, enlisted June 11, 1861, morocco finisher, age 29, married, residence Stoneham, born in Kerry, Ire. Mustered in June 11, 1861, term 3 years. Discharged for disability Jan. 10, 1863. Re-enlisted Nov. 25, 1863. Killed May 8, 1864, at Laurel Hill, Va.

Brown, Joseph, enlisted Aug. 21, 1863, farmer, age 30, single, residence New York, credited to Beverly. Mustered in Aug. 21, 1863. Wounded May 5, 1864, Wilderness, Va. Transferred to 32d Mass. Vols. June 9, 1864.

Britt, John, enlisted June 11, 1861, shoemaker, age 40, residence Reading, born in Waterford, Ire. Mustered in June 11, 1861, term 3 years. Discharged for disability Aug. 18, 1861.

Brickley, Patrick, enlisted June 11, 1861, painter, age 23, single, residence Boston, born in Cork, Ire. Mustered in June 11, 1861, term 3 years. Wounded May 5, 1864, Wilderness, Va.; wounded July 1, 1862, Malvern Hill, Va. Mustered out June 21, 1864, as Sergt.

Buckley, James, enlisted June 11, 1861, laborer, age 22, single, residence Boston, born in Co. Cork, Ire. Mustered in June 11, 1861, term 3 years. Discharged for disability Jan. 29, 1863.

Buchanan, William, enlisted Feb. 18, 1862, shoemaker, age 34, married, residence Quincy. Mustered in Feb. 18, 1862, term 3 years; transferred to Co. D. Wounded May 12, 1864, Spottsylvania, Va. Transferred to 32d Mass. Vols. June 9, 1864.

Burns, John, enlisted June 11, 1861, laborer, age 19, single, residence Lynn. Mustered in June 11, 1861, term 3 years. Deserted Jan. 28, 1863, Falmouth, Va.

Burns, John, enlisted June 11, 1861, shoemaker, age 25, single, residence Lowell, Mass. Mustered in June 11, 1861, term 3 years. Wounded June 27, 1862, Gaines' Mill, Va.; wounded May 12, 1864, Spottsylvania, Va. Mustered out June 21, 1864, as Corp.

Burns, William, enlisted June 11, 1861, shoemaker, age 19, single, residence Lynn, born in Providence, R.I. Mustered in June 11, 1861, term 3 years. Deserted Jan. 28, 1863, Falmouth, Va.

Bush, Otto, enlisted Aug. 21, 1863, clerk, age 21, single, residence New York, credited to Nahant. Mustered in Aug. 21, 1863, term 3 years. Wounded May 12, 1864, at Spottsylvania, Va. Transferred to 32d Mass. Vols. June 9, 1864, as " Busche."

Busse, William, enlisted Aug. 20, 1863, sailor, age 24, single, residence Taunton, credited to Abington. Mustered in Aug. 20, 1863, term 3 years; transferred to 32d Mass. Vols. June 9, 1864.

Butler, Hercules, enlisted Aug. 19, 1863, blacksmith, age 29, married, residence New York, credited to Colwain. Mustered in Aug. 19, 1863, term 3 years; transferred to 32d Mass. Vols. June 9, 1864.

Burke, John B., enlisted June 11, 1861, cotton-bleacher, age 22, married, residence Lowell, born in Co. Clare, Ire. Mustered in June 11, 1861, term 3 years. Wounded June 26, 1862, Mechanicsville, Va. Discharged for disability Aug. 30, 1862.

Burke, James, enlisted Dec. 17, 1863, seaman, age 35, married, residence Shelburne Falls, credited to Boston, Wd. 1, born in St. Johns, N.F. Mustered in Dec. 17, 1863, term 3 years. Wounded May 12, 1864, Spottsylvania, Va. Transferred to 32d Mass. Vols. June 9, 1864.

Carney, William, enlisted Aug. 5, 1862, laborer, age 26, single, residence Boston, born in Ireland. Mustered in Aug. 5, 1862, term 3 years. Killed May 9, 1864, at Laurel Hill, Va.

Collins, Dennis, enlisted June 11, 1861, shoemaker, age 19, single, residence Lynn, born in Lynn. Mustered in June 11, 1861, term 3 years. Wounded July 1, 1862, Malvern Hill, Va. Deserted July 3, 1862, Harrison Landing, Va.

Conlon, Andrew, enlisted June 11, 1861, laborer, age 18, single, residence Worcester, born in Ireland. Mustered in June 11, 1861, term 3 years. Killed June 27, 1862, Gaines' Mill, Va.

Connell, Peter, enlisted June 11, 1861, laborer, age 22, single, residence Boston, credited to Boston, Wd 3, born in Co. Cork, Ireland, term 3 years. Mustered out June 21, 1864.

Creighton, Micheal C., enlisted June 11, 1861, waiter, age 18, single, residence Boston, born in Ireland. Mustered in June 11, 1861, term 3 years; promoted Sergt. Sept. 1, 1862. Wounded June 27, 1862, Gaines' Mill, Va. Died from wounds received May 9, 1864, at Laurel Hill, Va., as Sergt.

Cullenan, John, enlisted Aug. 18, 1862, stovemaker, age 28, married, residence Boston, born in Ireland. Mustered in Aug 18, 1862, term 3 years. Mustered out June 21, 1864.

Cullinan, John W., enlisted June 11, 1861, laborer, age 29, married, residence E. Abington, born in Ireland. Mustered in June 11, 1861, term 3 years; promoted Sergt. Sept 1, 1863. Wounded June 27, 1862, at Gaines' Mill, Va., and May 23, 1864, at North Anna River, Va. Mustered out June 21, 1864.

Cullinan, John, enlisted June 11, 1861, shoemaker, age 18, single, residence New York, born in Co. Cork, Ireland. Mustered in June 11, 1861, term 3 years. Killed June 27, 1862, Gaines' Mill, Va.

Cummings, Martin, enlisted June 11, 1861, laborer, age 26, single, residence Roxbury, born in Ireland. Mustered in June 11, 1861, term 3 years. Wounded July 1, 1862, at Malvern Hill, Va. Mustered out June 21, 1864.

Curley, John, enlisted Aug 18, 1863, riveter, age 26, married, residence Pittsburg, Pa., credited to Shirley. Mustered in Aug. 18, 1863, term 3 years. Deserted Oct. 21, 1862, New Baltimore, Va.

Curran, John, enlisted June 11, 1861, morocco finisher, age 22, single, residence So. Danvers, born in Ipswich, Mass. Mustered in June 11, 1861, term 3 years. Wounded June 27, 1862, Gaines' Mill, Va. Mustered out June 21, 1864.

Daly, Daniel J., enlisted Nov. 9, 1861, laborer, age 25, single, residence Boston. Mustered in Nov. 9, 1861, term 3 years. Discharged for disability Oct. 30, 1862.

Denahey, Patrick, enlisted Aug. 8, 1862, laborer, age 34, married, residence Boston. Mustered in Aug. 8, 1862, term 3 years. Mustered out June 21, 1864, as "Danahay."

Dickinson, Daniel, enlisted Aug. 18, 1863, wool sorter, age 26, married, residence E. Troy, N.Y., credited to Shirley. Mustered in Aug. 18, 1863, term 3 years. Deserted Oct. 21, 1863, New Baltimore, Va.

Doherty, Daniel, enlisted June 11, 1861, laborer, age 30, married, residence Lynn, born in Ireland. Mustered in June 11, 1861, term 3 years. Killed June 27, 1862, Gaines' Mill, Va.

Doherty, Michael, enlisted Jan. 23, 1862, bootmaker, age 18, single, residence Boston, credited to Boston, Wd. 1. Mustered in Jan. 23, 1862, term 3 years. Re-enlisted Feb. 22, 1864. Transferred to 32d Mass. Vols. June 9, 1864.

Donahue, Patrick, professor, age 40, single, residence Ireland. Mustered in Oct. 9, 1862, term 3 years. No further record at A.-G. Office, Mass.

Donovan, John 2d, enlisted Aug. 8, 1862, laborer, age 40, residence Boston, born in Ireland. Mustered in Aug. 8, 1862, term 3 years. Discharged for disability Oct. 30, 1862.

Dooley, William, enlisted June 11, 1861, shoemaker, age 34, single, residence Randolph, born in Waterford, Ire. Mustered in June 11, 1861, term 3 years. Promoted Corp. Sept. 15, 1863. Mustered out June 21, 1864.

Driscoll, Dennis, enlisted July 24, 1862, laborer, age 39, married, residence Boston, born in Ireland. Mustered in July 24, 1862, term 3 years Wounded Dec. 13, 1862, Fredericksburg, Va. Mustered out June 21, 1864.

Driscoll, Timothy, enlisted June 11, 1861, currier, age 24, single, residence Salem, born in Co. Cork, Ireland. Mustered in June 11, 1861, term 3 years. Discharged for disability Sept. 30, 1862.

Dugan, William, enlisted July 25, 1862, teamster, age 24, single, residence Boston, born in Ireland. Mustered in July 25, 1862, term 3 years. Discharged for disability Nov. 11, 1863.

Emerson, Amos, enlisted Aug. 20, 1863, groom, age 32, single, residence Boston, credited to Boston. Mustered in Aug. 20, 1863, term 3 years. Discharged for disability Dec. 16, 1863.

Fallon, Edward, enlisted June 11, 1861, lather, age 23, single, residence W. Roxbury, born in Roxbury, Mass. Mustered in June 11, 1861, term 3 years. Deserted July 3, 1862.

Fallon, Michael, enlisted June 11, 1861, shoemaker, age 24, married, residence Lynn, born in Ireland. Mustered in June 11, 1861, term 3 years. Wounded Dec. 13, 1862, at Fredericksburg, Va. Mustered out as Corp. June 21, 1864.

Fallon, Daniel, enlisted June 11, 1861, laborer, age 19, single, residence W. Roxbury, born in Roxbury, Mass. Mustered in June 11, 1861, term 3 years. Mustered out as wagoner June 21, 1864.

Farley, Patrick, enlisted June 11, 1861, laborer, age 34, married, residence Chelsea, born in Ireland. Mustered in June 11, 1861, term 3 years. Discharged for disability June 15, 1863.

Farrell, Michael, enlisted July 12, 1862, harnessmaker, age 22, single, residence Boston, born in Boston. Mustered in July 12, 1862, term 3 years. No further record.

Farrell, Michael, enlisted Aug. 19, 1863, plumber, age 28, married, residence Brooklyn, N.Y., credited to Cummington. Mustered in Aug. 19, 1863, term 3 years. Deserted April 5, 1864, Bealton Station, Va.

Ferris, John, enlisted July 29, 1862, laborer, age 41, married, residence Boston, born in Ireland. Mustered in July 29, 1862, term 3 years. Killed May 5, 1864, at Wilderness, Va.

Fitzpatrick, John, enlisted June 11, 1861, laborer, age 26, married, residence Danvers, born in Ireland. Mustered in June 11, 1861, term 3 years. Transferred to Co. A. Deserted Sept. 12, 1862, at Washington, D C., in Co. A.

Gleason, Michael, enlisted June 11, 1861, currier, age 24, married, residence South Danvers, born in Ireland. Mustered in June 11, 1861, term 3 years. Wounded June 27, 1862, Gaines' Mill, Va. Discharged for disability Nov. 20, 1862.

Gleason, Michael, enlisted Dec. 28, 1863, currier, age 27, married, residence South Danvers, credited to South Danvers, born in Ireland. Mustered in Dec. 28, 1863, term 3 years. Wounded May 8, 1864, Laurel Hill, Va. Transferred to 32d Mass. Vols. June 9, 1864.

Giblin, James, enlisted Aug. 20, 1863, laborer, age 41, single, residence New York, credited to Roxbury. Mustered in Aug. 20, 1863, term 3 years. Wounded May 10, 1864, at Po River, Va. Transferred to 32d Mass. Vols. June 9, 1864.

Golden, David, enlisted June 11, 1861, morocco dresser, age 23, single, residence Boston, born in Co. Cork, Ireland. Mustered in June 11, 1861, term 3 years. Promoted Corp. Sept. 6, 1863. Mustered out June 21, 1864, as " Goulding."

Gordon, Joseph, enlisted June 11, 1861, chemist, age 32, married, residence Boston, born in Ireland. Mustered in June 11, 1861, term 3 years. Killed June 26, 1862, Mechanicsville, Va.

Grant, James, enlisted Aug. 21, 1863, fisherman, age 23, single, residence Nova Scotia, credited to Ipswich. Mustered in Aug. 21, 1863, term 3 years; transferred to 32d Mass. Vols. June 9, 1864.

Griffin, Michael, enlisted June 11, 1861, jeweller, age 20, single, residence Pawtucket, born in Ireland. Mustered in June 11, 1861, term 3 years. Wounded July 1, 1862, Malvern Hill, Va. Discharged for disability Feb. 2, 1863.

Griffin, John, enlisted June 11, 1861, clerk, age 22, single, residence Boston, born in Halifax, N.S. Mustered in June 11, 1861, term 3 years. Wounded June 27, 1862. Transferred to Invalid Corps Sept. 12, 1863.

Hackett, Patrick, enlisted June 11, 1861, laborer, age 20, single, residence Wareham Centre, born in Ireland. Mustered in June 11, 1861, term 3 years. Deserted March 4, 1862, Alexandria, Va.

Hall, William, bootmaker, age 18, single, residence Lynn. Mustered in Aug. 9, 1862, term 3 years. Discharged for disability Oct. 14, 1862.

Hall, Jacob, enlisted Aug. 20, 1863, shoemaker, age 27, single, residence New York, credited to Barnstable. Mustered in Aug. 20, 1863, term 3 years. Deserted Oct. 21, 1863.

Harney, William, enlisted June 11, 1861, carver, age 25, single, residence West Roxbury, born in Ireland. Mustered in June 11, 1861, term 3 years. Wounded June 27, 1862, Gaines' Mill, Va. Deserted from hospital in York, Va., June 30, 1862.

Harrington, Timothy, enlisted Aug. 5, 1862, laborer, age 30, married, residence Boston. Mustered in Aug. 5, 1862, term 3 years. Killed at Spottsylvania May 12, 1864.

Healy, John, enlisted June 11, 1861, laborer, age 25, married, residence East Braintree, born in Ireland. Mustered in June 11, 1861, term 3 years. Deserted Sept. 22, 1861, Arlington Heights, Va., as " Haley."

Hernon, John, enlisted June 11, 1861, teamster, age 19, single, residence North Bridgewater, born in Co. Galway, Ire. Mustered in June 11, 1861, term 3 years. Wounded June 27, 1862, at Gaines' Mill, Va. Discharged for disability Nov. 20, 1862, as " Herman."

Hines, Thomas, enlisted June 11, 1861, blacksmith, age 30, married, residence Boston, born in Ireland. Mustered in June 11, 1861, term 3 years. Deserted Aug. 17, 1863.

Hogan, Thomas, enlisted June 11, 1861, shoemaker, age 26, single, residence North Bridgewater, born in Ireland. Mustered in June 11, 1861, term 3 years. Killed June 27, 1862, Gaines' Mill, Va.

Hollaran, John, enlisted Aug. 9, 1862, laborer, age 29, single, residence Boston, born in Ireland. Mustered in Aug. 9, 1862, term 3 years. Deserted June 29, 1864, Frederick City, Md.

Horan, Dennis, enlisted Aug. 15, 1862, bootmaker, age 43, married, residence Boston, born in Ireland. Mustered in Aug. 16, 1862, term 3 years. Discharged for disability July 31, 1863.

Howard, Martin, enlisted Nov. 30, 1861, laborer, age 18, single, residence Worcester. Mustered in Nov. 30, 1861, term 3 years; transferred to 32d Mass. Vols. June 10, 1864, as missing.

Hyde, Dennis, enlisted June 11, 1861, shoemaker, age 22, single, residence Boston, born in Ireland. Mustered in June 11, 1861, term 3 years. Killed June 27, 1862, Gaines' Mill, Va.

Johnson, William, enlisted Aug 19, 1863, carpenter, age 22, single, residence New York, credited to Gardner. Mustered in Aug. 19, 1863, term 3 years. Deserted April 11, 1864, Bealton Station, Va.

Joyce, Taylor, enlisted Aug. 20, 1863, mariner, age 20, single, residence New York, credited to Plymouth. Mustered in Aug. 20, 1863, term 3 years; transferred to 32d Mass. Vols. June 9, 1864.

Keenan, Michael, enlisted June 11, 1861, currier, age 26, single, residence Salem, born in Ireland. Mustered in June 11, 1861, term 3 years. Killed June 27, 1862, Gaines' Mill, Va.

Kelly, Martin, enlisted Jan. 18, 1864, farmer, age 27, married, residence England, credited to Dennis, born in Galway, Ire. Mustered in Jan. 18, 1864, term 3 years. Deserted April 11, 1864, Bealton Station, Va.

Kelly, Patrick, enlisted June 11, 1861, shoemaker, age 18, single, residence Lynn, born in Ireland. Mustered in June 11, 1861, term 3 years. Killed May 8, 1864, at Laurel Hill, Va.

Kelleher, John, enlisted June 11, 1861, tinsmith, age 19, single, residence Boston, born in Co. Kerry, Ireland. Mustered in June 11, 1861, term 3 years Wounded at Gaines' Mill, Va., June 27, 1862. Discharged for disability Oct. 10, 1862.

Kenny, Thomas, enlisted Aug. 18, 1863, shoemaker, age 21, single, residence Roxbury, credited to Shirley. Mustered in Aug. 18, 1863, term 3 years. Transferred to 32d Mass. Vols. June 9, 1864

Lamb, Owen J., enlisted Aug. 21, 1862, laborer, age 34, married, residence Charlestown, born in Charlestown, Mass. Mustered in Aug 21, 1862, term 3 years. Discharged for disability Dec. 25, 1863.

Lane, Bernard, enlisted June 11, 1861, laborer, age 19, single, residence Roxbury, born in Boston. Mustered in June 11, 1861, term 3 years. Promoted Corp. Sept. 15, 1862. Wounded May 5, 1864, Wilderness, Va. Mustered out June 21, 1864, as Sergeant.

Leach, Elbridge L., enlisted Aug. 20, 1863, shoemaker, age 35, married, residence North Bridgewater, credited to Weymouth. Mustered in Aug. 20, 1863, term 3 years. Discharged for disability March 24, 1864.

Leary, Michael H., enlisted June 11, 1861, printer, age 22, single, residence Boston, born in Boston. Mustered in June 11, 1861, term 3 years. Deserted Jan 28, 1863, Falmouth, Va.

Leonard, Francis, enlisted July 22, 1862, spinner, age 45, married, residence Boston, born in Scotland. Mustered in July 22, 1862, term 3 years. No further record at A. G. office, Mass.

Little, Thomas, enlisted Aug. 4, 1862, cooper, age 43, married, residence East Boston, born in Ireland. Mustered in Aug. 4, 1862, term 3 years. Deserted June 29, 1863.

Longrien, Charles P., enlisted Aug. 20, 1863, farmer, age 25, single, residence New York, credited to Boston, Wd. 10. Mustered in Aug. 20, 1863, term 3 years. Transferred to 32d Mass. Vols. June 9, 1864.

Lyons, Charles, enlisted June 11, 1861, laborer, age 28, married, residence Foxboro, born in Co. Cork, Ire. Mustered in June 11, 1861, term 3 years. Wounded June 27, 1862, Gaines' Mill, Va.; July 1, 1862, Malvern Hill, Va. Discharged for disability Oct. 16, 1862.

Maibe, Francis, enlisted Aug. 20, 1863, sailor, age 25, single, residence New York, credited to Somerset. Mustered in Aug. 20, 1863, term 3 years; transferred to 32d Mass. Vols. June 9, 1864, as " Maybie."

Martin, John, enlisted June 11, 1861, currier, age 21, single, residence Boston, born in Ireland. Mustered in June 11, 1861, term 3 years. Wounded July 1, 1862, Malvern Hill, Va. Discharged for disability Jan. 12, 1863.

Mascus, Stephen I , enlisted Aug. 20, 1863, tailor, age 22, single, residence Boston, credited to Boston. Mustered in Aug. 20, 1863, term 3 years; transferred to 32d Mass. Vols. June 9, 1864, as " Marcus."

Murphy, Martin, enlisted June 11, 1861, shoemaker, age 28, married, residence Weymouth Landing, born in Co. Kerry, Ire. Mustered in June 11, 1861, term 3 years. Mustered out June 21, 1864.

Mulry, Daniel, enlisted Aug. 20, 1863, farmer, age 18, single, residence Concord, credited to Boston, Wd 11. Mustered in Aug. 20, 1863, term 3 years. Reported he died in rebel prison Andersonville, Ga., April 3, 1864.

McCarthy, Dennis, enlisted June 11, 1861, stereotyper, age 23, single, residence Boston, born in Boston, Mass. Mustered in June 11, 1861, term 3 years. Wounded June 27, 1862, at Gaines' Mill, Va. Mustered out June 21, 1864.

McCarthy, John, enlisted June 11, 1861, shoemaker, age 24, single, residence East Weymouth, born in Ireland. Mustered •in June 11, 1861, term 3 years. Mustered out June 21, 1864.

McCarthy, Florence, enlisted Feb. 20, 1862, printer, age 23, single, residence Boston, born in Ireland. Mustered in Feb. 20, 1862, term 3 years. Deserted from hospital.

McCoy, James, enlisted Jan. 18, 1864, laborer, age 23, single, residence Manchester, Eng., credited to Dennis, born in Ireland. Mustered in Jan. 18, 1864, term 3 years; transferred to 32d Mass. Vols., June 9, 1864.

McCurran, John, enlisted June 11, 1861, laborer, age 19, single, born in St. Johns, N.B. Mustered in June 11, 1861, term 3 years. Wounded May 23, 1864, at North Anna River, Va. Mustered out June 21, 1864, as " McKeincan."

McDonald, Donald, enlisted June 11, 1861, farmer, age 30, single, residence Chelsea, born in Sydney, N.S. Mustered in June 11, 1861, term 3 years. Discharged for disability Jan. 6, 1863.

McGaffany, Patrick, enlisted Feb. 11, 1862, laborer, age 25, single, residence Boston. Mustered in Feb. 11, 1862, term 3 years. Killed June 27, 1862, at Gaines' Mill, Va., as " McGaffigan."

McGline, Thomas, enlisted March 15, 1864, age 24, residence East Boston. Mustered in March 14, 1864, term 3 years; transferred from Co. B to Co. 100, 2d Batt., V.R.C., by order P.M.-Gen'l, Washington, D.C., dated March 25, 1865.

McGovern, Phillip, enlisted June 11, 1861, laborer, age 25, single, residence Lynn, born in Ireland. Mustered in June 11, 1861, term 3 years. Wounded July 1, 1862, Malvern Hill, Va. Discharged for disability Sept. 2, 1862.

McGuire, John, bricklayer, age 44, married, residence Boston. Mustered in June 30, 1861, term 3 years. Discharged for disability Dec. 21, 1863.

McGurn, Michael, enlisted June 11, 1861, machinist, age 30, single, residence Boston, born in Ireland. Mustered in June 11, 1861, term 3 years. Wounded July 1, 1862, Malvern Hill, Va. Mustered out June 21, 1864, as " McGurrien."

McIntire, William, enlisted June 11, 1861, bootmaker, age 35, married, residence Quincy, born in Ireland. Mustered in June 11, 1861, term 3 years. Deserted June 29, 1863.

McLaughlin, Patrick, enlisted June 11, 1861, shoemaker, age 20, single, residence Lynn, born in Ireland. Mustered in June 11, 1861, term 3 years. Wounded June 27, 1862, at Gaines' Mill, Va. Discharged for disability Jan. 19, 1863.

McQuade, John, enlisted June 11, 1861, papermaker, age 35, married, residence Lawrence, born in Co. Tyrone, Ire. Mustered in June 11, 1861, term 3 years. Killed June 27, 1862, at Gaines' Mill, Va.

Newton, Thomas, enlisted June 11, 1861, porter, age 30, married, residence Boston, born in Co. Cork, Ire. Mustered in June 11, 1861, term 3 years. Wounded June 27, 1862, Gaines' Mill, Va. Discharged for disability Feb. 24, 1863.

Norton, James, enlisted June 11, 1861, carpenter, age 28, married, residence South Boston, born in Ireland. Mustered in June 11, 1861, term 3 years. Discharged for disability Oct. 30, 1862, as " Naughton."

O'Brien, John, enlisted June 11, 1861, laborer, age 21, single, residence North Brighton, born in Ireland. Mustered in June 11, 1861, term 3 years. Killed June 27, 1862, at Gaines' Mill, Va.

O'Brien, Michael, enlisted June 11, 1861, laborer, age 26, single, residence Boston, born in Ireland. Mustered in June 11, 1861, term 3 years. Wounded in shoulder at Hanover Court House, Va , May 27, 1862; wounded Dec 13, 1862, at Fredericksburg, Va. Mustered out June 21, 1864.

O'Neil, Michael, enlisted June 11, 1861, shoemaker, age 24, single, residence Boston, born in Ireland. Mustered in June 11, 1861, term 3 years. Deserted from hospital.

O'Neil, James, enlisted June 11, 1861, bootmaker, age 34, married, residence Boston, born in Co. Cork, Ire Mustered in June 11, 1861, term 3 years; promoted 1st Sergt., Aug. 27, 1862; promoted 2d Lieut. June 27, 1863, and transferred to Co. E. Killed in action May 9, 1864, at Laurel Hill, Va.

O'Neil, Henry B., enlisted June 11, 1861, painter, age 22, single, residence Boston, born in Boston, Mass. Mustered in June 11, 1861, term 3 years; promoted 1st Sergt. May 9, 1864. Wounded May 5, 1864, Wilderness, Va. Mustered out June 21, 1864.

Phalen, Thomas, enlisted Aug. 12, 1862, laborer, age 30, residence Sherburn, born in Ireland. Mustered in Aug. 12, 1862, term 3 years; transferred to Invalid Corps Sept. 26, 1863.

Pierce, Charles E., enlisted Aug. 21, 1863, clerk, residence Grafton, credited to Boston. Mustered in Aug. 21, 1863, term 3 years. Discharged for disability Dec. 11, 1863.

Powers, Edward, enlisted June 11, 1861, laborer, age 30, married, residence Danvers, credited to Salem, born in Ireland. Mustered in June 11, 1861, term 3 years. Re-enlisted March 28, 1864. Transferred to 32d Mass. Vols. June 9, 1864.

Powers, Thomas, enlisted June 11, 1861, tailor, age 26, single, residence Boston, born in Ireland. Mustered in June 11, 1861, term 3 years. Wounded July 1, 1862, Malvern Hill, Va. Discharged for disability Feb. 9, 1863.

Quinlan, Thomas, enlisted June 11, 1861, shoemaker, age 23, single, residence Boston, born in Ireland. Mustered in June 11, 1861, term 3 years. Wounded at Gaines' Mill, Va., June 27, 1862. Discharged for disability Feb. 4, 1863.

Quinn, John, enlisted June 11, 1861, shoemaker, age 28, married, residence Lynn, born in Ireland. Mustered in June 11, 1861, term 3 years. Missing in action July 2, 1863, at Gettysburg.

Reagan, John, enlisted Nov. 9, 1862, laborer, age 32, married, residence Boston. Mustered in Nov. 9, 1862, term 3 years. Killed May 12, 1864, Spottsylvania, Va.

Reilly, James, enlisted June 11, 1861, shoemaker, age 21, single, residence North Bridgewater, born in Ireland. Mustered in June 11, 1861, term 3 years. Wounded June 27, 1862, at Gaines' Mill, Va. Deserted June 29, 1863, Frederick City, Md.

Remmick, James, enlisted June 11, 1861, shoemaker, age 22, married, residence Salem, born in Ireland. Mustered in June 11, 1861, term 3 years; promoted Corp. Sept. 15, 1862; Sergt. April 9, 1864. Wounded May 5, 1864, Wilderness, Va. Mustered out June 21, 1864.

Rice, Sylvester, enlisted July 28, 1862, tailor, age 38, married, residence Boston, born in Lewis Co., N.Y. Mustered in July 28, 1862, term 3 years. Mustered out June 21, 1864.

Scanlan, Joseph F., enlisted Feb. 11, 1862, laborer, age 20, single, residence Boston. Mustered in Feb. 11, 1862, term 3 years. Wounded June 27, 1862, Gaines' Mill, Va. Discharged for disability Feb. 23, 1863.

Scoffield, Peter, enlisted June 11, 1861, blacksmith, age 32, married, residence East Boston, born in Liverpool, Eng. Mustered in June 11, 1861, term 3 years. Wounded May 5, 1864, Wilderness, Va. Mustered out June 21, 1864.

Sheridan, Patrick, enlisted June 11, 1861, shoemaker, age 18, single, residence North Bridgewater, born in Ireland. Mustered in June 11, 1861, term 3 years. Wounded on picket. Discharged for disability March 10, 1862.

Sheehan, Martin, enlisted June 11, 1861, shoemaker, age 27, married, residence East Abington, born in Ireland. Mustered in June 11, 1861, term 3 years. Killed May 5, 1864, Wilderness, Va.

Smith, John C., enlisted July 17, 1863, sailor, age 22, single, residence Buffalo, N.Y., credited to Boston. Mustered in July 17, 1863, term 3 years. Deserted Oct. 21, 1863.

Smith, William, enlisted June 11, 1861, shoemaker, age 20, single, residence Dorchester, born in Germany. Mustered in June 11, 1861, term 3 years. Wounded June 27, 1862, at Gaines' Mill, Va. Discharged for disability Dec. 3, 1862.

Smith, Mathew, enlisted June 11, 1861, bootmaker, age 33, married, residence Grafton, born in Ireland. Mustered in June 11, 1861, term 3 years. Killed July 1, 1862, Malvern Hill, Va.

Stelfox, James F., enlisted Aug. 21, 1863, painter, age 21, single, residence Concord, credited to Watertown. Mustered in Aug. 21, 1863, term 3 years; transferred to 32d Mass. Vols. June 9, 1864.

Somerville, Alexander, enlisted June 11, 1861, tailor, age 35, married, residence Boston, born in Dunbarshire, Scot. Mustered in June 11, 1861, term 3 years. Discharged for disability Oct. 23, 1861.

Sullivan, Michael, enlisted July 26, 1862, laborer, age 34, married, residence Boston, born in Ireland. Mustered in July 26, 1862, term 3 years. On detached duty in Invalid Corps.

Sullivan, Timothy, enlisted Aug. 2, 1862, laborer, age 24, married, residence Boston, born in Ireland. Mustered in Aug. 2, 1862, term 3 years. On detached duty with 5th U.S. Art.

Thompson, William, enlisted June 11, 1861, laborer, age 23, single, residence Boston, born in Co Kerry, Ire. Mustered in June 11, 1861, term 3 years. Wounded in a scuffle, no date given. Discharged for disability Sept. 26, 1861.

Thompson, Charles, enlisted June 11, 1861, laborer, age 32, married, residence Worcester, born in Ireland. Mustered in June 11, 1861, term 3 years. Killed July 1, 1862, Malvern Hill, Va.

Toomay, Maurice, enlisted June 11, 1861, morocco dresser, age 40, married, residence Lynn, born in Co. Cork, Ire. Mustered in June 11, 1861, term 3 years. Mustered out June 21, 1864, as " Twomy."

Tracy, William, enlisted June 11, 1861, currier, age 23, married, residence Salem, born in Co. Kildare, Ire. Mustered in June 11, 1861, term 3 years. Mustered out June 21, 1864.

Turish, Hugh, enlisted June 11, 1861, glasscutter, age 22, single, residence South Boston, born in South Boston. Mustered in June 11, 1861, term 3 years. Discharged for disability Aug. 18, 1862.

Tynon, Timothy, enlisted June 11, 1861, laborer, age 25, single, residence Lowell, born in Ireland. Mustered in June 11, 1861, term 3 years. Deserted June 29, 1863.

Ward, James, enlisted July 14, 1863, operative, age 31, married, residence Lawrence, credited to Andover Mustered in July 14, 1863, term 3 years. Killed May 5, 1864, Wilderness, Va.

Welch, James N., enlisted Aug. 8, 1862, bootmaker, age 44, married, residence Reading, born in Ireland. Mustered in Aug. 8, 1862, term 3 years. Discharged for disability Oct. 30, 1862.

Welch, John, enlisted Aug. 19, 1863, seaman, age 25, single, residence New York, credited to Concord. Mustered in Aug. 19, 1863, term 3 years; transferred to 32d Mass. Vols. June 9, 1864.

Whelan, Michael, enlisted June 11, 1861, shoemaker, age 34, married, residence Salem, born in Ireland. Mustered in June 11, 1861, term 3 years. Mustered out June 21, 1864.

William, John, enlisted Aug 22, 1863, shoemaker, age 23, married, residence Taunton, credited to Rehoboth. Mustered in Aug. 22, 1863, term 3 years. Deserted April 1, 1864.

COMPANY C.

Madagan, William, Captain, printer, age 35, married, residence Boston, born in Boston. Mustered in June 11, 1861, term 3 years. Killed June 27, 1862, Gaines' Mill, Va.

Mahan, John W., 1st Lieut., counsellor, age 22, single, residence Boston, born in Boston. Mustered in June 11, 1861, term 3 years; promoted Capt. Oct. 25, 1861, Co. D; Major, March 30, 1863. Wounded July 1, 1862. Mustered out June 21, 1864.

McSweeney, Edward, 2d Lieut., clerk, age 21, single, residence Boston, born in Boston. Mustered in June 11, 1861, term 3 years. Promoted 1st Lieut. Oct. 25, 1861. Killed July 1, 1862, at Malvern Hill, Va.

Clancey, John, 1st Sergt., enlisted June 11, 1861, soldier, age 24, single, residence Boston, born in Ireland. Mustered in June 11, 1861, term 3 years. Wounded June 27, 1862, Gaines' Mill, Va. Re-enlisted March 28, 1864; transferred as Private to 32d Mass. Vols. June 9, 1864.

Kerr, William, Sergt , enlisted June 11, 1861, carpenter, age 31, single, residence Boston, born in Newtown, Ire. Mustered in June 11, 1861, term 3 years. Discharged for disability March 18, 1862. Wounded (no date given).

Lane, James, Sergt., enlisted June 11, 1861, blacksmith, age 22, single, residence Boston, born in Castle Island, Ire. Mustered in June 11, 1861, term 3 years. Deserted Nov. 29, 1861, Miner's Hill, Va.

Murphy, John P., Sergt., enlisted June 11, 1861, boot-treer, age 22, single, residence East Braintree, born in Ireland. Mustered in June 11, 1861, term 3 years. Wounded July 1, 1862, at Malvern Hill, Va. Mustered out June 21, 1864, as Private.

McDonald, Chas. N., Sergt., enlisted June 11, 1861, laborer, age 44, single, residence Boston, born in Ireland. Mustered in June 11, 1861, term 3 years. Discharged for disability March 8, 1862.

Lyons, Michael, Corp, enlisted June 11, 1861, cutler, age 28, single, residence Boston, born in Cork, Ire. Mustered in June 11, 1861, term 3 years. Wounded at Malvern Hill, Va, July 1, 1862, lost right arm. Discharged for disability Aug. 22, 1862.

McGee, Patrick, Corp., enlisted June 11, 1861, currier, age 26, single, residence Boston, born in Donegal, Ire. Mustered in June 11, 1861, term 3 years. Sergeant, killed June 27, 1862, Gaines' Mill, Va.

McCabe, Bernard, Corp, enlisted June 11, 1861, stonecutter, age 22, single, residence Providence, R.I., born in Ireland. Mustered in June 11, 1861, term 3 years. Deserted June 29, 1863, Frederick City, Md.

Gillis, James, Corp., enlisted June 11, 1861, laborer, age 23, single, residence Boston, born in Ireland. Mustered in June 11, 1861, term 3 years. Wounded July 1, 1862, at Malvern Hill, Va. Mustered out June 21, 1864, as Private.

Leary, Dana, Corp., enlisted June 11, 1861, stonemason, age 25, single, residence Boston, born in Cork, Ire. Mustered in June 11, 1861, term 3 years. Killed June 27, 1862, Gaines' Mill, Va. (as Daniel).

Kelly, James, Corp., enlisted June 11, 1861, laborer, age 32, married, residence Sandwich, born in Ireland. Mustered in June 11, 1861, term 3 years. Wounded Dec. 13, 1862, Fredericksburg, Va.; transferred to Invalid Corps Sept. 30, 1862, G.O. No. 32, W. Dept.

Cullen, Michael, Corp., enlisted June 11, 1861, shoemaker, age 28, married, residence Worcester, born in Ireland. Mustered in June 11, 1861, term 3 years. Discharged for disability Oct. 1, 1862.

Lord, Charles W., Corp., enlisted June 11, 1861, bootmaker, age 27, single, residence Philadelphia, born in Sand Town, N.J. Mustered in June 11, 1861, term 3 years. Discharged for disability Aug. 10, 1861.

McGirr, Patrick, Wagoner, enlisted June 11, 1861, glassblower, age 35, married, residence Boston, born in Tyrone, Ire. Mustered in June 11, 1861, term 3 years. Discharged for disability March 26, 1863.

Campbell, John, Musician, enlisted June 11, 1861, porter, age 26, single, residence Providence, R.I, born in Tyrone, Ire. Mustered in June 11, 1861, term 3 years. Wounded at Gettysburg July 3, 1863. Mustered out June 21, 1864.

Powers, John 1st. Musician, enlisted June 11, 1861, musician, age 38, married, residence Boston, born in Boston. Mustered in June 11, 1861, term 3 years. Discharged for disability March 10, 1862.

Bannon, Thos. A., enlisted Aug. 11, 1862, teamster, age 24, single, residence Boston, born in Braintree, Mass. Mustered in Aug. 11, 1862. Discharged (no date) for disability.

Barnes, Thomas, enlisted June 11, 1861, marble finisher, age 19, single, residence New York city, born in Co. Cork, Ire. Mustered in June 11, 1861, term 3 years. Corporal July 9, 1863. Wounded May 12, 1864, at Spottsylvania, Va. Mustered out June 21, 1864.

Boylston, Michael, enlisted Aug. 13, 1862, grocer, age 20, single, residence Boston, born in Boston.   Mustered in Aug. 14, 1862, term 3 years. Wounded Dec. 13, 1862, Fredericksburg, Va.   Mustered out June 21, 1864.

Breen, Jeremiah, enlisted June 11, 1861, spinner, age 22, single, residence Millbury, born in Ireland.   Mustered in June 11, 1861, term 3 years. Deserted June 15, 1863, Manassas, Va.

Britt, Michael, enlisted June 11, 1861, servant, age 38, married, residence Boston, born in Ireland.   Mustered in June 11, 1861, term 3 years.   Discharged for disability Oct. 13, 1862, Sharpsburg, Va.

Burke, William, enlisted Feb. 11, 1862, bootmaker, age 25, married, residence Quincy, born in Ireland.   Mustered in Feb. 11, 1862, term 3 years. Transferred to 32d Mass. Vols. June 9, 1864.

Burke, Richard, enlisted June 11, 1861, shoemaker, age 18, single, residence Salem, born in Galway, Ire.   Mustered in June 11, 1861, term 3 years. Deserted Aug. 27, 1862, Harrison Bar, Va.

Burk, Martin, enlisted June 11, 1861, stonemason, age 29, single, residence Bellingham, born in Galway, Ire.   Mustered in June 11, 1861, term 3 years.   Wounded at Gaines' Mill, Va , June 27, 1862.   Transferred to Invalid Corps Sept 30, 1863.

Campbell, William, enlisted Aug. 21, 1863, bricklayer, age 36, married, residence Salisbury, credited to Salisbury.   Mustered in Aug. 21, 1863, term 3 years.   Transferred to 32d Mass. Vols. June 9, 1864.

Casgrove, John, enlisted June 11, 1861, shoemaker, age 20, single, residence Southboro, born in Co. Cork, Ire.   Mustered in June 11, 1861, term 3 years.   Wounded on picket.   Discharged for disability, Oct. 28, 1861. Miners' Hill, Va.

Casey, Michael, enlisted Aug. 15, 1862, laborer, age 28, married, residence Boston, born in Ireland.   Mustered in Aug. 15, 1862, term 3 years. Transferred to Co. I.   Discharged for disability Dec. 30, 1862.

Casey, James, enlisted Aug. 8, 1862, moulder, age 24, married, residence Boston, born in England.   Mustered in Aug. 8, 1862, term 3 years.   Discharged for disability Oct. 29, 1862, Sharpsburg.

Clancy, William, enlisted July 26, 1862, cooper, age 38, married, residence Boston, born in Ireland.   Mustered in July 26, 1862, term 3 years.   Discharged for disability May 7, 1863, Alexandria, Va.

Cleary, Michael, enlisted June 11, 1861, laborer, age 35, single, residence Roxbury, born in Co. Cork, Ire.   Mustered in June 11, 1861, term 3 years. Deserted Jan. 26, 1862, Miners' Hill, Va.

Coffee, Michael, enlisted Aug. 20, 1863, clerk, age 25, single, residence Amherst, credited to New Bedford.   Mustered in Aug. 20, 1863, term 3 years.   Transferred to 32d Mass. Vols. July 9, 1864.

Coleman, Thomas W., enlisted Aug. 11, 1862, waiter, age 18, single, residence Boston, born in Boston, Mass.   Mustered in Aug. 11, 1862, term 3 years.   Mustered out June 21, 1864.

Connolly, Michael, enlisted Aug. 20, 1862, laborer, age 27, married, residence Lawrence, born in Ireland.   Mustered in Aug. 20, 1862, term 3 years. Mustered out June 21, 1864.

Conant, Daniel M., enlisted July 14, 1863, shoemaker, age 31, married, residence Northbridge, credited to Northbridge.   Mustered in July 14, 1863, term 3 years.   Discharged for disability Dec. 11, 1863.

Comally, Thomas, enlisted June 11, 1861, laborer, age 35, single, residence Boston, born in Galway, Ire. Mustered in June 11, 1861, term 3 years. Deserted Aug. 27, 1862, Harrison Bar, Va.

Cooney, Jeremiah, enlisted Aug. 8, 1862, mariner, age 27, married, residence Boston, born in Ireland. Mustered in Aug. 8, 1862, term 3 years. Transferred Oct. 3, 1863, to Invalid Corps.

Corcoran, Daniel, enlisted Aug. 11, 1862, tailor, age 30, married, residence Boston, born in Ireland. Mustered in Aug. 11, 1862, term 3 years. Mustered out June 21, 1864.

Coy, George H., enlisted July 10, 1863, machinist, age 31, married, residence East Cambridge, credited to Boston. Mustered in July 10, 1863, term 3 years. Transferred to 32d Mass. Vols June 9, 1864.

Coyne, John, enlisted June 11, 1861, laborer, age 24, married, residence South Boston, born in Galway, Ire. Mustered in June 11, 1861, term 3 years. Wounded May 8, 1864, at Laurel Hill, Va. Mustered out June 21, 1864.

Coyle, James, enlisted Aug. 20, 1863, seaman, age 22, single, residence Concord, N.H., credited to Shirley. Mustered in Aug. 20, 1863, term 3 years. Transferred to 32d Mass. Vols. June 9, 1864.

Craig, William, enlisted June 11, 1861, laborer, age 22, single, residence Lowell, born in Ireland. Mustered in June 11, 1861, term 3 years. Wounded May 5, 1864, Wilderness, Va.; wounded June 27, 1862, Gaines' Mill, Va. Mustered out June 21, 1864.

Crossin, Eugene, enlisted Aug. 19, 1862, laborer, age 21, single, residence Boston, born in New York, N.Y. Mustered in Aug. 19, 1862, term 3 years. Mustered out June 21, 1864.

Cunniff, John, enlisted Aug. 8, 1862, laborer, age 21, single, residence Boston, born in Ireland. Mustered in Aug. 8, 1862, term 3 years. Discharged for disability Oct. 27, 1862, Sharpsburg.

Cushing, Andrew G, enlisted Aug. 21, 1863, printer, age 25, single, residence East Abington, credited to Abington. Mustered in Aug. 21, 1863, term 3 years. Discharged for disability Dec 11, 1863.

Delaney, Michael, enlisted Aug. 19, 1863, laborer, age 29, married, residence Lawrence, credited to Methuen. Mustered in Aug. 19, 1863, term 3 years. Discharged for disability Dec. 11, 1863.

Denison, John D., enlisted Aug. 20, 1863, clerk, age 35, married, residence Boston, credited to New Bedford. Mustered in Aug. 20, 1863, term 3 years. Died of disease Nov. 7, 1863, Mt. Pleasant Hospital, Washington, D.C.

Dolan, Michael, enlisted Dec. 26, 1863, farmer, age 26, single, residence West Roxbury, credited to Boston, Wd. 3, born in Ireland. Mustered in Dec. 26, 1863, term 3 years. Killed May 5, 1864, Wilderness, Va.

Donavan, Daniel, enlisted June 11, 1861, ropemaker, age 18, single, residence Roxbury, born in Ireland. Mustered in June 11, 1861, term 3 years. Wounded Dec. 13, 1862, at Fredericksburg, Va. Reported transferred to V.R.C. April 26, 1864.

Donnelly, Peter B., enlisted June 11, 1861, confectioner, age 19, single, residence Boston, born in Glasgow, Scotland. Mustered in June 11, 1861, term 3 years. Deserted Dec. 13, 1863, Fredericksburg, Va.

Dudley, Henry E., enlisted June 11, 1861, printer, age 18, single, residence Boston, born in Houlton, Maine. Mustered in June 11, 1861, term 3 years. Died July 25, 1862, on U.S.S. Judge Torrence, near Vicksburg.

Duncan, Charles, enlisted June 11, 1861, dyer, age 28, married, residence Clinton, born in Glasgow, Scotland. Mustered in June 11, 1861, term 3 years Killed July 1, 1862, at Malvern Hill, Va.

Dwyer, Timothy, enlisted Aug. 20, 1863, shoemaker, age 21, single, residence Troy, N.Y., credited to Fall River. Mustered in Aug 20, 1863, term 3 years. Deserted Dec. 24, 1863, Bealton, Va.

Dyer, Daniel, enlisted June 11, 1861, carpenter, age 37, single, residence East Boston, born in Cork, Ire. Mustered in June 11, 1861, term 3 years. Transferred to Invalid Corps Oct. 1, 1863, G.O. No. 39.

Ellard, John, enlisted June 11, 1861, bootmaker, age 25, single, residence Hopkinton, born in Cork, Ire. Mustered in June 11, 1861, term 3 years. Deserted Aug. 27, 1862, Harrison Bar, Va.

Elliott, Geo. H., enlisted Aug. 20, 1863, tailor, age 32, single, residence Roxbury, credited to Roxbury. Mustered in Aug. 20, 1863, term 3 years. Wounded May 8, 1864, at Laurel Hill, Va. Transferred to 32d Mass. Vols. June 9, 1864.

Fagan, Lawrence, enlisted June 11, 1861, shoemaker, age 24, single, residence Worcester, born in Dublin, Ire. Mustered in June 11, 1861, term 3 years. Discharged for disability Nov. 3, 1862, Boston.

Fahy, William, enlisted July 31, 1862, laborer, age 26, single, residence Boston, born in Ireland. Mustered in July 31, 1862, term 3 years. Discharged for disability March 29, 1863.

Field, Simon, enlisted Aug. 18, 1863, shoemaker, age 40, single, residence South Boston, credited to Shirley. Mustered in Aug. 18, 1863, term 3 years. Wounded May 12, 1864, at Spottsylvania, Va. Transferred to 32d Mass. Vols. June 9, 1864.

Flanagan, Henry, enlisted July 14, 1863, machinist, age 20, single, residence Northbridge, credited to Northbridge. Mustered in July 14, 1863, term 3 years. Wounded May 5, 1864, Wilderness, Va. Transferred to 32d Mass. Vols. June 9, 1864.

Flanagan, John, enlisted Aug. 17, 1862, bootmaker, 24, married, residence Milford, born in Ireland. Mustered in Aug. 17, 1862, term 3 years. Killed May 5, 1864, Wilderness, Va.

Flemming, John, enlisted Aug. 22, 1862, tailor, age 21, single, residence Boston, born in Ireland. Mustered in Aug. 22, 1862, term 3 years. Wounded at Chancellorsville, Va. Deserted June 29, 1863, Frederick City, Md.

Flynn, William, enlisted June 11, 1861, carpenter, age 29, single, residence Boston, born in Cork, Ire. Mustered in June 11, 1861, term 3 years. Wounded at Gettysburg July 3, 1863. Mustered out June 21, 1864.

Ford, Edward, enlisted July 28, 1862, laborer, age 45, married, residence Boston, born in Ireland. Mustered in July 28, 1862, term 3 years. Discharged for disability March 30, 1863.

Ford, James, enlisted Aug. 1, 1862, printer, age 18, single, residence Boston, born in Boston. Mustered in Aug. 1, 1862, term 3 years. Deserted Aug. 28, 1862, Harrison Bar, Va.

Ford, Michael, enlisted Aug. 13, 1862, laborer, age 21, single, residence Boston, born in Ireland. Mustered in Aug. 13, 1862, term 3 years. Wounded Dec. 13, 1862, Fredericksburg, Va. Mustered out June 21, 1864.

Foye, William, enlisted Feb. 12, 1862, age 21. Mustered in Feb. 12, 1862, term 3 years. At Boston for duty. Wounded at Gettysburg, July 3, 1863. Transferred to 32d Mass. Vols. June 9, 1864.

Frost, Benjamin, enlisted July 17, 1863, stonecutter, age 38, single, residence Tyngsboro, credited to Tyngsboro. Mustered in July 17, 1863, term 3 years. Transferred to 32d Mass. Vols. June 9, 1864.

Gaffney, George, enlisted Aug. 4, 1862, carpenter, age 21, single, residence Boston, credited to Charlestown, born in Ireland. Mustered in Aug. 4, 1862, term 3 years. Transferred to 32d Mass. Vols. June 9, 1864. Re-enlisted March 28, 1864.

Gallagher, James D., enlisted June 11, 1861, clerk, age 22, single, residence Boston, born in Boston. Mustered in June 11, 1861, term 3 years. Promoted Sergt. June 11, 1861, reduced Oct. 16, 1861; again Sergt. May 8, 1864. Mustered out June 21, 1864.

Gleason, Spencer W., enlisted July 14, 1863, farmer, age 24, married, residence Northboro, credited to Northboro. Mustered in July 14, 1863, term 3 years. Transferred to 32d Mass. Vols. June 9, 1864.

Greaney, Charles, enlisted June 11, 1861, shoemaker, age 22, single, residence Hopkinton, born in Kerry, Ire. Mustered in June 11, 1861, term 3 years. Killed June 27, 1862, Gaines' Mill, Va.

Grier, George, enlisted June 11, 1861, confectioner, age 19, single, residence Cambridgeport, born in Longford, Ire. Mustered in June 11, 1861, term 3 years. Corporal Sept. 16, 1861; Sergeant March 21, 1862. Killed June 27, 1862, Gaines' Mill, Va.

Gosling, James, enlisted June 11, 1861, reedmaker, age 22, married, residence Fall River, born at sea, England. Mustered in June 11, 1861, term 3 years. Wounded June 27, 1862, Gaines' Mill, Va. Discharged for disability Nov. 3, 1862.

Gillday, Patrick, enlisted June 11, 1861, glassblower, age 20, single, residence Somerville, born in Charlestown, Mass. Mustered in June 11, 1861, term 3 years. Wounded June 27, 1862, Gaines' Mill, Va. Discharged for disability Feb. 2, 1863, Annapolis, Md.

Harrington, Andrew, enlisted June 11, 1861, painter, age 23, single, residence Boston, born in Cork, Ire. Mustered in June 11, 1861, term 3 years. Discharged for disability Oct. 30, 1861.

Harvey, John, enlisted June 11, 1861, mason, age 35, married, residence Boston, born in Moscow, Canada. Mustered in June 11, 1861, term 3 years. Discharged for disability Feb. 9, 1863, Falmouth. Wounded May 27, 1862, at Hanover Court House, Va.

Hatch, George E., enlisted July 14, 1863, shoemaker, age 27, married, residence Northbridge, credited to Northbridge. Mustered in July 14, 1863, term 3 years. Discharged for disability Dec. 11, 1863.

Healy, John, enlisted June 11, 1861, shoemaker, age 21, single, residence Abington, born in Ireland. Mustered in June 11, 1861, term 3 years. Deserted Aug. 27, 1862, Harrison Landing, Va., as "Feahy."

Hearty, Michael, enlisted June 11, 1861, laborer, age 24, single, residence Boston, born in Waterford, Ire. Mustered in June 11, 1861, term 3 years. Mustered out June 21, 1864, as "Harty."

Hennebry, John, enlisted June 11, 1861, laborer, age 21, single, residence Lowell, born in Cork, Ire. Mustered in June 11, 1861, term 3 years. Promoted Corp. Dec. 13, 1862, reduced Jan. 16, 1863. Mustered out June 21, 1864.

Howard, Thomas, enlisted June 11, 1861, bootmaker, age 22, single, residence Holliston, born in Clare, Ire. Mustered in June 11, 1861, term 3 years. Mustered out June 21, 1864.

Hughes, James, enlisted June 11, 1861, bootmaker, age 19, single, residence Hopkinton, born in Ireland. Mustered in June 11, 1861, term 3 years. Promoted Corp. Killed June 27, 1862, Gaines' Mill, Va.

Hurrell, John, enlisted Aug. 22, 1862, stonemason, age 22, single, residence Boston, credited to Salem, born in Kingston, N.Y. Mustered in Aug. 22, 1862, term 3 years. Re-enlisted Dec. 31, 1863. Killed May 19, 1864, Spottsylvania, Va.

Hyde, John, enlisted June 11, 1861, laborer, age 21, single, residence Dedham, born in Cork, Ire. Mustered in June 11, 1861, term 3 years. Killed June 27, 1862, Gaines' Mill, Va.

Jones, Patrick, enlisted Aug. 7, 1862, bootmaker, age 22, residence Boston, born in Ireland. Mustered in Aug. 7, 1862, term 3 years. Wounded May 12, 1864, at Spottsylvania, Va. Mustered out June 21, 1864.

Jones, William, enlisted March 1, 1864, laborer, age 21, single, residence Milford, credited to Boston, Wd. 11, born in Ireland. Mustered in March 1, 1864, term 3 years. Wounded May 8, 1864, at Laurel Hill, Va.; transferred to 32d Mass. Vols. June 9, 1864.

Kendall, John H , enlisted Aug. 17, 1863, farmer, age 33, married, residence Pepperell, credited to Pepperell. Mustered in Aug. 17, 1863, term 3 years. Discharged for disability Dec. 11, 1863.

Kenny, David, enlisted June 11, 1861, shoemaker, age 26, married, residence Webster, born in Ireland. Mustered in June 11, 1861, term 3 years. Deserted June 27, 1863, Frederick City, Md.

Kelleher, John, enlisted Dec. 7, 1863, laborer, age 38, single, residence Boston, credited to Boston, Wd. 7, born in Ireland. Mustered in Dec. 7, 1863, term 3 years. Wounded May 5, 1864, Wilderness, Va.; transferred to 32d Mass. Vols. June 9, 1864.

Lawler, Frank M., enlisted Aug. 12, 1862, student, age 25, single, residence Lawrence, born in Ireland. Mustered in Aug. 12, 1862, term 3 years. Promoted 2d Lieut. from Sergt. Feb. 13, 1863. Dismissed Aug. 3, 1863.

Leonard, John, enlisted June 11, 1861, bootmaker, age 18, single, residence Worcester, born in Manchester, Eng. Mustered in June 11, 1861, term 3 years. Wounded in shoulder at Hanover Court House, Va., May 27, 1862. Discharged for disability Jan. 25, 1863, Boston.

Lynch, John, enlisted June 11, 1861, shoemaker, age 21, single, residence Boston, born in County Meath, Ire. Mustered in June 11, 1861, term 3 years. Wounded at Malvern Hill, July 1, 1862. Mustered out June 21, 1864.

Macnamara, Michael H., enlisted Aug. 14, 1862, student, age 24, single, residence Boston, born in Boston. Mustered in Aug. 14, 1862, term 3 years. Promoted Sergt.; promoted Q.M.-Sergt. and transferred to N.C.S. July 1, 1863. Mustered out June 21, 1864, as Q M.-Sergt. (See Co. E.)

Maguire, Michael, enlisted June 11, 1861, teamster, age 26, single, residence Boston, born in Ireland. Mustered in June 11, 1861, term 3 years. Deserted March 21, 1862, as " McGane," Alexandria, Va.

Mahoney, Daniel O., enlisted Feb. 26, 1862, bootmaker, age 27, married, residence Quincy, born in Ireland. Mustered in Feb. 26, 1862, term 3 years. Transferred to 32d Mass. Vols. June 9, 1864, as " Daniel O'Mahoney."

Mahoney, Frank, enlisted June 11, 1861, laborer, age 19, single, residence Marlboro, born in Ireland. Mustered in June 11, 1861, term 3 years. Discharged for disability Dec. 11, 1863.

Maloney, Thomas, enlisted Nov. 25, 1863, cooper, age 44, married, residence Boston, credited to Boston, born in Ireland. Mustered in Nov. 25, 1863, term 3 years. Transferred to 32d Mass. Vols. June 9, 1864.

Marden, Erasmus D., enlisted July 13, 1863, expressman, age 30, married, residence Boston, credited to Boston, Wd. 10. Mustered in July 13, 1863, term 3 years. Killed May 5, 1864, Wilderness, Va., as " Madden."

Martin, Daniel, enlisted Nov. 9, 1861, painter, age 24, residence Boston. Mustered in Nov. 9, 1861, term 3 years. Wounded May 5, 1864, Wilderness, Va.; transferred to 32d Mass. Vols. June 9, 1864, as Corp.

Mathews, John F., enlisted June 11, 1861, hairdresser, age 22, single, residence Boston, born in Boston. Mustered in June 11, 1861, term 3 years. Discharged for disability March 8, 1862, Miners' Hill, Va.

Montague, Daniel, enlisted Aug. 1, 1862, potter, age 24, single, residence Charlestown, born in Charlestown, Mass. Mustered in Aug. 1, 1862, term 3 years. Discharged for disability March 5, 1863, Falmouth, Va.

Moynahan, Michael, enlisted June 11, 1861, laborer, age 22, single, residence Boston, born in Ireland. Mustered in June 11, 1861, term 3 years. Wounded July 1, 1862, Malvern Hill, Va ; transferred to 32d Mass. Vols.

Mullen, William, enlisted June 11, 1861, laborer, age 26, single, residence Webster, born in Limerick, Ire. Mustered in June 11, 1861, term 3 years. Wounded July 1, 1862, Malvern Hill, Va. Mustered out June 21, 1864.

Murray, Charles, enlisted June 11, 1861, laborer, age 25, single, residence Boston, born in Ireland. Mustered in June 11, 1861, term 3 years. Discharged March 11, 1863, because of wounds received at Gaines' Mill.

Murray, James, enlisted June 11, 1861, cooper, age 23, single, residence Hopkinton, born in Clare, Ire. Mustered in June 11, 1861, term 3 years. Corp. July 9, 1863; wounded May 5, 1864, Wilderness, Va. Mustered out June 21, 1864, as Corp.

Murphy, Cornelius, enlisted June 11, 1861, bootmaker, age 22, single, residence Hopkinton, born in Kerry, Ireland. Mustered in June 11, 1861, term 3 years. Deserted May 2, 1863, Chancellorsville, Va.

Murphy, Michael, enlisted Nov. 9, 1861, stonecutter, age 42, residence Boston. Mustered in Nov. 9, 1861, term 3 years. Discharged for disability Oct. 22, 1862.

Murphy, James, enlisted June 11, 1861, laborer, age 25, single, residence Boston, born in Ireland. Mustered in June 11, 1861, term 3 years. Discharged for disability Oct. 22, 1862, Fort McHenry, Md.

Murphy, Thomas, enlisted June 11, 1861, gardener, age 28, single, residence New Bedford, born in Ireland. Mustered in June 11, 1861, term 3 years. Wounded June 27, 1862, Gaines' Mill, Va. Discharged for disability Oct. 30, 1862.

Murphy, Jeremiah, enlisted June 11, 1861, laborer, age 22, single, residence New Bedford, born in Ireland. Mustered in June 11, 1861, term 3 years. Wounded July 1, 1862, at Malvern Hill, Va. Discharged for disability March 11, 1863.

McAuliff, Thomas, enlisted June 11, 1861, printer, age 18, single, residence Boston, born in Cork, Ire. Mustered in June 11, 1861, term 3 years. Wounded July 1, 1862, Malvern Hill, Va. Discharged for disability Dec. 22, 1862, Alexandria, Va.

McAuliff, John, enlisted June 11, 1861, marble polisher, age 21, single, residence South Boston, born in Cork, Ire. Mustered in June 11, 1861, term 3 years. Deserted Aug. 27, 1862, Harrison Bar, Va.

McCaffrey, John, enlisted Aug. 30, 1862, sailor, age 30. single, residence Lawrence, born in Lowell. Mustered in Aug. 30, 1862, term 3 years. Discharged for disability Oct. 3, 1862.

McCann, Hugh, enlisted June 11, 1861, boilermaker, age 26, single, residence Providence, R.I., born in St. John's, N.B. Mustered in June 11, 1861, term 3 years. Deserted Aug. 1, 1862, Arlington, Va.

McCarthy, James, enlisted Feb. 11, 1862, laborer, age 28, single, residence Natick. Mustered in Feb. 11, 1862, term 3 years. Wounded May 5, 1864, Wilderness, Va.; wounded June 27, 1862, Gaines' Mill, Va.; transferred as Sergt. to 32d Mass. Vols. June 9, 1864.

McCluskey, Michael, enlisted June 11, 1861, age 19, residence Boston. Mustered in June 11, 1861, term 3 years. Deserted June 18, 1861, Boston, Mass.

McGovern, James, enlisted June 11, 1861, tinner, age 20, single, residence Webster, born in Manchester, Eng. Mustered in June 11, 1861, term 3 years. Mustered out June 21, 1864.

McGuire, John D., enlisted June 11, 1861, bootmaker, age 22, single, residence Hopkinton, born in Kerry, Ire. Mustered in June 11, 1861, term 3 years. Wounded at Hanover Court House, Va., May 27, 1862. Discharged for disability March 6, 1863.

McLaughlin, Edward, enlisted June 11, 1861, painter, age 22, single, residence Boston, born in Donegal, Ire. Mustered in June 11, 1861, term 3 years. Sergt. July 7, 1863, from Private; prisoner of war since May 19, 1864, in Richmond. Died in Andersonville, Ga., July 9, 1864.

McMahan, Thomas, enlisted June 11, 1861, morocco dresser, age 22, single, residence Charlestown, born in Ireland. Mustered in June 11, 1861, term 3 years. Wounded July 1, 1862, Malvern Hill, Va. Discharged for disability Dec. 9, 1862.

McNamara, Michael T., enlisted June 11, 1861, cotton mill, age 18, single, residence Clinton, born in Ireland. Mustered in June 11, 1861, term 3 years. Wounded July 1, 1862, at Malvern Hill, Va. Discharged for disability Jan. 16, 1863.

McQueeney, William, enlisted June 11, 1861, boot-treer, age 37, married, residence Boston, born in Ireland. Mustered in June 11, 1861, term 3 years. Corp. March 28, 1862; Sergt. March 30, 1862; reduced Dec. 13, 1863. Mustered out June 21, 1864.

McTighe, Anthoney, enlisted June 11, 1861, butcher, age 19, single, residence Brighton, born in Mayo, Ire. Mustered in June 11, 1861, term 3 years. Wounded May 5, 1864, Wilderness, Va. Mustered out June 21, 1864.

Nannery, Michael, enlisted June 11, 1861, laborer, age 27, single, residence Boston, born in Longford, Ire. Mustered in June 11, 1861, term 3 years. Deserted March 21, 1862, Miners' Hill, Va.

O'Brien, William, enlisted Aug. 8, 1862, junk dealer, age 30, married, residence Boston, born in Ireland. Mustered in Aug. 8, 1862, term 3 years. Discharged for disability Oct. 11, 1862.

O'Brien, John, enlisted June 11, 1861, weaver, age 19, single, residence Webster, born in Ireland. Mustered in June 11, 1861, term 3 years. Discharged for disability March 18, 1862.

O'Brien, William, enlisted July 25, 1862, laborer, age 42, married, residence Boston, born in Ireland. Mustered in July 25, 1862, term 3 years. Wounded May 12, 1864, at Spottsylvania, Va. Mustered out June 21, 1864.

O'Brien, Timothy, enlisted July 26, 1862, laborer, age 36, married, residence Boston, born in Ireland. Mustered in July 26, 1862, term 3 years. Mustered out June 21, 1864.

O'Donnell, Maurice, enlisted June 11, 1861, shoemaker, age 20, single, residence Worcester, born in Waterford, Ire. Mustered in June 11, 1861, term 3 years. Wounded June 27, 1862, Gaines' Mill, Va.; Corp. July 9, 1863; wounded May 5, 1864, Wilderness, Va. Mustered out June 21, 1864, as Corp.

O'Neill, Patrick, enlisted June 11, 1861, stonecutter, age 22, single, residence Quincy, born in Cork, Ire. Mustered in June 11, 1861, term 3 years. Deserted Aug. 28, 1862, Harrison's Bar, Va.

O'Toole, Michael, enlisted June 11, 1861, ropemaker, age 21, single, residence Clinton, born in Ireland. Mustered in June 11, 1861, term 3 years. Wounded June 27, 1862, Gaines' Mill, Va. Mustered out June 21, 1864.

Parker, John H., enlisted Aug. 20, 1863, sailor, age 21, single, residence New York, credited to Medfield. Mustered in Aug. 20, 1863, term 3 years. Transferred to 32d Mass. Vols. June 9, 1864.

Parker, Warren, enlisted July 10, 1863, carpenter, age 22, married, residence Lawrence, credited to Lawrence. Mustered in July 10, 1863, term 3 years. Transferred to 32d Mass. Vols. June 9, 1864.

Parodi, Domingo, enlisted Nov. 9, 1861, soldier, age 42, residence Boston. Mustered in Nov. 9, 1861, term 3 years. Discharged for disability March 10, 1862.

Paterson, George T., enlisted June 11, 1861, clerk, age 18, single, residence Boston, born in Boston. Mustered in June 11, 1861, term 3 years. Discharged on writ of habeas corpus Dec. 13, 1862.

Peirce, John, enlisted July 14, 1863, bootmaker, age 26, married, residence Westboro, credited to Westboro. Mustered in July 14, 1863, term 3 years. Discharged for disability Dec. 11, 1863.

Pettee, Edward, enlisted Aug. 11, 1862, machinist, age 18, single, residence Boston, born in Frederickton, N.B. Mustered in Aug. 11, 1862, term 3 years. Killed May 5, 1864, Wilderness, Va.

Pettee, James, enlisted Aug. 7, 1862, grocer, age 20, residence Boston, born in Boston, Mass. Mustered in Aug. 7, 1862, term 3 years. Corp. Nov. 20, 1862; Sergt. Sept 1, 1863; 1st Sergt. May 5, 1864. Mustered out June 21, 1864, as Petty.

Phineys, Edwin, enlisted Aug. 22, 1862, tinsmith, age 24, married, residence Boston, credited to Salem. Mustered in Aug 22, 1862, term 3 years. Re-enlisted Dec. 31, 1863; wounded May 12, 1864, Spottsylvania, Va.; transferred as Corp. to 32d Mass. Vols. June 9, 1864.

Plunkett, William A., enlisted Aug. 14, 1862, clerk, age 22, married, residence Boston. Mustered in Aug. 14, 1862, term 3 years. Promoted 2d Lieut. from Sergt. Sept. 1, 1863; transferred to Co. F March 31, 1864. Mustered out June 21, 1864.

Plunkett, Christopher, enlisted Aug. 14, 1862, clerk, age 32, married, residence Boston, born in Ireland. Mustered in Aug. 14, 1862, term 3 years. Promoted 2d Lieut. Sept. 26, 1862, Co B; 1st Lieut. Jan. 8, 1863; wounded May 23, 1864, at North Anna river, Va., lost right arm. Mustered out June 21, 1864. (See Co. B.)

Powers, John 2d, enlisted June 11, 1861, bootmaker, age 19, single, residence Hopkinton, born in Ireland. Mustered in June 11, 1861, term 3 years. Deserted Dec. 13, 1862, Fredericksburg, Va.

Powers, Patrick, enlisted June 11, 1861, cotton spinner, age 19, single, residence North Webster, born in Kilkenny, Ire. Mustered in June 11, 1861, term 3 years. Discharged for disability March 10, 1862.

Pyne, William, enlisted June 11, 1861, bootmaker, age 26, single, residence Hopkinton, born in Ireland. Mustered in June 11, 1861, term 3 years. Wounded June 27, 1862, Gaines' Mill, Va. Discharged for disability March 21, 1862.

Regan, John, enlisted June 11, 1861, bootmaker, age 21, single, residence Hopkinton, born in Ireland. Mustered in June 11, 1861, term 3 years. Mustered out June 21, 1864.

Reynolds, William, enlisted June 11, 1861, marble cutter, age 22, single, residence New Haven, Conn., born in Ireland. Mustered in June 11, 1861, term 3 years. Promoted Sergeant from Private June 27, 1862. Mustered out June 21, 1864.

Ring, John, enlisted June 11, 1861, shoemaker, age 20, single, residence Hopkinton, born in Ireland. Mustered in June 11, 1861, term 3 years. Wounded June 27, 1862, Gaines' Mill, Va. Mustered out June 21, 1864.

Rogers, Michael, enlisted Aug. 7, 1862, bootmaker, age 44, married, residence Milford. Mustered in Aug 7, 1862, term 3 years. Discharged for disability Oct. 30, 1862, in Co. H.

Ryan, John 1st, enlisted June 11, 1861, baker, age 24, single, residence Hopkinton, born in Clare, Ire. Mustered in June 11, 1861, term 3 years. Discharged for disability Oct. 18, 1861.

Ryan, John 2d, enlisted June 11, 1861, teamster, age 25, single, residence Webster, born in Ireland. Mustered in June 11, 1861, term 3 years. Wounded July 1, 1862, Malvern Hill, Va. Mustered out June 21, 1864.

Ryan, John 3d, enlisted June 11, 1861, laborer, age 32, single, residence Portland, Me., born in Galway, Ire. Mustered in June 11, 1861, term 3 years. Wounded June 27, 1862, Gaines' Mill, Va.; May 12, 1864, at Spottsylvania, Va. Mustered out June 21, 1864.

Ryan, Patrick, enlisted June 11, 1861, weaver, age 22, single, residence Webster, born in Ireland. Mustered in June 11, 1861, term 3 years. Discharged for disability Oct. 15, 1861.

Sandow, Henry, enlisted June 11, 1861, shoemaker, age 20, single, residence Natick, born in England. Mustered in June 11, 1861, term 3 years. Discharged for disability March 6, 1863.

Shanahan, Robert, enlisted June 11, 1861, laborer, age 24, single, residence Webster, born in Isle of Man, Eng. Mustered in June 11, 1861, term 3 years. Mustered out June 21, 1864.

Shehan, James, enlisted June 11, 1861, bootmaker, age 22, single, residence Hopkinton, born in Tipperary, Ire. Mustered in June 11, 1861, term 3 years. Killed July 1, 1862, Malvern Hill, Va.

Shehan, Daniel J., enlisted June 11, 1861, shoemaker, age 18, single, residence Haverhill, born in Cork, Ire. Mustered in June 11, 1861, term 3 years, Wounded June 27, 1862, at Gaines' Mill, Va.; Dec. 13, 1862, Fredericksburg, Va. Transferred to Invalid Corps Feb. 27, 1864.

Sheehan, Cornelius, enlisted June 11, 1861, bootmaker, age 21, single, residence Hopkinton, born in Limerick, Ire. Mustered in June 11, 1861, term 3 years. Reported on detached duty with Battery D, 5th U.S. Art., January and February, 1863. Dropped from the rolls March and April.

Slattery, Michael, enlisted June 11, 1861, bootmaker, age 20, single, residence Hopkinton, born in Limerick, Ire. Mustered in June 11, 1861, term 3 years. Killed June 27, 1862, Gaines' Mill, Va.

Slattery, James, enlisted June 11, 1861, weaver, age 22, single, residence Webster, born in Tipperary, Ire. Mustered in June 11, 1861, term 3 years. Mustered out June 21, 1864.

Somerville, Alexander, enlisted Feb. 11, 1862, tailor, age 35, married, residence Boston. Mustered in Feb. 11, 1862, term 3 years. Wounded June 27, 1862, Gaines' Mill, Va.; wounded Dec. 13, 1862, Fredericksburg, Va. Transferred to Invalid Corps Dec. 16, 1863.

Sullivan, Dennis, enlisted Aug. 21, 1863, laborer, age 22, single, residence Fall River, credited to Plymouth. Mustered in Aug. 21, 1863, term 3 years. Transferred to V.R.C. Jan. 4, 1864.

Sullivan, Michael, enlisted June 11, 1861, bootmaker, age 20, single, residence Hopkinton, born in Tipperary, Ire. Mustered in June 11, 1861, term 3 years. Wounded Dec. 13, 1862, Fredericksburg, Va. Mustered out June 21, 1864.

Walder, Henry, enlisted June 11, 1861, brass finisher, age 20, single, residence Roxbury, born in Germany. Mustered in June 11, 1861, term 3 years. Wounded June 27, 1862, Gaines' Mill, Va. Killed May 12, 1864, Spottsylvania, Va.

Walsh, Daniel, enlisted Feb. 4, 1862, bootmaker, age 21, single, residence Boston, born in Ireland. Mustered in Feb. 4, 1862, term 3 years. Wounded May 5, 1864, Wilderness, Va. Transferred to 32d Mass. Vols. June 9, 1864, as Corp.

Waters, John, enlisted June 11, 1861, shoemaker, age 34, single, residence Stoneham, born in Ireland. Mustered in June 11, 1861, term 3 years. Wounded July 1, 1862, Malvern Hill, Va. Died of wounds Nov. 5, 1862, U.S. General Hospital, Chester, Pa.

Welch, Edward, enlisted Aug. 19, 1863, laborer, age 19, single, residence Boston, credited to Rowley. Mustered in Aug. 19, 1863, term 3 years. Transferred to 32d Mass. Vols. June 9, 1864.

Williams, George, enlisted Nov. 9, 1861, store-tender, age 18, single, residence Boston. Mustered in Nov. 9, 1861, term three years. Wounded May 27, 1862, at Hanover Court House, Va. Discharged for disability Oct. 22, 1862.

Wright, George, enlisted Aug. 20, 1863, sugar-boiler, age 29, single, residence New York, credited to Plymouth. Mustered in Aug. 20, 1863, term 3 years. Transferred to 32d Mass. Vols. June 9, 1864.

COMPANY D.

Guiney, Patrick R., Capt., lawyer, age 26, married, residence Roxbury, born in Ireland. Mustered in June 11, 1861, term 3 years. Promoted Maj. Oct. 26, 1862; Lieut.-Col. Jan 28, 1862; Col. July 26, 1862. Wounded May 5, 1864, at Wilderness, Va. Lost an eye. Brevetted Brig.-Gen. for gallant and meritorious service. Mustered out June 21, 1864.

Doherty, William W., 1st Lieut., age 24, single, residence Boston. Mustered in June 11, 1861, term 3 years. Honorable discharge, Nov. 1, 1861.

Rafferty, John H., 2d Lieut., age 25, single, residence East Cambridge, born in Ireland. Mustered in June 11, 1861, term 3 years. Promoted 1st Lieut. and transferred to Co. A, Feb. 1, 1862. Killed at Malvern Hill, Va., July 1, 1862.

Flaherty, Nicholas C., 1st Sergt., enlisted June 11, 1861, law student, age 25, married, residence Boston, born in Cork, Ireland. Mustered in June 11, 1861, term 3 years. Promoted 2d Lieut. Oct. 24, 1861; 1st Lieut. Sept. 26, 1862. Killed May 5, 1864, at the Wilderness.

Collins, Patrick, Sergt., enlisted June 11, 1861, stevedore, age 35, married, residence Boston, born in Ireland   Mustered in June 11, 1861, term 3 years. Promoted 1st Sergt. Oct. 26, 1861.   Killed June 27, 1862, at Gaines' Mill, Va.

Dealey, Frank, Sergt., enlisted June 11, 1861, soapmaker, age 33, married, residence Cambridge, born in Ireland. Mustered in June 11, 1861, term 3 years. Discharged for disability Sept 20, 1861, as "Daley."

Messer, Charles E., Sergt., enlisted June 11, 1861, stonecutter, age 38, single, residence Quincy Neck, born in Hudson, N.H. Discharged March 20, 1863. Reduced from Sergt.

Powers, Mathew E., Sergt., marbleworker, age 21, single, residence, Boston, born in Ireland. Mustered in June 11, 1861, term 3 years   Reduced from Sergt. to Private. Discharged for disability April 19, 1862.

Barber, Frank, Corp., enlisted June 11, 1861, gasfitter, age 18, single, residence Hoppington, R.I., born in Hoppington, R.I. Mustered in June 11, 1861, term 3 years. Deserted from Harrison Landing, Va., Aug. 12, 1862.

Doran, Peter, Corp., enlisted June 11, 1861, ship carpenter, age 23, single, residence Portland, born in Mayo, Ire. Mustered in June 11, 1861, term 3 years Mustered out June 21, 1864.

Duffey, Bernard, Corp., enlisted June 11, 1861, printer, age 20, single, residence Boston, born in Donegal, Ire. Mustered in June 11, 1861, term 3 years. Reduced from Corp. Wounded June 27, 1862, Gaines' Mill, Va. Discharged for disability Dec. 28, 1863.

Jameson, John E., Corp., enlisted June 11, 1861, combmaker, age 32, married, residence West Newbury, born in Ireland. Mustered in June 11, 1861, term 3 years. Wounded June 27, 1862, Gaines' Mill, Va.; July 1, 1862, Malvern Hill, Va. Mustered out June 21, 1864, as "John A.," Private.

Mallahan, Thomas, Corp., enlisted June 11, 1861, laborer, age 33, married, residence Somerville, born in Tyrone, Ire. Mustered in June 11, 1861, term 3 years. Wounded at Gaines' Mill, Va., June 27, 1862; 2d Bull Run, Va., Aug. 29, 1862, and North Anna River, Va., May 23, 1864. Mustered out June 21, 1864.

Mahoney, John, Corp., enlisted June 11, 1861, moulder, age 23, single, residence South Boston, born in Cork, Ire. Mustered in June 11, 1861, term 3 years. Discharged for disability Oct. 28, 1862.

Martial, James T., Corp., enlisted June 11, 1861, shoemaker, age 20, married, residence North Webster, born in Canada. Mustered in June 11, 1861, term 3 years. As "Marshall," absent sick.

McGinniskin, Chas. B., Corp., enlisted June 11, 1861, mariner, age 25, single, residence Boston, born in Boston. Mustered in June 11, 1861, term 3 years. Promoted Sergt., Commissioned 2d Lieut., April 25, 1863. Died June 7, 1864, of wounds received May 5, 1864, at Wilderness, Va.

Connell, John, Musician, enlisted June 11, 1861, shoemaker, age 19, single, residence Lynn, born in Co. Cork, Ire. Mustered in June 11, 1861, term 3 years. Deserted from Washington, D.C., Sept. 12, 1863, as "Crowell."

Benden, John J., Musician, enlisted June 11, 1861, lithographer, age 20, single, residence South Boston, born in Boston. Mustered in June 11, 1861, term 3 years. Re enlisted March 29, 1864, credited to Boston, Wd. 12. Transferred to 32d Mass. Vols. June 10, 1864.

O'Donnell, Owen, Wagoner, enlisted June 11, 1861, teamster, age 31, married, residence Boston. Mustered in June 11, 1861, term 3 years. Re-enlisted Dec. 31, 1863. Transferred to 32d Mass. Vols. June 9, 1864.

Baker, Charles, enlisted July 16, 1863, sailor, age 20, single, residence New York, credited to Springfield. Mustered in July 16, 1863, term 3 years. Transferred to 32d Mass. Vols. June 10, 1864. Sick at Hospital, Washington, D.C.

Baldwin, John H., enlisted June 11, 1861, shoe pegger, age 18, single, residence North Natick, born in Cambridgeport, Mass. Mustered in June 11, 1861, term 3 years. Mustered out June 21, 1864, as " George."

Barry, Michael, enlisted July 30, 1862, laborer, age 40, married, residence Brighton, born in Ireland Mustered in July 30, 1862, term 3 years. Deserted Aug. 1, 1862, Warrington, Va.

Bell, Richard, enlisted Feb. 23, 1863, clerk, age 22, residence Boston, born in Halifax, N.S. Mustered in Feb. 24, 1863, term 3 years. Transferred to Co. F, April 5, 1863. Discharged, no date or place.

Benway, Augustus, enlisted June 11, 1861, broom-maker, age 20, single, residence North Webster, born in Sovel, Canada. Mustered in June 11, 1861, term 3 years. Discharged from hospital, no date.

Blanchard, Henry, enlisted June 11, 1861, laborer, age 20, single, residence North Webster, born in St. Vincent, Canada. Mustered in June 11, 1861, term 3 years. Mustered out June 21, 1864.

Bourk, John H., enlisted Aug. 11, 1862, shoemaker, age 18, single, residence Boston, credited to Boston, Wd. 8, born in England. Mustered in Aug. 11, 1862, term 3 years. Transferred to Co. A. Transferred to 32d Mass. Vols. June 10, 1864.

Bower, John, enlisted June 11, 1861, confectioner, age 21, single, residence Roxbury, born in Germany. Mustered in June 11, 1861, term 3 years. On detached duty with Co. D, Battery 5th U.S. artillery. Deserted Feb. 15, 1863, from Battery.

Brennan, William, enlisted July 31, 1862, boilermaker, age 18, single, residence Boston, born in Charlestown, Mass. Mustered in July 31, 1862, term 3 years. Deserted from Co A, Sept. 12, 1863, Washington, D.C.

Brown, James, enlisted June 11, 1861, carver, age 23, single, residence South Danvers, born in County Cork, Ire. Mustered in June 11, 1861, term 3 years. Deserted Dec. 13, 1862, Fredericksburg, Va.

Brown, Dennis, enlisted June 11, 1861, bootmaker, age 31, single, residence Weymouth, born in Ireland. Mustered in June 11, 1861, term 3 years. Wounded June 27, 1862, Gaines' Mill, Va. Discharged for disability Oct. 17, 1862.

Burt, Thos. B , enlisted Feb. 10, 1862, bootmaker, age 23, single, residence Middleborough, born in Plymouth. Mustered in Feb. 10, 1862, term 3 years. No record at War Department March 8, 1867

Burt, Samuel, enlisted July 10, 1863, barkeeper, age 21, single, residence Springfield, credited to Springfield. Mustered in July 10, 1863, term 3 years. Discharged for disability Dec. 11, 1863.

Burns, Patrick, enlisted Nov. 9, 1861, laborer, age 24, single, residence Ireland. Mustered in Nov. 9, 1861, term 3 years. Wounded June 27, 1862, Gaines' Mill, Va Dropped as deserter Sept. 1, 1863.

Burk, Culbert, enlisted June 11, 1861, laborer, age 20, single, residence North Webster, born in Somerset, Canada. Mustered in June 11, 1861, term 3 years. Mustered out June 21, 1864.

Carnes, Nathaniel, enlisted, June 11, 1861, machine printer, age 21, single, residence Roxbury, born in Pawtucket. Mustered in June 11, 1861, term 3 years. Promoted Sergt. from Corp. Transferred by promotion to N.C.S., as Sergt.-Maj., April 1, 1863. Wounded at Malvern Hill, Va., July 1, 1862. Mustered out June 21, 1864.

Carr, James 1st, enlisted June 11, 1861, farmer, age 20, single, residence Boston, born in Ireland. Mustered in June 11, 1861, term 3 years. Wounded July 1, 1862, Malvern Hill, Va. Since absent.

Carr, James 2d, enlisted Aug. 11, 1862, laborer, age 35, married, residence Boston, credited to Boston, Wd. 12, born in Ireland. Mustered in Aug. 11, 1862, term 3 years. Re-enlisted Feb. 13, 1864. Transferred to 32d Mass. Vols. June 10, 1864.

Cassidy, Peter, enlisted Aug. 20, 1862, laborer, age 25, single, residence Lawrence, born in Ireland. Mustered in Aug. 20, 1862, term 3 years. Transferred to Invalid Corps. No date.

Cavanagh, James, enlisted June 11, 1861, tailor, age 21, single, residence Boston, born in Co. Cork, Ire. Mustered in June 11, 1861, term 3 years. Promoted Sergt. from Corp. Wounded at Malvern Hill, Va., July 1, 1862; Bethesda Church, Va., June 3, 1864. Mustered out June 21, 1864.

Childs, Albert F., enlisted June 11, 1861, engineer, age 23, single, residence Boston. Mustered in June 11, 1861, term 3 years. Was on detached duty with Battery D, 5th U.S. Artillery. Mustered out June 21, 1864.

Clancy, Jeremiah, enlisted June 11, 1861, tailor, age 31, married, residence Boston, born in Co. Cork, Ire. Mustered in June 11, 1861, term 3 years. Mustered out June 21, 1864.

Clancey, Michael, enlisted June 11, 1861, age 22. Mustered in June 11, 1861, term 3 years. Wounded July 1, 1862, Malvern Hill, Va. Discharged for disability Nov. 19, 1862.

Cleaveland, William, enlisted Feb. 11, 1864, seaman, age 22, single, residence Boston, credited to Sandwich, born in Dedford, England. Mustered in Feb. 11, 1864, term 3 years. Wounded May 5, 1864, Wilderness, Va. Transferred to 32d Mass. Vols. June 10, 1864.

Coakley, Dennis, enlisted June 11, 1861, bootmaker, age 20, single, residence Weymouth Landing, born in Co. Kerry, Ire. Mustered in June 11, 1861, term 3 years. Mustered out June 21, 1864.

Collins, John, enlisted June 11, 1861, upholsterer, age 22, single, residence Boston, born in Ireland. Mustered in June 11, 1861, term 3 years. Discharged for disability, no date.

Collins, Thomas, enlisted June 11, 1861, tailor, age 25, single, residence Boston, born in Ireland. Mustered in June 11, 1861, term 3 years. Promoted Sergt. from Corp. Jan. 15, 1864. Wounded at Malvern Hill, Va., July 1, 1862, and Wilderness, Va., May 5, 1864. Mustered out June 21, 1864.

Conlon, Charles, enlisted June 11, 1861, age 18, single. Mustered in June 11, 1861, term 3 years. No further record, A.G.O., Mass.

Condon, Michael, enlisted July 26, 1862, laborer, age 37, married, residence Groton, born in Ireland. Mustered in July 26, 1862, term 3 years. Discharged for disability, no date.

Conway, Michael, enlisted June 11, 1861, glassmaker, age 24, single, residence East Cambridge, born in Ireland. Mustered in June 11, 1861, term 3 years. Killed July 1, 1862, at Malvern Hill, Va.

Conlon, Michael, enlisted June 11, 1861, farmer, age 25, single, residence Boston, born in Co. Tyrone, Ire. Mustered in June 11, 1861, term 3 years. Discharged for disability Feb 2, 1862

Conlon, Thomas, enlisted June 11, 1861, bootmaker, age 26, married, residence Boston. Mustered in June 11, 1861, term 3 years Wounded May 12, 1864, Spottsylvania. Mustered out June 21, 1864.

NINTH MASSACHUSETTS VOLUNTEERS. 469

Cotey, William, enlisted June 11, 1861, age 22, residence Boston. Mustered in June 11, 1861, term 3 years. Deserted July 6, 1861, Washington, D.C.

Coughlan, Joseph, enlisted Aug. 25, 1862, laborer, age 19, single, residence Boston. Mustered in Aug. 25, 1862, term 3 years. Mustered out June 21, 1864.

Crowley, Jeremiah, enlisted June 11, 1861, bootmaker, age 23, single, residence Bangor, born in Co. Cork, Ire. Mustered in June 11, 1861, term 3 years. Discharged for disability Oct. 3, 1862.

Cummings, James, enlisted Aug. 25, 1862, tailor, age 39, married, residence Boston, born in Ireland. Mustered in Aug. 25, 1862, term 3 years. Discharged from hospital Feb. 9, 1864.

Curran, John, enlisted Nov. 9, 1863, painter, age 26, single, residence Boston, credited to Littleton, born in Ireland. Mustered in Nov. 9, 1863, term 3 years. Transferred to 32d Mass. Vols. June 9, 1864.

Daley, Martin, enlisted June 11, 1861, spinner, age 23, single, residence Brookline, born in Ireland. Mustered in June 11, 1861, term 3 years. Discharged to date Feb. 25, 1863.

Devlin, John (right name Tabler), enlisted June 11, 1861, currier, age 28, single, residence Roxbury, born in Germany. Mustered in June 11, 1861, term 3 years. Was on detached duty in 5th U.S. Artillery, Battery D, Mustered out June 21, 1864.

Doherty, Anthony, enlisted June 11, 1861, carpenter, age 24, single, residence East Boston, born in Ireland. Mustered in June 11, 1861, term 3 years. Absent sick.

Doherty, John D, enlisted June 11, 1861, carpenter, age 22, single, residence Roxbury, born in Ireland. Mustered in June 11, 1861, term 3 years. Promoted Sergt. from Corp., April 1, 1863. Wounded July 1, 1862, at Malvern Hill, Va. Killed May 30, 1864, at Totopotomy Swamp, Va.

Doherty, Edward, enlisted June 11, 1861, carpenter, age 35, single, residence Boston, born in Ireland Mustered in June 11, 1861, term 3 years. Wounded at Bealton, Va., March, 1864; leg amputated. Mustered out June 21, 1864.

Donahue, John, enlisted June 11, 1861, grocer, age 22, single, residence Boston, born in Co. Galway, Ire. Mustered in June 11, 1861, term 3 years. Discharged for disability Oct. 23, 1861.

Donavan, Timothy, enlisted July 30, 1862, laborer, age 42, married, residence Boston, born in Ireland. Mustered in July 30, 1862, term 3 years. Never joined the regiment and no record of his whereabouts and service subsequent to Aug. 13, 1862, has been found.

Dowd, Peter, enlisted June 11, 1861, weaver, age 22, single, residence Webster, born in England. Mustered in June 11, 1861, term 3 years. Wounded at Gaines' Mill, Va., June 27, 1862. Transferred to 32d Mass. Vols. June 10, 1864, to serve time lost by absence without leave.

Doyle, Patrick, enlisted June 11, 1861, age 18. Mustered in June 11, 1861, term 3 years. Wounded at Gaines' Mill, June 27, 1862. Deserted Oct. 5, 1862, Baltimore, Md.

Duggan, Dennis, enlisted Aug. 22, 1862, soldier, age 23, residence Lawrence, born in Ireland. Mustered in Aug. 22, 1862, term 3 years. Discharged for disability, Oct. 29, 1862.

Dunn, John, enlisted June 11, 1861, laborer, age 30, married, residence South Boston, born in Co. Cork, Ire Mustered in June 11, 1861, term 3 years. Transferred to Invalid Corps Dec. 18, 1863.

Durant, Charles, enlisted July 27, 1863, farmer, age 34, single, residence Pepperell, credited to Pepperell. Mustered in July 27, 1863, term 3 years. Transferred to 32d Mass. Vols. June 10, 1864.

Fairbanks, Charles L., enlisted July 16, 1863, machinist, age 24, single, residence Newton, credited to Newton. Mustered in July 16, 1863, term 3 years. Transferred to 32d Mass. Vols. June 10, 1864.

Farrell, James, enlisted June 11, 1861, hatter, age 18, single, residence East Cambridge, born in Boston, Mass. Mustered in June 11, 1861, term 3 years. Mustered out June 21, 1864.

Finan, Bernard F., enlisted June 11, 1861, clerk, age 18, single, residence Boston, born in Boston. Mustered in June 11, 1861, term 3 years. Discharged as 1st Sergt. Co. D, for promotion to 2d Lieut. Co. C, Sept. 26, 1862. Transferred as 1st Lieut. to Co. F, Feb. 13, 1863. Mustered out June 21, 1864, in Co. F.

Fleming, James, enlisted June 11, 1861, marble polisher, age 24, married, residence Boston, born in Co. Kerry, Ire. Mustered in June 11, 1861, term 3 years. Wounded May 30, 1864, Totopotomy Swamp, Va. Mustered out June 21, 1864.

Flynn, John, enlisted June 11, 1861, teamster, age 20, single, residence Boston, born in Ireland. Mustered in June 11, 1861, term 3 years. Killed June 27, 1862, Gaines' Mill, Va.

Fuller, Ezekiel, enlisted June 11, 1861, farmer, age 27, single, residence Berlin, Mass., born in Livermore, Me. Mustered in June 11, 1861, term 3 years. Was taken prisoner May 27, 1862, Hanover Court House. Transferred to Invalid Corps Nov. 28, 1863.

Giles, George, enlisted Aug. 22, 1862, laborer, age 23, residence Lawrence, born in Ireland. Mustered in Aug. 22, 1862, term 3 years. Mustered out June 21, 1864.

Gill, Joseph, enlisted June 11, 1861, factor, age 20, single, residence North Webster, born in St. Francis, Canada. Mustered in June 11, 1861, term 3 years. Transferred to V.R.C. Oct. 30, 1862.

Gilman, Peter, enlisted June 11, 1861, spinner, age 22, single, residence Lawrence, born in Ireland. Mustered in June 11, 1861, term 3 years. Deserted Oct. 5, 1862, Baltimore, Md.

Gleason, John, enlisted June 11, 1861, tailor, age 30, single, residence Boston, born in Ireland. Mustered in June 11, 1861, term 3 years. Discharged for disability Oct. 23, 1861.

Goode, John P., enlisted June 11, 1861, cigarmaker, age 21, single, residence Roxbury, born in Ireland. Mustered in June 11, 1861, term 3 years. Wounded July 1, 1862, Malvern Hill, Va. Discharged for disability, April 25, 1863.

Guiney, William, enlisted Feb. 29, 1863, laborer, age 21, single, residence Lewiston, Me., credited to Stoneham, born in Ireland. Mustered in Feb. 29, 1863, term 3 years. Transferred to 32d Mass. Vols. June 9, 1864.

Haggerty, John, enlisted Dec. 11, 1862, laborer, age 20, single, residence Wayland, credited to Boston, Wd. 6, born in Ireland. Mustered in Dec. 11, 1862, term 3 years. Wounded May 5, 1864, Wilderness, Va. Re-enlisted Dec. 31, 1863. Transferred to 32d Mass. Vols. June 10, 1864.

Hanglin, William, enlisted June 11, 1861, shoemaker, age 24, single, residence South Reading, born in Cork, Ire., Mustered in June 11, 1861, term 3 years. Mustered out June 21, 1864, as Corp.

Hanson, John, enlisted Aug. 21, 1863, sailor, age 29, single, residence Salisbury, credited to Salem. Mustered in Aug. 21, 1863, term 3 years. Transferred to navy April 21, 1864.

Havlin, Hugh, enlisted June 11, 1861, baker, age 30, single, residence Boston, born in Londonderry, Ire. Mustered in June 11, 1861, term 3 years. Discharged for disability, Feb. 15, 1863.

Healey, Dennis, enlisted Aug. 7, 1862, tanner, age 26, married, residence Salem, born in Ireland. Mustered in Aug. 7, 1862, term 3 years. Discharged for disability Oct. 29, 1863.

Healey, I. James, enlisted Aug. 9, 1862, carpenter, age 18, single, residence Boston, born in Ireland. Mustered in Aug. 9, 1862, term 3 years. Killed at the Wilderness, Va., May 5, 1864, as Corp.

Heenan, John C., enlisted June 11, 1861, mason, age 22, single, residence Lawrence, born in Ireland. Mustered in June 11, 1861, term 3 years. Discharged for disability Dec. 10, 1862.

Hegan, Edward, enlisted June 11, 1861, painter, age 21, single, residence South Boston, born in Digby, N.S. Mustered in June 11, 1861, term 3 years. Wounded June 27, 1862, Gaines' Mill, Va. Transferred to Invalid Corps, no date, as Sergt.

Hickey, Joseph, enlisted July 17, 1862, laborer, age 31, single, residence Boston, born in Ireland. Mustered in July 17, 1862, term 3 years. Deserted while on detached duty with 5th U.S. Art. Feb. 15, 1862.

Hickey, Simon P., enlisted Aug. 21, 1862, shoemaker, age 19, single, residence Lawrence, born in Ireland. Mustered in Aug. 21, 1862, term 3 years. Mustered out June 21, 1864, as Musician.

Hill, Thomas H., enlisted Aug. 22, 1863, clerk, age 23, single, residence New York, credited to Newburyport. Mustered in Aug. 22, 1863, term 3 years. Transferred to 32d Mass. Vols. June 10, 1864.

Hinckley, John, enlisted June 11, 1861, age 27. Mustered in June 11, 1861, term 3 years. Discharged for disability March 10, 1863.

Hughes, Edward, enlisted Aug. 19, 1862, shoemaker, age 23, married, residence Salem, born in Ireland. Mustered in Aug. 19, 1862, term 3 years. Transferred to V.R.C., no date.

Hughes, James, enlisted June 11, 1861, teamster, age 30, married, residence Boston, born in Ireland. Mustered in June 11, 1861, term 3 years. Mustered out June 21, 1864, as Wagoner.

Hunniff, John, painter, age 22, single, residence Boston. Mustered in Aug. 8, 1862, term 3 years. No further record at A.G.O., Mass.

Jackson, Andrew, enlisted Nov. 25, 1863, seaman, age 19, single, residence Liverpool, N.S., credited to Boston, Wd. 7, born in Liverpool, N.S. Mustered in Nov. 25, 1863, term 3 years. Transferred to 32d Mass. Vols. June 10, 1864.

Kane, Owen, enlisted June 11, 1861, shoemaker, age 21, single, residence Marlboro, born in Ireland Mustered in June 11, 1861, term 3 years. Deserted June 20, 1861, Long Island, Boston Harbor.

Keefe, John, enlisted June 11, 1861, painter, age 41, married, residence Boston, born in Co. Cork, Ire. Mustered in June 11, 1861, term 3 years. Discharged by order of War Dept. Detached on Western gunboat service.

Keenan, Richard, enlisted Aug. 16, 1863, laborer, age 25, married, residence Newton, credited to Concord. Mustered in Aug. 16, 1863, term 3 years. Transferred to 32d Mass. Vols. June 10, 1864.

Keenan, Thomas, enlisted Aug. 16, 1863, laborer, age 25, single, residence Newton, credited to Newton. Mustered in Aug. 16, 1863, term 3 years. Wounded May 5, 1864, Wilderness, Va. Transferred to 32d Mass. Vols. June 10, 1864

Kelleher, John, enlisted June 11, 1861, farmer, age 28, married, residence Salem, born in Co. Cork, Ire. Mustered in June 11, 1861, term 3 years. Discharged for disability Nov. 28, 1862.

Kenney, Michael, enlisted June 11, 1861, shoemaker, age 18, single, residence Roxbury, born in Ireland. Mustered in June 11, 1861, term 3 years. Deserted from Hospital, Point Lookout, Md., no date.

Kennedy, Dennis, enlisted Feb. 1, 1862, laborer, age 23, single, residence Boston. Mustered in Feb. 1, 1862, term 3 years. Transferred to 32d Mass. Vols. June 10, 1864.

Kinlan, Thomas, enlisted Dec. 9, 1863, minter, age 36, married, residence Boston, credited to Boston, Wd. 1, born in Ireland. Mustered in Dec. 9, 1863, term 3 years. Wounded May 5, 1864, Wilderness, Va. Transferred to 32d Mass. Vols. June 10, 1864, as " Kiflan."

Lancy, John, enlisted July 10, 1863, shoemaker, age 26, married, residence Marblehead, credited to Marblehead. Mustered in July 10, 1863, term 3 years. Transferred to navy, April 21, 1864, order Secretary of War.

Lee, Walter, enlisted June 11, 1861, farmer, age 35, married, residence Boston, born in Galway, Ire. Mustered in June 11, 1861, term 3 years. Deserted April 29, 1863.

Lee, Walter, enlisted March 28, 1864, mason, age 38, married, residence Boston, credited to Sudbury, born in Co. Galway, Ire. Mustered in March 28, 1864, term 3 years. Transferred to 32d Mass. Vols. June 10, 1864.

Leighton, Charles, enlisted June 11, 1861, currier, age 23, single, residence Lowell, born in Ireland. Mustered in June 11, 1861, term 3 years. Deserted June 30, 1862, Washington, D.C.

Leppert, John, enlisted Aug. 15, 1863, seaman, age 21, single, residence New York, credited to Newton. Mustered in Aug. 15, 1863, term 3 years. Transferred to 32d Mass. Vols. June 10, 1864.

Lynch, George, enlisted Feb. 10, 1862, painter, age 25, married, residence South Boston, born in Ireland. Mustered in Feb. 10, 1862, term 3 years. Wounded June 27, 1862, Gaines' Mill, Va. Discharged to date Oct. 2, 1862.

Lynch, William, enlisted Aug. 21, 1862, tailor, age 27, single, residence Boston, born in Ireland. Mustered in Aug. 21, 1862, term 3 years. Discharged Dec. 19, 1862, for disability.

McLaughlin, Patrick, enlisted June 11, 1861, jack spinner, age 21, single, residence Leicester, born in Ireland. Mustered in June 11, 1861, term 3 years. Wounded at Antietam, Sept. 17, 1862. Dropped from the rolls Sept. 1, 1863, as a deserter.

Magreal, Terrence, enlisted June 11, 1861, factory, age 19, single, residence Lowell, born in Ireland. Mustered in June 11, 1861, term 3 years. No further record at A.G.O. Mass.

Maloney, William, enlisted June 11, 1861, blacksmith, age 24, single, residence Cambridge, born in Co. Cork, Ire. Mustered in June 11, 1861, term 3 years. Wounded June 27, 1862, at Gaines' Mill, Va. Discharged for disability, no date.

Masterson, John, enlisted June 11, 1861, currier, age 23, married, residence Lowell, born in Longford, Ire. Mustered in June 11, 1861, term 3 years. Absent sick.

Medar, Albert, enlisted June 11, 1861, shoemaker, age 19, single, residence North Natick, born in New Hampshire. Mustered in June 11, 1861, term 3 years. Mustered out June 21, 1864, as "Meaden."

Mellen, William, enlisted June 11, 1861, glassblower, age 18, single, residence Charlestown, born in Charlestown, Mass. Mustered in June 11, 1861, term 3 years. Mustered out June 21, 1864.

Mitchell, Nathaniel, enlisted June 11, 1861, age 36, residence Boston. Mustered in June 11, 1861, term 3 years. Deserted June 21, 1863, while with Battery D, 5th U.S. artillery.

Murphy, Jeremiah, enlisted June 11, 1861, laborer, age 21, single, residence Great Falls, N.H., born in Cork, Ire. Mustered in June 11, 1861, term 3 years. Mustered out June 21, 1864.

Murray, Daniel A., enlisted Aug. 6, 1862, plumber, age 23, single, residence Boston. Mustered in Aug. 6, 1862, term 3 years. Mustered out June 21, 1864.

Murray, James, enlisted June 11, 1861, cotton dyer, age 21, single, residence Lawrence, born in Ireland. Mustered in June 11, 1861, term 3 years. Promoted Corp. Wounded July 1, 1862, at Malvern Hill, Va. Mustered out as Sergt. June 21, 1864.

McCann, James, enlisted June 11, 1861, jack spinner, age 20, single, residence Boston, born in Ireland. Mustered in June 11, 1861, term 3 years. Wounded July 1, 1862, at Malvern Hill, Va. Killed May 5, 1864, Wilderness, Va., as Corp.

McConolough, Neil, enlisted June 11, 1861, farmer, age 27, single, residence Boston, born in Ireland. Mustered in June 11, 1861, term 3 years. Killed June 27, 1862, Gaines' Mill, Va , as " McConologue "

McCormack, Thomas, enlisted Feb. 6, 1864, laborer, age 43, married, residence Boston, credited to Boston, Wd. 1, born in Ireland. Mustered in Feb. 6, 1864, term 3 years. Transferred to 32d Mass. Vols. June 10, 1864.

McDermott, William, enlisted June 11, 1861, laborer, age 28, single, residence Lowell, born in Co. Cavin, Ire. Mustered in June 11, 1861, term 3 years. Wounded May 5, 1864, Wilderness, Va. Mustered out June 21, 1864.

McDonough, James F., enlisted June 11, 1861, pressman, age 23, single, residence Boston, born in Ireland. Mustered in June 11, 1861, term 3 years. Transferred to Co. I. Killed June 27, 1862, Gaines' Mill, Va., as Corp. Co. I.

McFeeley, William, enlisted June 11, 1861, cooper, age 21, single, residence Boston, born in Ireland. Mustered in June 11, 1861, term 3 years. Killed June 27, 1862, at Gaines' Mill, Va.

McGowen, Thomas, enlisted Nov. 9, 1861, laborer, age 20, single, residence Boston. Mustered in Nov. 9, 1861, term 3 years. Transferred to 32d Mass. Vols. June 10, 1864.

McGrade, Terrence, enlisted June 11, 1861, age 23. Mustered in June 11, 1861, term 3 years. Died of wounds received June 27, 1862, Gaines' Mill, Va.

McKenna, Francis, enlisted June 11, 1861, blacksmith, age 20, single, residence Boston, born in St. Johns, N B. Mustered in June 11, 1861, term 3 years. Killed June 27, 1862, Gaines' Mill, Va.

McLaughlin, James, enlisted June 11, 1861, currier, age 19, single, residence Boston, born in Boston. Mustered in June 11, 1861, term 3 years, Wounded June 27, 1862, Gaines' Mill, Va. Deserted Aug. 14, 1862, Harrison Landing, Va.

McLaughlin, John, enlisted June 11, 1861, clerk, age 22, married, residence Charlestown, born in Donegal, Ire. Mustered in June 11, 1861, term 3 years. Died of wounds received July 1, 1862, at battle of Malvern Hill, Va.

Norton, Patrick G., enlisted June 11, 1861, bootmaker, age 18, single, residence Roxbury, born in Ireland. Mustered in June 11, 1861, term 3 years. Deserted May 13, 1863, Falmouth, Va., as Sergt.

O'Brien, John, enlisted June 11, 1861, bootmaker. age 20, single, residence Milford, credited to Milford, born in Kilkenny, Ire. Mustered in June 11, 1861, term 3 years. Wounded May 12, 1864, Spottsylvania, Va. Re-enlisted Dec. 31, 1863   Transferred to 32d Mass. Vols. June 10, 1864, as Corp.

O'Brien, Edward, enlisted June 11, 1861, baker, age 36, married, residence Charlestown, born in Co. Cork, Ire. Mustered in June 11, 1861, term 3 years. Wounded June 27, 1862, Gaines' Mill, Va. Discharged for disability, Feb. 6, 1863.

O'Donnell, James, enlisted Aug. 8, 1862, printer, age 21, single, residence Salem. Mustered in Aug 8, 1862, term 3 years. Promoted Sergt., 2d Lieut., Feb. 8, 1863, and transferred to Co. E; 1st Lieut., Oct. 22, 1863, transferred to Co. G. Mustered out June 21, 1864.

O'Hara, John, enlisted June 11, 1861, laborer, age 19, single, residence Boston, born in Boston, Mass. Mustered in June 11, 1861, term 3 years. Killed May 8, 1864, at Laurel Hill, Va.

Plant, Joseph, enlisted June 11, 1861, millman, age 18, single, residence, North Webster. Mustered in June 11, 1861, term 3 years. Mustered out June 21, 1864.

Provose, Mitchell, enlisted June 11, 1861, boatman, age 23, single, residence New York, born in Sancesyear, Canada. Mustered in June 11, 1861, term 3 years. Killed July 1, 1862, Malvern Hill, Va., as " Provost."

Quigley, James, enlisted July 31, 1862, laborer, age 23, single, residence Boston, born in Ireland. Mustered in July 31, 1862, term 3 years. Mustered out June 21, 1864.

Quigley, Martin, enlisted July 31, 1862, laborer, age 25, married, residence Boston, born in Ireland. Mustered in July 31, 1862, term 3 years. Mustered out June 21, 1864, as " James."

Ready, Andrew, enlisted Nov. 9, 1861, fisherman, age 23, married, residence Cambridge or Boston. Mustered in Nov. 9, 1861, term 3 years. Wounded July 1, 1862, at Malvern Hill, Va. Discharged for disability Oct. 12, 1862.

Reed, John, enlisted June 11, 1861, spinner, age 19, single, residence Lawrence, born in Ireland. Mustered in June 11, 1861, term 3 years. Wounded May 12, 1864, at Spottsylvania. Died of wounds May 18, 1864, as Corp.

Regan, Peter, enlisted June 11, 1861, ropemaker, age 18, single, residence Roxbury, born in Co. Mayo, Ire. Mustered in June 11, 1861, term 3 years. Died of disease Dec. 19, 1862, Falmouth, Va.

Roach, Michael, enlisted June 11, 1861, shoemaker, age 20, single, residence Lynn, born in Lowell. Mustered in June 11, 1861, term 3 years. Wounded May 12, 1864, Spottsylvania, left arm amputated; died of wounds.

Roberts, Frank, enlisted June 11, 1861, age 19, single, residence Boston. Mustered in June 11, 1861, term 3 years. No further record at A.G.O., Mass.

Rodgers, Peter, enlisted June 11, 1861, tailor, age 28, single, residence Boston, born in Tyrone, Ire. Mustered in June 11, 1861, term 3 years. Mustered out June 21, 1864, as Corp.

Russell, Michael, card grinder, age 20, single, residence Great Falls, N.H., born in Co. Cork, Ire. Mustered in June 11, 1861, term 3 years. Died of disease Dec. 9, 1862, Philadelphia, Pa.

Ryan, Thomas, enlisted June 11, 1861, shoemaker, age 23, single, residence Boston, born in Ireland. Mustered in June 11, 1861, term 3 years. Discharged for disability, no date.

Scott, Edward C., enlisted Aug. 20, 1861, age 25. Mustered in Aug. 20, 1861, term 3 years. Promoted Sergt. from Corp., Feb. 25, 1863, 1st Sergt., April 1, 1863. Wounded at Malvern Hill, Va., July 1, 1862; wounded at Wilderness, Va., May 5, 1864. Transferred to 32d Mass. Vols.

Shattuck, Charles F., enlisted July 17, 1863, shoemaker, age 40, single, residence Pepperell, credited to Pepperell. Mustered in July 17, 1863, term 3 years. Discharged for disability Dec. 8, 1863. (G. T. No. 4.)

Shea, Jeremiah, enlisted July 30, 1862, laborer, age 19, single, residence Boston, born in Boston, Mass. Mustered in July 30, 1862, term 3 years. Mustered out June 21, 1864.

Shea, James, enlisted Aug. 20, 1862, laborer, age 19, single, residence Lawrence, credited to Lawrence, born in Ireland. Mustered in Aug. 20, 1862, term 3 years; promoted Sergt. from Private, May 30, 1864. Re-enlisted, Dec. 31, 1863. Transferred to 32d Mass. Vols., June 10, 1864.

Shields, William, enlisted July 26, 1862, morocco finisher, age 26, married, residence Boston, born in Ireland. Mustered in July 26, 1862, term 3 years. Mustered out June 21, 1864.

Sullivan, Michael, enlisted Aug. 8, 1862, junk dealer, age 30, married, residence Boston, born in Ireland. Mustered in Aug. 8, 1862, term 3 years. Deserted June 29, 1863, Frederick, Md.

Sweeney, William, enlisted June 11, 1861, laborer, age 19, single, residence Boston, born in Cork, Ire. Mustered in June 11, 1861, term 3 years. Mustered out June 21, 1864

Teate, William I., enlisted June 11, 1861, laborer, age 19, single, residence Portsmouth, N.H., born in Kittery, Me. Mustered in June 11, 1861, term 3 years. Died of wounds received July 1, 1862.

Walsh, John, enlisted June 11, 1861, shoemaker, age 18, single, residence Boston, credited to Boston, Wd. 3, born in Ireland. Mustered in June 11, 1861, term 3 years. Re-enlisted Dec. 31, 1863. Killed May 5, 1864, Wilderness, Va.

Walsh, John, enlisted Feb. 17, 1864, mariner, age 31, single, residence Boston, credited to Medfield, born in Ireland. Mustered in Feb 17, 1864, term 3 years. Transferred to 32d Mass. Vols June 10, 1864.

Weimer, Conrad, enlisted Aug. 2, 1862, trader, age 21, single, residence Boston Mustered in Aug 2, 1862, term 3 years. Killed accidentally on the cars near Baltimore, Md., June 13, 1864.

Weimer, Rudolph, enlisted Aug. 5, 1862, shoemaker, age 44, married, residence Boston, born in Germany. Mustered in Aug. 5, 1862, term 3 years. Discharged Oct. 2, 1862.

Welch, Patrick 1st, enlisted Aug. 2, 1862, laborer, age 19, single, residence Boston, credited to Boston, Wd. 1, born in Boston. Mustered in Aug. 2, 1862, term 3 years Re-enlisted Dec. 31, 1863. Transferred to 32d Mass. Vols. June 9, 1864.

White, Stephen, enlisted June 11, 1861, seaman, age 20, single, residence New York, born in New York City. Mustered in June 11, 1861, term 3 years. Died of disease Jan. 14, 1863.

Young, Nicholas, enlisted Aug. 20, 1862, laborer, age 18, single, residence Lawrence, born in Ireland. Mustered in Aug. 20, 1862, term 3 years. Mustered out June 21, 1864.

COMPANY E..

Teague, John R., Capt., salesman, age 42, married, residence Boston, born in Salem, Mass. Mustered in June 11, 1861, term 3 years. Discharged Jan. 28, 1862.

Macnamara, Michael H., 1st Lieut., student, age 23, single, residence Boston, born in Boston. Mustered in June 11, 1861, term 3 years. Dismissed Sept. 1, 1861. Rejoined the regiment as a recruit in Co. C. (Which see.)

Lee, Timothy F., 2d Lieut., residence Boston, born in Ireland. Mustered in June 11, 1861, term 3 years Dismissed Nov. 2, 1861.

Macnamara, Daniel G., 1st Sergt., enlisted June 11, 1861, bookkeeper, age 21, single, residence Boston, born in Boston. Mustered in June 11, 1861, term 3 years. Appointed Commissary Sergt., March 10, 1862. Acting Lieut., July 2, 1862. Commissioned 2d Lieut., Sept. 26, 1862. Commissioned 1st Lieut., Aug. 27, 1862. Quartermaster, March 30, 1863. Mustered out June 21, 1864.

Macnamara, James W., Sergt., enlisted June 11, 1861, printer, age 25, single, residence Boston, born in Boston. Mustered in June 11, 1861, term 3 years. Promoted 1st Sergt. Co. I, Oct. 25, 1861, 2d Lieut. Oct. 20, 1862, 1st Lieut., Oct. 21, 1862, Capt. Aug. 4, 1863. Wounded June 27, 1862, Gaines' Mill, Va. Killed May 5, 1864, Wilderness, Va.

Mahler, Anthony, Sergt., enlisted June 11, 1861, brass finisher, age 32, married, residence Boston, born in Strasburg, France. Mustered in June 11, 1861, term 3 years. Mustered out June 21, 1864.

Ford, Daniel, Sergt., enlisted June 11, 1861, laborer, age 25, single, residence Cambridge, born in Ireland. Mustered in June 11, 1861, term 3 years. Wounded at Gaines' Mill, Va., June 27, 1862. Discharged for disability Feb. 27, 1863, Philadelphia, Pa.

Fogarty, William, Sergt., enlisted June 11, 1861, tailor, age 32, married, residence Brooklyn, N.Y, born in Ireland. Mustered in June 11, 1861, term 3 years Discharged Sept. 1, 1862, order War Dept.

McMullan, James, Corp., enlisted June 11, 1861, carpenter, age 24, single, residence Roxbury, born in Boston, Mass. Mustered in June 11, 1861, term 3 years. Promoted 1st Sergt. from Sergt., April 23, 1864. Mustered out June 21, 1864, as 1st Sergt.

Fuge, William H., Corp., enlisted June 11, 1861, farmer, age 38, married, residence Boston, born in Waterford, Ireland. Mustered in June 11, 1861, term 3 years. Discharged for disability Nov 19, 1862, at Warrington, Va. (Discharged as " Frye," right name Fuge.)

Lynn, Mathew, Corp., enlisted June 11, 1861, sailor, age 30, married, residence Salem, born in Dublin, Ire. Mustered in June 11, 1861, term 3 years. Discharged, to date Feb. 24, 1863.

Kelleher, Patrick, Corp., enlisted June 11, 1861, laborer, age 26, single, residence Boston, born in Ireland. Mustered in June 11, 1861, term 3 years. Deserted Feb. 27, 1863, Falmouth, Va.

O'Connor, Patrick, Corp., enlisted June 11, 1861, cooper, age 32, married, residence Boston. Mustered in June 11, 1861, term 3 years. Wounded July 1, 1862, Malvern Hill, Va. Transferred to V.R.C. Sept. 15, 1863.

Smith, Joseph, Corp., enlisted June 11, 1861, morocco dresser, age 37, married, residence Boston, born in Philadelphia, Pa. Mustered in June 11, 1861, term 3 years. Died of wounds received at Gaines' Mill, Va., June 29, 1862, as " Joseph F. Smyth," Savage's Station, Va.

Sullivan, John, Corp., enlisted June 11, 1861, tinner, age 22, single, residence Springfield, born in Springfield, Mo. Mustered in June 11, 1861, term 3 years. Wounded June 27, 1862, at Gaines' Mill, Va. Discharged for disability, Dec. 20, 1862, Fairfax Ferry, Va.

Roas, Henry, Corp., enlisted June 11, 1861, tinsmith, age 21, single, residence Boston, born in Detroit, Mich. Mustered in June 11, 1861, term 3 years. Died of wounds, Aug. 18, 1862, received either at Gaines' Mill or Malvern Hill, Va.

McPoland, Bernard, Musician, enlisted June 11, 1861, hostler, age 19, single, residence Lawrence, born in Charlestown, Mass. Mustered in June 11, 1861, term 3 years. Deserted Aug. 16, 1862, Harrison Landing, Va.

Powers, Benjamin, Musician, enlisted June 11, 1861, drummer, age 29, single, residence Boston, born in Boston, Mass. Mustered in June 11, 1861, term 3 years. Discharged as Private in Co. A for disability, Oct. 22, 1862, Sharpsburg, Md.

Denny, Edward, Wagoner, enlisted June 11, 1861, silver-plater, age 22, married. residence South Boston. Mustered in June 11, 1861, term 3 years, Wounded July 1, 1862, at Malvern Hill, Va. Discharged for disability Sept. 25, 1862.

Ash, Francis, enlisted June 11, 1861, cigarmaker, age 19, single, residence Springfield, born in Milltown, Ire. Mustered in June 11, 1861, term 3 years. Wounded May 12, 1864, at Spottsylvania, Va. Mustered out at Boston, Mass., as Private, Sept. 22, 1864.

Bannon, John, enlisted Aug. 8, 1862, tailor, age 36, married, residence Boston, born in Ireland. Mustered in Aug. 8, 1862, term 3 years. Mustered out June 21, 1864.

Barker, James, enlisted June 11, 1861, shoemaker, age 25, married, residence East Abington, born in Montreal, Can. Mustered in June 11, 1861, term 3 years. Discharged for disability Oct 25, 1861, Arlington, Va.

Barry, Patrick, enlisted Aug. 14, 1862, teamster, age 19 , single, residence Boston born in Boston, Mass. Mustered in Aug. 14, 1862, term 3 years. Wounded May 12, 1864, Spottsylvania, Va. Mustered out June 21, 1864.

Blakeney, James H., enlisted July 31, 1862, carpenter, age 23, single, residence Boston. Mustered in July 31, 1862, term 3 years. Mustered out June 21, 1864, as Sergeant.

Blood, William J., enlisted Aug. 14, 1862, trader, age 33, single, residence Boston, born in Galway, Ire. Mustered in Aug. 14, 1862, term 3 years. Promoted 2d Lieut. Sept. 26, 1862, and transferred to Co. G. Resigned Aug. 14, 1863.

Bloomis, William, enlisted June 11, 1861, soldier, age 40, married, residence Boston, born in Petersburg, Russia. Mustered in June 11, 1861, term 3 years. Wounded at Malvern Hill, Va., July 1, 1862. Discharged for disability Sept. 1, 1863, Philadelphia, Pa.

Boyle, Peter, enlisted June 11, 1861, laborer, age 37, single, residence Lynn, born in Ireland. Mustered in June 11, 1861, term 3 years. Wounded at Gaines' Mill, June 27, 1862. Discharged for disability Oct. 4, 1862, Baltimore, Md.

Boylan, Patrick, enlisted June 11, 1861, shoemaker, age 22, single, residence Marlboro, born in Ireland. Mustered in June 11, 1861, term 3 years. Wounded at Malvern Hill, July 1, 1862. Died of wounds July 13, 1862, Washington, D.C.

Brady, Patrick R., enlisted Feb. 22, 1864, currier, age 24, married, residence Salem, credited to Salem, Wd. 5. Mustered in Feb. 22, 1864, term 3 years. Transferred to 32d Mass. Vols. June 9, 1864.

Breed, Xenophon, enlisted Nov. 11, 1861, clerk, age 20, single, residence New York. Mustered in Nov. 11, 1861, term 3 years. Deserted April 10, 1862, Hampton Roads, Va.

Breen, John, enlisted Sept. 3, 1862, laborer, age 30, single, residence Boston, born in New York city. Mustered in Sept. 3, 1862, term 3 years. Slightly wounded May 10, 1864, at Po River, Va. Wounded June 3, 1864, at Bethesda Church, Va. Mustered out June 21, 1864.

Brenn, John, enlisted Aug. 23, 1862, teamster, age 25, married, residence Boston, born in Ireland. Mustered in Aug. 23, 1862, term 3 years. Wounded June 3, 1864, at Bethesda Church, Va. Mustered out June 21, 1864, as Corp. " Breen."

Buckley, Daniel, enlisted June 11, 1861, shoemaker, age 18, single, residence North Danvers, born in Cork, Ire. Mustered in June 11, 1861, term 3 years. Wounded at Gaines' Mill, June 27, 1862; Wilderness, Va., May 5, 1864; Bethesda Church, Va., June 3, 1864. Mustered out June 21, 1864.

Burns, Patrick, enlisted June 11, 1861, teamster, age 21, single, residence Roxbury, born in Longford, Ire. Mustered in June 11, 1861, term 3 years. Deserted Sept. 14, 1863, Falmouth, Va.

Bush, Richard, enlisted June 11, 1861, laborer, age 32, married, residence South Danvers, born in Cork, Ire. Mustered in June 11, 1861, term 3 years. Mustered out June 21, 1864.

Butler, Walter, enlisted June 11, 1861, laborer, age 22, single, residence Beverly, born in Ireland. Mustered in June 11, 1861, term 3 years. Died of disease at Gaines' Mill, Va., June 15, 1862.

Butcher, James, enlisted July 16, 1863, sailor, age 21, single, residence Springfield, credited to Springfield. Mustered in July 16, 1863, term 3 years. Wounded May 5, 1864, Wilderness, Va. Transferred to 32d Mass. Vols. June 9, 1864.

Cahill, Timothy, enlisted June 11, 1861, trunkmaker, age 18, single, residence Milford, born in Ireland. Mustered in June 11, 1861, term 3 years. Killed June 27, 1862, Gaines' Mill, Va.

Carney, Daniel, enlisted June 11, 1861, laborer, age 28, married, residence Boston, born in Ireland. Mustered in June 11, 1861, term 3 years. Wounded May 5, 1864, Wilderness, Va. Absent in hospital.

Carter, Thomas, enlisted June 11, 1861, currier, age 20, single, residence Roxbury, born in Galway, Ire. Mustered in June 11, 1861, term 3 years. Wounded June 3, 1864, at Bethesda Church, Va. Mustered out June 21, 1864, as Corp.

Carr, Joseph, enlisted Nov. 9, 1861, factory man, age 18, single, residence Lowell. Mustered in Nov. 9, 1861, term 3 years. Transferred to 32d Mass. Vols. June 9, 1864.

Carroll, John, enlisted June 11, 1861, laborer, age 25, single, residence East Abington, born in Ireland. Mustered in June 11, 1861, term 3 years. Discharged for disability Dec. 27, 1862, Washington, D.C.

Cassidy, John, enlisted June 11, 1861, laborer, age 25, single, residence Boston, born in Ireland. Mustered in June 11, 1861, term 3 years. Discharged for disability Feb. 5, 1863, Alexandria, Va.

Cluna, Michael, enlisted June 11, 1861, laborer, age 37, married, residence Boston, born in Clare, Ire. Mustered in June 11, 1861, term 3 years. Mustered out June 21, 1864.

Coburn, John, enlisted Aug. 21, 1863, lumberman, age 21, single, residence Lawrence, credited to Waltham. Mustered in Aug. 21, 1863, term 3 years. Deserted March 5, 1864, Bealton, Va.

Coffee, Jeremiah, enlisted June 11, 1861, bootmaker, age 22, single, residence Holliston, born in Kerry, Ire. Mustered in June 11, 1861, term 3 years. Wounded at Malvern Hill, Va., July 1, 1862. Discharged to date July 14, 1863.

Collins, Edward, enlisted June 11, 1861, varnisher, age 21, single, residence Boston, born in Ireland. Mustered in June 11, 1861, term 3 years. Wounded at Emmarts Farm, July, 1861. Died of wounds Nov. 28, 1861, Annapolis, Md.

Colton, Patrick, enlisted April 17, 1864, age 29. Mustered in April 17, 1864, term 3 years. Transferred to 32d Mass. Vols. June 9, 1864.

Conklin, Henry, enlisted Aug. 18, 1863, clerk, age 25, single, residence Boston, credited to North Hampton. Mustered in Aug. 18, 1863, term 3 years. Deserted Sept. 18, 1863, Beverly Ford, Va.

Connors, Thomas J., enlisted July 15, 1864, baker, age 19, single, residence Ireland, credited to Dennis, born in Ireland. Mustered in July 15, 1864, term 3 years. Transferred to 32d Mass. Vols. June 9, 1864.

Connors, Terrence, enlisted June 11, 1861, laborer, age 25, single, residence East Boston, born in Cork, Ire. Mustered in June 11, 1861, term 3 years. Wounded at Gaines' Mill, June 27, 1862. Mustered out June 21, 1864.

Connor, Thomas, enlisted Aug 20, 1863, laborer, age 20, single, residence New York, credited to Gloucester. Mustered in Aug. 20, 1863, term 3 years. Deserted April 7, 1864, Bealton, Va.

Conway, Bernard, enlisted June 11, 1861, shoemaker, age 24, married, residence East Cambridge, born in Ireland. Mustered in June 11, 1861, term 3 years. Wounded May 5, 1864, Wilderness, Va. Absent in hospital. Died July 29, 1864, hospital, Philadelphia, Pa.

Condon, James, enlisted June 11, 1861, shoemaker, age 20, single, residence East Abington, born in Cork, Ire. Mustered in June 11, 1861, term 3 years. Killed June 27, 1862, Gaines' Mill, Va.

Condon, Richard, enlisted June 11, 1861, glassblower, age 18, single, residence Cambridgeport, born in Ireland. Mustered in June 11, 1861, term 3 years. Killed May 5, 1864, Wilderness, Va., as Corp.

Crahan, Owen, enlisted June 11, 1861, laborer, age 19, single, residence Roxbury, born in Galway, Ire. Mustered in June 11, 1861, term 3 years. Wounded at Gaines' Mill, Va., June 27, 1862. Deserted Sept 14, 1863, Falmouth, Va.

Creeley, William, enlisted Nov. 18, 1863, mason, age 21, single, residence Boston, credited to Melrose, born in Ireland. Mustered in Nov. 18, 1863, term 3 years. Transferred to 32d Mass. Vols., June 9, 1864.

Cronin, Jeremiah, enlisted June 11, 1861, baker, age 22, single, residence Boston, born in Queenstown, Ire. Mustered in June 11, 1861, term 3 years. Discharged for disability October, 1861, Miner's Hill, Va.

Dady, Thomas, enlisted July 24, 1862, mason, age 42, married, residence Somerville, born in Ireland. Mustered in July 24, 1862, term 3 years. Wounded May 12, 1864, at Spottsylvania, Va. Mustered out June 21, 1864.

Daveron, Michael, enlisted June 11, 1861, bootmaker, age 26, single, residence Quincy, born in Galway, Ire. Mustered in June 11, 1861, term 3 years. Mustered out June 21, 1864.

Denney, John, enlisted June 11, 1861, seaman, age 29, single, residence Boston, born in Londonderry, Ire. Mustered in June 11, 1861, term 3 years. Wounded at Malvern Hill, Va., July 1, 1862. Deserted Aug. 14, 1862, Harrison Landing, Va.

Devine, John, enlisted June 11, 1861, tailor, age 32, single, residence East Boston. Mustered in June 11, 1861, term 3 years. Discharged for disability Dec. 23, 1861 (S. Crit.).

Dolan, Patrick, enlisted June 11, 1861, currier, age 32, married, residence Charlestown, born in Ireland. Mustered in June 11, 1861, term 3 years. Discharged for disability March 5, 1863, Miner's Hill, Va.

Doherty, George F., enlisted June 11, 1861, currier, age 26, single, residence Boston, born in Donegal, Ire. Mustered in June 11, 1861, term 3 years. Wounded May 12, 1864, at Spottsylvania, Va. Absent in hospital.

Doherty, Patrick, enlisted June 11, 1861, tailor, age 41, married, residence East Boston. Mustered in June 11, 1861, term 3 years. Mustered out June 21, 1864.

Danahy, John, enlisted June 11, 1861, shoemaker, age 18, single, residence Boston, born in Waterville, Ire. Mustered in June 11, 1861, term 3 years. Wounded June 27, 1862, Gaines' Mill, Va.; wounded May 5, 1864, Wilderness, Va. Mustered out June 21, 1864, as Corp.

Donavan, John, enlisted June 11, 1861, bootmaker, age 18, single, residence East Abington, born in Ireland. Mustered in June 11, 1861, term 3 years. No further record, A.G O., Mass.

Dorrington, Hugh, enlisted June 11, 1861, teamster, age 33, married, residence East Cambridge, born in Londonderry, Ire. Mustered in June 11, 1861, term 3 years. Mustered out June 21, 1864.

Durkin, Patrick, enlisted July 30, 1862, laborer, age 40, married, residence Boston, born in Ireland. Mustered in July 30, 1862, term 3 years Discharged for disability Dec. 29, 1863, Alexandria, Va.

Dwyer, Patrick, enlisted Aug. 18, 1862, tailor, age 28, married, residence Boston, born in Ireland. Mustered in Aug. 18, 1862, term 3 years. Discharged for disability Jan. 21, 1863, Annapolis.

Enright, Michael, enlisted June 11, 1861, bootmaker, age 37, single, residence Quincy, born in Halifax, N.S. Mustered in June 11, 1861, term 3 years. Died of disease Jan. 11, 1863, Washington, D.C.

Farmer, Charles, enlisted June 11, 1861, laborer, age 33, single, residence Chelsea, born in Ireland. Mustered in June 11, 1861, term 3 years. Promoted from Private to Sergt. May 12, 1864. Mustered out June 21, 1864, as Sergt.

Fenton, Michael, enlisted June 11, 1861, shoemaker, age 35, married, residence Quincy, born in Halifax, N.S. Mustered in June 11, 1861, term 3 years. Transferred to Co. D, 17th Mass. Vols.

Fitzgerald, Michael, enlisted June 11, 1861, bootmaker, age 23, single, residence Boston, born in St. Johns, N.B. Mustered in June 11, 1861, term 3 years. Killed June 27, 1862, Gaines' Mill, Va.

Frost, John, enlisted Aug. 18, 1863, painter, age 29, single, residence Brooklyn, N.Y., credited to Gardner. Mustered in Aug. 18, 1863, term 3 years. Deserted as "James Frost" April 16, 1864, Bealton Station, Va.

Gaffney, Patrick, enlisted June 11, 1861, laborer, age 40, married, residence Medford, born in Mucklin, N.B. Mustered in June 11, 1861, term 3 years. Discharged for disability Jan. 11, 1863, Falmouth, Va.

Gallagher, John, enlisted June 11, 1861, tailor, age 19, single, residence Boston, born in England. Mustered in June 11, 1861, term 3 years. Discharged for disability March 18, 1863, Point Lookout, Md.

Gallagher, Owen, enlisted June 11, 1861, bootmaker, age 22, single, residence Milford, born in Ireland. Mustered in June 11, 1861, term 3 years. Killed July 1, 1862, Malvern Hill, as Corp.

Garland, Owen W., enlisted June 11, 1861, farmer, age 19, single, residence Lowell, born in Ireland. Mustered in June 11, 1861, term 3 years. Drowned June 28, 1861, in Potomac River, Va.

Gordon, George, enlisted Aug. 20, 1863, laborer, age 25, single, residence New York, credited to Fall River. Mustered in Aug. 20, 1863, term 3 years. Transferred to 32d Mass. Vols. June 9, 1864, as Corp.

Grimes, Michael, enlisted Aug 22, 1862, blacksmith, age 18, single, residence Chelsea, born in Boston, Mass. Mustered in Aug. 22, 1862, term 3 years. Absent sick. Returned to duty from hospital June 17, 1863. No further information.

Halleran, John, enlisted June 11, 1861, laborer, age 19, single, residence Lowell, born in Co. Cork, Ire. Mustered in June 11, 1861, term 3 years. Wounded June 27, 1862, Gaines' Mill, Va.; wounded May 5, 1864, Wilderness, Va. As Corp., absent sick.

Hayes, Charles, enlisted June 11, 1861, currier, age 23, single, residence Woburn, born in Cork, Ire. Mustered in June 11, 1861, term 3 years. Wounded July 1, 1862, at Malvern Hill, Va. Discharged for disability Jan. 31, 1863, Providence, R.I.

Hennessy, Thomas, enlisted June 11, 1861, laborer, age 30, single, residence South Boston, born in Cork, Ire. Mustered in June 11, 1861, term 3 years. Discharged for disability Aug. 30, 1862, Philadelphia, Pa.

Hewitt, Francis, enlisted Aug. 20, 1863, sailor, age 28, single, residence New York, credited to Marblehead. Mustered in Aug. 20, 1863, term 3 years. Wounded May 5, 1864, Wilderness, Va. Transferred to 32d Mass. Vols. June 9, 1864.

Herrin, Michael, enlisted June 11, 1861, laborer, age 19, single, residence Boston, born in Waterford, Ire. Mustered in June 11, 1861, term 3 years. No further record, A.G.O.

Herrin, Patrick, enlisted June 11, 1861, shoemaker, age 25, married, residence Manchester, born in Galway, Ire. Mustered in June 11, 1861, term 3 years. Mustered out June 21, 1864.

Hill, William, enlisted July 16, 1863, sailor, age 27, single, residence New York, credited to Springfield. Mustered in July 16, 1863, term 3 years. Deserted April 16, 1864, Bealton Station, Va.

Horan, Michael, enlisted June 11, 1861, laborer, age 23, single, residence North Bridgewater, born in Ireland. Mustered in June 11, 1861, term 3 years. Died of wounds June 29, 1862, Savage's Station, Va.

Horrigan, Timothy, enlisted June 11, 1861, teamster, age 20, single, residence Boston, born in Ireland. Mustered in June 11, 1861, term 3 years. Wounded June 27, 1862, at Gaines' Mill, Va Discharged for disability, Nov. 17, 1862, Martinsville, Va.

Hunt, Peter, enlisted Aug. 1, 1862, boxmaker, age 45, married, residence Boston, born in Boston, Mass. Mustered in Aug. 1, 1862, term 3 years. Transferred to V.R.C. July 1, 1863.

Irish, Patrick, enlisted July 31, 1862, laborer, age 42, married, residence Boston, born in Ireland. Mustered in July 31, 1862, term 3 years Deserted Nov. 21, 1863, Beverly Ford, Va., and died in Richmond, March 3, 1864.

Ivers, Daniel, enlisted June 11, 1861, tailor, age 26, single, residence Boston, born in Ireland. Mustered in June 11, 1861, term 3 years. Mustered out June 21, 1864, as Corp.

Ivers, Thomas, enlisted June 11, 1861, soldier, age 33, married, residence Boston, born in Dublin, Ire. Mustered in June 11, 1861, term 3 years. Promoted Sergt. Captured at Miner's Hill, Va, Sept. 5, 1861. Discharged by order of Secretary of War, Sept. 1, 1862.

31

Jenkins, Martin, enlisted June 11, 1861, bootmaker, age 25, single, residence Milford, born in Galway, Ire. Mustered in June 11, 1861, term 3 years. Promoted to Sergt. Mustered out June 21, 1864, as Sergt.

Kane, Michael, enlisted June 11, 1861, bootmaker, age 25, single, residence Marlboro, born in Ireland. Mustered in June 11, 1861, term 3 years. Deserted Feb. 24, 1863, Falmouth.

Keating, John, enlisted, June 11, 1861, bootmaker, age 22, single, residence Malden, born in Ireland. Mustered in June 11, 1861, term 3 years. Wounded May 10, 1864, at Po River, Va. Mustered out June 21, 1864, as Corp.

Kelly, Michael, enlisted Aug. 12, 1862, laborer, age 29, married, residence Boston, born in Ireland. Mustered in Aug. 12, 1862, term 3 years. Discharged for disability Oct. 13, 1862, Sharpsburg, Va.

Kelly, Francis, enlisted June 11, 1861, laborer, age 33, single, residence Roxbury, born in Kilkenny, Ire. Mustered in June 11, 1861, term 3 years. Wounded July 1, 1862, at Malvern Hill, Va.; at Gettysburg, Va., July 3, 1863; June 3, 1864, at Bethesda Church, Va. Mustered out June 21, 1864.

Kinneally, David, enlisted Aug. 6, 1862, liquor dealer, age 33, married, residence Salem, born in Ireland. Mustered in Aug 6, 1862, term 3 years. Discharged May 5, 1865 (telegram from War Department).

Lambert, Joseph, enlisted June 11, 1861, hostler, age 21, married, residence Boston, born in Three Rivers, Can. Mustered in June 11, 1861, term 3 years. Killed June 27, 1862, Gaines' Mill, Va.

Lynch, Henry, enlisted June 11, 1861, tailor, age 30, single, residence Boston, born in Cork, Ire. Mustered in June 11, 1861, term 3 years. Discharged for disability Aug. 19, 1861, Arlington, Va.

Lynch, Martin, enlisted Aug. 21, 1862, tailor, age 43, married, residence Charlestown, born in Ireland. Mustered in Aug. 21, 1862, term 3 years. Wounded Dec. 13, 1862, Fredericksburg, Va. Died of wounds Dec. 31, 1863, Washington, D.C.

Lynch, Michael, enlisted Aug. 8, 1862, shoemaker, age 20, single, residence Marlboro. Mustered in Aug. 8, 1862, term 3 years. Died of wounds Dec. 31, 1862, at Washington, D.C.

Maher, Jeremiah, enlisted Aug 8, 1862, laborer, age 30, married, residence Boston, born in Ireland. Mustered in Aug 8, 1862, term 3 years. Discharged for disability March 25, 1863, Providence, R.I.

Malcolm, James, enlisted June 11, 1861, laborer, age 18, single, residence Pittsfield, born in Stephentown, N.Y. Mustered in June 11, 1861, term 3 years. Accidentally wounded at Emmarts Farm, July, 1861. Mustered out June 21, 1864.

Mann, John A., enlisted June 11, 1862, teamster, age 22, married, residence Boston, born in Boston. Mustered in June 11, 1862, term 3 years. Discharged for disability Feb. 14, 1863, Falmouth, Va.

Marrin, Thomas, enlisted June 11, 1861, teamster, age 25, married, residence Cambridgeport, born in Ireland. Mustered in June 11, 1861, term 3 years. Killed June 27, 1862, Gaines' Mill, Va.

McCann, Daniel, enlisted July 25, 1862, laborer, age 40, married, residence Boston, born in Ireland. Mustered in July 25, 1862, term 3 years. Discharged by order of General Morris, Nov. 20, 1862, Ft. McHenry, Md.

McDavitt, John, enlisted June 11, 1861, blacksmith, age 38, married, residence Boston, born in Ireland. Mustered in June 11, 1861, term 3 years. Transferred to V.R.C. April 9, 1864.

McGavisk, Thomas, enlisted June 11, 1861, laborer, age 29, single. residence Boston, born in Ireland. Mustered in June 11, 1861, term 3 years. Wounded June 27, 1862, Gaines' Mill, Va. Discharged for disability, Nov. 22, 1862, Philadelphia.

McKenner, Patrick, enlisted June 11, 1861, laborer, age 23, single, residence Providence, R.I., born in Cavan, Ire. Mustered in June 11, 1861, term 3 years. Discharged for disability, March 7, 1862, Miner's Hill, Va.

McLaughlin, Michael, enlisted Aug. 5, 1862, tailor, age 38, married, residence Boston, born in Ireland. Mustered in Aug. 5, 1862, term 3 years. Mustered out June 21, 1864.

Monahan, Bernard, enlisted June 11, 1861, bootmaker, age 26, single, residence Milford, born in Ireland. Mustered in June 11, 1861, term 3 years. Wounded June 27, 1862, Gaines' Mill, Va. Transferred to V.R.C. Aug. 1, 1863.

Morrison, John, enlisted June 11, 1861, house painter, age 26, married, residence New York, born in Ireland. Mustered in June 11, 1861, term 3 years. Mustered out June 21, 1864, as absent sick.

Moore, Richard, enlisted Aug. 1, 1862, laborer, age 34, residence Boston, born in Ireland. Mustered in Aug. 1, 1862, term 3 years. Was captured; released Aug. 12, 1864. Mustered out Oct. 10, 1864.

Mulroy, John, enlisted June 11, 1861, bookkeeper, age 21, single, residence Dublin, born in Dublin, Ire. Mustered in June 11, 1861, term 3 years. Captured at Yorktown, Va., April 6, 1861. Discharged Sept. 1, 1862, by order Secretary of War.

Mullen, Robert, enlisted Dec. 18, 1863, laborer, age 32, married, residence Cambridge, credited to Cambridge, born in Ireland. Mustered in Dec. 18, 1863, term 3 years. Transferred to 32d Mass. Vols. June 9, 1864.

Mullen, Robert, enlisted June 11, 1861, laborer, age 32, married, residence East Cambridge, born in Londonderry, Ire. Mustered in June 11, 1861, term 3 years. Discharged for disability March 19, 1863, Falmouth, Va.

Mullivan, Patrick, enlisted June 11, 1861, shoemaker, age 18, single, residence Lynn, born in Clare, Ire. Mustered in June 11, 1861, term 3 years. Mustered out June 21, 1864.

Mullooney, James, enlisted Aug. 20, 1863, laborer, age 19, single, residence Amesbury Mills, credited to Salisbury. Mustered in Aug 20, 1863, term 3 years. Killed May 5, 1864, at Wilderness.

Murphy, Thomas, enlisted June 11, 1861, boilermaker, age 20, single, residence Milford, born in Ireland. Mustered in June 11, 1861, term 3 years. Killed May 5, 1864, Wilderness, Va.

Neary, Patrick, enlisted June 11, 1861, age 22, residence Boston. Mustered in June 11, 1861, term 3 years. Discharged for disability Sept. 29, 1862, Washington, D C.

Newell, John B., enlisted July 24, 1862, printer, age 20, single, residence Boston, born in Massachusetts. Mustered in July 24, 1862, term 3 years. Killed May 12, 1864, at Spottsylvania, Va., as Sergt.

Nole, James P., enlisted Aug. 20, 1863, laborer, age 18, single, residence Philadelphia, credited to Quincy. Mustered in Aug. 20, 1863, term 3 years. Killed May 12, 1864, at Spottsylvania, Va.

Norton, Michael, enlisted June 11, 1861, marble-worker, age 19, single, residence Boston, born in Ireland. Mustered in June 11, 1861, term 3 years. Mustered out June 21, 1864.

O'Brien, James, enlisted Aug. 18, 1863, laborer, age 22, single, residence Boston, credited to Hatfield. Mustered in Aug. 18, 1863, term 3 years. Deserted Sept. 13, 1863, Beverly Ford, Va.

O'Callahan, Eugene, laborer, age 44, married, residence Salem. Mustered in Aug. 18, 1862, term 3 years. Absent sick.

O'Connor, Daniel, enlisted Nov. 19, 1863, laborer, age 35, single, residence East Boston, credited to Malden, born in Ireland. Mustered in Nov. 19, 1863, term 3 years. Wounded May 5, 1864, Wilderness, Va. Transferred to 32d Mass. Vols., June 9, 1864.

O'Connor, Patrick, enlisted June 11, 1861, cooper, age 32, married, residence Boston. Mustered in June 11, 1861, term 3 years. Wounded July 1, 1862, Malvern Hill, Va. Transferred to V.R.C. Sept 15, 1863.

O'Neil, John, enlisted Dec. 22, 1863, laborer, age 19, single, residence Boston, credited to Boston, Wd 7, born in Derry, Ire. Mustered in Dec. 22, 1863, term 3 years. Transferred to 32d Mass. Vols., June 9, 1864.

Punch, John, enlisted Aug. 21, 1862, laborer, age 35, married, residence Boston, born in Ireland. Mustered in Aug. 21, 1862, term 3 years. Mustered out June 21, 1864.

Quigley, Martin, enlisted Aug. 1, 1862, boilermaker, age 40, married, residence East Boston, born in Ireland. Mustered in Aug. 1, 1862, term 3 years. Mustered out June 21, 1864.

Quinlan, Thomas, enlisted Aug. 15, 1862, laborer, age 30, married, residence Salem or Boston, born in Ireland. Mustered in Aug. 15, 1862, term 3 years. Discharged for disability Dec. 18, 1862, Washington, D.C.

Redmond, Phillip E., enlisted Aug. 14, 1862, currier, age 25, married, residence Salem, born in Salem. Mustered in Aug. 14, 1862, term 3 years. Promoted 2d Lieut , June 6, 1863, and transferred to Co. K. Wounded at Chancellorsville, May 3, 1863. Died in Washington, D.C., Sept. 17, 1863. See Co. F.

Regan, Mathew, enlisted June 11, 1861, laborer, age 29, married, residence Boston, born in Cork, Ire. Mustered in June 11, 1861, term 3 years. Wounded July 1, 1862, at Malvern Hill, Va. Discharged by order of General Wadsworth, Aug. 7, 1862, Washington, D.C.

Regan, Timothy, enlisted June 11, 1861, mason, age 22, single, residence Boston, born in Cork, Ire. Mustered in June 11, 1861, term 3 years. Wounded June 27, 1862, Gaines' Mill, Va. Mustered out June 21, 1864.

Roach, Thomas, enlisted Aug. 20, 1863, laborer, age 21, single, residence New York, credited to New Bedford. Mustered in Aug. 20, 1863, term 3 years. Deserted Sept. 8, 1863, Beverly Ford, Va.

Robinson, James, enlisted Dec. 29, 1863, sailor, age 25, single, residence Pembroke, Me. Credited to Boston, Ward 12, born in Dublin, Ire. Mustered in Dec 29, 1863, term 3 years. Wounded May 5, 1864, Wilderness, Va. Transferred to 32d Mass. Vols. June 9, 1864, as " Robson."

Rourke, Dennis, enlisted June 11, 1861, currier, age 23, single, residence Lowell, born in Cork, Ire. Mustered in June 11, 1861, term 3 years. Died of disease Sept. 6, 1862, Washington, D.C.

Rooney, Thomas, enlisted June 11, 1861, tailor, age 26, married, residence Boston, born in Ireland. Mustered in June 11, 1861, term 3 years. Discharged Dec. 13, 1862, Washington, D.C., for disability.

Ryall, William, enlisted Aug. 7, 1862, teamster, age 37, single, residence Boston, born in Charlestown. Mustered in Aug. 7, 1862, term 3 years. Discharged for disability Jan. 21, 1864, Alexandria, Va.

Ryan, Timothy, enlisted June 11, 1861, farmer, age 22, single, residence North Andover, born in Kilkenny, Ire. Mustered in June 11, 1861, term 3 years. Wounded May 5, 1864, Wilderness, Va. Mustered out June 21, 1864, as "Regan."

Scanlan, Thomas, enlisted June 11, 1861, tailor, age 22, single, residence Boston, born in Limerick, Ire. Mustered in June 11, 1861, term 3 years. Transferred to gunboat service, February, 1862.

Smith, Charles D., enlisted Aug. 21, 1863, upholsterer, age 28, married, residence Boston, credited to Ipswich. Mustered in Aug. 21, 1863, term 3 years. Killed May 8, 1864, at Laurel Hill, Va.

Smith, James, enlisted July 16, 1863, sailor, age 22, single, residence New York, credited to Springfield. Mutered in July 16, 1863, term 3 years. Transferred to 32d Mass. Vols. June 9, 1864.

Smith, Samuel, enlisted June 11, 1861, teamster, age 19, single, residence Boston, born in Boston. Mustered in June 11, 1861, term 3 years. Wounded May 5, 1864, Wilderness, Va.; wounded in leg at Hanover Court House, May 27, 1862. Mustered out June 21, 1864, as Corp.

Spellman, John, enlisted June 11, 1861, bootmaker, age 22, single, residence Milford, born in Galway, Ire. Mustered in June 11, 1861, term 3 years. Wounded June 27, 1862, Gaines' Mill, Va. Discharged June 17, 1863, Baltimore, Md.

Spencer, Francis, enlisted June 11, 1861, tailor, age 23, single, residence Boston, born in New York. Mustered in June 11, 1861, term 3 years. Wounded July 1, 1862, as Malvern Hill, Va. Deserted Sept. 18, 1863, Beverly Ford, Va.

Sullivan, Daniel J., enlisted Feb. 2, 1862, carpenter, age 23, single, residence East Boston. Mustered in Feb. 2, 1862, term 3 years. Discharged for disability Feb. 26, 1863, Philadelphia, Pa.

Sullivan, Dennis, enlisted June 11, 1861, laborer, age 25, single, residence East Boston, born in Cork, Ire. Mustered in June 11, 1861, term 3 years. Mustered out June 21, 1864.

Sullivan, James, enlisted Aug. 10, 1863, laborer, age 22, single, residence New Bedford, credited to Westport. Mustered in Aug. 10, 1863, term 3 years. Deserted Sept. 18, 1863, Beverly Ford, Va.

Sullivan, Michael, enlisted June 11, 1861, spinner, age 18, single, residence Lawrence. Mustered in June 11, 1861, term 3 years. Died of wounds June 29, 1862, Savage's Station, Va.

Story, Nathaniel E., enlisted Aug. 20, 1863, seaman, age 25, married, residence Pepperell, credited to Pepperell. Mustered in Aug. 20, 1863, term 3 years. Transferred to 32d Mass. Vols June 9, 1864.

Sullivan, Thomas, enlisted June 11, 1861, slater, age 23, single, residence Boston, born in Miltown, Ire. Mustered in June 11, 1861, term 3 years. Wounded June 27, 1862, Gaines' Mill, Va. Discharged as Corporal, Nov. 17, 1862, Maconsville, Va.

Verricker, William, enlisted June 11, 1861, shoemaker, age 20, single, residence Bridgewater, born in Ireland. Mustered in June 11, 1861, term 3 years. Wounded July 1, 1862, Malvern Hill, Va. Discharged for disability Dec. 11, 1862, Washington, D.C.

Walsh, Edward, enlisted June 11, 1861, baker, age 27, single, residence Boston, born in Boyle, Ire. Mustered in June 11, 1861, term 3 years. Wounded June 27, 1862, Gaines' Mill, Va. Discharged for disability Feb. 4, 1863, Philadelphia, Pa.

Walsh, Patrick, enlisted Aug. 14, 1862, clerk, age 24, residence Boston, born in Cork, Ire. Mustered in Aug. 14, 1862, term 3 years. Mustered out June 21, 1864.

Webber, Louis, enlisted June 11, 1861, farmer, age 27, single, residence Roxbury, born in Germany. Mustered in June 11, 1861, term 3 years. Wounded at Chancellorsville, Va. Transferred to V.R.C., Sept. 1, 1863.

Welsh, James, enlisted June 11, 1861, bootmaker, age 32, single, residence North Milford, born in Waterford, Ire. Mustered in June 11, 1861, term 3 years. Discharged Aug. 3, 1863, Washington, D.C.

White, Thomas L., enlisted Aug. 7, 1862, lawyer, age 23, single, residence Boston, born in St. Johns, N.B. Mustered in Aug. 7, 1862, term 3 years. Wounded Dec. 13, 1862, Fredericksburg, Va. Discharged by order of War Department, Feb. 7, 1863.

Yates, Abram, enlisted Aug. 20, 1863, painter, age 21, married, residence Brooklyn, N.Y., credited to South Danvers. Mustered in Aug. 20, 1863, term 3 years. Deserted Nov. 14, 1863, Bealton Station, Va.

COMPANY F.

Fitzgerald, Edward, Capt., physician, age 35, married, residence Salem, born in Ireland. Mustered in June 11, 1861, term 3 years. Resigned Sept. 6, 1861, Arlington Heights, Va.

O'Leary, Timothy, 1st Lieut., tailor, age 30, married, residence Salem, born in Co. Cork, Ire. Mustered in June 11, 1861, term 3 years. Promoted Capt Sept 7, 1861. Transferred to Co. E April 1, 1864. Wounded May 5, 1864, at Wilderness, Va. Mustered out June 21, 1864, Capt. Co. E.

Redmond, Phillip E., 2d Lieut., currier, age 24, single, residence Salem, born in Salem. Mustered in June 11, 1861, term 3 years. Promoted 1st Lieut. Sept. 7, 1861. Cashiered Feb. 28, 1862. Rejoined the regiment as a recruit in Co. E.

Phalen, Michael, 1st Sergt., enlisted June 11, 1861, tanner, age 21, single, residence Salem, born in Halifax, Ire. Mustered in June 11, 1861, term 3 years. Promoted 2d Lieut. Sept. 7, 1861, 1st Lieut. Jan. 28, 1862, Co. D, Adjt. Aug. 28, 1862. Wounded June 27, 1862, Gaines' Mill, Va.; at Mine Run, Va., Nov. 30, 1863. Mustered out June 21, 1864, as Adjt.

Fallon, Thomas, Sergt., enlisted June 11, 1861, currier, age 25, single, residence Salem, born in Ireland. Mustered in June 11, 1861, term 3 years. Wounded June 27, 1862, Gaines' Mill; May 5, 1864, Wilderness, Va. Mustered out June 21, 1864.

Monaghan, Joseph H., Sergt., enlisted June 11, 1861, painter, age 23, single, residence Salem, credited to Salem, born in Ireland. Mustered in June 11, 1861, term 3 years. Promoted Commissary Sergeant, N.C. Staff. Wounded on picket, no date, 1861, near Arlington Heights. Reenlisted and transferred to 32d Mass. Vols. June 10, 1864.

Murphy, Michael, Sergt., enlisted June 11, 1861, engineer, age 22, married, residence Salem. Mustered in June 11, 1861, term 3 years. Transferred to Co. G.; 1st Sergt. Co. G, Oct. 1 1862. Wounded May 12, 1864, at Spottsylvania, Va. Mustered out June 21, 1864, as 1st Sergt. Co G.

O'Brien, Martin, Sergt., enlisted June 11, 1861, butcher, age 21, single, residence, Salem, born in Ireland. Mustered in June 11, 1861, term, 3 years. Promoted 1st Sergt. Sept. 7, 1861, acting Lieut. July 2, 1862; 2d Lieut. Sept 26, 1862, and transferred to Co. E; commissioned 1st Lieut. Oct. 20, 1863. Transferred to Co. K by reason of promotion to Capt. Oct. 22, 1863. Wounded May 12, 1864, Spottsylvania, Va. Mustered out June 21, 1864, as absent wounded.

Dowdell, Charles, Corp , enlisted June 11, 1861, vender, age 20, single, residence Salem, born in Dublin, Ire. Mustered in June 11, 1861, term 3 years. Mustered out June 21, 1864, as Private.

Hennessy, John, Corp., enlisted June 11, 1861, currier, age 27, married, residence Salem, born in Kilkenny, Ire. Mustered in June 11, 1861, term 3 years. Wounded July 1, 1862, at Malvern Hill, Va. Mustered out June 21, 1864, as Private.

Kelly, Simon P., Corp., enlisted June 11, 1861, butcher, age 20, single, residence Salem, born in Salem, Mass. Mustered in June 11, 1861, term 3 years. Mustered out June 21, 1864, as Private.

Lorigan, John, Corp., enlisted June 11, 1861, farmer, age 25, single, residence Salem, born in Ireland. Mustered in June 11, 1861. term 3 years, Wounded at Gettysburg, July 4, 1863. Mustered out June 21, 1864, as Sergt. "Lorrigan."

Murphy, Joseph, Corp., enlisted June 11, 1861, currier, age 21, single, residence Salem, born in Ireland. Mustered in June 11, 1861, term 3 years. Promoted 1st Sergt. Sept. 26, 1862. Q.-M Sergt., 2d Lieut., April 1, 1863. Transferred to Co. C March 16, 1863. 1st Lieut., Oct 22, 1863. Wounded May 5, 1864, Wilderness, Va. Mustered out June 21, 1864, 1st Lieut. Co. C.

Powers, James, Corp., enlisted June 11, 1861, currier, age 23, single, residence Salem, born in Waterford, Ire. Mustered in June 11, 1861, term 3 years. Killed June 3, 1864, at Bethesda Church, Va.

Ryan, John, Corp., enlisted June 11, 1861, age 26, residence Lowell, born in Dublin, Ire. Mustered in June 11, 1861, term 3 years. Mustered out June 21, 1864.

Timmins, Patrick, Corp., enlisted June 11, 1861, tanner, age 30, residence Salem, born in Kildare, Ire. Mustered in June 11, 1861, term 3 years. Mustered out June 21, 1864.

Walsh, Patrick, Musician, enlisted June 11, 1861, shoemaker, age 26, single, residence Salem, born in Kilkenny, Ire. Mustered in June 11, 1861, term 3 years. Mustered out June 21, 1864.

Barclay, Frank, Musician, enlisted June 11, 1861, seaman, age 25, single, residence Boston, born in Philadelphia, Pa. Mustered in June 11, 1861, term 3 years. Mustered out June 21, 1864.

Doherty, John, Wagoner, enlisted June 11, 1861, currier, age 22, single, residence Salem, born in Boston, Mass. Mustered in June 11, 1861, term 3 years. Promoted 2d Lieut., March 1, 1862. 1st. Lieut. Sept. 26, 1862. Wounded June 27, 1862, Gaines' Mill, Va. Discharged Feb. 12, 1863.

Allen, John, enlisted Aug. 21, 1863, sailor, age 25, single, residence Boston, credited to Wenham. Mustered in Aug. 21, 1863, term 3 years. Deserted Sept. 15, 1863, Beverly Ford, Va.

Anderson, William, enlisted Aug. 21, 1863, sailor, age 30, single, residence Boston, credited to Marblehead. Mustered in Aug. 21, 1863, term 3 years. Deserted August, 1863, Beverly Ford, Va.

Bailey, John, enlisted Aug. 22, 1863, boatman, age 26, single, residence West Vienna, N Y., credited to Ipswich. Mustered in Aug. 22, 1863, term 3 years. Deserted March, 1864, Bealton, Va.

Benjamin, Page, enlisted Aug. 27, 1863, age 21. Mustered in Aug. 27, 1863, term 3 years. Transferred to 32d Mass. Vols. June 10, 1864.

Boyd, Neil, enlisted Aug. 21, 1863, sailor, age 21, single, residence Boston, credited to Ipswich. Mustered in Aug. 21, 1863, term 3 years. Transferred to 32d Mass. Vols. June 10, 1864.

Boyle, Michael W., enlisted June 11, 1861, shoemaker, age 24, single, residence Salem, born in Ireland. Mustered in June 11, 1861, term 3 years. Wounded May 5, 1864, Wilderness, Va. Mustered out June 21, 1864, as 1st Sergt.

Broderick, Dennis, enlisted June 11, 1861, currier, age 30, married, residence Salem, born in Ireland. Mustered in June 11, 1861, term 3 years. Discharged for disability no date, Washington, D.C.

Burke, Charles, enlisted Nov. 9, 1861, servant, age 26, married, residence Boston. Mustered in Nov. 9, 1861, term 3 years. Discharged at Miner's Hill, Va., no date.

Burke, Alick, enlisted June 11, 1861, currier, age 24, single, residence South Danvers, born in Galway, Ire. Mustered in June 11, 1861, term 3 years. Discharged at Sharpsburg, Md., no date.

Burke, John, enlisted Aug. 21, 1863, teamster, age 20, single, residence Albany, N.Y., credited to Carver. Mustered in Aug. 21, 1863, term 3 years. Transferred to Invalid Corps, December, 1863.

Cain, Patrick, enlisted Aug. 13, 1862, laborer, age 18, single, residence Salem, born in Ireland. Mustered in Aug. 13, 1862, term 3 years. Mustered out June 21, 1864.

Callahan, Patrick, enlisted June 11, 1861, laborer, age 36, married, residence Salem, born in Cork, Ire. Mustered in June 11, 1861, term 3 years. Discharged at Sharpsburg, Md., no date.

Carney, Richard, enlisted June 11, 1861, blacksmith, age 24, single, residence Salem, born in Co. Cork, Ire. Mustered in June 11, 1861, term 3 years. Wounded at Malvern Hill, July 1, 1862. Mustered out June 21, 1864, as Corp.

Carey, Hugh, enlisted June 11, 1861, currier, age 21, single, residence Salem, born in Ireland Mustered in June 11, 1861, term 3 years. No record. Failed to elicit further information.

Cary, John, enlisted June 11, 1861, currier, age 24, single, residence Salem, born in Co. Cork, Ire. Mustered in June 11, 1861, term 3 years. Wounded at Malvern Hill, July 1, 1862. Discharged for disability, Miner's Hill, Va., no date.

Cashin, Robert, enlisted June 11, 1861, currier, age 29, married, residence Salem, born in Co. Cork, Ire. Mustered in June 11, 1861, term 3 years. Wounded May 5, 1864, Wilderness, Va. Mustered out June 21, 1864.

Cashin, David, enlisted June 11, 1861, currier, age 24, single, residence Salem, born in Ireland. Mustered in June 11, 1861, term 3 years. Wounded at Chancellorsville, May 2, 1863. Mustered out June 21, 1864, as Corp.

Clynes, John, enlisted June 11, 1861, farmer, age 22, single, residence Salem, born in Co. Galway, Ire. Mustered in June 11, 1861, term 3 years. Wounded at Malvern Hill, Va., July 1, 1862. Discharged for disability, Philadelphia, Pa., no date.

Cochran, Daniel, enlisted June 11, 1861, dresser, age 27, married, residence Salem, born in Ireland. Mustered in June 11, 1861, term 3 years. Discharged at Fort Monroe, no date.

Connor, James, enlisted Feb. 19, 1862, picture framer, age 19, single, residence Boston, born in Boston. Mustered in Feb. 19, 1862, term 3 years. Wounded July 1, 1862, at Malvern Hill, Va.; May 8, 1864, at Laurel Hill, Va. Died at Mt. Pleasant Hospital, Washington, D.C., June 7, 1864.

Connors, William, enlisted Aug. 20, 1863, patternmaker, age 21, single, residence Greenfield, credited to Hadley. Mustered in Aug. 20, 1863, term 3 years. Transferred to 32d Mass. Vols. June 10, 1864.

Connor, Thomas, enlisted Nov. 11, 1861, age 27. Mustered in Nov. 11, 1861, term 3 years. Wounded May 8, 1864, at Laurel Hill, Va. Transferred to V.R.C., no date.

Connor, John, enlisted Nov. 9, 1861, bookbinder, age 21, single, residence Boston. Mustered in Nov. 9, 1861, term 3 years. Transferred to 32d Mass. Vols. June 10, 1864.

Connolly, James, enlisted June 11, 1861, currier, age 25, married, residence Salem, born in Kilkenny, Ire. Mustered in June 11, 1861, term 3 years. Wounded at Malvern Hill, July 1, 1862. Mustered out June 21, 1864.

Coogan, John, enlisted June 11, 1861, painter, age 33, married, residence Salem, born in Cumberland, Eng. Mustered in June 11, 1861, term 3 years. Wounded July 1, 1862, at Malvern Hill, Va. Discharged for disability, Sharpsburg, no date.

Creden, Cornelious, enlisted June 11, 1861, currier, age 20, single, residence Salem, born in Co. Cork, Ire. Mustered in June 11, 1861, term 3 years. Wounded on picket, no date, in 1861; at Chancellorsville, May 2, 1863; at Laurel Hill, May 8, 1864. Mustered out June 21, 1864.

Cullinane, Patrick, enlisted Feb. 4, 1864, shoemaker, age 21, single, residence Boston. Credited to Cambridge, born in Ireland. Mustered in Feb 4, 1864, term 3 years. Wounded May 8, 1864, at Laurel Hill, Va. Transferred to 32d Mass. Vols. June 10, 1864.

Cullerton, Michael, enlisted June 11, 1861, laborer, age 36, married, residence Boston, born in Ireland. Mustered in June 11, 1861, term 3 years. Discharged at Falmouth, Va., no date.

Cunningham, Lawrence, enlisted Aug. 8, 1862, bootmaker, age 22, single, residence Salem, born in Ireland. Mustered in Aug. 8, 1862, term 3 years. Wounded May 12, 1864, at Spottsylvania, Va. Mustered out June 21, 1864.

Cusick, Patrick, enlisted June 11, 1861, currier, age 21, single, residence Salem, born in Ennis, Ire. Mustered in June 11, 1861, term 3 years. Wounded June 27, 1862, at Gaines' Mill, Va., and prisoner. Discharged, Fort Monroe, Va., no date.

Dailey, John 1st, enlisted June 11, '1861, baker, age 30, married, residence Salem, born in Cork, Ire. Mustered in June 11, 1861, term 3 years. Mustered out June 21, 1864.

Daley, John 2d, enlisted June 11, 1861, currier, age 27, married, residence South Danvers, born in Cork, Ire. Mustered in June 11, 1861, term 3 years. Wounded July 1, 1862, at Malvern Hill, Va.; July 4, 1863, at Gettysburg. Mustered out June 21, 1864.

Darcy, Thomas, enlisted June 11, 1861, currier, age 31, married, residence Salem, born in Galway, Ire. Mustered in June 11, 1861, term 3 years. Wounded July 1, 1862, Malvern Hill, Va. Discharged for disability, Sharpsburg, Md., no date.

Day, Eben F., enlisted Aug. 19, 1863, teamster, age 29, married, residence Boston, credited to Boston, Wd. 11. Mustered in Aug. 19, 1863, term 3 years. Prisoner of war since May 12, 1864. Transferred to 32d Mass. Vols. June 10, 1864.

Delany, Daniel, enlisted June 11, 1861, moulder, age 22, single, residence Fitchburg, born in Ireland. Mustered in June 11, 1861, term 3 years. Mustered out June 11, 1864, Wagoner, as "David."

Dempsey, James, enlisted June 11, 1861, age 24, residence Salem. Mustered in June 11, 1861, term 3 years. Wounded on picket, no date, 1861, near Arlington Heights. Mustered out June 21, 1864, as absent sick.

Denin, Michael, enlisted June 11, 1861, shoemaker, age 25, single, residence Lynn, born in Ireland. Mustered in June 11, 1861, term 3 years. Mustered out June 21, 1864.

Densmore, William, enlisted June 11, 1861, stonecutter, age 25, single, residence Westford, born in Ireland. Mustered in June 11, 1861, term 3 years. Wounded July 1, 1862, at Malvern Hill, Va. Absent sick. Wounded May 8, 1864, at Laurel Hill, Va. Died a prisoner in Andersonville, Ga.

Desmond, Dennis, enlisted June 11, 1861, currier, age 25, single, residence Salem, born in Cork, Ire. Mustered in June 11, 1861, term 3 years. Mustered out June 21, 1864.

Dolan, Patrick, enlisted June 11, 1861, currier, age 29, married, residence Salem, born in Co. Galway, Ire. Mustered in June 11, 1861, term 3 years. Wounded July 1, 1862, at Malvern Hill, Va. Discharged at Hampton, Va., for disability Jan. 26, 1863.

Donavan, John, enlisted June 11, 1861, sailor, age 37, single, residence Salem. Mustered in June 11, 1861, term 3 years. Mustered out June 21, 1864.

Doyle, James, enlisted June 11, 1861, servant, age 23, married, residence Boston, born in Co. Cork, Ire. Mustered in June 11, 1861, term 3 years. Discharged for disability, Washington, D.C., no date.

Duff, James, enlisted July 16, 1863, moulder, age 22, single, residence Dover, Me., credited to Springfield. Mustered in July 16, 1863, term 3 years. Deserted March, 1864, Bealton Station, Va.

Duggan, William, enlisted Aug. 8, 1862, laborer, age 42, married, residence Salem. Mustered in Aug. 8, 1862, term 3 years. Mustered out June 21, 1864.

Dunnings, Benjamin, joined regiment at Boston for duty. Transferred to gunboat service at Miner's Hill, no date.

Ensi, William, enlisted July 18, 1863. Mustered in July 18, 1863, term 3 years. Transferred to 32d Mass. Vols June 10, 1864.

Farrell, John, enlisted June 11, 1861, spinner, age 19, single, residence Salem, born in County Cork, Ire. Mustered in June 11, 1861, term 3 years. Discharged for disability Dec. 20, 1861.

Farrell, Robert, enlisted June 11, 1861, age 35. Mustered in June 11, 1861, term 3 years. Killed June 27, 1862, Gaines' Mill, Va.

Fillman, Bernard, enlisted Nov. 9, 1861, filemaker, age 25, single, residence Boston. Mustered in Nov. 9, 1861, term 3 years. Transferred from Co. F to Co. B, no date. Wounded July 1, 1862, Malvern Hill, Va. Deserted June 29, 1863, from Co. B, Frederick City, Md.

Finney, John F., enlisted Feb. 28, 1862, brass finisher, age 19, single, residence Boston. Mustered in Feb. 28, 1862, term 3 years. Wounded at Gaines' Mill, Va., June 27, 1862. Died of wounds, July 6, 1862.

Fitzgerald, John, enlisted Nov. 12, 1862, laborer, age 22, married, residence Salem, credited to Salem, born in Ireland. Mustered in Nov. 12, 1862, term 3 years. Transferred to 32d Mass. Vols. June 10, 1864.

Flaherty, Thomas, enlisted June 11, 1861, laborer, age 25, single, residence Salem, born in Mallow, Ire. Mustered in June 11, 1861, term 3 years. Mustered out June 21, 1864.

Ganley, John H., enlisted June 11, 1861, shoemaker, age 22, single, residence Salem, born in Co. Clare, Ire. Mustered in June 11, 1861, term 3 years. Killed July 1, 1862, at Malvern Hill, Va., as " Granby."

Gannop, John, enlisted June 11, 1861, currier, age 19, single, residence Salem, born in Ireland. Mustered in June 11, 1861, term 3 years. Mustered out June 21, 1864, as " Gunning."

Geigle, Edward, enlisted June 11, 1861, currier, age 24, single, residence Salem, born in Kilkenny. Ire. Mustered in June 11, 1861, term 3 years. Wounded July 1, 1862, at Malvern Hill, Va.; May 5, 1864, Wilderness, Va. Mustered out June 21, 1864, as Sergt.

Gorman, Thomas, enlisted Aug. 19, 1862, laborer, age 18, single, residence Salem, born in Salem, Mass. Mustered in Aug. 19, 1862, term 3 years. Wounded May 2, 1863, at Chancellorsville. Transferred to Invalid Corps March 15, 1864.

Gordon, Samuel, enlisted July 16, 1863, laborer, age 22, single, residence New Haven, credited to Springfield. Mustered in July 16, 1863, term 3 years. Transferred to 32d Mass. Vols. June 10, 1864.

Graham, William, enlisted June 11, 1861, currier, age 25, single, residence Salem, born in Ireland. Mustered in June 11, 1861, term 3 years. Wounded July 1, 1862, at Malvern Hill, Va. Mustered out June 21, 1864, as " Gocham."

Hayes, Benjamin, enlisted June 11, 1861, sailor, age 24, married, residence Salem, born in Dublin, Ire. Mustered in June 11, 1861, term 3 years. Mustered out June 21, 1864, as Corp.

Herlihy, Maurice, enlisted Feb. 8, 1862, tailor, age 34, married, residence Boston, born in Ireland. Mustered in Feb. 8, 1862, term 3 years. Died Dec 13, 1863, at Fredericksburg, Va.

Hurley, William, enlisted June 11, 1861, soldier, age 19, single, residence Salem, born in Cork, Ire. Mustered in June 11, 1861, term 3 years. Discharged at Hampton, Va., no date.

Hynes, John, enlisted June 11, 1861, laborer, age 21, single, residence Worcester, born in Co. Cork, Ire. Mustered in June 11, 1861, term 3 years. Wounded June 27, 1862, at Gaines' Mill, Va. Discharged at Harrison Landing, Va., no date.

Jenkins, James H., enlisted July 31, 1862, laborer, age 45, single, residence Boston. Mustered in July 31, 1862, term 3 years. Mustered out June 21, 1864.

Jennings, Benjamin, enlisted July 18, 1863, engineer, age 23, single, residence Boston, credited to Boston, Wd. 4. Mustered in July 18, 1863, term 3 years. Transferred to V.R.C. by P.M.G., Jan. 13, 1865.

Jordan, William, enlisted June 11, 1861, cordwainer, age 20, residence Salem, born in Glasgow, Scot. Mustered in June 11, 1861, term 3 years. Wounded May 5, 1864, Wilderness, Va. Mustered out June 21, 1864.

Joyce, William, enlisted Aug. 21, 1863, bootmaker, age 21, single, residence New York, credited to Manchester. Mustered in Aug. 21, 1863, term 3 years. Deserted Oct. 22, 1863, near Auburn, Va.

Keating, Michael, enlisted June 11, 1861, laborer, age 26, single, residence Salem, born in Meath, Ire. Mustered in June 11, 1861, term 3 years. Mustered out June 21, 1864.

Kelly, Charles D., enlisted Aug. 16, 1862, hostler, age 18, single, residence Salem, born in Providence, R.I. Mustered in Aug. 16, 1862, term 3 years. Discharged at Miner's Hill, Va., no date.

Kelly, James, enlisted June 11, 1861, currier, age 22, single, residence South Danvers, born in Dublin, Ire. Mustered in June 11, 1861, term 3 years. Discharged for disability, no date.

Kelly, John, enlisted June 11, 1861, currier, age 37, married, residence Salem, born in Waterford, Ire. Mustered in June 11, 1861, term 3 years. Mustered out June 21, 1864.

Kelley, John 2d, enlisted Aug. 15, 1862, dresser, age 38, married, residence Salem, born in Scotland. Mustered in Aug. 15, 1862, term 3 years. Mustered out June 21, 1864.

Kelly, Michael, enlisted June 11, 1861, soldier, age 20, single, residence Salem, born in Galway, Ire. Mustered in June 11, 1861, term 3 years. Discharged for disability at Harrison Landing, Va., no date.

Kennedy, Martin, enlisted June 11, 1861, shoemaker, age 21, single, residence Salem, born in Co. Cork, Ire. Mustered in June 11, 1861, term 3 years. Wounded June 27, 1862, Gaines' Mill, Va. Discharged for disability Dec. 26, 1862, Yorktown, Va.

Lane, Maurice, enlisted Aug. 14, 1863, tailor, age 35, married, residence East Boston, credited to Boston. Mustered in Aug 14, 1863, term 3 years. Transferred to 32d Mass. Vols. June 10, 1864, as "Martin Lane."

Leary, Timothy 2d, enlisted June 11, 1861, currier, age 35, married, residence Salem, born in Cork, Ire. Mustered in June 11, 1861, term 3 years. Discharged at Arlington Heights, Va., no date.

Legers, Phillip, enlisted Aug. 19, 1863, sailor, age 20, single, residence Boston, credited to Marblehead. Mustered in Aug. 19, 1863, term 3 years. Transferred to 32d Mass. Vols. June 10, 1864.

Leslie, James, enlisted June 11, 1861, shoemaker, age 20, single, residence Boston, born in Kilramey, Ire. Mustered in June 11, 1861, term 3 years. Wounded May 5, 1864, Wilderness, Va. Mustered out June 21, 1864.

Lynch, James 1st, enlisted June 11, 1861, pedler, age 29, married, residence Salem, born in Ireland. Mustered in June 11, 1861, term 3 years. Discharged at Arlington Heights, Va., no date.

Lynch, James 2d, enlisted July 22, 1862, cooper, age 32, married, residence Boston, born in Ireland. Mustered in July 22, 1862, term 3 years Discharged at Sharpsburg, Md., no date.

Lynch, William, enlisted June 11, 1861, pedler, age 38, married, residence Salem, born in Ireland. Mustered in June 11, 1861, term 3 years. Discharged at Arlington Heights, Va , no date.

Mahony, Dennis J. D., enlisted June 11, 1861, laborer, age 40, single, residence Salem, born in Cork, Ire. Mustered in June 11, 1861, term 3 years. Transferred to navy, Miner's Hill, Va , no date, as "Daniel D."

Martin, James P., enlisted July 17, 1862, carpenter, age 30, married, residence Boston, born in Ireland. Mustered in July 17, 1862, term 3 years. Discharged for disability at Miner's Hill, no date.

Mattox, Henry, enlisted Aug. 20, 1863, carpenter, age 43, married, residence Lynn, credited to Lynn. Mustered in Aug. 20, 1863, term 3 years. Transferred to 32d Mass. Vols. June 10, 1864.

McCarthy, Daniel, enlisted June 11, 1861, currier, age 24, married, residence Salem, born in Ireland. Mustered in June 11, 1861, term 3 years. Discharged for disability April 8, 1863.

McCarthy, Patrick, enlisted July 22, 1862, laborer, age 22, married, residence Boston, born in Ireland. Mustered in July 22, 1862, term 3 years. Mustered out June 21, 1864.

McCarthy, Patrick, enlisted June 11, 1861, teamster, age 30, married, residence Salem, born in Ireland. Mustered in June 11, 1861, term 3 years. Discharged for disability at Harrison Landing, Va , no date.

McFarland, James, enlisted July 28, 1862, moulder, age 23, single, residence Salem. Mustered in July 28, 1862, term 3 years. Mustered out ·June 21, 1864.

McGrath, John, enlisted June 11, 1861, age 29.   Mustered in June 11, 1861.
term 3 years.   Discharged for disability, no date, Washington, D.C.

McLaughlin, James, enlisted June 11, 1861, currier, age 23, single, residence
Danvers, born in Co. Cork, Ire.   Mustered in June 11, 1861, term 3
years.   Wounded in the thigh at Hanover Court House, Va. May 27,
1862; at Chancellorsville, Va., May 2, 1863; May 5, 1864, Wilderness, Va.
Mustered out June 21, 1864, as Corp.

McMahon, James, enlisted June 11, 1861, teamster, age 24, single, residence
Salem, born in Donegal, Ire.   Mustered in June 11, 1861, term 3 years.
Wounded at Gettysburg, July 4, 1863.   Mustered out June 21, 1864.

McNamara, Peter, enlisted June 11, 1861, currier, age 25, single, residence
Salem, born in Ireland.   Mustered in June 11, 1861, term 3 years   Killed
June 27, 1862, Gaines' Mill, Va.

Meagher, Patrick, enlisted June 11, 1861, laborer, age 25, single, residence
Providence, R I., born in Ireland. ;Mustered in June 11, 1861, term 3
years.   Killed June 27, 1862, Gaines' Mill, Va.

Morrisey, John, enlisted June 11, 1861, boot crimper, age 27, single, residence Milford, born in Kilkenny, Ire.   Mustered in June 11, 1861, term 3
years.   Wounded at Gaines' Mill, Va., June 27, 1862; Fredericksburg,
Va., Dec. 13, 1862.   Died of wounds March 2, 1863, Washington, D.C.

Moynihan, Humphrey, enlisted June 11, 1861, laborer, age 26, single, residence
South Danvers, born in Cork. Ire   Mustered in June 11, 1861, term 3
years.   Wounded July 1, 1862, at Malvern Hill, Va.   Mustered out June
21, 1864.

Neil, Edward, enlisted June 11, 1861, shoemaker, age 24, single, residence
Salem, born in Kilkenny, Ire.   Mustered in June 11, 1861, term 3 years.
Wounded July 1, 1862, Malvern Hill, Va.   Discharged for disability June
19, 1863.

Norton, John, enlisted June 11, 1861, laborer, age 21, married, residence Salem,
born in Ireland.   Mustered in June 11, 1861, term 3 years.   Wounded
July 1, 1862, at Malvern Hill, Va.   Discharged at Miner's Hill, Va., no
date.

O'Brien, Edward, enlisted June 11, 1861, servant, age 24, single, residence
Salem, born in Mallow, Ire.   Mustered in June 11, 1861, term 3 years.
Mustered out June 21, 1864.

O'Brien, John 1st, enlisted June 11, 1861, stonecutter, age 21, single, residence Beverly, born in Ireland.   Mustered in June 11, 1861, term 3
years.   Discharged at Miner's Hill, Va., no date.

O'Brien, John 2d, enlisted June 11, 1861, laborer, age 19, single, residence
Salem, born in Salem.   Mustered in June 11, 1861, term 3 years.   Discharged at Fort Monroe, Va , no date.

O'Brien, Thomas, enlisted June 11, 1861, currier, age 24, married, residence
Salem, born in Ireland.   Mustered in June 11, 1861, term 3 years.   Discharged at Miner's Hill, Va , no date.

O'Connor, James, enlisted June 11, 1861, cordwainer, age 23, married, residence Salem.   Born in Co Cork, Ire.   Mustered in June 11, 1861, term 3
years.   Discharged at Sharpsburg, Md., no date.

O'Donnell, Patrick, enlisted July 31, 1862, moulder, age 20, single, residence
Salem, born in Ireland.   Mustered in July 31, 1862, term β years.
Deserted at Falmouth, Va., no date.

O'Hara, Patrick, enlisted June 11, 1861, pedler, age 27, married, residence
Salem, born in Galway, Ire   Mustered in June 11, 1861, term 3 years.
Wounded June 27, 1862, at Gaines' Mill, Va.   Discharged for disability
Sept. 16, 1862.

O'Keeffe, John, enlisted June 11, 1861, soldier, age 25, single, residence Beverly, born in Co. Cork, Ire. Mustered in June 11, 1861, term 3 years. Mustered out June 21, 1864.

O'Keeffe, Patrick, enlisted June 11, 1861, currier, age 30, married, residence Salem, born in Kilkenny, Ire. Mustered in June 11, 1861, term 3 years. Mustered out June 21, 1864.

O'Roarke, John, enlisted July 26, 1862, clerk, age 22, residence Salem, born in Ireland. Mustered in July 26, 1862, term 3 years. Mustered out June 21, 1864.

O'Shea, Timothy, enlisted July 31, 1862, blacksmith, age 18, residence Salem, born in Ireland. Mustered in July 31, 1862, term 3 years. Wounded June 3, 1864, at Bethesda Church, Va. Mustered out June 21, 1864.

Pender, John, enlisted June 11, 1861, currier, age 35, married, residence Salem, born in Ireland. Mustered in June 11, 1861, term 3 years. Wounded July 1, 1862, Malvern Hill, Va. Discharged at Miner's Hill, no date.

Regan, Dennis, enlisted June 11, 1861, age 25. Mustered in June 11, 1861, term 3 years. Discharged, Washington, D.C., no date.

Regan, Edmund, enlisted June 11, 1861, soldier, age 20, single, residence Salem, born in Co. Cork, Ire. Mustered in June 11, 1861, term 3 years. Wounded July 1, 1862, Malvern Hill, Va. Unofficially reported died, Aug. 22, 1862, Philadelphia, Pa., S.G.O.

Regan, James, enlisted June 11, 1861. Mustered in June 11, 1861, term 3 years. Killed June 27, 1862, Gaines' Mill, Va.

Regan, William, enlisted June 11, 1861, shoemaker, age 21, residence Salem, born in County Cork, Ire. Mustered in June 11, 1861, term 3 years. Died as "Rogan" Long Island, Boston Harbor, no date.

Richmond, William B., enlisted July 13, 1863, machinist, age 29, married, residence Mattapoisett, credited to Boston, Wd. 11. Mustered in July 13, 1863, term 3 years. Transferred to navy as "Redmond," no date, at Bealton, Va.

Rogan, Cornelious, enlisted June 11, 1861, shoemaker, age 21, single, residence Salem, born in Co. Cork, Ire. Mustered in June 11, 1861, term 3 years. Wounded June 27, 1862, Gaines' Mill, Va. Discharged at Washington, D.C., no date.

Sculley, John, enlisted July 28, 1862, shoemaker, age 18, single, residence Salem, born in Salem, Mass. Mustered in July 28, 1862, term 3 years. Mustered out June 21, 1864.

Shakleton, Joseph, enlisted Aug. 19, 1863, spinner, age 24, married, residence Lawrence, credited to Boston, Wd. 10. Mustered in Aug. 19, 1863, term 3 years. Transferred to 32d Mass. Vols. June 10, 1864.

Sherlock, Thomas T., enlisted June 11, 1861, laborer, age 21, married, residence Salem, born in Ireland. Mustered in June 11, 1861, term 3 years. Died of disease Jan. 2, 1864, Bealton Station, Va.

Shea, Daniel, enlisted Aug. 7, 1862, currier, age 30, married, residence Salem, born in Ireland. Mustered in Aug 7, 1862, term 3 years. Mustered out June 21, 1864.

Shea, Patrick, enlisted June 11, 1861, shoemaker, age 20, single, residence No. Danvers, born in Co. Cork, Ire. Mustered in June 11, 1861, term 3 years. Wounded July 1, 1862, at Malvern Hill, Va.; May 5, 1864, at Wilderness, Va. Died of wounds received May 31, 1864.

Shortell, James, enlisted June 11, 1861, shoemaker, age 26, married, residence Salem, born in Kilkenny, Ire. Mustered in June 11, 1861, term 3 years. Mustered out June 21, 1864.

Smith, George B., enlisted Feb. 22, 1862, age 28, residence Salem. Mustered in Feb. 22, 1862, term 3 years. Discharged, Sharpsburg, Md., no date.

Stephens, Joseph F., enlisted June 11, 1861, spinner, age 30, married, residence Swanton Falls, Vt., born in Vermont. Mustered in June 11, 1861, term 3 years. Discharged, Sharpsburg, Va., no date.

Sullivan, Patrick, enlisted June 11, 1861, soldier, age 20, residence Salem, born in Ireland. Mustered in June 11, 1861, term 3 years. Re-enlisted Dec. 7, 1863. Wounded May 8, 1864, at Laurel Hill, Va. Died in Andersonville, Ga., Sept. 8, 1864.

Sweeney, Daniel, enlisted June 11, 1861, cordwainer, age 20, single, residence Beverly, born in Co. Cork, Ire. Mustered in June 11, 1861, term 3 years. Wounded June 27, 1862, Gaines' Mill, Va. Mustered out June 21, 1864.

Sweeney, Morgan, enlisted Feb. 11, 1862, currier, age 19, single, residence Salem, born in Ireland. Mustered in Feb. 11, 1862, term 3 years. Wounded July 1, 1862, Malvern Hill, Va. Discharged for disability Harrison Landing, Va., no date.

Sweeney, Patrick, enlisted Aug. 19, 1863, sailor, age 29, sailor, residence Buffalo, N.Y., credited to North Hampton. Mustered in Aug. 19, 1863, term 3 years. Transferred to navy, no date, at Bealton, Va.

Tierney, Patrick, enlisted June 11, 1861, currier, age 21, single, residence Salem, born in Tipperary, Ire. Mustered in June 11, 1861, term 3 years. Wounded July 1, 1862, Malvern Hill, Va.; May 8, 1864, Laurel Hill, Va. Mustered out June 21, 1864, Corp.

Timmins, Garrett, enlisted June 11, 1861, shoemaker, age 19, single, residence Salem, born in Kildare, Ire. Mustered in June 11, 1861, term 3 years. Mustered out June 21, 1864, as Sergt.

Tracy, John, enlisted June 11, 1861, currier, age 22, single, residence Salem, born in Kildare, Ire. Mustered in June 11, 1861, term 3 years. Died of disease at hospital, Philadelphia, Pa., Sept. 16, 1862.

Treanor, Edward, enlisted July 21, 1862, machinist, age 31, residence Boston. Mustered in July 21, 1862, term 3 years. Mustered out June 21, 1864.

Twohig, John, enlisted June 11, 1861, spinner, age 20, single, residence Salem, born in Co. Cork, Ire. Mustered in June 11, 1861, term 3 years. Discharged at Harrison Landing, Va.

Walsh, John, enlisted June 11, 1861, spinner, age 19, single, residence Salem, born in Co. Cork, Ire. Mustered in June 11, 1861, term 3 years. Wounded June 27, 1862, Gaines' Mill, Va. Deserted June 29, 1863, Frederick City, Md.

Whelan, John, enlisted June 11, 1861, currier, age 30, single, residence Salem, born in Kilkenny, Ire. Mustered in June 11, 1861, term 3 years. Unofficially reported. Discharged for disability, Aug. 19, 1861.

COMPANY G.

Carey, John, Capt., shoemaker, age 25, single, residence Marlboro, born in Ireland. Mustered in June 11, 1861, term 3 years. Killed June 27, 1862, Gaines' Mill, Va.

Tobin, John M., 1st Lieut., age 24, residence Boston, born in Kilkenny, Ire. Mustered in June 11, 1861, term 3 years. Capt. Aug. 28, 1862, from Adjt.; wounded May 8, 1864. Mustered out June 21, 1864.

Simpson, Archibald, 2d Lieut., blindmaker, age 26, married, residence Boston, born in Ireland. Mustered in June 11, 1861, term 3 years. Promoted 1st Lieut. Sept. 20, 1862; transferred to Co. K March 20, 1864. Killed May 12, 1864, at Spottsylvania.

Finnotty, Edward, 1st Sergt., enlisted June 11, 1861, shoemaker, age 27, married, residence Boston, born in Boston. Mustered in June 11, 1861, term 3 years. Promoted 2d Lieut. and transferred to Co. K Sept. 1, 1861. Resigned Feb. 28, 1863.

Regan, Daniel J., Sergt., enlisted June 11, 1861, shoemaker, age 21, single, residence Marlboro, born in Cork, Ire. Mustered in June 11, 1861, term 3 years. Mortally wounded May 27, 1862, at battle of Hanover Court House, Va. Died of wounds received May 27, 1862, at Hanover Court House, Va.

Goodwin, James M., Sergt., enlisted June 11, 1861, age 30, married, residence Boston, born in Boston. Mustered in June 11, 1861, term 3 years. Discharged for disability July 1, 1862, as " James H."

Dempsey, Timothy, Sergt., enlisted June 11, 1861, varnisher, age 27, single, residence Boston, born in Cork, Ire. Mustered in June 11, 1861, term 3 years. Discharged for disability Aug 31, 1862, as Private.

Clark, Michael, Sergt., enlisted June 11, 1861, shoemaker, age 21, single, residence, Marlboro, born in Galway, Ire. Mustered in June 11, 1861, term 3 years. Wounded May 12, 1864, at Spottsylvania, Va. Died of wounds June 10, 1864. Mustered out as absent, wounded, June 21, 1864.

Buckley, John, Corp., enlisted June 11, 1861, shoemaker, age 27, single, residence Marlboro, born in Cork, Ire. Mustered in June 11, 1861, term 3 years. Wounded at Gaines' Mill, Va , June 27, 1862; May 12, 1864, at Spottsylvania, Va. Died of wounds received May 12, 1864.

Carey, Francis, Corp, enlisted June 11, 1861, shoemaker, age 22, single, residence Randolph, born in Longford, Ire. Mustered in June 11, 1861, term 3 years. Sergt. May 28, 1862; mustered out June 21, 1864.

Cowhey, Edward, Corp., enlisted June 11, 1861, shoemaker, age 27, single, residence Marlboro, born in Cork, Ire. Mustered in June 11, 1861, term 3 years. Mustered out June 21, 1864.

Daley, Robert, Corp., enlisted June 11, 1861, shoemaker, age 23, single, residence Marlboro, born in Cork, Ire. Mustered in June 11, 1861, term 3 years. Killed July 1, 1862, Malvern Hill, Va., as 1st Sergt

Feeley, John, Corp., enlisted June 11, 1861, shoemaker, age 26, single, residence Marlboro, born in Mayo, Ire. Mustered in June 11, 1861, term 3 years. Discharged for disability May 5, 1863; discharge papers say Feb. 12, 1863.

Keating, William, Corp., enlisted June 11, 1861, shoemaker, age 20, single, residence Marlboro, born in Boston, Mass. Mustered in June 11, 1861, term 3 years. Died of disease Sept. 17, 1863, Fort Monroe, Va.

Linehan, Dennis, Corp., enlisted June 11, 1861, shoemaker, age 30, married, residence Marlboro, born in Cork, Ire. Mustered in June 11, 1861, term 3 years. Mustered out June 21, 1864, as Private.

Mahoney, James, Corp., enlisted June 11, 1861, shoemaker, age 24, married, residence Marlboro, born in Cork, Ire. Mustered in June 11, 1861, term 3 years. Discharged for disability, Jan. 21, 1862.

Murphy, Richard F., Corp., enlisted June 11, 1861, residence Boston. Mustered in June 11, 1861, term 3 years. Absent wounded.

Philbin, Thomas, Musician, enlisted June 11, 1861, shoemaker, age 20, single, residence Marlboro, born in Mayo, Ire. Mustered in June 11, 1861, term 3 years. Mustered out June 21, 1864.

Curran, Charles, Musician, enlisted June 11, 1861, carmaker, age 18, single, residence Brighton, born in St. Johns, N.B. Mustered in June 11, 1861, term 3 years. Discharged for disability Dec. 19, 1862, Washington, D.C.

Armstrong, William H., Wagoner, enlisted June 11, 1861, shoemaker, age 33, married, residence Milford, born in Galway, Ire. Mustered in June 11, 1861, term 3 years. Promoted Sergt. Oct. 1, 1862. Wounded at Hanover Court House, Va., May 27, 1862; May 5, 1864, Wilderness, Va. Mustered out June 21, 1864.

Ahearn, Michael, enlisted June 11, 1861, shoemaker, age 25, married, residence Marlboro, born in Ireland. Mustered in June 11, 1861, term 3 years. Accidentally shot Sept. 2, 1862, near Washington, D.C.

Allen, John, enlisted June 11, 1861, shoemaker, age 23, single, residence Marlboro, born in Waterford, Ire. Mustered in June 11, 1861, term 3 years. Promoted Corp. January, 1862. Discharged for disability Oct. 18, 1862.

Allen, Michael, enlisted June 11, 1861, shoemaker, age 23, single, residence Marlboro, born in Waterford, Ire. Mustered in June 11, 1861, term 3 years. Mustered out June 21, 1864.

Bailey, Samuel, enlisted June 11, 1861, shoemaker, age 22, single, residence Marlboro, born in Ireland. Mustered in June 11, 1861, term 3 years. Deserted Feb. 13, 1862, Falls Church, Va.

Barry, Thomas, enlisted July 30, 1862, laborer, age 29, single, residence Boston. Mustered in July 30, 1862, term 3 years. Mustered out June 21, 1864.

Brigham, Thomas B., enlisted June 11, 1861, shoemaker, age 21, single, residence Marlboro, born in Marlboro, Mass. Mustered in June 11, 1861, term 3 years. Wounded at Gaines' Mill, Va., June 27, 1862; May 5, 1864, Wilderness, Va Mustered out June 21, 1864.

Bryne, Edward, enlisted June 11, 1861, printer, age 23, single, residence Southbridge, born in England. Mustered in June 11, 1861, term 3 years. Deserted Aug. 14, 1862, Harrison Landing, Va., as "Ryan."

Bumpus, Jedediah, enlisted July 17, 1863, farmer, age 29, married, residence Plymouth, credited to Plymouth. Mustered in July 17, 1863, term 3 years. Killed May 5, 1864, Wilderness.

Burke, Patrick, enlisted June 11, 1861, shoemaker, age 30, single, residence Marlboro, born in Waterford, Ire. Mustered in June 11, 1861, term 3 years. Discharged for disability Dec. 18, 1861.

Burns, Eugene, enlisted June 11, 1861, shoemaker, age 25, single, residence Marlboro, born in Cork, Ire. Mustered in June 11, 1861, term 3 years. Died of disease Sept. 8, 1862.

Burnes, Michael, enlisted June 11, 1861, shoemaker, age 19, single, residence Marlboro. Mustered in June 11, 1861, term 3 years. Missing May 8, 1864, at Laurel Hill, Va. Subsequently reported mustered out of service.

Callahan, Dennis, enlisted Aug. 9, 1862, laborer, age 30, married, residence Taunton. Mustered in Aug. 9, 1862, term 3 years. Discharged for disability Jan. 29, 1863.

Carey, James, enlisted June 11, 1861, shoemaker, age 22, single, residence Marlboro, born in Ireland. Mustered in June 11, 1861, term 3 years. Discharged for disability, Aug. 14, 1862.

Cary, Daniel, enlisted July 16, 1863, bookbinder, age 19, single, residence Springfield, credited to Springfield. Mustered in July 16, 1863, term 3 years. Deserted Oct. 27, 1863, Warrington, Va.

Carroll, John, enlisted Nov. 27, 1863, laborer, age 30, single, residence Albany, N.Y., credited to Boston, Wd. 7, born in Ireland. Mustered in Nov. 27, 1863, term 3 years. Deserted May 12, 1864..

Cassidy, Lawrence, enlisted Aug. 21, 1863, shoemaker, age 20, single, residence Troy, N.Y. Mustered in Aug. 21, 1863, term 3 years. Wounded May 5, 1864, Wilderness, Va. Transferred to 32d Mass. Vols. June 10, 1864.

Clancy, Thos., enlisted June 11, 1861, shoemaker, age 19, single, residence Marlboro, born in Ireland. Mustered in June 11, 1861, term 3 years. Absent sick, no record.

Clark, Patrick, enlisted June 11, 1861, shoemaker, age 23, single, residence Marlboro, born in Ireland. Mustered in June 11, 1861, term 3 years. Killed June 27, 1862, Gaines' Mill, Va.

Clark, Peter, enlisted June 11, 1861, shoemaker, age 25, single, residence Marlboro, born in Galway, Ire. Mustered in June 11, 1861, term 3 years. Mustered out June 21, 1864.

Cleary, James, enlisted Feb. 5, 1862, bootmaker, age 28, single, residence Abington. Mustered in Feb. 5, 1862, term 3 years. Transferred to 32d Mass. Vols. June 10, 1864.

Clements, Francis, enlisted June 11, 1861, painter, age 19, single, residence New York, born in New York City. Mustered in June 11, 1861, term 3 years. Discharged for disability Feb. 19, 1862.

Clifford, John, enlisted Nov. 9, 1861, shoemaker, age 21, single, residence Roxbury. Mustered in Nov. 9, 1861, term 3 years. Transferred to 32d Mass. Vols. May 10, 1864.

Collins, William, enlisted July 16, 1863, painter, age 22, married, residence Philadelphia, credited to Long Meadow. Mustered in July 16, 1863, term 3 years. Deserted Sept. 19, 1863, Beverly Ford, Va.

Collins, James, enlisted June 11, 1861, chairmaker, age 24, single, residence South Boston, born in Glasgow, Scot. Mustered in June 11, 1861, term 3 years. Mustered out June 21, 1864.

Conklin, Joseph, enlisted Aug. 21, 1863, laborer, age 21, single, residence Roundout, N.Y., credited to Hadley. Mustered in Aug. 21, 1863, term 3 years. Deserted Aug. 27, 1863. Returned Oct. 1, 1863.

Conboy, Thomas, enlisted June 11, 1861, shoemaker, age 26, single, residence Lynn, born in Ireland. Mustered in June 11, 1861, term 3 years. Wounded May 5, 1864, Wilderness, Va. Mustered out June 21, 1864.

Connors, Williams, enlisted June 11, 1861, carpenter, age 37, married, residence Marlboro, born in Limerick, Ire. Mustered in June 11, 1861, term 3 years. Deserted as Sergt. Sept. 12, 1862, on march to Antietam.

Conners, John, enlisted June 11, 1861, shoemaker, age 22, single, residence Marlboro, born in Ireland. Mustered in June 11, 1861, term 3 years. Killed May 5, 1864, as 1st Sergt., Wilderness.

Coughlin, Michael, enlisted June 11, 1861, shoemaker, age 21, single, residence Marlboro, born in Cork, Ire. Mustered in June 11, 1861, term 3 years. Discharged for disability Aug 1, 1862.

Cotter, Cornelius, enlisted June 11, 1861, shoemaker, age 21, single, residence Marlboro, born in Cork, Ire. Mustered in June 11, 1861, term 3 years. Wounded at Gaines' Mill June 27, 1862. Discharged for disability Nov. 14, 1862.

Cotter, Michael, enlisted June 11, 1861, shoemaker, age 18, single, residence Marlboro, born in Cork, Ire. Mustered in June 11, 1861, term 3 years. Discharged for disability Oct. 28, 1861.

Cowan, John, enlisted Aug. 21, 1863, laborer, age 22, single, residence Jersey City, credited to Hadley. Mustered in Aug. 21, 1863, term 3 years. Deserted Oct. 27, 1863, Warrington, Va.

Cramer, Lawrence, enlisted June 11, 1861, shoemaker, age 29, married, residence Marlboro, born in Cork, Ire. Mustered in June 11, 1861, term 3 years. Mustered out June 21, 1864.

Creed, John, enlisted June 11, 1861, shoemaker, age 25, single, residence North Bridgewater, born in Cork, Ire. Mustered in June 11, 1861, term 3 years. Discharged for disability March 8, 1862.

Crotty, Patrick J., enlisted Aug. 9, 1862, marble worker, age 21, single, residence Boston, born in Ireland. Mustered in Aug. 9, 1862, term 3 years. Deserted Jan. 1, 1863; returned May 11, 1863. Deserted June 27, 1863.

Crowley, John, enlisted June 11, 1861, shoemaker, age 20, single, residence Marlboro, born in Co. Cork, Ire. Mustered in June 11, 1861, term 3 years. Unofficially reported Died of wounds June 27, 1862, Gaines' Mill, Va.

Cunningham, Wm., enlisted Aug. 9, 1862, shoemaker, age 36, married, residence Marlboro, born in Ireland. Mustered in Aug. 9, 1862, term 3 years. Mustered out June 21, 1864.

Cutter, A. O. W., enlisted July 9, 1863, machinist, age 21, single, residence Charlestown, credited to Charlestown. Mustered in July 9, 1863, term 3 years. Died of disease March 4, 1864, Bealton, Va.

Daly, Felix, enlisted July 19, 1861, baker, age 27, single, residence Boston. Mustered in July 19, 1861, term 3 years. Wounded at Gaines' Mill June 27, 1862. Discharged from 9th Mass Vols. for expiration of service, July 18, 1864.

Davis, William, enlisted Aug. 12, 1862, glassmaker, age 26, single, residence Boston, born in Ireland. Mustered in Aug. 12, 1862, term 3 years. Mustered out June 21, 1864.

Devlin, Patrick, enlisted July 19, 1861, age 22, residence Lynn. Mustered in July 19, 1861, term 3 years. Deserted June 27, 1863, Frederick, Md.

Dinneen, Thomas, enlisted Aug. 7, 1862, laborer, age 35, single, residence Malden, born in Ireland. Mustered in Aug. 7, 1862, term 3 years. Wounded May 5, 1864, Wilderness, Va. Mustered out June 21, 1864, as " Dineen."

Doherty, Patrick, enlisted Aug. 8, 1862, shoemaker, age 30, married, residence Boston, born in Ireland. Mustered in Aug. 8, 1862, term 3 years. Mustered out June 21, 1864.

Dolan, John, enlisted June 11, 1861, shoemaker, age 22, single, residence Marlboro, born in Dublin, Ire. Mustered in June 11, 1861, term 3 years. Mustered out June 21, 1864.

Donavan, John, enlisted Aug. 11, 1862, laborer, age 35, married, residence Fall River, born in Ireland. Mustered in Aug. 11, 1862, term 3 years. Mustered out June 21, 1864.

Donavan, John, enlisted June 11, 1861, shoemaker, age 35, single, residence Marlboro, born in Cork, Ire. Mustered in June 11, 1861, term 3 years. Discharged for disability March 8, 1862.

Donavan, John E., enlisted June 11, 1861, shoemaker, age 24, single, residence Marlboro, born in Cork, Ire. Mustered in June 11, 1861, term 3 years. Mustered out June 21, 1864.

Dooley, Thomas, enlisted June 11, 1861, shoemaker, age 18, single, residence Lynn, born in Galway, Ire. Mustered in June 11, 1861, term 3 years. Discharged for disability Aug. 22, 1861.

Duffy, Charles F., enlisted Aug. 21, 1862, stevedore, age 28, married, residence Boston, born in Fall River, Mass. Mustered in Aug. 21, 1862, term 3 years. Died of disease Aug. 26, 1863, Washington, D.C.

Dugan, Patrick W., enlisted July 22, 1862, sailor, age 35, single, residence Boston, born in Ireland. Mustered in July 22, 1862, term 3 years. Discharged for disability, Dec. 13, 1862, Washington, D.C., as "Patrick Duggan."

Duggan, Mathew, enlisted June 11, 1861, shoemaker, age 22, single, residence Marlboro, born in Cork, Ire. Mustered in June 11, 1861, term 3 years. Discharged for disability Feb. 5, 1862.

Driscoll, John D., enlisted July 24, 1862, painter, age 29, married, residence Boston, born in Ireland. Mustered in July 24, 1862, term 3 years. Discharged for disability from Co. F; time not known.

Driscoll, John, enlisted Aug. 15, 1862, laborer, age 40, married, residence Salem, born in Ireland. Mustered in Aug. 15, 1862, term 3 years. Mustered out June 21, 1864.

Fahey, Martin, enlisted June 11, 1861, shoemaker, age 18, single, residence Marlboro, born in Galway, Ire. Mustered in June 11, 1861, term 3 years. Wounded Malvern Hill, July 1, 1862. Discharged for disability Dec. 13, 1862.

Farley, Michael, enlisted June 11, 1861, carpenter, age 29, married, residence Lynn, born in Ireland. Mustered in June 11, 1861, term 3 years. Wounded at Malvern Hill, Va., July 1, 1862. Discharged for disability Jan. 2, 1863.

Feeley, Richard, enlisted June 11, 1861, shoemaker, age 22, single, residence Holliston, born in Kilkenny, Ire. Mustered in June 11, 1861, term 3 years. Promoted Sergt. Missing May 18, 1864, at Laurel Hill, Va. Investigation fails to elicit any further information in this case.

Fleming, John, enlisted July 15, 1862, tailor, age 35, married, residence Boston, born in Ireland. Mustered in July 15, 1862, term 3 years. Discharged for disability March 17, 1863.

Flynn, David, enlisted Aug. 9, 1862, harnessmaker, age 19, married, residence Boston, born in Ireland. Mustered in Aug. 9, 1862, term 3 years. Missing May 12, 1864, at Spottsylvania, Va. He was taken prisoner, transferred to 32d Mass. Vols. and discharged Feb. 27, 1865, City of Boston.

Flynn, John M., enlisted May 16, 1864, carpenter, age 30, residence Ex. of Washington, D.C., credited to Worcester. Mustered in May 16, 1864, term 3 years. Transferred to 32d Inf. (Taken from enlistment papers served in 5th U.S. Art. and discharged April 30, 1864, from same.)

Finnerty, Bartholomew, enlisted June 11, 1861, shoemaker, age 25, single, residence Marlboro, born in Ireland Mustered in June 11, 1861, term 3 years. Killed June 27, 1862, Gaines' Mill, Va.

Fitzgerald, John, enlisted June 11, 1861, shoemaker, age 20, single, residence Natick. Mustered in June 11, 1861, term 3 years. Died of disease March 2, 1862, Miner's Hill, Va.

Foley, John, enlisted Feb. 5, 1862, bootmaker, age 21, single, residence Randolph. Mustered in Feb. 5, 1862, term 3 years. Missing and reported killed May 12, 1864, at Spottsylvania, Va.

Fullard, Owen, enlisted June 11, 1861, tailor, age 28, single, residence Marlboro, born in Ireland. Mustered in June 11, 1861, term 3 years. Wounded at Malvern Hill, July 1, 1862. Deserted July 9, 1862, Washington, D C. (So says letter War Dept.)

Furfey, Richard, enlisted June 11, 1861, weaver, age 19, single, residence Braintree, born in Ireland. Mustered in June 11, 1861, term 3 years. Wash. not on file. Wounded June 27, 1862, at Gaines' Mill, Va.; May 5, 1864, at Wilderness, Va. Supposed to be killed May 12, 1864, Spottsylvania, Va.

Furfey, Cornelius, enlisted June 11, 1861, weaver, age 22, single, residence Braintree, born in Ireland. Mustered in June 11, 1861, term 3 years. Killed at Malvern Hill, Va , July 1, 1862.

Gammon, Lorenzo, enlisted Aug. 21, 1863, farmer, age 21, single, residence Boston, credited to Boston, Wd. 11. Mustered in Aug. 21, 1863, term 3 years. Transferred to 32d Mass. Vols. June 10, 1864.

Garrity, Patrick, enlisted Aug. 22, 1862, laborer, age 34, married, residence West Roxbury, born in Ireland. Mustered in Aug. 22, 1862, term 3 years. Mustered out June 21, 1864.

Green, George L., enlisted July 15, 1863, farmer, age 24, married, residence East Sheffield, credited to Sheffield. Mustered in July 15, 1863, term 3 years. Wounded May 5, 1864, Wilderness, Va. Died of wounds received May 12, 1864.

Hackett, Thomas, enlisted June 11, 1861, chandler, age 21, single, residence Cambridgeport, credited to Boston, Wd. 1, born in Clare, Ire. Mustered in June 11, 1861, term 3 years. Wounded May 5, 1864, Wilderness, Va. Mustered out June 21, 1864, as Corp.

Hagerty, John, enlisted June 11, 1861, shoemaker, age 20, single, residence Southboro, born in Cork, Ire. Mustered in June 11, 1861, term 3 years. Wounded June 27, 1862, at Gaines' Mill, Va. Died of wounds received June 27, 1862.

Hagerty, Michael, enlisted June 11, 1861, shoemaker, age 19, single, residence Southboro, born in Cork, Ire. Mustered in June 11, 1861, term 3 years. Mustered out June 21, 1864.

Hayes, William, enlisted June 11, 1861, shoemaker, age 24, single, residence Marlboro, born in Cork, Ire. Mustered in June 11, 1861, term 3 years. Discharged for disability Oct. 31, 1862.

Higgins, Timothy, enlisted Aug. 15, 1862, carpenter, age 42, married, residence Boston, born in Ireland. Mustered in Aug. 15, 1862, term 3 years. Discharged for disability Oct. 31, 1862.

Howard, William, enlisted Nov. 9, 1861, butcher, age 30, single, residence Boston. Mustered in Nov. 9, 1861, term 3 years. Transferred to Invalid Corps Nov. 11, 1863.

Hughes, Peter, enlisted Aug. 21, 1863, laborer, age 21, married, residence Greenfield, credited to Irving. Mustered in Aug. 21, 1863, term 3 years. Killed May 5, 1864, Wilderness, Va.

Kallaher, Cornelius, enlisted Aug. 6, 1862, carpenter, age 40, married, residence Boston. Mustered in Aug 6, 1862, term 3 years. Died of disease Sept. 27, 1862, Washington, D.C.

Kane, Henry, enlisted June 11, 1861, shoemaker, age 22, single, residence Lynn. Mustered in June 11, 1861, term 3 years. Discharged for disability Oct. 25, 1861.

Kelliher, William, enlisted June 11, 1861, laborer, age 27, married, residence Boston, born in Kerry, Ire. Mustered in June 11, 1861, term 3 years. Discharged for disability Aug. 8, 1862.

Kelley, Lawrence, enlisted June 11, 1861, shoemaker, age 20, single, residence Marlboro, born in Galway, Ire. Mustered in June 11, 1861, term 3 years. Wounded July 1, 1862, at Malvern Hill, Va. Discharged for disability Aug. 8, 1862.

Kenney, Bryan, enlisted June 11, 1861, shoemaker, age 20, single, residence Marlboro, born in Galway, Ire. Mustered in June 11, 1861, term 3 years. Discharged for disability Aug. 8, 1862.

Lanagan, James, enlisted Aug. 9, 1862, fireman, age 19, single, residence Boston, born in Ireland. Mustered in Aug. 9, 1862, term 3 years. Wounded May 5, 1864, Wilderness, Va. Mustered out June 21, 1864.

Lavery, William, enlisted July 19, 1861, shoemaker, age 27, residence Lynn. Mustered in July 19, 1861, term 3 years. Wounded June 27, 1862, Gaines' Mill, Va. Re-enlisted March 28, 1864. Transferred to 32d Mass. Vols. June 9, 1864.

Leavitt, Charles W., enlisted June 11, 1861, shoemaker, age 18, single, residence Marlboro, born in Maine. Mustered in June 11, 1861, term 3 years. Discharged for disability Oct. 25, 1861 (deafness), as "Lovett."

Long, Cornelius, enlisted June 11, 1861, shoemaker, age 20, single, residence Marlboro, born in Cork, Ire. Mustered in June 11, 1861, term 3 years. Killed June 27, Gaines' Mill, Va.

Lowe, George, enlisted Aug. 20, 1862, laborer, age 18, single, residence Lawrence, born in Ireland. Mustered in Aug. 20, 1862, term 3 years. Mustered out June 21, 1864.

Low, John, enlisted Aug 20, 1862, operative, age 19, single, residence Lawrence, born in Ireland. Mustered in Aug. 20, 1862, term 3 years. Wounded May 12, 1864, at Spottsylvania, Va. Mustered out June 21, 1864.

Lydon, Martin, enlisted Feb. 5, 1862, bootmaker, age 21, single, residence Boston. Mustered in Feb. 5, 1862, term 3 years. Wounded July 1, 1862, at Malvern Hill, Va.; May 5, 1864, Wilderness, Va. Transferred to 32d Mass. Vols. June 10, 1864.

Maguire, Thomas, enlisted June 11, 1861, age 34. Mustered in June 11, 1861, term 3 years. Mustered out June 21, 1864, as "McGuire."

Mahoney, William, enlisted June 11, 1861, shoemaker, age 30, single, residence Boston, born in Cork, Ire. Mustered in June 11, 1861, term 3 years. Discharged for disability Feb. 19, 1864.

Mahoney, John, enlisted June 11, 1861, shoemaker, age 23, single, residence Boston, born in Cork, Ire. Mustered in June 11, 1861, term 3 years. Killed July 1, 1862, Malvern Hill, Va.

Mulloy, Patrick, enlisted Dec. 3, 1863, laborer, age 21, single, residence Boston, credited to Boston, Wd. 7. Mustered in Dec. 3, 1863, term 3 years. Killed May 5, 1864, Wilderness, Va., as "Maloy."

Marnane, William, enlisted June 11, 1861, shoemaker, age 22, single, residence Boston, born in Cork, Ire. Mustered in June 11, 1861, term 3 years. Wounded July 1, 1862, Malvern Hill, Va.; May 12, 1864, at Spottsylvania, Va. Mustered out as absent without leave, June 21, 1864.

Murphy, John, enlisted June 11, 1861, age 19, single, residence Boston, born in Cork, Ire. Mustered in June 11, 1861, term 3 years. Wounded May 14, 1864, at Spottsylvania, Va. Mustered out as absent wounded, June 21, 1864. Discharged Aug. 20, 1864, for wounds received May 14, 1864.

Murphy, Christopher, enlisted Aug. 16, 1862, plumber, age 27, married, residence Salem, born in Ireland. Mustered in Aug. 16, 1862, term 3 years. Deserted Jan. 21, 1863, Falmouth, Va.

Murray, Patrick, enlisted June 11, 1861, shoemaker, age 20, residence Marlboro, born in Cork, Ire. Mustered in June 11, 1861, term 3 years. Discharged for disability Aug. 8, 1864.

McCann, Michael, enlisted June 11, 1861, shoemaker, age 20, single, residence Boston. Mustered in June 11, 1861, term 3 years. Wounded June 27, 1862, at Gaines' Mill, Va. Mustered out June 21, 1864.

McCarthy, Jeremiah, enlisted June 11, 1861, age 21. Mustered in June 11, 1861, term 3 years. Deserted June 16, 1861, Boston.

McCarty, Owen, enlisted June 11, 1861, shoemaker, age 26, single, residence Boston, born in Cork, Ire. Mustered in June 11, 1861, term 3 years. Deserted June 16, 1861, Boston, Mass., as "John."

McCurdy, John, enlisted June 11, 1861, shoemaker, age 19, single, residence Boston, born in Kerry, Ire. Mustered in June 11, 1861, term 3 years. Wounded June 27, 1862, Gaines' Mill, Va.; wounded July 1, 1862, Malvern Hill, Va. Deserted Oct. 16, 1862.

McDermott, Patrick, enlisted June 11, 1861, shoemaker, age 18, single, residence Marlboro, born in Galway, Ire. Mustered in June 11, 1861, term 3 years. Discharged for disability, Aug 22, 1861.

McEnerny, William, enlisted Nov. 9, 1861, shoemaker, age 18, single, residence Boston. Mustered in Nov. 9, 1861, term 3 years. Transferred to Co. F, 32d Mass. Vols. June 10, 1864.

McEneny, John, enlisted Nov. 9, 1861, plasterer or shoemaker, age 21, single, residence Boston. Mustered in Nov. 9, 1861, term 3 years. Wounded July 1, 1862, at Malvern Hill, Va. Discharged for disability March 30, 1863, Falmouth, Va.

McGann, John, enlisted Feb. 5, 1862, bootmaker, age 35, married, residence Quincy, born in Ireland. Mustered in Feb. 5, 1862, term 3 years. Discharged for disability March 6, 1863.

McGrath, Michael, enlisted June 11, 1861, shoemaker, age 19, single, residence Lakeville, born in Cork, Ire. Mustered in June 11, 1861, term 3 years. Deserted June 16, 1861, Boston, Mass.

McGuire, Thomas, enlisted Aug. 21, 1862, currier, age 32, single, residence Salem. Mustered in Aug. 21, 1862, term 3 years. Wounded June 27, 1862, at Gaines' Mill, Va. Deserted June 27, 1863, Frederick, Md.

McHugh, Patrick H., enlisted Aug. 7, 1862, shoemaker, age 28, single, residence Salem, born in Ireland. Mustered in Aug. 7, 1862, term 3 years. Wounded May 12, 1864, at Spottsylvania, Va. Mustered out June 21, 1864.

McHugh, Cornelius, enlisted June 11, 1861, shoemaker, age 18, single, residence Marlboro, born in Leitrim, Ire. Mustered in June 11, 1861, term 3 years. Mustered out June 21, 1864.

McLaughlin, James, weaver, age 35, single, residence Boston. Mustered in Aug. 12, 1862, term 3 years. Discharged for disability Feb. 16, 1863.

McQueeney, Peter, enlisted June 11, 1861, shoemaker, age 21, single, residence Marlboro, born in Ireland. Mustered in June 11, 1861, term 3 years Wounded May 5, 1864, Wilderness, Va. Absent wounded; mustered out as such, June 21, 1864.

Nevins, Edward, enlisted June 11, 1861, shoemaker, age 19, single, residence Marlboro, born in Ireland. Mustered in June 11, 1861, term 3 years. Discharged for disability Feb. 9, 1863.

O'Brien, Patrick, enlisted July 30, 1862, porter, age 19, single, residence Boston, born in Ireland. Mustered in July 30, 1862, term 3 years. Mustered out June 21, 1864.

O'Brien, Richard, enlisted June 11, 1861, shoemaker, age 35, single, residence
Weymouth Landing. Mustered in June 11, 1861, term 3 years. Discharged
for disability Oct. 28, 1861.

O'Donnell, John, enlisted Aug. 22, 1863, burnisher, age 26, single, residence
Boston, credited to Salisbury. Mustered in Aug. 22, 1863, term 3 years.
Deserted March 14, 1864, Bealton, Va.

Ola, Oscar, enlisted Aug. 9, 1862, fisherman, age 38, single, residence Gloucester,
born in Norway. Mustered in Aug. 9, 1862, term 3 years. Wounded May
5, 1864, Wilderness, Va. Mustered out June 21, 1864.

Prusia, Joseph, enlisted June 11, 1861, baker, age 41, married, residence Marlboro. Mustered in June 11, 1861, term 3 years. Discharged for disability May 5, 1863 as Corp. " Prushia."

Purbeek, John H., enlisted June 11, 1861, showman, age 25, married, residence
Salem. Mustered in June 11, 1861, term 3 years. Discharged for disability May 7, 1862, letter W.D.

Quinn, Timothy, enlisted July 25, 1861, shoemaker, age 27, single, residence
Marlboro. Mustered in July 25, 1861, term 3 years. Wounded July 1,
1862, Malvern Hill, Va. Mustered out June 21, 1864, as Corp.

Quinn, Charles, enlisted June 11, 1861, farmer, age 20, single, residence
Marlboro, born in Cork, Ire. Mustered in June 11, 1861, term 3 years.
Killed June 27, 1862, at Gaines' Mill, Va.

Rice, Thomas, enlisted June 11, 1861, shoemaker, age 24, single, residence
Marlboro, born in Houlton, Me. Mustered in June 11, 1861, term 3
years. Absent without leave.

Riley, Maurice, enlisted Aug. 9, 1862, fisherman, age 44, residence Gloucester.
Mustered in Aug. 9, 1862, term 3 years. Mustered out June 21, 1864.

Riordon, Michael, enlisted Nov. 4, 1863, shoemaker, age 36, married, residence
Marlboro, credited to Marlboro, born in Co. Cork, Ire. Mustered in
Nov. 4, 1863, term 3 years. Transferred to 32d Mass. Vols. June 10,
1864.

Ryan, James, enlisted Dec. 3, 1863, laborer, age 33, married, residence Philadelphia, credited to Boston, Wd. 7, born in Ireland. Mustered in Dec. 3,
1863, term 3 years. Deserted March 20, 1864, Bealton, Va.

Ryan, Andrew, enlisted June 11, 1861, shoemaker, age 21, single, residence
Abington, born in Ireland. Mustered in June 11, 1861, term 3 years.
Deserted March 19, 1864, Bealton, Va.

Sanborn, James D., enlisted June 11, 1861, bootmaker, age 27, single, residence
Abington. Mustered in June 11, 1861, term 3 years. Deserted Aug.
14, 1863.

Scollard, Patrick, enlisted June 11, 1861, bootmaker, age 20, single, residence
Boston, born in Cork, Ire. Mustered in June 11, 1861, term 3 years.
Killed June 27, 1862, Gaines' Mill, Va.

Shaughnessy, Michael, enlisted Aug. 8, 1862, laborer, age 40, married, residence Salisbury, born in Ireland. Mustered in Aug. 8, 1862, term 3
years. Discharged for disability Oct. 13, 1862, as " O'Shaughnessy."

Shea, Cornelieus, enlisted June 11, 1861, shoemaker, age 20, married, residence
Marlboro, born in Cork, Ire. Mustered in June 11, 1861, term 3 years.
Deserted June 27, 1863.

Sheehan, John, enlisted June 11, 1861, shoemaker, age 20, single, residence
Marlboro, born in Cork, Ire. Mustered in June 11, 1861, term 3 years.
Deserted June 16, 1861, Boston.

Sheenan, James, enlisted June 11, 1861, shoemaker, age 19, single, residence Marlboro, born in Ireland   Mustered in June 11, 1861, term 3 years. Died of disease Jan. 3, 1863, as Corp. "Sheshan" at Falmouth, Va.

Skelly, Daniel, enlisted Aug. 21, 1863, laborer, age 20, single, residence Jersey City, credited to Hadley. Mustered in Aug. 21, 1863, term 3 years. Deserted Oct. 29, 1863, at Frederick, Md , as " Scally."

Smith, Bernard, enlisted June 11, 1861, shoemaker, age 18, single, residence Marlboro, born in Cavan, Ire. Mustered in June 11, 1861, term 3 years. Mustered out June 24, 1864.

Smith, John, enlisted June 11, 1861, shoemaker, age 19, single, residence Marlboro, born in Ireland. Mustered in June 11, 1861, term 3 years. Discharged on S.C. of D. Nov. 12, 1862, letter War Dept.

Smith, Thomas, enlisted July 15, 1863, cook, age 41, single, residence Wilbraham, credited to Wilbraham. Mustered in July 15, 1863, term 3 years. Transferred to 32d Mass Vols. June 10, 1864.

Stewart, George A., enlisted June 11, 1861, clerk, age 20, married, residence Boston, born in Boston. Mustered in June 11, 1861, term 3 years. Discharged Aug. 22, 1861.

Stiles, Lewis H., enlisted Aug. 14, 1863, mechanic, age 20, single, residence Greenfield, credited to Greenfield. Mustered in Aug. 14, 1863, term 3 years. Accidentally shot Feb. 29, 1864, Bealton, Va.

Stone, Lewis, enlisted June 11, 1861, shoemaker, age 20, single, residence Marlboro. Mustered in June 11, 1861, term 3 years. Wounded Dec. 13, 1862, Fredericksburg, Va. Mustered out June 21, 1864.

Strachan, William M., enlisted Aug. 18, 1862, last maker, age 37, married, residence East Boston, born in Edinburgh, Scot. Mustered in Aug. 18,'1862, term 3 years. Promoted Sergt.-Maj., Oct 28, 1862. Discharged for disability as a Private, near Stoneman's Switch, Va. See Non-Commissioned Staff.

Sullivan, Jeremiah, enlisted June 11, 1861, laborer, age 27, residence Marlboro. Mustered in June 11, 1861, term 3 years. Discharged for disability, Oct. 17, 1863.

Sullivan, Daniel, enlisted June 11, 1861, shoemaker, age 20, single, residence Marlboro, born in Cork, Ire. Mustered in June 11, 1861, term 3 years. Wounded June 27, 1862, at Gaines' Mill, Va.; Dec. 13, 1862, at Fredericksburg, Va. Discharged Feb. 19, 1863, for disability, at Washington, D.C.

Sullivan, Maurice, enlisted June 11, 1861, shoemaker, age 19, single, residence Marlboro, born in Cork, Ire. Mustered in June 11, 1861, term 3 years. Wounded May 5, 1864, Wilderness, Va. Mustered out June 21, 1864, as Corp.

Sweeney, Edward, enlisted June 11, 1861, shoemaker, age 18, single, residence Marlboro, born in Cork, Ire. Mustered in June 11, 1861, term 3 years. Mustered out June 21, 1864.

Tighe, Patrick, enlisted June 11, 1861, age 23, single, residence Boston. Mustered in June 11, 1861, term 3 years. Deserted Sept. 6, 1863, Miner's Hill, Va.

Tobin, Michael, enlisted June 11, 1861, shoemaker, age 26, single, residence Marlboro, born in Cork, Ire. Mustered in June 11, 1861, term 3 years. Mustered out June 21, 1864.

Walker, Silas, enlisted July 16, 1863, operative, age 26, single, residence Monson, credited to Monson. Mustered in July 16, 1863, term 3 years. Missing in action May 8, 1864, Laurel Hill, Va. Unofficially reported as killed.

Walsh, Martin, enlisted Aug. 12, 1862, shoemaker, age 21, single, residence Salem.   Mustered in Aug. 12, 1862, term 3 years.   Discharged April 22, 1863.

Walsh, Walter, enlisted Aug. 9, 1862, laborer, age 22, residence Boston, born in Ireland.   Mustered in Aug. 9, 1862, term 3 years.   Wounded May 5, 1864, Wilderness, Va.   Mustered out June 21, 1864.

Whalan, Mathew, enlisted Feb. 13, 1862, bootmaker, age 35, married, residence Dorchester, credited to Dorchester.   Mustered in Feb. 13, 1862, term 3 years.   Re-enlisted Feb. 22, 1864.   Transferred to 32d Mass. Vols. June 10, 1864.

Williams, William, enlisted Aug. 20, 1863, laborer, age 21, single, residence Jersey City, credited to Hatfield.   Mustered in Aug. 20, 1863, term 3 years.   Deserted Sept. 13, 1863, Beverly Ford, Va.

Winter, Lawrence, enlisted Aug. 16, 1862, laborer, age 43, married, residence Salem, born in Ireland   Mustered in Aug. 16, 1862, term 3 years.   Died of disease Dec. 6, 1862, Falmouth, Va.

COMPANY H.

O'Neil, Jeremiah, Capt., bootmaker, age 22, single, residence Milford, born in Co. Cork, Ire.   Mustered in June 11, 1861, term 3 years.   Killed June 27, 1862, Gaines' Mill, Va.

Roach, Thomas K., 1st Lieut., bootmaker, age 25, single, residence Milford, born in Ireland.   Mustered in June 11, 1861, term 3 years.   Promoted Capt. July 8, 1862.   Dismissed Sept. 30, 1863.

Burke, Timothy, 2d Lieut., bootmaker, age 25, single, residence Milford, born in Co Cork, Ire.   Mustered in June 11, 1861, term 3 years.   Promoted 1st Lieut. Jan. 28, 1862; Capt. Aug. 27, 1862.   Wounded June 27, 1862, Gaines' Mill, Va.; wounded May 5, 1864, Wilderness, Va.   Mustered out June 21, 1864.

Murphy, Patrick E., 1st Sergt., enlisted June 11, 1861, bootcutter, age 20, single, residence Milford, born in Co. Cork, Ire.   Mustered in June 11, 1861, term 3 years.   Promoted Commissary Sergt. March 1, 1862; Q.M.-Sergt. March 10, 1862; promoted Sergt.-Maj.; acting Lieut. July 2, 1862; 2d Lieut. Co. K, Sept. 26, 1862; 1st Lieut. Feb. 8, 1863; mustered March 1, 1863, Co. E.   Wounded July 1, 1862, Malvern Hill, Va.; wounded May 5, 1864, Wilderness, Va., lost left arm.   Mustered out June 21, 1864.

Burke, William R., Sergt., enlisted June 11, 1861, bootmaker, age 21, single, residence Milford.   Mustered in June 11, 1861, term 3 years.   Promoted Sergt.-Maj. to Jan. 8, 1863; 2d Lieut. Jan. 8, 1863; 1st Lieut. Aug. 4, 1863.   Mustered out June 21, 1864.

Doherty, Patrick, Sergt., enlisted June 11, 1861, bootmaker, age 20, single, residence Milford.   Mustered in June 11, 1861, term 3 years.   1st Sergt. Jan. 8, 1863.   Wounded June 4, 1864, Bethesda Church, Va.   Mustered out June 21, 1864.

Hubon, Thomas, Sergt., enlisted June 11, 1861, bootmaker, age 25, single, residence Milford, born in Ireland   Mustered in June 11, 1861, term 3 years.   Wounded July 1, 1862, Malvern Hill, Va.   Died July 22, 1862, as Corp., of wounds received.

Finnerty, Michael A., Sergt., enlisted June 11, 1861, clerk, age 22, single, residence Milford, born in Mayo, Ire.   Mustered in June 11, 1861, term 3 years.   Promoted Sergt.-Maj.; 2d Lieut. Co. H, Nov. 3, 1861; 1st Lieut. Sept. 26, 1862; Capt. March 30, 1863.   Transferred to Co. D, Oct. 22, 1863.   Mustered out June 21, 1864, as Capt. Co. D.

Callahan, Daniel, Corp., enlisted June 11, 1861, bootmaker, age 23, married, residence Milford, born in Ireland. Mustered in June 11, 1861, term 3 years. Wounded June 27, 1862, Gaines' Mill, Va. Discharged for disability Oct. 1, 1862 (wounded).

Rowe, Patrick, Corp., enlisted June 11, 1861, bootmaker, age 27, single, residence Milford, born in Co. Galway, Ire. Mustered in June 11, 1861, term 3 years. Discharged for disability Oct. 30, 1862.

O'Neil, Dennis, Corp., enlisted June 11, 1861, bootmaker, age 18, single, residence Milford, born in Cork, Ire. Mustered in June 11, 1861, term 3 years. Sergt., March 1, 1862. Discharged for disability as Sergt. Sept. 17, 1862.

Donavan, John H., Corp., enlisted June 11, 1861, bootmaker, age 18, single, residence Milford, born in Randolph, Mass. Mustered in June 11, 1861, term 3 years. Sergt., Sept. 16, 1862. Mustered out June 21, 1864, as Sergt.

Rowe, James, Corp., enlisted June 11, 1861, bootmaker, age 22, single, residence Milford, born in Co. Galway, Ire. Mustered in June 11, 1861, term 3 years. Wounded June 27, 1862, Gaines' Mill, Va. Discharged for disability Oct. 22, 1862.

Blunt, Patrick, Corp., enlisted June 11, 1861, bootmaker, age 25, single, residence Milford, born in Mayo, Ire. Mustered in June 11, 1861, term 3 years. Promoted Sergt. Jan. 15, 1863. Mustered out June 21, 1864.

Cosgrove, Michael, Corp., enlisted June 11, 1851, bootmaker, age 18, single, residence Milford, born in Blackstone. Mustered in June 11, 1861, term 3 years. No further record at A.G.O., Mass

McGovern, James, Corp., enlisted June 11, 1861, bootmaker, age 21, single, residence Milford, born in Holliston, Mass. Mustered in June 11, 1861, term 3 years. Wounded June 27, 1862, Gaines' Mill, Va. Died of wounds received Aug. 7, 1862.

Mooney, Thomas, Musician, enlisted June 11, 1861, age 16, single, residence Worcester, born in Worcester. Mustered in June 11, 1861, term 3 years. Deserted Sept., 1863, from hospital.

Pratt, Andrew, Musician, enlisted June 11, 1861, gilder, age 26, single, residence Boston, born in Cork, Ire. Mustered in June 11, 1861, term 3 years. Sergt., Jan. 8, 1863. Mustered out June 21, 1864.

Conoughton, Timothy, Wagoner, enlisted June 11, 1861, bootmaker, age 25, single, residence Milford, born in Galway, Ire. Mustered in June 11, 1861, term 3 years. Mustered out June 21, 1864.

Adams, Thomas H., enlisted July 10, 1863, shoemaker, age 25, single, residence Marblehead. Mustered in July 10, 1863, term 3 years. Wounded June 3, 1864, Bethesda Church, Va. Transferred to 32d Mass. Vols. June 10, 1864.

Binder, John W. H., enlisted Aug. 21, 1863, clerk, age 31, single, residence Boston, credited to Boston, Wd. 12. Mustered in Aug. 21, 1863, term 3 years. Transferred to 32d Mass. Vols. June 10, 1864.

Brady, Peter, enlisted June 11, 1861, bootmaker, age 20, single, residence Randolph, born in Ireland. Mustered in June 11, 1861, term 3 years. Mustered out June 21, 1864.

Bradley, Peter, enlisted June 11, 1861, bootmaker, age 24, married, residence Milford, born in Ireland. Mustered in June 11, 1861, term 3 years. Deserted Feb 22, 1863, Falmouth, Va.

Broderick, William, enlisted June 11, 1861, bootmaker, age 18, single, residence Milford, born in Maine. Mustered in June 11, 1861, term 3 years. Wounded July 1, 1862, Malvern Hill, Va. Mustered out June 21, 1864.

Burke, Michael, enlisted Aug. 21, 1863, seaman, age 24, single, residence Boston, credited to Boston, Wd. 11. Mustered in Aug. 21, 1863, term 3 years. Wounded July 1, 1862, Malvern Hill, Va. Transferred to 32d Mass. Vols. June 10, 1864, as " Bourke, Michael J."

Burke, David, enlisted June 11, 1861, bootmaker, age 36, married, residence Milford, born in Mayo, Ire. Mustered in June 11, 1861, term 3 years. Wounded July 1, 1862, Malvern Hill, Va. Mustered out June 21, 1864.

Burk, Michael D., enlisted July 26, 1862, shoemaker, age 24, married, residence Boston. Mustered in July 26, 1862. Mustered out June 21, 1864.

Burke, Michael, enlisted June 11, 1861, bootmaker, age 22, married, residence Lynn, born in Galway. Mustered in June 11, 1861, term 3 years. Wounded June 27, 1862, Gaines' Mill, Va. Mustered out June 21, 1864.

Bourk, Samuel, enlisted Aug. 10, 1862, bootmaker, age 29, residence Holliston, born in Ireland. Mustered in Aug. 11, 1862, term 3 years. Wounded May 12, 1864, Spottsylvania, Va. Absent wounded.

Cahill, Maurice, enlisted June 11, 1861, bootmaker, age 20, single, residence Lawrence, born in Ireland. Mustered in June 11, 1861, term 3 years. Wounded July 1, 1862, Malvern Hill, Va. Discharged for disability Oct. 14, 1862.

Cain, John, enlisted June 11, 1861, bootmaker, age 25, single, residence Milford, born in Co. Galway, Ire. Mustered in June 11, 1861, term 3 years. Discharged for disability Nov. 8, 1862. Wounded July 1, 1862, Malvern Hill, Va.

Carey, William J., enlisted June 11, 1861, bootmaker, age 30, married, residence Milford, born in Galway, Ire. Mustered in June 11, 1861, term 3 years. Mustered out June 21, 1864.

Carr, John W., enlisted June 11, 1861, bootmaker, age 21, single, residence Milford, born in Galway, Ire. Mustered in June 11, 1861, term 3 years. Mustered out June 21, 1864.

Carr, John, enlisted June 11, 1861, bootmaker, age 24, single, residence Milford, born in Galway, Ire. Mustered in June 11, 1861, term 3 years. Mustered out June 21, 1864.

Carmody, Cornelius, enlisted June 11, 1861, bootmaker, age 21, single, residence Haverhill, born in Limerick, Ire. Mustered in June 11, 1861, term 3 years. Transferred to Co. A, Aug. 9, 1861. Wounded, Malvern Hill, Va., July 1, 1862; Fredericksburg, Va., Dec. 13, 1862. Mustered out June 21, 1864, in Co. A.

Cashman, John C., enlisted June 11, 1861, laborer, age 20, single, residence East Boston, born in Ireland. Mustered in June 11, 1861, term 3 years. Deserted Sept. 20, 1861, Arlington Heights, Va.

Clifford, John, enlisted June 11, 1861, bootmaker, age 23, single, residence Abington, born in Ireland. Mustered in June 11, 1861, term 3 years. Wounded June 27, 1862, Gaines' Mill, Va. Discharged for disability Oct. 27, 1862.

Coakley, Michael, enlisted Feb. 19, 1862, laborer, age 21, single, residence Somerville, born in Halifax, N S. Mustered in Feb. 19, 1862, term 3 years Wounded July 1, 1862, Malvern Hill, Va.; Dec. 13, 1862, Fredericksburg, Va. Discharged for disability, no date.

Collins, Patrick, enlisted June 11, 1861, bootmaker, age 22, single, residence Milford, born in Ireland. Mustered in June 11, 1861, term 3 years. Died of disease Oct. 21, 1862.

Connors, James, enlisted June 11, 1861, bootmaker, age 18, single, residence Milford, born in Cork, Ire. Mustered in June 11, 1861, term 3 years. Wounded July 1, 1862, Malvern Hill, Va.; wounded May 5, 1864, Wilderness, Va. Mustered out June 21, 1864.

Connor, William, enlisted June 11, 1861, baker, age 19, single, residence Boston, born in Cork, Ire. Mustered in June 11, 1861, term 3 years. Mustered out June 21, 1864.

Convoy, John, enlisted June 11, 1861, laborer, age 35, married, residence East Boston, born in Galway, Ire. Mustered in June 11, 1861, term 3 years. Mustered out June 21, 1864.

Connell, Bryan, enlisted June 11, 1861. Mustered in June 11, 1861, term 3 years. Transferred to Invalid Corps July 27, 1863.

Corcoran, James, enlisted Aug. 20, 1862, engraver, age 32, married, residence Lawrence, born in Ireland. Mustered in Aug. 20, 1862, term 3 years. Wounded Dec. 13, 1862, Fredericksburg, Va. Transferred to Invalid Corps Oct. 5, 1863, Washington, D.C.

Coy, James, enlisted June 11, 1861, bootmaker, age 21, single, residence Milford, born in Ireland. Mustered in June 11, 1861, term 3 years. Deserted Aug. 14, 1862, Harrison Landing, Va.

Cowells, Merrick, enlisted June 11, 1861, bootmaker, age 21, single, residence Milford, born in Worcester. Mustered in June 11, 1861, term 3 years. Discharged for disability Oct. 29, 1861.

Cummings, Thos., enlisted June 11, 1861, laborer, age 19, single, residence Milford, born in Co. Clare, Ire. Mustered in June 11, 1861, term 3 years. Killed June 27, 1862, Gaines' Mill, Va.

Curley, Simon, enlisted June 11, 1861, bootmaker, age 22, single, residence Brookfield, born in Ireland. Mustered in June 11, 1861, term 3 years. Killed June 27, 1862, Gaines' Mill, Va.

Curley, Malachi, enlisted June 11, 1861, bootmaker, age 21, single, residence Milford, born in Galway, Ire. Mustered in June 11, 1861, term 3 years. Wounded at Gainesville June 27, 1862; Sergt. Jan. 4, 1863; wounded May 5, 1864, Wilderness, Va. Mustered out June 21, 1864, as Sergt.

Cronin, John, enlisted June 11, 1861, bootmaker, age 22, single, residence Milford, born in Kerry, Ire. Mustered in June 11, 1861, term 3 years. Mustered out June 21, 1864.

Davoren, Patrick, enlisted June 11, 1861, bootmaker, age 32, residence Milford, born in Ireland. Mustered in June 11, 1861, term 3 years. Transferred to Invalid Corps Oct. 5, 1863, by order Secretary of War.

Day, Samuel, enlisted June 11, 1861, bootmaker, age 24, married, residence Milford, born in Ireland. Mustered in June 11, 1861, term 3 years. Killed June 27, 1862, Gaines' Mill, Va.

Desmond, Timothy, enlisted Aug. 15, 1862, bootmaker, age 24, single, residence Hopkinton. Mustered in Aug. 15, 1862, term 3 years. Promoted Corp. Sept. 18, 1862. Mustered out June 21, 1864.

Dillon, Jeremiah, enlisted June 11, 1861, bootmaker, age 22, single, residence Milford, born in Kerry, Ire. Mustered in June 11, 1861, term 3 years. Mustered out June 21, 1864.

Dodd, Nehemiah S., enlisted July 10, 1863, shoemaker, age 24, married, residence Marblehead, credited to Marblehead. Mustered in July 10, 1863, term 3 years Wounded June 2, 1864, Bethesda Church, Va. Transferred to 32d Mass. Vols. June 10, 1864.

Doherty, John, enlisted June 11, 1862, bootmaker, age 32, married, residence Boston, born in Cork, Ireland. Mustered in June 11, 1861, term 3 years. Mustered out June 21, 1864.

Doherty, Hugh, enlisted June 11, 1861, bootmaker, age 20, single, residence Milford, born in Ireland. Mustered in June 11, 1861, term 3 years. Drowned Sept 26, 1861, Potomac river.

Doherty, Patrick, enlisted June 11, 1861, bootmaker, age 21, single, residence Boston, born in Ireland. Mustered in June 11, 1861, term 3 years. Mustered out June 21, 1864.

Doherty, Patrick B., enlisted July 19, 1862, teamster, age 35, married, residence Boston, born in Ireland. Mustered in July 19, 1862, term 3 years. Discharged with Co., Boston, June 21, 1864.

Donnelly, John, enlisted June 11, 1861, bootmaker, age 22, single, residence Weymouth, born in Limerick, Ire. Mustered in June 11, 1861, term 3 years. Wounded May 3, 1863, Chancellorsville, Va. Transferred to Invalid Corps Dec. 29, 1863.

Donavan, John F., enlisted June 11, 1861, bootmaker, age 22, single, residence Boston, born in Boston, Mass. Mustered in June 11, 1861, term 3 years. Wounded at Malvern Hill, Va., July 1, 1862. Corp. Jan 4, 1863. Mustered out June 21, 1864, as Corp.

Donnelly, James, enlisted Feb. 7, 1862, laborer, age 34, married, residence Boston, born in Ireland. Mustered in Feb. 7, 1862, term 3 years. Transferred to 32d Mass. Vols. June 3, 1864.

Dooley, James, enlisted July 29, 1862, laborer, age 27, single, residence Boston, born in Ireland. Mustered in July 29, 1862, term 3 years. Wounded Dec. 13, 1862, Fredericksburg, Va. Died of wounds received Dec. 20, 1862.

Driscoll, Michael, enlisted June 11, 1861, bootmaker, age 22, single, residence Milford, born in Cork, Ire. Mustered in June 11, 1861, term 3 years. Mustered out June 21, 1864.

Fahy Cornelius, enlisted July 26, 1862, shoemaker, age 22, married, residence Boston, born in Ireland. Mustered in July 26, 1862, term 3 years. Discharged for disability Dec. 27, 1862.

Finton, Thomas, enlisted June 11, 1861, bootmaker, age 30, married, residence Milford, born in Ireland. Mustered in June 11, 1861, term 3 years. Mustered out June 21, 1864.

Finnerty, Francis, enlisted Aug. 6, 1862, bootmaker, age 25, single, residence Milford, credited to Milford, born in Ireland. Mustered in Aug. 6, 1862, term 3 years. Re-enlisted Dec. 31, 1863. Killed May 5, 1864, Wilderness, Va. Certificate on file from 2d Aud. Officer.

Finnerty, Michael, enlisted March 17, 1864, bootmaker, age 29, single, residence Milford, credited to Milford, born in Ireland. Mustered in March 17, 1864, term 3 years. Wounded June 3, 1864, Bethesda Church, Va., May 5, 1864, Wilderness, Va. Transferred to 32d Mass. Vols. June 10, 1864.

Fitzsimmons, Patrick, enlisted Dec. 10, 1863, bootmaker, age 18, single, residence Milford, credited to Milford, born in Limerick, Ire. Mustered in Dec. 10, 1863, term 3 years. Transferred to 32d Mass. Vols. June 10, 1864.

Fitzpatrick, Edward, enlisted June 11, 1861, bootmaker, age 20, single, residence Milford, born in Killdare, Ire. Mustered in June 11, 1861, term 3 years. Wounded July 1, 1862, at Malvern Hill. Mustered out June 21, 1864.,

Flemming, Alexander, enlisted Aug. 4, 1862, laborer, age 26, residence Boston, born in St. Johns, N.B. Mustered in Aug. 4, 1862, term 3 years. Deserted July 1, 1863, Maryland.

Flynn, Patrick, enlisted June 11, 1861, bootmaker, age 27, single, residence Milford, born in Ireland. Mustered in June 11, 1861, term 3 years. Wounded June 27, 1862, Gaines' Mill. Discharged for disability Sept. 26, 1862.

Foley, Francis, enlisted June 11, 1861, bootmaker, age 24, single, residence Milford, born in Ireland. Mustered in June 11, 1861, term 3 years. Discharged for disability Jan. 26, 1863.

Foley, John, enlisted Aug. 21, 1863, laborer, age 28, single, residence New York, credited to Braintree. Mustered in Aug. 21, 1863, term 3 years. Wounded May 5, 1864, Wilderness, Va. Transferred to 32d Mass. Vols. June 10, 1864.

Ford, John J., enlisted Jan. 1, 1864, bootmaker, age 29, married, residence Milford, credited to Milford, born in Ireland. Mustered in Jan. 1, 1864, term 3 years. Wounded May 5, 1864, Wilderness, Va. Transferred to 32d Mass. Vols. June 10, 1864.

Ford, William, enlisted June 11, 1861, bootmaker, age 24, single, residence Milford, born in Galway, Ire. Mustered in June 11, 1861, term 3 years. Promoted to Corp. Jan. 1, 1862. Mustered out June 21, 1864.

Gilbride, Hugh, enlisted June 11, 1861, bootmaker, age 26, single, residence Milford, born in Ireland. Mustered in June 11, 1861, term 3 years. Prisoner July 20, 1862. Discharged for disability Jan. 13, 1863, wounded.

Goss, John R., enlisted July 10, 1863, shoemaker, age 23, single, residence Marblehead, credited to Marblehead. Mustered in July 10, 1863, term 3 years. Killed May 12, 1864, Spottsylvania, Va.

Greene, Edward, enlisted June 11, 1861, bootmaker, age 25, single, residence Milford, born in Ireland. Mustered in June 11, 1861, term 3 years. Deserted Sept. 20, 1861, Arlington Heights, Va.

Griffin, John, enlisted June 11, 1861, bootmaker, age 19, single, residence Milford, born in Galway, Ire. Mustered in June 11, 1861, term 3 years. Mustered out June 21, 1864.

Griffin, John W., enlisted June 11, 1861, bootmaker, age 19, single, residence Milford, born in Tipperary, Ire. Mustered in June 11, 1861, term 3 years. Promoted Corp. Oct. 16, 1862. Mustered out June 21, 1864, as Corp.

Hart, Henry, enlisted June 11, 1861, laborer, age 18, single, residence Lowell, born in England. Mustered in June 11, 1861, term 3 years. Mustered out June 21, 1864.

Hayes, Michael, enlisted Aug. 19, 1862, laborer, age 32, married, residence Boston, born in Ireland. Mustered in Aug. 10, 1862, term 3 years. Deserted July 1, 1863, Maryland.

Healy, John, enlisted Aug. 21, 1863, tailor, age 26, married, residence New York city, credited to Boston, Wd. 11. Mustered in Aug. 21, 1863, term 3 years. Transferred to 32d Mass. Vols. June 10, 1864.

Holien, Patrick, enlisted June 11, 1861, bootmaker, age 20, single, residence Milford, born in Co. Mayo, Ire. Mustered in June 11, 1861, term 3 years. Killed July 1, 1862, Malvern Hill, Va.

Holmes, John, enlisted July 13, 1863, shoemaker, age 33, married, residence Methuen, credited to Methuen. Mustered in July 13, 1863, term 3 years. Wounded May 5, 1864, Wilderness, Va. Transferred to 32d Mass. Vols. June 10, 1864.

Houran, Patrick, enlisted June 11, 1861, bootmaker, age 26, single, residence Milford, born in Ireland. Mustered in June 11, 1861, term 3 years. Wounded June 27, 1862, Gaines' Mill, Va.; wounded July 1, 1862, Malvern Hill, Va. Deserted from hospital September, 1863.

Jackson, William, enlisted June 11, 1861, blacksmith, age 25, residence Boston, born in Ireland. Mustered in June 11, 1861, term 3 years. Deserted Aug. 14, 1862, Harrison Landing, Va.

Jordan, Michael, enlisted June 11, 1861, bootmaker, age 26, single, residence Milford, born in Ireland. Mustered in June 11, 1861, term 3 years. Died of disease June 1, 1862.

Kavanay, Paul, enlisted July 22, 1862, baker, age 28, married, residence Boston, born in Ireland. Mustered in July 22, 1862, term 3 years. Deserted at Fredericksburg, Va., Dec. 13, 1862, as '' Kavanagh.''

Keenan, James, enlisted June 11, 1861, laborer, age 21, single, residence Boston, born in Ireland. Mustered in June 11, 1861, term 3 years. Wounded June 27, 1862, Gaines' Mill, Va. Deserted July 1, 1863, Maryland.

Keliell, Edward S., enlisted June 11, 1861, bootmaker, age 21, single, residence Boston. Mustered in June 11, 1861, term 3 years. Deserted September, 1863, from hospital, as '' Skehill.''

Kelley, Patrick, enlisted June 11, 1861, bootmaker, age 25, single, residence Milford, born in Galway, Ire. Mustered in June 11, 1861, term 3 years. Discharged July 1, 1863.

Kennedy, Patrick, enlisted June 11, 1861, bootmaker, age 29, single, residence Milford, born in Galway, Ire. Mustered in June 11, 1861, term 3 years. No further record A.-G.O.

Leydon, Patrick, enlisted Aug. 21, 1863, manufacturer, age 26, single, residence Dobb's Ferry, N.Y., credited to Boston, Wd. 11. Mustered in Aug. 21, 1863, term 3 years. Transferred to 32d Mass. Vols. June 10, 1864.

Leonard, John, enlisted Aug. 20, 1863, lumberman, age 26, single, residence Salem, credited to West Newbury. Mustered in Aug. 20, 1863, term 3 years. Deserted May 1, 1864, Bealton, Va.

Lewis, Edmund, enlisted July 10, 1863, mason, age 34, single, residence Marblehead, credited to Marblehead. Mustered in July 10, 1863, term 3 years. Transferred to 32d Mass. Vols. June 10, 1864.

Lynch, Patrick, enlisted Feb. 3, 1862, laborer, age 33, married, residence South Weymouth. Mustered in Feb. 3, 1862, term 3 years. Wounded June 27, 1862, Gaines' Mill, Va. Transferred to 32d Mass. Vols. June 10, 1864.

Melvin, John, enlisted July 10, 1863, cordwainer, age 25, single, residence Marblehead, credited to Marblehead. Mustered in July 10, 1863, term 3 years. Wounded May 5, 1864, Wilderness, Va. Transferred to 32d Mass. Vols. June 10, 1864.

Mitchell, George, enlisted Jan. 4, 1864, farmer, age 21, single, residence Scarboro, credited to Boston, Wd. 3, born in Waterbury, Vt. Mustered in Jan. 4, 1864, term 3 years. Transferred to 32d Mass. Vols. June 10, 1864.

Mooney, Dennis, enlisted June 11, 1861, bootmaker, age 26, single, residence Milford, born in Ireland. Mustered in June 11, 1861, term 3 years. Discharged for disability Oct. 30, 1862.

Mullan, Thomas, enlisted June 11, 1861, laborer, age 21, single, residence Abington, born in Ireland. Mustered in June 11, 1861, term 3 years. Wounded in the head by shell Oct. 16, 1862, on Sheppardstown reconnoissance. Discharged to date Nov. 25, 1864, by reason of insanity.

Mullen, John, enlisted June 11, 1861, bootmaker, age 30, married, residence Milford, born in Ireland. Mustered in June 11, 1861, term 3 years. Killed May 8, 1864, at Laurel Hill, Va.

Mullen, Thomas, enlisted Feb 9, 1864, bootmaker, age 21, single, residence Milford, credited to Milford. Mustered in Feb. 9, 1864, term 3 years. Wounded May 5. 1864, Wilderness, Va. Transferred to 32d Mass. Vols. June 10, 1864.

Murry, Francis, enlisted Dec. 7, 1863, bootmaker, age 37, married, residence Hopkinton, credited to Milton, born in Galway, Ire. Mustered in Dec. 7, 1863, term 3 years. Wounded May 8, 1864, Laurel Hill, Va Transferred to 32d Mass. Vols. June 10, 1864.

Murray, John, enlisted June 11, 1861, bootmaker, age 19, single, residence Milford, born in Co. Cork, Ire. Mustered in June 11, 1861, term 3 years. Wounded June 27, 1862, Gaines' Mill, Va. Discharged for expiration of term of service.

Murphy, Jeremiah, enlisted June 11, 1861, bootmaker, age 23, single, residence Milford, born in Ireland. Mustered in June 11, 1861, term 3 years. Killed June 27, 1862, at Gaines' Mill, Va.

Murphy, Michael, enlisted June 11, 1861, bootmaker, age 20, single, residence Southboro, born in Kerry, Ire. Mustered in June 11, 1861, term 3 years. Mustered out June 21, 1864.

McAnnany, John, enlisted June 11, 1861, bootmaker, age 25, single, residence Milford, born in Ireland. Mustered in June 11, 1861, term 3 years. Discharged for disability Oct. 29, 1861.

McBrine, William, enlisted Nov. 9, 1861, polisher, age 19, single, residence Boston. Mustered in Nov. 9, 1861, term 3 years. Killed June 27, 1862, Gaines' Mill, Va.

McCarthy, Daniel, enlisted July 29, 1862, sailor, age 19, married, residence Boston, born in Ireland. Mustered in July 29, 1862, term 3 years. Deserted March 1, 1863, Falmouth, Va.

McCarthy, Owen, enlisted Jan. 2, 1864, bootmaker, age 42, married, residence Hopkinton, credited to Hopkinton, born in Ireland. Mustered in Jan. 2, 1864, term 3 years. Transferred to 32d Mass. Vols. June 10, 1864.

McCarthy, Patrick, enlisted June 11, 1861, bootmaker, age 21, single, residence Milford, born in St. Johns, N.B. Mustered in June 11, 1861, term 3 years. Mustered out June 21, 1864.

McCormack, James, enlisted Aug. 12, 1862, shoemaker, age 35, married, residence Boston, born in Ireland. Mustered in Aug. 12, 1862, term 3 years. Mustered out June 21, 1864.

McDonald, William, enlisted Aug 20, 1863, sailor, age 20, married, residence Washington, N.C., credited to Ipswich. Mustered in Aug. 20, 1863, term 3 years. Transferred to 32d Mass. Vols June 10, 1864.

McGowen, James, enlisted June 11, 1861, bootmaker, age 22, single, residence Milford, born in Ireland. Mustered in June 11, 1861, term 3 years. Wounded July 1, 1862, Malvern Hill, Va.; prisoner July 20, 1862. Discharged for disability, March 25, 1863, Corp.

McGrath, William, enlisted June 11, 1861, laborer, age 20, single, residence Boston, born in Ireland. Mustered in June 11, 1861, term 3 years. Wounded in leg at Hanover Court House, Va., May 27, 1862. Deserted Sept. 18, 1863, from hospital.

McGulleon, Patrick, enlisted June 11, 1861, laborer, age 20, single, residence Milford, born in Kerry, Ire. Mustered in June 11, 1861, term 3 years. Promoted Corp. Jan. 24, 1862. Mustered out June 21, 1864.

McLaughlin, William, enlisted Aug. 7, 1862, laborer, age 34, single, residence Boston, born in Ireland. Mustered in Aug. 7, 1862, term 3 years. Died of disease Jan. 2, 1863.

McLoughlin, Edward, enlisted June 11, 1861, bootmaker, age 20, single, residence Boston, born in Ireland. Mustered in June 11, 1861, term 3 years. Mustered out June 21, 1864.

McMahan, Michael B., enlisted June 11, 1861, bootmaker, age 21, single, residence Milford, born in Ireland. Mustered in June 11, 1861, term 3 years. Discharged for disability, March 1, 1862.

McMurray, Timothy, enlisted Feb. 5, 1862, butcher, age 23, single, residence Woburn, born in Ireland. Mustered in Feb. 5, 1862, term 3 years. Deserted Feb. 21, 1863, Falmouth, Va.

McNamara, Owen, enlisted Aug. 8, 1862, moulder, age 39, married, residence Boston, born in Ireland. Mustered in Aug. 9, 1862, term 3 years. Transferred to Invalid Corps.

McNeal, James, enlisted June 11, 1861, bootmaker, age 19, single, residence Milford, born in Scotland. Mustered in June 11, 1861, term 3 years. Wounded June 27, 1862, Gaines' Mill, Va; July 1, 1862, Malvern Hill, Va. Mustered out June 21, 1864.

Nugent, Thomas, enlisted July 26, 1862, tailor, age 28, married, residence Boston, born in Ireland   Mustered in July 26, 1862, term 3 years. Accidentally killed, March 17, 1864, on railroad.

O'Connell, James, enlisted Dec. 9, 1863, laborer, age 40, married, residence Boston, credited to Boston, Wd. 3.   Mustered in Dec. 9, 1863, term 3 years. Wounded May 5, 1864, Wilderness, Va. A.G.O. died of starvation and exposure while a prisoner of war Oct. 7, 1864.

O'Grady, John, enlisted June 11, 1861, laborer, age 24, single, residence Boston, born in Ireland. Mustered in June 11, 1861, term 3 years. Wounded June 27, 1862, Gaines' Mill, Va. Discharged for disability Dec. 31, 1862.

O'Keeffe, John, enlisted Nov. 9, 1861, hod-carrier, age 42, married, residence Boston. Mustered in Nov. 9, 1861, term 3 years. Wounded June 27, 1862, Gaines' Mill, Va. ; July 1, 1862, Malvern Hill, Va. Discharged Nov. 2, 1862.

O'Neil, John, enlisted June 11, 1861, bootmaker, age 22, single, residence Milford, born in Ireland. Mustered in June 11, 1861, term 3 years. Killed June 27, 1862, Gaines' Mill, Va.

Peachey, William, enlisted July 10, 1863, cordwainer, age 24, married, residence Marblehead, credited to Marblehead. Mustered in July 10, 1863, term 3 years. Killed May 5, 1864, Wilderness, Va.

Reagon, Joseph, enlisted June 11, 1861, bootmaker, age 20, single, residence Milford, born in Limerick. Ire. Mustered in June 11, 1861, term 3 years. Mustered out June 21, 1864.

Riley, John F., enlisted Aug. 12, 1862, shoemaker, age 32, married, residence Randolph, born in Ireland. Mustered in Aug. 12, 1862, term 3 years. Died of disease Dec. 15, 1862.

Riley, John O., enlisted Nov. 9, 1861, blacksmith, age 25, single, residence Boston. Mustered in Nov. 9, 1861, term 3 years. Deserted Aug. 14, 1862, Harrison Landing, Va., as " O'Reilly."

Ring, Jeremiah, enlisted June 11, 1861, bootmaker, age 27, single, residence Milford, born in Co. Cork, Ire. Mustered in June 11, 1861, term 3 years. Killed Dec. 13, 1862, Fredericksburg, Va.

Rix, James J., enlisted July 10, 1863, cordwainer, age 26, single, residence Marblehead, credited to Marblehead. Mustered in July 10, 1863, term 3 years. Wounded May 5, 1864, Wilderness, Va. Transferred to 32d Mass. Vols. June 10, 1864.

Roach, Patrick, enlisted June 11, 1861, bootmaker, age 24, single, residence Hopkinton, born in Ireland. Mustered in June 11, 1861, term 3 years. Wounded July 1, 1862, Malvern Hill, Va. Deserted Aug. 14, 1862, Harrison Landing, Va.

Rowley, Edward, enlisted June 11, 1861, bootmaker, age 23, single, residence Weymouth, born in Ireland. Mustered in June 11, 1861, term 3 years. Deserted July 1, 1863, Maryland, as " Raleigh "

Salkins, John B., enlisted July 10, 1863, farmer, age 20, single, residence Marblehead, credited to Marblehead. Mustered in July 10, 1863, term 3 years. Wounded June 3, 1864, Bethesda Church, Va. Transferred to 32d Mass. Vols. June 10, 1864.

Savage, John, enlisted June 11, 1861, bootmaker, age 21, single, residence Worcester, born in Ireland. Mustered in June 11, 1861, term 3 years. Deserted Aug. 14, 1862, Harrison Landing, Va.

Scahill, Edward, enlisted June 11, 1861, laborer, age 21, single, residence Boston, born in Ireland. Mustered in June 11, 1861, term 3 years. Deserted September, no date, 1863, from hospital.

Shea, Maurice, enlisted Aug. 19, 1862, shoemaker, age 29, married, residence Boston, born in Ireland. Mustered in Aug. 19, 1862, term 3 years. Deserted July 1, 1863, Maryland.

Shea, John, enlisted June 11, 1861, bootmaker, age 20, single, residence Milford, born in Kerry, Ire. Mustered in June 11, 1861, term 3 years Wounded May 5, 1864, Wilderness, Va Mustered out June 21, 1864.

Shields, John, enlisted June 11, 1861, laborer, age 21, single, residence Boston, born in Ireland. Mustered in June 11, 1861, term 3 years. Deserted Aug. 14, 1862, Harrison Landing, Va.

Slattery, Thomas, enlisted June 11, 1861, bootmaker, age 21, single, residence Milford, born in Limerick, Ire. Mustered in June 11, 1861, term 3 years. Wounded June 27, 1862, Gaines' Mill, Va. Mustered out June 21, 1864.

Slattery, David, enlisted June 11, 1861, bootmaker, age 20, single, residence Milford, born in Limerick, Ire. Mustered in June 11, 1861, term 3 years. Corp. Oct. 16, 1862. Wounded July 1, 1862, Malvern Hill, Va. Mustered out June 21, 1864, as Corp.

Smith, Patrick, enlisted July 9, 1861, laborer, age 35, married, residence Boston, born in Ireland. Mustered in July 9, 1862, term 3 years. Transferred to Invalid Corps Dec. 14, 1863.

Sweeney, Daniel, enlisted June 11, 1861, factory, age 22, single, residence Asabet or Stowe, born in Co Cork, Ire. Mustered in June 11, 1861, term 3 years. Wounded June 27, 1862, Gaines' Mill, Va. Discharged for disability Sept. 22, 1862

Sweeney, Patrick, enlisted Dec. 3, 1863, pedler, age 38, married, residence Boston, credited to Boston, Wd. 3, born in Mayo, Ire. Mustered in Dec. 3, 1863, term 3 years. Transferred to 32d Mass. Vols June 10, 1864.

Sweeney, Dolty, enlisted June 11, 1861, bootmaker, age 19, single, residence Milford, born in St. Johns. Mustered in June 11, 1861, term 3 years. Wounded June 27, 1862, Gaines' Mill, Va. Transferred to Battery D, 5th U.S Art., June 10, 1864.

Sullivan, John, enlisted June 11, 1861, laborer, age 25, single, residence Boston, born in Ireland. Mustered in June 11, 1861, term 3 years. Discharged for disability Jan. 31, 1863.

Sullivan, Daniel, enlisted Aug. 7, 1862, bootmaker, age 29, married, residence Milford, born in Ireland. Mustered in Aug. 7, 1862, term 3 years. Corp. Oct. 20, 1862; wounded June 3, 1864, Bethesda Church, Va. Mustered out June 21, 1864.

Tiernan, Mark, enlisted June 11, 1861, bootmaker, age 22, residence Milford, born in Galway, Ire. Mustered in June 11, 1861, term 3 years. Mustered out June 21, 1864, as " Marcus."

Tobin, James W., enlisted June 11, 1861, bootmaker, age 30, single, residence Milford, born in Ireland. Mustered in June 11, 1861, term 3 years. Sergt. May 6, 1862; wounded June 27, 1862, Gaines' Mill, Va. Discharged for disability as Sergt. April 6, 1863.

Tobin, John, enlisted Oct. 22, 1863, glassmaker, age 20, single, residence Milford, credited to Worcester. Mustered in Oct 22, 1863, term 3 years. Wounded May 12, 1864, Spottsylvania, Va. Transferred to 32d Mass. Vols. June 10, 1864.

Toomey, John F., enlisted Aug. 5, 1862, laborer, age 42, married, residence Boston, born in Ireland. Mustered in Aug. 5, 1862, term 3 years. Discharged for disability, Oct. 25, 1862.

Tynon, Thomas, enlisted June 11, 1861, bootmaker, age 28, single, residence Milford, born in Ireland. Mustered in June 11, 1861, term 3 years. Died of disease June 15, 1862.

Warren, Michael M , enlisted Jan. 7, 1862, gardener, age 23, single, residence Watertown, credited to Watertown. Mustered in Jan. 7, 1862, term 3 years. Wounded June 27, 1862, Gaines' Mill, Va; July 1, 1862, Malvern Hill, Va. Re-enlisted Feb. 16, 1864. Deserted May 1, 1864, Boston, Mass.

Welden, Hugh, enlisted Aug. 14, 1862, bootmaker, age 23, married, residence Boston, born in England. Mustered in Aug. 15, 1862, term 3 years. Transferred to Invalid Corps July 1, 1863.

Whalan, John, enlisted Aug. 4, 1862, forger, age 40, married, residence South Boston, born in Ireland. Mustered in Aug. 4, 1862, term 3 years. Discharged for disability, Oct. 15, 1862

White, Patrick, enlisted June 11, 1861, farmer, age 25, single, residence Milford, born in Kerry, Ire. Mustered in June 11, 1861, term 3 years. Wounded June 27, 1862, Gaines' Mill, Va ; Corp. Jan. 9, 1863. Mustered out June 21, 1864.

Willis, Charles, enlisted June 11, 1861, farmer, age 22, single, residence Milford, born in Milford. Mustered in June 11, 1861, term 3 years. Transferred to Invalid Corps Dec. 29, 1863.

Young, Henry, enlisted Aug. 21, 1863, carpenter, age 29, married, residence Cambridgeport, credited to Boston, Wd. 8. Mustered in Aug. 21, 1863, term 3 years. Wounded May 5, 1864, Wilderness, Va   Transferred to 32d Mass. Vols. June 10, 1864.

COMPANY I.

McCafferty, James E. Jr., Capt., gas engineer, age 25, residence Boston. Mustered in June 11, 1861, term 3 years. Killed June 27, 1862, Gaines' Mill, Va.

Walsh, John H., 1st Lieut., age 30, married, residence Boston, born in Boston, Mustered in June 11, 1861, term 3 years. Promoted Capt. Feb. 28, 1862, and transferred to Co. D. Resigned Jan. 8, 1863.

Nugent, Richard P., 2d Lieut., printer, age 23, married, residence Boston, born in Bethany, Wayne Co., Pa. Mustered in June 11, 1861, term 3 years. Promoted 1st Lieut. Feb. 10, 1862. Killed June 27, 1862, Gaines' Mill,Va.

Flynn, Michael, 1st Sergt., enlisted June 11, 1861, clerk, age 21, single, residence Boston, born in Dublin, Ire. Mustered in June 11, 1861, term 3 years. 2d Lieut. Oct. 25, 1861; 1st Lieut. June 28, 1862; Capt. Feb. 28, 1863. Transferred to Co. F, March 31, 1864. On detached duty, Gallops Island, Boston Harbor, since March 28, 1864. Mustered out June 21, 1864.

Conlin. Lawrence, Sergt., enlisted June 11, 1861, carpenter, age 33, married, residence Boston, born in Boston, Mass. Mustered in June 11, 1861, term 3 years. Wounded May 27, 1862, at Hanover Court House, Va. Discharged for disability Oct. 15, 1862, Alexandria, Va.

McDonald, Edward, Sergt., enlisted June 11, 1861, plumber, age 36, married residence East Boston, born in Ireland. Mustered in June 11, 1861, term 3 years. Transferred to Co. D, Sept. 1, 1861. Discharged in Co. D, March 23, 1863, as Sergt.

Cook, Thomas, Sergt., enlisted June 11, 1861, cooper, age 31, married, residence Boston, born in Dublin, Ire. Mustered in June 11, 1861, term 3 years. Deserted Aug. 27, 1862, Centerville, Va., as Corp.

Spillane, John, Sergt., enlisted June 11, 1861, carpenter, age 25, single, residence Lawrence, born in Ireland. Mustered in June 11, 1861, term 3 years. Wounded May 27, 1862, Hanover Court House, Va. Discharged for disability, Oct. 22, 1862, Sharpsburg, Md.

Gillis, William, Corp., enlisted June 11, 1861, ship sawyer, age 32, married, residence Charlestown, born in Ireland. Mustered in June 11, 1861, term 3 years. Wounded June 27, 1862, Gaines' Mill, Va. Died of wounds received at the battle of the Wilderness, May 5, 1864.

Dacey, Timothy, Corp., enlisted June 11, 1861, hatter, age 21, single, residence Lawrence, born in Ireland. Mustered in June 11, 1861, term 3 years. Promoted 2d Lieut. Sept. 26, 1862, from Sergt.; and 1st Lieut. June 6, 1863. Slightly wounded May 9, 1864, near Laurel Hill, Va. Mustered out June 21, 1864.

McGuire, Michael, Corp., enlisted June 11, 1861, printer, age 19, single, residence Chelsea, born in Ireland. Mustered in June 11, 1861, term 3 years. Wounded June 27, 1862, Gaines' Mill, Va. Deserted June 27, 1863, Frederick, Md.

Rabbit, Patrick, Corp., enlisted June 11, 1861, currier, age 26, single, residence South Boston, born in Ireland. Mustered in June 11, 1861, term 3 years. Sergt. Oct. 15, 1861. Wounded at Malvern Hill, Va., July 1, 1862. Died of wounds received in battle, Spottsylvania, Va., May 12, 1864.

Murphy, James, Corp., enlisted June 11, 1861, baker, age 30, single, residence Lawrence, born in Cork, Ire. Mustered in June 11, 1861, term 3 years. Promoted Sergt. Dec. 15, 1862 Reduced July 6, 1863. Mustered out June 21, 1864, as Private.

Flynn, Thomas, Corp., enlisted June 11, 1861, miller, age 25, married, residence Boston, born in Ireland. Mustered in June 11, 1861, term 3 years. Promoted Corp. June 11, 1861. Reduced July 20, 1861. Corp. Dec. 14, 1862; Sergt. March 24, 1864. Wounded, Malvern Hill, July 1, 1862; Gettysburg, July 3, 1863. Mustered out June 21, 1864, as Sergt.

Kearney, Charles, Corp., enlisted June 11, 1861, mule spinner, age 22, single, residence Blackstone, born in Ireland. Mustered in June 11, 1861, term 3 years. Killed June 27, 1862, Gaines' Mill, Va.

Cotter, Maurice, Corp., enlisted June 11, 1861, laborer, age 22, single, residence Boston, born in Ireland. Mustered in June 11, 1861, term 3 years. Killed June 27, 1862, Gaines' Mill, Va.

McPoland, William, Musician, enlisted June 11, 1861, sailor, age 19, single, residence Lawrence, born in Charlestown. Mustered in June 11, 1861. Deserted March 26, 1862, Alexandria, Va.

Cox, Patrick, Musician, enlisted June 11, 1861, blacksmith, age 27, married, residence Winthrop, born in Ireland. Mustered in June 11, 1861, term 3 years. No further record, A.G.O.

Keenan, John, Wagoner, enlisted June 11, 1861, teamster, age 36, married, residence Boston, born in Ireland. Mustered in June 11, 1861, term 3 years. Discharged Feb. 21, 1862, Boston, on account of disability.

Alcorn, Thomas, enlisted Nov. 9, 1861, painter, age 35, single, residence Boston. Mustered in Nov. 9, 1861, term 3 years. Discharged for disability Oct. 10, 1862.

Angell, John, enlisted Aug. 21, 1863, sailor, age 25, single, residence Providence, R.I., credited to Boston, Wd. 11. Mustered in Aug. 21, 1863, term 3 years. Transferred to United States Navy.

Barry, Joseph, enlisted June 11, 1861, hatter, age 19, single, residence Lawrence, born in Calais, Me. Mustered in June 11, 1861, term 3 years. Promoted Corporal. Wounded July 1, 1862, Malvern Hill, Va. Not heard from since. Dropped from Co. Rolls Oct. 12, 1862.

Beaman William A., enlisted July 14, 1863, shoemaker, age 24, married, residence Athol, credited to Athol. Mustered in July 14, 1863, term 3 years. Transferred to 32d Mass. Vols. June 9, 1864.

Blake, George, enlisted Aug. 7, 1862, seaman, age 25, single, residence Boston, born in Scotland. Mustered in Aug. 7, 1862, term 3 years. Discharged Oct. 23, 1862, Sharpsburg, Md., G.O.War Dept.

Blake, Stephen, enlisted June 11, 1861, boilermaker, age 27, single, residence South Boston, born in Manchester, Eng. Mustered in June 11, 1861, term 3 years. Wounded at Gaines' Mill, June 27, 1862. Killed at the battle of the Wilderness, Va., May 5, 1864.

Boylan, Henry, enlisted June 11, 1861, carpenter, age 30, single, residence New York, born in Ireland. Mustered in June 11, 1861, term 3 years. Wounded July 1, 1862, Malvern Hill, Va. Mustered out June 21, 1864, as "Boyland."

Bresnihan, Cornelius, enlisted June 11, 1861, laborer, age 27, single, residence East Cambridge, born in Ireland. Mustered in June 11, 1861, term 3 years. Deserted July 2, 1862, Harrison Landing, Va.

Brickley, David, enlisted June 11, 1861. Mustered in June 11, 1861, term 3 years. Promoted Corp., Oct. 13, 1863. Mustered out June 21, 1864.

Buckley, Michael, enlisted June 11, 1861, laborer, age 25, married, residence Moscow, Me., born in Cork, Ire. Mustered in June 11, 1861, term 3 years. Wounded at Gaines' Mill, June 27, 1862. Deserted June 22, 1863, Aldie, Va.

Buckley, James, enlisted June 11, 1861, farmer, age 20, single, residence Charlestown, born in Ireland. Mustered in June 11, 1861, term 3 years. Wounded at Gaines' Mill, June 27, 1862. Discharged for disability, Nov. 28, 1862.

Butterfield, Zenas A., enlisted July 15, 1863, farmer, age 27, single, residence Burniston or Bernardston, credited to Burniston. Mustered in July 15, 1863, term 3 years. Wounded May 5, 1864, Wilderness, Va. Transferred to 32d Mass. Vols. June 9, 1864.

Burns, William, enlisted June 11, 1861, shoemaker, age 20, single, residence Lawrence, born in Donegal, Ire. Mustered in June 11, 1861, term 3 years. Wounded June 27, 1862, Gaines' Mill, Va. Wounded at Chancellorsville, Va., May 3, 1863. Discharged for disability, Sept. 1, 1863.

Burns, James, enlisted June 11, 1861, currier, age 22, married, residence Boston, born in Ireland. Mustered in June 11, 1861, term 3 years. Shot by Officer of Day at Harrison Landing, Va., July 6, 1862. Died from wounds received from Officer of Day, July 13, 1862.

Burke, Patrick B., enlisted June 11, 1861, clerk, age 20, single, residence Boston, born in Ireland. Mustered in June 11, 1861, term 3 years. Reduced from Corp Dec. 14, 1862. Mustered out June 21, 1864.

Bystram, Sayer, enlisted Nov. 9, 1861, glasscutter, age 35, married, residence Boston. Mustered in Nov. 9, 1861, term 3 years. Discharged for disability, date unknown, surgeon certificate as " Berrystron, Charles."

Carney, Martin, enlisted June 11, 1861, carpenter, age 31, married, residence Groton Junction, born in Ireland. Mustered in June 11, 1861, term 3 years. Discharged for disability July 18, 1862, Harrison Landing, Va.

Carney, Thomas, enlisted June 11, 1861, chairmaker, age 20, single, residence Boston, born in Boston, Mass. Mustered in June 11, 1861, term 3 years. Transferred to 32d Mass. Vols. June 9, 1864.

Carney, Thos. S., enlisted July 26, 1862, laborer, age 21, married, residence Boston. Mustered in July 26, 1862, term 3 years. Transferred to 32d Mass. Vols. June 10, 1864.

Carroll, William, enlisted Aug. 13, 1862, carpenter, age 22, married, residence Boston, born in Ireland. Mustered in Aug. 13, 1862, term 3 years. Promoted Corp. March 18, 1863. Wounded May 5, 1864, Wilderness, Va. Mustered out June 21, 1864.

Carroll, Patrick, enlisted June 11, 1861, reedmaker, age 19, single, residence Lawrence, born in Ireland. Mustered in June 11, 1861, term 3 years. Promoted Sergt. June 8, 1864 Wounded at Wilderness, Va., May 5, 1864. Mustered out June 21, 1864, as absent wounded.

Cartwright, John, enlisted June 11, 1861, carpenter, age 19, single, residence East Boston, born in Ireland. Mustered in June 11, 1861, term 3 years. Transferred to Co. D, Aug 10, 1861, Arlington Heights, Va. Died of wounds June 27, 1862, Gaines' Mill, Va.

Caughlin, James, enlisted June 11, 1861, laborer, age 19, single, residence Lawrence, born in Ireland. Mustered in June 11, 1861, term 3 years. Mustered out June 21, 1864.

Church, Spencer Jr., enlisted July 14, 1863, painter, age 41, single, residence Amherst, credited to Amherst. Mustered in July 14, 1863, term 3 years. Wounded May 8, 1864, Laurel Hill, Va. Transferred to 32d Mass. Vols. June 9, 1864.

Conlon, Michael P., enlisted Aug. 14, 1862, gasfitter, age 19, single, residence Boston, born in Ireland. Mustered in Aug. 14, 1862, term 3 years. Died at Falmouth, Va., at division hospital, April 16, 1863, chronic diarrhœa.

Connors, John, enlisted June 11, 1861, farmer, age 30, married, residence South Danvers, born in Kilkenny, Ire. Mustered in June 11, 1861, term 3 years. Discharged for disability Jan. 27, 1863, Alexandria, Va

Connell, William, enlisted June 11, 1861, currier, age 26, single, residence South Danvers, born in Cork, Ire. Mustered in June 11, 1861, term 3 years. Wounded June 27, 1862, Gaines' Mill, Va. Discharged for disability July 16, 1862, Washington, D.C.

Connell, Bryan, enlisted June 11, 1861, age 32, single, residence Boston. Mustered in June 11, 1861, term 3 years. Transferred to Invalid Corps July 27, 1863, from Co. H.

Cook, Thomas 2d, enlisted Aug. 20, 1863, plumber, age 21, single, residence New York, credited to Irving. Mustered in Aug. 20, 1863, term 3 years. Deserted April 19, 1864, Bealton, Va.

Coy, Henry, enlisted Aug. 18, 1863, painter, age 32, single, residence New
York, credited to East Hampton.   Mustered in Aug. 18, 1863, term 3
years.   Wounded May 5, 1864, Wilderness, Va.   Transferred to 32d
Mass. Vols. June 9, 1864.

Cronan, Jeremiah, enlisted June 11, 1861, currier, age 23, married, residence
Salem, born in Ireland.   Mustered in June 11, 1861, term 3 years.   Promoted Sergt. Sept. 26, 1862; 1st Sergt. Oct. 26, 1862.   Wounded May 5,
1864, Wilderness, Va.   Mustered out June 21, 1864.

Cullen, John, enlisted June 11, 1861, stonecutter, age 30, single, residence
Quincy, born in Ireland.   Mustered in June 11, 1861, term 3 years.
Wounded at Malvern Hill, July 1, 1862.   Discharged for disability Nov.
19, 1862, Washington, D.C.

Cunningham, William, enlisted Aug. 21, 1862, shoemaker, age 23, married,
residence Marlboro, born in Ireland.   Mustered in Aug. 22, 1862, term
3 years.   Mustered out June 21, 1864.

Cunningham, John J , enlisted Aug. 20, 1863, bootmaker, age 20, single, residence Plymouth, credited to Townsend.   Mustered in Aug. 20, 1863,
term 3 years.   Captured Oct. 3, 11 or 13; paroled Nov. 17, 1863.   Present
at camp parole, Annapolis, Md., April 30, 1864; sent to camp distribution
May 14, 1864.   Transferred June 10, 1864, to 32d Mass. Vols.

Curran, Francis, enlisted June 11, 1861, morocco dresser, age 24, single, residence South Danvers, born in Westboro, Mass.   Mustered in June 11,
1861, term 3 years.   Transferred to Invalid Corps March 15, 1864.

Curran, Patrick, enlisted June 11, 1861, laborer, age 20, single, residence
Lawrence, born in Ireland.   Mustered in June 11, 1861, term 3 years.
Killed June 27, 1862, Gaines' Mill, Va.

Curtin, Daniel, enlisted June 11, 1861, laborer, age 41, married, residence
Boston, born in Ireland.   Mustered in June 11, 1861, term 3 years.
Discharged for disability Nov. 24, 1862.

Dacey, Cornelius, enlisted June 11, 1861, hatter, age 19, single, residence
Lawrence, born in Ireland.   Mustered in June 11, 1861, term 3 years.
Wounded July 1, 1862, Malvern Hill and May 5, 1864, Wilderness, Va.
Mustered out June 21, 1864.

Delacy, John, enlisted July 16, 1863, shoemaker, age 23, single, residence
Newburgh, N.Y., credited to Long Meadow.   Mustered in July 16, 1863,
term 3 years.   Transferred to 32d Mass. Vols. June 9, 1864.

Dempsey, Michael, enlisted Aug. 15, 1862, hostler, age 20, single, residence
Boston, born in Ireland.   Mustered in Aug. 15, 1862, term 3 years.
Promoted Corp. July 1, 1863.   Mustered out June 21, 1864.

Dolan, Thomas, enlisted July 22, 1862, tailor, age 30, married, residence
Boston.   Mustered in July 22, 1862, term 3 years.   Transferred to
Battery D, 5th U.S. Art., Oct. 18, 1862.   Mustered out June 21, 1864.

Donavan, Patrick, enlisted June 11, 1861, shoemaker, age 19, single, residence
Abington, born in Ireland.   Mustered in June 11, 1861, term 3 years.
Transferred to Co. A Sept. 1, 1861.   Discharged for disability in Co. A,
Miner's Hill, Va.

Donnelly, Peter, enlisted June 11, 1861, laborer, age 19, single, residence
Lonsdale, R.I., born in Ireland.   Mustered in June 11, 1861, term 3 years.
Wounded Gaines' Mill, Va., June 27, 1862.   Deserted July 5, 1863, Get-
tysburg, Pa.

Dwyer, Thomas, enlisted June 11, 1861, bootmaker, age 22, single, residence
Lawrence, born in Ireland.   Mustered in June 11, 1861, term 3 years.
Deserted Sept. 23, 1861, Arlington Heights, Va

Doran, **Andrew**, enlisted June 11, 1861, bootmaker, age 22, single, residence Quincy, born in Ireland. Mustered in June 11, 1861, term 3 years. Wounded Gaines' Mill, June 27, 1862. Discharged for disability Feb. 12, 1863, Alexander, Va., as Corp.

Duffy, **Michael**, enlisted June 11, 1861, blacksmith, age 20, single, residence West Roxbury, born in Ireland. Mustered in June 11, 1861, term 3 years. Wounded June 27, 1862, Gaines' Mill, Va., since not heard from. Dropped from the Co. Rolls, Sept. 26, 1862.

Earley, **Thomas**, enlisted Nov. 9, 1861, hackman, age 40, married, residence Boston. Mustered in Nov. 9, 1861, term 3 years. Wounded Gaines' Mill, Va., June 27, 1862. Deserted Nov. 18, 1863.

Eddy, **David**, enlisted Aug. 25, 1862, laborer, age 19, single, residence Lawrence, born in Ireland. Mustered in Aug. 25, 1862, term 3 years. Discharged for disability, April 15, 1863, Falmouth, Va.

Fahy, **Thomas**, enlisted July 24, 1862, farmer, age 29, married, residence Boston, born in Ireland. Mustered in July 24, 1862, term 3 years. Mustered out June 21, 1864.

Fallon, **Thomas**, enlisted June 11, 1861, laborer, age 28, single, residence Roxbury, born in Ireland. Mustered in June 11, 1861, term 3 years. Mustered out June 21, 1864.

Fitzgibbon, **John**, enlisted June 11, 1861, laborer, age 21, single, residence South Danvers, born in Ireland. Mustered in June 11, 1861, term 3 years. Died of wounds July 7, 1862, received June 27, 1862, Gaines' Mill, Va.

Flynn, **John**, enlisted Jan. 29, 1862, bootmaker, age 28, married, residence East Bridgewater. Mustered in Jan. 29, 1862, term 3 years. Wounded May 8, 1864, at Laurel Hill, Va.; wounded June 3, 1864, Bethesda Church, Va. Transferred to 32d Mass. Vols. June 9, 1864.

Flynn, **Edmund**, enlisted Aug. 14, 1862, bootmaker, age 30, residence Randolph, born in Ireland. Mustered in Aug. 14, 1862, term 3 years. Wounded Dec. 13, 1862, Fredericksburg, Va.; wounded at Gettysburg, Pa., July 3, 1863; wounded May 12, 1864, Spottsylvania, Va. Mustered out June 21, 1864.

Flynn, **Nicholas**, enlisted Aug. 11, 1862, bootmaker, age 40, married, residence Fall River, born in Ireland. Mustered in Aug. 11, 1862, term 3 years. Mustered out June 21, 1864.

Gallagher, **Patrick**, enlisted Aug. 5, 1862, teamster, age 19, single, residence Boston, born in Ireland. Mustered in Aug. 5, 1862, term 3 years. Wounded at Gettysburg, Va., July 3, 1863. Mustered out June 21, 1864.

Gallagher, **John**, enlisted June 11, 1861, laborer, age 32, married, residence Lexington, born in Ireland. Mustered in June 11, 1861, term 3 years. Wounded May 5, 1864, Wilderness, Va. Mustered out June 21, 1864.

Garritty, **Michael**, enlisted June 11, 1861, laborer, age 22, single, residence Boston. Mustered in June 11, 1861, term 3 years. Wounded June 27, 1862, Gaines' Mill, Va.; wounded May 5, 1864, Wilderness, Va. Absent, wounded; died of wounds.

Garvey, **Patrick**, enlisted June 11, 1861, currier, age 22, single, residence East Boston, born in Ireland. Mustered in June 11, 1861, term 3 years. Wounded June 27, 1862, Gaines' Mill, Va. Discharged for disability Oct. 28, 1862, Washington, D.C.

Garrity, **John**, enlisted June 11, 1861, shoemaker, age 19, married, residence Boston, born in Roxbury, Mass. Mustered in June 11, 1861, term 3 years. Missing in action June 27, 1862, Gaines' Mill, Va.

Green, Thomas, enlisted Aug. 6, 1862, shoemaker, age 29, married, residence Salem, born in Ireland. Mustered in Aug. 7, 1862, term 3 years. Promoted Corp. July 1, 1863; wounded May 5, 1864, Wilderness, Va. Mustered out as absent, wounded, June 21, 1864.

Griffin, Patrick, enlisted Aug. 14, 1862, laborer, age 32, married, residence Boston, born in Ireland. Mustered in Aug. 14, 1862, term 3 years. Wounded May 12, 1864, Spottsylvania. Mustered out June 21, 1864.

Hackett, Thomas, enlisted Aug. 12, 1862, moulder, age 23, married, residence Boston, born in Ireland. Mustered in Aug. 12, 1862, term 3 years. Re-enlisted Dec. 31, 1863. Killed at battle of the Wilderness, Va., May 5, 1864.

Hale, John H., enlisted July 15, 1862, carpenter, age 26, married, residence Bernardstown, credited to Bernardstown. Mustered in July 15, 1862, term 3 years. Killed at battle of Laurel Hill, Va., May 8, 1864.

Hayes, Michael, enlisted June 11, 1861, farmer, age 24, single, residence Fitchburg, born in Ireland. Mustered in June 11, 1861, term 3 years. Wounded June 27, 1862, Gaines' Mill, Va. Deserted June 27, 1863, Frederick, Md.

Hayes, Bernard, enlisted June 11, 1861, worm cutter, age 32, married, residence East Boston, born in Ireland. Mustered in June 11, 1861, term 3 years. Wounded June 27, 1862, Gaines' Mill, Va. Killed at the battle of the Wilderness May 5, 1864, as Corp.

Heaney, Richard, enlisted Aug. 8, 1862, currier, age 32, married, residence Salem, born in Ireland. Mustered in Aug. 8, 1862, term 3 years. Discharged for disability March 25, 1863, Falmouth, Va.

Herlehy, Patrick, enlisted Aug. 16, 1862, hostler, age 22, single, residence Boston, born in Ireland. Mustered in Aug. 16, 1862, term 3 years. Promoted Corp. March 21, 1864; wounded May 5, 1864, Wilderness, Va. Mustered out June 21, 1864.

Hermania, Louis, enlisted Aug. 22, 1863, cooper, age 20, single, residence Boston, credited to Boston. Mustered in Aug. 22, 1863, term 3 years. Transferred to navy, no date.

Hurley, Daniel, enlisted Aug. 15, 1862, laborer, age 21, single, residence Boston, born in Ireland. Mustered in Aug. 15, 1862, term 3 years. Mustered out June 21, 1864.

Jones, John, enlisted Aug. 6, 1862, machinist, age 33, residence Boston, born in England. Mustered in Aug. 6, 1862, term 3 years. Discharged for disability April 13, 1864, Washington, D.C.

Kelley, Daniel, enlisted June 11, 1861, currier, age 23, single, residence Spencer, born in Ireland. Mustered in June 11, 1861, term 3 years. Died of disease Oct. 23, 1862, Fairfax Seminary Hospital, Va.

Kelly, John, enlisted June 11, 1861, ropemaker, age 29, single, residence Roxbury, born in Ireland. Mustered in June 11, 1861, term 3 years. Died of fever at Miner's Hill, Va., Nov. 16, 1861.

Kelley John 2d, enlisted June 11, 1861, laborer, age 26, single, residence Worcester, born in Ireland. Mustered in June 11, 1861, term 3 years. No further record A.G.O.

Kelley, Timothy, enlisted June 11, 1861, hatter, age 19, single, residence Lawrence, born in Ireland. Mustered in June 11, 1861, term 3 years. Discharged for disability March 2, 1862, Miner's Hill, Va.

Kiernan, John, enlisted June 11, 1861, mule spinner, age 18, single, residence Lowell, born in Lowell. Mustered in June 11, 1861, term 3 years. Wounded July 1, 1862, Malvern Hill, Va. Deserted Sept. 12, 1862, Washington, D.C.

Kirby, Michael H., enlisted June 11, 1861, laborer, age 18, single, residence East Boston. Mustered in June 11, 1861, term 3 years. Wounded, Malvern Hill, July 1, 1862. Discharged Oct. 23, 1862, Sharpsburg, Md., G O. War Dept. to enlist 5th U.S. Art.

Kohlbrand, Charles H., enlisted Aug. 21, 1863, seaman, age 23, single, residence Boston, credited to Watertown. Mustered in Aug. 21, 1863, term 3 years. Transferred to 32d Mass. Vols. June 9, 1864.

Lane, Patrick, enlisted June 11, 1861, laborer, age 19, single, residence Boston, born in Boston, Mass. Mustered in June 11, 1861, term 3 years. Wounded June 27, 1862, Gaines' Mill, Va. Discharged for disability March 25, 1863, Philadelphia, Pa.

Lavin, Thomas, enlisted Aug. 14, 1862, laborer, age 18, single, residence Boston, credited to Boston, born in Ireland. Mustered in Aug. 14, 1862, term 3 years. Wounded Dec. 13, 1862, Fredericksburg, Va. Wounded at Gettysburg, July 3, 1863. Re-enlisted Dec. 31, 1863. Transferred to 32d Mass. Vols. June 9, 1864.

Leahey, Thomas, enlisted June 11, 1861, shoemaker, age 18, single, residence East Abington, born in Ireland. Mustered in June 11, 1861, term 3 years. Deserted Nov. 18, 1863.

Leslie, James, enlisted June 11, 1861, bootmaker, age 18, single, residence Waterbury, Conn., born in Ireland. Mustered in June 11, 1861, term 3 years. Mustered out June 21, 1864.

Lewellen, Thomas J., enlisted Aug. 6, 1862, farmer, age 18, single, residence Salem, born in Ireland. Mustered in Aug. 6, 1862, term 3 years. Transferred to 1st Ohio Art., May 27, 1863. Returned to regiment, April 10, 1864. Wounded May 5, 1864, Wilderness, Va. Mustered out June 21, 1864 as "Llewellen."

Loughlin, Terrance O., enlisted Aug. 21, 1863, pressman, age 29, married, residence Lowell, credited to Hamilton. Mustered in Aug. 21, 1863, term 3 years. Wounded June 3, 1864, Bethesda Church, Va. Transferred to 32d Mass. Vols. June 9, 1864.

Mahoney, Dennis, enlisted July 28, 1861, laborer, age 44, married, residence Boston, born in Ireland. Mustered in July 28, 1861, term 3 years. Mustered out June 21, 1864.

Mathews, Lawrence, enlisted June 11, 1861, laborer, age 23, single, residence Salem, born in Boston. Mustered in June 11, 1861, term 3 years. Died of wounds received at Wilderness May 5, 1864.

Moore, Patrick, enlisted June 11, 1861, currier, age 25, single, residence Roxbury, born in Ireland. Mustered in June 11, 1861, term 3 years. Discharged for disability Jan. 2, 1862, Arlington Heights, Va.

Moran, Martin, enlisted June 11, 1861, currier, age 18, single, residence Chelsea, born in Ireland. Mustered in June 11, 1861, term 3 years. Deserted Aug. 27, 1862, Centreville, Va.

Morris, John, enlisted June 11, 1861, sailor, age 19, single, residence Boston, born in Dublin, Ire. Mustered in June 11, 1861, term 3 years. Wounded July 1, 1862, Malvern Hill. Discharged for disability Sept. 12, 1862, Washington, D.C.

Mulcahy, David, enlisted June 11, 1861, currier, age 22, single, residence South Danvers, born in Cork, Ire. Mustered in June 11, 1861, term 3 years. Died July 14, 1862, of wounds received at Malvern Hill.

Mundy, Bernard, enlisted June 11, 1861, stone-cutter, age 21, single, residence Quincy, born in Ireland. Mustered in June 11, 1861, term 3 years. Discharged for disability Sept. 21, 1861, Arlington Heights, Va.

Manyan, Thomas, enlisted June 11, 1861, laborer, age 28, single, residence Boston, born in Galway, Ire. Mustered in June 11, 1861, term 3 years. Absent, wounded, May 12, 1864, Spottsylvania, Va. Reported killed in action, May 12, 1864.

Murphy, Francis, enlisted June 11, 1861, carriage finisher, age 22, single, residence New York, born in Ireland. Mustered in June 11, 1861, term 3 years. Wounded at Gaines' Mill, June 27, 1862. Deserted Aug. 11, 1862, Washington, D.C.

McAuliff, Dennis, enlisted Aug. 16, 1862, cordwainer, age 27, married, residence East Weymouth, born in Ireland. Mustered in Aug. 16, 1862, term 3 years. Wounded at Chancellorsville, Va. Deserted near Falmouth, Va., Feb. 11, 1863.

McCarron, Daniel, enlisted June 11, 1861, teamster, age 21, single, residence Charlestown, born in Ireland. Mustered in June 11, 1861, term 3 years. Wounded June 27, 1862, Gaines' Mill, Va.; at Chancellorsville, Va., May, 1863. Mustered out June 21, 1864.

McCarthy, John, enlisted June 11, 1861, shoemaker, age 17, single, residence Natick, born in East Cambridge. Mustered in June 11, 1861, term 3 years. Deserted Aug. 28, 1862, Centreville, Va.

McCarthy, Charles, enlisted June 11, 1861, shoemaker, age 20, single, residence Lynn, born in Wethersfield, Conn. Mustered in June 11, 1861, term 3 years. Wounded May 9, 1864, Po River, Va. Mustered out June 21, 1864.

McCormack, John, enlisted Aug. 8, 1862, mason, age 33, married, residence Salem, born in Ireland. Mustered in Aug. 8, 1862, term 3 years. Discharged for disability Oct. 26, 1862, Annapolis, Md

McDermot, John, enlisted Aug. 14, 1862, laborer, age 20, single, residence Roxbury. Mustered in Aug. 14, 1862. Mustered out June 21, 1864.

McDonald, Michael, enlisted June 11, 1861, laborer, age 27, single, residence Lawrence, born in Ireland. Mustered in June 11, 1861, term 3 years. Deserted Sept. 26, 1862.

McGarrity, John, enlisted June 11, 1861, bolter, age 28, married, residence East Boston, born in Ireland. Mustered in June 11, 1861, term 3 years. Wounded June 27, 1862, Gaines' Mill, Va. On M.O. rolls, in pencil, says "drowned in Potomac river Aug. 25, 1862."

McGuire, Thomas, enlisted Aug. 15, 1862, currier, age 34, single, residence Salem. Mustered in Aug 15, 1862, term 3 years. Mustered out June 21, 1864.

McHugh, Hugh, enlisted June 11, 1861, laborer, age 22, single, residence Boston, born in Ireland. Mustered in June 11, 1861, term 3 years. Discharged for disability Nov. 24, 1862.

McKliget, James, enlisted Aug. 18, 1862, laborer, age 37, married, residence Salem, born in Ireland. Mustered in Aug. 18, 1862, term 3 years. Mustered out June 21, 1864.

McKever, James, enlisted Nov. 9, 1861, laborer, age 20, single, residence Boston. Mustered in Nov. 9, 1861, term 3 years. Wounded May 8, 1864, Laurel Hill, Va.; wounded June 27, 1862, Gaines' Mill, Va. Transferred to 32d Mass. Vols. June 9, 1864, as "McKeever."

McLaughlin, Hugh, enlisted June 11, 1861, clerk, age 18, single, residence East Boston, born in East Boston. Mustered in June 11, 1861, term 3 years. Wounded June 27, 1862, Gaines' Mill, Va.; not heard from since, and dropped from the Co. Rolls Sept. 26, 1862, as a deserter.

McLauglin, Bernard, enlisted June 11, 1861, laborer, age 20, single, residence East Boston, born in Ireland. Mustered in June 11, 1861, term 3 years. Corp. Oct. 18, 1862; Sergt. July 6, 1863. Mustered out June 21, 1864, as Sergt.

McNeil, James, enlisted Aug. 21, 1863, sailor, age 23, single, residence Ipswich, credited to Ipswich. Mustered in Aug. 21, 1863, term 3 years. Wounded May 5, 1864, Wilderness, Va. Transferred to 32d Mass Vols. June 9, 1864.

Nagle, Patrick, enlisted Nov. 9, 1861, laborer, age 23, single, residence Boston. Mustered in Nov. 9, 1861, term 3 years. Killed June 27, 1862, Gaines' Mill, Va.

Nevens, William L., enlisted Aug. 2, 1862, currier, age 42, single, residence Boston, born in Chelsea. Mustered in Aug. 2, 1862, term 3 years. Discharged March, 1863.

Norton, Thomas, enlisted June 11, 1861, teamster, age 26, married, residence Roxbury, born in Athlone, Ire. Mustered in June 11, 1861, term 3 years. Mustered out June 21, 1864.

Oakes, James, enlisted Nov. 9, 1861, printer, age 19, single, residence Boston. Mustered in Nov. 9, 1861, term 3 years. Died of disease on board transport bound to N.Y., no date.

O'Brien, Daniel A., enlisted June 11, 1861, printer, age 19, single, residence Boston, born in Co. Cork, Ire. Mustered in June 11, 1861, term 3 years. Reduced from Corp. March 18, 1863. Mustered out June 21, 1864.

O'Niel, Patrick, enlisted June 11, 1861, baker, age 27, single, residence Watertown, N.Y., born in Ireland. Mustered in June 11, 1861, term 3 years. Discharged for disability Dec. 29, 1862, Alexandria, Va.

Palmer, John, enlisted Aug 20, 1863, cooper, age 23, single, residence Halifax, N.S., credited to Irving. Mustered in Aug. 20, 1863, term 3 years. Wounded May 5, 1864, Wilderness, Va. Transferred to 32d Mass. Vols. June 9, 1864.

Palmer, William A., enlisted June 11, 1861, hatter, age 25, single, residence Lawrence, born in Ireland. Mustered in June 11, 1861, term 3 years. Wounded June 27, 1862, Gaines' Mill, Va. Absent sick in Co. E as " Wm. E " This man was transferred to Co. E and served in Co. E.

Pealey, Stephen, enlisted July 13, 1863, laborer, age 22, single, residence Charlestown, credited to Charlestown. Mustered in July 13, 1863, term 3 years. Wounded May 9, 1864, Po River, Va. Transferred to 32d Mass. Vols. June 9, 1864.

Phalon, William, enlisted June 11, 1861, cabinet-maker, age 40, married, residence East Cambridge. Mustered in June 11, 1861, term 3 years. Wounded Gaines' Mill, Va., June 27, 1862. Mustered out June 21, 1864.

Phelan, William, enlisted June 11, 1861, cabinet-maker, age 40, married, residence East Cambridge, born in Ireland. Mustered in June 11, 1861, term 3 years, Promoted Sergt.-Maj., 2d Lieut. Co. A, Feb. 26, 1862, 1st Lieut. Jan. 5, 1863. Co. E, Capt. and transferred to Co. C, April 1, 1864. Wounded June 27, 1862, Gaines' Mill, Va. Killed May 5, 1864, Wilderness, Va.

Quinn, John, enlisted June 11, 1861, blacksmith, age 19, single, residence Lawrence, born in Birmingham, Eng. Mustered in June 11, 1861, term 3 years. Wounded June 27, 1862, Gaines' Mill, Va.; May 5, 1864, Wilderness, Va. Mustered out June 21, 1864.

Regan, Andrew, enlisted June 11, 1861, currier, age 27, single, residence Lowell, born in Ireland. Mustered in June 11, 1861, term 3 years. Wounded June 27, 1862, Gaines' Mill, Va. Discharged for disability Sept. 27, 1862, Alexandria, Va.

Riley, Patrick, enlisted June 11, 1861, laborer, age 25, single, residence, South Boston, born in Ireland. Mustered in June 11, 1861, term 3 years. Deserted Sept. 12, 1862, Washington, D.C.

Riley, William, enlisted Aug. 13, 1862, sailor, age 27, married, residence Charlestown, born in Charlestown, Mass. Mustered in Aug. 16, 1862, term 3 years. Deserted July 9, 1863, Maryland.

Roach, Edward, enlisted June 11, 1861, blacksmith, age 25, single, residence Boston, born in Ireland. Mustered in June 11, 1861, term 3 years. Deserted Sept. 22, 1861, Arlington Heights, Va.

Roach, Michael, enlisted June 11, 1861, currier, age 22, single, residence South Danvers, born in Mallow, Ire. Mustered in June 11, 1861, term 3 years. Promoted Corp. Oct. 15, 1862. Wounded Dec. 13, 1862, Fredericksburg, Va. Reduced July 1, 1863, again Corp. Jan. 18, 1864. Mustered out June 21, 1864, as Corp.

Rock, Michael, enlisted July 3, 1862, tailor, age 23, single, residence Boston, born in Ireland. Mustered in July 3, 1862, term 3 years. Deserted April 27, 1864, Washington, D.C.

Ryan, William P., enlisted Nov. 9, 1861, brass finisher, age 21, single, residence Boston. Mustered in Nov. 9, 1861, term 3 years. Deserted July 1, 1862, Harrison Landing, Va.

Shields, Peter, enlisted June 11, 1861, ship carpenter, age 18, single, residence East Boston, born in Ireland. Mustered in June 11, 1861, term 3 years. Wounded July 1, 1862, Malvern Hill, Va. Discharged for disability Aug. 21, 1862, Washington, D.C.

Sheridan, Thomas, enlisted July 28, 1862, laborer, age 21, married, residence Boston, credited to Boston, Wd. 3. Mustered in July 28, 1862, term 3 years. Wounded May 5, 1864, Wilderness, Va. Re-enlisted Dec. 31, 1863. Transferred to 32d Mass. Vols. June 9, 1864.

Sherlock, Thomas, enlisted Aug. 19, 1862, tinsmith, age 27, married, residence Boston. Mustered in Aug. 19, 1861, term 3 years. Mustered out June 21, 1864.

Sliney, Edward, enlisted Feb. 4, 1862, bootmaker, age 30, married, residence Boston. Mustered in Feb. 4, 1862, term 3 years. Wounded June 27, 1862, Gaines' Mill, Va.; Dec. 13, 1862, Fredericksburg, Va. Discharged to date April 18, 1864.

Slyman, John, enlisted June 11, 1861, laborer, age 25, single, residence South Boston, born in Ireland. Mustered in June 11, 1861, term 3 years. Mustered out June 21, 1864.

Spring, Patrick, enlisted Aug. 7, 1862, laborer, age 43, single, residence Salem, born in Ireland. Mustered in Aug. 7, 1862, term 3 years. Mustered out June 21, 1864.

Smith, John, enlisted Aug. 21, 1863, blacksmith, age 23, single, residence New York, credited to Shirley. Mustered in Aug. 21, 1863, term 3 years. Deserted April 19, 1864, Bealton, Va.

Sullivan, Bernard, enlisted June 11, 1861, baker, age 24, single, residence Charlestown, born in Ireland. Mustered in June 11, 1861, term 3 years. Mustered out June 21, 1864.

Sullivan, John P., enlisted June 11, 1861, laborer, age 19, single, residence Biddeford, Me, born in Ireland. Mustered in June 11, 1861, term 3 years. Wounded June 27, 1862, Gaines' Mill, Va. Discharged for disability, Oct. 28, 1862, Pennsylvania.

Sullivan, Lawrence, enlisted June 11, 1861, shoemaker, age 20, single, residence Boston, born in Ireland. Mustered in June 11, 1861, term 3 years. Discharged for disability, July 15, 1863, Alexandria, Va.

Sullivan, James, enlisted June 11, 1861, laborer, age 25, single, residence South Boston, born in Ireland   Mustered in June 11, 1861, term 3 years. Wounded June 27, 1862; Gaines' Mill, Va.; since not heard from, dropped from the Co. rolls Nov. 18, 1863.

Sullivan, Cornelius, enlisted June 11, 1861, bootmaker, age 21, single, residence South Boston, born in Ireland.   Mustered in June 11, 1861, term 3 years. Wounded June 27, 1862, Gaines' Mill, Va.; since not heard from, dropped from the Co. rolls Nov. 18, 1863.

Sweeney, Owen, enlisted June 11, 1861, laborer, age 36, single, residence North Bridgewater, born in Ireland.   Mustered in June 11, 1861, term 3 years. Discharged for disability April 16, 1863, Washington, D C.

Thompson, Andrew, enlisted Aug. 21, 1863, laborer, age 27, single, residence Boston, credited to Shirley.   Mustered in Aug. 21, 1863, term 3 years. Transferred to 32d Mass. Vols. June 9, 1864.

Thompson, Peter, enlisted June 11, 1861, sailor, age 23, single, residence Boston, born in Malaga, Portugal.   Mustered in June 11, 1861, term 3 years. Discharged Oct. 23, 1863, Sharpsburg, Md , G.O. War Dept , to enlist in 5th U.S. Art.

Tierney, William, enlisted June 11, 1861, spinner, age 29, married, residence Biddeford, Me., born in Ireland.   Mustered in June 11, 1861, term 3 years.   No further record A.G.O.

Walsh, John, enlisted July 30, 1862, teamster, age 26, married, residence Boston, born in Eastport, Me.   Mustered in July 30, 1862, term 3 years. Wounded Dec. 13, 1862, Fredericksburg, Va.   Discharged for disability Dec. 26, 1863, Washington, D.C.

Way, George, enlisted Aug. 21, 1863, seaman, age 21, single, residence Boston, credited to Taunton.   Mustered in Aug. 21, 1863, term 3 years.   Transferred to 32d Mass. Vols. June 9, 1864.

Whelan, James, enlisted June 11, 1861, laborer, age 42, single, residence South Boston, born in Kildare, Ire.   Mustered in June 11, 1861, term 3 years Discharged for disability March 25, 1863, Falmouth, Va.

Winn, William, enlisted June 11, 1861, laborer, age 21, single, residence Boston, born in Ireland.   Mustered in June 11, 1861, term 3 years.   Killed June 27, 1862, Gaines' Mill, Va.

COMPANY K.

Dutton, George W., Capt., machinist, age 24, married, residence Stoughton, born in Cambridge.   Mustered in June 11, 1861, term 3 years.   Wounded July 1, 1862, Malvern Hill, Va.   Promoted Major Aug. 26, 1862.   Resigned on account of wounds.   Discharged March 27, 1863.

McGuinegle, James F., 1st Lieut., bootmaker, age 26, married, residence Boston, born in Boston, Mass.   Mustered in June 11, 1861, term 3 years. Transferred to Co. B.   Commissioned Capt. June 28, 1862.   Wounded July 1, 1862, Malvern Hill, Va.   Transferred to Co A, Sept. 28, 1862, as Capt.   Wounded May 12, 1864, Spottsylvania, Va   Mustered out June 21, 1864.

Willey, John C., 2d Lieut., turnkey, age 43, married, residence East Cambridge, born in Tolland, Conn.   Mustered in June 11, 1861, term 3 years.   1st Lieut. Co. E, Oct. 3, 1861; Capt. Jan. 28, 1862.   Dismissed the service Feb. 7, 1863.

McGunnigle, Hugh, 1st Sergt., enlisted June 11, 1861, bootmaker, age 23, married, residence Stoughton, born in Boston, Mass. Mustered in June 11, 1861, term 3 years. Promoted 2d Lieut. Oct. 21, 1862, in Co. E. Resigned March 1, 1863.

Downey, Michael, Sergt., enlisted June 11, 1861, bootmaker, age 22, single, residence Stoughton, born in Ireland. Mustered in June 11, 1861, term 3 years. Wounded July 1, 1862, Malvern Hill, Va. Deserted Sept. 12, 1862.

Toomey, John, Sergt., enlisted June 11, 1861, bootmaker, age 23, single, residence Stoughton, born in Ireland. Mustered in June 11, 1861, term 3 years. Wounded July 1, 1862, Malvern Hill, Va. Died of wounds Jan. 1, 1863, as "James."

Butler, James, Sergt., enlisted June 11, 1861, bootmaker, age 26, married, residence Stoughton, born in Ireland. Mustered in June 11, 1861, term 3 years. Wounded July 1, 1862, Malvern Hill, Va. Discharged for disability Oct. 20, 1862, as Private.

Rice, John B., Sergt., enlisted June 11, 1861, age 21, single, residence Stoughton, born in Ireland. Mustered in June 11, 1861, term 3 years. Wounded June 27, 1862, Gaines' Mill, Va. Discharged for disability Oct. 28, 1862.

Kelley, Richard, Corp., enlisted June 11, 1861, bootmaker, age 44, married, residence Stoughton, born in Ireland. Mustered in June 11, 1861, term 3 years. Wounded July 1, 1862, Malvern Hill, Va. Deserted Oct. 1, 1863, from hospital. Gained from desertion Feb. 20, 1864. Discharged for disability April 29, 1864.

Long, John, Corp., enlisted June 11, 1861, bootmaker, age 27, married, residence Stoughton, born in Ireland. Mustered in June 11, 1861, term 3 years. Discharged for disability Nov. 11, 1862, order Colonel Day.

Gilbride, James, Corp,, enlisted June 11, 1861, bootmaker, age 19, single, residence, Bridgewater, born in Ireland. Mustered in June 11, 1861, term 3 years. Discharged for disability Oct. 14, 1862.

O'Brien, Edward, Corp., enlisted June 11, 1861, bootmaker, age 27, single, residence Stoughton, born in Ireland. Mustered in June 11, 1861, term 3 years. Deserted June 29, 1863.

Murray, Neil, Corp., enlisted June 11, 1861, clerk, age 26, single, residence Ticonderoga, N.Y., born in Ticonderoga, N.Y. Mustered in June 11, 1861, term 3 years. Wounded June 27, 1862, Gaines' Mill, Va. Discharged for disability Nov. 24, 1862, order General Montgomery.

Clark, Michael, Corp., enlisted June 11, 1861, bootmaker, age 26, single, residence North Bridgewater, born in Ticonderoga, N.Y. Mustered in June 11, 1861, term 3 years. Wounded June 27, 1862, Gaines' Mill, Va. Discharged for disability Oct. 15, 1862, order Major-General Porter.

Ford, Joseph, Corp., enlisted June 11, 1861, bootmaker, age 22, single, residence Stoughton, born in Ireland. Mustered in June 11, 1861, term 3 years. Wounded at Malvern Hill, Va , July 1, 1862. Killed July 2, 1863, Gettysburg, Va.

Rice, James, Corp., enlisted June 11, 1861, bootmaker, age 19, single, residence Stoughton, born in Ireland. Mustered in June 11, 1861, term 3 years. Wounded June 27, 1862, Gaines' Mill, Va. Deserted Nov. 5, 1862.

McGuire, David, Musician, enlisted June 11, 1861, age 24, married, residence North Bridgewater, born in New York city. Mustered in June 11, 1861, term 3 years. Discharged for disability Nov. 3, 1861, Miner's Hill, Va.

McCarthy, James, Musician, enlisted June 11, 1861, bootmaker, age 22, married, residence St. Johns, N.B., born in St. Johns, N.B. Mustered in June 11, 1861, term 3 years. Deserted Oct. 1, 1862.

Dempsey, Patrick, Wagoner, enlisted June 11, 1861, spinner, age 28, married, residence Athol, born in Ireland. Mustered in June 11, 1861, term 3 years. Mustered out June 21, 1864, as Private.

Armor, George, enlisted June 11, 1861, laborer, age 30, married, residence Boston, born in Ireland. Mustered in June 11, 1861, term 3 years. Deserted Oct. 11, 1862.

Barlow, Robert, enlisted June 11, 1861, bootmaker, age 21, married, residence Stoughton, born in Ireland. Mustered in June 11, 1861, term 3 years. Mustered out June 21, 1864.

Barry, Michael, enlisted June 11, 1861, bootmaker, age 19, single, residence Stoughton, born in Ireland. Mustered in June 11, 1861, term 3 years. Wounded May 5, 1864, Wilderness, Va. Mustered out June 21, 1864.

Blair, Robert, enlisted Aug. 21, 1863, sailor, age 21, single, residence New York, credited to Boston. Mustered in Aug. 21, 1862, term 3 years. Deserted Dec. 25, 1863, Bealton, Va.

Breen, John J , enlisted Aug. 12, 1862, bootmaker, age 40, residence Boston, born in Hingham, Mass. Mustered in Aug. 12, 1862, term 3 years. Wounded May 5, 1864, Wilderness, Va.; May 12, 1864, Spottsylvania, Va. Mustered out June 21, 1864, as Corp.

Burke, James, enlisted June 11, 1861, tailor, age 26, single, residence Boston, born in Ireland. Mustered in June 11, 1861, term 3 years. Mustered out June 21, 1864.

Butler, John, enlisted June 11, 1861, laborer, age 30, single, residence Boston, born in Ireland. Mustered in June 11, 1861, term 3 years. Killed Gaines' Mill, Va., June 27, 1862.

Callahan, Daniel, enlisted June 11, 1861, age 23. Mustered in June 11, 1861, term 3 years. At Boston for duty. Deserted March 24, 1863.

Callahan, Hugh, enlisted June 11, 1861, farmer, age 19, single, residence Stoughton, born in Ireland. Mustered in June 11, 1861, term 3 years. No further record at A.G.O.

Carroll, Thomas, enlisted Aug. 8, 1862, bootmaker, age 38, married, residence Boston, born in Ireland. Mustered in Aug. 8, 1862, term 3 years. Mustered out June 21, 1864.

Carney, John, enlisted June 11, 1861, bootmaker, age 21, single, residence Stoughton, born in Ireland. Mustered in June 11, 1861, term 3 years, Deserted July 1, 1863.

Connell, Michael, enlisted June 11, 1861, laborer, age 23, single, residence North Bridgewater, born in Ireland. Mustered in June 11, 1861, term 3 years. Killed May 5, 1864, Wilderness, Va.

Cogger, John, enlisted Oct. 26, 1863, laborer, age 40, single, residence Lawrence, credited to Lawrence. Mustered in Oct. 26, 1863, term 3 years. Killed at Laurel Hill, Va., May 8, 1864.

Clifford, Thomas, enlisted June 11, 1861, bootmaker, age 25, married, residence Stoughton, born in Ireland. Mustered in June 11, 1861, term 3 years. Wounded at Gaines' Mill, Va., July 27, 1862; at Chancellorsville, Va. Mustered out June 21, 1864.

Columbus, Anthony, enlisted Aug. 22, 1863, marble cutter, age 32, single, residence Chelsea, credited to Braintree. Mustered in Aug. 22, 1863, term 3 years. Transferred to 32d Mass. Vols. June 9, 1864.

Cochlin, John, enlisted Aug. 12, 1862, currier, age 34, married, residence Salem, born in Ireland. Mustered in Aug. 12, 1862, term 3 years. Discharged for disability May 12, 1864, order Maj.-Gen. Augur.

34

Condon, Morris, enlisted June 11, 1861, bootmaker, age 20, single, residence Randolph, born in Ireland. Mustered in June 11, 1861, term 3 years. Mustered out June 21, 1864, 1st Sergt.

Collins, Charles O., enlisted June 11, 1861, bootmaker, age 23, single, residence North Bridgewater, born in Ireland. Mustered in June 11, 1861, term 3 years. Mustered out June 21, 1864.

Connelly, Michael, enlisted June 11, 1861, bootmaker, age 22, single, residence Stoughton. Mustered in June 11, 1861, term 3 years. Wounded at Gaines' Mill, June 27, 1862; Sergt. from Private May 8, 1864. Mustered out June 21, 1864.

Crane, Dominick, enlisted June 11, 1861, bootmaker, age 21, single, residence Stoughton, born in Ireland. Mustered in June 11, 1861, term 3 years. Wounded May 18, 1864, near Spottsylvania, Va. Mustered out June 21, 1864.

Cunningham, Rodger, enlisted June 11, 1861, bootmaker, age 22, single, residence West Bridgewater, born in Ireland. Mustered in June 11, 1861, term 3 years. Wounded at Gaines' Mill June 27, 1862. Mustered out June 21, 1864.

Cunningham, Patrick, enlisted June 11, 1861, bootmaker, age 24, single, residence West Bridgewater, born in Ireland. Mustered in June 11, 1861, term 3 years. Wounded Malvern Hill, Va., July 1, 1862; May 5, 1864, Wilderness, Va. Mustered out June 21, 1864, Corp.

Cullen, James, enlisted June 11, 1861, laborer, age 24, single, residence Boston, born in Ireland. Mustered in June 11, 1861, term 3 years. Mustered out June 21, 1864.

Dani, Emanuel, enlisted July 22, 1863, sailor, age 20, single, residence South Danvers, credited to South Danvers. Mustered in July 22, 1863, term 3 years. Transferred to navy April 21, 1864, as "Daney."

Deery, Lawrence E., enlisted June 11, 1861, bootmaker, age 22, single, residence Stoughton, born in Ireland. Mustered in June 11, 1861, term 3 years. Mustered out June 21, 1864 as "Deary."

Dermody, Patrick, enlisted June 11, 1861, bootmaker, age 25, married, residence Stoughton, born in Ireland. Mustered in June 11, 1861, term 3 years. Killed July 1, 1862, Malvern Hill, Va.

Denison, Patrick, enlisted June 11, 1861, bootmaker, age 19, single, residence Stoughton, born in Ireland. Mustered in June 11, 1861, term 3 years. Killed June 27, 1862, Gaines' Mill, Va.

Dorrien, Christian, enlisted Aug. 20, 1863, clerk, age 25, single, residence New York, credited to Marblehead. Mustered in Aug. 20, 1863, term 3 years. Transferred to 32d Mass. Vols. June 9, 1864.

Donohue, John, enlisted June 11, 1861, bootmaker, age 18, single, residence Stoughton, born in Ireland. Mustered in June 11, 1861, term 3 years. Mustered out June 21, 1864, as Corp.

Doherty, James, enlisted June 11, 1861, laborer, age 43, married, residence Stoughton, born in Ireland. Mustered in June 11, 1861, term 3 years. Discharged for disability Nov. 8, 1862.

Dooley, John, enlisted June 11, 1861, bootmaker, age 23, married, residence Stoughton, born in Boston. Mustered in June 11, 1861, term 3 years. Wounded Gaines' Mill, Va., June 27, 1862. Discharged Aug. 26, 1862, order Brig.-Gen. Montgomery, for disability.

Donavan, Malachi, enlisted June 11, 1861, bootmaker, age 21, single, residence Stoughton, born in Ireland. Mustered in June 11, 1861, term 3 years. Deserted Sept. 12, 1863, as "Michael."

Eberhard, Justin, enlisted Aug. 22, 1863, pianist, age 21, single, residence New York, credited to Boston. Mustered in Aug. 22, 1863, term 3 years. Wounded May 5, 1864, Wilderness, Va. Transferred to 32d Mass. Vols. June 9, 1864, as "Ebberhardt."

Farrell, William, enlisted June 11, 1861, bootmaker, age 18, single, residence Bridgewater, born in Bridgewater. Mustered in June 11, 1861, term 3 years. Deserted Sept. 1, 1863.

Fulton, Thomas, enlisted Aug. 21, 1863, mason, age 26, single, residence Newport, R.I., credited to Plymouth. Mustered in Aug. 21, 1863, term 3 years. Wounded June 3, 1864, Bethesda Church, Va. Transferred to 32d Mass. Vols. June 10, 1864.

Finn, Patrick, enlisted June 11, 1861, bootmaker, age 22, single, residence Bridgewater, born in Ireland. Mustered in June 11, 1861, term 3 years. Mustered out June 21, 1864, as "Flynn."

Flynn, Joseph, enlisted June 11, 1861, bootmaker, age 35, single, residence Quincy, born in Ireland. Mustered in June 11, 1861, term 3 years. Wounded at Mechanicsville, Va., June 26, 1862; Gaines' Mill, June 27, 1862. Killed May 5, 1864, Wilderness, Va.

Flynn, James, enlisted June 11, 1861, bootmaker, age 21, single, residence Boston. Mustered in June 11, 1861, term 3 years. Wounded May 12, 1864, Spottsylvania, Va. Mustered out June 21, 1864.

Ford, Alexander, enlisted June 11, 1861, bootmaker, age 20, single, residence Stoughton, born in Ireland. Mustered in June 11, 1861, term 3 years. Wounded at Malvern Hill, Va., July 1, 1862. Transferred to Invalid Corps, no date.

Gateley, Martin, enlisted June 11, 1861, bootmaker, age 31, married, residence Clinton, born in Ireland. Mustered in June 11, 1861, term 3 years. Discharged for disability Dec. 22, 1862, order General Martindale.

Gallagher, Owen, enlisted June 11, 1861, bootmaker, age 27, single, residence Stoughton, born in Ireland. Mustered in June 11, 1861, term 3 years. Deserted Sept. 12, 1863.

Gartlin, John, enlisted June 11, 1861, bootmaker, age 24, married, residence Stoughton, born in Ireland. Mustered in June 11, 1861, term 3 years. Wounded Gaines' Mill, Va., June 27, 1862. Mustered out June 21, 1864, as "Gartland."

Geary, John, enlisted June 11, 1861, bootmaker, age 21, single, residence Stoughton, born in Boston, Mass. Mustered in June 11, 1861, term 3 years. Mustered out June 21, 1864, as "Garcy."

Goward, James A., enlisted June 11, 1861, bootmaker, age 28, married, residence Stoughton, born in Stoughton. Mustered in June 11, 1861, term 3 years. Discharged for disability Dec. 31, 1862, order General Martindale.

Gulle, Hugo, enlisted Aug. 22, 1863, teacher, age 21, single, residence New York, credited to Salisbury. Mustered in Aug. 22, 1863, term 3 years. Reported deserted Dec. 12, 1863, returned March 4, 1864, Bealton, Va. Transferred to 32d Mass. Vols. June 9, 1864.

Hayes, James, enlisted June 11, 1861, bootmaker, age 21, single, residence Stoughton, born in Ireland. Mustered in June 11, 1861, term 3 years. Died of wounds received May 5, 1864, Wilderness, Va. No record at A G.O., Mass.

Harris, James, enlisted June 11, 1861, bootmaker, age 24, single, residence North Bridgewater, born in Ireland. Mustered in June 11, 1861, term 3 years. Discharged for disability Feb. 9, 1863, by order General Montgomery.

Healey, John D., enlisted Aug. 20, 1862, tailor, age 44, married, residence Cambridge, born in Ireland Mustered in Aug. 20, 1862, term 3 years. Discharged for disability Oct. 30, 1862, order General Porter, as " John D Haley."

Hennessy, James, enlisted June 11, 1861, laborer, age 20, single, residence New York, born in Ireland. Mustered in June 11, 1861, term 3 years. Deserted Oct. 11, 1862.

Holcraft, Patrick, enlisted June 11, 1861, bootmaker, single, residence Stoughton, born in Ireland. Mustered in June 11, 1861, term 3 years. Deserted July 1, 1863.

Holman, John, enlisted Aug. 12, 1862, cigarmaker, age 19, residence Boston, born in Jersey City, N.J. Mustered in Aug. 12, 1862, term 3 years. Deserted Oct. 1, 1863.

Hogan, James, enlisted Dec. 1, 1863, laborer, age 44, single, residence Boston, credited to Boston, Wd. 7, born in Waterford, Ire. Mustered in Dec. 1, 1863, term 3 years. Transferred to 32d Mass. Vols. June 9, 1864.

Howard, Simon, enlisted June 11, 1861, tailor, age 29, single, residence Boston, born in Ireland. Mustered in June 11, 1861, term 3 years. Wounded at Malvern Hill, July 1, 1862. Died of wounds Sept. 14, 1862.

Horan, Patrick, enlisted Aug. 21, 1862, hostler, age 39, married, residence Boston, born in Ireland. Mustered in Aug. 21, 1862, term 3 years. Mustered out June 21, 1864.

Hughes, James, enlisted Aug. 7, 1862, teamster, age 25, residence Boston, born in Ireland. Mustered in Aug. 7, 1862, term 3 years. Charge of desertion removed. Discharged March 28, 1863.

Jackson, John, enlisted Nov. 27, 1863, seaman, age 29, single, residence Boston, credited to Boston, Wd. 1, born in Dublin, Ire. Mustered in Nov. 27, 1863, term 3 years. Transferred to Invalid Corps, no date.

Johnson, Edward, enlisted June 11, 1861, bootmaker, age 24, married, residence Stoughton. Mustered in June 11, 1861, term 3 years. Mustered out June 21, 1864.

Johnson, William E., enlisted Aug. 7, 1862, tailor, age 25, married, residence Milford. Mustered in Aug. 7, 1862, term 3 years. Discharged for disability Nov. 1, 1862, order Colonel Day.

Keegan, John, enlisted June 11, 1861, bootmaker, age 33, married, residence Stoughton, born in Ireland. Mustered in June 11, 1861, term 3 years. Discharged for old age Nov. 5, 1862

Kerns, John, enlisted June 11, 1861, bootmaker, age 38, single, residence Stoughton, credited to Stoughton, born in Ireland. Mustered in June 11, 1861, term 3 years. Re-enlisted Dec. 31, 1863. Transferred to 32d Mass. Vols.

Kenney, Patrick, enlisted Aug. 15, 1862, porter, age 40, married, residence Boston, born in Ireland. Mustered in Aug. 15, 1862, term 3 years. Wounded May 14, 1864, near Spottsylvania, Va. Absent wounded in Washington, D.C. Mustered out Aug. 22, 1864.

Kelleher, Patrick, enlisted June 11, 1861, bootmaker, age 34, single, residence Stoughton, born in Ireland. Mustered in June 11, 1861, term 3 years. Killed May 12, 1864, Spottsylvania, Va.

Kelley, Martin, enlisted June 11, 1861, bootmaker, age 24, single, residence Stoughton, born in Ireland. Mustered in June 11, 1861, term 3 years. Discharged for disability Oct. 29, 1862.

Kelly, Patrick, enlisted Aug. 21, 1863, laborer, age 22, married, residence Lee, credited to Newburg   Mustered in Aug. 21, 1863, term 3 years. Transferred to 32d Mass. Vols. June 9, 1864.

Koche, Christian, enlisted Aug. 21, 1863, cooper, age 25, single, residence New York, credited to Boston.   Mustered in Aug 21, 1863, term 3 years. Transferred to 32d Mass. Vols. June 9, 1864.

Landy, Patrick, enlisted June 11, 1861, bootmaker, age 24, single, residence Stoughton, born in Ireland.   Mustered in June 11, 1861, term 3 years. Discharged for disability July 5, 1862, order General Montgomery.

Lanagan, Patrick, enlisted July 29, 1862, carpenter, age 32, single, residence Boston, born in Provinces.   Mustered in July 30, 1862, term 3 years. Discharged for disability Aug. 19, 1863, order Captain Dryer, Boston.

Lawless, John, enlisted Aug. 27, 1862, cooper, age 27, married, residence Boston, born in Ireland.   Mustered in Aug. 27, 1862, term 3 years.   Wounded Dec. 13, 1862, Fredericksburg, Va.   Deserted May 27, 1863.

Lee, Robert, enlisted June 11, 1861, bootmaker, age 26, married, residence Lynn, born in Ireland.   Mustered in June 11, 1861, term 3 years.   Wounded July 1, 1862, Malvern Hill, Va.   Mustered out June 21, 1864.

Lenahan, William, enlisted June 11, 1861, bootmaker, age 18, single, residence North Bridgewater, born in Bridgewater, Mass.   Mustered in June 11, 1861, term 3 years.   Wounded June 27, 1862, Gaines' Mill, Va.   Mustered out June 21, 1864, Sergt., as "Linnehan."

Lingner, Adolph, enlisted Aug. 21, 1863, clerk, age 29, single, residence New York, credited to Boston, Wd. 11.   Mustered in Aug. 21, 1863, term 3 years. Transferred to 32d Mass. Vols. June 9, 1864.

Lunergan, John, enlisted June 11, 1861, bootmaker, age 31, married, residence North Bridgewater, credited to Boston, Wd. 12, born in Ireland.   Mustered in June 11, 1861, term 3 years.   Transferred to Invalid Corps as "John Lundergreen."

Mahoney, James, enlisted June 11, 1861, bootmaker, age 21, single, residence Stoughton, born in Ireland.   Mustered in June 11, 1861, term 3 years. Wounded July 1, 1862, Malvern Hill, Va.   Mustered out June 21, 1864.

Maloney, David, enlisted June 11, 1861, bootmaker, age 25, single, residence Stoughton, born in Ireland.   Mustered in June 11, 1861, term 3 years. Deserted Feb. 25, 1863.

Maloney, Charles, enlisted Aug. 7, 1862, laborer, age 23, residence Boston, born in England.   Mustered in Aug. 7, 1862, term 3 years.   Discharged for disability March 9, 1863, Frederick, Md

Manning, Patrick, enlisted Aug. 4, 1862, teamster, age 42, married, residence Boston, born in Ireland.   Mustered in Aug. 4, 1862, term 3 years.   Discharged for disability June 2, 1863, Baltimore, Md.

Martin, Michael, enlisted June 11, 1861, laborer, age 21, single, residence Providence, born in Ireland.   Mustered in June 11, 1861, term 3 years. Wounded June 27, 1862, Gaines' Mill, Va.; Dec. 13, 1862, Fredericksburg, Va.   Transferred to V.R.C. Feb. 20, 1864.

Meier, Louis, enlisted Aug. 21, 1863, carpenter, age 28, married, residence Long Island, credited to Newton.   Mustered in Aug. 21, 1863, term 3 years. Deserted Oct. 25, 1863.

Miller, Michael, enlisted Aug. 21, 1863, operative, age 29, married, residence New York, credited to Sudbury.   Mustered in Aug. 21, 1863, term 3 years. Deserted Oct. 25, 1863.

Mitchel, William, enlisted June 11, 1861, boilermaker, age 20, single, residence Bridgewater, born in Ireland. Mustered in June 11, 1861, term 3 years. Wounded May 8, 1864, Laurel Hill, Va. Mustered out June 21, 1864, as Sergt.

Mooney, William, enlisted June 11, 1861, bootmaker, age 20, single, residence Stoughton, born in Ireland. Mustered in June 11, 1861, term 3 years. Mustered out June 21, 1864.

Murphy, James, enlisted June 11, 1861, bootmaker, age 20, single, residence Stoughton, born in Ireland. Mustered in June 11, 1861, term 3 years. Deserted Sept. 1, 1863.

Murphy, John, enlisted June 11, 1861, bootmaker, age 22, married, residence Stoughton, born in Ireland. Mustered in June 11, 1861, term 3 years. Deserted Sept. 12, 1863.

Murphy, Miles, enlisted Aug. 23, 1862, gilder, age 22, single, residence Boston, born in Ireland. Mustered in Aug. 23, 1862, term 3 years. Taken prisoner at Spottsylvania and paroled April 30, 1865, Jacksonville, Fla. Discharged, order A.G.O., Washington, D.C., May 12, 1865, S.M.R.O.

Murtagh, Thomas J., enlisted Aug. 5, 1862, bootmaker, age 26, single, residence Boston, credited to Hopkinton, born in Ireland. Mustered in Aug. 5, 1862, term 3 years Re-enlisted Dec. 31, 1863. Killed May 8, 1864, Laurel Hill, Va.

McGowan, John, enlisted Aug. 25, 1862, gardener, age 43, married, residence Boston, born in Scotland. Mustered in Aug. 25, 1862, term 3 years. Wounded May 5, 1864, Wilderness, Va Mustered out June 21, 1864.

McGuire, Michael, enlisted June 11, 1861, bootmaker, age 24, single, residence Stoughton, born in Ireland. Mustered in June 11, 1861, term 3 years. Wounded June 3, 1864, Bethesda Church, Va. Mustered out June 21, 1864.

McGuire, Patrick F., enlisted June 11, 1861, bootmaker, age 24, single, residence Stoughton, born in Ireland. Mustered in June 11, 1861, term 3 years. Mustered out June 21, 1864, as Corp

McKenna, Phillip, enlisted June 11, 1861, bootmaker, age 25, single, residence Stoughton, born in Ireland. Mustered in June 11, 1861, term 3 years. Wounded July 1, 1862, Malvern Hill, Va. Mustered out Feb. 3, 1865. (War Dept. letter.)

McLaughlin, James, enlisted June 11, 1861, laborer, age 27, single, residence Boston, born in Glasgow, Scot. Mustered in June 11, 1861, term 3 years. Wounded July 1, 1862, Malvern Hill, Va. Died of wounds Nov. 12, 1863.

Nally, James, enlisted June 11, 1861, bootmaker, age 19, single, residence Stoughton, born in Ireland. Mustered in June 11, 1861, term 3 years. Deserted June 27, 1863.

Nally, Patrick, enlisted June 11, 1861, bootmaker, age 24, married, residence Stoughton, born in Ireland. Mustered in June 11, 1861, term 3 years. Discharged for disability April 26, 1862.

Nolde, William, enlisted Aug. 20, 1863, farmer, age 33, single, residence Uncas, N.Y., credited to Lynn. Mustered in Aug. 20, 1863, term 3 years. Transferred to 32d Mass. Vols. June 9, 1864.

Naphut, Mathias, enlisted Aug. 21, 1863, teamster, age 22, single, residence New York, credited to Quincy. Mustered in Aug. 21, 1863, term 3 years. Wounded May 5, 1864, Wilderness, Va. Transferred to 32d Mass. Vols. June 9, 1864.

Noonan, Thomas, enlisted June 11, 1861, bootmaker, age 32, single, residence West Randolph, born in South Boston, Mass. Mustered in June 11, 1861, term 3 years. Mustered out June 21, 1864.

O'Hare, Hugh, enlisted June 11, 1861, bootmaker, age 20, married, residence Stoughton, born in Ireland. Mustered in June 11, 1861, term 3 years. Killed at Gaines' Mill, Va., June 27, 1862.

O'Sullivan, James, enlisted June 11, 1861, bootmaker, age 25, married, residence Stoughton, born in Ireland. Mustered in June 11, 1861, term 3 years. Wounded at Malvern Hill, Va., July 1, 1862. Discharged for disability Jan. 5, 1863, New York.

O'Sullivan, Thomas A., enlisted Aug. 21, 1862, plumber, age 19, single, residence Boston, born in Ireland. Mustered in Aug. 21, 1862, term 3 years. Discharged Oct. 30, 1862, disability, order General Porter.

Peck, Francis, enlisted Aug. 22, 1863, barkeeper, age 24, single, residence Jersey City, credited to Boston. Mustered in Aug. 22, 1863, term 3 years. Deserted Oct. 24, 1863.

Pryor, George, enlisted Aug. 20, 1863, sailor, age 27, single, residence Boston, credited to Marblehead. Mustered in Aug. 20, 1863, term 3 years. Deserted Oct. 28, 1863.

Ragon, Michael, enlisted June 11, 1861, bootmaker, age 22, single, residence Stoughton, born in Ireland. Mustered in June 11, 1861, term 3 years. Deserted Sept. 1, 1862.

Reynolds, Michael, enlisted Aug. 25, 1862, shoemaker, age 23, married, residence Upton, born in Ireland. Mustered in Aug. 25, 1862, term 3 years. Discharged to date Jan. 25, 1863.

Reilly, Alexander, enlisted June 11, 1861, farmer, age 18, single, residence Randolph, born in Randolph, Mass. Mustered in June 11, 1861, term 3 years. Deserted Feb. 19, 1863.

Ready, Andrew, enlisted Aug. 6, 1862, tailor, age 39, married, residence Milford, born in England. Mustered in Aug. 6, 1862, term 3 years. Discharged for disability October 30, order General Wadsworth.

Ready, Patrick, enlisted Aug. 27, 1862, laborer, age 31, married, residence Boston. Mustered in Aug. 29, 1862, term 3 years. Discharged for disability March 22, 1863, Falmouth.

Reilly, Thomas, enlisted June 11, 1861, bootmaker, age 19, single, residence Stoughton, born in Ireland. Mustered in June 11, 1861, term 3 years. Discharged for disability April 26, 1862, Georgetown, D.C.

Rieorden, Daniel 1st, enlisted June 11, 1861, bootmaker, age 21, single, residence Stoughton, born in Ireland. Mustered in June 11, 1861, term 3 years. Killed June 27, 1862, Gaines' Mill, Va.

Rieorden, Daniel 2d, enlisted June 11, 1861, bootmaker, age 33, married, residence Randolph, born in Ireland Mustered in June 11, 1861, term 3 years. Killed June 27, 1862, Gaines' Mill, Va.

Riordon, Edward, enlisted June 11, 1861, bootmaker, age 19, single, residence Stoughton, born in Stoughton, Mass. Mustered in June 11, 1861, term 3 years. Promoted Sergt. from Private, May 8, 1864. Wounded at Malvern Hill, Va., July 1, 1862. Mustered out June 21, 1864.

Roza, George, enlisted Aug. 20, 1863, sailor, age 21, single, residence New York, credited to South Danvers. Mustered in Aug. 20, 1863, term 3 years. Transferred to 32d Mass. Vols. June 9, 1864.

Scannell, John, enlisted Aug. 21, 1863, fireman, age 25, single, residence New York, credited to Hadley. Mustered in Aug. 21, 1863, term 3 years. Wounded May 12, 1864, Spottsylvania, Va. Transferred to 32d Mass. Vols. June 9, 1864.

Scannell, John, enlisted June 11, 1861, shoemaker, age 26, married, residence North Bridgewater, born in Ireland. Mustered in June 11, 1861, term 3 years. Died of wounds July 1, 1862, Malvern Hill, Va.

Schaffer, William, enlisted Aug. 21, 1863, cabinet-maker, age 23, single, residence Philadelphia, credited to Ipswich. Mustered in Aug. 21, 1863, term 3 years. Transferred to 32d Mass. Vols. June 9, 1864.

Schmidt, George, enlisted Aug. 20, 1863, clerk, age 22, single, residence New York, credited to Shirley. Mustered in Aug. 20, 1863, term 3 years. Transferred to 32d Mass. Vols. June 9, 1864.

Schmidt, William, enlisted Aug. 21, 1863, miner, age 26, single, residence New York, credited to Salisbury. Mustered in Aug. 21, 1863, term 3 years. Killed May 5, 1864, Wilderness, Va.

Sheridan, Philip, enlisted June 11, 1861, machinist, age 24, single, residence Providence, born in New York City. Mustered in June 11, 1861, term 3 years. Discharged for disability Dec. 1, 1862, Washington, D.C.

Sherer, John, enlisted Aug. 21, 1863, cooper, age 29, single, residence New York, credited to Watertown. Mustered in Aug. 21, 1863, term 3 years. Wounded June 3, 1864, Bethesda Church, Va. Transferred to 32d Mass. Vols. June 9, 1864.

Shultz, William, enlisted Aug. 22, 1863, book-keeper, age 31, single, residence Philadelphia, Pa. Term 3 years. Prisoner of war. Transferred to 32d Mass. Vols. June 10, 1864.

Smith, Patrick, enlisted June 11, 1861, bootmaker, age 22, single, residence Stoughton, born in Ireland. Mustered in June 11, 1861, term 3 years. Deserted June 29, 1863.

Smith, David, enlisted Aug. 12, 1862, butcher, age 39, single, residence Boston, born in Scotland. Mustered in Aug. 12, 1862, term 3 years. Wounded Dec. 13, 1862, Fredericksburg, Va. Discharged for disability May 15, 1863, order General Martindale.

Sullivan, Richard, enlisted June 11, 1861, bootmaker, age 20, single, residence Stoughton, born in Boston, Mass. Mustered in June 11, 1861, term 3 years. Mustered out June 21, 1864.

Spellman, Patrick, enlisted June 11, 1861, laborer, age 26, single, residence Boston, born in Ireland. Mustered in June 11, 1861, term 3 years. Mustered out June 21, 1864.

Steward, John, enlisted Nov. 22, 1863, laborer, age 32, married, residence Boston, credited to Boston, Wd. 1, born in Derry, Ire. Mustered in Nov. 22, 1863, term 3 years. Wounded May 12, 1864, Spottsylvania, Va. Transferred to 32d Mass. Vols. June 9, 1864.

Sweeney, John, enlisted June 11, 1861, bootmaker, age 21, single, residence North Bridgewater, born in Ireland. Mustered in June 11, 1861, term 3 years. Discharged for disability Oct. 30, 1862, order of Major-General Porter.

Thede, William, enlisted Aug. 21, 1863, clerk, age 21, single, residence New York, credited to Rowley. Mustered in Aug. 21, 1863, term 3 years. Transferred to 32d Mass. Vols. June 9, 1864.

Toomey, Jeremiah, enlisted June 11, 1861, bootmaker, age 22, single, residence Bridgewater, born in Ireland. Mustered in June 11, 1861, term 3 years. Mustered out June 21, 1864.

Tully, Bartlett, enlisted June 11, 1861, bootmaker, age 21, single, residence Bridgewater, born in Ireland. Mustered in June 11, 1861, term 3 years. Killed June 27, 1862, Gaines' Mill, Va.

Trainor, Francis, enlisted July 29, 1862, shoemaker, age 18, residence East Boston, born in Boston, Mass. Mustered in July 29, 1862, term 3 years. Discharged for disability, Jan. 25, 1863, order Colonel Belknap.

Walsh, Michael, enlisted June 11, 1861, bootmaker, age 20, single, residence Stoughton. Mustered in June 11, 1861, term 3 years. Discharged for disability, Dec. 1, 1862, Washington, D.C., as "Welsh."

Walsh, Michael, enlisted June 11, 1861, bootmaker, age 18, single, residence Stoughton, born in Ireland. Mustered in June 11, 1861, term 3 years. Wounded May 8, 1864, Spottsylvania, Va. Taken prisoner May 29, 1864, near Cold Harbor, Va. Released at Savannah, Ga., May 6, 1865. Reported at Boston, May 22, 1865, and mustered out.

Webb, James, enlisted June 11, 1861, bootmaker, age 28, single, residence North Bridgewater, born in Madaras, East India. Mustered in June 11, 1861, term 3 years. Mustered out June 21, 1864.

Welch, Patrick, enlisted Aug. 4, 1862, laborer, age 38, single, residence Boston, born in Ireland. Mustered in Aug. 4, 1862, term 3 years. Mustered out June 21, 1864.

Whalen, Dennis, enlisted June 11, 1861, bootmaker, age 21, single, residence North Bridgewater, born in Ireland. Mustered in June 11, 1861, term 3 years. Deserted Sept. 12, 1862.

Willey, Charles, enlisted June 11, 1861, conductor, age 20, single, residence East Cambridge, born in Cambridge, Mass. Mustered in June 11, 1861, term 3 years. Discharged for disability Oct. 12, 1862, order Colonel Day, Boston.

UNASSIGNED RECRUITS.

NO RECORD IN THE ADJUTANT-GENERAL'S OFFICE AND NEVER JOINED
THE NINTH MASSACHUSETTS VOLUNTEERS.

Anglin, James, sailor, age 44, married, residence Boston. Mustered in Aug. 1, 1862, term 3 years.

Barry, John, shoemaker, age 29, married, residence Wayland. Mustered in Dec. 9, 1862, term 3 years.

Barry, Michael, laborer, age 21, single, residence Boston. Mustered in Aug. 13, 1862, term 3 years.

Basso, James, enlisted July 21, 1862, gasfitter, age 22, single, residence Boston. Mustered in July 21, 1862, term 3 years.

Blake, Moses, enlisted Aug. 12, 1862, laborer, age 35, married, residence Boston. Mustered in Aug. 12, 1862, term 3 years.

Birmingham, Michael, enlisted Feb. 16, 1864, fisherman, age 22, single, residence South Danvers, credited to Taunton. Mustered in Feb. 16, 1864, term 3 years. Transferred to 32d Mass. Vols. (See Co. C Rolls.)

Buckley, Michael, enlisted June 4, 1864, laborer, residence New York, credited to Ludlow. Mustered in June 4, 1864. Drafted.

Burke, Thos., machinist, age 21, married, residence Boston. Mustered in Aug. 19, 1862, term 3 years.

Burns, John, enlisted Aug. 4, 1862, laborer, age 32, married, residence Salem. Mustered in Aug. 4, 1862, term 3 years.

Burns, John, laborer, age 24, single, residence Tyngsboro. Mustered in Dec. 17, 1862, term 3 years.

Burnham, John, enlisted Aug. 7, 1862, shoemaker, age 42, married, residence Salem. Mustered in Aug. 7, 1862, term 3 years.

Callahan, Eugene O , enlisted Aug. 19, 1862, laborer, age 44, married, residence Boston. Mustered in Aug. 19, 1862, term 3 years.

Calhoun, Patrick, enlisted July 22, 1862, laborer, age 33, married, residence Boston. Mustered in July 22, 1862, term 3 years.

Campbell, John, stonecutter, age 20, residence Boston. Mustered in Aug. 12, 1862, term 3 years.

Campbell, Daniel, enlisted Aug. 6, 1862, laborer, age 30, residence Boston. Mustered in Aug. 6, 1862, term 3 years.

Carr, Albert, farmer, age 21, married, residence Boston. Mustered in Aug. 22, 1862, term 3 years.

Carr, Patrick, enlisted Aug. 19, 1862, laborer, age 28, married, residence Boston. Mustered in Aug. 19, 1862, term 3 years. Deserted, no date, Boston.

Carroll, Chas., enlisted Aug. 18, 1862, laborer, age 21, residence Boston. Mustered in Aug. 18, 1862, term 3 years.

Connor, William, seaman, age 23, single, residence Wayland. Mustered in Dec. 8, 1862, term 3 years.

Crampton, Demetrius, trader, age 39, married, residence Boston. Mustered in July 23, 1862, term 3 years. Discharged for disability Feb. 17, 1863, at Boston.

Crother, John, spinner, age 40, single, residence Wayland. Mustered in Dec. 11, 1862, term 3 years.

Cully, Peter, enlisted July 28, 1862, bricklayer, age 31, married, residence Boston. Mustered in July 28, 1862, term 3 years.

Cummings, James, enlisted March 26, 1864, tailor, age 42, residence Boston, credited to Boston, Wd. 3. Mustered in March 26, 1864, term 3 years. Unofficially reported. Discharged Galloups Island, April 15, 1864.

Dean, Albert, teamster, age 21, single, residence Wayland. Mustered in Dec. 10, 1862, term 3 years.

Delany, John, enlisted Aug. 6, 1862, laborer, age 37. Mustered in Aug. 6, 1862, term 3 years.

Donavan, Daniel O., enlisted Feb. 10, 1862, bootmaker, age 33, residence Boston. Mustered in Feb. 10, 1862, term 3 years. Deserted Feb. 22, 1862.

Donavan, William, sailor, age 21, married, residence Boston. Mustered in Aug. 12, 1862, term 3 years.

Dorsey, John, enlisted Aug. 19, 1862, sailor, age 25, residence Boston. Mustered in Aug. 19, 1862, term 3 years.

Dunn, Timothy, enlisted Aug. 21, 1862, laborer, age 30, married, residence Boston. Mustered in Aug. 21, 1862, term 3 years.

Doyle, Thomas, enlisted Aug 6, 1862, laborer, age 21, residence Boston. Mustered in Aug. 7, 1862, term 3 years.

Fayane, Thomas, stonecutter, age 22, married, residence Boston. Mustered in Aug. 12, 1862, term 3 years.

Fogerly, John, laborer, age 25, married, residence Boston. Mustered in Aug. 25, 1862, term 3 years.

Foren, James, enlisted Feb. 26, 1862, machinist, age 33, residence Boston. Mustered in Feb. 26, 1862, term 3 years. Transferred to 1st Cavalry.

Garrigan, Nicholas, enlisted Aug. 6, 1862, mariner, age 39, single, residence Boston. Mustered in Aug. 6, 1862, term 3 years. Unofficially reported as discharged for disability April, 1863.

Garslin, Daniel, enlisted Aug. 2, 1862, fisherman, age 25, residence Boston. Mustered in Aug. 2, 1862, term 3 years.

Garvey, James, laborer, age 22, single, residence Wayland. Mustered in Dec. 10, 1862, term 3 years.

Gibbons, John G., enlisted Nov. 9, 1862, age 21, residence Boston. Mustered in Nov. 9, 1862, term 3 years.

Gorman, Daniel, enlisted Aug. 20, 1863, hostler, age 21, single, residence Nashua, N.H., credited to Boston, Wd. 11. Mustered in Aug. 20, 1863, term 3 years.

Gurney, Michael, blacksmith, age 18, single, residence Boston. Mustered in Aug. 25, 1862, term 3 years.

Hastings, Patrick, hostler, age 22, single, residence Boston. Mustered in Aug. 18, 1862, term 3 years.

Higgins, John, enlisted Aug. 19, 1864, clerk, age 19, single, residence Boston. Mustered in Aug. 19, 1862, term 3 years. Deserted, no date, Boston.

Higgins, Lorenzo S., enlisted Aug. 4, 1862, mariner, age 29, residence Boston. Mustered in Aug. 4, 1862, term 3 years.   Discharged Dec. 6, 1862, on Sergt. Certificate of Discharge.

Hogan, Michael, enlisted Aug. 9, 1862, tailor, age 26, residence Boston. . Mustered in Aug. 9, 1862, term 3 years.

Holaran, Edward J., enlisted Aug. 5, 1862, shoemaker, age 25, residence Boston. Mustered in Aug. 5, 1862, term 3 years.

Houston, Frank, teamster, age 33, married, residence Boston.   Mustered in Aug. 8, 1862, term 3 years.

Hughes, John, enlisted July 22, 1862, laborer, age 35, married, residence Boston.   Mustered in July 22, 1862, term 3 years.

Irvine, John, enlisted Aug. 14, 1862, laborer, age 35, married, residence Boston. Mustered in Aug. 14, 1862, term 3 years. Deserted, no date, Boston.

Ivers, Henry, enlisted Feb. 13, 1863, seaman, age 20, residence Boston. Mustered in Feb. 13, 1863, term 3 years.

Johnson, George, enlisted Aug. 22, 1862, machinist, age 39, single, residence Boston. Mustered in Aug. 22, 1862, term 3 years.

Jones, John, enlisted Aug. 20, 1863, seaman, age 24, single, residence Boston, credited to Marblehead.   Mustered in Aug. 20, 1863, term 3 years.   Sub.

Keen, Hugh, enlisted Aug. 2, 1862, boilermaker, age 27, residence Boston. Mustered in Aug. 2, 1862, term 3 years.

Kelley, Michael, shoemaker, age 21, residence Boston. Mustered in July 28, 1862, term 3 years.

Kelley, James, enlisted July 29, 1862, laborer, age 28, married, residence Boston.   Mustered in July 29, 1862, term 3 years.

Kelly, John, enlisted Aug. 25, 1863, cigarmaker, age 21, single, residence Brooklyn, N.Y., credited to Irving.   Mustered in Aug. 25, 1863, term 3 years.   Sub. for A. A. Thompson.

Kelly, John J., enlisted July 28, 1862, printer, age 19, single, residence Boston. Mustered in July 28, 1862, term 3 years.

Kirk, Joseph, soldier, age 25, single, residence Malden.   Mustered in Aug. 8, 1862, term 3 years.

Lynase, Benjamin, enlisted Aug. 6, 1862, painter, age 21, single, residence Malden.   Mustered in Aug. 6, 1862, term 3 years.

Lynch, Patrick, enlisted Aug. 12, 1862, shoemaker, age 23, married, residence Salem.   Mustered in Aug. 12, 1862, term 3 years.

Lynn, James, enlisted March 1, 1862, bootmaker, age 32, single, residence Boston.   Mustered in March 1, 1862, term 3 years.   Deserted, no date, Boston.

Mahoney, Cornelius, enlisted Feb. 27, 1862, soapstone worker, age 22, residence Boston.   Mustered in Feb. 27, 1862, term 3 years.

Mead, Alonzo, enlisted Aug. 21, 1863, machinist, age 27, single, residence Albany, N.Y., credited to Ewing.   Mustered in Aug. 21, 1863, term 3 years.

Mehan, Michael, tailor, age 27, married, residence Boston.   Mustered in July 21, 1862, term 3 years.   Discharged for disability Oct. 29, 1862.

Millican, James, enlisted July 30, 1862, laborer, age 33, married.   Mustered in July 30, 1862, term 3 years.

Morris, Henry, clerk, age 31, married, residence Boston.   Mustered in Aug. 29, 1862, term 3 years.

Murphy, Michael, horseshoer, age 29, single, residence Wayland.   Mustered in Dec. 5, 1862, term 3 years.

Murphy, Thomas, enlisted Nov. 30, 1863, glassblower, age 30, residence Cambridge. Mustered in Nov. 30, 1863, term 3 years.

Murphy, John, enlisted Aug. 14, 1862, tailor, age 38, residence Boston. Mustered in Aug. 14, 1862, term 3 years.

McCabe, John, seaman, age 24, single, residence Tyngsboro. Mustered in Dec. 17, 1862, term 3 years.

McCauley, Patrick, enlisted Aug. 18, 1862, laborer, age 28, married, residence Boston, born in Ireland. Mustered in Aug. 18, 1862, term 3 years. Unassigned recruit. Deserted, date unknown.

McCluskey, Edward, enlisted Aug. 25, 1862, sailor, age 24, married, residence Boston. Mustered in Aug. 25, 1862, term 3 years.

McDonnell, James, enlisted Aug. 21, 1862, varnisher, age 25, residence Charlestown. Mustered in Aug. 21, 1862, term 3 years.

McGinnys, William, enlisted Feb. 11, 1862, laborer, age 21, residence Boston. Mustered in Feb. 11, 1862, term 3 years.

McGray, Lorenzo D., enlisted July 31, 1862, baker, age 32, residence Boston. Mustered in July 31, 1862, term 3 years. Deserted, no date, Boston.

McGowan, James, sailor, age 19, single, residence Boston. Mustered in Aug. 25, 1862, term 3 years.

McGrath, John, currier, age 30, married, residence Boston. Mustered in Aug. 17, 1862, term 3 years.

McKeefe, James, potter, age 27, single, residence East Boston. Mustered in Aug. 8, 1862, term 3 years.

McLaughlin, Richard, sailor, age 38, married, residence Boston. Mustered in Aug. 6, 1862, term 3 years.

O'Brien, John, enlisted Aug. 20, 1863, laborer, age 35, single, residence New Bedford, credited to New Bedford. Mustered in Aug. 20, 1863, term 3 years. Sub. for Francis A. Butts, Jr. Deserted Aug. 22, 1863, Long Island, Boston Harbor.

Parkhurst, Charles F., mariner, age 35, single, residence Blackstone. Mustered in Aug. 2, 1862, term 3 years.

Roach, John, clerk, age 22, single, residence Boston. Mustered in Aug. 5, 1862, term 3 years.

Ryerson, Thomas J., enlisted Aug. 7, 1862, seaman, age 25, residence Boston. Mustered in Aug. 7, 1862, term 3 years.

Ruston, Richard W., seaman, age 23, single, residence Wayland. Mustered in Dec. 12, 1862, term 3 years.

Sandford, Joseph F., enlisted Aug. 8, 1862. Mustered in Aug. 8, 1862, term 3 years.

Sawyer, George, enlisted July 22, 1862, laborer, age 26, married, residence Boston. Mustered in July 22, 1862, term 3 years.

Shedd, Dennis, laborer, age 30, married, residence Boston. Mustered in Aug. 24, 1862, term 3 years.

Sheehey, John, enlisted Aug. 8, 1862, bootmaker, age 38, residence Boston. Mustered in Aug. 8, 1862, term 3 years.

Sherry, James, tailor, age 28, single, residence Boston. Mustered in Aug. 7, 1862, term 3 years.

Smith, Albert P., enlisted Aug. 13, 1863, machinist, age 20, single, residence Salem, credited to Salem. Mustered in Aug 13, 1863, term 3 years. Discharged for disability Sept. 17, 1863. See roll of drafted men.

Smith, Charles, hostler, age 32, single, residence Boston.   Mustered in Aug. 19, 1862, term 3 years.

Sorrell, James, printer, age 18, single, residence Boston.   Mustered in Aug. 1, 1862, term 3 years.

Spougbery, Carl Johnn, machinist, age 41, single, residence Wayland.   Mustered in Dec 8, 1862, term 3 years.

Strange, Thomas, enlisted Aug. 21, 1862, laborer, age 25, residence Boston. Mustered in Aug. 21, 1862, term 3 years.

Sullivan, Patrick, enlisted Aug. 19, 1862, shoemaker, age 30, married, residence Boston.   Mustered in Aug. 19, 1862, term 3 years.

Taylor, Oliver F., enlisted Aug. 6, 1862, seaman, age 33, residence Boston. Mustered in Aug. 6, 1862, term 3 years.

Thompson, James, enlisted Aug. 1, 1862, shoemaker, age 18, single, residence Boston.   Mustered in Aug. 1, 1862, term 3 years.

Tiernan, Michael, enlisted July 17, 1862, tailor, age 39, married, residence Boston.   Mustered in July 17, 1862, term 3 years.

Tombley, William, seaman, age 21, single, residence Wayland.   Mustered in Dec. 8, 1862, term 3 years.

Turner, Terrence, tinman, age 45, married, residence Boston.   Mustered in July 12, 1862, term 3 years.   Discharged for disability April 4, 1863, S.B. June 30, 1866, War Dept.

Twoling, Timothy, age 22, single, residence Milford.   Mustered in Aug. 4, 1862, term 3 years.

Waters, Henry, painter, age 32, single, residence Wayland.   Mustered in Dec. 11, 1862, term 3 years.

Webster, Francis, farmer, age 24, married, residence Boston.   Mustered in July 30, 1862, term 3 years.

Wilson, Francis, enlisted July 13, 1863, shoemaker, age 30, married, residence Lynn, credited to Lynn.   Mustered in July 13, 1863, term 3 years.

Wright, Charles, seaman, age 20, single, residence Wayland.   Mustered in Dec. 12, 1862, term 3 years.

NUMERICAL STRENGTH, CASUALTIES
AND MUSTER-OUT

IN THE

NINTH MASSACHUSETTS VOLUNTEERS

(INCLUDING ASSIGNED RECRUITS)

FROM JUNE 11, 1861, TO JUNE 21, 1864.

Field and Staff Officers 14
Non-Commissioned Staff 7
Band 24

COMPANIES,
INCLUDING COMMISSIONED OFFICERS.

Company A 179
" B 169
" C 172
" D 164
" E 159
" F 152
" G 169
" H 162
" I 166
" K 154

Total — Officers and men 1,691

CASUALTIES AND MUSTER-OUT.

Killed and mortally wounded 211
Died 69
Discharged for disability 387
Commissioned officers discharged 28
Missing 24
Deserted 195
Transferred 300
Band discharged 16
Expiration of term of service 461

Total — Officers and men 1,691

INDEX.